THE DIARY OF
SAMUEL PEPYS

THE DIARY
OF
SAMUEL PEPYS

A new and complete
transcription edited by

ROBERT LATHAM
AND
WILLIAM MATTHEWS

CONTRIBUTING EDITORS
WILLIAM A. ARMSTRONG · MACDONALD EMSLIE
SIR OLIVER MILLAR · T. F. REDDAWAY

VOLUME IV · 1663

HarperCollins*Publishers*

University of California Press
Berkeley and Los Angeles

Published in the UK by
HarperCollins*Publishers*
77-85 Fulham Palace Road
Hammersmith, London W6 8JB
www.**fire**and**water**.com

UK paperback edition 1995
Reissued 2000

Published in the USA by
University of California Press
Berkeley and Los Angeles, California

First US paperback edition 2000

1 3 5 7 9 8 6 4 2

First published by Bell & Hyman Limited 1971

© The Master, Fellows and Scholars of Magdalene College, Cambridge,
Robert Latham and the Executors of William Matthews 1983

Robert Latham and William Matthews assert the moral right
to be identified as the editors of this work.

ISBN 0 00 499024 2 (UK)
ISBN 0 520 22694 1 (USA)

Library of Congress Catalog Card No. 70-96950

Printed and bound in Great Britain by
Omnia Books Limited, Glasgow

CONTENTS

LIST OF ILLUSTRATIONS

READER'S GUIDE

This section is meant for quick reference.   More detailed information about the editorial methods used in this edition will be found in the Introduction and in the section 'Methods of the Commentary' in vol. I, and also in the statement preceding the Select Glossary at the end of each text volume.

I. THE TEXT

The fact that the MS. is mostly in shorthand makes exact reproduction (e.g. of spelling, capitalisation and punctuation) impossible.

Spelling is in modern British style, except for those longhand words which Pepys spelt differently, and words for which the shorthand indicates a variant pronunciation which is also shown by Pepys's longhand elsewhere.   These latter are given in spellings which reflect Pepys's pronunciations.

Pepys's capitalisation is indicated only in his longhand.

Punctuation is almost all editorial, except for certain full-stops, colons, dashes and parentheses.   Punctuation is almost non-existent in the original since the marks could be confused with shorthand.

Italics are all editorial, but (in e.g. headings to entries) often follow indications given in the MS. (by e.g. the use of larger writing).

The **paragraphing** is that of the MS.

Abbreviations of surnames, titles, place names and ordinary words are expanded.

Single **hyphens** are editorial, and represent Pepys's habit of disjoining the elements of compound words (e.g. Wh. hall/White-hall).   Double hyphens represent Pepys's hyphens.

Single **angle-brackets** mark additions made by Pepys in the body of the MS.; double angle-brackets those made in the margins.

Light **asterisks** are editorial (see below, Section II); heavy asterisks are Pepys's own.

Pepys's **alterations** are indicated by the word 'replacing' ('repl.') in the textual footnotes.

II. THE COMMENTARY

1. **Footnotes** deal mainly with events and transactions.   They also

identify MSS, books, plays, music and quotations, but give only occasional and minimal information about persons and places, words and phrases. The initials which follow certain notes indicate the work of the contributing editors. Light asterisks in the text direct the reader to the Select Glossary for the definition of words whose meanings have changed since the time of the diary.

2. The **Select List of Persons** is printed unchanged in each text volume. It covers the whole diary and identifies the principal persons, together with those who are described in the MS. by titles or in other ways that make for obscurity.

3. The **Select Glossary** is printed at the end of each text volume. It gives definitions of certain recurrent English words and phrases, and identifications of certain recurrent places.

4. The **Companion** (vol. X) is a collection of reference material. It contains maps, genealogical tables, and a Large Glossary, but consists mainly of articles, printed for ease of reference in a single alphabetical series. These give information about matters which are dealt with briefly or not at all in the footnotes and the Select Glossary: i.e. persons, places, words and phrases, food, drink, clothes etc. They also treat systematically the principal subjects with which the diary is concerned: Pepys's work, interests, health etc. References to the *Companion* are given only rarely in the footnotes.

III. DATES

In Pepys's time two reckonings of the calendar year were in use in Western Europe. Most countries had adopted the New Style – the revised calendar of Gregory XIII (1582); Britain until 1752 retained the Old Style – the ancient Roman, or Julian, calendar, which meant that its dates were ten days behind those of the rest of Western Europe in the seventeenth century. 1 January in England was therefore 11 January by the New Style abroad. On the single occasion during the period of the diary when Pepys was abroad (in Holland in May 1660) he continued to use the Old Style, thus avoiding a break in the run of his dates. In the editorial material of the present work dates relating to countries which had adopted the new reckoning are given in both styles (e.g. '1/11 January') in order to prevent confusion.

It will be noticed that the shortest and longest days of the year occur in the diary ten days earlier than in the modern calendar. So, too, does Lord Mayor's Day in London – on 29 October instead of 9 November.

For most legal purposes (from medieval times until 1752) the new year in England was held to begin on Lady Day, 25 March.   But in accordance with the general custom, Pepys took it to begin on 1 January, as in the Julian calendar.   He gives to all dates within the overlapping period between 1 January and 24 March a year-date which comprehends both styles – e.g. 'January 1 16$\frac{59}{80}$.'   In the present commentary a single year-date, that of the New Style, has been used: e.g. '1 January 1660'.

THE DIARY
1663

JANUARY [16$\frac{62}{63}$]

1. Lay with my wife at my Lord's lodgings,[1] where I have been these two nights, till 10 a-clock with great pleasure talking; and then I rose. And to White-hall, where I spent a little time walking among the Courtiers, which I perceive I shall be able to do with great confidence, being now beginning to be pretty well-known among them.

Then to my wife again and dined, Mrs. Sarah with us, in the[a] chamber we lay in. Among other discourse, Mrs. Sarah tells us how the King sups at least four or [five] times every week with my Lady Castlemayne;[2] and most often stays till the morning with her and goes home through the garden all alone privately, and that so as the very Centry's take notice of it and speak of it.

She tells me that about a month ago she quickened at my Lord Gerrards at dinner and cried[b] out that she was undone; and all the lords and men were fain to quit the room, and women called to help her.[3]

In fine, I find that there is nothing almost but bawdry at Court from top to bottom, as if it were fit I could instance, but it is not necessary. Only, they say my Lord Chesterfield, Groom of the Stole to the Queene, is either gone or put away from Court upon the score of his lady's having smitten the Duke of York, so as that he is watched by the Duchesse of Yorke and the lady is retired into the country upon it.[4] How much of this is true, God knows, but it is common talk.

After dinner I did reckon with Mrs. Sarah for what we have eat and drank here, and gave her a crowne; and so took coach and to the Duke's house, where we saw *The Villaine*[5] again; and the more I see it, the more I am offended at my first undervaluing the

a repl. 'our'   b MS. 'cry'

---

1. In Whitehall Palace.
2. Sarah was Sandwich's house-keeper. Lady Castlemaine's house was in King St, Westminster, next door to Sandwich's.

3. Lady Castlemaine's second son (cr. Duke of Grafton) by Charles II was not born until 2 September 1663.
4. See above, iii. 248 & n. 2.
5. See above, iii. 230 & n. 1. (A).

play, it being very good and pleasant and yet a true and allowable Tragedy.[1]   The house was full of Citizens and so the less pleasant, but that I was willing to make an end of my gaddings and to set to my business for all the year again tomorrow.   Here we saw the old Roxalana[2] in the chief box, in a velvet gowne as the fashion is and very handsome, at which I was glad.

Thence by coach home, where I finde all well.   Only, Sir W. Penn they say ill again.   So to my office to set down these two or three days' journall and to close the last year therein. And so that being done, home to supper and to bed – with great pleasure talking and discoursing with my wife of our late observations abroad.

2.   Lay long in bed, and so up and to the office, where all the morning alone doing something or another.   So dined at home with my wife and in the afternoon to the Treasury office, where Sir W. Batten was paying of tickets, but so simply and arbitrarily (upon a dull pretence of doing right to the King, though to the wrong of poor people, when I know there is no man that means the King less right then he or would trouble himself less about it, but only that he sees me stir and so he would appear doing something, though to little purpose), that I was weary of it.   At last we broke up and walk home together; and I to see Sir W. Penn, who is fallen sick again.   I stayed a while talking with him, and so to my office, practising some arithmetique;[3] and so home to supper and bed – having sat up late talking with my poor wife with great content.

3.   Up and to the office all the morning and dined alone with my wife at noon; and then to my office all the afternoon till night, putting business in order with great content in my mind – having nothing now in my mind of trouble in the world, but quite the contrary, much joy, except only the ending of our difference with my Uncle Tho.[4] and the getting of the bills well

1. For Pepys's views on what was 'allowable Tragedy', see above, i. 236, 239.

2. Mrs Hester Davenport, formerly an actress at this theatre: above, iii. 32 & n. 6. (A).

3. Cf. above, iii. 160–1.

4. The dispute about the Brampton estate of Robert Pepys: see below, p. 42 & n. 3. Thomas Pepys was the heir-at-law to the estate.

over for my building of my house here; which, however, are as small and less then any of the others.[1] Sir W. Penn it seems is fallen very ill again.

So to my Arithmetique again tonight, and so home to supper – and to bed.

4. *Lords day.* Up and to church, where a lazy sermon. And so home to dinner to a good piece of powdered beef, but a little too salt. At dinner my wife did propound my having of my sister Pall at my house again to be her Woman, since one we must have – hoping that in that quality possibly she may prove better then she did before.[2] Which I take very well of her, and will consider of it – it being a very great trouble to me that I should have a sister of so ill a nature that I must be forced to spend money upon a stranger, when it might better be upon her if she were good for anything.

After dinner I and she walked, though it was dirty, to White-hall (I in the way calling at the Wardrobe to see how Mr. Moore doth, who is pretty well but not currant yet),[3] being much afeared of being seen by anybody and was, I think, of Mr. Coventry, which so troubled me that I made her go before and I ever after loytered behind. She to Mr. Hunts and I to White-hall Chappell. And then up to walk up and down the House; which now I am well known there, I shall forbear to do, because I would not be a-thought a lazy body by Mr. Coventry and others, by being seen, as I have lately been, to walk up and down doing nothing. So to Mr. Hunts[4] and there was most prettily and kindly entertained by him and her – who are two so good people as I hardly know any, and so neat and kind one to another. Here we stayed late, and so to my Lord's to bed.

5. Up and to the Duke – who himself told me that Sir J Lawson was come home to Portsmouth from the Streights.

---

1. For the work and its cost, see above, iii. 59, n. 2.

2. She had served the Pepyses as a maid from January to September 1661.

3. Henry Moore (lawyer and Sandwich's man of business) had been ill since the previous October.

4. John Hunt (an excise officer) lived in Axe Yard near Pepys's old home.

Who is now come, with great renowne among all men; and I
perceive mightily esteemed at Court by all.[1] The Duke did not
stay long in his chamber, but to the King's chamber, whither by
and by the Russia Embassadors came; who it seems have a
custome that they will not come to have any treaty with our or
any King's Comissioners but they will themselfs see at that
time the face of the King himself, be it 40 days one after another;
and so they did today, only go in and see the King, and so out
again to the Council-chamber.[2]

The Duke returns to his chamber and so to his closet, where
Sir G. Carteret, Sir J. Mennes, Sir W. Batten, Mr. Coventry and
myself attended him about the business of the Navy, and after
much discourse and pleasant talk he went away. And I took
Sir W. Batten and Captain Allen into the wine-cellar to my
tenant (as I call him, Serjeant Dalton)[3] and there drank a great deal
of variety of wines, more then I have drunk at one time, or shall
again a great while when I come to return to my oaths, which I
entend in a day or two. Thence to my Lord's lodging, where
Mrs. Hunt and Mr. Creede dined with us, and were very merry.
And after dinner he and I to White-hall, where the Duke and the
Commissioners for Tanger met, but did not do much; my Lord
Sandwich not being in Towne, nobody making it their business.
So up, and Creede and I to my wife again; and after a game or
two at Cards, to the Cocke=pitt, where we saw *Claracilla*,[4] a poor
play, done by the King's house (but the King nor Queen were
there, but only the Duke and Duchesse, who did show some
impertinent and methought unnatural dalliances there before the
whole world, such as kissing of hands and leaning upon one
another) but to my very little content, they not acting in any

1. The new standing of this ex-
Anabaptist and ex-Republican was
due to his treaties with the Moors:
above, iii. 89, 263 & nn. On
29 December 1662 he had been
granted a pension of £500 p.a.:
CSPD 1661–2, p. 605.

2. For the embassy, see above, iii.
267 & n. 2. Russian protocol required their envoys to see the King
before negotiating with his agents:

see Sir J. Finett, *Finetti Philoxenis*
(1656), p. 47.

3. Richard Dalton, Sergeant of the
King's wine cellar, had leased Pepys's
old house in Axe Yard.

4. A tragicomedy by Thomas
Killigrew (q.v. above, ii. 132 & n. 2)
now being played at the royal private
theatre adjoining Whitehall Palace,
at which evening performances were
given. (A).

degree like the Dukes people.[1] So home (there being here this night Mrs. Turner and Mrs. Martha Batten of our office) to my Lord's lodgings again and to a game at Cards, we three and Sarah; and so to supper and some apples and ale,[2] and to bed – with great pleasure – blessed be God.

6. ⟨*Twelfth=day.*⟩ Up, and Mr. Creede brought a pot of Chocolatt ready made for our morning draught. And then he and I to the Dukes; but I was not very willing to be seen at this end of the towne and so retired to our lodgings and took my wife by coach to my brother's; where I set her down, and Creede and I to St. Paul's churchyard to my Booke-seller's and looked over several books with good discourse. And then into St. Paul's church; and there finding Elborough (my old schoolfellow at Pauls, now a parson, whom I know to be a silly fellow), I took him out and walked with him, making Creede and myself sport with talking with him; and so sent him away and we to my office and house to see all well. And thence to the Exchange, where we met with Major Thomson,[3] formerly of our office, who doth talk very highly of Liberty of conscience, which now he hopes for by the King's declaracion, and that he doubts not but if he will give it,[a] he will find more and better friends then the Bishops can be to him. And that if he do not, there will many thousands in a little time go out of England where they may have it.[4] And I do believe it is true – but the Bishopps will never give way to it. But he says that they are well contented that if the King thinks it good, the papists may have the same liberty with them. He tells me, and so do others, that Dr. Calamy is this day sent to Newgate for preaching, Sunday was sennit, without leave; though he did it only to supply the place, which otherwise the people

a MS. 'him'

---

1. It is generally agreed that the Duke of York's Company were superior to the King's Company. (A).

2. Lamb's-wool, a hot spiced drink.

3. Robert Thomson, Navy Commissioner under the Protectorate.

4. The declaration of 26 December 1662 had promised liberty of conscience to all peaceable dissenters (including Papists), but was subject to parliamentary confirmation. A bill introduced in the Lords for this purpose in February 1663 was defeated in the Commons: below, p. 58 & n. 3. But there was little emigration on this account.

must have gone away without ever a sermon, they being dis-
appointed of a Minister.   But the Bishop of London will not take
that as an excuse.[1]   Thence into Woodstreete and there bought a
fine table for my dining roome, costs me 50s.   And while we were
buying it, there was a scare=fire in an ally over against us, but they
quenched it.   So to my brother's, where Creed and I and my
wife dined with Tom.   And after dinner to the Dukes house
and there saw *Twelfth night* acted well, though it be but a silly
play and not relating at all to the name or day.[2]   Thence Mr.
Battersby (the apothecary), his wife and I and mine by coach
together, and setting him down at his house, he paying his share,
my wife and I home and find all well.   Only, myself somewhat
vexed at my wife's neglect in leaving of her scarfe, waistcoat, and
night-dressings in the coach today that brought us from Westminster, though I confess she did give them to me to look after –
yet it was her fault not to see that I did take them out of the coach.
I believe it might be as good as 25s loss or thereabouts.

So to my office, however, to set down my last three days'
Journall, and writing to my Lord Sandwich to give him an
account of Sir J. Lawsons being come home – and to my father
about my sending him some wine and things this week for his
making an entertainment of some friends in the country, and so
home.   This night making an end wholly of Christmas, with a
mind fully satisfyed with the great pleasures we have had by
being abroad from home.   And I do find my mind so apt to
run to its old wont of pleasures, that it is high time to betake
myself to my late vows, which I will tomorrow, God willing,
perfect and bind myself to, that so I may for a great while do my
duty, as I have well begun, and encrease my good name and
esteem in the world and get[a] money, which sweetens all things

a repl. 'good'

---

1. Edmund Calamy, sen., a leading
Presbyterian, had preached in St
Mary's Aldermanbury, from which
he had been extruded in August 1662
for nonconformity. He was released from Newgate on 13 January
on the ground that he had acted with
the approval of several privy coun-
cillors, and not in contempt of the
law: *CSPD 1663–4*, p. 10.   The Act
of Uniformity made dissenting clergy-
men liable to three months' imprisonment for public preaching. This
was the first prosecution under the
act. Cf *CSPVen. 1661–4*, p. 229.
The Bishop was Gilbert Sheldon.

2. Cf. Pepys's similar opinion:
above, ii. 177. (A).

and whereof I have much need. So home to supper and to bed – blessing God for his mercy to bring me home, after much pleasure, to my house and business, with health and resolution to fall hard to work again.

7. Up pretty earely; that is, by 7 a-clock, it being not yet light before or then. So to my office all the morning, signing the Treasurers ledger, part of it where I have not put my hand. And then eat a mouthful of pie at home to stay my stomach; and so with Mr. Waith by water to Deptford and there, among other things, viewed old pay-books and find that the Comanders did never heretofore receive any pay for the Rigging-time but only for Sea time, contrary to what Sir J. Minnes and Sir W. Batten told the Duke the other day.[1] I also searched all the ships in the Wett docke for fire and found all in good order – it being very dangerous for the King that so many of his ships lie together there. I was among the Canvas in stores also with Mr. Harris the Saylmaker, and learnt the difference between one sort and another to my great content.[2] And so by water home again – where my wife tells me stories how she hears that by Sarahs going to live at Sir W. Penn's,[3] all our affairs of my family are made known and discoursed of there, and theirs by my people – which doth trouble me much, and I shall take a time to let Sir W. Penn know how he hath dealt in taking her without our full consent. So to my office, and by and by home to supper. And so to prayers and bed.

8. Up pretty earely and sent my boy to the Carriers with some wine for my father, for to make his feast[4] among his Brampton friends this Christmas – and my Muffe to my mother, sent as from my wife. But before I sent my boy out with them, I beat him for a lie he told me – at which his sister (with whom we have of late been highly displeased, and warned her to be gone) was

1. Cf. Pepys to Coventry, 7 January: *Further Corr.*, pp. 2–3. Pepys had searched over 100 pay-books and proved that, until the First Dutch War, commanders (Mennes and Batten themselves included) had never been paid for the period when their ships were being rigged.

2. Cf. Pepys's notes (22 June 1664) of Harris's discourse about canvas: NWB, p. 24.

3. See above, iii. 295.

4. Possibly for his birthday (14 January).

angry; which vexed me, to see the girl I loved so well, and my wife, should at last turn so much a fool and unthankful to us.[1]

So to the office and there all the morning; and though without and a little against the advice of the officers, did to gratify him send Tho. Hater today towards Portsmouth a day or two before the rest of the clerks, against the pay next week.

Dined at home; and there being the famous new play acted the first time today,[a] which is call[ed] *The Adventures of five houres*, at the Duke's house, being they say made or translated by Collonell Tuke,[2] I did long to see it and so made my wife to get her ready, though we were forced to send for a smith to break open her Trunke, her maid Jane being gone forth with the keyes. And so we went; and though earely, were forced to sit almost out of sight at the end of one of the lower formes,[3] so full was the house. And the play, in one word, is the best, for the variety and the most excellent continuance of the plot to the very end, that ever I saw or think ever shall. And all possible, not only to be done in that time, but in most other respects very admittible and without one word of ribaldry. And the house, by its frequent plaudites, did show their sufficient approbacion. So home, with much ado in an hour getting a coach home; and after writing letters at my office, I went home to supper and to bed – now resolving to set up my rest as to plays till Easter, if not Whitsuntide next, excepting plays at Court.

a   repl. 'this was'

---

1. Jane Birch (sister of the incorrigible boy Wayneman, who was sent to Barbados in the following November) had been with the Pepyses since 1658.

2. This was an adaptation of a Spanish comedy, *Los empeños de seis horas*, once attributed to Calderon but probably by Don Antonio Coello y Ochoa (d. 1682). It was made by Samuel Tuke (d. 1673) after Charles II had suggested that he should adapt a Spanish play for the English stage.

This is one of the earliest records of a performance, though Evelyn had seen it on 23 December 1662, and was present on this occasion. The cast listed by Downes (pp. 22–3) includes Betterton as Don Henriq, Harris as Antonio, Smith as the Corregidor and Mrs Betterton as Portia. Tuke's comedy was published in 1663 under the title given here. (A).

3. The backless benches near the front of the pit. (A).

9.   Waking in the morning, my wife I found also awake, and
begun to speak to me with great trouble and tears; and by
degrees, from one discourse to another, at last it appears that
Sarah hath told somebody that hath told my wife of my meeting
her at my brother's and making her set down by me while she
told me stories of my wife, about her giving her Scallop to her
brother and other things[1] – which I am much vexed at, for I am
sure I never spoke anything of it, nor could anybody tell her
but by Sarahs own words.   I endeavoured to excuse my silence
herein hitherto, by not believing anything she told me; only that
of the Scallop,*a* which she herself told me of.   At last we were
pretty good friends and my wife begun to speak again of the
necessity of her keeping somebody to bear her company; for
her familiarity with her other servants is it that spoils them all, and
other company she hath none (which is too true); and called for
Jane to reach her out of her trunk, giving her the keys to that
purpose, a bundle of papers; and pulls out a paper, a copy of
what, a pretty while since, she had writ in a discontent to me,
which I would*b* not read but burned.[2]   She now read it, and was
so picquant, and wrote in English and most of it true, of the
retirednesse of her life and how unpleasant it was, that being writ
in English and so in danger of being*c* met with and read by others,
I was vexed at it and desired her and then commanded her to
teare it – which she desired to be excused it; I forced it from
her and tore it, and withal took her other bundle of papers from
her and leapt out of the bed and in my shirt clapped them into
the pockets of my breeches, that she might not get them from
me; and having got on my stockings and breeches and gown,
I pulled them out one by one and tore them all before her face,
though it went against my heart to do it, she crying and desiring
me not to do it.   But such was my passion and trouble to see the
letters of my love to her, and my Will, wherein I had given her
all I have in the world when I went to sea with my Lord Sandwich,[3] to be joyned with a paper of so much disgrace to me and

a l.h. repl. s.h. 'hand'   *b* MS. 'could'   *c* l.h. repl. s.h. 'me'-

1. Cf. above, iii. 285.
2. See above, iii. 257–8.
3. In March 1660: see above,

i. 90. He had then promised her all
his possessions except most of his
books.

dishonour if it should have been found by anybody.   Having
tore them all, saving a bond of my uncle Robts. which she hath
long had in her hands, and our Marriage=licence and the first letter
that ever I sent her when I was her servant,* I took up the pieces
and carried them into my chamber, and there, after many disputes
with myself whether*a* I should burn them or no, and having
picked up the pieces of the paper she read today and of my Will
which I tore, I burnt all the rest.   And so went out to my office –
troubled in mind.

Hither comes Major Tolhurst, one of my old acquaintance in
Cromwell's time and sometimes of our clubb,[1] to see me, and I
could do no less then carry him to the Miter; and thither having
sent for Mr. Beane, a merchant, a neighbour of mine, we sat and
talk – Tolhurst telling me the manner of their Collierys in the
North.   We broke up, and I home to dinner.

And to see my folly, as discontented as I am, when my wife
came I could not forbear smiling all dinner, till she begun to speak
bad words again; and then I begun to be angry again, and so to
my office.

Mr. Bland came in the evening to me hither, and sat talking to
me about many things of Merchandize; and I should be very
happy in his discourse, durst I confess my ignorance to him, which
is not so fit for me to do.[2]

There coming a letter to me from Dr.*b* Pierce the Surgeon, by
my desire appointing his and Dr Clerkes coming to dine with
me next Monday, I went to my wife and agreed upon matters;
and at last, for my honour am forced to make her presently a new
Moyre gown to be seen by Mrs. Clerke; which troubles me to
part with so much money, but however it sets my wife and I
to friends again, though I and she never were so heartily angry in
our lives as today almost, and I doubt the heart-burning will not
soon over.   And the truth is, I am sorry for the tearing of so
many poor loving letters of mine from Sea and elsewhere to her.

a followed by two blank pages stuck together   *b* l.h. repl. l.h. 'Mr.'

---

1. Jeremiah Tolhurst, an excise
farmer for Northumberland under
the Commonwealth and now a
customs officer in Newcastle, active in
the coal-trade and a member of the
Company of Hostmen. For the
club, see above, i. 208 & n. 4.

2. John Bland traded with Tangier;
Pepys was a member of the committee controlling its government.

So to my office again, and there the Scrivener brought me the end of my Manuscript which I am going*a* to get together of things of the Navy[1] – which pleases me much. So home – mighty friends with my wife again, and so to bed.

10. Up and to the office; from whence, before we sat, Sir W. Penn sent for me to his bedside to talk (endeed, to reproach me with my not owning to Sir J. Mennes that he had my advice in the blocking-up the garden door the other day, which is now by him, out of fear to Sir J. Mennes, opened again), to which I answered him so indifferently that I think he and I shall be at a distance, at least to one another, better then ever we did and love one another less – which for my part I think I need not care for. So to the office and sat till noon; then rise and to dinner and then to the office again, where Mr. Creede sat with me till late, talking very good discourse, as he is full of it, though a cunning knave in his heart; at least, not to be too much trusted – till Sir J. Mennes came in, which at last he*b* did; and so, beyond my expectation, he was willing to sign his accounts,[2] notwithstanding all his objections, which really were very material; and yet now like a doting coxcomb he signs the accounts without the least satisfaccion – for which we both sufficiently laughed at him and Sir W. Batten after they had signed them and were gone; and so sat talking together till 11 a-clock at night, and so home and to bed.

11. *Lords day.* Lay long, talking pleasant with my wife; then up and to church, the pew being quite full with strangers come along with Sir W. Batten and Sir J. Mennes. So after a pitiful

a l.h. repl. s.h. 'bind'   *b* repl. 'I'

---

1. Untraced: first mentioned at 20 June 1662; possibly inspired by Coventry's appointment (cf. above, iii. 103). Pepys had it bound and made many entries in it during the next few months, but he never appears to mention it after 6 August 1663. Referred to variously as his 'Sea Manuscript', 'Navy Manuscript', 'Book Manuscript', 'Manuscript Book', 'Manuscript' and 'Navy Collections', it was a work of reference, with, e.g., lists of ships, comparable to (and possibly replaced by) the book of 'Naval Precedents' he made in retirement after 1688 (PL 2867).

2. See above, iii. 278–9 & n.; below, p. 16 & n. 2.

sermon of the young Scott,[1] home to dinner.   After dinner comes a footman of my Lord Sandwiches (my Lord being come to town last night) with a letter from my father in which he presses me to carry on the business for Tom with his late Mistrisse;[2] which I am sorry to see my father do, it being so much out of our power or for his advantage, as it is clear to me it is – which I shall think of and answer in my next.   So to my office, all the afternoon writing orders myself to have ready against tomorrow, that I might not appear negligent to Mr. Coventry.

In the evening to Sir W. Penn's, where Sir J. Mennes and Sir W. Batten, and afterward came Sir G. Carteret; there talked about business, and afterward to Sir W. Batten's, where we stayed talking and drinking Syder; and so I went away to my office a little, and so home – and to bed.

12.   Up, and to Sir Wm. Battens to bid him and Sir J. Mennes Adieu, they going this day toward Portsmouth; and then to Sir W. Penn's to see Sir John Lawson, who I heard was there; where I found him the same plain man he was, after all his successe in the Streights with which he is come loaded home.   Thence to Sir G. Carteret and with him in his coach to White-hall; and first I to see my Lord Sandwich (being come now from Hinching-brooke) and after talking a little with him, he and I to the Duke's chamber, where Mr. Coventry and he and I in the Duke's Closett and Sir John Lawson, discoursing upon business of the Navy; and perticularly got his consent to the ending some difficultys in Mr. Creedes accounts.

Thence to my Lord's Lodgeings and with Mr. Creede to the Kings-head ordinary; but people being sat down, we went to two or three places; at last found some meat at a welch cook's at Charing-cross and there dined, and our boys.

After dinner to the Change to buy some linen for my wife; and going back, met our two boys; mine had struck down Creedes boy in the dirt, with his new suit on in the dirt, all over dirty, and the boy taken by a gentlewoman into a house to make

---

1. Pepys suffered much from this visiting preacher; e.g., 'the Scott preached and I slept': below, p. 348. He is never named in the diary, and his identity can only be conjectured: see *Comp.*: 'The Scot'.

2. See above, iii. 232–3.

clean, but the poor boy was in a pitiful taking and pickle; but I
basted my rogue soundly. Thence I to my Lord's Lodgeings
and Creede to his for his papers against the Comittee. I find my
Lord within, and he and I went out through the garden toward
the Duke's chamber to sit upon the Tanger matters; but a lady
called to my Lord out of my Lady Castlemaynes lodging, telling
him that the King was there and would speak with him. My
Lord could not tell what to bid me say at the Comittee to excuse
his absence, but that he was with the King; nor would suffer
me to go into the privy garden (which is now a through-passage,
and common), but bid me to go through some other way, which
I did; so that I see he is a servant of the King's pleasures too, as
well as business. So I went to the Comittee, where we spent all
this night attending to Sir J. Lawsons description of Tanger and
the place for the molde, of which he brought a very pretty draught.
Concerning the making of the molle, Mr. Cholmely did also
discourse very well, having had some experience in it.[1]

Being broke up, I home by coach to Mr. Blands, and there
discoursed about sending away of the Merchant-ship which hangs
so long on hand for Tanger.[2]

So to my Lady Battens and sat with her a while, Sir W. Batten
being gone out of towne; but I did it out of design to get some
oranges for my feast tomorrow of her – which I did.

So home, and find my wife's new gowne come home and she
mightily pleased with it. But I appeared very angry that there
was no more things got ready against tomorrow's feast, and in
that passion sat up long and went discontented to bed.

13. So my poor wife rose by 5 a-clock in the morning,
before day, and went to market and bought fowle and many
other things for dinner – with which I was highly pleased. And
the chine of beef was done also before 6 a-clock, and my own
Jacke, of which I was doubtful, doth carry it very well. Things
being put in order and the Cooke come, I went to the office,
where we sat till noon; and then broke up and I home – whither

---

1. Lawson was one of the contractors for the mole's construction;
Hugh Cholmley (who had built
Whitby pier) the principal engineer.
2. Cf. above, iii. 300 & n. 1.

by and by comes Dr. Clerke and his lady – his sister and a she-Cosen, and Mr. Pierce and his wife, which was all my guest[s].

I had for them, after oysters – at first course, a hash of rabbits and lamb, and a rare chine of beef – next, a great dish of roasted fowl, cost me about 30s, and a tart; and then fruit and cheese. My dinner was noble and enough.*a*   I had my house mighty clean and neat, my room below with a good fire in it – my dining-room above, and my chamber being made a withdrawing-chamber, and my wife's a good fire also.   I find my new table very proper, and will hold nine or ten people well, but eight with great room.   After dinner, the women to Cards in my wife's chamber and the Doctor [and] Mr. Pierce in mine, because the dining-room smokes unless I keep a good charcole fire, which I was not then provided with.   At night to supper; had a good sack-posset and cold meat and sent my guests away about 10 a-clock at night – both them and myself highly pleased with our management of this day.   And endeed, their company was very fine and Mrs. Clerke a very witty, fine lady, though a little conceited and proud.   So weary to bed.   I believe this day's feast will cost me near 5*l*.

14.   Lay very long in bed – till with shame forced to rise, being called up by Mr. Bland about business.   He being gone, I went and stayed upon business at the office and then home to dinner.   And after dinner stayed a little, talking pleasant with my wife – who tells me of another woman offered her by her brother, that is pretty and can sing;[1] to which I do listen but will not appear over-forward; but I see I must keep somebody for company sake to my wife, for I am ashamed she should live as she doth.   So to the office till 10 at night upon business, and numbering and examining part of my Sea=manuscript[2] with great pleasure – my wife sitting working by me.   So home to supper and to bed.

15.   Up, and to my office preparing things. By and by we met and sat, Mr. Coventry and I, till noon.   Then I took him in to dine with me, I having a wild goose roasted and a cold chine of beef and a barrel of oysters.   We dined alone in my chamber,

a   repl. 'enough' written too high

---

1. Mary Ashwell: below, p. 16.   2. See above, p. 11, n. 1.

and then he and I to fit ourselfs for horseback, he having brought me a horse; and so to Debtford, the ways being very dirty. There we walked up and down the yard and wet-dock and did our main business, which was to examine the proof of our new way of the Call=bookes,[1] which we think will be of great use. And so to horse again and I home with his horse, leaving him to go over the fields to Lambeth – his boy at my house taking home his horse.

I vexed, having left my key in my other pocket in my chamber and my door is shut, so that I was forced to set my boy in at the window; which done, I shifted myself, and so to my office till late. And then home to supper – my mind being troubled about Fields business[2] – and my Uncles,[3] which, the Terme coming on, I must now think to fallow again. So to prayers and to bed. And much troubled in mind this night in my dreams about my uncle Thomas and his son going to law with us.

16. Lay long, talking in bed with my wife. Up, and Mr. Battersby the Apothecary coming to see me, I called for the cold chine of beef and made him eat and drink wine, and talked; there being with us Captain Brewer the paynter,[4] who tell me how highly the Presbyters do talk in the Coffee-houses still, which I wonder at. They being gone, I walk two or three hours with my brother Tom, telling him my mind how it is troubled about my father's concernments, and how things would be with them all if it should please God I should die; and therefore desire him to be a good husband* and fallow his business, which I hope he doth. At noon to dinner, and after dinner my wife begun to talk of a woman again; which I have a mind to have, and would be glad Pall might please us, but she is quite against having her; nor have I any great mind to it, but only for her good and to save money flung away upon a stranger. So to my office till 9 a-clock about my Navy=manuscript. And then, troubled in my mind more and more about my uncles business, from a letter come this day from my father that tells me that all his tenants are sued by my uncle,[5] which will cost me some new trouble, I went home to supper, and so to bed.

1. See above, iii. 289, n. 2.
2. See above, iii. 23, n. 2.
3. See *Comp.*: 'Pepys, Robert'.
4. William Brewer; in charge of the painting at Pepys's house and other buildings at the Navy Office.
5. For this dispute, see above, p. 2, n. 4.

17. Waked early, with my mind troubled about our law matters; but it came into my mind that of Epictetus about his ἐκ ἡνῖν καὶ οὐκ ¹&c., which did put me to a great deal of ease, it being a saying of great reason.

Up and to the office, and there sat Mr. Coventry, Mr. Pett (now come to town) and I. I was sorry for signing of a bill and guiding*a* Mr. Coventry*b* to sign a bill to Mr. Creed for his pay as Deputy-Treasurer to this day, though the service ended five or six months ago;² which he perceiving did blot out his name afterwards – but I will clear myself to him from design in it. Sat till 2 a-clock and then home to dinner, and Creed with me. And after dinner, to put off my mind's trouble, I took Creed by coach and to the Dukes playhouse, where we did see the *Five houres* entertainment again³ – which endeed is a very fine play; though, through my being out of order, it did not seem so good as at first; but I could discern it was not any fault in the play. Thence with him to the China ale house and there drank a bottle or two, and so home, where I find my wife and her brother discoursing about Mr. Ashwells daughter, which we are like to have for my wife's woman; and I hope it may do very well, seeing there is a necessity of having one. So to the office to write letters and then home. To supper and to bed.

18. *Lords day.* Up; and after the barber had done and I had speak with Mr. Smith (whom I sent for on purpose to speak of Filds business, who stands upon 250*l* before he will release us,⁴ which doth trouble me highly), and also Major Allen of the victualling-Office about his ship to be hired for Tanger, I went to church. And thence home to dinner alone with my wife, very pleasant; and after dinner to church again and heard a dull, drowzy sermon; and so home and to my office, perfecting my vowes again for the next year, which I have now done and sworn

a l.h. repl. s.h. 'get'-   *b* l.h. repl. l.h. 'Cov'-

1. 'Some things are in our power, others are not'. See above, iii. 194 & n. 1.

2. The bill authorised payment to Creed of £160 for his services to Sandwich's fleet in the Mediterranean voyage of 1661–2, from 5 May 1661 to the date of the bill: cf. PRO, Adm. 20/4, p. 429 (14 January).

3. See above, p. 8 & n. 2. (A).

4. See above, iii. 23 & n. 2; 281 & n. 1.

to in the presence of Almighty God to observe upon the respective penalties thereto annexed. And then to Sir W. Penn's to see how he doth (though much against my will, for I cannot love him, but only to keep him from complaint to others that I do not see him), and find him pretty well and ready to go abroad again. Then home and to supper and prayers and bed.

19. Up and to White-hall; and while the Duke is dressing himself, I went to wait on my Lord Sandwich, whom I find not very well, and Dr Clerke with him. He is feverish and hath sent for Mr. Pierce to let him blood; but not being in the way, he puts it off till night – but he stirs not abroad today. Then to the Duke and in his closet discoursed as we use to do, and then broke up. That done, I singled out Mr. Coventry into the Matted Gallery and there I told him the complaints I meet every day about our Treasurers or his people's paying no money but at the goldsmiths shops, where they are forced to pay 15, or 20 sometimes, per cent for their money – which is a most horrid shame and that which must not be suffered. Nor is it likely that the Treasurer (at least his people) will suffer Maynell the goldsmith to go away with 10000*l* per annum, as he doth now get by making people pay after this manner for their money. We were interrupted by the Duke, who called Mr. Coventry aside for half an hour, walking with him in the gallery and then in the garden; and then going away, I ended my discourse with Mr. Coventry. But by the way Mr. Coventry was saying that there remained nothing now in our office to be amended but what would do of itself every day better and better, for as much as he that was slowest, Sir W. Batten, doth now begin to look about him and to mind business – at which, God forgive me, I was a little moved with envy; but yet I am glad and ought to be, though it doth lessen a little my care to see that the King's service is like to be better attended then it was heretofore.

Thence by coach to Mr. Povys,[1] being invited thither by*a* a messenger this morning from him – where really, he made a most excellent and large dinner of their variety, even to admiration; he bidding us in a frolique to call for what we had a mind and

a MS. 'by came'

---

1. In Lincoln's Inn Fields.

he would undertake to give it us – and we did, for prawns – Swan – venison after I had thought the dinner was quite done, and he did immediately produce it, which I thought great plenty.   And he seems to set off his rest in this plenty and the neatness of his house; which he after dinner showed me from room to room, so beset with delicate pictures, and above all, a piece of per[s]pec-tive¹ in his closet in the low parler.   His stable, where was some most delicate horses, and the very racks painted, and mangers, with a neat leaden painted cistern and the walls done with Dutch tiles like my chimnies.   But still, above all things, he bid me go down into his wine-cellar, where upon several shelves there stood bottles of all sorts of wine, new and old, with labells pasted upon each bottle, and in that order and plenty as I never saw books in a bookseller's shop.²   And herein, I observe, he puts his highest content and will accordingly commend all that he hath, but still they deserve to be so.   Here dined with me Dr. Whore and Mr. Scawen.

Thence with him and Mr. Bland (whom we met by the way) to my Lord Chancellors, where the King was to meet my Lord Treasurer, &c., many great men, to settle the Revenue of Tanger. I stayed talking a while there; but the King not coming, I walked to my brother's, where I met my Cosen Scotts (Tom not being at home) and sent for a glass of wine for them; and having

1. An early reference to the current liking, very marked in Pepys's tastes, for illusionist paintings and paintings of feigned perspectives. Povey's pic-ture was probably the illusionist picture painted in 1662 by Samuel van Hoogstraten (d. 1678) and measuring 104 × 53¾ ins., which later passed into the collection of his nephew William Blathwayt, and is still at Dyrham Park, Glos. (exhibited *17th century art in Europe*, R.A., 1938 (no. 160)). Hoogstraten was working in London, 1662-3, and portraits painted by him in England in 1667 are also recorded. He also painted perspective pieces, of a rather more grandiose nature, for the Finch family. (OM).

2. Normally wines were drunk 'new', and wooden casks were used for the short maturing process they were allowed. Bottles were used simply for the serving of the wine at table or for its carriage and storage over short periods. Their stoppers were of oiled hemp or of glass covered with wax. The use of cork (which made storage in horizontal bottles possible) was introduced into England in the early 18th century, for port. A. L. Simon, *Bottlescrew Days*, pp. 234+; *The Times*, 14 November 1964, p. 11; cf. below, p. 346 & n. 1. In 1672 some of Povey's wines were stolen: Mdx R.O., Sessions Bks 296, pp. 8-28.

drunk, we parted and I to the Wardrobe, talking with Mr. Moore about my law businesses, which I doubt will go ill for want of time for me to attend them.

So home, where I find Mrs. Lodum speaking with my wife about her kinswoman which is offered my wife to come as a woman to her.

So to the office and put things in order; and then home and to bed – it being my great comfort that every day I understand more and more the pleasure of fallowing of business and the credit that a man gets by it, which I hope at last too will end in profit.

This day, by Dr Clerke, I was told the occasion of my Lord Chesterfield's going and taking his lady (my Lord Ormonds daughter) from Court.[1] It seems he not only hath been long jealous of the Duke of Yorke, but did find them two talking together, though there was others in the room and the lady by all opinions a most good, virtuous woman. He, the next day (of which the Duke was warned by somebody that saw the passion my Lord Chesterfield was in the night before), he went and told the Duke how much he did apprehend himself wronged in his picking out his lady of the whole Court to be the subject of his dishonour – which the Duke did answer with great calmnesse, not seeming to understand the reason of complaint, and that was all past; but my Lord did presently pack his lady into the country in Derbyshire, near the peake; which is become a proverb at Court – to send a man's wife to the Devil's Arse a-Peak[2] when she vexes him.

This noon I did find out Mr. Dixon at White-hall and discoursed with him about Mr. Wheatelys daughter for a wife for my Brother Tom, and have committed it to him to enquire the pleasure of her father and mother concerning it. I demanded 300*l*.

20. Up betimes and to the office, where all the morning. Dined at home, and Mr. Deane of Woolwich with me, talking about the abuses of the yard. Then to the office about business all the afternoon, with great pleasure seeing myself observed by

1. See above, iii. 248 & n. 2.
2. A cave near Castelton, Derby; alias Devil's Hole or Peak Cavern; one of the 'Seven Wonders of the Peak'. The 'proverb' appears to have had a short life and does not occur e.g., in John Ray's *Coll. Engl. proverbs* (1670).

everybody to be the only man of business of us all, but Mr. Coventry. So till late at night, and then home to supper and bed.

21. Up early, leaving my wife very ill in bed *de ses Mois*, and to my office till 8 a-clock – there coming Ch. Pepys to demand his legacy of me, which I denied him upon the good reason of his father and brother's suing us, and so he went away.[1] Then came Commissioner Pett, and he and I by agreement went to Deptford, and after a turn or two in the yard, to Greenwich[a] and thence walked to Woolwich; here we did business, and I on board the *Tanger=Merchant*, a ship freighted by us that hath long lain on hand in her dispatch to Tanger but is now ready for sailing.[2]   Back and dined at Mr. Ackworths,[3] where a pretty dinner and she a pretty, modest woman; but above all things, we saw her Rocke, which is one of the finest things done by a woman that ever I saw – I must have my wife to see it.   After dinner, on board the *Elias* and found the timber brought by her from the Forrest of Deane to be exceeding good.   The Captain gave each of us two barrels of pickled oysters, put up for the Queene-Mother.

So to the Docke again, and took in Mrs. Ackworth and another gentlewoman and carried them to London, and at the Globe taverne in Eastchip did give them a glass of wine and so parted. I home, where I find my wife ill in bed all day, and her face swelled with pain.   My Will hath received my last two Quarters salary,[4] of which I am glad.   So to my office till late and then home; and after the barber had done, to bed.

a   repl. 'Wool'-

---

1. Charles Pepys and his brother Thomas (the turner) had been left £35 each under the will of their uncle Robert Pepys of Brampton, of which Pepys was the executor.

2. See above, iii. 291, n. 6; 300, n. 1; *CSPD 1663*, pp. 38, 48, 354. John Bland later paid Pepys £20 for his services in connection with this ship: below, v. 139.

3. William Ackworth, Storekeeper, Woolwich yard.

4. Cf. PRO, Adm. 20/3, p. 311; ib., 20/4, p. 412 (warrants dated 29 September 1662, 25 December 1663; £87 10s. salary, plus £15 for clerks, for each quarter).

22. To the office, where Sir W. Batten and Sir J. Mennes are come from Portsmouth; we sat till dinner time. Then home and Mr. Dixon by agreement came to dine with me, to give me an account of his successe with Mr. Wheately for his daughter for my brother; and in short, it is that his daughter cannot fancy my brother because of his imperfection in his speech – which I am sorry for, but there that business must die and we must look out for another.

There came in also Mrs. Lodum, with an answer about her brother Ashwells daughter who is likely to come to me, and with her my wife's brother; and I carried Comissioner Pett in with me, so I feared want of victuals, but I had a good dinner and mirth; and so rise and broke up, and I with the rest of the officers to Mr. Russells buriall – where we had wine and rings, and a great good company of Aldermen and the livery of the Skinners Company.[1] We went to St. Dunstans-in-the-East church, where a sermon,[2] but I stayed not but went home; and after writing letters, I took coach and to Mr. Povys; but he not within, I left a letter there of Tanger business and so to my Lord's. And there find him not sick, but expecting his fit tonight of an ague. Here was Sir W. Compton – Mr. Povy, Mr. Bland, Mr. Gawden and myself; we were very busy about getting provisions sent forthwith to Tanger, fearing that by Mr. Gaudens neglect they might want bread. So among other ways thought of to supply them, I was impowered by the three Comissioners of Tanger that were present to write to Plimouth and direct Mr. Lanyon to take up vessels great or small, more or less to the Quantity of 150 tons, and fill them with bread of Mr. Gaudens lying ready there for Tanger – which they undertake to bear me out in and to see the freight paid. This I did. About 10 a-clock we broke up, and my Lord's Fitt was coming upon him and so we parted, and I with Mr. Creed, Dr Pierce, W. Howe and Captain Ferrer (who was got almost drunk this afternoon, and

1. Robert Russell, sen., ship's-chandler to the navy, was a livery-man of the Skinners' Company, a common councilman and deputy of Tower Ward, and for at least 30 years a parishioner of St Dunstan-in-the-East. (R).

2. His will asked that his funeral sermon be preached by his 'dear friend' Rev. George Gifford or, failing him, Dr Daniel Milles. (R).

was mighty capricious and ready to fall out with everybody)
supped together in the little chamber that was mine heretofore,
upon some fowles*a* sent by Mr. Sheply;[1] so we were very merry
till 12 at night and so away; and I lay with Mr. Creede at his
lodgings and sleep well.

23. Up, and hastened him in despatching some business
relating to Tanger; and I away homewards, hearing that my
Lord had a bad fit tonight. Called at my brother's and find him
sick in bed of a pain in the sole of one of his feet, without swelling; knowing not how it came, but it will not suffer him to stand
these two days. So to Mr. Moore; and Mr. Loven[2] our proctor
being there, discoursed of my law business. Thence to Mr. Grant
to bid him come for money for Mr. Barlow,[3] and he and I to a
Coffee-house where Sir J. Cutler was; and in discourse, among
other things, he did fully make it out that the trade* of England is
as great as ever it was, only in more hands; and that of all trades
there is a greater number then ever there was, by reason of men's*b*
taking more prentices, because of their having more money then
heretofore.[4] His discourse was well worth hearing.

Coming by Temple-bar, I bought Audlys *Way to be rich*, a
serious pamphlett and some good things worth my minding.[5]
Thence homeward; and meeting Sir W. Batten, turned back
again to a Coffee-house and there drunk more, till I was almost
sick.[6] And here much discourse, but little to be learned – but of
a design in the North of a riseing which is discovered among some

a l.h. repl. l.h. 'fowle'   *b* repl. ? 'means'

1. Steward at Hinchingbrooke.
2. *Recte* Lovell: cf. below, p. 33.
3. Pepys's predecessor as Clerk of
the Acts, to whom Pepys paid a life-
annuity of £100. John Graunt's
friend William Petty normally acted
as his agent.
4. Graunt had recently noted in his
Natural and political observations (1662,
pp. 42+) that population was increasing (despite the common view
to the contrary), and that the increase
was particularly great in the towns.
5. *The way to be rich, according to*

the practice of the great Audley, who
begun with two hundred pound, in the
year 1605 and dyed worth four hundred
thousand pound ... November 1662
(1662); not in the PL. It includes a
collection of Audley's sayings: e.g.
'they cannot thrive, who take no care
of their little Expences'; 'they cannot
thrive who have not an exact Account
of their Expences and Incoms'. For
Hugh Audley, see above, iii. 264, n. 2.
6. Cf. Audley's warning (op. cit.,
p. 26): 'Drink not the third glass'.

men of condition, and they sent for up.[1] Thence to the Change, and so home with him by coach and I to see how my wife doth, who is pretty well again, and so to dinner to Sir W. Batten to a codd's head; and so to my office and after stepping to see Sir W. Penn, where was Sir J. Lawson and his lady and daughter (which is pretty enough), I came back to my office and there set to business pretty late – finishing the Margenting my Navy= manuscript;[2] so home and to bed.

24. Lay pretty long; and by lying with my sheet upon my lip, as I have of old observed it, my upper lip was blistered in the morning. To the office all the morning. Sat till noon. Then to the Exchange to look out for a ship for Tanger, and delivered my manuscript to be bound at the Stacioner's. So to dinner at home, and then down to Redriffe to see a ship hired for Tanger what readiness she was in, and find her ready to sail. Then home, and so by coach to Mr. Povys, where Sir W. Compton, Mr. Bland, Gawden, Sir J. Lawson and myself met to settle the victualling of Tanger for the time past (which with much ado we did) and for a six month supply more.[3]

So home in Mr. Gawden's coach, and to my office till late about business; and find that it is business that must and doth every day bring me to something. So home to supper and to bed.

25. *Lords day.* Lay till 9 a-bed; then up, and being trimmed by the barber, I walked toward White-hall, calling upon Mr. Moore, whom I find still very ill of his ague. I discoursed with him about my Lord's estate against I spoke with my Lord this day. Thence to the King's-head ordinary at Charing-crosse and sent for Mr. Creed, where we dined very finely – and good

1. A group of alleged conspirators had just been arrested in Yorkshire, among them Luke Robinson (who had sat for several Yorkshire constituencies since 1640), two members of the Lascelles family, Capt. Matthew Beckwith, Richard Cholmeley and Thomas Dickenson, Alderman of York: *CSPD 1663–4*, pp. 16, 18.

2. See above, p. 11, n. 1.

3. This was a meeting of the Tangier committee, of which Thomas Povey was Treasurer. 3500 men were to be supplied at 8*d.* per day; victuals for six months would cost c. £19,660, and transportation c. £8500. Estimates etc. in BL, Sloane 1956, f. 75*v*.

company, good discourse. I understand the King of France is
upon consulting his devines upon the old Question, what the power
of the Pope is; and doth intend to make war against him unless
he do right him for the wrong his Embassador received[1] and
banish the Cardinall Imperiall, which I understand this day is not
meant the Cardinall belonging or chosen by the Emperor, but the
name of his family is Imperiali.[2]

Thence to walk in the park, which we did two hours, talking;
it being a pleasant sunshine day though cold. Our discourse
upon the rise of most men that we know, and observing them to
be the results of chance, not policy, in any of them – perticularly
Sir J. Lawsons, from his declaring against Ch. Stuart in the river
of Thames and for the Rump.[3]

Thence to my Lord, who had his ague fit last night but now is
pretty well; and I stayed talking with him an hour alone in his
chamber about sundry public and private matters. Among
others, he wonders what the project should be of the Dukes going
down to Portsmouth just now with his Lady, at this time of the
year – it being no way, we think, to encrease his popularity, which
is not great; nor yet safe to do it for that reason, if it would have

1. An affray in Rome between the
Duc de Créqui (French Ambassador)
and the Pope's Corsican guards had
occurred on 10/20 August 1662. Louis
XIV used the incident to provoke a
quarrel. He broke off diplomatic
relations, made extravagant demands,
seized Avignon and threatened to
march into Italy. On 27 October/6
November at an extraordinary council he had made known the views of
some of his clergy, who maintained
that the Pope's powers should be
limited by the cardinalate, and that
Louis had, like Charlemagne, a pre-
eminent authority in the church.
Grimaldi, Archbishop of Aix, was the
foremost exponent of this Gallican
view. The dispute was settled in
February 1664 by the abject surrender
of the Pope, who sent a legate to
Paris to apologise, and erected a
monument in Rome which recorded
his humiliation. C. Gérin, *Louis
XIV et le Saint-Siège*, i. 283+ (esp.
p. 371); L. Pastor, *Hist. Popes* (trans.),
xxxi. 91+. Cf. above, iii. 253, n. 3.

2. Lorenzo Imperiale (Imperiali),
Cardinal-Governor of Rome since
1654, had been transferred to the
legateship of the Marches as a result of
the quarrel with France. But the
consistory refused to accede to Louis'
wishes and banish him. In consequence, de Créqui sailed for France on
14/24 December 1662. Imperiale
came of a distinguished Genoese
family: Louis extorted from Genoa
a decree exiling both him and his
household.

3. On 13 December 1659. For his
recent reputation, see above, p. 4 &
n. 1.

any such effect.[1] By and by comes in my Lady Wright, and so I went away; and after talking with Captain Ferrers, who tells me of my Lady Castlemaynes and Sir Ch. Barkelys being the great favourites at Court and growing every day more and more. And that upon a late dispute between my Lord Chesterfield, that is the Queens Lord chamberlain, and Mr. Edwd. Mountagu, her Maister of the Horse, who should have the precedence in taking the Queens upper hand abroad out of the house, which Mr. Mountagu challenges, it was given to my Lord Chesterfield – so that I perceive he goes down the wind, in honour as well as everything else, every day. So walk to my brother's and talked with him; who tells me that this day a messenger is come that tells us how Collonell Honiwood,[2] who was well yesterday at Canterbury, was flung by his horse in getting up, and broke his skull and so is dead. So home and to the office despatching some business; and so home to supper, and then to prayers and to bed.

26. Up, and by water with Sir W. Batten to White-hall (drinking a glass of wormewood-wine at the Stillyard); and so up to the Duke and with the rest of the officers did our common service.[3] Thence to my Lord Sandwiches, but he was in bed and had a bad fit last night; and so I went to Westminster-hall, it being terme-time, it troubling me to think that I should have any business there to trouble myself and thoughts with. Here I met with Monsieur Raby, who is lately come from France; tells me that my Lord Hinchingbrooke and his brother do little improve there, and are much neglected in their habitt and other things;[4] but I do believe he hath a mind to go over as their Tutour and so

---

1. The Duke of York (feared by many as a militarist) was Governor of Portsmouth, 1661–73 (Sir Charles Berkeley, jun., being his deputy). It is possible that this projected visit was connected with the repairs then being made to the fort: *CSPD 1663–4*, p. 30. Whether he went is uncertain: he was at Whitehall on 26 January and on 2 February: see below. For his unpopularity at this time, see,

e.g., *CSPD 1660–1*, p. 471; cf. above, ii. 95 & n. 1.

2. Henry Honywood of West Hawkes, Kingsworth, Kent; brother of Peter Honywood who lodged at Tom Pepys's house in Salisbury Court.

3. I.e. the regular Monday morning meeting with the Duke.

4. For their European tour, see above, ii. 142 & n. 2.

I am not apt to believe what[a] he says therein. But I had a great deal of very good discourse with him concerning the difference between the French and the Pope, and the occasion, which he told me very perticularly and to my great content – and of most of the chief affairs of France which I did enquire. And that the King is a most excellent Prince, doing all business himself; and that it is true he hath a Mistresse, Madamoiselle La Valiere,[1] one of the Princesse Henriette's women, that he courts for his pleasure every other day, but not so as to make him neglect his public affairs. He tells me how the King doth carry himself nobly to the relations of the dead Cardinall and will not suffer one pasquill to come forth against him. And that he acts by what directions he received from him before his death.[2]

Having discoursed long with him, I took him by coach and set him down at my Lord Crews and myself went and dined at Mr. Povys, where Orlando Massam, Mr Wilkes a wardrobe man, myself and Mr. Gawden, and had just such another dinner as I had the other day there.

But above all things, I do the most admire his piece of perspective especially, he opening me the closet door and there I saw that there is nothing but only a plain picture hung upon the wall.[3]

After dinner Mr. Gawden and I to settle the business of the Tanger=victualling, which I perceive none of them yet have hitherto understood but myself.

Thence by coach to White-hall and met upon the Tanger Commission, our greatest business the discoursing of getting things ready for my Lord Rutherford[4] to go about the middle of March next – and a proposal of Sir J. Lawson's and Mr. Cholmely's

a   repl. 'them'

---

1. Françoise Louise de la Vallière, in 1667 cr. Duchesse de la Vallière (d. 1710); the King's mistress for about ten years from 1661.

2. Cardinal Mazarin had died on 27 February/9 March 1661. He left no *testament politique*, but in his last few weeks gave advice to Louis XIV, which the young King dictated to a secretary, and which is printed in *Lettres, instructions et mémoires de* *Colbert* (ed. P. Clément), i. 535. See also A. Chéruel, *Hist. de France sous Mazarin*, iii. 395+. Many pasquils (i.e. lampoons later known as *mazarinades*) had been issued against him during his lifetime. See below, p. 412 & n. 1.

3. See above, p. 18 & n. 1. (OM).

4. Governor, 1663–4.

concerning undertaking the molle, which is referred to another time.

So by coach home, being melancholy, overcharged with business, and methinks I fear that I have some ill offices done to Mr. Coventry, or else he observes that of late I have not des-patch[ed] business so as I did use to do, which I confess I do acknowledge. But it may be it is but my*a* fears; only he is not so fond as he used to be of me. But I do believe that Sir W. Batten hath made him believe that I do too much crow upon having his kindness, and so he may, on purpose to countenance him, seem a little more strange to me. But I will study hard to bring him back again to the same degree of kindness.

So home; and after a little talk with my wife, to the office and did a great deal of business there till very late; and then home to supper and to bed.

27. Up and to the office, where sat till 2 a-clock; and then home to dinner, whither by and by comes in Creede and he and I talked of our Tanger business and do find that there is nothing in the world done with true integrity but there is design along with it; as in my Lord Rutherford, who designs to have the profit of victualling of the garrison*b* himself, and others to have the benefit of making the molle. So that I am almost discouraged from coming any more to the Committee, were it not that it will possibly hereafter bring me to some acquaintance of the great men. Then to the office again, where very busy till past 10 at night; and so home to supper and bed.

I have news this day from Cambridge that my brother hath had his Bachelors cap put on.[1] But that which troubles me is that he hath the pain of the stone and makes bloody water with great pain, it beginning just as mine did. I pray God help him.

28. Up, and all the morning at my office doing business – and at home seeing my painters' work measured.[2] So to dinner

a l.h. repl. s.h. 'his'   *b* l.h. repl. s.h. 'sea'-

---

1. Bachelors' degrees were nor-mally conferred at General Admission in January.
2. Measurements for the outside paintwork of the building are given in

PRO, Adm. 20/5, p. 363 (February 1663). Three coats of oil paint were given to 168 yards of pales and posts, and 181 'lights'.

and abroad with my wife, carrying her to Unthankes, where she lights and I to my Lord Sandwichs, whom I find missing his ague fit today and is pretty well, playing at dice (and by this I see how time and example may alter a man; he being now acquainted with all sorts of pleasures and vanities which heretofore he never thought of nor loved, or it may be, hath allowed) with Ned Pickering and his page Loud. Thence to the Temple to my Cosen Roger Pepys, and thence to Serjeant Bernard to advise with him and retain him against my uncle – my heart and head being very heavy with the business. Thence to Wottons the shoemaker and there bought another pair of new boots for the other I bought my last journey, that would not fit me.[1] And here I drank with him and his wife, a pretty woman, they broaching a vessel of Cyder a-purpose for me. So home, and there find my wife come home and seeming to cry; for bringing home in a coach her new Ferrandin waistcoat, in Cheapside a man asked her whether that was the way to the tower, and while she was answering him, another on the other side snatched away her bundle out of her lap, and could not be recovered – but ran away with it – which vexes me cruelly, but it cannot be helped.

So to my office and there till almost 12 at night with Mr. Lewes, learning to understand the manner of a pursers account[2] – which is very hard and little understood by my fellow-officers, and yet mighty necessary.[a] So at last with great content broke up, and home to supper and bed.

29. Lay chiding and then pleased with my wife in bed, and did consent to her having a new waistcoat made her for that which she lost yesterday. So to the office and sat all the morning. At noon dined with Mr. Coventry at Sir J. Mennes his lodgings, the first time that ever I did yet; and am sorry for doing it now, because of obliging me to do the like to him again. Here dined old Captain Marsh of the Tower with us. So to visit Sir W. Penn; and then to the office and there late upon business by myself, my Will being sick today. So home and to supper and to bed.

a repl. 'nothing'

1. See above, iii. 217.   2. See above, iii. 181 & n. 1.

30. *A solemne Fast for the King's murther.*[1] And we were forced to keep it more then we would have done, having forgot to take any victuals into the house.

I to church in the forenoon, and Mr. Mills made a good sermon upon David's heart smiting him for cutting off the garment of Saule.[2]

Home and whiled away some of the afternoon at home, talking with my wife. So to my office, and all alone making up my month's accounts; which to my great trouble I find that I am got no further then 640*l* – but I have had great expenses this month. I pray God the next may be a little better, as I hope it will. In the evening my manuscript[3] is brought home, handsomely bound to my full content; and now I think I have a better collection in reference to the Navy, and shall have by the time I have filled it, then any of my predecessors. So home to eat something, such as we have, bread and butter and milk; and so to bed.

31. Up and to my office, and there we sat till noon. I home to dinner and there find my plat of the *Soverayne*, with the Table to it,[4] come from Mr. Chr. Pett, of which I am very glad. So to dinner, late and not very good; only a rabbit not half-roasted, which made me angry with my wife. So to my office and there till late, busy all the while. In the evening examining my wife's letter entended to my Lady and another to Madamoiselle;[5] they were so false-spelt that I was ashamed of them and took occasion to fall out about them with my wife, and so she writ none; at which, however, I was sorry, because it was in answer to a letter of Madamoiselle – about business. Late home to supper and to bed.

1. For the fast, see above, ii. 26, n. 1.
2. I Sam., xxiv. 5.
3. See above, p. 11 & n. 1.
4. There were several drawings of the *Royal Sovereign*, the largest ship in the navy. The best-known was that by John Payne: *The true portraicture of his Majesties royall ship The Soveraigne of the Seas built in the yeare 1637; Capt. Phineas Pett being superuisor and Peter Pett his sonne Mr Builder* (1637); see Sir G. Callender, *Portrait of Peter Pett*, pl. iv. Pepys now hung the print in his Green Chamber: below, p. 43. He preserved a copy of Payne's drawing in his library (PL 2972, pp. 271–2). No 'table' (key) has been traced there or elsewhere. Presumably it was a MS.
5. Mlle Le Blanc, governess to Sandwich's daughters.

FEBRUARY.

1. *Lords day.* Up and to church, where Mr. Mills; a good sermon. And so home and had a good dinner with my wife, with which I was pleased to see it neatly done; and this troubled me, to think of parting with Jane, that is come to be a very good Cooke. After dinner walked to my Lord Sandwich and stayed with him in the chamber talking almost all the afternoon, he being not yet got abroad since his sickness. Many discourses we had; but among others, how Sir R. Bernard is turned out of his Recordership of Huntington by the Comissioners for Regulacion, &c.,[1] at which I am troubled because he thinking it is done by my Lord Sandwich, will act some of his revenge, it is likely, upon me in my business – so that I must cast about me to get some other good counsel to rely upon.

In the evening came Mr. Povey and others to see my Lord; and they gone, my Lord and I and Povey fell to the business of Tanger – as to the victualling, and so broke up; and I, it being a fine frost, my boy lighting me I walked home. And after supper, up to prayers and then alone with my wife and Jane did fall to tell her what I did expect would become of her, since after so long being my servant she hath carried herself so as to make us be willing to put her away; and desired God to bless, but bid her never to let me hear of her what became of her, for that I could never pardon ingratitude. So to bed – my mind much troubled for the poor girl that she leaves us; and yet she not submitting herself for some words she spoke boldly and yet I believe innocently and out of familiarity to her mistress about six weeks ago, I could not recall my words that she should not stay with me./ ⟨This day Creed and I, walking in White-hall garden, did see the King coming privately from my Lady Castlemayns; which is a poor thing for a Prince to do. And I expressed my sense of

---

1. Local commissioners for the regulation of municipalities had been appointed under the Corporation Act passed in December 1661, and were armed with extensive powers of dismissal. Sandwich was one of those appointed for Huntingdon, and he himself was appointed Recorder in Bernard's place: below, p. 62.

it to Creed in termes which I should not have done, but that I
believe he is trusty in that point.⟩*a*

2.   Up; and after paying Jane her wages, I went away because
I could hardly forbear weeping; and she cried, saying it was not
her fault that she went away.   And endeed, it is hard to say what
it is but only her not desiring to stay, that she doth now go.[1]

By coach with Sir J. Mennes and Sir W. Batten to the Duke;
and after discourse as usual with him in his closet, I went to my
Lord's – the King and Duke being gone to chapel, it being
Coller-day, it being Cand[l]emas-day – where I stayed with him
a while till toward noon, there being Jonas Moore talking about
some Mathematical businesses; and thence I walked at noon to
Mr. Povey's, where Mr. Gauden met me.   And after a neat and
plentiful dinner, as is usual, we fell to our victualling business till
Mr. Gawden and I did almost fall out, he defending himself in
the readiness of his provision when I know that the ships everywhere stay for them.

Thence Mr. Povey and I walked to White-hall, it being a
great frost still; and after a turn in the parke, seeing them slide –
we met at the Comittee for Tanger, a good full Comittee, and
agreed how to proceed in the dispaching my Lord Rutherford
and treating about this business of Mr. Cholmely and Sir J.
Lawson's proposal for the Molle.

Thence with Mr. Coventry down to his chamber; where
among other discourse, he did tell me how he did make it not
only his desire but as his greatest policy to make himself an interest
by doing business truly and justly, though he thwarts others
greater then*b* himself, not striving to make himself friends by
addresses.   And by this he thinks and observes he doth live as
contentedly (now he finds himself secured from fear of want)
and, take one time with another, as void of fear or cares, or more,
then they that (as his own termes were) have "quicker pleasures
and sharper agonys" then he.

Thence walking with Mr. Creed homewards, we turned into a

a   addition crowded in between entries   *b*   MS. 'them'

1. See above, p. 8 & n. 1.

house and drank a cup of Cocke ale and so parted; and I to the
Temple, where at my Cosen Rog. chamber I met Madam
Turner; and after a little stay led her home and there left her, she
and her daughter having been at the play today at the Temple,
it being a Revelling time with them.[1]

Thence called at my brother's, who is at church at the buriall
of young Cumberland[2] – a lusty young man.

So home[a] and there find Jane gone, for which my wife and I
are very much troubled and myself could hardly forbear shedding
tears – for fear the poor wench should come to any ill condition
after her being so long with me.

So to my office and setting papers to rights, and then home to
supper and to bed. This day at my Lord's I sent for Mr Ashwell,
and his wife came to me; and by discourse I perceive their
daughter is very fit for my turn if my family may be as much for
hers, but I doubt it will be to her loss to come to me for so small
wages, but that will be considered on.

3.   To the office all the morning; at noon to dinner, where
Mr. Creede dined with me – and Mr. Ashwell, with whom after
dinner I discoursed concerning his daughter coming to live with
us. I find that his daughter will be very fit, I think as any for
our turn. But the conditions, I know not what they will be,
he leaving it wholly to her, which will be agreed on a while
hence when my wife sees her. After an hour's discourse after
dinner with them, I to my office again and there about businesses
of the office till late; and then I home to supper and to bed.

a l.h. repl. s.h. 'to'

1. Private performances were given by the King's Company and the Duke of York's Company at the Inner Temple on festive occasions. The play was Samuel Tuke's *The adventures of five hours*, performed by the Duke of York's company: see above, p. 8 & n. 2; W. J. Lawrence in *RES*, 9/221. (A).

2. Henry Cumberland, 'Tayler in Salisbury Court', buried at St Bride's this day: GL, MS. 6540/1, St Bride's Reg., 1653-73.

4. Up earely and to Mr. Moore, and thence to Mr. Lovell about my law businesses, and from him to Pauls schoole, it being opposicion-day there.[1] I heard some of their speeches, and they were just as schoolboys used to be, of the seven Liberall Sciences;[2] but I think not so good as ours were in our time.   Away thence and to Bow church to the Court of Arches;[3] where a judge sits and his proctors about him in their habitts, and their pleadings all in Latin.   Here I was sworn to give a true answer to my uncles Libells.*   And so paid my fee for swearing and back again to Paul's schoole and went up to see the head forms posed in Latin, Greek and Hebrew,[4] but I think they do not answer in any so well as we did; only in Geography they did pretty well.   Dr. Wilkins and Outram[5] were examiners.   So down to the school, where Mr. Crumlum did me much honour by telling many what a present I had made to the school, showing my *Stephanus* in four volumes, cost me 4*l*. 10*s*.[6] He also showed us, upon my desire, an old edicion of the grammer of Coletts – where his epistle to the children is very pretty.   And in rehearsing the Creed it is said

1. Apposition Day had been held every Candlemas since at least 1567 or 1568. Declamations were made in the learned tongues, and every form was examined by visiting scholars appointed by the Mercers' Company, trustees of the school. The High Master's annual re-appointment was still theoretically dependent on the success of the occasion. The name 'Opposition' or 'Apposition' (the latter still surviving as the title of the school's summer Speech-day) derives from the work of the examiners, who posed ('apposed') questions to the pupils.

2. The *trivium* (grammar, logic, rhetoric) and the *quadrivium* (arithmetic, geometry, music and astronomy – including geography); the traditional curriculum of medieval and early modern grammar schools and universities.

3. The archbishop's court dealing,

inter alia, with testamentary disputes like this between Pepys and his uncle Thomas Pepys. For the case, see above, iii. 275 & n. 3.

4. For the teaching of Hebrew in schools, see Foster Watson, *Engl. grammar schools to 1660*, ch. xxxii, esp. p. 529; W. A. L. Vincent, *The state and school education, 1640–60*, pp. 17–19.   It had been taught at St Paul's in Pepys's time by John Langley. Pepys never uses it in the 'secret' passages of the diary, but he retained several Hebrew books in his library. The Posing Chamber, where this examination took place, was in the High Master's house.

5. John Wilkins (mathematician, one of the founders of the Royal Society, later Bishop of Chester), and William Owtram (rabbinical scholar). Both held city livings.

6. See above, ii. 239 & n. 3.

"borne of the cleane virgin Mary."[1] Thence with Mr. Elborough[2] (he being all of my old acquaintance that I could meet with here) to a Cookes shop to dinner, but I find him a fool as he ever was, or worse. Thence to my Cosen Roger Pepys and Mr. Phillips about my law businesses, which stand very bad. And so home to the office; where after doing some business, I went home, where I find our new mayd Mary, that is come in Janes place.[3]

5. Up and to the office, where we sat all the morning; and then home to dinner – and find it so well done, above what I did expect from my maid Susan now Jane is gone, that I did call her in and give her six-pence. Thence walked to the Temple and there at my Cosen Roger Pepys's chamber met by appointment with my uncle Tho and his son Tho; and there, I showing them a true state of my uncles estate[4] as he hath left it with the debts &c. left upon it, we did come to some quiet talk and fair offers toward an agreement on both sides – though I do offer quite to the losing of the profit of the whole estate for eight or ten years together; yet if we can gain peace and set my mind at a little liberty, I shall be glad of it. I did give them a copy of this state, and we are to meet tomorrow with their answer.

So walk home, it being a very great frost still, and to my office; there late writing letters of office business, and so home to supper and to bed.

6. Up and to my office about business, examining people what they could swear against Field; and the whole is, that he hath called us cheating rogues and cheating knaves – for which we hope to be even with him.[5]

Thence to Lincolns Inn fields; and it being too soon to go to dinner, I walked up and down and looked upon the outside of the new Theatre now a-building in Covent garden, which will be

1. John Colet's edition of William Lily's *Epigramma* (1534), p. ii (The Creed, art. 3). Pepys's spelling is slightly inaccurate. Cromleholme gave Pepys a copy of the book on 9 March 1665: probably PL 424 (1). Lily had been the first High Master of St Paul's (1512–22); Dean Colet the founder. This grammar was much

used both at St Paul's and elsewhere: cf. C. G. Allen in *The Library* (ser. 5), 9/85+, 14/49+.

2. Robert Elborough, in 1664 priest-in-charge, St Laurence Pountney, London.

3. She stayed until 27 April.
4. See above, iii. 275, n. 3.
5. See above, iii. 23 & n. 2.

very fine;[1] and so to a bookseller's in the Strand and there bought *Hudibras* again, it being certainly some ill humour to be so set against that which all the world cries up to be the example of wit[2] – for which I am resolved once again to read him and see whether I can find it or no.   So to Mr. Povys and there find them at dinner and dined there – there being, among others, Mr Williamson, Latin Secretary, who I perceive is a pretty knowing man and a scholar, but it may be thinks himself to be too much so.[3]   Thence after dinner to the Temple to my Cosen Roger Pepys, where met us my uncle Tho. and his son; and after many high demands, we at last came to a kind of agreement upon very hard terms, which are to be prepared in writing against Tuesday next.   But by the way, promising them to pay my Cosen Marys Legacys at the time of her Marriage, they afterward told me she was already married, and married very well, so that I must be forced to pay that in some time.[4]

My Cosen Roger was so sensible of our coming to agreement that he could not forbear weeping; and endeed, though it be very hard, yet I am glad to my heart that we are like to end our trouble.   So we parted for tonight.

And I to my Lord Sandwich and there stayed, there being a Comittee to sit upon the Contract for the Molle, which I dare say none of us that were there understood; but yet they agreed of

---

1. The Theatre Royal, which was being built for Thomas Killigrew between Drury Lane and Bridges St, and which was burnt down in 1672. (A).

2. The first part of Butler's poem had appeared in 1662; for Pepys's dislike of it, see above, iii. 294. Made popular by its wit and its satire against Puritans, it went through several editions in 1663. The second part came out in November 1663 (see below, p. 400 & n. 1); the third in 1678. Pepys later bought all three parts: PL 889 (1689 ed.). Clarendon had a portrait of Hudibras, and the King carried a copy in his

pocket: Evelyn, *Diary and corr.*, ed. Wheatley, iii. 444; *Poet. works S. Butler*, ed. Johnson, vol. i, p. xiii.

3. Joseph Williamson, an ex-Fellow of Queen's, Oxford, was Secretary Bennet's principal secretary, Keeper of the King's Library, and Latin Secretary, responsible for drafting certain diplomatic correspondence. His learning lay chiefly in history and genealogy. Evelyn (22 July 1674) also criticised his manner.

4. Mary, daughter of Thomas Pepys of London, and the diarist's first cousin, had married Samuel de Santhune, a weaver, in 1662.

things as Mr Cholmly and Sir J Lawson demanded,*a* who are
the undertakers;[1] and so I left them to go on to agree, for I
understood it not.

So home; and being called by a coachman who had a fare in
him, he carried me beyond the Old Exchange and there set down
his fare, who would not pay him what was his due because he
carried a stranger with him; and so after wrangling, he was
fain to be content with 6*d*.; and being vexed, the coachman
would not carry me home a great while, but set me down there
for the other 6*d*. But with fair words he was willing to it;
and so I came home and to my office, setting business in order;
and so home to supper and to bed – my mind being in disorder
as to the greatness of this day's business that I have done, but yet
glad that my trouble therein is like to be over.

7. Up and to my office, whither by agreement Mr. Coventry
came before the time of setting to confer about preparing an
account of the extraordinary charge[2] of the Navy since the
King's coming, more then is properly to be applied and called the
Navy=charge.

So by and by we sat, and so till noon. Then home to dinner;
and in the afternoon some of us met again upon something
relating to the Victualling; and thence to my writing of letters
late, and making my Alphabet to my new Navy=booke,[3] very
pretty. And so after writing to my father by the post about the
endeavour to come to a composition with my uncle, though a
very bad one, desiring him to be contented therewith – I went
home to supper and bed.

8. *Lords day.* Up; and it being a very great frost, I walked
to White-hall and to my Lord Sandwiches; by the fireside till
chapel time and so to chapel, where there preached little Dr.

a repl. 'offered'

1. See below, p. 88 & n. 3.
Pepys later learned that the contractors had given £1500 to Sandwich to gain his support: below,
viii. 592–3.
2. E.g. charges for garrisons, and

freightage payable by merchants,
which the Navy Board accounted for
but which were not strictly naval
expenses: NMM, LBK/8, p. 41.
See below, p. 49.
3. See above, p. 11, n. 1.

Duport of Cambrige upon Josiahs words, "But I and my house, we will serve the Lord."[1]   But though a great scholar, he made the most flat, dead sermon, both for matter and manner of delivery, that ever I heard; and very long beyond his hour, which made it worse.[2]

Thence with Mr. Creede to the King's-head ordinary, where we dined well; and after dinner Sir Tho. Willis[3] and another stranger and Creede and I fell a-talking – they of the errours and corruptions of the Navy* and great expense thereof, not knowing who I was – which at last I did undertake to confute and disabuse them; and they took it very well and I hope it was to good purpose, they being Parliament-men.   By and by to my Lord's and with him a good while, talking upon his want of money and ways of his borrowing some, &c.   And then by other visitants, I withdrew and away; Creede and I and Captain Ferrers to the parke – and there walked finely, seeing people slide – we talking all the while and Captain Ferrers telling me, among other Court passages – how about a month ago, at a Ball at[a] Court, a child was dropped by one of the ladies in dancing; but nobody knew who, it being taken up by somebody in their handkercher.   The next morning all the Ladies of Honour appeared early at Court for their vindication, so that nobody could tell whose this mischance should be.   But it seems Mrs. Wells fell sick that afternoon and hath disappeared ever since, so that it is concluded it was her.[4]   Another story was how my Lady Castlemayne, a few days since, had Mrs. Stuart to an entertainment, and at night begun a frolique that they two must be married; and married they were, with ring and all other ceremonies of church service, and

a repl. 'before'

---

1. Dr James Duport, chaplain to the King, was Fellow and Vice-Master of Trinity, Cambridge; lately Regius Professor of Greek; Master of Magdalene from 1668 to 1679. He often made jokes about his small stature: R. North, *Life of . . . John North* (1744), p. 255. Pepys makes a mistake about the text; the words were Joshua's (Josh., xxiv. 5).

2. Cf. Evelyn (15 September 1672): 'no greate preacher, but a very worthy & learned man.'

3. M.P. for Cambridgeshire, 1659, and for Cambridge borough, 1660.

4. Winifred Wells was a Maid of Honour to the Queen.   The King was said to have been the father: Gramont, p. 369. For this story, see below, p. 48 & n. 3.

ribbands and a sack-posset in bed and flinging the stocking.*a*1   But in the close, it is said that my Lady Castlemayne, who was the bridegroom, rose, and the King came and took her place with pretty Mrs. Stuart.   This is said to be very true.

Another story was how Captain Ferrers and W. Howe both have often seen through my Lady Castlemayne's windows, seen her go to bed and Sir Ch. Barkely in the chamber all the while with her.   But the other day, Captain Ferrers going to Sir Charles to excuse his not being so timely at his armes the other day, Sir Charles, swearing and cursing, told him before a great many other gentlemen that he would not suffer any man of the King's guards to be absent from his lodging a night without leave; "not but that," says he, "once a week or so, I know a gentleman must go to his whore, and I am not for denying it to any man; but however, he shall be bound to ask leave to lie abroad and to give account of his absence, that we may know what guard the King hath to depend upon."

The little Duke of Monmouth, it seems, is ordered to take place of all Dukes, and so doth fallow Prince Robert now, before the Duke of Buckingham or any else.²

Whether the wind and the cold did cause it or no, I know not; but having been this day or two mightily troubled with an iching all over my body, which I took to be a louse or two that might bite me – I find this afternoon that all my body is inflamed and my face in a sad redness and swelling and pimpled; so that I was, before we had done walking, not only sick but ashamed of myself to see myself so changed in my countenance; so that after we had thus talked, we parted and I walked home with much ado (Captain Ferrars with me as far as Ludgate-hill, toward Mr.

a l.h. repl. l.h. 'gart'-

---

1. Frances Stuart (aged about 19) had been appointed Maid of Honour to the Queen at about this time.   The King was for long infatuated with her, but she seems to have resisted his advances.   Lady Castlemaine was for a while her intimate friend and is said to have encouraged the King's interest in her in order to distract his attention from her intrigue with Jermyn: Gramont, pp. 110–11. Gramont tells of Frances Stuart's 'taste for infantile diversions' (p. 137) such as the one Pepys here describes. She eloped with the Duke of Richmond in 1667.

2. See the similar report (10 November 1662) in HMC, *Rep.*, 7/1/463.

Moore at the Wardrobe), the ways being so full of ice and water by people's trampling. At last got home and to bed presently and had a very bad night of it, in great pain in my stomach and great fever.

9. Could not rise and go to the Duke, as I should have done with the rest, but keep my bed; and by the apothecary's advice, Mr. Battersby, I am to sweat soundly and that will carry all this matter away; which nature would of itself eject, but this will assist nature – it being some disorder given the blood; but by what I know not, unless it be by my late great Quantitys of Dantzicke=girkins that I have eaten.[1]

In the evening came Sir J. Mennes and Sir W. Batten to see me. And Sir J. Mennes advises me to the same thing; but would[a] not have me take anything from the apothecary, but from him, his Venice Treakle being better then the others;[2] which I did consent to and did anon take and fell into a great sweat; and about 10 or 11 a-clock came out of it, and shifted myself and

《10.》 slept pretty well alone (my wife lying in the red chamber above); and in the morning, most of my disease, that is, itching and pimples, was gone. In the morning visited by Mr. Coventry and others, and very glad I am to see that was so much enquired after and my sickness taken notice of as I did. I keep my bed all day and sweat again at night, by which I expect to be very well tomorrow.

This evening Sir W Warren came himself to the door and left a letter and box for me – and went his way. His letter mentions his giving me and my wife a pair of gloves. But opening the box, we find a pair of plain white gloves for my hand and a fair State-dish of Silver and cup with my armes ready-cut

a MS. 'could'

---

1. Dr C. E. Newman writes: 'Pepys was probably suffering from an allergical disorder caused by something he had eaten; possibly the gherkins, as he suggests.'

2. This was a favourite and costly panacea, and every apothecary claimed to make the best. It was used particularly in cases of colic. Mennes also claimed to have a cure for the pox: below, v. 242.

upon them, worth I believe about 18*l* – which is a very noble present and the best I ever had yet.[1]

So after some contentful talk with my wife, she to bed and I to rest.

11. Took a glister in the morning and rise in the afternoon. My wife and I dined on a pullet and I eat heartily – having eat nothing since Sonday but water-gruel and posset-drink. But must needs say that our new maid Mary hath played her part very well, in her readiness and discretion in attending me, of which I am very glad.

In the afternoon several people came to see me – my uncle Thomas, Mr. Creede and*ª* Sir J. Mennes (who hath been, God knows to what end, mighty kind to me and careful of me in my sickness); at night my wife read *Sir H. Vanes trial*[2] to me, which she begun last night, and I find it a very excellent thing, worth reading, and him to have been*ᵇ* a very wise man.

So to supper and to bed.

12. Up, and find myself pretty well; and so to the office and there all the morning. Rise at noon and home to dinner – in my green chamber, having a good fire – whither there came my wife's brother and brought Mary Ashwell with him, whom we find a very likely person to please us both for person, discourse, and other qualities. She dined with us, and after dinner went away again, being agreed to come to us about three weeks or a

a repl. '&'   *b* repl. 'be'

---

1. Warren was soon to conclude contracts with the office: below, pp. 232, 304. The identification of this cup with one which survived in the possession of the Pepys Cockerell family until 1931 (*Country Life*, 4 June 1927, p. 922) is disproved by the 1671 hallmark of the latter: Sotheby's *Catalogue*, 1 April 1931, no. 2. For Pepys's arms, see above, iii. 50, n. 3.

2. *The tryal of Sir Henry Vane, Kt., at the Kings Bench, Westminster, June the 2nd and 6th, 1662, together with what he intended to have spoken the day of his sentence (June 11) for arrest of judgment (had he not been interrupted and over-ruled by the court) and his bill of exceptions. With other occasional speeches etc. also his speech and prayer etc. on the scaffold* (1662); not in the PL.

month hence.[1] My wife and I well pleased with our choice, only I pray God I may be able to maintain it.

Then came an[a] old man from Mr. Povey to give me some advice about his experience in the Stone, which I [am] beholden to him for and was well pleased with it – his chief remedy being Castle Sope[2] in a posset.

Then in the evening to the office late, writing letters and my Journall since Saturday; and so home to supper and to bed.

13. Lay very long with my wife in bed, talking with great pleasure – and then rise. This morning Mr. Cole our Timber merchant[3] sent me five couple of Duckes. Our maid Susan is very ill, and so the whole trouble of the house lies upon our maid Mary; who doth it very contentedly and mightily well, but I am sorry she is forced to it.

Dined upon one couple of ducks today; and after dinner my wife and I by coach to Toms, and I to the Temple to discourse with my cousin Roger Pepys about my law business; and so back again, it being a monstrous thaw after this long great frost, so that there is no passing but by coach in the streets, and hardly that.

Took my wife home, and I to my office; find myself pretty well but fearful of cold; and so to my office, where late upon business – Mr. Bland setting with me, talking of my Lord Windsor's being come home from Jamaica unlooked-for;[4] which makes us think that these young Lords are not fit to do any service abroad, though it is said that he could not have his health there, but hath raced a fort of the King of Spain's upon Cuba, which is considerable, or said to be so, for his honour.[5]

a MS. 'and'

---

1. She served Mrs Pepys from 12 March to 25 August 1663.
2. Castile soap.
3. Christopher Cole(s), a leading timber merchant of Hampshire. He had recently fallen short in the completion of a contract: *CSPD 1663-4*, p. 29.
4. Windsor, Governor of Jamaica, had embarked for England in October 1662 after only ten weeks at his post. His return may have been due not only to illness but also to his financial troubles: *Hatton Corr.* (ed. E. M. Thompson), i. 46. Cf. Pepys's remarks below, pp. 54-5.

5. In October 1662 a force o eleven ships sent by Windsor, commanded by Capt. Christopher Myngs, had raided Santiago de Cuba and rased the fortifications to the ground: *CSPCol.* (*America and W. Indies*) *1661-8*, p. 114; HMC, *Heathcote*, pp. 34-5; *EHR*, 14/536+.

So home to supper and to bed.   This day I bought the second part of Dr. Bates's *Elenchus*, which reaches to the fall of Richard and no further, for which I am sorry.[1] ⟨This evening my wife had a great mind to choose Valentins against tomorrow.   I, Mrs. Clerke or Pierce; she, Mr. Hunt or Captain Ferrers, but I would not because of begetting charge both to me for mine, and to them men for her – which did not please her.⟩[a]

14.   Up and to my office, where we met and sat all the morning (only Mr. Coventry, which I think is the first or second time he hath missed since he came to the office, was forced to be absent); so home to dinner, my wife and I, upon a couple of Duckes and then by coach to the Temple, where my Uncle Thomas[b] and his sons both and I did meet at my Cosen Roger's and did sign and seal to an agreement;[2] wherein I was displeased at nothing but my Cosen Roger's insisting upon my being obliged to settle upon them, as the Will doth, all my uncles estate that he hath left, without power of selling any for payment of debts; but I would not yield to it without leave of selling, my Lord Sandwich himself and my cousin Tho. Pepys being judges of the necessity thereof – which was done.   One thing more that troubles me was my being forced to promise to give half of what personal estate could be found, more then 372*l*, which I reported to them; which though I do not know it to be less then what we really have found, yet he could have been glad to have[c] been at liberty for that;[3] but at last I did agree to it under my own

<hr>

a addition crowded in between entries   *b* repl. '&'   *c* MS. 'be'

1. George Bate, *Elenchi motuum nuperorum in Anglia pars secunda* ... (1663); PL 1056; a royalist history of the rebellion written in Latin for the international market. Pepys had bought the first part on 25 February 1660. The second part, telling the story as far as the fall of Richard Cromwell in the spring of 1659, was published both in London and in Amsterdam in 1663. It was the last part to be written by Bate himself. Pepys also bought the third part (to 1669), later added by Thomas Skinner and published in 1676: PL 538.

2. PL (unoff.), Freshfield MSS, no. 4 (10 February). Thus ended one of the worst of the disputes about the estate of Robert Pepys of Brampton: for details of the agreement, see *Comp.*: s.n.

3. Sc. Uncle Thomas would once have been only too pleased to settle for a half-share of £372 (the amount of personalty declared by the executors at the time of death). Now he wanted also half of any personal estate in excess of that figure.

handwriting on the backside of the report I did make and did give them of the estate, and have taken a copy of it upon the backside of one that I have.[1] All being done, I took the father and his son Tho home by coach and did pay them 30*l*, the arreares of the father's annuity, and with great seeming love parted – and I presently to bed, my head akeing mightily with the hot dispute I did hold with my Cosen Rogr and them in that business.

15. *Lords day.* This morning my wife did wake me, being frighted with the noise I made in my sleep, being a dream that one of our sea-maisters did desire to see the St. John's Isle of my drawing;[2] which methought I showed him, but methought he did handle it so hard that it put me to very horrid pain; and what should this be but my cods, which after I woke were in very great pain for a good while – what a strange extravagant dream it was.*a*

So to sleep again and lay long in bed, and then trimmed by the barber; and so sending Will to church, myself stayed at home, hanging up in my green chamber my picture of the *Soveraigne*[3] and putting some things in order there.

So to dinner to three more Duckes and two Teales, my wife and I. Then to church, where a dull sermon; and so home and after walking about the house a while, discoursing with my wife, I to my office, there to set down something and prepare businesses for tomorrow – having in the morning read over my vowes, which through sickness I could not do the last Lord's day, and not through forgetfulness or negligence; so that I hope it is no breach of my vowe not to pay my forfeiture. So home, and after prayers to bed – talking long with my wife and teaching her things in Astronomy.

16. Up, and by coach with Sir Wm. Batten and Sir J. Mennes to White-hall; and after we had done our usual business with the Duke, to my Lord Sandwich and by his desire to Sir Wm. Wheeler (who was brought down in a sedan-chair from his chamber, being lame of the goute) to borrow 1000*l* of him for

a MS. 'which what it a strange . . .'

---

1. These reports not traced.   3. See above, p. 29 & n. 4.
2. Untraced. (OM).

my Lord's occasions;[1] but he gave me a very kind denial that he
could not, but if anybody else would, he would be bond[a] with
my Lord for it. So to Westminster-hall and there find great
expectation what the parliament will do, when they come two
days hence to sit again, in matters of Religion. The great Question
is whether the presbyters will be contented to have the papists
have the same liberty of conscience with them or no, or rather be
denied it themselfs; and the papists, I hear, are very busy designing
how to make the presbyters consent to take their liberty and to let
them have the same with them, which some are apt to think they
will.[2]

   It seems a priest was taken in his vests officiating somewhere in
Holborne the other day, and was committed by Secretary Morrice
according to law; and they say the Bishopp of London did give
him thanks for it.[3]

   Thence to my Lord Crews and dined there, there being much

a   ? 'bound'

1. Wheler was an old friend and
rich, and had lent money to Sandwich
before: above, i. 46, n. 1.
   2. The King's declaration of 26
December 1662 promised that he
would obtain from Parliament a
measure of liberty for dissenters: see
above, p. 5 & n. 3. Possibly the
Catholics aimed at preventing a
union of Presbyterians and Anglicans,
and at gaining the alliance of the
Protestant dissenters for their own
policy (cf. Burnet, i. 344–5, 349); but,
according to Baxter, the Presbyterians
resisted all proposals of a general
toleration from which Papists would
benefit, willing though some of the
Independent leaders were to accept
it: *Reliq. Baxt.* (1695), bk i, pt ii. 430.
In any case the Presbyterian party in
the Commons appears to have opposed the royal declaration, for only
30 votes were mustered in its favour
when the House divided on the
question later in the month: see

below, p. 58. They could usually
mobilise 40–60 votes: K. Feiling,
Hist. Tory party, 1640–1714, p. 106.
The Independents had almost no
voting strength in parliament.
   3. No trial of any such priest has
been traced, but the records for the
Old Bailey and Guildhall are incomplete for this period. Possibly
this arrest was timed so as to convince
Parliament that the royal policy of
indulgence to Catholics held no
dangers to the establishment. Two
days later, in his speech to the
Houses, the King said, of the Catholics: 'I desire some Laws may be
made, to hinder the Growth and Progress of their Doctrine': *LJ*, xi. 478.
The Bishop of London (Sheldon) and
his colleagues were active at this
moment in using their influence with
members of Parliament against toleration: *CSPD 1663–4*, p. 64. Morice
had been politically associated with
the Presbyterians.

company, and the above-said matter is now the present public discourse.

Thence about several businesses to Mr. Phillips my atturny, to stop all proceedings at law; and so to the Temple, where at the Sollicitor Generalls I find Mr. Cholmely and Creed reading to him the agreement for him to put into form about the contract for*a* the Molle at Tanger – which is done at 13*s* the Cubicall yard, though upon my conscience not one of the Comittee besides the parties concerned do understand what they do therein, whether they give too much or too little.[1]

Thence with Mr. Creed to see Mr. Moore, who continues sick still within doors; and here I stayed a good while after him, talking of all the things, either business or no, that came into my mind; and so home and to see Sir W. Penn, and sat and played at cards with him, his daughter and Mrs. Rooth; and so to my office a while and then home*b* and to bed.

17. Up and to my office, and then we sat all the morning; and at noon (my wife being gone to Chelsey with her brother and sister and Mrs. Lodum to see the Wassell at the schoole where Mary Ashwell is)[2] I took home Mr. Pett and he dined with me all alone, and much discourse we had upon the business of the office and so after dinner broke up. And with much ado, it raining hard (which it hath not done a great while now, but only frosts a great while) I got a coach and so to the Temple, where discoursed with Mr. Wm Mountagu about borrowing some money for my Lord; and so by water (where I have not been a good while through cold) to Westminster to Sir W. Wheelers, whom I find busy at his own house with the Comissioners of

a MS. 'from'   *b* repl. 'to'

---

1. See below, p. 88 & n. 3.
2. She worked as 'a kind of a mistress' over little children: below, p. 72. Two Chelsea schools were advertised in J. Houghton's *Coll. for*

improvement of husbandry and trade, 27 July and 24 August 1694. For the wassail (entertainment), see below, pp. 58–9.

Sewers.[1]   But I spoke to him about my Lord's business of borrowing money, and so to my Lord of Sandwich to give him an
account of all – whom I find at Cards with Pickering, but he
made an end soon and so all alone, he and I; after I had given
him an account, he told me he had a great secret to tell me, such
as no flesh knew but himself, nor ought – which was this: that
yesterday morning, Eschar, Mr. Edwd. Mountagu's man, did
come to him from his Maister with some of the Clerkes of the
Exchequer, for my Lord to sign to their books for the Embassy[2]
money;   which my Lord very civilly desired not to do till he
had spoke with his maister himself.   In the afternoon, my Lord
and my Lady Wright being at Cards in his chamber, in comes
Mr. Mountagu;   and desiring to speak with my Lord at the
window in his chamber, he[a] begun to charge my Lord with the
greatest ingratitude in the world – that he that had received his
Earldome, Garter, 4000*l* per annum and whatever he is in the world
from him, should now study him all the dishonour that he could;[3]
and so fell to tell my Lord that if he should speak all that he knew
of him, he could do so and so.   In a word, he did rip up all that
could be said that was unworthy, and in the basest terms they
could be spoke in.   To which my Lord answered with great
temper,* justifying himself but endeavouring to lessen his heat;
which was a strange temper in him – knowing that he did owe
all that he hath in the world to my Lord and that he is now all
that he is by his means and favour.   But my Lord did forbear
to encrease the quarrel, knowing that it would be to no good
purpose for the world to see a difference in the family, but did
allay him so as that he fell to weeping.   And after much talk
(among other things, Mr. Mountagu telling him that there was a
fellow in the towne, naming me, that had done ill offices;   and that

a   repl. 'they'

---

1. There were eight courts of commissioners in charge of the streams,
ditches and surface water drainage in
the London area outside the city.
   2. Sandwich's embassy to Portugal,
1661–2.   Edward Mountagu, Sandwich's first cousin once removed,

had been in charge of his affairs in
England during his absence.
   3. Mountagu (now Master of the
Horse to the Queen Mother) had
acted as intermediary between Sandwich and the royalists in the summer
of 1659: Harris, i. 139+.

if he knew it to be so, he would have him cudgelled), my Lord did promise him that, if upon account he saw that there was not many tradesmen unpaid, he would sign the books; but if there was, he could not bear with taking too great a debt upon him. So this day he sent him an account and a letter assuring him there was not above 200*l* unpaid; and so my Lord did sign to the Exchequer books. Upon the whole, I understand fully what a rogue he is and how my Lord doth think and will think of him for the future – telling me that thus he had served his father – my Lord Manchester – and his whole family, and now himself. And which is worst, that he hath abused and in speeches every day doth abuse my Lord Chancellor, whose favour he hath lost; and hath no friend but Sir H. Bennett and that (I knowing the rise of that friendship) only from the likeness of their pleasures and acquaintance and concernments they have in the same matters of lust and baseness[1] – for which God forgive them. But he doth flatter himself, from promises of Sir H Bennet, that he shall have a pension of 2000*l* per annum and be made an Earle.[2] My Lord told me he expected a challenge from him, but told me there was no great fear of him, for there was no man lies under such an imputation as he doth in the business of Mr. Cholmely,[3] who though a simple sorry fellow, doth brave him and struts before him with the Queene, to the sport and[a] observation of the whole Court.

He did keep my Lord at the Window, thus reviling and braveing him above an houre, my Lady Wright being by; but my Lord tells me she could not hear every word, but did well know what their discourse was; she could hear enough to know that. So that he commands me to keep it as the greatest secret in the world, and bids me beware of speaking words against Mr. Mountagu, for fear I should suffer by his passion thereby.

After he had told me this, I took coach and home; where I

a   repl. 'of the'

---

1. Mountagu appears like Bennet to have had strong Catholic leanings: Harris, ii. 141. Bennet's sexual morals were generally held to be above reproach: V. Barbour, *Arlington*, p. 97.

2. For Bennet as 'bribe-master-general', see below, viii. 185–6 & n.

3. The duel mentioned at 6 August 1662.

find my wife come home and in bed, with her sister in law¹ in the
chamber with her – she not being able to stay to see the Wassell,
being so ill of her termes – which I was sorry for.   Hither we sent
for her sister's Viall,² upon which she plays pretty well for a
girl; but my expectation is much deceived in her, not only for
that but in her spirit, she being I perceive a very subtle, witty
jade and one that will give her husband trouble enough, as little
as she is – whereas I took her heretofore for a very child and a
simple fool.   I played also, which I have not done this long time
before upon any instrument; and at last broke up and I to my
office a little while, being fearful of being too much taken with
musique, for fear of returning to my old dotage thereon and so
neglect my business as I used to do.

Then home and to bed.

Coming home, I brought Mr. Pickering as far as the Temple;
who tells me the story is very [true] of a child being dropped at the
Ball at Court; and that the King had it in his closet a week after,
and did dissect it; and making great sport of it, said that in his
opinion it must have been a month and three houres old and that
whatever others think, he had the greatest loss (it being a boy,
as he says), that had lost a subject by the business.³

He tells me too, that the other, of my Lady Castlemaynes and
Stuarts marriage, is certain; and that it was in order to the King's
coming to Stuart, as is believed generally.   He tells me that Sir
H. Bennet is a Catholique, and how all the Court almost is changed
to the worse since his coming in, they being afeared of him.⁴
And that the Queene-Mother's Court is now the greatest of all;

1. Esther, wife of Balty St Michel.
2. A bass viol: see above, iii. 286.
(E).
3. Cf. above, p. 37 & n. 3.   The
ball was possibly that described at
31 December 1662: for two similar
births, see above, iii. 117 & n. 1.
For the King's laboratory 'under his
closet', see below, ix. 416 & n. 1.
This story appears to lack confirmation.   Gramont (pp. 273-6) tells of a
court ball at Tunbridge Wells a few

summers later at which Lady Mus-
kerry dropped a cushion which the
wags pretended to mistake for a newborn baby.
4. Bennet had been made a
Secretary of State in October 1662.
He was now no more than a Catholic
sympathiser, but Pepys later repeats
from a different source the story
that he was Papist: below, p. 224.
Like Charles II, he was received into
the church on his death-bed in 1685.

and that our own*a* Queene hath little or no company come to her, which I know also to be very true – and am sorry to see it.

18. Up, leaving my wife sick, as last night, in bed. I to my office, all the morning casting up with Captain Cocke their accounts of 500 Tons of hemp brought from Riga, and bought by him and parteners upon account,[1] wherein are many things worth my knowledge. So at noon to dinner, taking Mr. Hater with me because of losing time; and in the afternoon he and I alone at the office, finishing our account of the Extra charge of the Navy not properly belonging to the Navy since the King's coming in to Christmas last; and all extra things being abated, I find that the true charge of the Navy to that time hath been after the rate of 374743*l.* a year.[2] I made an end by 11 a-clock at night, and so home to bed, almost weary.

This day the Parliament met again after their long prorogacion;[3] but I know not anything what they have done, being within doors all day.

19. Up and to my office, where abundance of business all the morning. Dined by my wife's bedside, she not being yet well.*b* We fell out almost upon my discourse of delaying the having of Ashwell come, my wife believing that I have a mind to have Pall; which I have not, though I could wish she did deserve to be had. So to my office, where by and by we sat, this afternoon being the first that we have met upon a great while – our times being changed because of the parliament sitting.[4] Being rose, I to my office till 12 at night, drawing out Copys of the Overcharge of the Navy – one to send to Mr. Coventry early tomorrow. So

a MS. 'and'   *b* repl. 'weak'

1. Cf. above, iii. 114, 129–30. The partners were Rider and Cutler.

2. A copy (by Hewer and Pepys) of these accounts (24 June 1660–31 December 1662), with a copy of a covering letter from Pepys to Coventry (19 February), is in NMM, LBK/8, pp. 41–3.

3. Since 19 May 1662.

4. They met on Tuesday and Thursday afternoons during the present parliamentary session: PRO, Adm. 106/3520, f. 11*v*.

home and to bed, being weary, sleepy, and my eyes begin to fail me, looking so long by candlelight upon white paper.[1]

This day I read the King's speech to the parliament yesterday;[2] which is very short and not very obliging, but only telling them his desire to have a power of indulging tender consciences, not that he will yield to have any mixture in the uniformity of the Church discipline.   And says the same for the papist, but declares against their ever being admitted to have any offices or places of trust in the kingdom – but God knows, too many have.[3]

20.   Up and by water with Comissioner Pett to Deptford and there looked over the yard and had a call, wherein I am very highly pleased with our new manner of Call=bookes, being my invencion.[4]   Thence, thinking to have gone down to Woolwich in the *Charles* pleasure-boat, but she run aground, it being almost low water; and so by oares to the towne and there dined; and then to the yard at Mr. Acworths, discoursing with the officers of the yard about their stores of masts, which was our chief business; and having done something therein, took boat and to the pleasure-boat which was come down to fetch us back; and I could have been sick if I would in going, the wind being very fresh.   But very pleasant it was and the first time I have sailed in any one of them.   It carried us to Cuckold's poynt, and so by oares to the Temple, it raining hard; where missed of speaking with my Cosen Roger, and so walked home and to my office; there spent the night till bed-time, and so home to supper and to bed.

21.   Up and to the office, where Sir John Minnes (most of the rest being at the Parliament-house); all the morning [an]swering petitions and other business.   Towards noon there comes a man in, as if upon ordinary business, and shows me a Writt from the

1. The first mention (? apart from that at 25 April 1662) of the eye trouble which plagued Pepys for much of the rest of his life.   Probably a combination of hypermetropia and astigmatism, it caused him eventually to discontinue this diary, and to fear (needlessly, as it turned out) that he would go blind.

2. *His Majesties gracious speech to both Houses of Parliament on Wednesday, February the 18th 1662* (1662/3); reprinted, e.g., in *LJ*, xi. 478–9.

3. Cf. Pepys's comments on Secretary Bennet and Governor Rutherford: above, p. 48; iii. 283.

4. See above, iii. 289, n. 2.

Exchequer, called a Comission of Rebellion,[1] and tells me that I am his prisoner – in Fields business. Which*a* methought did strike me to the heart, to think that we could not sit safe*b* in the middle of the King's business. I told him how and where we were imployed and bid him have a care; and perceiving that we were busy, he said he would and did withdraw for an houre – in which time Sir J. Minnes took coach and to Court to see what he could do from thence; and our*c* Sollicitor against Field came by chance and told me that he would go and satisfy the fees of the Court and would end the business. So he went away about that, and I stayed in my closet, till by and by the man and four more of his fellows came to know what I would do; I told them stay till I heard from the King or my Lord Chief Baron, to both whom I had now sent. With that they consulted and told me that if I would promise to stay in the house they would go and refresh themselfs, and come again and know what answer I had. So they away and I home to dinner – whither by chance in comes Mr. Hawly and dined with me.

Before I had dined, the Baylys came back again with the Constable, and at the office knock for me but found me not there; and I hearing in what manner they were come, did forbear letting them know where I was. So they stood knocking and enquiring for me.

By and by at my parlour-window comes Sir W. Batten's Mingo to tell me that his Maister and Lady would have me come to their house through Sir J. Mennes's lodgings, which I could not do; but however, by lathers did get over the pale between our yards and so to their house, where I find them (as they have reason) to be much concerned for me – my Lady especially.

The fellows stayed in the yard swearing with one or two constables; and some time we locked them into the yard and by and by let them out again, and so keeped them all the afternoon, not letting them see me or know where I was. One time, I went up to the top of Sir W. Batten's house and out of one of

---

a MS. 'where'   *b* MS. 'sat'   *c* repl. 'my'

---

1. A writ used to secure the appearance of a defendant; abolished in 1860. It was now issued by the court of Exchequer Pleas in Field's action against the Navy Board: q.v. above, iii. 23, n. 2.

their windows spoke to my wife out of one of ours – which methought, though I did it in mirth, yet I was sad to think what a sad thing it would be for me to be really in that condition. By and by comes Sir J. Mennes, who (like himself and all that he doth) tells us that he can do no good, but that my Lord Chancellor wonders that we did not cause the seamen to fall about their eares – which we wished we could have done without our being seen in it; and Captain Grove being there, he did give them some affront and would have got some seamen to have drubbed them, but he had not time nor did we think it fit to have it done, they having executed their commission. But there was occasion given that he did draw his sword upon one of them and he did complain that Grove had pricked him in the breast – but no hurt done; but I saw that Grove would have done our business to them if we had bid him. By and by comes Mr. Clerke our Sollicitor, who brings us a release from our adverse atturny, we paying the fees of the Comission, which comes to five markes, and pay the charges of these fellows, which are called the Comissioners (but are the most rake-shamed rogues that ever I saw in my life); so he showed them his release and [they] seemed satisfied and went away with him to their atturny to be paid by him. But before they went, Sir W. Batten and my Lady did begin to taunt them; but the rogues answered them as high as themselfs and swore they would come again, and called me rogue and Rebell and they would bring the Sheriffe and untile his house before he should harbour a Rebell in his house – and that they would be here again shortly.

Well, at last they went away; and I by advice took occasion to go abroad, and walked through the street to show myself among the neighbours, that they might not think worse then the business is. Being met by Captain Taylor and Bowry, whose*a* ship we have hired for Tanger, they walked along with me to Cornhill, talking about their business; and after some difference about their price, we agreed;[1] and so they would have me to the

a repl. 'who'

1. The contract was dated 20 February. The *William and Mary* (Capt. John Taylor, part owner, and John Bowry, master) was to be hired to carry goods at 25s. a ton: *CSPD Add. 1660–85*, p. 86; see also below, p. 414 & n. 1.

taverne and there I drank one glass of wine and discoursed of something about freight of a ship that may bring me a little money; and so broke up and I home to Sir W. Batten again – where Sir J Lawson, Captain Allen, Spragg and several others, and all our discourse about the disgrace done to our office to be liable to this trouble,*a* which we must get removed.

Hither came Mr. Clerke by and by, and tells me that he hath paid the fees of the Court for the commission, but the men are not contented with under 5*l* for their charges, which he will not give them; and therefore advises me not to stir abroad till Munday that he comes or sends to me again, whereby I shall not be able to go to White-hall to the Duke of Yorke, as I ought.

Here I stayed, vexing and yet pleased to see everybody, man and woman, my Lady and Mrs. Turner especially, for me, till 10 at night; and so home, where my people are mightily surprised to see this business, but it troubles me not very much, it being nothing touching my perticular person or estate.

Being in talk today with Sir W. Batten, he tells me that little is done yet in the parliament-house; but only this day it was moved and ordered that all the members of the House do subscribe to the renouncing of the Covenant, which is thought will try some of them.[1]

There is also a bill brought in for the wearing of nothing but cloath or stuffs of our own manufacture and is likely to be passed.[2]

Among other talk this evening, my Lady did speak concerning Comissioner Pett's calling the present king "bastard", and other high words heretofore; and Sir W. Batten did tell us*b* that he

---

a repl. 'fear'   *b* repl. 'me'

---

1. There is no trace of any such order in the journals of the House. Presumably it was a vote passed by the Committee of Elections and Privileges appointed on the 18th: *CJ*, viii. 436–7. (Batten was not a member.) It never became law. Renunciation of the presbyterian Covenant of 1643 was already re-quired of municipal officers by the Corporation Act (1661) and of the clergy by the Act of Uniformity (1662). The Covenant had been publicly burnt by order of the Commons in May 1661: *CJ*, viii. 254.

2. A committee to draft the bill was appointed on this day, but the bill was not passed: ib., p. 438.

did give the Duke or Mr. Coventry an account of that and other like matters in writing, under oath; of which I was ashamed and for which I was sorry.[1] But I do see there is an absolute hatred never to be altered there, and Sir J. Mennes, the old coxcomb, hath got it by the end – which troubles me for the sake of the King's service, though I do truly hate the expressions laid to him. To my office and set down this day's Journall; and so home with my mind out of order, though not very sad with it but ashamed for myself something, and for the honour of the office much more. So home and to bed.

22. *Lords day.* Lay long in bed and went not out all day; but after dinner to Sir W. Batten and Sir W. Penn's, where discoursing much of yesterday's trouble and scandal; but that which troubled me most was Sir J. Mennes coming from Court at night and instead of bring[ing] great comfort from thence (but I expected no better from him) he tells me that the Duke and Mr. Coventry make no great matter of it. So at night, discontented,*a* to prayers and to bed.

23. Up betimes, and not daring to go by land, did (Griffin going along with me for fear) slip to White-hall by water; where to Mr. Coventry and, as we used to do, to the Duke, the other of my fellows being come. But we said nothing of our business, the Duke being sent for to the King, that he could not stay to speak with us. This morning came my Lord Windsor to kiss the Dukes hand, being returned from Jamaica.[2] He tells the Duke that from such a degree of Latitude going thither, he begun to be sick and was never well till his coming so far back again, and then presently begun to be well. He told the Duke of their taking the Fort of St. Jago upon Cuba by his men; but upon the whole, I believe that he did matters like a young lord, and was weary of being upon service out of his own country, where he

a repl. 'to'

---

1. Nothing has been traced of this affair. Batten had probably made the accusation in order to scotch the proposal to make Pett his assistant in the Surveyor's business: above, iii.

237. Pett's services to the revolutionary governments laid him open to this sort of attack.

2. See above, p. 41 & n. 4.

might have pleasure – for methought it was a shame to see him this very afternoon, being the first day of his coming to town, to be at a playhouse.

Thence to my Lord Sandwich; who though he hath been abroad again two or three days, is falling ill again and is let blood this morning, though I hope it is only a great cold that he hath got.

It was a great trouble to me (and I had great apprehensions of it) that my Lord desired me to go to Westminster-hall to the parliament-house door about business and to Sir Wm. Wheeler; which I told him I would do, but durst not go for fear of being taken by these rogues; but was forced to go to White-hall and take boat and so land below the Tower at the Iron-gate and so the back way over little Tower-hill; and with my cloak over my face, took one of the watermen along with me and stayed behind a wall in the New=buildings behind our garden while he went to see whether anybody stood within the Merchants gate, under which we pass to go into our garden;[1] and there standing but a little dirty boy before the gate, did make me quake and sweat to think that he might be a Trapan; but there was nobody, and so I got safe into the garden; and coming to open my office door, something behind it fell in the opening, which made me start. So that God knows in what a sad condition I should be in if I were truly in the condition that many a poor man is for debt – and therefore ought to bless God that I have no such real reason, and to endeavour to keep myself by my good deportment and good husbandry out of any such condition.

. At home I find Mr. Creed with my wife and so he dined with us. And finding by a note that Mr. Clerke in my absence had left here that I am free, and that he had stopped all matters in Court, I was very glad of it and immediately had a light thought of taking pleasure to rejoice my heart; and so resolved to take my wife to a play at Court tonight[2] and the rather because it is my birth day, being this day thirty year old – for which let me praise God.

While my wife dressed herself, Creed and I walked out to see

---

1. Though the normal entrance to the Navy Office was in Seething Lane, its garden stretched eastwards almost to Tower Hill, and a narrow tongue of ground from that Hill gave access to a gate in the garden wall. (R).

2. Cf. the terms of his recent vow against play-going: above, p. 8. (A).

what play was acted today, and we find it *The Sleighted mayde*.[1] But Lord, to see that though I did know myself to be out of danger, yet I durst not go through the street, but round by the garden into towerstreete.

By and by took coach and to the Dukes house, where we saw it well acted, though the play hath little good in it – being most pleased to see the little girl[2] dance in boy's apparel, she having very fine legs; only, bends in the hams as I perceive all women do. The play being done, we took coach and to Court and there got good places and saw *The Wilde gallant*[3] performed by the King's house; but it was ill acted and the play so poor a thing as I never saw in my life almost, and so little answering the name, that from beginning to the end I could not, nor can at this time, tell certainly which was the wild gallant. The King did not seem pleased at all, all the whole play, nor anybody else, though Mr. Clerke whom we met here did commend it to us. ⟨My Lady Cast[l]emayne was all worth seeing tonight, and little Steward.[4] Mrs. Wells doth appear at Court again and looks well, so that it may be the late report of laying the dropt child to her was not true.⟩[a][5]

It being done, we got a coach and got well home about 12 at night. Now, as my mind was but very ill-satisfied with these two plays themselfs, so was I in the midst of them sad to think of my spending so much money and venturing upon the breach of my vowe; which I find myself sorry for, I bless God, though my nature could well be contented to fallow that pleasure still. But I did make payment[b] of my forfeiture presently, though I

a addition crowded in between paragraphs   *b* repl. 'place'

---

1. Playbills were fixed to posts in various parts of London. This play was a comedy by Sir Robert Stapylton, published in 1663. This is the first recorded performance. The cast listed by Genest (i. 46) includes Betterton as Iberio, Harris as Salerno, Sandford as Vindex and Mrs Betterton as Pyramena. (A).

2. Probably Ann Gibbs, afterwards Mrs Thomas Shadwell. According to the 1663 edition of the play (A3*v*), she played the part of Ericina, who disguises herself as her brother. (A).

3. Dryden's first comedy; published in 1669. The play was now performed by the King's Company in the Great Hall, Whitehall, which stood between the Banqueting House and the Thames. In December 1662 stepping for seats and a stage 27 ft wide were constructed there: E. Boswell, *Restoration court stage*, pp. 25–6. (A).

4. Frances Stuart, later Duchess of Richmond.

5. Cf. above, p. 37 & n. 4.

hope to save it back again by forbearing two plays at Court for this one at the Theatre, or else to forbear that to the Theatre which I am to have at Easter. But it being my birth day and my day of Liberty regained to me, and lastly, the last play that is likely to be acted at Court before Easter, because of the Lent coming in, I was the easier contented to fling away so much money.[1]

So to bed.

⟨This day I was told that my Lady Castlemaine had all the King's Christmas presents made him by the Peeres[2] given to her, which is a most abominable thing; and that at the great Ball[3] she was much richer in Jewells then the Queene and Duchesse put both together.⟩[a]

24. Slept hard till 8 a-clock; then waked by Mr. Clerkes being come to consult me about Fields business, which we did by calling him up to my bedside, and he says we shall trounce him.

Then up and to the office, and at 11 a-clock by water to Westminster and to Sir W Wheelers about my Lord's borrowing of money that I was lately upon with him; and then to my Lord, who continues ill but will do well I doubt not.

Among other things, he tells me that he hears the Commons will not agree to the King's late declaracion, nor will yield that the Papists have any ground given them to raise themselfs up again in England – which I perceive by my Lord was expected at Court.[4] Thence home again by water presently; and with a bad dinner, being not looked for, to the office; and there we sat and then Captain Cocke and I upon his Hempe accounts till 9 at night; and then, I not very well, home to supper and bed – my late distemper of heat and Itching being come upon me again, so that I must think of sweating again as I did before.

a   addition crowded in between paragraphs

---

1. I.e. on the visit to the LIF. It was not until 1675 that the King allowed a company to charge for admission to a court performance at Whitehall – much to Evelyn's disgust (29 September): E. Boswell, *Restoration court stage*, p. 121. (A.)

2. These New Year gifts were usually of plate: above, ii. 5 & n. 4.

3. Above, iii. 300-1.

4. For the Declaration, see above, p. 5 & n. 3. The King had asked for Parliament's concurrence in his speech at the opening of the new session on 18 February. The Commons had given it a cool reception and on the 21st appointed the 25th for a debate: *CJ*, viii. 438. See below, p. 58.

25. Up and to my office, where with Captain Cocke making an end of his last night's accounts till noon. And so home to dinner, my wife being come in from laying out about 4*l.* in provision of several things against Lent. In the afternoon to the Temple, my brother's, the Wardrobe, to Mr. Moore and other places, called at about small businesses; and so at night home to my office and then to supper and to bed.

The Commons in parliament, I hear, are very high to stand to the act of uniformity, and will not indulge the papists (which is endeavoured by the court party) nor the Presbyters.*ᵃ* [1]

26. Up, and drinking a draught of wormwood wine with Sir W. Batten at the Steelyard, he and I by water to the parliament-house. He went in and I walked up and down the hall. All the news is the great odds yesterday in the votes between them that are for the indulgence to the papists and presbyters and those that are against it, which did carry it by 200 against 30.[2] And pretty it is to consider how the King would appear to be a stiff Protestant and son of the Church, and yet would appear willing to give a liberty to these people because of his promise at Breda.[3] And yet all the world doth believe that the King would not have this liberty given them at all.

Thence to my Lord's, who I hear hath his ague again, for which I am sorry. And Creed and I to the King's-head ordinary, where much good company – among the rest, a young gallant lately come from France who was full of his French; but methought not very good, but he had enough to make him think himself a wise man a great while. Thence by water from the New Exchange home to the Tower; and so sat at the office and then writing letters till 11 at night.

Troubled this evening that my wife is not come home from

a l.h. repl. l.h. 'p'-

---

1. The Commons this day resolved that no indulgence be granted to dissenters: *CJ*, viii. 440.

2. There was no division on this resolution. A previous vote on the same day (to discuss the King's Declaration) passed by 269 to 30: *CJ*, loc. cit.

3. In the Declaration of Breda (April 1660) the King had promised a liberty to tender consciences, which was to be confirmed by Parliament. Parliament had, instead, passed the Act of Uniformity of 1662.

Chelsey, whither she is gone to see the Play at the Schoole where Ashwell is. But she came at last, it seems by water, it being cold and dark; but came well and tells me she is much pleased with Ashwells acting and carriage, which I am glad of.

So home and to supper and bed.

27. Up and to my office, whither several persons came to me about office business. About 11 a-clock Comissioner Pett and I walked to Chyrurgeons hall (we being all invited thither and promised to dine there), where we were led into the Theatre; and by and by came the Reader, Dr Tearne, with the Maister and Company, in a very handsome manner; and all being settled, he begun his lecture, this being the second upon the Kidnys, Ureters, and yard, which was very fine;[1] and his discourse being ended, we walked into the hall; and there being great store of company we had a fine dinner and good learned company, many Doctors of Physique, and we used with extraordinary great respect.

Among other observables, we drank the King's health out of a gilt cupp given by King Henry the 8th to this Company, with bells hanging at it, which every man is to ring by shaking after he hath drunk up the whole cup.[2] There is also a very excellent piece of the King done by Holben stands up in the hall, with the officers of the Company kneeling to him to receive their charter.[3]

After dinner Dr. Scarborough took some of his friends, and I went along with them, to see the body alone; which we did;

1. Anatomy lectures were often given in public. The Company (whose Hall was in Monkwell St; the Master, 1662–3, being Thomas Lisle) had the right to claim annually the bodies of four executed felons; it would then arrange four 'public anatomies' by its reader (in this case Christopher Terne, F.R.C.P.); guests were invited and dinner provided. There were in addition 'private anatomies' at which guests were also present, besides other lectures, sometimes held almost weekly. See Sidney Young, *Annals of Barber Surgeons*, pp. 361+.

2. The grace cup, presented by the King in 1540 to mark the passage in that year of the act of union between the Barbers' Company and the Guild of Surgeons; still in the possession of the Company. See illust. in Young, op. cit., p. 499.

3. The painting represents the passage of the act of 1540, not the grant of a charter (though the painter has included one). Description and reproduction in Young, pp. 80+; still in the possession of the Company. For the picture and Pepys's intention to buy it, see below, ix. 293 & n. 1.

he was a lusty fellow, a seaman that was hanged for a*ᵃ* robbery. I did touch the dead body with my bare hand; it felt cold, but methought it was a very unpleasant sight.

It seems one Dillon, of a great family, was, after much endeavours to have saved him, hanged with a silken halter this Sessions (of his owne preparing) not for honour only, but it seems, it being saft and slick, it doth slip close and kills, that is, strangles presently; whereas a stiff one doth not come so close together and so the party may live the longer before killed.[1] But all the Doctors at table conclude that there is no pain at all in hanging, for that it doth stop the circulacion of the blood and so stops all sense and motion in an instant.

Thence we went into a private room, where I perceive they prepare the bodies, and there was the Kidnys, Ureters, yard, stones and semenary vessels upon which he read today. And Dr Scarborough, upon my desire and the company's, did show very clearly the manner of the disease of the stone and the cutting and all other Questions that I could think of, and the manner of the seed, how it comes into the yard, and how the water into the bladder, through the three skinnes or coats,[2] just as poor Dr Jolly[3] had heretofore told me.

Thence, with great satisfaccion to me, back to the Company, where I heard good discourse; and so to the afternoon Lecture upon the heart and lungs, &c. And that being done, we broke up, took leave, and back to the office we two (Sir W. Batten, who dined here also, being gone before).

a   accidental long line under symbol

---

1. It was the practice both now and in the 18th century to allow to criminals of gentle birth the privilege of being hanged by silken ropes if they petitioned for it: cf. William Andrews, *Bygone Punishments*, p. 17. In this case William Dillon, gent., of St Martin-in-the-Fields, had been sentenced with two others (also gentlemen) on 18 February for the murder of Matthew Webb: *Middlesex county records* (ed. J. C. Jeaffreson), iii. 331. Both he and his companion Garsfield came of good Irish stock.

2. Dr C. E. Newman writes: 'This follows the description in William Harvey's *Praelectiones*, in which he himself followed Bauhin in describing three coats: the peritoneum, and the two solid, thick, hard coats (probably transverse and oblique muscular coats). The effect is to form a flap-valve which prevents the reflux of urine.'

3. George Jolliffe, who had attended Pepys after his operation for the stone in 1658 and had died shortly afterwards at an early age.

Here late, and to Sir W. Batten to speak upon some business; where I find Sir J. Mennes pretty well fuddelled I thought. He took me aside to tell me how being at my Lord Chancellors today, my Lord told him that there was a Great Seal passing for Sir W. Penn, through the impossibility of the Comptroller's duty to be performed by one man, to be as it were joynt-controller with him;[1] at which he is stark mad and swears he will give up his place – and doth rail at Sir W. Penn the cruellest; which[a] I made shift to increase as much as I could, but it pleased me heartily to hear him rail against him, so that I do see thoroughly that they are not like to be great friends, for he cries out against him for his house and yard and God knows what. For my part, I do hope, when all is done, that my fallowing my business will keep me secure against all their envys; but to see how the old man doth strut and swear that he understands all his duty as easily as crack a nut; and easier, he told my Lord Chancellor, for his teeth are gone – and that he understands it as well as any man in England; and that he will never leave to Record that he should be said to be unable to do his duty alone; though God knows, he cannot do it no more then a child. All this I am glad to see fall out between them, and myself safe; and yet I hope the King's service will [be] done for all this, for I would not that should be hindered by any of our private differences.

So to my office, and then home to supper and to bed.

28. Waked with great pain in my right eare (which I find myself much subject to), having taken cold. Up and to my office, where we sat all the morning, and I dined with Sir W. Warren[b] by chance, being in business together about a bargain of New=England Masts.[2]

a MS. 'with' – possibly another instance of the audial factor in Pepys's method of composition. Cf. above, vol. i, p. cii.

b MS. 'Batten'

---

1. The Duke's warrant to the law-officers had been issued on 6 January (PRO, Adm. 2/1733, f. 34*v*), but Mennes's resistance was successful until January 1667, when two assistants – Penn and Brouncker – were appointed.

2. Possibly the bargain concluded on 10 September whereby Warren was to deliver 150 Gothenburg and 300 Norwegian masts, with three shiploads of New England masts: *CSPD 1663–4*, p. 270. For supplies from New England, see above, iii. 268, n. 1.

Then to the Temple to meet my uncle Tho., who I find there; but my Cosen Roger not being come home, I took boat and to Westminster, where I find him in Parliament this afternoon – the House having this noon been with the King to give him their reasons for refusing to grant any indulgence to presbyters or Papists – which he with great content and seeming pleasure took, saying that he doubted not but he and they should agree in all things, though there may seem a difference in judgement, he having writ and declared for an indulgence; and that he did believe never prince was happier in a House of Commons then he was in them.[1]

Thence he and I to my Lord Sandwich, who continues troubled with his Cold. Our discourse most upon the outing of Sir R Bernard and my Lord's being made Recorder[2] in his stead, which he seems well contented with, saying that it may be for his convenience to have the chief officer of the towne dependant upon him, which is very true.

Thence he and I to the Temple; but my uncle being gone, we parted and I walked home and to my office. And at 9 a-clock had a good supper of a Oxes cheek of my wife's dressing and baking; and so to my office again till past 11 at night, making up my month's account; and I find that I am at a stay with what I was last, that is 640*l*. So home and to bed.

Coming by, I put in at White-hall and at the Privy Seale I did see the Docquet[3] by which Sir W. Penn is made the Comptroller's Assistant, as Sir J. Mennes told me last night – which I must endeavour to prevent.[a]

a followed by two blank pages

---

1. The Commons' address and the King's answer are given in *CJ*, viii. 442–4; *LJ*, xi. 474.

2. For this affair of the recordership of Huntingdon, see above, p. 30 & n. 1. The 'chief officer' mentioned later is the mayor. Sandwich was probably here referring to the usefulness of having the mayor (as parliamentary returning officer) dependent upon him in the contests between his interest and that of Bernard for control of the borough. Bernard had won in the election of 1660, Sandwich in that of 1661. Cf. VCH, *Hunts.*, ii. 25+.

3. Cf. PRO, Index 6751, n.p. See above, p. 61, n. 1.

1. *Lords day.* Up and walked to White-hall to the chapel –
where preached one Dr. Lewes, said heretofore to have been a
great wit; but he read his sermon every word, and that so
brokenly and so low that nobody could hear at any distance;
nor I anything worth hearing, that sat near.[1] But which was
strange, he forgot to make any prayer before sermon; which all
wonder at, but they impute it to his forgetfulness.

After sermon, a very fine Anthemne.

So I up into the House among the Courtiers, seeing the fine
ladies, and above all, my Lady Castlemayne who is above all,
the only she I can observe for true beauty. The King and
Queen being sat to dinner, I went to Mr. Foxes[2] and there dined
with him. Much genteel company; and among other things,
I hear for certain that peace is concluded between the King of
France and the Pope.[3] And also I heard the reasons given by our
Parliament yesterday to the King why they dissent from him in
matter of Indulgence, which are very good quite through and
which I was glad to hear.

Thence to my Lord Sandwich, who continues with a great cold,
locked up; and being alone we fell into discourse of my Uncle
the Captain's death and estate;[4] and I took the opportunity of
telling my Lord how matters stand, and read his Will and told
him all, what a poor estate[a] he hath left; at all which he wonders
strangely, which he may well do.

Thence, after singing some new tunes with W. Howe, I walked
home – whither came Will Joyce (whom I have not seen here a
great while), nor desire it a great while again, he is so impertinent

a MS. 'what a poor a state'

---

1. William Lewis, chaplain both
to Charles I and to Charles II, was
now an old man of 71. He had
been a prebendary of Winchester
since 1627.

2. Stephen Fox, Comptroller of
the King's Household.

3. A mistake: diplomatic relations
had not yet been resumed, and the
peace was not made until February
1664. For the dispute, see above,
iii. 253 & n. 3; below, v. 60 & n. 2.

4. See *Comp.*: 'Pepys, Robert'.

a coxcomb – and yet good-natured, and mightily concerned for my brother's late folly in his wooing at that charge, to no purpose nor could in any probability expect it.

He gone, we all to bed without prayers, it being washing day tomorrow.

2. Up early; and by water with Comissioner Pett to Deptford and there took the *Jemmy* yacht (that the King and the Lords virtuosos built the other day)[1] down to Woolwich, where we discoursed of several matters both there and at the Ropeyard; and so to the Yacht again and went down four or five mile with extraordinary pleasure, it being a fine day and a brave gale of wind. And had some oysters brought us aboard, newly-taken, which were excellent and eat with great pleasure.

There also coming into the river two Duchmen,*a* we sent a couple of men on board and bought three hollands cheeses, cost 4*d* a pound, excellent cheese, whereof I had two and Comissioner Pett one.

So back again to Woolwich; and going aboard the Hulke to see the manner of the Iron bridles which we are making of for to save cordage to put to the chain,[2] I did fall from the ship-side into the Ship (*Kent*) and had like to have broke my left hand; but I only sprained some of my fingers, which when I came ashore, I sent to Mrs. Ackworth for some balsam and put to my hand, and I was pretty well within a little while after.

We dined at the White hart, with several officers with us. And after dinner went and saw the *Royall Jame[s]* brought down to the stern of the Docke (the main business we came for); and then to the Ropeyard and saw a trial between Riga hemp and a sort of Indian grasse,[3] which is pretty strong but no comparison between it and the other for strength – and it is doubtful whether it will take tarre or no.

So to the Yacht again and carried us almost to London; so by our oares home to the office, and thence Mr. Pett and I to Mr.

a l.h. repl. s.h. 'D'-

---

1. See above, iii. 164 & n. 4.
2. The bridles connected the ship to the mooring-chain which was stretched between anchors fixed on either side of the river.

3. Probably jute. Of all hemps, that from Riga was generally accounted the best: below, p. 259 & n. 4.

Grant's Coffee-house, whither he and Sir J. Cutler came to us and had much discourse, mixed discourse, and so broke up. And so home, where I find my poor wife all alone at work and the house foul, it being washing-day; which troubled me because that tomorrow I must be forced to have friends at dinner.

So to my office, and then home to supper and to bed.

3. *Shrovetuesday.* Up and walked to the Temple; and by promise calling Comissioner Pett, he and I to White-hall to give Mr. Coventry an account of what we did yesterday. Thence I to the Privy Seale Office and there got a copy of Sir W. Penn's grant to be assistant to Sir J. Mennes Comptroller; which, though there be not much in it, yet I entend to stir up Sir J. Mennes to oppose – only to vex Sir W. Penn. Thence by water home; and at noon, by promise, Mrs. Turner and her daughter and Mrs. Morrice comes along with Rogr Pepys to dinner. We were as merry as I could be, having but a bad dinner for them; but so much the better, because of the dinner which I must have at the end of this month. And here Mrs. The showed me my name upon her breast as her valentin,[1] which will cost me 20s. After dinner I took them down into the wine-cellar and broached my Terce of Clarret for them. Toward the evening we parted, and I to the office a while and then home to supper and to bed; the sooner, having taken some cold yesterday upon the water, which brings me my usual pain. This afternoon Rogr Pepys tells me that for certain the King is, for all this, very highly incensed at the Parliaments late opposing the Indulgence; which I am sorry for and fear it will breed great discontent.[a]

4. Lay long, talking with my wife about ordering things in our family; and then rose and to my office, there collecting an Alphabet for my Navy-Manuscript;[2] which after a short dinner I returned to and by night perfected to my great content. So to other business till 9 at night, and so home to supper and to bed.

a entry crowded into bottom of page.

1. Theophila Turner was aged 10 or 11. She had drawn Pepys's name by lot.

2. See above, p. 11 & n. 1.

5. Rise this morning early only to try, with intentions to begin my last summers course in rising betimes. So to my office a little; and then to Westminster by coach with Sir J. Mennes and Sir W. Batten, in our way talking of Sir W. Penn's business of his patent, which I think I have put a stop to wholly, for Sir J. Mennes swears he will never consent to it.

Here to the Lobby and spoke with my Cosen Rogr., who is going to Cambrige tomorrow. In the hall I do hear that the Catholiques are in great hopes for all this, and do set hard upon the King to get Indulgence. Matters, I hear, are all naught in Ireland; and that the parliament hath voted and the people, that is the papists, do cry out against the Comissioners sent by the King; so that they say the English interest will be lost there.[1] Thence I went to see my Lord Sandwich, who I find very ill; and by his cold being several nights hindered from sleep, he was hardly able to open his eyes, and is very weak and sad upon it – which troubled me much. So after talking with Mr. Cooke,[2] whom I find there, about his folly for looking and troubling me and other friends in getting him a place (that is, Storekeeper of the Navy at Tanger) before there is any such thing, I returned to the hall and thence back with the two knights home again by coach – where I find Mr. Moore got abroad and dined with me;[a] which I was glad to see, he having not been able to go abroad a great while. Then came in Mr. Hawly and dined with us; and after dinner I left them and to the office, where we sat late; and I do find that I shall meet with nothing to oppose my growing great in the office but Sir W. Penn, who is now well again and comes into the office very briscke, and thinks to get up his time that he hath been out of the way by being mighty diligent at the office –

a repl. 'him'

---

1. Commissioners appointed by the King had sat as a Court of Claims since September 1662, settling the complex disputes which arose from the aftermath of the Cromwellian land settlement in Ireland. On 10 February 1663 the Irish House of Commons had unanimously passed a vote (in defiance of the government's wishes) which made alterations in the Court's procedure to the injury of Catholic claimants and demanded power to treat with the Privy Council. *CSP Ireland 1663-5*, pp. 22-7; Lister, iii. 239-43; R. Bagwell, *Ireland under Stuarts*, iii. 30-2.

2. A servant of Sandwich's.

which I pray God he may be; but however, I hope by mine to weary him out, for I am resolved to fall to business as hard as I can drive – God giving me health.

At my office late, and so home to supper and to bed.

6. Up betimes; and about 8 a-clock by coach with four horses with Sir J. Mennes and Sir W. Batten to Woolwich, a pleasant day. There at the yard we consulted and ordered several matters, and thence to the ropeyard and did the like; and so into Mr. Falconers, where we had some fish which we brought with us dressed; and there dined with us his new wife, which had been his maid but seems to be a gentile*a* woman, well enough bred and discreet.

Thence after dinner back to Deptford, where we did as before, and so home. Good discourse in our way, Sir J. Mennes being good company, though a simple man enough as to the business of his office. But we did discourse at large again about Sir W. Penn's patent to be his assistant, and I perceive he is resolved never to let it pass.

To my office and thence to Sir W. Batten, where Major Holmes was lately come from the Streights; but doth tell*b* me strange stories of the faults of Cooper, his master, put in by me;[1] which I do not believe but am sorry to hear, and must take some Course to have him removed, though I believe that the Captain[2] is proud and the fellow is not supple enough to him. So to my office again to set down my Journall, and so home and to bed. This evening my boy Waynman's brother was with me, and I did tell him again that I must part with the boy, for I will not keep him; he desires my keeping him a little longer, till he can provide for him; which I am willing for a while to do.

This day it seems the House of Commons hath been very high against the Papists, being incensed by the stir which they make for

a or 'gentle'-   *b* l.h. repl. s.h. 'make'

1. Cooper had taught arithmetic etc. to Pepys, who had had him made sailing master in the *Reserve*: above, iii. 160–1. For this affair, see R. Ollard, *Pepys*, pp. 124–6; below, p. 84.

their having a Indulgence;[1] which without doubt is a great folly
in them to be so hot upon at this time, when they see how
averse already the House have showed themselfs from it.

This evening Mr. Povy was with me at my[a] office, and tells
me that my Lord Sandwich is this day so ill that he is much
afeared of him; which puts me to great pain, not more for my
own sake then for his poor family.

7. Up betimes and to the office, where some of us sat all the
morning. At noon Sir W. Penn begun to talk with me, like a
counterfeit rogue, very kindly about his house and getting bills
signed for all our works;[2] but he is a cheating fellow and so I
let him talk and answered nothing. So we parted.

I to dinner and there at home met The Turner, who is come on
foot in a frolic to beg me to get a place at Sea for John their man,
which is a rogue. But however, it may be the sea may do him
good in reclaiming him and therefore I will see what I can do.
She dined with me; and after dinner I took coach and carried
her home, in our way, in Cheapside, lighting and giving her a
Dozen pair of white gloves as my valentine. Thence to my Lord
Sandwich, who is gone to Sir W. Wheelers for his more quiet
being; where he slept well last night and I took him very merry
playing at Cards and much company with him. So I left him,
and Creed and I to Westminster-hall and there walked a good
while. He told me how for some words of my Lady Gerards
against my Lady Castlemayne to the Queene, the King did the
other day affront her in going out to dance with her at a Ball
when she desired it as the ladies do, and is since forbid attending
the Queene by the King.[3] Which is much talked of, my Lord
her husband being a great favourite.

Thence by water home and to my office; wrote by the post,
and so home to bed.

a l.h. repl. s.h. 'the'

1. A bill 'to hinder the further
growth of Popery' was debated,
though its drafting (by a committee)
was not yet completed: CJ, viii. 445.
For the attempted royal indulgence,
see above, p. 5 & n. 3.

2. See below, p. 293 & n. 1.
3. Cf. the similar incident reported
by de Cominges to de Lionne earlier
on 5/15 January: Pepysiana, p. 289.
Lord Gerard commanded the King's
Lifeguards.

8. *Lords day*. Being sent to by Sir J. Mennes to know whether I would go with him to White-hall today, I rose but could not get ready before he was gone; but however, I walked thither and*a* hear Dr. King, Bishopp of Chichester, make a good and eloquent sermon upon these words, "They that sow in tears, shall reap in joy."[1]

Thence (the chapel in Lent being hung with black and no Anthemne sung after sermon as at other times) to my Lord Sandwich at Sir W Wheelers. I find him out of order, thinking himself to be in a fit of an ague, but in the afternoon he was very cheery. I dined with Sir William, where a good but short dinner, not better then one of mine commonly of a Sunday.

After dinner, up to my Lord, there being Mr. Rumball. My Lord, among other discourse, did tell us of his great difficultys passed in the business of the Sound, and of his receiving letters from the King there, but his sending them by Whetstone was a great folly;[2] and the story how my Lord, being at dinner with Sydny, one of his fellow Plenipotenciarys and his mortal ennemy, did see Whetstone and put off his hat three times to him, but the fellow would not be known; which my Lord imputed to his coxcombly humour (of which he was full) and bid Sydny take notice of him too; when at that very time he had letters in his pocket from the King – as it proved afterward. And Sydny afterward did find it out at Copenhagen, the Duch Comissioners telling him how my Lord Sandwich had hired one of their Shipps to carry back Whetstone to Lubeck, he being come from Flanders from the King. But I cannot but remember my Lord's equinimity in all these affairs with admiration.

a repl. 'on' or 'one'

1. Ps. cxxvi. 5.
2. This took place at Copenhagen in late July 1659 when Sandwich (in command of the fleet) and Algernon Sidney (one of the parliamentary commissioners) were attempting to mediate in the Swedish–Danish war. Thomas Whetstone (royalist nephew of Oliver Cromwell) had been sent by the royalists to get in touch with Sandwich, using the latter's namesake and cousin, Edward Mountagu, as intermediary. Sandwich knew that he was being watched by someone among the republicans, and had already asked Whetstone not to allow himself to be seen. Whetstone was well known to both Sandwich and Sidney. Above, i. 285 & n. 3; *Naval Minutes*, p. 387; *CSP Clar.*, iv. 255–6 etc.; M. Noble, *House of Cromwell* (1787), ii. 206–7; Harris, i. 143–5.

Thence walked home, in my way meeting Mr. Moore, with whom I took a turn or two in the street among the Drapers in Pauls churchyard, talking of business; and so home – to bed.

9. Up betimes to my office, where all the morning. About noon Sir J. Robinson, Lord Mayor, desiring way through the garden from the Tower, called in at the office and there invited me (and Sir W. Penn, who happened to be in the way) to dinner, which we did. And there had a great Lent dinner of fish, little flesh. And thence he and I in his coach, against my will (for I am resolved to shun too great fellowship with him) to White-hall; but came too late, the Duke having been with our fellow-officers before we came, for which I was sorry. Thence he and I to walk one turn in the parke and so home by coach, and I to my office, where late; and so home to supper and bed.

There dined with us today Mr. Slingsby of the Mint, who showed us all the new pieces, both gold and silver (examples of them all), that are made for the King by Blondeaus way, and compared them with those made for Oliver[1] – the pictures of the latter made by Symons,[2] and of the King by one Rotyr,[3] a German I think, that dined with[a] us also. He extolls these of Rotyrs above the others; and endeed, I think they are the better, because the sweeter of the two; but upon my word, those of the Pro-tectors are more like in my mind then the King's – but both very well worth seeing.[4] The Crownes of Cromwell's are now sold it seems for 25s and 30s. a-piece.[5]

10.   Up and to my office all the morning, and great pleasure

a repl. 'us'

1. For the recoinage of 1662–3 and Blondeau's introduction of milling, see above, iii. 265 & n. 2; below, p. 147. Illustrations both of these coins and those of Cromwell are in G. C. Brooke, *Engl. Coins*, pls 51, 59, 60. Cf. also G. Vertue, *Medals, coins of Thomas Simon* (1793); *Numis. Chron.* (ser. 4), 9/56+.
2. Thomas Simon, chief graver to the Mint, 1645–60.
3. Roettier: there were three

brothers of this name acting as gravers at the Mint. The reference here is probably to John.
4. Most numismatists regard Simon's work as superior, and his coins to be among the most beautiful ever struck in England: *The Times*, 26 October 1957, p. 9.
5. The Commonwealth coinage had been completely demonetised since 1 March 1662. Cf. above, ii. 224 & n. 3.

it is to be doing my business betimes. About noon Sir J. Mennes came to me and stayed half an hour with me in my office, talking about his business with Sir W. Penn and (though he be an old doter) yet he told me freely how sensible he is of Sir W. Penn's treachery in this business and what poor ways all along he hath taken to ingraciate himself, by making Mr. Turner write out things for him and then he give them to the Duke; and how he decoyed him to give Mr. Coventry 100*l* for his place – but that Mr. Coventry did give him 20*l* back again. All this I am pleased to hear, that his knavery is found out. Dined upon a poor Lenten dinner at home, my wife being vexed at a fray this morning with my Lady Batten about my boy's going thither to turn the water-cock, with their maids leave, but my Lady was mighty high upon it, and she would teach his mistress better manners; which my wife answered aloud, that she might hear, that she could learn little manners of her. After dinner to my office, and then we sat all the afternoon till 8 at night; and so wrote my letters by the post, and so before 9 home, which is rare with me of late, I staying longer; but with multitude of business, my head akes and so I can stay no longer, but home to supper and to bed.

11. Up betimes, and to my office all the morning. Walked a little in the garden with Sir W. Batten, talking about the difference between his Lady and my wife yesterday, and I doubt my wife is to blame. About noon, had news by Mr. Wood that Butler, our chief witness against Field,[1] was sent by him to New-England, contrary to our desire, which made me mad almost; and so Sir J. Mennes, Sir W. Penn, and I dined together at Trinity-house and thither sent for him to us and told him our minds; which he seemed not to value much, but went away. I wrote and sent an express to Walthamstow to Sir W. Batten[2] (who is gone thither this morning) to tell him of it. However, in the afternoon Wood sends us word that he hath appointed another to go, who shall overtake the ship in the Downes. So I was late at the office; among other things, writing to the Downes to the commander-in-chief and putting things into the surest course I could to help that business. So home and to bed.

1. See above, iii. 23 & n. 2.   2. MS. 'Sir W. Penn'.

12.*ᵃ* Up betimes and to my office all the morning with
Captain Cocke, ending their account of their Riga Contract for
Hemp.¹ So home to dinner, my head full of business against the
office. After dinner comes my uncle Thomas with a letter to
my father, wherein, as we desire, he and his son do order their
Tenants to pay their rents to us; which pleases me well.² In
discourse he tells me my uncle Wight thinks much that I do
never see them, and they have reason; but I do apprehend their
hav[ing] been too far concerned with my uncle Tho. against
us, so that I have had no mind hitherto; but now I will go see
them. He being gone, I to the office; where at the choice of
Maisters and Chyrurgeons for the fleet now going out,³ I did my
business as I could wish, both for the persons I have a mind to
serve and in getting the warrants signed drawn by my clerks,
which I was afeared of.⁴

Sat late; and having done, I went home; where I find Mary
Ashwell come to live with us, of whom I hope well and pray
God she may please us – which though it cost me something,
yet will give me much content. So to supper and to bed. And
find by her discourse and carriage tonight, that she is not proud
but will do what she is bid; but for want of being abroad,
knows not how to give that respect to her mistress as*ᵇ* she will
do when she is told it – she having been used only to little
children, and there was a kind of a mistress over them.

Troubled all night with my cold, I being quite hoarse with it,
that I could not speak to be heard at all almost.

13. Up pretty earely and to my office all the morning busy.

a figure smudged   *b* MS. 'is'

1. See above, p. 49, for the contract with George Cocke and his
partners.
2. PL (unoff.), Freshfield MSS,
no. 7, dated this day from St Paul's
Churchyard, and addressed to their
'Loving Unkell'; endorsed on the
same day by Pepys himself. This
concerned the Brampton and Buck-
den lands of the estate of Robert
Pepys: see above, p. 42 & n. 2.

3. This squadron sailed to Portugal and the Mediterranean in early
May, more than a month later than
expected: PRO, Adm. 106/7, no. 199;
HMC, *Heathcote*, pp. 65–6, 80; *CSPD
1663–4*, p. 130.
4. Fees or gratuities would thereby
accrue to Pepys and his clerks: cf.
below, p. 74.

At noon home to dinner, expecting Ashwells father, who was here in the morning and promised to come, but he did not; but there came in Captain Grove and I find him to be a very stout man, at least in his discourse he would be thought so; and I do think he is and one that bears me great respect and deserves to be encouraged for his care in all business.[1]

Abroad by water with my wife and Ashwell and left them at Mrs. Pierces, and I to White-hall and St.*a* James parke (there being no Commission for Tanger sitting today as I looked for), where I walked an hour or two with great pleasure, it being a most pleasant day. So to Mrs. Hunts and there find my wife; and so took them up by coach and carried them to Hide parke, where store of coaches and good faces. Here till night, and so home and to my office to write by the post; and so to supper and to bed.

14. Up betimes. And to my office, where we sat all the morning; and a great rant I did give to Mr. Davis of Deptford and others about their hard usage of Michell in his*b* Bewpers, which he serves in for flags – which did trouble me, but yet it was in defence of what was truth.[2] So home to dinner, where Creed dined with me and walked a good while in the garden with me after dinner; talking, among other things, of the poor service which Sir J Lawson did really do in the Streights, for which all this great fame and honour done him is risen.[3] So to

a l.h. repl. s.h. 'the'   *b* repl. 'the'

---

1. Edward Grove, naval captain, acted as a river agent for the Navy Board – an efficient one, but fussy and boastful, to judge by his correspondence. On 21 February (above, p. 52) he had impressed Pepys by his willingness to defend the Board against the Exchequer's bailiffs. In 1665 he was guilty of cowardice during the battle of Lowestoft, when Pepys wrote him off as a 'prating coxcombe... of no courage': below, vi. 130. In 1664 Pepys had considered him as a possible husband for his sister Paulina: below, v. 42–3.

2. John Davis (Storekeeper, Deptford) had complained that the flags provided by John Mitchell, the contractor, did not correspond with the pattern he had submitted, and Mitchell had later to accept a reduced sum in payment: *CSPD 1663–4*, p. 39; ib., *Add. 1660–85*, p. 107. Pepys had reason to believe that Davis favoured Whistler, a rival contractor: NWB, pp. 19, 48.

3. Cf. above, pp. 3–4 & n.

my office, where all the afternoon giving Maisters their warrants for this voyage, for which I hope hereafter to get something at their coming home.

In the evening my wife and I and Ashwell walked in the garden, and I find she is a very pretty ingenuous* girl at all sorts of fine works; which pleases me very well and I hope will be very good entertainment for my wife, without much cost. So to write by the post, and so home to supper and to bed.

15. *Lords=day.* Up and with my wife and her woman Ashwell, the first time, to church; where our pew so full with Sir J. Mennes's sister and her daughter, that I perceive when we come all together some of us must be shut out – but I suppose we shall come to some order what to do therein. Dined at home, and to church again in the afternoon; and so home and I to my office till the evening, doing one thing or other and reading my vowes*a* as I am bound every Lord's day, and so home to supper and talk; and Ashwell is such good company that I think we shall be very lucky in her. So to prayers and to bed.

This day, the weather, which of late hath been very hot and fair, turns very wet and cold, and all the church-time this afternoon it thundered mightily, which I have not heard a great while.

16. Up very betimes and to my office; where, with several Masters of the King's ships, Sir J. Mennes and I advising upon the business of Slopps, wherein the seaman is so much abused by the pursers;[1] and that being done, then I home to dinner and so carried my wife to her mother's, set her down and Ashwell to my Lord's lodging, there left her, and I to the Duke, where we

a l.h. repl. s.h. 'weekly'

1. Since the 1620s seamen's clothes had been stored on board ship under the control of the purser, who often forced expensive items on the sailors. On 26 March 1663 the Duke of York issued instructions regulating their number and cost, and removing control from the pursers: PRO, Adm. 2/1733/61 (printed *Mem. (naval),* pp. 75–9); cf. Tedder, pp. 69–70; Ehrman, pp. 122–3. It was an old abuse (Oppenheim, p. 286), and persistent: in 1668 Edward Barlow complained of it (*Journal,* ed. B. Lubbock, i. 151–2).

met of course* and talked of our Navy matters. Then to the Commission of Tanger and there, among other things,*a* had my Lord Peterborough's commission read over; and Mr. Secretary Bennet did make his Queerys upon it, in order to the drawing one for my Lord Rutherford more regularly, that being a very extravagant thing.[1]

Here long discoursing upon my Lord Rutherfords despatch, and so broke up. And going out of the Court, I met with Mr. Coventry and so he and I walked half an hour in the long Stone Gallery – where we discoursed of many things. Among others, how the Treasurer doth*b* entend to come to pay in course[2] – which is the thing of the world that will do the King the greatest service in the Navy, and which joys my heart to hear of. He tells me of that business of Sir J. Mennes and Sir W. Penn, which I knew before but took no notice, or little, that I did know it. But he told me it was chiefly to make Mr. Petts being joined with Sir W. Batten to go down the better. And doth tell me how he well sees that neither one nor the other can do their duties without help.[3] But however, will let it fall at present without doing more in it, to see whether they will do their duties themselfs – which he well sees, and saith, they do not. We discoursed of many other things to my great content; and so parted and I to my wife at my Lord's lodgings, where I heard Ashwell play first upon the Harpsicon, and I find she doth play pretty well – which pleaseth me very well. Thence home by

a repl. 'think'   *b* l.h. repl. s.h. 'did'

---

1. Peterborough's commission as Governor (16 September 1661) was couched in full-flowing English, and looked forward to an ambitious extension of the territory. Extracts in Routh, pp. 17–18.

2. I.e. to pay the navy's creditors in the order in which the debts had been contracted. Carteret never did so; no doubt the intention had been inspired by a letter from the Duke (12 March) asking for a full review before 25 March of the existing state of accounts and for preparations for future expenditure: PRO, Adm. 2/1745, n.p. Other attempts to pay in course were made later: Pepys, in a wry letter to Coventry (9 November 1665) made it clear that it was impossible, for it 'implies an income in some near proportion to the expense': *Further Corr.*, p. 76.

3. Nothing came of the proposal to join Pett with Batten. They had in any case recently quarrelled: above, pp. 53–4. For the scheme to associate Penn with Mennes in a joint comptrollership, see above, p. 61 & n. 1.

coach, buying at the Temple the printed virginall-book[1] for her, and so home and to my office a while; and so home to supper and to bed.

17. Up betimes and to my office a while, and then home and to Sir Wm. Batten; with whom by coach to St. Margaretts-hill in Southworke, where the Judge of the Admiralty came and the rest of the Doctors of the Civill law and some other Comissioners; whose Commission of Oyer and Terminer was read, and then the charge given by Dr Exton – which methought was somewhat dull, though he would seem to entend it to be very Rhetoricall, saying that Justice had two wings, one of[a] which spread itself over the land and the other over the water, which was this Admiralty court. That being done and the Jury called, they broke up and to dinner to a Taverne hard by, where a great dinner, and I with them; but I perceive that this Court is yet but in its infancy (as to its rising again)[2] and their design and consultation was, I could overhear them, how to proceed with the most solemnity and spend time, there being only two businesses to do, which of themselfs would not spend much time. In the afternoon to the Court again, where first Abraham, the Boatswain of the King's pleasure-boat, was tried for drowning a man;[3] and next, Turpin accused by our wicked rogue Field for stealing the King's timber.[4] But after full examinacion they were both

a MS. 'when'

---

1. Probably Playford's *Musicks Hand-maide* (1663), sold at his shop there. (E).

2. The Court of Admiralty had never been abolished, but had lost, and was still losing, a great deal of its jurisdiction to the courts of common law: Sir W. Holdsworth, *Hist. Engl. law*, i (1922), 556–7. An act of 1662 had restored to it all prize jurisdiction, but achieved slow results: Duke of York, *Mem. (naval)*, pp. 95+. The judges and officers received dwindling fees, and were soon complaining that it was diffi-

cult to pay for meals such as this: HMC, *Eliot Hodgkin*, pp. 174–5.

3. John Abraham, waterman, once of Greenwich, had been indicted for killing Gilbert Bradshawe in a fight on 28 July: PRO, HCA 1/9/45.

4. William Turpin, labourer, of Wapping, was accused of having in his possession three pieces of timber, marked with the King's broad arrow, worth £15: PRO, HCA 1/9/44, 57, 58. Edward Field, who had informed against him, had also informed against the Navy Board on another matter: above, iii. 23 & n. 2.

acquitted; and as I was glad of the first for the saving the man's life, so did I take the other as a very good fortune to us; for if Turpin had been found guilty, it would have sounded very ill in the eares of all the world in the business between Field and us.

So home, with my mind at very great ease, over the water to the Tower; and thence, there being nobody at the office, we being absent and so no office could be kept – Sir W. Batten and I to my Lord Mayors, where we found my Lord with Collonell Strangways and Sir Rd. Floyd, Parliament men, in the cellar drinking; where we sat with them and then up, and by and by comes in Sir Rd. Ford. In our drinking, which was alway going, we had many discourses; but from all of them, I do find Sir R. Ford a very able man of his brains and tongue, and a Scholler.[1] But my Lord Mayor I find to be a talking, bragging Bufflehead,[2] a fellow that would be thought to have led all the City in the great business of bringing in the King; and that nobody understood his plots and the dark lanthorn he walked by, but led them and plowed with them as oxen and Asses (his own words) to do what he had a mind – when in every discourse, I observe him to be as very a coxcomb as I could have thought had been in the City. But he is resolved to do great matters in pulling down the Shops quite through the City, as he hath done in many places, and will make a through-passage quite through the City, through Canning-street, which endeed will be very fine.[3] And then his precept which he in vain-glory said he had drawn up himself and had printed it, against Coachmen and Carrmen affronting of the gentry in the street, it is drawn so like a fool, and some faults

1. Sir Richard Ford, Spanish merchant, M.P. for Southampton and later (1670-1) Lord Mayor of London, had been educated at Oxford and was to be elected F.R.S. in 1673. He was responsible for the publication in 1664 of Thomas Mun's *England's treasure by foreign trade*: see *CSPD 1663-4*, p. 527.

2. According to the Venetian Resident, Sir John Robinson was 'a rich and talented man': *CSPVen. 1661-4*, p. 200.

3. The city was suffering from traffic congestion and this reference is presumably to one-storey shops built between the frontages of churches and public buildings and the thoroughfare. These tended to encroach on the thoroughfare. Cf. below, p. 191; 5 May 1667 & n. (R).

was found openly in it, that I believe he will have so much wit as not to proceed upon it, though it be printed.[1]

Here we stayed talking till 11 at night – Sir Rd. Ford breaking to my Lord our business of our patent to be Justices of the Peace in the City,[2] which he stuck at mightily; but however, Sir R. Ford knows him to be a fool, and so in his discourse he made him appear and cajolled him into a consent to it; but so as I believe, when he comes to his right mind tomorrow, he will be of another opinion; and though Sir R Ford moved it very weightily and neatly, yet I had rather it had been spared now.

But to see how he doth rant and pretend to sway all the City in the Court of Aldermen, and says plainly that they do nor can do nor will he suffer them to do anything but what he pleases; nor is there any officer of the City but of his putting in, nor any man that could have kept the City for the King thus well and long but him – and if the country can be preserved, he will undertake that the City shall not dare to stir again – when I am confident there is no man almost in the City cares a turd for him, nor hath he brains to out-wit any ordinary tradesman.

So home and wrote a letter to Comissioner Pett to Chatham, by all means to compose the business between Major Holmes and Cooper his Maister;[3] and so to bed.

18. Wake betimes and talked a while with my wife about a wench*a* that she had*b* hired yesterday, which I would have enquired after before she comes, she having lived in great fami-

---

a MS. 'wife'   *b* repl. 'would'

---

1. Issued on 3 March, it complained that 'Noblemen, Ladies, Gentlemen and persons of quality' were being discouraged from shopping in the city by reason of the 'rudeness, affronts and insolent behaviour' of, among others, 'Hackney-coachmen, Carmen, Draymen, Colliers'. 'The unruely & meaner sort of people,' said the Mayor, had 'under the late usurped powers, been encouraged & borne up in their undutifulnesse & contempt of their Superiors'. City constables were admonished to apprehend the offenders. LRO, Journals 45, f. 264*v*. No printed copies have been traced.

2. See below, p. 82, n. 1.

3. See above, p. 67, n. 1.

lies;[1] and so up and to my office – where all the morning; and at noon home to dinner and after dinner by water to Redriffe, my wife and Ashwell with me, and so walked; I left them at Halfway-house and I to Deptford, where up and down the store-houses and on board two or three ships now getting ready to go to sea; and so back and finde[a] my wife walking in the way, so home again, merry with our Ashwell, who is a merry jade; and so a while to my office and then home to supper and to bed. This day, my Tryangle[2] (which was put in tune yesterday) did please me very well, Ashwell playing upon it pretty well.

19. Up betimes and to Woolwich all alone by water, where took the officers most a-bed. I walked and enquired how all matters and businesses go. And by and by to the Clerk of the Cheques house and there eat some of his good Jamaica brawne, and so walked to Greenwich[b] – part of the way Deane[3] walking with me, talking of the pride and corruption of most of his fellow officers of the yard (and which I believe to be true). So to Deptford, where I did the same to great content, and see that people begin to value me as they do the rest. At noon Mr. Wayth[4] took me to his house, where I dined and saw his wife, a pretty woman, and had a good fish dinner; and after dinner he and I walked to Redriffe, talking of several errors in the Navy; by which I learned a great deal and was glad of his company. So by water home, and by and by to the office, where we sat till almost 9 at night. So after doing my own business in my office, writing letters &c., home to supper and to bed, being weary and vexed that I do not find other people so willing to do business as myself when I have taken pains to find out what in the yards is wanting and fitting to be done.

a l.h. repl. s.h. 'there'   *b* repl. 'D'-

---

1. One of the families was that of Albemarle: below, p. 86. The practice of requiring testimonials was just coming in: cf. D. M. Stuart, *Engl. Abigail*, pp. 61+.
2. Perhaps the 'Triangle virginall' of 14 June 1661. (E).

3. Anthony Deane, Assistant-Shipwright, Woolwich.
4. Robert Waith, Paymaster to the Navy Treasurer.

20. Up betimes; and over the water and walked to Deptford, where up and down the yard and met the two Clerks of the Cheque to conclude [by] our method their Call=bookes,[1] which we have done to great perfection. And so walked home again, where I find my wife in great pain abed of her months; I stayed and dined by her. And after dinner walked forth and by water to the Temple, and in Fleet Street bought me a little sword with gilt handle, cost 23s[2] – and silk stockings to the colour of my riding cloth suit, cost 15s. And bought me a belt there too, cost 15s. And so calling at my Brothers, I find he hath got a new maid, very likely girl; I wish he do not play the fool with her. Thence homeward; and meeting with Mr. Kirton's kinsman in Paul's churchyard, he and I to a Coffee-house,[3] where I hear how there had like to have been a surprizall of Dublin by some discontented protestants, and other things of like nature; and it seems the Comissioners have carried themselfs so high for the papists that the others will not endure it. Hewlett and some others are taken and clapped up. And they say the King hath sent over to dissolve the parliament there, who went very high against the Comissioners.[4] Pray God send all well. Thence

1. Cf. above, iii. 289 & n. 2. The Clerks were Thomas Cowley of Deptford and William Sheldon of Woolwich.

2. A low price: cf. J. D. Aylward, *Smallsword in Engl.*, p. 24. Smallswords (originally French) were now in fashion: cf. above, ii. 29 & n. 2. The hilt would probably be bound in gilt wire.

3. Possibly 'the coffee-house at west end of St Paul's, London' (Boyne, no. 2730), kept by Luke Petley and known as the Turk's Head: BL, Add. 5071 (28). Joseph Kirton, of St Paul's Churchyard, was Pepys's bookseller. (R).

4. The Commissioners were those adjudging land claims: see above, p. 66, n. 1. Ormond, the Lord Lieutenant, was empowered to dissolve the parliament if he thought it necessary. In fact, it was adjourned and then prorogued on no fewer than thirty-four occasions, and did not meet again for more than two years – until 26 October 1665. A plot to take Dublin Castle and kidnap the Lord Lieutenant had been discovered (see Ormond's reports, 7 and 28 March, in *CSP Ireland 1663–5*, pp. 34–51). William Hewlett (Hulet), one of the two leaders of the small party who were to execute the plot, was imprisoned, but for lack of evidence could not be arraigned. He was reported to have boasted that he had been the executioner of Charles I: op. cit., p. 34. See T. Carte, *Ormond*, iv. 123+.

home and in comes Captain Ferrer and by and by Mr. Bland to
see me, and sat talking with me till 9 or 10 at night and so good-
night – the Captain to bid my wife to his child's christening.
So my wife being pretty well again and Ashwell there, we
spent the evening pleasantly, and so to bed.

21. Up betimes and to my office, where busy all the morning.
And at noon, after a little dinner, to it again; and by and by,
by appointment, our full board met, and Sir Phillip Warwicke
and Sir Robt. Long came from my Lord Treasurer to speak with
us about the state of the debts of the Navy and how to settle it,
so as to begin upon the new Foundacion of 200000*l* per annum[1]
which the King is now resolved not to exceed. This discourse
done and things put in a way of doing – they went away; and
Captain Holmes being called in, he begun his high complaint
against his Master, Cooper, and would have him forthwith
discharged[2] – which I opposed, not in his defence but for the
justice of proceeding, not to condemn a man unheard. Upon
[which] we fell from one word to another that we came to very
high Termes, such as troubled me, though all and the worst I ever
said was that that was insolently and illmannerdly spoken
– which he told me it was well it was here that I said it. But all
the officers, Sir G. Carteret, Sir J. Mennes, Sir W. Batten, and
Sir W. Penn cried shame of it. At last he parted, and we resolved
to bring the dispute between him and his Master to a trial next
week – wherein I shall not at all concern myself in defence of
anything that is unhandsome on the Maister's part, nor willingly
suffer him to have any wrong. So we rose and I to my office
troubled, though sensible that all the officers are of opinion that
he hath carried himself very much unbecoming him.
So wrote letters by the post, and home to supper and to bed.

22. *Lords day.* Up betimes, and in my office wrote out our
Bill for the Parliment, about our being made Justices of Peace

1. See above, iii. 297 & n. 1. The
Duke of York had on 12 March commanded the Navy Board to meet the
officers of the Exchequer sometime
before the end of the quarter: PRO,
Adm. 2/1745, f. 88*v*. Warwick was

secretary to the Lord Treasurer;
Long an Auditor of the Receipt in the
Exchequer.
2. See above, p. 67, n. 1; below,
p. 84.

in the City.[1] So home and to church, where a dull formall
fellow that prayed for the Right Honourable John, Lord Barkely,
Lord President of Conought &c.[2]

So home to dinner; and after dinner, my wife and I and her
woman by coach to Westminster; where being come too soon
for the Christening, we took up Mr. Creede and went out to take
some ayre as far as Chelsey and further – I lighting there and
letting them go on with the coach, which while I went to the
church, expecting to see the young ladies of the schoole, Ashwell
desiring me; but I could not get in far enough and so came out
and at the coach's coming back went in again; and so back
to Westminster and led my wife and her to Captain Ferrers,
and I to my Lord Sandwich and with him talking a good while.
I find the Court would have this indulgence go on, but the parliament are against it.[3] Matters in Ireland are full of discontent.

Thence with Mr. Creede to Captain Ferrers, where many fine
ladies. The house well and prettily furnished. She lies in in
great state.[4] Mr. G. Mountagu, Collonell Williams (Cromwell

1. This bill was not a parliamentary
bill but an office memorandum which
led to legislation. Two copies survive. One (in Pepys's hand) is dated
21 March and endorsed 'Papers
relating to the Bill to be preferred in
Parliament for empowering the Principal Officers and Commissioners to
act as Justices of Peace in the Citty';
PRO, SP 29/70/6; calendared in
CSPD 1663-4, p. 82. The other, in
a clerk's hand, undated but identical
except for the title, is in NMM,
LBK/8, pp. 48-9; printed in *Further
Corr.*, pp. 3-5. It resulted in an act of
1664 (16 Car. II c. 5), amended in
1667 (18-19 Car. II c. 12), by which
the officers of the Board, or any two
of them, were empowered to punish
by a fine of not more than 20*s.*, and
by imprisonment not exceeding one
week, anyone making 'any disturbance, fighting, or quarrelling in the
yards, stores, or offices aforesaid, at
pay-days, or on other occasions relating to the naval services'. Batten
and Pepys were already J.P.'s in four
counties where the royal dockyards
were situated (cf. above, i. 252), but
neither they nor their colleagues had
similar powers in the City, within
whose jurisdiction their office lay.
Hence Field had been able to prosecute them: cf. above, iii. 23.
Powers were needed to keep order
during the public pays, and to ad-
minister oaths in the course of the
examination of the accounts of pursers, boatswains etc. For an example
of their use, see below, p. 292 & n. 2.

2. Berkeley was a Navy Commissioner, 1660-4.

3. See above, p. 68, n. 1.

4. Ann Ferrer was the daughter of
a Scottish earl (and had been cut off
by her family for marrying beneath
her): Carte 74, f. 365*v*.

that was),[1] and Mrs. Wright as proxy for my Lady Jemimah, were Witnesses. Very pretty and plentiful entertainment. Could not get away till 9 at night, and so home. My coach cost me 7s. So to prayers and to bed.

This day, though I was merry enough, yet I could not get yesterday's quarrel out of my mind and a natural fear of being challenged by Holmes for the words I did give him,[2] though[a] nothing but what did become me as a Principall Officer.[b]

23. Up betimes and to my office. Before noon my wife and I eat something, thinking to have gone abroad together; but in comes Mr. Hunt, who we were forced to stay to dinner; and so while that was got ready, he and I abroad about two or three small business of mine and so back to dinner; and after dinner he went away and my wife and I and Ashwell by coach, set my wife down at her mother's and Ashwell at my Lord's, she going to see her father and mother, and I to White-hall, being fearful almost, so poor a spirit I have, of meeting Major Holmes. By and by the Duke comes and we with him about our usual business; and then the Committee for Tanger – where after reading my Lord Rutherfords commission[3] and consented to, Sir R. Ford, Sir W. Rider and I were chosen to bring in some Laws for the Civill government of it; which I am little able to do but am glad to be joined with them, for I shall learn something of them.[4]

Thence to see my Lord Sandwich, and who should I meet at the doore but Major Holmes. He would have gone away, but I

a s.h. repl. s.h. and l.h. 'on Sa'-   *b* l.h. repl. l.h. 'Officers'

---

1. Henry Cromwell, of Ramsey, Hunts., cousin of the Protector, but a royalist, changed his surname (as did many of his relatives) at the Restoration, and adopted that of his early 16th-century ancestor, Richard Williams, who had assumed the name Cromwell out of compliment to his patron, Thomas Cromwell, Earl of Essex. VCH, *Hunts.*, ii. 70.
2. Holmes fought a duel with a fellow-officer in 1666: below, vii.

348. He had once shown what Pepys thought to be an improper interest in Mrs Pepys: above, ii. 237.
3. As Captain-General, Commander-in-Chief and Vice-Admiral of Tangier: see below, p. 116 & n. 1.
4. Tangier was not incorporated as a municipality until 4 June 1668. Until then civil government was in the hands of the military. Cf. below, p. 89, n. 1.

told him I would not spoil his visitt and would have gone; but however, we fell to discourse and he did as good as desire excuse for the high words that did pass in his heat the other day, which I was willing enough to close with; and after telling him my mind, we parted – and I left him to speak with my Lord. And I by coach home – where I find Will Howe come home today with my wife and stayed with us all night, staying late up singing songs; and then he and I to bed together in Ashwells bed and she with my wife. This the first time that I ever lay in that room. ⟨This day, Greatorex brought me a very pretty Weather glasse for heat and cold.⟩*a*

24.*b* Lay pretty long, that is, till past 6 a-clock; and then up and W. Howe and I very merry together, till having eat our breakfast, he went away and I to my office. By and by Sir J. Mennes and I to the Victualling Office by appointment to meet several persons upon stating the demands of some people of money from the King.

Here we went into their Bakehouse and saw all the ovens at work – and good bread too, as ever I would desire to eat.

Thence Sir J. Mennes and I homeward, calling at Brownes the Mathematician[1] in the Minnerys with a design of buying Whites ruler[2] to measure timber with, but could not agree on the price. So home and to dinner, and so to my office.

Where we sat anon; and among other things, had Cooper's business tried against Captain Holmes.[3] But I find Cooper a fudling, troublesome fellow, though a good artist;* and so am contented to have him turned out of his place. Nor did I see reason to say one word against it, though I know what they did against him was with great envy and pride.

So anon broke up, and after writing letters, &c., home to supper and to bed.

---

a paragraph crowded into bottom of page   *b* repl. '25'

---

1. John Brown, maker of mathematical instruments.
2. A type of early slide-rule, inscribed with logarithmic scales; used e.g. for calculation of area or volume. See below, p. 85, n. 1.
3. See above, p. 67 & n. 1.

25. *Lady day.* Up betimes and to my office, where all the morning. At noon dined and to the Exchange; and thence to the Sun taverne to my Lord Rutherford and dined with him and some other his officers and Scotch gentlemen of fine discourse and educacion. My Lord used me with great respect and discoursed upon his business as with one that he did esteem of. And indeed, I do believe that this guarrison is now likely to come to something under him. ⟨By and by he went away, forgetting to take leave of me, my back being turned looking upon the Aviary, which is there very pretty and the Birds begin to sing well this spring.⟩*a*

Thence home and to my office till night, reading over and consulting upon the book and Ruler that I bought this morning of Browne concerning the Lyne of Numbers, in which I find much pleasure.[1]

This evening came Captain Grove about hiring ships for Tanger. I did hint to him my desire that I could make some lawfull profit thereof – which he promises, that he will tell me of all that he gets and that I shall have a share – which I did not demand, but did silently consent to it – and money, I perceive something will be got thereby.

At night Mr. Bland came and sat with me at my office till late, and so I home and to bed. This day being washing-day and my maid Susan ill, or would be thought so, puts my house so out of order that we have no pleasure almost in anything, my wife being troubled thereat for want of a good cook-maid, and moreover I cannot have my dinner tomorrow as I ought in memory of my being cut of the Stone.[2] But I must have it a day or two hence.

26. Up betimes and to my office – leaving my wife in bed to take her physique; myself also not being out of some pain today, by some cold that I have got by the sudden change of the weather from hot to cold.

    a   addition crowded in between paragraphs

---

1. John Brown, *The use of the line of numbers, on a sliding (or glasiers) rule . . . for the measuring of timber, either round or square . . . first drawn by Mr. White, and since much inlarged . . . by* John Brown; printed as second part of his *Description and use of the carpenters-rule* (1662; PL 85).

2. Cf. above, i. 97 & n. 3. The feast was this year held on 4 April.

This day is five years since it pleased God to preserve me at my being cut of the Stone; of which, I bless God, I am in all respects well – only, now and then upon taking cold I have some pain, but otherwise in very good health alway. But I could not get my feast to be keeped today as it used to be, because of my wife's being ill and other disorders by my servants being out of order.

This morning came a new Cooke-maid[1] at 4*l* per annum, the first time I ever did give so much – but we do hope it will be nothing lost by keeping a good cook. She did live last at my Lord Monkes house. And endeed, at dinner did get what there was very prettily ready and neat for me, which did please[a] me much.

This morning my uncle Thomas was with me according to our agreement and I paid him the 50*l*,[2] which went against my heart to part with and yet I must be contented. I used him very kindly and desire to continue so, voyd of any discontent as to my estate, that I may fallow my business the better.

At the Change I met him again, with intent to have met with my uncle Wight to have made peace with him, with whom by my long absence I fear I shall have a difference; but he was not there and so we missed. All the afternoon sat at the office about business, till 9 or 10 at night; and so despatch business and home to supper and to bed.

My mayde Susan went away today, I giving her something for her lodging and diet somewhere else a while, that I might have room for my new mayde.

27. Up betimes, and at my office all the morning; at noon to the Exchange and there by appointment met my uncles Thomas and Wight, and from thence with them to a Taverne and there paid my Uncle Wight three pieces of gold for himself, my aunt, and their son that is dead, left by my Uncle Robt.,[3] and read over our agreement with my uncle Tho. and the state of our debts and Legacys. And so good friendship, I think, is made up between us all, only we have the worst of it in having

a MS. 'place'

---

1. This was Hannah: she left on 17 August.
2. See above, p. 42.
3. The Wights had been left 20*s.* each to buy rings.

so much money to pay. Thence I to the Exchange again; and thence with Creede into Fleetstreete, and calling at several places about business in passing; at the Hercules pillers, he and I dined though late; and thence with one that we found there, a friend of Captain Ferrers I used to meet at the playhouse;[1] they would have gone to some gameing-house – but I would not, but parted; and staying a little in Paul's churchyard at the forreigne booksellers, looking over some Spanish books and with much ado keeping myself from laying out money there; as also with them, being willing enough to have gone to some idle house with them; I got home; and after a while at my office, home to supper and to bed.[a]

28. Up betimes and to my office, where all the morning. Dined at home and Creede with me. And though a very cold day and high wind, yet I took him by land to Detford, my common walk, where I did some little businesses; and so home again, walking both forward and backwards, as much along the streets as we could, to save going by water.

So home; and after being a little while hearing Ashwell play of the Triangle,* to my office and there late, writing a chiding letter[2] to my poor father about his being so unwilling to come to an account with me; which I desire he might do, that I may know what he spends and how to order the estate so as to pay debts and legacies – as far as may be. So late home to supper and to bed.

29. *Lords=day.* Waked as I use to do, betimes; but being Sunday and very cold, I lay long, it rayning and snowing very hard, which I did never think it would have done any more this year.

Up and to church. Home to dinner. After dinner, in comes Mr. Moore and sat and talked with us a good while – among other things, telling me that my Lord nor he are under no apprehensions of the late discourse in the House of Commons

a entry crowded into bottom of page

1. See below, p. 179 & n. 2.   2. Untraced.

concerning Resumpcion of Crowne Lands – which I am very glad of.[1]

He being gone – up to my chamber, where my wife and Ashwell and I all the afternoon, talking and laughing; and by and by I a while to my office, reading over some papers which I find in my man Wms. chest of drawers; among others, some old precedents concerning the practice of this office heretofore, which I am glad to find and shall make use of. Among others, an Oath which the Principall Officers were bound to swear at their entrance into their offices, which I would be glad were in use still.[2]

So home and fell hard to make up my monthly accounts – letting my family go to bed after prayers. I stayed up long, and find myself, as I think, fully worth 670*l*. So with good comfort to bed, finding that though it be but little, yet I do get ground every month. I pray God it may continue so with me.

30. Up betimes and find my weatherglasse sunk again just to the same position which it was last night, before I had any fire made in my chamber – which had made it rise in two hours time above half a degree. So to my office – where all the morning ⟨and at the Glasse house⟩; and after dinner by coach with Sir W. Penn, I carried my wife and her woman to Westminster, they to visit Mrs. Ferrer and Clerke, we to the Duke, where we did our usual business, and afterward to the Tanger Comittee, where among other thing, we all of us sealed and signed the Contract for building the Molle with my Lord Tiviott, Sir J. Lawson, and Mr. Cholmely – a thing I did with a very ill will, because a thing which I did not at all understand, nor any or few of the whole board.[3] We did also read over the proposicions for the Civill government and Law merchant of the towne, as they

1. A committee had been appointed on 23 March to enquire into alienations of Crown land. On 19 May the grants made by the King to Sandwich and Albemarle were exempted: *CJ*, viii. 456, 487. Henry Moore, a lawyer, was Sandwich's man of business.

2. Only the Treasurer now took an oath. John Hollond in 1659 had also

urged the revival of this practice: *Discourses* (ed. Tanner), pp. 277–8. For the papers Pepys now read, see below, p. 96 & n. 4.

3. The 'heads of agreement' between the Commissioners and the three undertakers named here are in BM, Sloane 3509, ff. 18+; a copy of the contract is in Rawl. C 423, ff. 74+. Cf. Routh, p. 344 & n.

were agreed on this morning at the glasse-house by Sir R. Ford and Sir W Rider (who drow them); Mr. Povy and myself as a Comittee appointed to prepare them – which were in substance but not in the manner of executing them, independent wholly upon [what] the Governor consented to.¹

Thence to see my Lord Sandwich, who I find very merry and every day better and better. So to my wife, who waited my coming at my Lord's Lodgeings, and took her up and by coach home – where no sooner come, but to bed, finding myself just in the same condition I was lately by the extreme cold weather, my pores stopped and so my body all inflamed and itching. So keeping myself warm and provoking myself to a moderate sweat, 《31.》 and so somewhat better in the morning. And to that purpose I lay long, talking with my wife about my father's coming; which I expect today, coming up with the horses brought up for my Lord.

Up and to my office, where doing business all the morning; and at Sir W. Batten's, whither Mr. Gauden and many others came to us about business. Then home to dinner, where W. Joyce came, and he still a talking, impertinent fellow.

So to the office again; and hearing by and by that Madam Clerke, Pierce, and others were come to see my wife, I stepped in and stayed a little with them; and so to the office again, where late; and so home to supper and to bed.

1. Cf. above, p. 83 & n. 4. The instructions now issued to Teviot (27 April) included an assurance that the city would be treated as a free port, and referred to instructions about the courts maritime which were to be sent to him by the Duke of York. In civil cases the Governor was to follow the precedents established by his predecessors. Rawl. C 423, ff. 71*v*+.

APRILL. 1663./

1. Up betimes and abroad to my brother's; but he being gone out, I went to the Temple to my Cosen Roger Pepys to see and talk with him a little – who tells me that with much ado the parliament doth agree to throw down popery; but he says it is with so much spite and passion and an endeavour of bringing all nonconformists into the same condition, that he is afeared matters will not yet go so well as he could wish.[1]

Thence back to my brother's, in my way meeting Mr. Moore and talking with him about getting me some money; and calling at my brother's, they tell me that my brother is still abroad and that my father is not yet up – at which I wondered, not thinking that he was come, though I expected him, because I looked for him at my house. So I up to his bedside and stayed an hour or two talking with him. Among other things, he tells me how unquiett my mother is grown, that he is not able to live almost with her, if it were not for Pall.

All other matters are as well as upon so hard conditions with my Uncle Tho. we can expect them.

I left him in bed, being very weary – to come to my house tonight or tomorrow when he please; and so I home, calling on the virginall-maker[2] – buying a Rest for myself to tune my Tryangle* and taking one of his people along with me to put it in tune once more; by which I learned how to go about it myself for the time to come.

So to dinner, my wife being lazily in bed all this morning. Ashwell and I dined below together, and a pretty girl she is and I hope will give my wife and myself good content, being very humble and active. My Cooke-maid also doth dress my meat very well and neatly.

1. A bill to prevent the growth of Popery had just reached committee stage, and a joint address of both Houses had been presented to the King on 31 March for the expulsion of priests and Jesuits: *CJ*, viii. 460; *LJ*, xi. 502–4. Cf. above, p. 68, n. 1. The Commons' feeling against Protestant dissent soon found expression in a Conventicle Bill: below, pp. 159–60.

2. Possibly Thatcher: above, ii. 44. (E).

So to my office all the afternoon till night. And then home – calling at Sir W. Batten, where was Sir J. Mennes and Sir W. Penn – I telling them how by my letter this day from Comissioner Pett, I hear that his Stempeece he undertook for for the new ship at Woolwich, which we have been so long to our shame in looking for, doth prove knotty and not fit for service.[1] Lord, how Sir J. Mennes, like a mad coxcomb, did swear and stamp, swearing that Comissioner Pett hath still the old heart against the King that ever he had, and that this was his envy against his brother that was to build that ship – and all the damnable reproaches in the world – at which I was ashamed but said little. But upon the whole, I find him still a fool, led by the nose with stories told by Sir W. Batten, whether with or without reason. So, vexed in my mind to see things ordered so unlike gentlemen or men of reason, I went home and to bed.

2. Up by very betimes and to my office, where all the morning till towards noon, and then by coach to Westminsterhall with Sir W. Penn; and while he went up to the House, I walked in the hall with Mr. Pierce the surgeon, that I met there – talking about my business the other day with Holmes, whom I told all my mind and did freely tell how I do depend upon my care and diligence in my imployment to bear me out against the pride of Holmes or any man else in things that are honest, and much to that purpose; which I know he will make good use of.[2] But he did advise me to take as few occasions as I*a* can of disobliging Comanders, though this is one that everybody is glad to hear that he doth receive a cheque.

By and by the House rises, and I home again with Sir W. Penn, all the way talking of the same business; to whom I did on purpose tell my mind freely and let him see that it must be a

a repl. symbol rendered illegible

---

1. The stempiece was the main vertical timber of the bow. On 2 April Pepys wrote to Commissioner Pett despairing of getting another: NMM, LBK/8, p. 54. The ship was the *Royal Catherine*; for her launch, see below, v. 306. The builder was Pett's brother, Christopher.

2. Pearse was surgeon to the Duke of York.

wiser man then Holmes (in those very words) that shall do me any hurt while I do my duty. I took occasion to remember him of Holmes's words against Sir J. Mennes, that he was a Knave, Rogue, Coward, and that he will kick him and pull him by the eares;[1] which he remembered all of them and may have occasion to do it hereafter to his own shame, to suffer them to be spoke in his presence without any reply but what I did give him, which hath caused all this fewd. But I am glad of it, for I would now and then take[a] occasion to let the world know that I will not be made a novice.

Sir W. Penn took occasion to speak about my wife's strangenesse to him and his daughter; and that believing at last that it was from his taking of Sarah to[b] be his maid,[2] he hath now put her away – at which I am glad.

He told me that this day the King hath sent to the House his concurrence wholly with them against the Popish priests, Jesuits, &c., which gives great content and I am glad of it.[3] So home, whither my father comes and dines with us. And being willing to be merry with him, I made myself so as much as I could; and so to the[c] office, where we sat all the afternoon; and at night, having done all my business, I went home to my wife and father and supped, and so to bed – my father lying with me in Ashwells bed in the red chamber.

3. Waked betimes and talked half an hour with my father, and so I rose and to my office. And about 9 a-clock by water from the Old Swan to White-hall and to Chappell; which being most monstrous full, I could not go into my pew but sat among the Quire. Dr. Creeton the Scotch-man preached a most admirable, good, learned, honest and most severe Sermon, yet Comicall – upon the words of the woman concerning the virgin, "Blessed is the womb that bore thee" (meaning Christ) "and the

a l.h. repl. s.h. 'took'   *b* repl. 'off' or 'of'   *c* l.h. repl. s.h. 'my'

---

1. Above, ii. 229; iii. 14.
2. See above, iii. 295.
3. The King had made an oral answer when the parliamentary ad-

dress was presented on 31 March; he now sent a written reply, dated 1 April: *LJ*, xi. 502–4.

paps that gave thee suck." And he answered, "Nay; rather is he blessed that heareth the word of God and keeps it."[1]

He railed bitterly ever and anon against John Calvin and his brood, the presbyterians, and against the present terme now in use, of "Tender consciences."[2] He ripped up Hugh Peters (calling him "that execrable Skellum") his preaching and[a] stirring up the maids of the city to bring in their bodkins and thimbles.[3]

Thence going out of White-hall, I met Captain Grove, who did give me a letter directed to myself from himself; I discerned money to be in it and took it, knowing, as I found it to be, the proceed of the place I have got him, to have[b] the taking up of vessells for Tanger. But I did not open it till I came home to my office; and there I broke it open, not looking into it till all the money was out, that I might say I saw no money in the paper if ever I should be Questioned about it. There was a piece in gold and 4*l* in silver.

So home to dinner with my father and wife. And after dinner up to my Tryangle, where I find that above[c] my expectation Ashwell hath very good principles of Musique and can take out a lesson[4] herself with very little pains – at which I am very glad. Thence away back again by water to White-hall and there to the Tanger Committe, where we find ourselfs at a great stand – the establishment being but 70000*l* per annum – and the[d] forces to be kept in the town, at the least estimate that my Lord Rutherford

a repl. 'up'   *b* repl. ? 'is with'
c l.h. repl. symbol rendered illegible   *d* l.h. repl. s.h. 'men'

---

1. A loose recollection of Luke, xi. 27–8. The preacher was Robert Creighton, Dean of Wells and chaplain to the King. He was often outspoken in the pulpit.

2. The phrase was at least as old as James I's reign, but had been given new currency by its use in the controversial Declaration of Breda (1660). It now referred to the scruples of puritan ministers who would not conform to the terms of the Act of Uniformity of 1662.

3. Peters, the Independent minister, had been the leading preacher of the

New Model army, and had often preached begging sermons. The army became known as the 'Thimble and Bodkin Army'. Cf. W. Yonge, *England's Shame* (1663), p. 35; Butler, *Hudibras*, pt i, canto 2. See also the story about his collection of gold rings in *Tales and jests of Mr. Hugh Peters* (1660), pp. 23–4. Richard Baxter, too, was accused of cajoling 'bodkins and thimbles' from his female admirers: *Autobiography* (Everyman ed.), p. 259.

4. Learn how to perform a piece. (E).

can be got to bring it, is 5300*l*. The charge of this year's work of the Molle will be 13000*l* – besides 1000*l* a year to my Lord Peterburgh as a pension,[1] and the fortificacions and contingencys – which puts us to a great stand. And so, unsettled what to do therein, we rose, and I to see my Lord Sandwich, whom I find merry at Cards; and so by coach home, and after supper a little to my office and so home and to bed.

I find at Court that there is some bad newes from Ireland of an insurreccion of the Catholiques there, which puts them into an alarme.[2]

I hear also in the City that for certain there is an embargo upon all our ships in Spayne, upon this action of my Lord Windsors at Cuba; which signifies little or nothing, but only he had a mind to say that he had done something before he came back again.[3]

Late tonight I sent to invite my uncle Wight and aunt to dinner with Mrs. Turner tomorrow.

4. Up betimes and to my office. By and by to Lumbard-streete by appointment, to meet Mr. Moore; but the business not being ready, I returned to the office, where we sat a while; and being sent for, I returned to him and there signed to some papers in the conveying of some lands morgaged by Sir Rob. Parkehurst in my name to my Lord Sandwich[4] – which I having done, I returned home to dinner.

Whither by and by comes Roger Pepys, Mrs. Turner, her daughter, Joyce Norton and a young lady, a daughter of Collonell

---

1. Peterborough had resigned his government of Tangier after a few months' service in 1661-2, in return for a life-pension of £1000 p.a. on the establishment there. Its payment was to give Pepys some difficulty.

2. A number of 'Tories' (Catholic peasants) had risen in protest against decisions of the Court of Claims: HMC, *Ormonde*, n.s., iii. 48-9. Cf. above, p. 80, n. 4. See below, pp. 100, 168.

3. See above, p. 41 & n. 5. Cf. Joseph Williamson to Sir R. Fanshawe

(14 May): 'Letters from Cadiz say they are much dejected there at hearing from the West Indies of our hostile carriage towards them, which has wholly ruined their trade': HMC, *Heathcote*, p. 88. Partly as a result of the raid on Santiago, the English government now forbade privateering expeditions of this sort: A. P. Thornton, *West-India policy under Restoration*, p. 79. Charles II disavowed Windsor's action: ib., p. 81; *CSPVen. 1661-4*, pp. 243, 247-8.

4. See above, i. 310.

Cockes – my uncle Wight – his wife and Mrs. Anne Wight – this being my feast, in lieu of what I should have had a few days ago, for my cutting of the Stone,[1] for which the Lord make me truly thankful.

Very merry before, at, and after dinner, and the more for that my dinner was great and most neatly dressed by our own only mayde. We had a Fricasse of rabbets and chicken – a leg of mutton boiled – three carps in a dish – a great dish of a side of lamb – a dish roasted pigeons – a dish of four lobsters – three tarts – a Lampry pie, a most rare pie – a dish of anchoves – good wine of several sorts; and all things mighty noble and to my great content.

After dinner to Hide parke; my aunt, Mrs. Wight, and I in one Coach, and all the rest of the women in Mrs.*ᵃ* Turners – Roger being gone in haste to the parliament about the carrying this business of the papists, in which it seems there is great contest on both sides.[2] And my uncle and father staying together behind. At the parke was the King, and in another coach my Lady Castlemayne, they greeting one another at every Tour.[3] Here about an hour; and so leaving all by the way, we home and find the house as clean as if nothing had been done there today from top to bottom – which made us give the Cooke 12*d* a piece, each of us.

a repl. 'another'

1. See above, p. 85 & n. 2.

2. The bill to prevent the growth of Popery was now recommitted and the committee was appointed to meet on the afternoon of this day: *CJ*, vii. 462, 464.

3. It was the custom in spring and summer for members of the fashionable world of London to drive in coaches in the 'Ring' –an internal road within Hyde Park. Cf. Monconys, ii. 21 (May 1663): 'Le cours se fait en rond; ainsi on ne voit pas tous les carrosses si l'on ne change pas son tour. Le Roy & la Reyne y vinrent ensemble dans une fort belle Caliche attelée de six beaux chevaux pies: ils

y demeurent peu, y estant venus tard, & quand ils partirent tous les carrosses suivirent . . .'. Sorbière, in 1664, thought the coaches too numerous and not sufficiently elegant: *Relation d'un voyage en Angleterre* (Cologne, 1667), p. 119. Cf. also H. Misson de Valbourg, *Mémoires et observations faites par un voyageur en Angleterre* (The Hague, 1698), p. 239. The habit had begun as soon as the park was thrown open to the public in the 1620s, and was to continue throughout the 18th and 19th centuries – as long in fact as the horse-drawn carriage remained modish. J. Ashton, *Hyde Park*, pp. 50+.

So to my office about writing letters by the post – one to my brother John at Brampton, telling him (hoping to work a good effect by it upon my mother) how melancholly my father is, and bidding him use all means to get my mother to live peaceably and quietly, which I am sure she neither doth nor I fear can ever do – but frighting her with his coming down no more and the danger of her condition if he should die, I trust may do good.

So home and to bed.

5. *Lords day.* Up and spent the morning till the Barber came in reading in my chamber part of Osborne's *Advice to his Son*[1] (which I shall not never enough admire for sense and language); and being by and by trimmed – to church, myself, wife, Ashwell, &c; and home to dinner, it raining. While that was prepared, to my office to read over my vowes,[2] with great affection* and to very good purpose. So to dinner, and very well pleased with it.

Then to church again, where a simple bawling young Scott[3] preached.

So home to my office alone till dark, reading some part of my old *Navy precedents*, and so home to supper. And after some pleasant talk, my wife, Ashwell and I – to prayers and to bed.

6. Up very betimes; to my office and there made an end of reading my book that I have of Mr. Barlows, of the Journall of the Comissioners of the Navy who begun to act in the year 1618 and continued six years; wherein is fine observations and precedents, out of which I do purpose to make a good collection.[4]

By and by much against my Will, being twice sent for, to Sir G Carterets to pass his accounts there – upon which Sir J.

1. See above, ii. 199, n. 1.
2. See above, p. 8; also ii. 242, n. 1.
3. See above, p. 12, n. 1.
4. The commission of 1618 had been established to rectify the maladministration of the navy under the *régime* of Sir Robert Mansell (Treasurer, 1604–18). The journal here referred to was probably the report of their proceedings, of which a copy remains in Pepys's collection in Rawl. A 455, ff. 76+. Hewer was responsible for making the copy mentioned in this entry: *Naval Minutes*, pp. 95–6. There is a later copy (made from Sir W. Coventry's transcript) in PL 2735.

Mennes, Sir W. Batten, Sir W. Penn and myself all the morning, and again after dinner to it – being vexed at the heart to see a thing of that importance done so slightly and with that neglect, for which God pardon us – and I would I could mend it. Thence, leaving them, I made an excuse and away home; and took my wife by coach and left her at Madam Clerkes to make a visit there, and I to the Comittee of Tanger, where I find to my great joy my Lord Sandwich, the first time I have seen him abroad these some months. And by and by he rose and took leave, being it seems this night to go to Kensington or Chelsey, where he hath taken a lodging for a while to take the ayre.

We stayed; and after business done, I got Mr. Coventree into the matted gallery and told him my whole mind concerning matters of our office, all my discontent to see things of so great trust carried so neglectfully, and what pitiful service the Controller and Surveyor make of their duties. And disburdened my mind wholly to him and he to me his, of many things, telling me that he is much discouraged by seeing things not to grow better and better, as he did well hope they would have done. Upon the whole, after a full houres private discourse, telling one another our minds, we with great content parted; and I, with very great satisfaction for my [having] thus cleared my conscience, went to Dr Clerkes and thence fetched my wife and by coach home. To my office a little to set things in order; and so home to supper and to bed.

7. Up very betimes; and angry with Will that he made no more haste to rise after I called him. So to my office and all the morning there. At noon to the Exchange and so home to dinner, where I find my wife hath been with Ashwell at La Roches[1] to have her tooth drawn, which it seems akes much. But my wife could not get her to be contented to have it drawn after the first twich, but would let it alone; and so they came home with it undone, which made my wife and me good sport. After dinner to the office, where Sir J. Mennes did make a great complaint to me alone, how my clerk Mr. Hater had entered in one of the Seabookes a ticket to have been signed by

1. Peter de la Roche, Mrs Pepys's dentist (and also the King's), seems to have had his surgery near to Fleet Bridge.

him before it had been examined; which makes the old foole mad almost, though there was upon enquiry the greatest reason in the world for it – which though it vexes me, yet it is most [?plain] to see from day to day what a coxcomb he is, and that so great a trust should lie in the hands of such a foole.

We sat all the afternoon; and I late at my office, it being post night; and so home to supper, my father being come again to my house. And after supper to bed; and after some talk, to sleep.

8. Up betimes and to my office; and by and by, about 8 a-clock, to the Temple to Comissioner Pett, lately come to town, and discoursed about the affairs of our office; how ill they go through the corruption and folly of Sir W. Batten and Sir J. Mennes.

Thence by water to White-hall to chapel, where preached Dr. Pierce, the famous man that preached the sermon so much cried up, before the King against the papists.¹

His matter was the Devil tempting*ᵃ* our saviour, being carried into the wilderness by the spirit. And hath as much of natural eloquence as most men that ever I heard in my life, mixed with so much learning.

After sermon I went up and saw the ceremony of the Bishop of Peterborough's paying homage upon the knee to the King, while Sir H. Bennet, Secretary, read the King's grant of the Bishopric of Lincolne, to which he is translated – his name is

a repl. 'carrying'

---

1. Thomas Pierce, chaplain to the King, President of Magdalen, Oxford, and Canon of Canterbury, was a busy disputant against both Papists and Dissenters. The sermon to which Pepys refers had been delivered at Whitehall on 1 February 1663, shortly after the King had issued a declaration of indulgence to the Papists. Printed as *The primitive rule of reformation*, it passed through eight editions before the year was over, and started a European controversy. His style was a little old-fashioned, marked by 'quotations and references to authorities often quaintly applied': W. Fraser Mitchell, *Engl. pulpit oratory*, p. 309.

Dr. Lany.[1] Here I also saw the Duke of Monmouth with his order of the garter – the first time I ever saw it.[2]

I am told that the University of Cambrige did treat him a little while since with all the honour possible – with a Comedy at Trinity College and banquet – and made him Maister in arts there.[3] All which they say the King took very well – Dr Raynbow, Maister of Magdalen, being now Vicechancellor.

Home by water to dinner; and with my father,[a] wife, and Ashwell after dinner, by water toward Woolwich; and in our way I bethought myself that we had left our poor little dog, that fallowed us out a-doors, at the waterside and God knows whether he be not lost; which did not only strike my wife into a great passion, but I must confess, myself also, more then was becoming me. We immediately returned, I taking another boat, and with my father went to Woolwich while they went back to find the dog.

I took my father on board the King's pleasure-boat – and down to Woolwich and walked to Greenwich[b] thence; and turning into the parke to show my father the steps up the hill,[4] we find my wife, her woman, and dog attending us, which made us all merry again, and so took boats – they to Deptford and so by land to Halfway-house, I into the King's yard and overtook them[c] there and eat and drank with them – and saw a company of seamen play drolly at nine-pins, and so home by water. I a little at the office, and so home to supper and to bed – after having Ashwell play my father and me a lesson upon her Tryangle.*

9. Up betimes and to my office, and anon we met upon finishing the Treasurer's accounts. At noon dined at home, and am

a repl. 'm'-   *b* repl. 'D'-   *c* repl. 'themselfs'

---

1. On 18 March royal assent had been given for the election to Lincoln of Benjamin Laney, Bishop of Peterborough since 1660: *CSPD 1663-4*, p. 78.

2. Monmouth had been appointed to the order on 28 March and was installed on 22 April. Pepys had already seen the insignia belonging to Sandwich: above, i. 161.

3. He had received the degree (by royal mandate) on 16 March, together with 34 gentlemen of his nomination. Details of the ceremony in C. H. Cooper, *Annals of Cambridge* (1845), iii. 509.

4. The steps were part of the recent landscaping of the park: see above, iii. 63 & n. 4.

vexed to hear my wife tell me how our mayd Mary doth endeavour to corrupt our cook-maid, which did please me very well.   But I am resolved to rid the house of her as soon as I can.

To the office and sat all the afternoon till 9 at night; and an hour after home to supper and bed – my father lying at Toms tonight, he dining with my Uncle Fenner and his sons and a great many more of that gang at his own cost today.

To bed, vexed also to think of Sir J. Mennes's finding fault with Mr. Hater for what he had done the other day[1] – though there be no hurt in the thing at all, but only the old fool's jealousy – made worse by Sir W. Batten.

10.   Up very betimes and to my office, where most hard at business alone all the morning.   At noon to the Exchange, where I hear that after great expectation from Ireland and long stop of letters, there is good news come that all is quiet – after our great noise of troubles there, though some stir hath been as was reported.[2]

Off the Exchange with Sir J. Cutler and Mr. Grant to the Royall Oake Taverne in Lumbard-street, where ⟨Alexander⟩ Broome the poet was, a merry and witty man I believe, if he be not a little conceited.[3]   And here drank a sort of French wine called *Ho Bryan*,[4] that hath a good and most perticular taste that I never met with.

Home to dinner, and then by water abroad to White-hall. My wife to see Mrs. Ferrers.   I to White-hall and the park, doing no business.   Then to my Lord's lodgings, met my wife, and walked to the New Exchange; there laid out 10s upon pendents and painted leather-gloves, very pretty and all the mode. So by coach home and to my office till late, and so to supper and bed.

11.   Up betimes and to my office – where we also sat all the morning till noon; and then home to dinner, my father being there but not very well.   After dinner, in comes Captain Lambert

1. See above, pp. 97–8.
2. See above, p. 94 & n. 2.
3. Aubrey (i. 126) records that he had been a precocious scholar, being 'in his accedence [Latin grammar] at four years old and a quarter.'   He was a writer of lyrics and epigrams, an anthologist and a dramatist.
4. *Haut Brion*, a red Bordeaux.

of the *Norwich*, this day come from Tanger, whom I am glad to see. There came also with him Captain Wager, and afterwards in came Captain Allen to see me, of the *Resolucion*. All stayed a pretty while; and so away, and I a while to my office; then abroad into the street with my father and left him to go to see my aunt Wight and uncle, entending to lie at Toms tonight or my Cosen Scotts, where it seems he hath hitherto lain and is most kindly used there. So I home and to my office very late, making up my Lord's Navy accompts, wherein I find him to stand Debtor 1200*l*.[1] So home to supper and to bed.[a]

12. *Lords day.* Lay till 8 a-clock in bed, which I have not done a great while. Then up and to church, where I find our pew altered by taking some of the hind pew to make ours bigger, because of the number of women; more by Sir J. Mennes's company then we used to have.

Home to dinner; and after dinner, entending to go to Ch[e]lsey to my Lord Sandwich, my wife would needs go with me, though she walked a-foot to White-hall – which she did, and stayed at my Lord's lodgings while Creede and I took a turn at Whitehall; but no coach to be had and so I returned to them and sat talking till evening; and then got a coach and to Grayes Inne walks – where some handsome faces. And so home and there to supper; and a little after 8 a-clock, to bed – a thing I have not done God knows when.

Coming home tonight, a drunken boy was carrying by our Constable to our new pair of stocks – to handsel them – being a new pair and very handsome.

13. Up by 5 a-clock and to my office – where hard at work till towards noon, and home and eat a bit; and so going out, met with Mr. Mount, my old acquaintance, and took him in and drunk a glass of wine or two to him and so parted, having not time to talk together; and I with Sir W. Batten to the Stylyard and there eat a Lobster together; and Wyne the King's Fish-

a entry crowded into bottom of page

---

1. See below, pp. 114, 116–17. The accounts were those of the voyage of 1661–2 to Tangier and Lisbon.

monger coming in, we were very merry half an hour; and so by
water to White-hall, and by and by, being all met, we went in to
the Duke and there did our business.   And so away, and anon
to the Tanger Committee – where we had very fine discourse
from Dr. Walker and Wiseman, Civilians, against our erecting a
Court=merchant at Tanger,[1] and well answered in many things by
my Lord Sandwich (whose speaking I never till now observed so
much to be very good) and Sir Rd. Ford.

By and by, the discourse being ended, we fell to my Lord
Rutherfords despatch; which doth not please him, he being a
Scott and one resolved to scrape every penny that he can get by
any way, which the Comittee will not agree to.   He took offence
at something and rose away without taking leave of the board;
which all took ill, though nothing said but only by the Duke of
Albemarle, who said that we ought to settle things as they ought
to be; and if he will not go upon those termes, another man will
no doubt.[2]   Here late, quite finishing of things against his going,
and so rose; and I walked home, being accompanied by Creed to
Templebarr, talking of this afternoon's passages; and so I called
at the Wardrobe in my way home and there spoke at the Horne-
taverne with Mr. Moore a word or two, but my business was
with Mr. Townsend (who is gone this day to his country house)[3]
about sparing Charles Pepys some money of his bills due to him
when he can.[4]   But missing him, lost my labour.

So walked home, finding my wife abroad at my aunt Wights;
who coming home by and by, I home to supper and to bed.

14.   Up betimes to my office, where busy till 8 a-clock, that
Sir W. Batten, Sir J. Mennes, Sir W. Penn and I down by barge

1. The civil (Roman) lawyers (practising in mercantile, admiralty and international law) had an interest in keeping this jurisdiction in the hands of the Governor, to whom the Lord Admiral deputed powers of admiralty. For this argument, see above, p. 89 & n. 1. A mayoral court merchant was established in 1668.

2. Rutherford left for Tangier without reaching any agreement with the committee: below, p. 116. He was already one of the contractors for the mole.

3. At Elvetham, Hants. Thomas Townshend, sen., was Sandwich's principal assistant at the Wardrobe.

4. According to the Wardrobe accounts, £150 was owed to Charles Pepys, joiner ('*conjugator*'): PRO, LC 9/107, f. 102r. He was Pepys's cousin.

to Woolwich to see the *Royall James* lanched, where she hath been under repair a great while. We stayed in the yard till almost noon, and then to Mr Falconer's to a dinner of fish of our own sending. And when it was just ready to come upon the table, word is brought that the King and Duke are come, so they all went away to show themselfs, while[a] I stayed and had a little dish or two by myself, resolving to go home; and by the time I had dined, they came again, having gone to little purpose, the King I believe taking little notice of them. So they to dinner, and I stayed a little with them and so good-bye. I walked to Greenwich, studying my slide-rule for measuring of timber,[1] which is very fine. Thence to Deptford by water and walked through the yard, and so walked to Redriffe and so home, pretty weary, and to my office; where anon they all came home, the ship[b] well lanched, and so sat at the office till 9 at night – and I longer, doing business at my office; and so home to supper, my father being come, and to bed.

Sir G. Carteret tells me tonight that he perceives the Parliament is likely to make a great bustle before they will give the King any money – will call all things into Question; and above all, the expenses of the Navy. And doth enquire into the King's expenses everywhere and into the truth of the report of people's being forced to sell their bills at 15 per cent losse in the Navy.[2] And lastly, that they are in a very angry pettish mood at present, and not likely to be better.[3]

15. Up betimes; and after talking with my father a while, I to my office and there hard at it till almost noon; and then went down the River with Mayres the pourveyor[4] to see[c] a ship's loading of Norway goods; and called at Sir W. Warrens yard[5] and so home to dinner.

After dinner, up with my wife and Ashwell a little to the Tryangle;* and so I down to Deptford by land, about looking out a couple of Catches fittest to be speedily set forth, in answer to a

a repl. 'where'   *b* MS. 'shipped'   *c* MS. 'she'

---

1. See above, p. 84 & n. 2.   on the revenue: *CJ*, viii. 453, 471.
2. Cf. above, p. 17.   4. Robert Mayer(s), purveyor of
3. For almost a month committees   timber to the navy, Woolwich.
and sub-committees had been at work   5. At Wapping.

letter of Mr. Coventrys to me[1] – which done, I walked back again, all the way reading of my book of Timber measure,[2] comparing it with my new Sliding rule, brought home this morning, with great pleasure.

Taking boat again, I went to Shishes yard; but he being newly gone out toward Deptford, I fallowed him thither again; and there seeing him, I went and with him pitched upon a couple; and so by water home, it being late, past 8 at night, the wind cold and I a little weary. So home to my office; then to supper and bed.

16. Up betimes and to my office. Anon met to pass Mr. Pitts (Sir J. Lawson's Secretary and Deputy Treasurer) accounts for the voyage last to the Streights[3] – wherein the demands are strangely irregular; and I dare not oppose it alone, for making an enemy, and both no good but only bring a review upon my Lord Sandwiches; but God knows, it troubles my heart to see it and to see the Comptroller, whose duty it is, to make no more matter of it. At noon home[a] for an hour to dinner, and so to the office, public and private, till late at night; so home to supper and bed with my father.

17. Up by 5 a-clock, as I have long done, and to my office all the morning; at noon home to dinner with my father with us. Our dinner, it being Goodfriday, was only sugar sopps and fish; the only time that we have had a Lenten dinner all this Lent.[4]

This morning Mr. Hunt the instrument-maker brought me home a Basse-viall to see whether I like it, which I do not very well; besides, I am under a doubt whether I had best buy one

a preceded by small blot

---

1. Duke of York to Navy Board, 15 April, requiring immediate provision of two ketches, one for the Downs, and another for Tangier: PRO, Adm. 106/7, f. 471r. Warrants for the *Giles* and the *Eaglet* were issued on the 16th: ib., loc. cit.

2. Probably John Brown's *Description and use of the carpenter's rule* (1662): above, p. 85, n. 1.

3. In 1662, when Lawson had imposed treaties on Algiers, Tunis and Tripoli. He had returned in January 1663. For some of the accounts (1 April 1661–15 January 1663), see PRO, Adm. 20/4, p. 427.

4. They had had a 'poor Lenten dinner' on 10 March.

yet or no – because of spoiling my present mind and love to business.[1]

After dinner my father and I walked into the city a little and parted; and I to Pauls churchyard to cause the title of my English *Mare Clausum* to be changed and the new title, dedicated to the King, to be put to it, because I am ashamed to have the other seen dedicate[d] to the Commonwealth.[2]

So home and to my office till night; and so home to talk with my father, and sup and to bed – I having not had yet one Quarter of an hour's leisure to sit down and talk with him since he came to towne. Nor do I know till the holidays when I shall.

18. Up betimes and to my office, where all the morning. At noon to dinner. With us was Mr. Creed, who hath been deeply engaged at the office this day about the ending his accounts; wherein he is most unhappy to have to do with a company of Fooles, who after they had signed his accounts and made bills upon them, yet dare not boldly assert to the Treasurer that they are satisfyed with his accounts. Hereupon all dinner and walking in the garden the afternoon, he and I talking of the ill-management of our office, which God knows is very ill; for the King's advantage, I would I could make it better.

In the evening to my office; and at night home to supper and bed.

19. *Easterday.* Up, and this day put on my close-kneed colourd suit; which, with new stockings of that colour, with belt and new gilt-handle sword, is very handsome.

1. Pepys later had one made by Wise of Bishopsgate St: below, pp. 232, 252, 282–4. (E).

2. John Selden's *Mare Clausum seu De dominio maris libri*, first published in 1635, had been dedicated to Charles I. The translation of 1652, by Marchamont Needham, had been dedicated to 'the Supreme Autoritie of the Nation – the Parliament of the Commonwealth of England'. This was re-issued in April 1663, with a new title: *Mare Clausum, the right and* *dominion of the sea. ...* In addition, owners of the 1652 edition could buy – as Pepys did – separate pages containing a frontispiece with the royal arms, the new title, the original dedication of 1635 and an advertisement to the reader. The bookseller selling it was Robert Walton, at the Globe and Compasses, on the n. side of St Paul's Yard. Cf. *Trans. Stat. Reg.*, ii. 322. The PL has copies of the editions of 1635 and 1652: PL 2048, 2131.

To church alone. And so to dinner, where my father and brother Tom dined with us. And after dinner to church again, my father sitting below in the chancel. After church done (where the young scotch man preaching, I slept all the while) my father and I to see my uncle and aunt Wight; and after a stay of an hour there, my father to my brothers and I home to supper. And after supper fell in discourse of dancing, and I find that Ashwell hath a very fine carriage, which makes my wife almost ashamed of herself to see herself so outdonne; but to-morrow she begins to learn to dance for a month or two.

So to prayers and to bed – my Will being gone with my leave to his father's this day for a day or two, to take physique these holidays.

20. Up betimes as I use to do, and in my chamber begun to look over my father's accounts, which he brought out of the country with him by my desire, whereby I may see what he hath received and spent. And I find that he is not anything extravagant, and yet it doth so far outdo his estate that he must either think of lessening his charge or I must be forced to spare money out of my purse to help him through; which I would willing do, as far as 20*l* goes.

So to my office the remaining part of the morning, till towards noon, and then I went to Mr. Grants;[1] there saw his prints which he showed me, and endeed are the best collection of any things almost that ever I saw, there being the prints of most of the greatest houses, churches and antiquitys in Italy and France, and brave cutts.[2] I had not time to look them over as I ought, and which I will take time hereafter to do, and therefore left them and home to dinner.

After dinner, it raining very hard, by coach to White-hall; where after Sir G. Carteret, Sir J. Mennes, Mr. Coventry, and I had been with the Duke, we to the Committee of Tanger and did matters there – despatching wholly my Lord Tiviott; and so broke up.

With Sir G. Carteret and Sir J. Mennes by coach to my Lord Treasurers, thinking to have spoke about getting money

1. John Graunt, shopkeeper and demographer, of Birchin Lane.
2. An early indication of Pepys's

lasting interest in topographical prints. Nothing is known of Graunt's collection. (OM).

for paying the yards, but we found him with some ladies at
Cards; and so it being a bad time to speak, we parted and Sir
J. Mennes and I home. And after walking with my wife in the
garden late – to supper and to bed – being somewhat troubled
at Ashwell's desiring and insisting over-eaguerly upon her going
to a ball to meet some of her old companions at a dancing school
here in town next Friday; but I am resolved she shall not go.
So to bed.

This day the little Duke of Munmouth was marryed at White-
hall in the King's*a* chamber.[1] And tonight is a great supper and
dancing at his lodgings near chearing-cross. I observed his coate
at the tail of his coach. He gives the armes of England, Scott-
land, and France, quartered, upon some other fields; but what it
is that speaks his being a bastard I know not.[2]

21. Up betimes and to my office, where first I ruled with red
Inke my English *Mare clausum*; which, with the new Orthodox
title, makes it now very handsome.[3] So to business and then
home to dinner; and after dinner to sit at the office in the afternoon and thence to my study late and so home to supper – to
play a game at cards with my wife, and so to bed. Ashwell
plays well at cards, and will teach us to play; I wish it do not lose
too much of my time and put my wife too much upon it.

22. Up betimes and to my office; very busy all the morning
there, entering things into my book Manuscript,[4] which pleases
me very much. So to the Change and thence to my uncle

a preceded by small blot

---

1. The bride was Anne Scott, *suo
jure* Countess of Buccleuch; she was
12 and the Duke 14. According to
GEC the marriage took place at the
house of her stepfather, the Earl of
Wemyss, but the Venetian Resident
confirms Pepys's statement: *CSPVen.
1661–4*, p. 245.

2. Monmouth's grant of arms of
8 April 1663 did not include the
baton-sinister, which was added, with
other alterations, in a second grant of
22 April: GEC; John Woodward,
Heraldry (1896 ed.), ii. 181–2.

3. See above, p. 105, n. 2. This
copy (now PL 2131) has red lines
around the edges of the margins and
underneath words of the frontispiece,
title-page and preface. There are
none in the body of the work. For
Pepys's love of such embellishments,
see the instructions attached to the
codicil of his will, 13 May 1703:
Pepysiana, pp. 265–6.

4. See above, p. 11 & n. 1.

Wights by invitacion; whither my father, wife and Ashwell came – where we had but a poor dinner and not well dressed; besides, the very sight of my aunts hands and greasy manner of carving did almost turn my stomach.   After dinner, by coach to the King's Playhouse, where we saw*a* but part of *Witt without mony*[1] – which I do not much like; but coming late put me out of tune, and it costing me four half-Crownes for myself and company.[2]   So the play done, home and to my office a while; and so home, where my father (who is not very currant and so very melancholy) and we played at cards; and so to supper and to bed.

23.   *St. George's day and Coronacion*: the King and Court being at Windsor, at the installing of the Prince of Denmarke by proxy[3] and the Duke of Monmouth —

I up betimes and with my father, having a fire made in my wife's new closet above, it being a wet and cold day; we sat there all the morning, looking over his country accounts ever since his going into the country.   I find his spending hitherto hath been (without extraordinary charges) at full a 100*l* per annum – which troubles me and I did let him apprehend it, so as that the poor man wept, though he did make it well appear to me that he could not have saved a farthing of it.   I did tell him how things stand with us and did show my distrust of Pall, both for her good nature and housewifery; which he was sorry for, telling me that, endeed, she carries herself very well and carefully; which I am glad to hear, though I doubt it was but his doting and not being able to find her miscarriages so well nowadays as he could heretofore have done.

We resolve upon sending for Will Stankes up to town, to give us a right understanding in all that we have in Brampton; and before my father goes, to settle*b* everything, so as to resolve how to find a living for my father and to pay debt and legacies – and

---

a repl. 'sit'   *b* repl. 'sit'-

1. A comedy by John Fletcher (q.v. above, i. 267 & n. 2); now at the TR, Vere St.   According to Langbaine (p. 216), Mohun played the leading role of Valentine for the King's Company.   (A).

2. Seats in the pit cost *2s. 6d.*   (A).

3. Christian, Prince of Denmark (King Christian V, 1670-99), who had visited England in the previous autumn.   Sir George Carteret acted as his proxy.   *Kingd. Intell.*, 27 April, pp. 270-2; *CSPVen. 1661-4*, p. 193.

also to understand truly how Tom's condition is in the world, that we may know what we are like to expect of his doing, ill or well.

So to dinner; and after dinner to the office, where some of us met and did a little business. And so to Sir W. Batten to see a little picture drawing of his by a Duchman, which is very well done.

So to my office and put a few things in order; and so home to spend the evening with my father. At Cards till late; and being at supper, my boy being sent for some mustard to a neat's tongue, the rogue stayed half an hour in the streets, it seems at a Bonefire; at which I was very angry and resolve to beat him tomorrow.

24. Up betimes; and with my salt Eele went down in the pa[r]ler, and there got my boy and did beat him till I was fain to take breath two or three times; yet for all, I am afeared it will make the boy never the better, he is grown so hardened in his tricks; which I am sorry for, he being capable of making a brave man and is a boy that I and my wife love very well. So made me ready and to my office – where all the morning; and at noon home, whither came Captain Holland, who is lately come home from Sea and hath been much harassed in law about the ship which he hath bought; so that it seems, in a despaire he endeavoured to cut his own throat, but is recovered it; and it seems, whether by that or any other's persuasion (his wife's mother being a great zealot), he is turned almost a Quaker, his discourse being nothing but holy, and that impertinent that I was weary of him. At last, pretending to go to the Change, we walked thither together; and there I left him and home to dinner, sending my boy by the way to enquire after two dancing*a*-masters at our end of the towne for my wife to learn of – of whose names the boy brought word.[1]

After dinner, all the afternoon at home, fidling upon my viallin (which I have not done many a day) while Ashwell danced above in my upper best chamber, which is a rare room for Musique.[2] Expecting this afternoon my father to bring my Cosen Scott and Stradwicke, but they came not; and so in the evening, we by our-

a symbol smudged

1. Pembleton was chosen: below, p. 111. (E).
2. This room (below, p. 126)

seems to have become 'our dancing room' by the following 6 May. (E).

selfs to Halfway-house to walk; but did not go in there, but only
a walk; and so home again and to supper, my father with us, and
had a good Lobster, entended for part of our entertainment to
those people today; and so to cards and then to bed – being the
first day that I have spent so much to my pleasure a great while.

25. Up betimes and to my Vyall*a* and song book a pretty while;
and so to my office. And there we sat all the morning. Among
other things, Sir W. Batten had a mind to cause Butler (our chief
witnesse in the business of Field, whom we did force back from
an imployment going to sea to come back to attend our law-
Sute) to be borne as a Mate on the *Raynbow* in the Downes, in
compensacion of his loss for our sakes. This he orders an order
to be drawn by Mr. Turner for; and after Sir J. Mennes, Sir
W. Batten and Sir W. Penn had signed it, it came to me and I
was going to put it up into my book, thinking to consider of it
and give them my opinion upon it before I parted with it; but
Sir W. Penn told me I must sign it or give it him again, for it
should not go without my hand. I told him what I meant to do
– whereupon Sir W. Batten was very angry, and in a great heat
(which will bring out anything that he hath in his mind; and I
am glad of it, though it is base in him to have a thing so long in
his mind without speaking of it, though I am glad this is the
worst; for if he had worse, it would out as well as this some time
or other) told me that I should not think as I have heretofore
done, make them sign orders and not sign them myself – which,
what ignorance or worse it implies is easy to judge, when he shall
sign (and the rest of the board too, as appears in this business)
to things for company and not out of their justice; for after
some discourse, I did convince them that it was not fit to have
it go; and so Sir W. Batten first, and then the rest, did willingly
cancel all their hands and tore the order. For I told them,
Butler being such a rogue as I know him and we have all signed
him to be to the Duke, it will be in his power to publish this to
our great reproach, that we should take such a course as this to
serve ourself in, wronging the King by putting him into a place
he is nowise capable of, and that in an Admirall ship.
   At noon we rise, Sir W. Batten ashamed and I vexed, and so
home to dinner. And after dinner, walked to the old exchange

a l.h. repl. l.h. ? 'Vo'-

and so all along to Westminster-hall [and] White-hall, my Lord
Sandwich's lodgings; and going by water back to the Temple,
did pay my debts in several places in order to my examining my
accounts tomorrow, to my great content. So in the evening
home; and after supper (my father at my brother's) and merrily
practising to dance, which my wife hath begun to learn this day
of Mr. Pembleton; but I fear will hardly do any great good at it,
because she is conceited that she doth well already, though I
think no such thing.[1]
So to bed.

At Westminster-hall this day I buy a book lately printed and
licensed by Dr. Stradling, the Bishop of Londons Chaplin, being
a book discovering the practices and designs of the Papists, and the
fears of some of our own fathers of the Protestant church heretofore of the return to popery – as it were, prefacing it.[2]

The book is a very good book; but forasmuch as it touches one
of the Queen-Mothers fathers-confessors, the Bishop (which
troubles many good men and members of parliament) hath called
it in[3] – which I am sorry for.

Another book I bought,[a] being a collection of many expressions of the great Presbyterian preachers upon public occasions in
the late times, against the King and his party (as some of Mr.
Marshall, Case, Calamy, Baxter, &[c.]),[4] which is good reading

a repl. 'buy'

1. The lessons continued until the
following 27 May. (E).
2. *Fair-warning: the second part.
Or XX prophecies concerning the return
of Popery. By Archbishop Whitgift,
Archbishop Laud, Archbishop Bancroft,
Bishop Sanderson, Bishop Gauden, Mr.
Hooker and others. With the several
plots laid by Campella, Contzen, and
others of late, in private letters for
restoring Papacy, now discovered. . .* ;
not in the PL. Stradling's impri-
matur is dated 31 March 1663.
3. The passage to which objection
was taken is at p. 47, where Father
Sarabras, confessor to Queen Henrietta Maria, is alleged to have
attended the King's execution in 1649,
and to have tossed his cap in the air for
joy as the head fell. The story was a
common one. The Bishop was
Sheldon.
4. *Evangelium Armatum.* A speci-
men; or short collection of several
doctrines & positions destructive to our
government, both civil and ecclesiastical,
preached and vented by the known
leaders & abetters of the pretended
reformation, such as Mr. Calamy, Mr.
Jenkins, Mr. Case, Mr. Baxter, Mr.
Caryll, Mr. Marshall and others etc.
(1663); not in the PL. It consists
of extracts from sermons mostly
preached before Parliament.

now, to see what they then did teach and the people believe, and what they would seem* to be now.

Lastly, I did hear that the Queene is much grieved of late at the King's neglecting her, he having not supped once with her this Quarter of a year, and almost every night with my Lady Castlemayne, who hath been with him this St. Geo[r]ges feast at Windsor and came home with him last night; and which is more, they say is removed, as to her bed, from her house to a chamber in White-hall next to the King's owne – which I am sorry to hear, though I love her much.

26. *Lords=day.* Lay pretty long in bed, talking with my wife; and then up and set to the making up of my month's accounts; but Tom coming (with whom I was angry for his botching my camelott coat) to tell me that my father and he would dine with me and that my father was at our church, I got me ready and heard a very good sermon of a country Minister, upon "How blessed a thing it is for Brethren to live together in unity."*a*[1] So home and all to dinner, and then would have gone by coach to have seen my Lord Sandwich at Chelsy, if the man would have taken us; but he denying it, we stayed at home. And I all the afternoon upon my accounts, and find myself worth full 700*l*, for which I bless God, it being the most I was ever yet worth in money.

In the evening (my father being gone to my brother's to lie tonight) my wife, Ashwell, and the boy and I, and the dog, over the water and walked to Halfway house and beyond, into the fields gathering of Cowslipps; and so to Halfway-house with some cold lamb we carried with us, and there supped; and had a most pleasant walk back again – Ashwell all along telling us some parts of their maske at Chelsy school,[2] which was very pretty; and I find she hath a most prodigious memory, remembering so much of things acted six or seven years ago.

So home; and after reading my vowes, being sleepy, without prayers to bed; for which God forgive me.

a Here, and occasionally elsewhere, Pepys writes the text of a sermon in large symbols.

---

1. A loose recollection of Ps. cxxxiii. 1.

2. Cf. above, pp. 45, 58–9. For masques at Chelsea schools, see Eric W. White, *Rise Engl. opera*, pp. 41–2. (E).

27. Up betimes and to my office; where doing businesses alone a good while, till people came about business to me.

Will Griffin tells me this morning that Captain Browne (Sir W. Batten's brother-in-law) is dead of a blow given him two days ago by a seaman, a servant of his, being drunk, with a Stone striking him on the forehead; for which I am sorry, he having a good woman and several small children.

At the office all the morning; at noon dined at home with my wife, merry. And after dinner by water to White-hall but find the Duke of Yorke gone to St. James's for this summer,[1] and Mr. Coventry, to whose chamber I went, and thence with him and Sir W. Penn up to the Dukes closet – and a good while with him about our Navy business. And so I to White-hall and there alone a while with my Lord Sandwich, discoursing about his debt to the Navy; wherein he hath given me some things to resolve him in. Thence to my Lord's lodging; and thither came Creed to me and he and I walked a great while in the garden; and thence to an alehouse in the market-place[2] to drink fine Lambeth ale; and so to Westminster-hall, and after walking there a great while, home by coach – where I find Mary[3] gone from my wife, she being too high for her, though a very good servant; and my boy too will be going in a few days; for he is not for my family, he is grown so out of order and not to be ruled, and doth himself, against his brother's counsel, desire to be gone; which I am sorry for, because I love the boy and would be glad to bring him to good.

At home with my wife and Ashwell, talking of her going into the country this year; wherein we had like to have fallen out, she thinking that I have a design to have her go, which I have not; and to let her stay here I perceive will not be convenient, for she expects more pleasure then I can give her here, and I fear I have done very ill in letting her begin to learn to dance.

The Queene (which I did not know) it seems, was at Windsor at the late St. Geo[r]ges feast there. And the Duke of Monmouth

---

1. His usual practice.
2. Probably the market-place between King St and Cannon (Channel) Row: see map above, vol. i, p. xxv. (R).

3. The chambermaid: she had been with the Pepyses only since the previous 4 February.

dancing with her with his hat in his hand, the King came in and kissed him and made him put on his hat, which everybody took notice of.

After being a while at my office, home to supper and to bed – my Will being come home again, after being at his father's all the last week, taking physique.

28. Up betimes and to my office, and there all the morning. Only stepped up to see my wife and her dancing-maister at it, and I think after all she will do pretty well at it. So to dinner, Mrs. Hunt dining with us; and so to the*ᵃ* office, where we sat late; and then I to my office, casting up my Lord's sea accounts[1] over again and putting them in order for payment; and so home to supper and to bed.

29. Up betimes, and after having at my office settled some accounts for my Lord Sandwich, I went forth; and taking up my father at my brother's, took coach and towards Chelsey – lighting at an alehouse near the gatehouse at Westminster to drink our morning draught; and so up again and to Chelsey, where we find my Lord all alone at a little table, with one joynt of meat*ᵇ* at dinner. We sat down and very merry, talking – and mightily extolling the manner of his retirement and the goodness of his diet; which endeed is so finely dressed, the mistress of the house, Mrs. Becke, having been a woman of good condition heretofore, a merchant's wife, and hath all things most excellently dressed. Among others, her cheeks*ᶜ* admirable, and so good that my Lord's words were that they were fit to present to my Lady Castlemaine.

From ordinary*ᵈ* discourse, my Lord fell to talk of other matters to me – of which, chiefly the second part of the fray, which he told me a little while since of, between Mr. Edwd. Mountagu and himself.[2] Which is, that after that – he had since been with him three times and no notice taken at all of any difference between them; and yet since that, he hath forborne coming to him almost two months and doth speak not only slightly of my

a l.h. repl. s.h. 'my'   *b* repl. 'meal'   *c* ? an error for 'cakes'
          d repl. ? 'this'

1. See above, p. 101 & n. 1.   2. See above, pp. 46–7.

Lord everywhere, but hath complained to my Lord Chancellor of him, and arrogated all that ever my Lord hath done to be only by his direction and persuasion. Whether he hath done the like to the King or no, my Lord knows not; but my Lord hath been with the King since and finds all things fair; and my Lord Chancellor hath told him of it, but with so much contempt of Mr. Mountagu as my Lord knows himself very secure against anything the fool can do; and notwithstanding all this, so noble is his nature, that he professes himself ready to show kindness and pity to Mr. Mountagu on any occasion.

My Lord told me of his presenting Sir H. Bennet with a gold cup of 100*l* – which he refuses with a compliment; but my Lord would have been glad he had taken it, that he might have had some obligations upon him – which he thinks possible the other may refuse, to prevent it; not that he hath any reason to doubt his kindness. But I perceive great differences there are at Court, and Sir H. Bennet and my Lord Bristoll and their faction are likely to carry all things before them (which my Lord's judgment is, will not be for the best) and perticularly against the Chancellor, who he tells me is irrecoverably lost.[1] But however, that he will not actually joyne in anything against the Chancellor, whom he doth own to be his most sure friend and to have been his greatest – and therefore will not openly act in either, but passively carry himself even.

The Queene, my Lord tells me, he thinks he hath incurred some displeasure with for his kindness to his[a] neighbour, my Lady Castlemayne; with whom[b] my Lord tells me he hath no reason to fall [out] for her sake, whose wit, management, nor interest is not likely to hold up any man; and therefore he thinks it not his obligation to stand for her against his own interest.

The Duke and Mr. Coventry, my Lord says he is very well with, and fears not but they will show themselfs his very good friends; especially at this time, he being able to serve them and they needing him, which he did not tell me wherein.

Talking of the business of Tanger, he tells me that my Lord

a repl. 'my'   *b* MS. 'him'

---

1. An unsuccessful attempt to im-   below, pp. 222–5.
peach Clarendon soon followed:

Tiviott is gone away without the least respect paid to him, nor endeed to any man, but without his commission[1] and (if it be true what he says) having laid out 7 or 8000*l* in commodities for the place; and besides, having not only disobliged all the Commissioners for Tanger, but also Sir Ch. Barkely[2] the other day, who speaking in behalfe of Collonell FitzGerard, that having been Deputy-Governor there already, he ought to have expected and had the Governorship upon the death or removall of the former governor.   And whereas it is said that he and his men are Irish (which is endeed the main thing that hath moved the King and Council to put in Tiviott, to prevent the Irish having too great and the whole command there under Fitzgerard), he further said that there was never an Englishman fit to command Tanger.   My Lord Tiviott answered "Yes", that there were many more fit then himself, or Fitzgerard either.   So that Fitzgerard being so great with the Duke of Yorke, and being already made Deputy-Governor, independent on my Lord Tiviott, and he being also left here behind him for a while, my Lord Sandwich doth think that putting all these things together, the few friends he hath left and the ill posture of his affairs, my Lord Tiviott is not a man of the conduct and management that either people take him to be, or is fit for the command of that place.

And here, speaking of the Duke of Yorke and Sir Ch. Barkely, my Lord tells me that he doth very much admire the good management and discretion and nobleness of the Duke, that whatever he may be led by him or Mr. Coventry singly in private, yet he did not observe that in public matters but he did give as ready hearing and as good acceptance to any reasons offered by any other man against the opinions of them, as he did to them; and would concur in the prosecution of it.   Then wee came to discourse upon his own Sea=accompts and came to a resolution what and how to proceed in them; wherein he resolved, though I offered him a way of evading the greatest part of his debt honestly, by making himself debtor to the Parliament before the King's time, which he might justly do, yet he resolved

1. The commission was issued finally on 2 May. His instructions had been drafted on 27 April: Rawl. C 423, ff. 71*v*–73*r* (copy).

2. The Duke of York's confidant.

to go openly and nakedly in it, and put himself to the kindness of the King and Duke[1] – which humour, I must confess and so did tell him (with which he was not a little pleased), had thriven very well with him, being known to be a man of candid and open dealing, without any private trickes or hidden designs as other men commonly have in what they do.

From that, we had discourse of Sir G Carteret (who he finds kind to him, but it may be a little envious, and most other men are) and of many others; and upon the whole, do find that it is a troublesome thing for a man of any condition at Court to carry himself even and without contracting enemies or envyers; and that much discretion and dissimulacion is necessary to do it.

My father stayed a good while at the window and then sat down by himself while my Lord and I were thus an hour together or two after dinner discoursing. And by and by he took his leave and told me he would stay below for me.

Anon I took leave; and coming down, find my father unexpectedly in great pain and desiring for God sake to get him a bed to lie upon; which I did, and W. How and I stayed by him, in so great pain as I never saw, poor wretch, and with that patience, crying only: "Terrible.: terrible pain, God help me, God help me!' – with that mournful voice, that made my heart ake. He desired to rest a little alone, to see whether it would abate; and W. How and I went down and walked in the gardens, which are very fine, and a pretty fountayne, with which I was finely wetted – and up to a banqueting-house with a very fine prospect. And so back to my father, who I find in such pain that I could not bear*a* the sight of it without weeping, never thinking that I should be able to get him from thence; but at last, finding it like to continue, I got him to go to the coach, with great pain; and driving hard, he all the while in a most unsufferable torment (meeting in the way with Captain Ferrer, going to my Lord to tell him that my Lady Jemimah is come to

a repl. 'endure'

---

1. He owed £1200: above, p. 101. The restored monarchy honoured the debts owed by the revolutionary governments. The Duke's orders for the making out of bills on Sandwich's accounts were issued on 29 and 30 May: BL, Add. 9314, f. 5*r*. For the payments, see PRO, Adm. 20/4, pp. 248–9, 251.

town and that W. Stankes is come with my father's horses), not
staying the coach to speak with anybody; but once, in Pauls
churchyard, we were forced to stay, the jogging and pain making
my father vomit – which it never had done before. At last we
got home; and all helping him, we got him to bed presently;
and after half an hour's lying in his naked bed (it being a rupture
which he is troubled [with] and hath been this 20 years, but never
in half the pain and with so great swelling as now, and how this
came but by drinking of cold small beer and sitting long upon a
low stool and then standing long after it, he cannot tell), his
bowells went up again into his belly, being got forth into his cod,
as it seems is usual with very many men – after which he was
at good ease and so continued – and so fell to sleep and we went
down; whither W. Stankes was come with his horses. But it is
very pleasant to hear how he rails at the rumbling and ado that
is in London over it is in the country, that he cannot endure it.

He supped with us, and very merry. And then he to his
lodgings at the Inne with the horses, and so we to bed – I to my
father, who is very well again, and both slept very well.

30. Up; and after drinking my morning draught with my
father and W. Stankes, I went forth to Sir W. Batten, who is
going (to no purpose, as he uses to do) to Chatham upon a
Survey.

So to my office, where till towards noon; and then to the
Exchange and back home to dinner, where Mr. Hunt, my father,
and W. Stankes; but Lord, what a stir Stankes makes with his
being crowded in the streets and wearied in walking in London,
and would not be woo'd by my wife and Ashwell to go to a play
nor to White-hall or to see the Lyons,[1] though he was carried
in a coach. I never could have thought there had been upon
earth a man so little curious in the world as he is.

At the office all the afternoon till 9 at night; so home – to
cards with my father, wife and Ashwell, and so to bed.

1. In the Tower menagerie.

MAY.

1. Up betimes and my father with me, and he and I all the morning and Will Stankes private in my wife's Closet above, settling our matters concerning our Brampton estate &c.; and I find that there will be, after all debts paid within 100*l*, 50*l* per annum clear coming towards my father's maintenance, besides 25*l* per annum annuitys to my Uncle Tho and Aunt Perkins[1] – of which, though I was in my mind glad, yet I thought it not fit to let my father to know it thoroughly (but after he had gone out to visit my uncle Thomas and brought him to dinner with him; and after dinner I got my father, brother Tom, and myself together), I did make the business worse to them and did promise 20*l* out of my own purse to make it up 50*l* a year to my father, propounding that Sturtlow may be sold to pay 200*l* for his satisfaccion therein and the rest to go toward payment of debts and legacies.[2] The truth is, I am fearful lest my father should die before debts are paid, and then the Land goes to Tom and the burden of paying all debts will fall upon the rest of the land – not that I would do my brother any real hurt. I advised*a* my father to good husbandry and to living within the compass of 50*l* a year; and all in such kind words as made not only both them but myself to weep – and I hope it will have a good effect. That being done, and all things agreed on, we went down; and after a glass of wine, we all took horse and I (upon a horse hired of Mr. Game) saw him out of London at the end of Bishop-gate street; and so I turned and rode with some trouble*b* through the fields and then Holborne &c. toward Hide parke, whither all the world I think are going; and in my going (almost thither) met W. How coming, galloping upon a little

---

a preceded by small blot   *b* l.h. repl. s.h. 'through'

---

1. This was the total of the two annuities.

2. See Pepys's letter to his father, 16 May: below, p. 141 & n. 3. Stankes managed the Brampton lands for Pepys, and he reckoned that

Stirtloe would fetch £480. Pepys represented that its sale would reduce the net value of their share of the estate to £29 p.a. besides the house.

crop black nag (it seems one that was taken in some ground of my
Lord's, by some mischance being left by his maister, a Thiefe;
this horse being found with black cloth eares on and a false
mayne, having none of his owne); and I back again with him to
the Chequer at Charing-cross, and there put up my own dull jade
and by his advice saddled a delicate stone-horse of Captain
Ferrers.[1] And with that rid in state to the park – where none
better mounted then I almost; but being in a throng of horses,
seeing the King's Riders showing tricks with their managed-
horses, which were very strange, my stone-horse was very troublesome and begun to fight with other horses, to the endangering
him and myself; and with much ado I got out and kept myself
out of harm's way.

Here I saw nothing good, neither the King nor my Lady
Castlemayne nor any great ladies or beauties being there, there
being more pleasure, a great deal, at an ordinary day – or else
those few good faces that there were, were choked up with the
many bad ones, there being people of all sorts in coaches there,
to some thousands I think.

Going thither in the highway, just by the park-gate I met a boy
in a Sculler-boat (carried by a dozen people at least) rowing as
hard as he could drive, it seems upon some wager.

By and by, about 7 or 8 a-clock, homeward; and changing
my horse again, I rode home, coaches going in great crowd to
the further end of the town almost. In my way in Leadenhall-
street there was morris dancing, which I have not seen a great
while. So set up my horse at Games's, paying 5s for him, and so
home to see Sir J Minnes, who is well again; and after staying
talking with him a while, I took leave and went to hear Mrs.
Turner's daughter (at whose house Sir J. Mennes lies) play on
the Harpsicon; but Lord, it was enough to make any man sick
to hear her; yet was I forced to commend her highly.

So home to supper and to bed, Ashwell playing upon the
Tryangle* very well before I went to bed.

This day Captain Grove sent me a side of porke, which was
the oddest present, sure, that was ever made to any man; and the
next, I remember I told my wife, I believe would be a pound of
candles or a shoulder of mutton. But the fellow doth it in
kindness and is one I am beholding to.

1. Master of the Horse to Sandwich.

So to bed, very weary and a little galled for lack of riding –
praying to God for a good Journy to my father, of whom I am
afeared, he being so lately ill of his pain.

2.   Being weary last night, I slept*ª* till almost 7 a-clock, a thing
I have not done many a day.   So up and to my office (being
come to some angry words with my wife about neglecting the
keeping of the house clean, I calling her "beggar" and she me
"prick-louse",¹ which vexed me) and there all the morning; so
to the Exchange and then home to dinner, and very merry and
well pleased with my wife; and so to the office again, where we
met extraordinary upon drawing up the debts of the Navy to my
Lord Treasurer.²

So rose, and up*ᵇ* to Sir W. Penn to drink a glass of bad Syder
in his new, fair, low dining-room, which is very noble; and so
home, where Captain Ferrer and his lady are come to see my
wife – he being to go the beginning of the next week to France
to see, and I think to fetch over, my young Lord Hinchingbrooke.³
They being gone, I to my office to write letters by the post; and
so home to supper and bed.

3.   *Lords day.*   Up before 5 a-clock, and alone at setting my
Brampton papers to rights according to my father's and my
computation and resolution the other day, to my good content – I
finding that there will be clear saved to us, 50*l* per annum; only
a debt of it may be 100*l*.

So made myself ready and to church – where Sir W. Penn
showed me the young lady which young Dawes, that sits in the
new corner-pew in the church, hath stole*ᶜ* away from Sir Andrew
Rickard her guardian, worth 1000*l* per annum present good land

---

a   repl. 'st'-   *b*   repl. 'then'   *c*   s.h. repl. l.h. 'r'-

---

1. She having brought no dowry,
and he being a tailor's son.

2. A statement was sent on 18 May.
The Treasurer ·had asked for 'an
account of the whole navy debt, the
present state and needful supply of
the stores, and the proposed distribution of the £200,000 a year for the
navy': *CSPD 1663-4*, p. 143.

3. See above, ii. 142 & n. 3.

and some money, and a very well-bred and handsome lady.[1]
He, I doubt but a simple fellow; however, he got this good luck
to get her, which methinks I could envy him with all my heart.
Home to dinner with my wife, who not being very well, did not
dress herself but stayed at home all day; and so I to church in the
afternoon; and so home again and up to teach Ashwell the
grounds of time[2] and other things on the Tryangle,* and made her
take out a psalm very well, she having a good eare and hand.
And so a while to my office and then home to supper – and
prayers, to bed – my wife and I having a little falling-out because
I would not leave my discourse below with her and Ashwell to
go up and talk with her alone upon something*a* she hath to say.
She reproached me that I had rather talk with anybody then her –
by which I find I think she is jealous of my freedom with Ashwell
– which I must avoid giving occasion of.*b*

4. Up betimes, and to setting my Brampton papers in order
and looking over my Wardrobe against summer and laying things
in order to send to my brothers to alter. By and by took boat,
entending to have gone down to Woolwich; but seeing I could
not get back time enough to dinner, I returned and home –
whither by and by the Dancing Maister[3] came; whom standing
by seeing him instructing my wife, when he had done with her
he would needs have me try the steps of a *Coranto*; and what with
his desire and my wife's importunity, I did begin, and then was
obliged to give him entry-money, 10*s* – and am become his
Scholler. The truth is, I think it is a thing very useful for any
gentleman and sometimes I may have occasion of using it; and

a repl. 'business'   *b* small blot at bottom of page

---

1. The marriage licence of John
Dawes of St Olave's, Hart St (bachel-
or, aged 30) and Christian Hawkins
(spinster, aged 16) is dated 21 April
1663. It states that the bride's
parents were dead and that consent
had been given by her aunt, the wife
of [Sir Andrew]Rickard of St Olave's:
J. L. Chester, *London marriage licences*
(ed. Foster), col. 386. A petition
from Dawes to the King about the

disputed guardianship is given in
CSP Add. 1660–85, p. 83. He was
the son and heir of Sir Thomas
Dawes (who had been ruined by his
loyalty in the wars), and was created
a baronet on 1 June 1663.
2. The rudiments of mensural
notation – still elaborate at this period.
(E).
3. Pembleton. (E).

though it cost me, which I am heartily sorry it should, besides that I must by my oath give half as much more to the poor, yet I am resolved to get it up some other way; and then it will not be above a month or two in a year. So though it be against my stomach, yet I will try it a little while; if I see it comes to any great inconvenience or charge, I will fling it off.

After I had begun with the steps of half a *coranto*, which I think I shall learn well enough, he went away and we to dinner.

And by and by out by coach and set my wife down at my Lord Crews, going to see my Lady Jem Mountagu, who is lately come to town; and I to St James,*ᵃ* where Mr. Coventry, Sir W. Penn and I stayed a good while for the Duke's coming in; but not coming, we walked to White-hall. And meeting the King,*ᵇ* we fallowed him into the parke; where Mr. Coventry and he talking of building a new Yacht, which the King is resolved to have built out of his privy purse, he having some contrivance of his own.[1] That talk being done, we fell off to White-hall, leaving the King in the Park; and going back, met the Duke going toward St. James's to meet us. So he turned back again and to his Closet at White-hall; and there, my Lord Sandwich present, we did our weekly arrand and so broke up. And I down into the garden with my Lord Sandwich (after we had sat an hour at the Tanger Committee); and after talking largely of his own businesses, we begun to talk how matters are at Court; and though he did not flatly tell me any such thing, yet I do suspect that all is not kind between the King and the Duke, and that the King's fondness to the little Duke[2] doth occasion it; and it may be that there is some fear of his being made heire to the crown – but this my Lord did not tell me, but is my guess only.[3] And that my Lord Chancellor is without doubt falling past hopes.[4] He being gone to Chelsey by coach, I to his lodgings,

a repl. 'Wh.'   *b* repl. 'Duke'

---

1. This was the *Henrietta* built to replace the *Jemmy*. For the latter's defeat in a race against the *Bezan*, see above, iii. 188. Burnet (i. 167) referred to the King's interest in naval architecture as being 'exact rather more than became a prince'. Pepys himself was to argue that it led to some unwelcome interference with the professionals: *Naval Minutes*, p. 194.

2. Monmouth.

3. Cf. above, iii. 303, n. 1.

4. Cf. below, p. 173, n. 3.

where my wife stayed for me; and she from thence to see Mrs. Pierce and called me at White-hall stairs (where I went before by land, to know whether there was any play at Court tonight) and there being none, she and I and Mr. Creed to the Exchange, where she bought something; and from thence by water to White-Fryers, and wife to see Mrs. Turner and then came to me to my brother's, where I did give him order about my summer clothes; and so home by coach and after supper to bed with my wife, with whom I have not lain since I used to lie with my father till tonight.

5. Up betimes and to my office – and there busy all the morning. Among other things, walked a good while up and down with Sir J. Mennes, he telling me many old stories of the Navy – and of the state of the Navy at the beginning of the late troubles, and am troubled at my heart to think and shall hereafter cease to wonder at the bad success of the King's cause, when such a knave*a* as he (if it be true what he says) had the whole management of the fleet and the design of putting out of my Lord of Warwicke and carrying the fleet to the King; wherein he failed most fatally, to the King's ruine.[1]

Dined at home and after dinner up to try my dance; and so to the office again, where we sat all the afternoon. In the evening Deane of Woolwich[2] went home with me and showed me the use of a little Sliding ruler, less then that I bought the other day, which is the same with that but more portable; however, I did not seem to understand or even to have seen anything of it before. But I find him an ingenious*b* fellow and a good servant in his place to the King.

Thence to my office, busy late, writing letters; and then came Sir W Warren, staying for a letter in his business by the post, and while that was writing, he and I talk about merchandise, trade

a MS. 'navy'   *b* or 'ingenuous' (abbrev. l.h.)

1. In late June 1642 the King made an attempt to win over the fleet (then in the Downs) from Warwick, the parliamentary commander. After its failure, Mennes (Rear-Admiral, in the *Victory*) was one of the five pro-royalist commanders dismissed by Warwick. He appears to have played no leading part in the plot. See Penn, i. 41-2; Clarendon, *Hist.*, ii. 216+.

2. Anthony Deane, the shipwright.

and getting of money. I made it my business to enquire what way there is for a man bred like me to come to understand anything of trade. He did most discretely answer me in all things, showing me the danger for me to meddle either in ships or merchandise of any sort, or common Stockes, but what I have, to keep at interest, which is a good, quiet and easy profit and once in a little while something offers that with ready money you may make use of money to good profit – wherein I concur much with him, and parted late with great pleasure and content in his discourse; and so home to supper and to bed. ⟨It hath been this afternoon very hot, and this evening also; and about 11 at night, going to bed, it fell a-thundering and lightning, the greatest flashes, enlightening the whole body of the yard, that ever I saw in my life.⟩

6. Up betimes and to my office; a good while at my new rulers, then to business. And towards noon to the exchange with Creede, where we met with Sir J. Minnes coming in his coach from Westminster; who tells us in great heat that, by God, the parliament will make mad work; that they will render all men incapable of any military or Civill imployment that have borne arms in the late troubles against the King, excepting some persons[1] – which if it be so, as I hope it is not, will give great cause of discontent, and I doubt will have but bad effects.

I left them at the Exchange and I walked to Pauls churchyard to look upon a book or two, and so back and thence to the Trinity-house and there dined – where, among other discourse worth hearing among the old Seamen, they tell us that they have ketched often in Greenland in fishing Whales, with the Iron grapnells that had formerly been struck into their bodies covered over with fat – that they have had eleven hogsheadds of Oyle out of the Tongue of a Whale.

Thence after dinner home to my office and there busy till the

1. On 5 May the Commons had appointed a committee to bring in a bill 'for disposing all Offices, military and civil, into the Hands of such persons as have been loyal Subjects, and conformable to the *Church of England*': *CJ*, viii. 476. But (as a result of government pressure) the bill was never introduced: cf. below, p. 196. Disgruntled cavaliers had been urging some such measure for a long time: cf. *An humble representation of the sad condition of many of the King's party . . .* (1661) in *Somers Tracts* (ed. Scott), vii. 516–20.

evening. Then home and to supper; and while at Supper comes Mr. Pembleton; and after supper, we up to our dancing room and there danced three or four country dances, and after that, a practice of my *coranto* I begun with him the other day; and I begin to think that I shall be able to do something at it in time. Late and merry at it; and so, weary to bed.

7. Up betimes and to my office a while; and then by water with my wife, leaving her at the new Exchange, and I to see Dr Williams and speak with him about my business with Tom Trice.[1] And so to my brother's, who I find very careful nowadays, more then ordinary, in his business, and like to do well. From thence to Westminster and there up and down, from the Hall to the Lobby, the Parliament sitting; and so by coach to my Lord Crews and there dined with him. He tells me of the order the House of Commons hath made for the drawing an act for the rendering none capable of preferment or imployment in the State but who have been Loyall and constant to the King and Church – which will be fatal to a great many, and makes me doubt lest I myself, with all my innocence during the late times, should be brought in, being imployed in the Exchequer. But I hope God will provide for me.

This day the new Theatre Royall begins to act with scenes *The Humorous Lieutenant*,[2] but I have not time to see it. Nor could stay to see my Lady Jemimah, lately come to town, and who was here in the house but dined above with her grandmother.[3] But taking my wife at my brother's home by coach, and the officers being at Deptford at a pay, we had no office; but I took

1. A dispute over Robert Pepys's will: see above, ii. 215 & n. 1.
2. The theatre was Thomas Killigrew's new playhouse, situated between Drury Lane and Bridges St, built at a cost of £2400. Downes states (p. 3) that 'the New Theatre in *Drury Lane*' was opened 'on *Thursday* [*sic*] in *Easter* week, being the 8th Day of April 1663', but Pepys's dating here and at the following entry is almost certainly the correct one. 8 April 1663 was not in Easter Week

nor did it fall on a Thursday. Moreover, Pepys saw a performance by the King's Company on 22 April 1663, but does not mention its having taken place at the new Theatre Royal in Bridges St, as he probably would have done if it had then been in use. The play was a tragicomedy by John Fletcher: see above, ii. 80 & n. 3. Killigrew had not used movable painted scenery in his productions at the first Theatre Royal in Vere St. (A).

3. Lady (Ann) Mountagu.

my wife by water and so spent the evening; and so home with
great pleasure to supper, and then to bed.

《Sir Tho. Crew this day tells me that the Queene hearing
that there was 40000*l* per annum brought into, among the other
expenses of the Crown, to the Committee of Parliament, she
took order to let them know that she hath yet for the payment of
her whole family* received but 4000*l*[1] – which is a notable act of
spirit, and I believe is true.》*a*

8. Up very earely and to my office, there preparing letters to
my father, of great import in the settling of our affairs and
putting him upon a way [of] good husbandry – I promising
him to make out of my own purse him up 50*l* per annum, till
either by my Uncle Thomas's death or the fall of the Wardrobe
place he be otherwise provided.[2]

That done, I by water to the Strand and there viewed the
Queene-Mother's works at Somerset-house;[3] and thence to the
new playhouse, but could not get in to see it; so to visit my Lady
Jemimah, who is grown much since I saw her – but lacks
mightily to be brought into the fashion of the Court to set her off.

Thence to the Temple and there sat till one a-clock, reading at
Playford's in Dr Ushers *Body of Divinity* his discourse of the
Scripture;[4] which is as much, I believe, as is anywhere said by any
man, but yet there is room to cavill, if a man would use no faith
to the tradition of the Church in which he is born; which I think

a This addition appears in the margin, without any indication of its proper
place; but since the paragraph beginning 'This day' is crowded into the
bottom of a page, it seems to be the conclusion.

1. The letters patent granting the
£40,000 p.a. to the Queen had not
yet passed, and on 16 April the
Treasurer had issued a warrant for the
payment of £10,000, a quarter's
income: *CTB*, i. 509, 585. The
parliamentary committee had been
at work since 23 March: *CJ*, viii.
456.

2. For the letter, see below, p. 141
& n. 3. For the place at the Wardrobe, see above, ii. 42 & n. 1.

3. The new work included a
watergate and a refurbished chapel:
see below, v. 63 & n. 2.

4. James Ussher's *A body of divini-
tie* (1645, folio; several times re-
issued; not in the PL). Published
against Ussher's wishes and not fairly
representative of his views, it argued
strongly for the superiority of scripture over the church's tradition.

to be as good an argument as most is brought for many things, and it may be for that, among others.

Thence to my brother's, and there took up my wife and Ash-well to the Theatre Royall, being the second day of its being opened. The house is made with extraordinary good con-trivance; and yet hath some faults, as the narrowness of the passages in and out of the pit, and the distance from the stage to the boxes, which I am confident cannot hear.[1] But for all other things it is well. Only, above all, the Musique being below,[2] and most of it sounding under the very stage, there is no hearing of the bases at all, nor very well of the trebles, which sure must be mended.[3]

The play was *The Humorous Lieutenant* – a play that hath little good in it, nor much in that very part which, by the King's command, Lacey now acts instead of Clun.[4] In the dance, the Tall Devil's actions was very pretty.[5]

The play being done, we home by water, having been a little ashamed that my wife and woman were in such a pickle, all the ladies being finer and better dressed in the pit then they use I think to be.

To my office to set down this day's passage. And though my oath against going to plays[6] doth not oblige me against this house,

---

1. There were two entrances to the pit, one at either side of the audito-rium, each being close to the apron stage. The pit sloped upwards to the base of the first tier of seats (the boxes), and was furnished with rows of backless benches. Though this theatre was not large by modern standards – its site measured 112 ft × 59 ft – Pepys's criticism is supported by the fact that Killigrew enlarged the stage early in 1666: see below, vii. 76 & n. 4. (A).

2. I.e. at the front of the stage, where the orchestra pit is situated nowadays. This was an innovation; in most Restoration theatres the musicians played in the music room, which was a small gallery above the proscenium arch. A gallery of this kind is depicted in the illustrations which accompany the text of Elkaneh Settle's dramatic opera, *The Empress of Morocco* (1673). (A).

3. Pepys's criticism was a valid one, for Killigrew subsequently moved his orchestra to a gallery above the proscenium arch. He probably constructed this gallery as part of his alterations to the Theatre Royal in the spring of 1666. (A).

4. Walter Clun, who had played the title-role, was an actor much admired by Pepys; John Lacy was one of Charles II's favourite comed-ians. (A).

5. In IV, 3 a magician conjures diabolical spirits who dance around a bowl and distil a love potion. (A).

6. See above, p. 8. (A).

because it was not then in being, yet believing that at that time my meaning was against all public houses, I am resolved to deny myself the liberty of two plays at Court which are in arreare to me for the months of March and Aprill; which will more then countervail this excess. So that this month of May is the first that I must claim a liberty of going to a Court play, according to my oath.

So home to supper. And at supper comes Pembleton; and afterward we all up to dancing till late, and so broke up and to bed; and they say that I am like to make a dancer.

9. Up betimes and to my office; whither sooner then ordinary comes Mr. Hater, desiring to speak a word to me alone, which I was from the disorder of his countenance amused* at; and so the poor man begun telling me that by Providence being the last Lord's day at a meeting of some Friends upon doing of their duties, they were surprized and he carried to the Counter, but afterward released; however, hearing that Sir W. Batten doth hear of [it], he thought it good to give me an account of it, lest it might tend to any prejudice to me.[1] I was extraordinary surprized with it and troubled for him, knowing that now it is out, it is impossible for me to conceal it, or keep him in imployment under me without danger to myself. I cast about all I could and did give him the best advice I could; desiring to know if I should promise that he would not for the time to come commit the same, he told me he desired that I would rather forbear to promise that; for he durst not do it, what[ever] God in His providence shall do with him; and that for my part, he did bless God and thank me for all the love and kindness I have showed him hitherto. I could not, without tears in my eyes, discourse with him further, but at last did pitch upon telling the truth of the whole to Mr. Coventry as soon as I could; and to that end did use means to prevent Sir W. Batten (who came to town last night) from going to that end today, lest he might doe*a*

a l.h. repl. '2' ('to')

---

1. Thomas Hayter was one of Pepys's two clerks. Pepys refers to him at 15 May as an Anabaptist.   For the Duke of York's decision about this case, see below, p. 135.

it to Sir G. Carteret or Mr. Coventry before me – which I did prevail, and kept him at the office all the morning.

At noon dined at home with a heavy heart for the poor man. And after dinner went out to my brother's, and thence to Westminster; where at Mr. Jervas my old Barber I did try two or three borders and periwiggs, meaning to wear one; and yet I have no stomach, but that the pains of keeping my hair clean is so great. He trimmed me; and at last I parted, but my mind was almost altered from my first purpose, from the trouble that I foresee will be in wearing them also. Thence by water home and to the office, where busy late. And so home to supper and bed – with my mind much troubled about T Hater.

10. *Lords=day.* Up betimes and put on a black cloth suit with white Lynings under all, as the fashion is to wear, to appear under the breeches. So being ready, walked to St. James – where I sat talking with Mr. Coventry while he made himself ready, about several businesses of the Navy. And after the Duke being gone out, he and I walked to White-hall together over the parke, I telling him what had happened about Tom Hater; at which he seems very sorry, but tells me that if it is not made very public it will not be necessary to put him away at present, but give*a* him good caucion for the time to come. However, he will speak to the Duke about it and know his pleasure.

Parted with him there; and I walked back to St. James's and was there at Masse, and was forced in the croud to kneel down;[1] and Masse being done, to the King's-head ordinary,[2] whither I sent for Mr. Creed and there we dined; where many parliament-men and most of their talk was about the news from Scotland that the Bishop of Galloway was besieged in his house by some women and had like to have been outraged, but, I know not how, he was secured – which is bad news and looks just as it did in

a small blot in margin

1. This same mass was attended by Monconys: Monconys, ii. 21–2. For the Queen's chapel at St James's, see above, iii. 202, n. 1. Pepys asserted in 1674 that he had never been to mass: see above, loc. cit.
2. At Charing Cross. (R).

the beginning of the late troubles.[1] From thence they talked of rebellion; and I perceive they make it their great maxime to be sure to Maister the City of London, whatever comes of it or from[a] it. After that, to some other discourse; and among other things, talking of the way of ordinaries, that it is very convenient because a man knows what he hath to pay, one did wish that among many bad, we could learn two good things of France – which were that we would not think it below the gentleman or person of honour at a taverne to bargain for his meat before he eates it; and next, to take no servants without Certificate from some friend or gentleman of his good behaviour and abilities.[2]

Thence with Creed into St. James parke and there walked all the afternoon; and thence on foot home. And after a little while at my office, walked in the garden with my wife. And so home to supper and after prayers to bed. My brother Tom supped with me and should have brought my aunt Ellen[3] with him; she was not free to go abroad.

11. Up betimes and by water to Woolwich on board the *Royall James* to see in what dispatch she is to be carried about to Chatham. So to the yard a little and thence on foot to Greenewich; where going, I was set upon by a great dog, who got hold of my garters and might have done me hurt; but Lord, to see in what a maze I was, that having a sword about me, I never thought of it or had the heart to make use of it, but might for want of that courage have been worried.

Took water there and home; and both coming and going, did

a MS. 'for'

---

1. These disorders were provoked by the restoration of the bishops to full powers in Scotland by an act of May 1662. Galloway and Kircudbright were in the heart of the Covenanting country, and Pepys was now reminded of similar troubles which had led to the national rising of 1637. The Bishop of Galloway was James Hamilton, appointed in 1661. He was placed under the protection of the magistrates, and many of the 'amazons' who attacked him were pilloried and imprisoned. Cf. Henry Coventry to Ormond, 12 May, in HMC, *Ormonde*, n.s., iii. 52; *Reg. Privy Counc. Scot. 1661–4*, esp. pp. 372–6; R. Wodrow, *Hist. sufferings Church of Scotland* (1829–30), i. 363–9.

2. For this practice, see above, p. 79, n. 1.

3. Ellen Kite.

con my lessons upon my Ruler to measure timber, which I think I can well undertake now to do.

At home, there being Pembleton, I danced, and I think shall come on to do something in a little time.   And after dinner, by coach with Sir W. Penn (setting down his daughter at Clerkenwell)[1] to St James, where we attended the Duke of Yorke; and among other things, Sir G. Carteret and I had a great dispute about the different value of the peeces-of-eight, rated by Mr. Creed at 4s-5d and by Pitts at 4s. 9d, which was the greatest husbandry to the King, he persisting that the greatest sum was; which is so ridiculous a piece of ignorance as could be imagined.[2] However, it is to be argued at the Board and reported to the Duke next week; which I shall do with advantage I hope.

Thence to the Tanger Comittee, where we should have concluded in sending Captain Cuttance and the rest to Tanger to deliberate upon the design of the Molle before they begin to work upon it; but there being not a committee[a] (my Lord entending to be there but was taken up at my Lady Castlemayn's), I parted and went homeward, after a little discourse with Mr. Pierce the surgeon, who tells me that my Lady Castlemayne hath now got lodgings near the King's chamber at Court.[3]   And that the other day Dr. Clerke and he did dissect two bodies, a man and a woman, before the King, with which the King was highly pleased.

By water and called upon Tom Trice, by appointment with Dr Williams; but the Doctor did not come, it seems by T. Trice's desire, not thinking he should be at leisure.   However, in general we talked of our business and I do not find that he will come to any lower terms then 150l; which I think I shall not give him but by law.[4]   And so we parted and I called upon Mr. Crumlum

a followed by 'coming' struck through

---

1. Where Margaret Penn was at school.

2. 4s. 9d. was the official rate fixed by proclamation (29 January 1661) and prevailing at Tangier, where Pitts had worked as Deputy-Treasurer to Lawson's fleet: R. Ruding, *Annals of coinage* (1840), ii. 3; Routh, p. 33 n.

3. The Queen was in June forced to accept her as a lady of her bed-chamber: G. S. Steinman, *Mem. Duchess of Cleveland*, Add. etc., p. 1.

4. For the settlement of this dispute (about Robert Pepys's estate), see below, p. 352. Pepys had reckoned his debt to Trice at £126 in the accounts he drew up at about this time: the figure is difficult to explain, but may represent interest plus legal charges.

and did give him the 10s. remaining not laid out of the 5l. I promised him for the school[1] – with which he will buy strings and golden letters upon the books I did give them. I sat with him and his wife a great while talking; and she is [a] pretty woman, never yet with child, and methinks looks as if her*ᵃ* mouth watered now and then upon some of her boys.

Then up [to] Tom Pepys the Turner desiring his father and his letter to Piggott, signifying his*ᵇ* consent to the selling of his land for the paying of us his money.[2] And so home; and finding Pembleton there, we did dance till it was late, and so to supper and to bed.

12. Up between 4 and 5; and after dressed myself, then to my office to prepare business against the afternoon – where all the morning and dined at noon at home, where a little angry with my wife for minding nothing now but the dancing-maister, having him come twice a day, which is a folly.

Again to my office, where we sat till late – our chief business being the reconciling the business of the peeces-of-eight mentioned yesterday before the Duke of Yorke; wherein I have got the day and they are all brought over to what I said, of which I am proud.

Late, writing letters; and so home to supper and to bed. Here I find Creed staying for me; and*ᶜ* so after supper I stayed him all night and lay with me – our great discourse being the folly of our two doting knights,[3] of which I am ashamed.

13. Lay till 6 a-clock and then up; and after a little talk and mirth – he went away and I to my office, where busy all the morning; and at noon home to dinner; and after dinner, Pembleton came and I practised. But Lord, to see how my wife will not be thought to need telling by me or Ashwell and yet will plead that she hath learned but a month; which causes many short fallings-out between us. So to my office, whither one-eyed Cooper came to see me and I made him to show me the

---

a repl. 'she'   *b* repl. 'their'   *c* '13' struck through in margin

---

1. St Paul's. For this gift, see above, ii. 239 & n. 3.

2. See below, p. 237 & n. 4.
3. Batten and Penn.

use of platts and to understand the lines and how to find how lands* bear &c., to my great content.

Then came Mr. Barrow, storekeeper of Chatham, who tells me many things how basely Sir W. Batten hath carried himself to him, and in all things else, like a passionate dotard, to the King's great wrong. God mend all, for I am sure we are but in an ill condition in the Navy, however the King is served in other places.

Home to supper. To cards and to bed.

14.*a* Up betimes and put up some things to send to Brampton. Then abroad to the Temple and up and down about business. And met Mr. Moore and with him to an alehouse in Holborne; where in discourse he told me that he fears the King will be tempted to endeavour the setting the crown upon the little Duke,[1] which may cause troubles; which God forbid, unless it be his due. He told me my Lord doth begin to settle to business again; which I am glad of, for he must not sit out now he hath done his own business by getting his estate settled.[2] And that the King did send for him the other day to my Lady Castlemayns the other day, to play at cards, where he lost 50*l*; for which I am sorry, though he says my Lord was pleased at it and said he would be glad at any time to lose 50*l* for the King to send for him to play; which I do not so well like.

Thence home; and after dinner to the office, where we sat till night and then made up my papers and letters by the post; and so home to dance with Pembleton.

This day we received a basket from my sister Pall, made by her of paper, which hath a great deal of labour in it for country innocent work.

After supper to bed. And going to bed, received a letter from Mr. Coventry, desiring my coming to him tomorrow morning; which troubled me to think what the business should be, fearing it might be some bad news in Tom Haters business.

a repl. '12'

1. Monmouth. There were re-current rumours of the King's intention to make Monmouth his heir: see above, iii. 303 & n. 1.

2. See above, i. 285, n. 4.

15. Up betimes and walked to St. James's; where Mr Coventry being in bed, I walked in the park, discoursing with the keeper of the Pell Mell who was sweeping of it – who told me of what the earth is mixed that doth floor the Mall, and that over all there is Cockle-shells powdered and spread, to keep it fast; which however, in dry weather turns to dust and deads the ball.[1] Thence to Mr. Coventry; and sitting by his bedside, he did tell me that he sent for me to discourse upon my Lord Sandwiches allowances for his several pays, and what his[a] thoughts are concerning his[b] demands; which he could not take the freedom to do face to face, it being not so proper as by me; and did give me a most friendly and ingenuous account of all, telling me how unsafe at this juncture, while every man's, and his actions perticularly, are descanted upon, it is either for him to put the Duke upon doing or my Lord himself to desire anything extraordinary, especially, the King having been so bountiful already; which the world takes notice of even to some repinings. All which he did desire me to discourse with my Lord of; which I have[c] undertook to do.

We talked also of our office in general; with which he told me that he was nowadays nothing so satisfyed as he was wont to be. I confess I told him things are ordered in that way that we must of necessity break in a little time a-pieces.

After done with him about[d] those things, he told me that for Mr. Hater, the Dukes word was, in short, that he found he had a good servant, an Anabaptist; and unless he did carry himself more to the scandall of the office, he would bear with his opinion till he heard further[2] – which doth please me very much.

Thence walked to Westminster and there up and down in the hall and the parliament-house all the morning. And at noon by coach to my Lord Crews, hearing that my Lord Sandwich did

---

a repl. 'is'   *b* repl. 'my'   *c* repl. 'shall'   *d* repl. 'with'

---

1. For the game, see above, ii. 64, n. 2.

2. The Duke of York often showed toleration of this sort. Military men in all European states at this period were more inclined than other public servants to judge of loyalty by actions rather than beliefs: armed forces often included men of differing nationalities and creeds. Moreover, in England the Catholics and their friends (James was to become an open Catholic in 1673) supported toleration as long as it protected their rights as a minority.

dine there; where I told him what had passed between Mr. Coventry and myself; with which he was contented, though I could perceive not very well pleased; and I do believe that my Lord doth find some other things go against his mind in the House, for in the motion made the other day in the House by my Lord Bruce, that none be capable of imployment but such as have been Loyall and constant to the King and Church, the Generall and my Lord were mentioned to be excepted;[1] and my Lord Bruce did come since to my Lord to clear himself, that he meant nothing to his prejudice nor could it have any such effect if he did mean it. After discourse with my Lord, to dinner with him, there dining there my Lord Mountagu of Boughton, Mr Wm. Mountagu his brother, the Queen's Sollicitor, &c.; and a fine dinner.

Their talk about a ridiculous falling-out two days ago at my Lord of Oxfords house at an entertainment of his, there being there my Lord of Albemarle, Lynsey, two of the Porters, my Lord Bellasse[s], and others; where there was high words[a] and some blows and pulling off of perriwiggs – till my Lord Monke took away some of their swords and sent for some soldiers to guard the house till the fray was ended. To such a degree of madness the nobility of this age is come.

After dinner I went up to Sir Tho. Crew, who lies there not very well in his head, being troubled with vapours and fits of dizzinesse; and there I sat talking with him all the afternoon, from one discourse to another. The most was upon the unhappy posture of things at this time; that the King doth mind nothing but pleasures and hates the very sight or thoughts of business.[2] That my Lady Castlemayne rules him; who he says hath all the tricks of Aretin[3] that are to be practised to give pleasure – in

a repl. 'blown'

1. Bruce had moved the order for the drafting of this (abortive) bill. See above, p. 125 & n. 1. The *Commons' Journals* (having no information about proceedings in committee) do not report the proposal to make exceptions for Sandwich and Albemarle. But they were exempted under another bill (also abortive) which aimed at cancelling certain grants of Crown lands: *CJ*, viii. 487.

2. Cf. the collection of evidence about his indolence in *AHR*, 43/535, n. 8.

3. Pietro Aretino (d. 1557), whose erotic writings had become well-known in England in the 1650s: D. Foxon in *The Book Collector*, Summer 1963, pp. 163+.

which he is too able, hav[ing] a large ——;[a][1] but that which is
the unhappiness is that, as the Italian proverb says, *Cazzo dritto non
vuolt consiglio.* If any of the Sober counsellors give him good
advice and move him in anything that is to his good and honour,
the other part, which are his counsellors of pleasure, take him
when he [is] with my Lady Castlemayne and in a humour of delight and then persuade him that he ought not to hear or listen to
the advice of those old dotards or counsellors that were heretofore
his enemies, when God knows it is they that nowadays do most
study his honour. It seems the present favourites now are my
Lord Bristoll, Duke of Buckingham, Sir H. Bennet, my Lord
Ashley, and Sir Ch. Berkely; who among them have cast
my Lord Chancellor upon his back, past ever getting up again;
there being now little for him to do, and waits at court
attending to speak to the King as others do – which I pray God
may prove of good effects, for it is feared it will be the same
with my Lord Treasurer shortly. But strange to hear how my
Lord Ashly, by my Lord Bristolls means (he being brought over
to the Catholique party against the Bishops, whom he hates to the
death and publicly rails against them; not that he is become a
Catholique, but merely opposes the Bishopps; and yet for aught I
hear, the Bishop of London[2] keeps as great with the King as ever)
is got into favour so much, that being a man of great business
and yet of pleasure and drolling too, he is thought will be made

a   *sic* in MS.

---

1. Cf. Rochester's verse (for which he was banished the court in 1676): *Collected Works* (ed. Hayward), p. 104.
2. Gilbert Sheldon. The bishops (together with Clarendon and Southampton the Lord Treasurer) had been out of favour with the King since February, when they had opposed an indulgence bill for the relief of Catholics which both Buckingham and Ashley had supported. 'From that time,' Clarendon wrote, 'the King never treated any of them [the bishops] with that respect as he had done formerly, and often spake of them too slightly; which easily encouraged others not only to mention their persons very negligently, but their function and religion itself': *Life*, ii. 351. It is possible that Ashley had been sarcastic at the expense of the bishops in the debate (8 May) on the fees they paid on translation: *LJ*, xi. 519.

Lord Treasurer upon the death or Removall of the good old man.[1]

My Lord Albemarle, I hear, doth bear through and bustle among them and will not be removed from the King's good opinion and favour, though none of the Cabinett; but yet he is envied enough.

It is made very doubtful whether the King doth not entend the making of the Duke of Monmouth legitimate; but surely the Commons of England will never do it nor the Duke of Yorke suffer it – whose lady I am told is very troublesome to him by her jealousy. But it is wonderful that Sir Ch. Barkely should be so great still, not [only] with the King, but Duke also; who did so stiffly swear that he had lain with her;[2] and another,[a] one Armorer, that he rid before her on horseback, in Holland I think, and she rid with her hand upon his ——.[b]

No care is observed to be taken of the main chance, either for maintaining of trade or opposing of factions, which God knows are ready to break out if any of them, which God forbid, should dare to begin; the King and every man about him minding so much their pleasures or profits.

My Lord Hinchingbrooke, I am told, hath had a mischance to kill his boy by his birding-piece going off as he was a-fouling. The gun was charged with small shot and hit the boy in the face and about the Temples, and [he] lived four days.

Scotland: it seems, for all the news-book tells us every week that they are all so quiet and everything in the Church settled,[3] the old women had like to have killed the other day the Bishop of Galloway, and not half the churches of the whole kingdom conforms.

a repl. 'that'   *b*   *sic* in MS.

---

1. This is contrary to Clarendon's view (recorded in 1671–2) that Ashley by now had 'got no ground': *Life*, ii. 351. Southampton was just 55, and ill with gout and the stone. Rumours of his resignation or dismissal were current throughout 1662–4, partly because he had delegated most of his work to his secretary, Sir Philip Warwick. Cf. above, iii. 263. The French ambassador, de Cominges, noted the rising reputa-tion of Ashley as Chancellor of the Exchequer, in a despatch of 30 March/9 April: PRO, PRO 31/3, no. 111, f. 91r. But Southampton retained office until his death in 1667.

2. See above, i. 315 & n. 2.

3. E.g. the report from Edinburgh in *Kingd. Intell.*, 6 April, p. 209: 'this country is in all peace and quietness, and most willing to submit to his Majestie in everything'. Cf. above, p. 131, n. 1.

Strange were the effects of the late Thunder and lightening about a week since at Northampton, coming with great rain – which caused extraordinary floods in a few houres, bearing away bridges, drowning houses, men, and cattle. Two men passing over a bridge on horseback, the Arches before and behind them were borne away and that left which they were upon. But however, one of the horses fell over and was drowned. Stacks of faggots carried as high as a steeple, and other dreadful things; which Sir Tho. Crew showed me letters to him about, from Mr. Freemantle and others – that it is very true.[1]

The Portugalls have choused us, it seems, in the Island of Bombay in the East Indys; for after a great charge of our fleets being sent thither with full commission from the King of Portugall to receive it, the Governor by some pretence or other will not deliver to Sir Abraham Shipman, sent from the King, nor to my Lord of Marlborough[2] – which the King takes highly ill, and I fear our Queene will fare the worse for it.

The Dutch decay there exceedingly, it being believed that their people will revolt from them there, and they forced to give over their trade. This is talked of among us, but how true I understand not.

Sir Thomas showed me his picture and Sir Anth. Vandikes, in Croyon in little, done exceeding well.[3]

1. The storm occurred on 6 May: both the West Bridge and the South Bridge were badly damaged. See *Hist. Northampton* (1815); cf. C. A. Markham and J. C. Cox (ed.), *Records of Northampton*, ii. 538. Cf. Wood, *L. & T.*, i. 474. The Crews' country house was near Brackley, Northants. For the Freemantles, see *Comp.*

2. A small squadron had been sent in April 1662 under the Earl of Marlborough (Governor-designate), to take possession of Bombay, ceded in the marriage treaty of 1661. Shipman was in command of the troops. But on their arrival in December 1662, the Portuguese Governor (D. Antonio de Mello de Castro) refused to surrender it on the ground that Shipman had not brought formal authority to take possession. The extent of the boundaries was also a matter of dispute, since the English claimed the two neighbouring islands as well as Bombay itself. Charles II made a strong protest against de Castro's action, and the whole territory claimed was ceded in February 1665. See Shafaat Ahmed Khan in *Journ. Indian Hist.*, 1/419+.

3. Crew's portrait in chalk does not survive; the portrait of Van Dyck was presumably a small copy of one of the painter's self-portraits. The taste for portrait-drawings in pastel was developing rapidly at this period: J. Woodward, *Tudor and Stuart drawings*, pp. 27+; Whinney and Millar, pp. 99–102. (OM).

Having thus freely talked with him and of many more things, I took leave; and by coach to St. James's and there told Mr. Coventry what I had done with my Lord, with great satisfaction; and so, well pleased, home – where I find it almost night and my wife and the Dancing Maister alone above, not dancing but walking.   Now, so deadly full of jealousy I am, that my heart and head did so cast about and fret, that I could not do any business possibly, but went out to my office; and anon late home again, and ready to chide at everything; and then suddenly to bed and could hardly sleep, yet durst not say anything; but was forced to say that I had bad*a* news from the Duke concerning Tom Hater, as an excuse to my wife – who by my folly hath*b* too much opportunity given her with that man; who is a pretty neat black man, but married.   But it is a deadly folly and plague that I bring upon myself to be so jealous; and by giving myself such an occasion, more then my wife desired, of giving her another month's dancing – which however shall be ended as soon as I can possibly.   ⟨But I am ashamed to think what a course I did take by lying to see whether my wife did wear drawers[1] today as she used to do, and other things to raise my suspicion of her; but I found no true cause of doing it.⟩*c*

16.   Up, with my mind disturbed and with my last night's doubts upon me.

For which I deserve to be beaten, if not really served as I am fearful of being; especially since, God knows, that I do not find honesty enough in my own mind but that upon a small temptation I could be false to her, and therefore ought not to expect more justice from her – but God pardon both my sin and my folly herein.

To my office and there setting all the morning; and at noon dined at home.   After dinner comes Pembleton again; and I being out of humour, would not see him, pretending business; but Lord, with what jealousy did I walk up and down my chamber, listening to hear whether they danced or no or what

a l.h. repl. s.h. 'news'   *b* repl. 'is'   *c* addition crowded in between entries

---

1. Not commonly worn by Englishwomen; 'habitually worn by French ladies from the middle of the 16th century. . . . Mrs Pepys . . . may have acquired the habit before her marriage': C. W. and P. Cunnington, *Hist. Underclothes*, p. 65.

they did; notwithstanding I afterwards knew, and did then believe, that Ashwell was with them. So to my office awhile; and my jealousy still reigning, I went in and, not out of any pleasure but from that only reason, did go up to them to practise; and did make an end of *La Duchesse*,[1] which I think [I] should with a little pains do very well. So broke up and saw him gone.

Then Captain Cocke coming to me to speak about my seeming discourtesy to him in the business of his Hemp,[2] I went to the office with him and there discoursed it largely, and I think to his satisfaction.

Then to my business, writing letters and other things till late at night; and so home to supper and bed. My mind in some better ease – resolving to prevent matters for the time to come as much as I can, it being to no purpose to trouble myself for what is past; being occasiond, too, by my own folly.

17. *Lords day.* Up and in my chamber all the morning, preparing my great letters to my father, stating to him the perfect condition of our estate.[3] My wife and Ashwell to church; and after dinner, they to church again and I all the afternoon making an end of my morning's work, which I did about the evening, and then to talk with my wife till after supper; and so to bed – having another small falling-out, and myself vexed with my old fit of jealousy about her dancing-master – but I am a fool for doing it. So to bed by daylight – I having a very great cold, so as I doubt whether I shall be able to speak tomorrow at our attending the Duke, being now so hoarse.

18. Up; and after taking leave of Sir W. Batten, who is gone this day toward Portsmouth (to little purpose, God knows) upon his Survey, I home and spent the morning at Dancing. At noon Creede dined with us and Mr. Deane of Woolwich; and so after dinner came[a] Mr. Howe, who however had enough for his dinner; and so having done, by coach to Westminster, she to

---

a repl. 'carried'

---

1. *The complete country dancing master* (1718, p. 191) has a dance in 6/4 time called 'Dutchess'. (E).

2. Possibly the accounts mentioned above, at e.g. p. 49.

3. This letter (16 May) is in Rawl. A 191, ff. 244r–6r; printed in *Family*

Letters, pp. 1–5. It has a detailed statement of the Brampton rents annexed. Cf. above, p. 119 & n. 2; and the earlier statements of account in PL (unoff.), Freshfield MSS, nos 8 and 9.

Mrs. Clerke and I to St. James's; where the Duke being gone down by water today with the King, I went thence to my Lord Sandwich's lodgings, where Mr Howe and I walked a while; and going toward White-hall through the garden, Dr Clerke and Creed called me across the Bowling greene and so I went thither and after a stay went up to Mrs. Clerke, who was dressing herself to go abroad with my wife; but Lord, in what a poor condition her best chamber is and things about her, for all the outside and show that she makes, that I find her just such a one as Mrs. Pierce, contrary to my expectation; so much that I am sick and sorry to see it.

Thence for an hour Creede and I walked to White-hall and into the parke, seeing the Queene and maids of honour passing through the house going to the parke. But above all, Mrs. Stuart is a fine woman, and they say now a common mistress*ᵃ* to the King, as my Lady Castlemayne is; which is great pity.[1] Thence taking a coach to Mrs. Clerkes, took her and my wife and Ashwell and a French[man], a kinsman of hers, to the parke; where we saw many fine faces and one exceeding handsome, in a white dress off her head – with many others very beautiful. Staying there till past 8 at night, I carried Mrs. Clerke and her Frenchman (who sings well) home; and thence home ourselfs, talking much of what we had observed today of the poor household stuff of Mrs. Clerke and mere show and flutter that she makes in the world. And pleasing myself in my own house and manner of living more then ever I did, by seeing how much better and more substantially I live then others do.

So to supper and bed.

19. Up pretty betimes; but yet I observe how my dancing, and lying a morning or two longer then ordinary for my cold, doth make me hard to rise as I used to do, or look after my business as I am wont.

To my chamber to make ⟨an⟩ end of my papers to my father to be sent by the post tonight, and taking copies of them; which

a repl. 'whore'

---

1. Gramont (p. 146) has a story – probably unfounded – that after long resistance she finally capitulated to Charles on being given the first ride in a new *calèche* which arrived from France.

was a great work but I did it this morning, and so to my office. And thence with Sir John Minnes to the tower and by Mr. Slingsby and Mr. Howard,[1] Controller of the Mint, we were shown the method of making this new money from the beginning to the end; which is so pretty that I did take notes of every part of it and set them down by themselfs for my remembrance hereafter. That being done, it was dinner-time, and so the Comptroller would have us dine with him and his company, the King giving them a dinner every day; and very merry, and good discourse about the business we have been upon; and after dinner went to the Essay-Office and there saw the manner of essaying of gold and Silver, and how silver melted down with gold doth part again being put into aqua fartis, the silver turning into water[2] and the gold lying whole in the very form it was put in, mixed of gold and silver; which is a miracle – and to see no silver at all, but turned into water; which they can bring again into itself out of that water.[3]

And here I was made thoroughly to understand the business of the finenesse and coursenesse of metals, and have put down my lessons with my other observations therein.

At table, among other discourse, they told us of two cheats, the best I ever heard. One of a labourer discovered to convey away the bits of silver cut for pence[4] by swallowing them down into his belly, and so they could*a* not find him, though of course they search all the labourers. But having reason to doubt him, they did by threates and promises get him to confess, and did find 7*l* of it in his house at one time.

The other, of one that got a way of coining money as good and passable and large as the true money is, and yet saved 50 per cent to himself; which was by getting moulds made to stamp groats like old groats,[5] which is done so well (and I did beg two of them, which I keep for rarities) that there is not better in the world; and is as good, nay better, then those*b* that commonly

a repl. 'came'   *b* repl. 'they'

---

1. *Recte* [James] Hoare, sen.
2. I.e. dissolving.
3. I.e. it can be recovered from the solution.
4. Both threepenny-pieces and pennies were of silver.

5. The old groats then current were the silver fourpenny-pieces issued under Mary Tudor and in the early years (1558–61) of Elizabeth. The next issue was in 1670.

go; which was the only*ᵃ* thing that they could find out to doubt
them by, besides the number that the party doth go to put off;
and then coming to the Controller of the Mint, he could not,
I say, find any other thing to raise any doubt upon, but only
their being so truly round or near it; though I should never
have doubted that thing neither.   He was neither hanged nor
burned,¹ the cheat was thought so ingenious and being*ᵇ* the first
time they could ever trap him in it, and so little hurt to any man
in it, the money being as good as commonly goes.

Thence to the office till the evening; we sat and then by water
(taking Pembleton with us) over the water to the Halfway-house,
where we played at nine-pins; and there my damned jealousy
took fire, he and my wife being of a side and I seeing of him
taking her by the hand in play; though I now believe he did
only in passing and sport.   Thence home; and being 10 a-clock,
was forced to land beyond the Custome-house and so walked
home and to my office; and having despatched my great letters
by the post to my father, of which I keep copies to show by me
and for my future understanding, I went home to supper and bed,*ᶜ*
being late.

The most observables in the making of money which I observed
today is the steps of their doing it.²   *tu[r]ne over*ᵈ

1. Before they do anything, they essay the Bullion – which is
   done, if it be gold, by taking an equall weight of that and of
   Silver; of each a small weight, which they reckon to be six
   ounces or half a pound Troy; this they wrap up in thin leade.
   If it be Silver, they put such*ᵉ* a quantity of that alone and

a repl. 'first'   *b* repl. 'thence'   *c* repl. '2' ('to')
d following page written in small hand
e repl. 'an [s.h.] equall [l.h.]'

1. Counterfeiting the coinage was
high treason, punishable by hanging
in the case of men and burning in the
case of women.
2. This detailed account of the
manufacture of English coins has a
special interest. In theory the
methods used were secret, and nothing was published on the subject.
But some knowledge leaked out,

since the secrets were shared among
so many individuals. Moreover, the
methods were essentially the same as
those used by other countries (such
as France) which had no inhibitions
about publication. Sandwich, in his
MS. journal, has a similar but less
detailed account of the Mint at
Madrid: Mapperton, Sandwich
MSS, Journal, ii. 241 +.

wrap it up in lead; and then putting them into little earthen cupps made of Stuffe like tobacco pipes and put them into a burning hot Furnace; where after a while the whole body is melted and at last the lead in both is sunk*ᵃ* into the body of the cup, which carries away all the copper or dross with it and left the pure gold and silver embodyed together, of that which hath both [been] put into the cup together, and the silver alone in those where it was put alone in the leaden case. And to part*ᵇ* the silver and the gold*ᶜ* in the first experiment, they put the mixed body into a glass of boyling aqua fortis, which separates them by spitting out the silver into such small parts that you cannot tell what it becomes; but turns into the very water and leaves the gold at*ᵈ* the bottom clear of itself, with the silver wholly spewed out; and yet the gold in the form that it was double[d] together in when it was a mixed body of gold and silver – which is a great mystery; after all this is done, to get the silver together out of the water is as strange.

But the nature of the Essay is thus. The piece of gold that goes into the Furnace, 12 ounces, if it comes out again, 11 ounces; and the piece of silver which goes in, 12, and comes out again 11 and 2 penny-weight, are just of the allay of the*ᵉ* standard of England.¹ If it comes out, either of them, either the gold above 11, as very fine will sometimes within very little of what it went in, or the silver about 11 and 2 pennyweight, as that also will sometimes come out 11 and 10 pennyweight or more, they are so much above the goodness of the standard; and so they know what proportion of worse gold*ᶠ* or silver to put to such a quantity of the Bullion to bring to the exact standard. And on the contrary, [if] they comes out lighter, then such a weight is beneath the standard and so requires such a proportion of fine mettall to be put to the Bullion to bring it to standard. And this is the

a repl. 'sung'   b repl. 'get'   c MS. 'leade'
d l.h. repl. s.h. ? 'dry'   e repl. 'England'   f repl. 'silver to'

---

1. Sterling silver had to be 11 oz 2 dwt in the pound weight (or 925 parts of pure silver to 75 parts of alloy). This was the normal English standard for coins from Norman times until 1920. Sir A. E. Feavearyear, *Pound Sterling*, p. 8.

difference of good and bad, better and worse then the standard, and also the difference of standards, that of Sivill being the best and that of Mexico worse; and I think they said none but Sivill is better then ours.

2. They melt it into long plates; which, if the mould do take ayre, then that plate is not of an equal heavynesse in every part of it, as it often falls out.

3. They draw these plates between rollers, to bring them to an even thickness all along and every plate of the same thickness. And it is very strange how the drawing it twice easily between the rowlers will make it as hot as fire, you cannot touch it.

4. They bring it to another pair of Rowlers, which they call adjousting it – which brings it to a greater exactnesse in its thickness then the first could do.

5. They cut them into round pieces, which they do with the greatest ease, speed and exactness in the world.

6. They weigh these; and where they find any to be too heavy, they file them 〈which they call Sizeing them〉; or light, they lay them by; which is very seldom but they are of a most exact weight. But however, in the melting, all parts by some accident not being close alike, now and then a difference will be. And this fyling being done, there shall not be any imaginable difference almost between the weight of 40 of these against another 40 chosen by chance out of all their heapes.

7. These round pieces having been cut out of the plates, which in passing the rollers are bent, they are sometimes a little crooked or swelling out or sinking in; and therefore they have a way of clapping a hundred or two together into an engine, which with a screw presses them so hard that they come out as flat as is possible.

8. They blanch them.

9. They mark the letters on the edges, which is kept as the great secret by Blondeau (who was not in the way and so I did not speak with him today).[1]

10. They mill them; that is, put on the marks on both sides at once, with great exactness and speed – and then the money is perfect.

   The Mill is after this manner; one of the dyes, which hath one side of the piece cut, is fastened to a thing fixed below; and the other dye (and they tell me a payre of Dyes will last the marking of 10000*l* before it be worn out, they and all other their tools being made of hardened steel, and the Duchman[2] who makes them is an admirable artist, and hath so much by the pound for every pound that is coyned, to find a constant supply of dyes) to an engine above, which is moveable by a screw which is pulled by men; and then a piece being clap[ped] by one sitting below between the two dyes, when they meet the impression is set; and then the man with his finger strikes off the piece and claps another on; and then the other men they pull again and that is marked; and then another and another, with great speed.

   They say that this way is more charge to the King then the old way. But it is neater, freer from clipping or counterfeiting, the putting of the words upon the edges being not to be done (though counterfeited) without an engine of that charge and noise that no counterfeit will be at or venture upon. And it imploys as many men as the other, and speedier.

   They now coyne between 16 and 24000*l* in a week.

   At dinner they did discourse very finely to us of the probability that there is a vast deal of money hid in the land, from this:

---

1. Pierre Blondeau, the French-born engineer of the Mint, had been employed to produce this new issue (the first coins appearing in February 1663). He was now allowed to use a machine of his invention which stamped the edges to discourage clipping and counterfeiting. Cf. Magalotti's praise: p. 176. On Blondeau's previous visit, 1649–56, he had been unable to overcome the resistance of the officials to his ideas. Sir A. E. Feavearyear, *Pound Sterling*, pp. 85–6; Sir John Craig, *The Mint*, p. 158.

2. Roettier, a Fleming.

That in King Cha[r]les's time there was near 10 millions of money coyned[1] – besides what was then in being of King James's and Queen Elizabeths, of which there is a good deal at this day in being.

Next, that there was but 750000*l* coyned of the harp and Crosse=mony,[2] and of this there was 500000*l* brought in upon its being called in, and from very good arguments they find that there cannot be less of it in Ireland and Scotland then 100000*l*; so that there is but 150000*l* missing; and of that, suppose that there should be not above 50000*l* still remaining, either ⟨melted down⟩, hid or lost or hoarded up in England, there will then be but 100000*l* left to be thought to have been transported.[3]

Now, if 750000*l* in twelve yeares time lost but a 100000*l* in danger of being transported, then 10000000*l* in 35 Years time will have lost but 3888880*l* and odd pounds.   And as there is 650000*l* remaining after 12 years' time in England, so after 35 years' time, which was within this two years, there ought in proportion to have been resting 6111120*l* or thereabouts ⟨besides King James and Queen Elizabeth mony⟩.

Now, that most of this must be hid is evident as they reckon, because of the dearth of money immediately upon the calling-in of the State's money,[4] which was 500000*l* that came in; and yet there was not any money to be had in this City – which they say to their own observation and knowledge was so.   And therefore, though I can say nothing in it myself, I do not dispute it.[5]

20.   Up and to my office; and anon home and to ⟨see my wife⟩ dancing with Pembleton about noon, and I to the Trinity-house to dinner; and after dinner home and there met Pembleton, who I perceive had dined with my wife, which she takes

---

1. Probably an exaggeration: see Feavearyear, op. cit., p. 83.
2. Commonwealth coins, demonetised in 1661–2; so-called from the English cross and the Irish harp represented in shields on the reverse. For the reliability of the figures which follow, see below, vi. 326 & n. 1.
3. I.e. taken abroad – either in the

course of trade (since England imported more than she exported), or to be sold to foreign mints, which paid higher prices than England for silver.
4. See above, ii. 224 & n. 3.
5. Cf. Pepys's own habit of hoarding: below, v. 269 & n 1.

no notice of; but whether that proceeds out of design or fear to displease me, I know not, but it put me into a great disorder again, that I could mind nothing but vexing; but however, I continued my resolution of going down by water to Woolwich and took my wife and Ashwell; and going out, met Mr. Howe come to see me, whose horse we caused to be set up and took him with us; but tide against us, so I went ashore at Greenwich before and did my business at the yard about putting things in order as to their proceeding to build the new Yacht ordered to be built by Chr. Pett;[1] and so to Woolwich town, where at a alehouse I find them ready to attend my coming; and so took boat again, it being cold and I sweating with my walk (which was very pleasant along the green corne and peas); and most of the way sang, he and I, and eat some cold meat we had and with great pleasure home, and so he took horse again; and Pembleton coming, we danced a country dance or two and so broke up and to bed – my mind restless and like to be so while she learns to dance. God forgive my folly.

21. Up; but cannot get up so early as I was wont, nor my mind to business as it should be and used to be before this dancing. However, to my office, where most of the morning talking with Captain Cox of Chatham about his and the whole yard's difference against Mr. Barrow the Storekeeper;[2] wherein I told him my mind clearly, that he would be upheld against the designs of any to ruin him; he being, we all believed but Sir W. Batten his mortal enemy, as good a servant as any the King hath in that yard.

After much good advice and other talk – I home and danced with Pembleton and then the barber trimmed me; and so to dinner – my wife and I having high words about her dancing, to that degree that I did retire and make a vowe to myself, not to oppose her or say anything to dispraise or correct her therein as long as her month lasts, in pain of *2s-6d* for every time; which if

---

1. The *Henrietta*: see above, p. 123 & n. 1.
2. Cf. above, iii. 155. The dispute continued into 1665. One issue was the question of precedence between Barrow as Storekeeper and Gregory as Clerk of the Cheque: *CSPDAdd. 1660–85*, p. 136. Cox was Master-Attendant.

God please, I will observe, for this roguish business hath brought us more disquiet then anything hath happened a great while.

After dinner to my office, where late, and then home; and Pembleton being there again, we fell to dance a country dance or two, and so to supper and bed. But being at supper, my wife did say something that caused me to oppose her in; she used the word "Devil," which vexed me; and among other things, I said I would not have her to use that word, upon which she took me up most scornefully; which before Ashwell and the rest of the world, I know not nowadays how to check as I would heretofore, for less then that would have made me strike her. So that I fear, without great discretion, I shall go near to lose too my command over her; and nothing doth it more then giving her this occasion of dancing and other pleasure, whereby her mind is taken up from her business and finds other sweets besides pleasing of me, and so makes her that she begins not at all to take pleasure in me or study to please me as heretofore. But if this month of her dancing were but out (as my first was this *a* night, and I paid off Pembleton for myself), I shall hope with a little pains to bring her to her old wont. This day, Susan *b* that lived with me lately [1] being out of service, and I doubt a simple wench, my wife doth *c* take her for a little time to try her, at least till she goes into the country; which I am yet doubtful whether it will be best for me to send her or no, for fear of her running on in her liberty before I have brought her to her right temper again.

22. Up pretty betimes; and shall I hope come to myself and business again after a small playing the truant, for I find that my interest and profit do grow daily, for which God be praised and keep me to my duty.

To my office. And anon one tells me that Rundall the house-carpenter of Deptford hath sent me a fine Blackebird *d* – which I went to see. He tells me he was offered 20s for him as he came along, he doth so whistle.

So to my office, and busy all the morning. Among other

a repl. 'last'
b A blank was originally left in the MS., the name being added later.
c repl. 'did'   d l.h. repl. 'Blackeburd'

1. She had been cookmaid from December 1662 to March 1663.

things, learning to understand the course of the tides, and I think I do now do it.

At noon Mr. Creede comes to me, and he and I to the Exchange, where I had much discourse with several merchants; and so home with him to dinner and then by water to Greenwich; and calling at the little alehouse at the end of the town to wrap a rag about my little left toe, being new-sore with walking, we walked pleasantly to Woolwich, in our way hearing the Nightingales sing. So to Woolwich yard; and after doing many things there, among others preparing myself for a dispute against Sir W. Penn in the business of Bewpers, wherein he is guilty of some corruption to the King's wrong, we walked back again without drinking there; which I never do, because I would not make my coming troublesome to any, nor would become obliged too much to any. In our going back we were overtook by Mr. Steventon, a purser and uncle to my clerk Will, who told me how he was abused in the passing of his accounts by Sir J. Mennes, to the degree that I am ashamed to hear it and resolve to retrive the matter if I can, though the poor man hath given it over. And however, am pleased enough to see that others do see his folly and dotage as well as myself, though I believe in my heart the man in general means well. Took boat at Greenwich and to Deptford, where I did the same thing and find Davis, the Storekeeper, a knave and shuffling in the business of Bewpers, being of the party with Young and Whistler to abuse the King; but I hope I shall be even with them.[1] So walked to Redriffe, drinking at the Halfway-house; and so walk and by water to White-hall, all our way by water, both coming and going, reading a little book said to be writ by a person of Quality concerning English Gentry to be preferred before Titular honours; but the most silly nonsense, no sense nor grammar, yet in as good words that ever I saw in all my life, that from beginning to end you meet not with one entire and regular sentence.[2]

1. In September 1662 a contract for flags with John Young and Henry Whistler had been the subject of a dispute at the Board. Pepys had found on enquiry that Davis had never on any count rejected flags served in by Young and Whistler: NWB, p. 48.

2. *A vindication of the degree of gentry in opposition to titular honours, and the humour of riches being the measure of honours. Done by a Person of Quality* (1662); duodecimo; 300 pp.; not in the PL. Much of the book is unintelligible.

At White-hall Sir G. Carteret was out of the way; and so returned back presently and home by water and to bed.

23. Waked this morning between 4 and 5 by my black-Bird, which whistles as well as ever I heard any; only it is the beginning of many tunes very well, but there leaves them and goes no further. So up and to my office, where we sat; and among other things, I had a fray with Sir J. Mennes in defence of my Will in a business where the old coxcomb would have put a fault upon him; which was only in Jack Davis and in him a downright piece of knavery, in procuring a double ticket and getting the wrong one paid, as well as the second was to the true party.[1] But it appeared clear enough to the board that Will was true in it. Home to dinner; and after dinner by water to the temple and there took my Lyra viall book, bound up with blank paper for new lessons.*[2] Thence to Greatorex's; and there, seeing Sir J. Mennes and Sir W. Penn go by by coach, I went in to them and to White-hall, where, in the ⟨matted⟩ gallery, Mr. Coventry was; who told us how the parliament hath required of Sir G. Carteret and him an account what money shall be necessary to be settled upon the Navy for the ordinary charge, which they intend to report 200000*l* per annum;[3] and how to allot this, we met this afternoon and took their papers for our perusal, and so we parted. Only, there was walking in the gallery some of the Barba[r]y company; and there we saw a draught of the armes of the company, which the King is of and so is called the Royall company – which is, in a field argent a Elephant proper, with a Canton on which England and France is Quartered – Supported by two Moores; the Crest, an Anchor Winged I think it is, and the Motto

---

1. For a similar case, see below, viii. 215. Another variety of double ticket was one by which a single person was paid in two capacities: see J. Hollond, *Discourses* (ed. Tanner), p. 142. Davis was a clerk (probably Mennes's) in the Navy Office.

2. The book was perhaps entirely in MS., but it was not unknown for printed music to be bound up with MS. pages (e.g. PL 2803). 'Lyra viall book' suggests Playford's *Musicks recreation: on the lyra viol* (? 1652) or his *Musicks recreation on the viol, lyra-way* (1661). Playford's shop was by the Temple. (E)

3. See above, iii. 297 & n. 1; above, p. 121 & n. 2. A Commons' committee on the King's revenue was now at work.

too tedious – *Regio floret patrocinio Commercium, commercioque Regnum.*[1]

Thence back by water to Greatorex's, and there he showed me his Varnish which he hath invented, which appears every whit as good, upon a stick which he hath done, as the Indian, though it did not do very well upon my paper rules with Musique lines, for it sunk and did not shine.[2] Thence home by water; and after a dance with Pembleton, to my office and wrote by the post to Sir W. Batten at Portsmouth, to send for him up against next Wednesday; being our triall day against Field at Guild-hall, in which God give us good end.[3] So home to supper and bed.[a]

24. *Lords day.* Having taken one of Mr. Holliards pills last night, it brought a stool or two this morning; and so I forebore going to church this morning, but stayed at home, looking over my papers about T. Trices business;[4] and so at noon dined, and my wife telling me that there was a pretty lady come to church with Pegg Pen today, I against my intention had a mind to go to church to see her, and did so – and she is pretty handsome. But over against our gallery I espied Pembleton and saw him leer upon my wife all the sermon, I taking no notice of him, and my wife upon him; and I observed she made a curtsey to him at coming out, without taking notice to me at all of it; which,

     a   followed by two blank pages stuck together

---

1. The company was more usually known as the Guinea or African Company; incorporated on 10 January 1663 as 'the Company of Royal Adventurers trading into Africa'. (A previous charter had been issued in December 1660). The King had a venture of £6000 in it, which he never paid. C. T. Carr (ed.), *Select charters of trading companies*, pp. 177+; K. G. Davies, *Royal African Co.*, p. 42. For the arms and motto (about which Pepys is substantially correct), see Stow, *Survey* (ed. Strype, 1720), bk v. 268. The enterprise was reorganised in 1672 as the Royal African Company.

2. For methods of varnishing and japanning in England at this time, see J. Stalker, *A treatise of japaning and varnishing* (1688; PL 2719; repr. 1960, ed. Molesworth); F. W. Gibbs in *Annals of Science*, 7/401; 9/88. The Royal Society had gathered information about 'China varnish' in October and November 1661: Birch, i. 51-2, 54.

3. *Recte* next Wednesday but one: below, p. 172. For the case, see above, iii. 23 & n. 2.

4. See above, ii. 215 & n. 1.

with the consideration of her being desirous these two last Lord's-days to go to church both forenoon and afternoon, doth really*a* make me suspect something more then ordinary, though I am loath to think the worst; but yet it put and doth still keep me at a great loss in my mind, and makes me curse the time that I consented to her dancing, and more, my continuing it a second month, which was more then she desired, even after I had seen too much of her carriage with him. But I must have patience and get her into the country, or at*b* least to make an*c* end of her learning to dance as soon as I can. After sermon, to Sir W Pens with Sir J. Mennes to do a little business to answer Mr. Coventry tonight. And so home and with my wife and Ashwell into the garden, walking a great while discoursing what this pretty wench should be by her garb and deportment; with respect to Mrs. Pen, she might be her woman but only that she sat in the pew with her – which I believe he[1] would not let her do.

So home and read to my wife a Fable or two in Ogleby's *Æsop*;[2] and so to supper and then to prayers and to bed – my wife this evening discoursing of making clothes for the country; which I seem against, pleading lack of money, but I am glad of it in some respects, because of getting her out of the way from this fellow, and my own liberty to look after my business more then of late I have done. So to prayers and to bed.

This morning it seems Susan, who I think is distracted, or however is since she went from me taught to drink and so gets out of doors two or three times a day without leave to the ale-house, did go before 5 a-clock today, making Griffin rise in his shurt to let her out to the alehouse, she said to warm herself. But her mistress falling out with her about it, turned her out of doors this morning, and so she is gone like an idle slut. I took a pill also this night.

25. Up; and my pill working a little, I stayed within most of the morning; and by and by the barber came, and Sarah Kite my cosen, poor woman, came to see me and to borrow 40s of me, telling me she will pay it at Michaelmas again to me. I was

a repl. ? 'truly'   *b* MS. 'all'   MS. 'and'

---

1. Sir William Penn, Peg's father.   2. See above, ii. 6 & n. 4.

glad it was no more, being indifferent whether she pays it me or no; but it will be a good excuse to lend her nor give her any more; so I did freely, at first word, do it and gave her a Crowne more freely to buy her child something – she being a good-natured and painful wretch, and one that I would do good for, as far as I can that I might not be burdened.

My wife was not ready; and she coming pretty early, did not see her, and I was glad of it.

She gone, I up and there hear that my wife and her maid Ash-well had between them spilt the pot of piss and turd upon the floor and stool and God knows what, and were mighty merry washing of it clean. I took no great notice, but merrily.

Ashwell*ᵃ* did by and by come to me with an errand from her mistress, to desire money to buy a country suit for her against she goes as we talked last night; and so I did give her 4*l* and believe it will cost me the best part of 4 more to fit her out; but with peace and honour, I am willing to spare anything so as to be able to keep all ends together and my power over her undisturbed.

So to my office. And by and by home, where my wife and her Maister*ᵇ* were dancing; and so I stayed in my chamber till they had done and set down myself to try a little upon the Lyra viall,[1] my hand being almost out, but easily brought to again. So by and by to dinner and then carried my wife and Ashwell to St. James's, and there they sat in the coach while I went in; and finding nobody there likely to meet with the Duke, but only Sir J. Mennes with my Lord Barkely (who speaks very kindly and invites me with great compliment to come now and then and eat with him; which I am glad to hear, though I value not the thing, but it implies that my esteem doth encrease rather then fall) and so I stayed not, but into the coach again; and taking up my wife's Taylor,[2] it raining hard, they set me down at (and who should our Coachman be but Carelton, the Vintener that should have had Mrs. Sarah at Westminster) my Lord Chancellors, and they to Pater noster row. I stayed there to speak with my Lord Sandwich; and in my staying, meeting Mr. Lewes Phillips of Brampton, he and afterward others tell me that news came

a repl. 'Ashell'   *b* symbol smudged

1. See above, i. 295 & n. 4. (E).   2. John Unthank.

last night to Court that the King of France is sick of the Spotted feavour and that they[1] are struck in again; and this afternoon my Lord Mandeville is gone from the King to make him a visitt – which will be great news and of great import through Europe.[2]

By and by out comes my Lord Sandwich, and he and I talked a great while about his business of his accounts for his pay; and among other things, he told me that this day a vote hath passed that the King's grants of land to my Lord Monke and him should be made good; which pleases him very well.[3]

He also tells me that things don't go right in the House with Mr. Coventry, I suppose he means in the business of selling of places, but I am sorry for it.[4]   Thence by coach home, where I find Pembleton; and so I up to dance with them till the evening, when there came Mr. Alsopp the King's Brewer and Lanyon of Plimouth to see me.   Mr. Alsop tells me of a horse of his[a] that lately, after four days' pain, voided at his fundament four stones, bigger then that I was cut of, very heavy and in the middle of each of them either a piece of Iron or wood.   The King hath two of them in his closet, and a third, the College of Physicians to keep for rarities; and by the King's command he causes the turd of the horse to be every day searched to find more.

At night to see Sir W. Batten come home this day from Portsmouth; I met with some that say the King of France is poisoned,

a   repl. 'is

---

1. The spots.
2. Mandeville's pass (as Ambassador-Extraordinary) is dated this day: *CSPD 1663–4*, p. 249. Louis XIV, who had caught the measles from his wife, was well and back at work after dinner on 23 May/2 June (de Lionne to de Cominges, 24 May/ 3 June): J. J. Jusserand, *French Ambassador*, p. 211. 'Spotted fever' was a vague phrase: it could sometimes mean typhus. See below, p. 342; Evelyn, ii. 522 & n. 4. The Venetian Ambassador to France believed that Mandeville had been sent to enquire after the health of the Queen Mother: *CSPVen. 1661–4*, p. 249.

3. *CJ*, viii. 487; cf. above, p. 136, n. 1.

4. A bill 'for the discovery, punishment and preventing Frauds and abuses in buying and selling of offices' had received its second reading in the Commons on 18 May: *CJ*, viii. 486.   It was never passed. See V. Vale in *Camb. Hist. Journ.*, 12/107+.   Coventry sold certain offices in his gift but only warrant-offices, not commissions, and never in excess of what was customary.

but how true that is is not known.[1]   So home to supper and to bed, pleasant.

26. Lay long in bed, talking and pleasing myself with my wife.   So up and to my office a while and then home, where I find Pembleton; and by many circumstances I am led to conclude that there is something more then ordinary between my wife and him; which doth so trouble me that I know not, at this very minute that I now write this almost, what either I write or am doing nor how*a* to carry myself to my wife in it, being unwilling to speak of it to her for making of any breach and other inconveniences, nor let it pass for fear of her continuing to offend me and the matter grow worse thereby.   So that I am grieved at the very heart, but I am very unwise in being so.

There dined with me Mr Creed and Captain Grove; and before dinner, I had much discourse in my chamber with Mr. Deane, the Builder of Woolwich, about building of ships.   But nothing could get the business out of my head, I fearing that this afternoon, by my wife's sending every[one] abroad and knowing that I must be at the office, she hath appointed him to come. This is my devilish jealousy; which I pray God may be false, but it makes a very hell in my mind; which the God of heaven remove, or I shall be very unhappy.   So to the office, where we sat a while.

By and by, my mind being in great trouble, I went home to see how things were; and there I find as I doubted, Mr. Pembleton with my wife and nobody else in the house, which made me almost mad; and going up to chamber, after a turn or two I went out again and called somebody, upon pretence of business, and left him in my little room at the door (it was the Duchman,[2] commander of one of the King's pleasure-boats; who having been beat by one of his men sadly, was come to the office today to complain), telling him I would come again to him to speak with him about his business; so in great trouble and doubt to the office; and Mr. Coventry nor Sir G. Carteret being there,

a   repl. symbol rendered illegible

---

1. It was not true, but none the less a good story: cf. HMC, *Portland*, iii. 273.   The sudden illness of a royal person was in England often attributed to poisoning, especially if he were foreign, and especially if he had quarrelled with the Pope.

2. Jan de Gens, Captain of the *Mary*.

I made a quick end of our business and desired leave to be gone, pretending to go to the Temple, but it was home; and so up to my chamber and, as I think, if they had any intentions of hurt, I did prevent doing anything at that time; but I continued in my chamber vexed and angry till he went away, pretending aloud, that I might hear, that he could not stay, and Mrs. Ashwell not being within they*a* would not dance. And Lord, to see how my jealousy wrought so far, that I went saftly up to see whether any of the beds were out of order or no, which I found not; but that did not content me, but I stayed all the evening walking, and though anon my wife came up to me and would have spoke of business to me, yet I construed it to be but impudence; and though my heart was full, yet I did say nothing, being in a great doubt what to do. So at night suffered them to go all to bed, and late put myself to bed in great discontent, and so to sleep.

27. So I waked by 3 a-clock, my mind being troubled; and so took occasion by making water to wake my wife, and after having lain till past 4 a-clock, seemed going to rise, though I did it only to see what she would do; and so going out of the bed, she took hold of me and would know what ayled me; and after many kind and some cross words, I begun to tax her discretion in yesterday's business, but she quickly told me my owne, knowing well enough that it was my old disease of Jealousy; which I disowned, but to no purpose. After an hour's discourse, sometimes high and sometimes kind, I find very good reason to think that her freedom with him was very great and more then was convenient,* but with no evil intent. And so after a while I caressed her and parted seeming friends, but she crying and in a great discontent.*b* So I up and by water to the Temple, and thence with Comissioner Pett to St. James's, where an hour with Mr. Coventree, talking of Mr. Petts proceedings lately in the Forrest of Sherwood;[1] and thence with Pett to my Lord Ashly, Chancellor of the Exchequer, where we met the Auditors about settling the business of the accounts of persons to whom

a repl. 'he'　　　　*b* repl. 'heat'

1. For Commissioner Pett's report (26 May) on the costs of felling and transporting timber from Sherwood Forest, see *CSPD 1663–4*, p. 151.

money is due before the King's time in the Navy, and the clearing
of their imprests for what little of their debts they have received.[1]
I find my Lord as he is reported, a very ready, quick and diligent
person.   Thence I to Westminster-hall, where terme and parliament make the Hall full of people.   No further*a* news yet of the
King of France, whether he be dead or not.

Here I met with my Cosen Roger Pepys and walked a good
while with him; and among other discourse, as a secret he hath
committed to nobody yet but myself, he tells me that his sister
Claxton now resolving to give over the keeping of his house at
Impington, he thinks it fit to marry again; and would have me,
by the help of my uncle Wight or others, to look him out a
widow between 30 and 40 year old, without children and with a
fortune, which he will answer in any degree with a Joynture fit
for her fortune.[2]   A woman sober and no high flyer as he calls
it.

I demanded his estate; he tells me (which he says also he hath
not done to any) that his estate is not full 800*l* per annum, but it is
780*l* per annum – of which 200*l* is by the death of his last wife;
which he will allot for a Joynture for a wife, but the rest, which
lies in Cambrigeshire, he is resolved to leave entire for his eldest
son.   I undertook to do what I can in it, and so I shall.   He
tells me that the King hath sent to them to hasten to make an
end by Midsummer, because of his going into the country; so
they have set upon four bills to despatch[3] – the first of which is,
he says, too devilish a severe act against conventicles; so beyond

a repl. 'certain'

---

1. These debts were due to be
stated before Lady Day: PRO, Adm.
2/1745, f. 88*v*.

2. Already thrice widowed, Roger
Pepys was not married again until
February 1669. But he was then
still of the same mind, and married a
widow (Esther Dickenson) of about
40.

3. The King had given notice on
the 26th of his intention to permit a
recess by midsummer. The reason
he gave was that the members (not
he himself) ought by then to be free

to go into the country: *CJ*, viii. 493.
Upon which the House voted that
priority should be given to four bills:
those concerning the revenue, the
militia, conventicles and the growth
of Popery. Parliament was not
prorogued until 27 July. The bills
against conventicles and Popery
(which the Upper House had shown
no great hurry to deal with) thereupon lapsed, the measure against
conventicles being passed in May 1664
(16 Car. II c. 4).

all moderation, that he is afeared it will ruin all.[1] Telling me that it is matter of the greatest grief to him in the world that he should be put upon this trust of being a parliament-man, because he says nothing is done, that he can see, out of any truth and sincerity, but mere envy and design.

Thence by water to Chelsy, all the way reading a little book I bought of Improvement of trade,* a pretty book and many things useful in it.[2]

So walked to Little Chelsy, where I find my Lord Sandwich with Mr. Becke, the maister of the house, and Mr. Creed at dinner. And I sat down with them, and very merry. After dinner (Mr. Gibbons being come in also before dinner done) to Musique; they played a good Fancy,[3] to which my Lord is fallen again and says he cannot endure a merry tune – which is a strange turn of his humour, after he hath for two or three years flung off the practice of Fancies and played only fiddlers tunes.[4] Then into the great garden up to the banquetting-house; and there by his glass we drow in the Species[5] very pretty.

Afterward to nine-pins, where I won a shilling – Creed and I playing against my Lord and Cooke. ⟨This day there was great thronging to Bansted downes, upon a great horse-race and foot-race;[6] I am sorry I could not go thither.⟩[a]

a addition crowded in between paragraphs

---

1. See below, p. 243 & n. 3.
2. Of the many books on this subject, Pepys retained *The trades increase* (1615), by I. R.: PL 1079 (5). But that mentioned here may well be Samuel Fortrey, *Englands interest and improvement consisting in the increase of . . . trade* (46 pp., Cambridge, 1663: not in PL). Or possibly *short notes and observations drawn from the present decaying condition of this kingdom in point of trade* . . . (14 pp., 1662; not in PL), which offered a twelve-point programme for the revival of trade.
3. Fantasia: a piece for viols in a highly contrapuntal style, having 'a strange tranquill harmony in [it] – nothing of hurry, but as a temperate air flowing': North (ed. Wilson), p. 11, n. Christopher Gibbons (son of

Orlando) held a court post for virginals and was organist of Westminster Abbey. (E).
4. Light, tuneful melodies, such as country or tavern fiddlers played: e.g. those for the violin in Playford's *Brief introduction to the skill of musick* (1660, 1662), pp. 88–90. (E).
5. Sc. 'we used his telescope to magnify the views'.
6. Horse-races had been run at Banstead (the most popular course near London) since at least 1625: VCH, *Surrey*, iii. 253, 272. For a description of a race there, at which most of the spectators seem to have been on horseback, see Z. C. von Uffenbach, *London in 1710* (ed. Quarrell and Mare), pp. 105–9.

So home, back as I came, to London-bridge and so home – where I find my wife in a musty humour, and tells me before Ashwell that Pembleton had been there and she would not have him come in unless I was there, which I was ashamed of; but however, I had rather it should be so then the other way.

So to my office to put things in order there. And by and by comes Pembleton and word is brought me from my wife thereof, that I might come home; so I sent word that I would have her go dance, and I would come presently. So being at a great loss whether I should appear to Pembleton or no, and which would most proclaim my jealousy to him, I at last resolved to go home; and took Tom Hater with me and stayed a good while in my chamber, and there took occasion to tell him how I hear that parliament is putting an act out against all sorts of Conventicles[1] and did give him good counsel, not only in his own behalfe but my own, that if he did hear or know anything that could be said to my prejudice, that he would tell me; for in this wicked age (especially Sir W. Batten being so open to my reproches and Sir J. Mennes, for the neglect of their duty, and so will think themselfs obliged to scandalize me all they can to right themselfs if there shall be any enquiry into the matters of the Navy, as no doubt there will) a man ought to be prepared to answer for himself in all things that can be enquired concerning him.

After much discourse of this nature to him, I sent him away and then went up; and there we danced country dances and single, my wife and I, and my wife paid him off[a] for this month also, and so he is cleared.

After dancing, we took him down to supper and were very merry; and I made myself so and kind to him as much as I could, to prevent his discourse; though I perceive to my trouble that he knows all, and my doty doth me the disgrace to publish it as much as she can. Which I take very ill, and if too much provoked shall witness it to her. After supper and he gone, we to bed.

28. ·Up this morning; and my wife, I know not for what

a l.h. repl. s.h. 'for'

1. For Hayter's conventicling, see above, pp. 129-30 & n.

cause, being against going to Chelsey today, it being a holy day
(Ascension day) and I at leisure, it being the first holy-day almost
that we have observed ever since we came to this office – we did
give Ashwell leave to go by herself.   And I out to several places
about business.   Among other, to Dr Williams to reckon with
him for Physique that my wife hath had for a year or two,
coming to almost 4*l*.   Then to the Exchange, where I hear that
the King had letters yesterday from France that the King there
is in a [way] of living again, which I am glad to hear.

At the Coffee-house in*a* Exchange=ally I bought a little book,
Counsell to Builders, written by Sir Balth. Gerbier;[1] it is dedicated
almost to all the men of any great condition in England, so that
the epistles are more then the book itself;[2] and both it and them
not worth a turd, that I am ashamed that I bought it.

Home and there find Creede, who dined with us; and after
dinner, by water to the Royall Theatre[3] but that was so full they
told us we could have no room; and so to the Dukes house
and there saw *Hamlett* done, giving us fresh reason never to think
enough of Baterton.[4]

Who should we see come upon the Stage but Gosnell, my wife's
maid, but neither spoke, danced nor sung; which I was sorry
for.   But she becomes the stage very well.[5]

Thence by water home, after we had walked to and fro, backward and forward, six or seven times in the Temple walks,
disputing whether to go by land or water.   By land*b* home, and
thence by water to Halfway-house and there eat some supper
we carried with us, and so walked home again; it being late,
we were forced to land at the Docke, my wife and they; but I
in a humour, not willing to daub my shoes, went round by the

---

a repl. 'against'   *b* repl. 'water'

---

1. *Counsel and advise to all builders;
for the choice of their surveyours . . .
Together with several epistles to eminent
persons, who may be concerned in building* (1663); not in the PL.
2. A pardonable exaggeration.
3. The TR, Drury Lane. (A).
4. Some interesting details of Betterton's fine interpretation of Hamlet
are provided by Colley Cibber in his

Apology, ch. iv (1740). For *Hamlet*
(now at the LIF), see above, ii. 161
& n. 1. (A).
5. Cf. above, iii. 276, where Pepys
praises Gosnell's singing. She was a
member of his household for a few
days only and appears to have become
eventually one of the leading actresses
in the Duke of York's company.
(A).

Custome-house. So home, and by and by to bed – Creed lying with me in the red chamber all night.

29. This day is kept strictly as a holy-day, being the King's Coronacion.*ᵃ¹* We lay long in bed. And it rained very hard, rain and hail almost all the morning. By and by Creed and I abroad and called at several churches; and it is a wonder to see, and by that to guess, the ill temper of the City at this time, either to religion in general or to the King, that in some churches there was hardly ten people in the whole church, and those poor people.

So to a Coffee-house, and there in discourse hear the King of France is likely to be well again.

So home to dinner and out by water to the Royall Theatre, but they not acting today; then to the Dukes house and there saw *The Slighted mayde*, wherein Gosnell acted Peromena, a great part,² and did it very well and I believe will do it better and better and prove a good actor.

The play is not very excellent, but is well acted; and in general the actors in all perticulars are better then at the other house.³

Thence to the Cocke alehouse; and having there drunk, sent them with Creede to see the German princesse at the gate house at Westminster;⁴ and I to my brother and thence to my uncle Fenners to have seen my aunt James⁵ (who hath been long in

a MS. l.h. 'Cronoucon'

---

1. *Recte* the King's birthday and the anniversary of his restoration.
2. In this comedy by Sir Robert Stapylton (q.v. above, p. 56 & n. 1) the important role of Pyramena was usually played by Mrs Betterton: see Genest, i. 46. (A).
3. Cf. above, p. 5 & n. 1. (A).
4. This was Mary Moders, a fiddler's daughter from Canterbury, who had recently married John Carleton and was now indicted for bigamy, the penalty for which could be death. The public imagination had been caught by the extraordinary story of how she had successfully posed as a German noblewoman, compelled to flee her native land by

the prospect of a forced marriage with an old man of 80. People flocked to see her in prison: Rugge, ii, f. 73*v*. Pepys approved of her subsequent acquittal because it was earned by her 'wit and spirit': below, p. 177. On 15 April 1664 he saw a play about her in which she herself acted. Her career of fraud and theft ended on the gallows at Tyburn in 1673. For the pamphlets and plays about her, see E. Bernbaum, *The Mary Carleton narratives*.
5. Unidentified; probably a relative of Pepys's mother; apparently from Wales (below, v. 266), and very pious.

town and goes away tomorrow, and I not seen her) but did find none of them within, which I was glad of; and so back to my brother's to speak with him, and so home and in my way did take two turns forward and backward through the Fleete ally to see a couple of pretty whores that stood off the doors there; and God forgive me, I could scarce stay myself from going into their houses with them, so apt is my nature to evil, after once, as I have these two days, set upon pleasure again.

So home, and to my office to put down these two days' journalls. Then home again and to supper; and then Creed and I to bed with good discourse, only my mind troubled about my spending my time so badly for these seven or eight days; but I must impute it to the disquiet that my mind hath been in of late about my wife – and for my going these two days to plays, for which I have paid the due forfeit, by money and abating the times of going to plays at Court; which I am now to remember that I have cleared all my times that I am to go to Court Plays to the end of this month, and so June is the first time that I am to begin to reckon.[1]

30. Up betimes and Creed and I by water to*a* Fleetestreete; and my brother not being ready, he and I walked to the New Exchange and there dranke our morning draught of Whay, the first I have done this year. But I perceive the lawyers come all in as they go to the hall, and I believe it is very good.[2]

So to my brother's and there I find my aunt James, a poor, religious, well-meaning, good humble soul, talking of nothing but God Almighty, and that with so much innocence that mightily pleased me. Here was a fellow that said grace so long, like a prayer; I believe the fellow is a cunning fellow, and yet I by my brother's desire did give him a crowne, he being in great want and it seems a parson among the fanatiques and a cousin of my poor aunts – whose prayers, she told me, did do me good among the many good souls that did by my father's desires pray for me when I was cut of the stone, and which God did hear; which I

a repl. 'the'

---

1. See above, p. 8. (A).
2. Whey was held to be more wholesome than cold milk, which was

drunk at this period chiefly by infants and old people.

also in complaisance did owne, but God forgive me, my mind was otherwise. I had a couple of lobsters and some wine for her; and so she going out of town today and being not willing to come home with me to dinner, I parted and home, where we sat at the office all the morning, and after dinner, all the afternoon till night there at my office, getting up the time that I have of late lost by not fallowing my business. But I hope now to settle my mind again very well to my business.

So home; and after supper did wash my feet, and so to bed.

31. *Lords day.* Lay long in bed, talking with my wife. And I do plainly see that her distaste (which is beginning only in her yet) against Ashwell arises from her jealousy of me and her for my neglect of herself; which indeed is true and I to blame, but for the time to come I will take care to remedy all.

So up and to church, where I think I did see Pembleton; but whatever the reason is, I did not perceive him to look up toward my wife, nor she much toward him; however, I could hardly keep myself from being troubled that he was there – which is a madness not to be excused, now that his coming to my house is past and, I hope, all likelihood of her having occasion to converse with him again.

Home to dinner. And after dinner, up and read part of the new play of *The Five houres adventures*;[1] which though I have seen it twice, yet I never did admire or understand it enough – it being a play of the greatest plot that ever I expect to see, and of great vigour quite through the whole play, from beginning to the end.

To church again after dinner (my wife finding herself ill of her months did not go); and there the Scot preaching, I slept most of the sermon.

This day, Sir W. Batten's son's child is christened in the country,[2] whither Sir J. Mennes and Sir W. Batten and Sir W. Penn are all gone. I wonder, and take it highly ill, that I am not invited by the father, though I know his father and mother, with whom I am never likely to have much kindness but rather I study the contrary, are the cause of it, and in that respect I am

1. See above, p. 8 & n. 2; not in the PL.

2. At Walthamstow, Essex; the child's father was William, elder son of Sir William. The child, too, was named William.

glad of it.   Being come from church, I to make up my month's accounts and find myself clear worth 726*l* – for which God be praised.   But yet I might have been better by 20*l* almost had I forborne some layings-out in dancing and other things upon my wife, and going to plays and other things merely to ease my mind as to the business of the dancing maister; which I bless God is now over and I falling to my quiet of mind and business again, which I have for a fortnight neglected too much.

This month, the greatest news is the heighth and heat that the Parliament is in enquiring into the Revenue, which displeases the Court, and their backwardness to give the King any money. Their enquiring into the selling of places doth trouble a great many; among the chief, my Lord Chancellor (against whom perticularly it is carried) and Mr. Coventry, for which I am sorry. The King of France was given out to be poisoned and dead; but it proves to be the meazles and is well, or likely to be soon well again.

I find myself growing in the esteem and credit that I have in the office, and I hope falling to my business again will confirm me in it, and the saving of money – which God grant.

So to supper – prayers and bed.

My whole family lying longer this morning then was fit, and besides, Will having neglected to brush my cloak as he ought to do till I was ready to go to church, and not then till I bid him, I was very angry; and seeing him make little matter of it, but seeming to make a matter indifferent whether he did it or no, I did give him [a] box on the eare, and had it been another day had done more.   This is the second time I ever struck him.[1]

1. He had struck him on 8 June and 27 August 1662.

JUNE

1. Begun again to rise betimes, by 4 a-clock. And made an end of *The Adventures of five houres*, and it is a most excellent play.

So to my office – where a while and then abroad about several businesses in my way to my brother's, where I dined (being invited) with Mr. Peter and Deane Honiwood[1] – where Tom did give us a very pretty dinner – and we very pleasant but not very merry, the Deane being but a weak man, though very good.

I was forced to rise, being in haste to St. James's to attend the Duke, and left them to end their dinner. But the Duke having been a-hunting today and so lately come home and gone to bed, we could not see him;[2] and Mr. Coventry being out of the house too, we walked away to White-hall and there took coach; and I with Sir J. Mennes to the Strand May pole and there I light out of his coach and walked to the New=theatre, which, since the King's players are gone to the Royall one, is this day begun to be imployed by the Fencers to play prizes at.[3] And here I came and saw the first prize I ever saw in my life; and it was between one Mathews, who did beat at all weapons, and one Westwicke, who was soundly cut several times both in the head and legs, that he was all over bloody. And other deadly blows they did give and take in very good earnest, till Estwicke[4] was in a most sad pickle. They fought at eight weapons, three boutes at each weapon. It was very well worth seeing, because I did till this day think that it had only been a cheat; but this being upon a private quarrell, they did it in good earnest; and I felt one

1. Peter Honywood and his brother Michael, Dean of Lincoln. The former lodged at Tom Pepys's.
2. Cf. Reresby, *Memoirs* (ed. Browning), p. 45: '[June 1663]. This Sommer the Duke took a fancy (and sometimes the King) to buck-hunt in Enfield Chace and the Forest . . .'.
3. The King's Company had left the former TR, Vere St, and were now (after 7 May 1663) at the TR, Drury Lane.
4. *Sic.*

of their swords and find it to be very little, if at all, blunter on the edge then the common swords are. Strange to see what a deal of money is flung to them both upon the stage between every boute. But a woeful rude rabble there was and such noises, made my head ake all this evening. So, well pleased for once with this sight, I walked home, doing several businesses by the way – in my way calling to see Comissioner Pett, who lies sick at his daughter's,[1] a pretty woman, in Gracious-street, but is likely to be abroad again in a day or two. At home I find my wife in bed all this day of her months.

I went to see Sir[a] William Pen, who hath a little pain of his goute again but will do well. So home to supper and to bed.

This day I hear at Court of the great plot which was lately discovered in Ireland, made among the presbyters and others, designing to cry up the Covenant and to secure Dublin Castle – and other places; and have debauched a good part of the army there, promising them ready money.[2] Some of the parliament there, they say, are guilty, and some withdrawn upon it. Several persons taken; and among others, a son of Scotts that was executed here for the King's murder.[3]

What reason the King hath, I know not, but it seems he is doubtful of Scotland: and this afternoon when I was there, the Councell was called extraordinarily and they were opening the letter this last post, coming and going between Scotland and us

a l.h. repl. s.h. 'Mr.'

---

1. Probably Agnes, wife of Rowland Crisp. (R).
2. The Castle Plot; a conspiracy of discontented soldiers and settlers threatened with the loss of the land they had been granted during the Interregnum. It was joined by several M.P.'s, and aimed at the seizure of the person of the Lord-Lieutenant and the proclamation of a Protestant *régime*. But it was disclosed on 19 May, two days before it was timed to begin. Lt Thomas Blood (who as Col. Blood made the famous attack on Ormond in 1670, and the even more famous raid on the Crown Jewels in 1671) was the leader of the party which was to assault Dublin Castle. T. Carte, *Ormond,* iv. 132+; *CSP Ireland 1663–5,* passim; R. Bagwell, *Ireland under Stuarts,* iii. 35+.
3. Thomas, son of Thomas Scott, the republican Secretary of State. He turned King's evidence and was pardoned in 1666: *CSP Ireland 1663–5,* p. 691; ib., *1666–9,* p. 150.

and other places.[1] Blessed be God, my head and hands are clear, and therefore my sleep safe. The King of France is well again.

2. Up and by water to White-hall; and so to St. James to Mr. Coventry, where I had an*a* hour's private talk with him. Most of it was discourse concerning his own condition, at present being under the censure*b* of the House, being concerned with others in the Bill for selling of offices.[2] He tells me that though he thinks himself to suffer much in his fame hereby, yet he values nothing more of evil to hang over him; for that it is against no Statute as is pretended, nor more then what his predecessors time out of mind have taken. And that so soon as he found himself to be in an errour, he did desire to have his fees set, which was done and since that he hath not taken a token more.[3] He undertakes to prove that he did never take a token of any Captain to get him imployed in his life beforehand, or demanded anything. And for the other accusacion, that the Cavaliers are not imployed, he looked over the list of them now in the service, and of the 27 that are imployed, 13 have been heretofore alway under the King. Two, Neutralls; and the other 12 men of great courage and such as had either the King's perticular command or great recomendacion to put them in, and none by himself. Besides that, he says it is not the King's nor Dukes opinion that the whole party of the late officers should be rendered desperate; and lastly, he confesses that the more of the Cavaliers are put in, the less of discipline hath fallowed in the fleet; and that whenever there comes occasion, it must be the old ones that must do any

a repl. 'our'   *b* l.h. repl. s.h. 'censure'

---

1. For the recent discontent in Scotland, see above, p. 131, n. 1. It was feared that a rising there had been timed to coincide with that in Ireland. Two letters addressed to Secretary Bennet on the subject are summarised in *CSPD 1663-4*, p. 152. See *Coll. state letters of . . . Orrery* (1742), pp. 69-71; *AHR*, 14/518-19. There is no account of this meeting in the Privy Council Register.
2. The bill on this subject (above,

p. 156, n. 4) reached report stage in the Commons this day. It was agreed that the King should have the nomination of commissioners to enquire into abuses. But nothing further was heard of it.
3. In April 1661 a list of authorised fees was issued by the Duke of York. Copies in PL 488; NMM, MS. 51/064/4; Longleat, Coventry MSS, 98, f. 80r.

good – there being none,*a* he says, but Captain Allen good for anything of them all.[1]

He tells me that he cannot guess whom all this should come from, but he suspects Sir G. Carteret; as I also do, at least that he is pleased with it.   But he tells me that he will bring Sir G. Carteret to be the first adviser and instructor of him what to make his place of benefitt to him – telling him that Smith did make his place worth 5000 and he believed 7000*l* to him the first year – besides something else greater then all this, which he forbore to tell me.[2]

It seems one Sir Tho. Tomkins[3] of the House, that makes many mad motions, did bring it into the House, saying that a letter was left at his lodgings, subscribed by one Benson (which is a feigned name, for there is no such man in the Navy),* telling how many places in the Navy have been sold.   And by another letter, left in the same manner since, nobody appearing, he writes him that there is one Hughs and another Butler (both rogues that have for their roguery been turned out of their places)[4] that will swear that Mr. Coventry did sell their places and other things.

I offered him my service and will with all my heart serve him; but he tells me he doth not think it convenient to meddle, or to any purpose, but is sensible of my love*b* therein.

So I bid him good-morrow, he being out of order to speak anything of our office business; and so away to Westminster-hall – where I hear more of the plot from Ireland; which it seems hath been hatching and known to the Lord-Lieutenant*c* a great while, and kept close till within three days that it should have taken effect.   The Terme ended yesterday, and it seems the*d* Courts rise sooner, for want*e* of causes, then it is remembered to have done in the memory of man.

----

a MS. 'one'   *b* repl. 'service'   *c* MS. l.h. 'Lieuetenant'
        d l.h. repl. ? 'a'   *e* MS. 'for what want'

----

1. On this question of the merits of 'old' and 'new' officers, see above, iii. 122 & n. 3.

2. Thomas Smith had been secretary to the Lord Admiral (the Earl of Northumberland, 1638–42) at about the same time as Carteret had been Comptroller (1639–42), and in 1640 had had to defend himself against the charge of receiving money for an appointment: Oppenheim, p. 286.

3. M.P. for Weobley, Hereford; a fierce critic of the court.

4. For the dismissal of William Hughes, ropemaker, see above, iii. 101 & n. 3.   Moses Butler appears to have been a shipwright: his dismissal has not been traced.

Thence up and down about businesses in several places; as, to speak with Mr. Phillips; but missed him and so to Mr. Beacham the goldsmith, he being one of the Jury tomorrow in Sir W. Batten's case against Field; I have been telling him our case, and believe he will do us good service there.[1]

So home; and seeing my wife had^a dined, I went, being invited, and dined with Sir W. Batten, Sir J. Mennes, and others at Sir W. Batten's, Captain Allen giving them a foy=dinner, he being to go down to lie Admirall in the Downes this Summer. I cannot but think it a little strange that having been so civil to him as I have been, he should not invite me to dinner; but I believe it was but a sudden motion, and so I heard not of it.

After dinner to the office, where all the afternoon till late; and so to see Sir W Pen, and so home to supper and to bed.

Tonight I took occasion with the Vintener's man, who came by my direction to taste again my terce of Claret, to go down into the cellar with him to consult about the drawing of it; and there to my great vexation I find that the cellar door hath long been kept unlocked and above half my wine drunk. I was deadly mad at it and examined my people round. But nobody would confess it; but I did examine the boy, and afterward Will, and told him of his setting up, after we were in bed, with the maids, but as to that business, he denies it – which I can remedy, but I shall endeavour to know how it went.

My wife did also this evening tell me a story of Ashwells stealing some new ribbon from her, a yard or two; which I am sorry to hear and I fear my wife doth take a displeasure against her, that they will hardly stay together – which I should be sorry for, because I know not where to pick such another out anywhere.

3. Up betimes and studying of my Double Horizontall diall[2]

a MS. 'he had'

---

1. For the case, see above, iii. 23, n. 2. A list of the jurors, with Pepys's shorthand notes on all of them (except James Beecham), is in PRO, SP 29/75, no. 17. Most were described (presumably as a result ot Beecham's information) as 'good', 'honest', 'discreet' etc.

2. An instrument for astronomical calculation.

against Deane Honiwood comes to me, who dotes mightily upon it and I think I must give it him.

So after talking*a* with Sir W. Batten, who is this morning gone to Guild Hall to his trial with Field, I to my office and there read all the morning in my Statute-book, consulting among others the statute against selling of offices,[1] wherein Mr. Coventry is so much concerned. And though he tells me that the statute doth not reach him, yet I much fear that it will.

At noon, hearing that the triall is done and Sir W. Batten come to the Sun behind the Exchange, I went thither; where he tells me that he had much ado to carry it on his side, but that at last he did; but the Jury, by the Judges favour, did give us but 10*l* damages and the charges of the suit – which troubles me, but it is well it went not against us, which would have been much worse.

So to the Exchange and thence home to dinner, taking Deane of Woolwich along with me; and he dined alone with me, [my] wife being undressed, and he and I spent all the afternoon finely, learning of him the method of drawing the lines of a ship, to my great satisfaction; and which is well worth my spending some time in, as I shall do when my wife is gone into the country. In the evening to the office and did some business. Then home and, God forgive me, did from my wife's unwillingness to tell me whither she had sent the boy, presently suspect that he was gone to Pembleton's, and from that occasion grew so discontented that I could hardly speak or sleep all night.

4. Up betimes, and my wife and Ashwell and I whiled away the morning up and down, while they got themselfs ready; and I did so watch to see my wife put on drawers, which poor soul she did,[2] and yet I could not get off my suspicion, she having a mind to go into Fanchurch-street before she went out for good and all with me; which I must needs construe to be to meet Pembleton, when she afterward told me it was to buy a fan that she had not a mind that I should know of, and I believe it is so. Especially, I did by a wile get out of my boy that he did not

a repl. 'p'-

1. The much-evaded act of 1552 against corrupt buying and selling of offices (5–6 Ed. VI c. 16). It was the defects of this act which had now suggested the need for another bill: *CJ*, viii. 471.

2. Cf. above, p. 140, n. 1.

yesterday go to Pembleton's or thereabouts, but only was sent at that time for some starch; and I did see him bring home some – and yet all this cannot make my mind quiet.

At last, by coach I carried her to Westminster-hall, and they two to Mrs. Bowyer, to go from thence to my wife's father's and Ashwell to hers. And by and by, seeing my wife's father in the hall and being loath that my wife should put me to another trouble and charge by missing him today, I did imploy a porter[1] to go, from a person unknown, to tell him that his daughter was come to his lodgings. And I at a distance did observe him; but Lord, what a company of Questions he did aske him; what kind of man I was and God knows what. So he went home; and after I had stayed in the hall a good while, where I heard that this day the Archbishop of Canterbury, Juxon, a man well spoken of by all for a good man, is dead and the Bishop of London is to have his seat[2] – home by water – where by and by comes Deane Honywood and I showed him my double Horizontall Diall and promise to give him one, and that shall be it. So, without eating or drinking, he went away to Mr. Turner's, where Sir J. Mennes doth treat my Lord Chancellor and a great deal of guesse today with a great dinner, which I thank God I do not pay for; and besides, I doubt it is too late for a man to expect any great service from my Lord Chancellor; for which I am sorry and pray God a worse doth not come in his room.[3]

So I to dinner alone, and so to my chamber and then to the office alone, my head akeing and my mind[a] in trouble for my wife, being jealous of her spending the day, though God knows I have no great reason. Yet my mind is troubled. By and by comes Will Howe to see us, and walked with me an hour in the

a MS. 'mine'

---

1. For porters, see above, i. 38, n. 2.

2. Sheldon of London had been the power behind the archiepiscopal throne ever since the Restoration; he was raised to the primacy in July. Juxon, enfeebled by age, was always respected, even by his opponents. He had died on this day.

3. Illness and the rise of rivals (particularly Bennet and Bristol) combined to reduce Clarendon's power from the spring or summer of 1663 onwards, but he did not lose office until the autumn of 1667.

garden, talking of my Lord's falling to business again, which I am glad of, and his coming to lie at his lodgings at White-hall again.[1]

The match between Sir J. Cutts and my Lady Jemimah, he says, is like to go on, for which I am glad.[2]

In the hall today, Dr. Pierce tells me that the Queene begins to be briske and play like other ladies, and is quite another woman[a] from what she was, of which I am glad – it may be it may make the King like her the better and forsake his two mistresses, my Lady Castlemaine and Steward.

He gone, we sat at the office till night; and then home, where my wife is come and hath been with her father all the afternoon; and so home and she and I to walk in the garden, giving eare to her discourse of her father's affairs, and I find all well.

So after putting things in order in my office, home to supper and to bed.

5.   Up and to read a little; and by and by, the Carver coming, I directed him how to make me a neat head for my viall that is making.[3]   About 10 a-clock my wife and I, not without some discontent, abroad by coach, and I set her at her father's; but their condition is such that she will not let me see where they live – but goes by herself when I am out of sight.[4]   Thence I to my brother's, taking care for a passage for my wife the next week in a coach to my father's.   Thence to Pauls churchyard, where I find several books ready bound for me; among others, the new *Concordance* of the Bible,[5] which pleases me much and is a book I hope to make good use of.   Thence, taking the little history of

a   repl. incorrect symbol

1. He had been living in Chelsea. Will told Pepys the reason why on 10 August.

2. Lady Jemima Mountagu (Sandwich's daughter) married Philip Carteret in 1665; Sir John Cutts died unmarried in 1670.

3. Peg-boxes of stringed instruments were not infrequently ornamented with carved heads (e.g. of lions): see illust. in C. Simpson, *The division-violist* (1659), pp. 1, 3; Day and Murrie, pp. 3, 5, figs. 2, 10.   (E).

4. In 1662 the St Michels had moved to Covent Garden: above, iii. 232 & n. 2.

5. S. N., *A concordance to the Holy Scriptures* (Cambridge, 1662); re-issued 1672 etc.; attributed (by BM and Bodl. catalogues and Wing) to Samuel Newman, compiler of *A large and complete concordance* (1643; reissued 1650, 1658 etc.).   The work published in 1662 became known as the Cambridge concordance.

England[1] with me, I went by water to Deptford, where I (Sir J. Mennes and Sir W. Batten, they attending the pay) dined with them; and there was Dr. Britton, parson of the town, a fine man and good company, dined with us, and good discourse. After dinner I left them and walked to Redriffe; and thence to White-hall, and at my Lord's lodgings find my wife and thence carried her to see my Lady Jemimah, but she was not within; so to Mrs. Turners and there saw Mr. Edwd. Pepys's lady, who my wife concurs with me to be very pretty – as most women we ever saw. So home; and after a walk in the garden (a little troubled to see my wife take no more pleasure with Ashwell, but neglect her and leave her at home) home to supper and to bed.[a]

6. Lay in bed till 7 a-clock, yet rise with an opinion that it was not 5; and so continued, though I heard the clock strike, till noon and could not believe that it was so late as it truly was. I was hardly ever so mistaken in my life before.[2]

Up and to Sir G. Carteret at his house and spoke to him about business; but he being in a bad humour, I had no mind to stay with him, but walked (drinking my morning draught of Whey by the way) to Yorke-house, where the Russia Embassador[3] doth lie; and there I saw his people go up and down louseing themselfs; they are all in a great hurry, being to be gone the beginning of next week. But that that pleased me best was the remains of the noble soul of the late Duke of Buckingham,[4] appearing in his house in every place in the door-cases and the windows.

By and by comes Sir John Hebden the Russia Resident to me, and he and I in his coach to White-hall to Secretary Morrices, to see the orders about the Russia Hemp that is to be fetched from Archangell for our King;[5] and that being done, to coach again

a entry crowded into bottom of page

1. Possibly [W.G.], *The abridgement of the English history* . . . (1660); not in the PL; a duodecimo telling of 'the wonders and remarkable passages' in the lives of rulers, from William I to Richard Cromwell.

2. Pepys acquired a pocket-watch on 17 April 1665: below, vi. 83 & n. 2.

3. See above, iii. 267, n. 2.

4. The first Duke (d. 1628; favourite of James I and Charles I), who had rebuilt York House.

5. Cf. *CSPD 1663-4*, p. 271 (bills of lading for 436 bundles of hemp, Archangel, 14 September). Hebden was a merchant of the Muscovy Company who acted as agent of the Czar in England.

and he brought me into the City; and so I home, and after dinner abroad by water and met by appointment Mr. Deane in the Temple church; and he and I over to Mr. Blackburys yard and thence to other places; and after that, to a drinking house; in all which places I did so practise and improve my measuring of timber, that I can now do it with great ease and perfection, which doth please me mightily.

This fellow Deane is a conceited fellow and one that means the King a great deal of service, more of disservice to other people that go away with profits which he cannot make; but however, I learn much of him and he is, I perceive, of great use to the King in his place, and so I shall give him all the encouragement I can.

Home by water; and having wrote a letter for my wife to my Lady Sandwich, to copy out to send this night's post, I to the office and wrote there myself several things; and so home to supper and bed – my mind being troubled to think into what a temper of neglect I have myself flung my wife into, by my letting her learn to dance, that it will require time to cure her of, and I fear her going into the country will but make her worse. But only, I do hope in the meantime to spend my time well in my office, with more leisure then while she is here.

Hebden did today in the coach tell me how he is vexed to see things at Court ordered as they are; by nobody that attends business, but every man himself or his pleasures. He cries up my Lord Ashley to be almost the only man that he sees to look after business; and with that ease and mastery that he wonders at him. He cries out against the King's dealing so much with goldsmiths, and suffering himself to have his purse kept and commanded by them.

He tells me also with what exact care and order the States of Hollands stores are kept in their Yards, and everything managed there by their builders with such husbandry as is not imaginable[1] – which I will endeavour to understand further, if I can by any means learn.

7. 《*Whitsunday.*》 *Lords day.* Lay long, talking with my wife, sometimes angry; and ended pleased and hope to bring our matters to a better posture in a little time, which God send. So

1. Hebden had been the Tsar's agent in Holland.

up and to church, where Mr. Mills preached; but I know not how, I slept most of the sermon. Thence home and dined with my wife and Ashwell and after dinner discoursed very pleasantly; and so I to church again in the afternoon. And the Scott[1] preaching again, slept all the afternoon. And so home and by and by to Sir W. Batten's to talk about business; where my Lady Batten enveighd mightily against the German princesse and I as high in the defence of her wit and spirit, and glad that she is cleared at the Sessions.[2a]

Thence to Sir W. Penn, who I find ill again of the goute. He tells me that now Mr. Castle and Mrs. Martha Batten do own themselfs to be married, and have been this fortnight.[3] Much good may [it] do him, for I do not envy him his wife. So home, and there my wife and I had an angry word or two upon discourse of our boy compared with Sir W. Penn's boy that he hath now, which I say is much prettier then ours and she the contrary. It troubles me to see that every small thing is enough nowadays to bring a difference between us.

So to my office and there did a little business; and then home to supper and to bed. Mrs. Turner, who is often at Court, doth tell me today that for certain the Queene hath much changed her humour, and is become very pleasant and sociable as any; and they say is with child, or believed to be so.[4]

8. Up and to my office a while, and thence by coach with Sir J. Mennes to St. James to the Duke, where Mr. Coventry and us[b] two did discourse with the Duke a little about our office business, which saved our coming in the afternoon; and so to rights* home again – and to dinner. After dinner my wife and I had a little jangling, in which she did give me the lie, which vexed me; so that finding my talking did but make her worse and that

a smudge at end of line   *b* repl. 'my'

1. See above, p. 12, n. 1.

2. Cf. above, p. 163 & n. 4. For the trial, see *State Trials* (ed. Howell), vi. 274+. She had conducted her own case, and had made great play with a fan.

3. A mistake: they were married on 5 July: below, pp. 217–18 & n. William Castle, a widower of 34, was a shipwright; Martha Batten a spinster of 26.

4. The rumour that she was pregnant was untrue: cf. above, iii. 217 & n. 2. See HMC, *Portland*, iii. 276 for the same rumour in August. Mrs Turner (wife of Thomas Turner of the Navy Office) does not appear to have held any post at court. But she had a talent for gossip: see e.g. below, viii. 225–9.

her spirit is lately come to be other then it used to be, and now depends upon her having Ashwell by her, before whom she thinks I shall not say nor do anything of force to her, which vexes me and makes me wish that I had better considered all that I have of late done concerning my bringing my wife to this condition of heat – I went up vexed to my chamber and there fell examining my new *Concordance* that I have bought with Newmans, the best that ever was out before,[1] and I find mine altogether as copious as that and something larger, though the order in some respects not so good, that a man may think a place is missing, when it is only put in another place.

Up; by and by my wife comes and good friends again; and to walk in the garden and so anon to supper and to bed – my Cosen John Angier, the son, of Cambrige coming to me late to see me, and I find his business is that he would be sent to sea; but I dissuaded him from it, for I will not have to do with it without his friends consent.

9. Up; and after ordering some things toward my wife's going into the country, to the office; where I spent the morning upon my measuring rules very pleasant, till noon; and then comes Creed and he and I talked about mathematiques and he tells me of a way found out by*a* Mr. Jonas Moore, which he calls Duodecimall arithmetique,[2] which is properly applied to measuring, where all is ordered by inches, which are 12 in a foot; which I have a mind to learn.

So he with me home to dinner and after dinner walk in the garden; and then we met at the office, Mr. Coventry, Sir J. Mennes and I; and so in the evening, business done, I went home. Spent my time till night with my wife.

Presently after my coming home comes Pembleton, whether

                    a repl. 'of'

---

1. See above, p. 174 & n. 5. Pepys kept a first edition of Newman (1643; PL 2535), and on the title page inscribed: 'Price 1l 7s 0d yet bought of a friend for 1l 5s 6d.'

2. A system of numeration in which 12 is the base instead of 10 – i.e. '14' would be sixteen (12 + 4). Moore did not publish on the subject.

by appointment or no I know not, or whether by a former promise that he would come once before my wife's going into the country. But I took no notice, but*a* let them go up and Ashwell with them to dance; which*b* they did, and I stayed below in my chamber; but Lord, how I listened and laid my eare to the door, and how I was troubled when I heard them stand still and not dance. Anon they made an end and had done, and so I suffered him to go away and spoke not to him, though troubled in my mind; but showed no discontent to my wife, believing that this is the last time I shall be troubled with him.

So my wife and I to walk in the garden, and so home and to supper and to bed.

10. Up, and all the morning helping my wife to put up her things towards her going into the country and drawing the wine out of my vessel also to send.

This morning came my Cosen Tho. Pepys, to desire me to furnish him with some money; which I could not do till his father hath wrote to Piggott his consent to the sale of his lands.[1] So by and by we parted, and I to the Exchange a while; and so home and to dinner, and thence to the Royall Theatre by water; and landing, met with Captain Ferrer's his friend,[2] the little man that used to be with him, and he with us and sat by us while we saw *Love in a maze*.[3] The play is pretty good, but the life of the play is Lacy's*c* part, the Clowne,*4 which is most admirable. But for the rest, which are counted such old and excellent actors, in my life I never heard both men and women so ill pronounce their parts, even to my making myself sick therewith.

Thence, Creed happening to be with us, we four to the Half-Moone taverne, I buying some Sugar and carrying it with me, which we drank with wine; and thence to the Whay-house

a MS. 'of'   *b* repl. 'that'   *c* l.h. repl. l.h. 'Lacey'

1. The letter was written on 20 July: below, p. 237 & n. 4. Pepys had agreed in the settlement made with his uncle Thomas to pay him £50: above, p. 42 & n. 3.
2. Unidentified: possibly Emanuel Luffe, a 'German': above, ii. 228.
3. A comedy by Shirley (q.v. above,

iii. 88 & n. 4); now at the TR, Drury Lane. (A).
4. John Lacy played Johnny Thumpe, a country bumpkin. He probably added many gags to his part, as was his wont, for the role provided by the text is a small one. (A).

and drank a great deal of Whay; and so by water home, and thence I to see Sir Wm Pen, who is not in much pain, but his legs swoln and so immoveable that he cannot stir them but as they are lifted by other people, and I doubt will have another fit of his late pain. Played a little at cards with him and his daughter, who is grown every day a finer and finer lady; and so home to supper and to bed.

When my wife and I came first home, we took Ashwell and all the rest below in the cellar with the vintener, drawing out my wine;*a* which I blamed Ashwell much for and told her my mind, that I would not endure it, nor was it fit for her to make herself equall with the ordinary servants of the house.

11. Up, and spent most of the morning upon my measuring Ruler; and with great pleasure I have found out some things myself of great despatch, more then my book teaches me, which pleases me mightily.[1] Sent my wife's things and the wine today by the Carrier to my father. But stayed my boy from a letter of my father's, wherein he desires that he may not come to trouble his family as he did the last year.

Dined at home and then to the office, where we sat all the afternoon. And at night home and spent the evening with my wife, and she and I did jangle mightily about her cushions that she wrought with worsteds the last year, which are too little for any use; but were good friends by and by again. But one thing I must confess I do observe, which I did not before; which is, that I cannot blame my wife to be now in a worse humour then she used to be, for I am taken up in my talk with Ashwell, who is a very witty girle, that I am not so fond of her as I used and ought to be; which now I do perceive, I will remedy. But I would to the Lord I had never taken any, though I cannot have a better then her. To supper and to bed. The consideration that this is the longest day in the year[2] is very unpleasant to me. This

a MS. 'wife'

---

1. For the ruler and the book, see above, p. 84, n. 2; p. 85, n. 1. Pepys designed his own slide-rule for measuring timber, and had it made by Brown: below, p. 266.

2. I.e. by the Old Style: see above, vol. i, p. clii.

afternoon my wife had a visitt from my Lady Jemimah and Mrs. Ferrer.

12. Up and my office, there conning my measuring-Ruler, which I shall grow a master of in a very little time. At noon to the Exchange, and so home to dinner and abroad with my wife by water to the Royall Theatre and there saw *The Comittee*, a merry but an indifferent play; only Lacy's part, an Irish footman, is beyond imagination.[1] Here I saw my Lord Falconbrige and his Lady, my Lady Mary Cromwell,[2] who looks as well as I have known her and well-clad; but when the House begun to fill, she put on her vizard[3] and so kept it on all the play – which is of late become a great fashion among the ladies, which hides their whole face.

So to the Exchange to buy things with my wife; among others, a vizard for herself; and so by water home and to my office to do a little business, and so to see Sir W. Penn. But being going to bed and not well, I could not see him. So home and to supper and bed, being mightily troubled all night and next morning with the palate of my mouth being down from some cold I took today, sitting sweating in the playhouse and the wind blowing through the windows upon my head.

13. Up, and betimes to Thames-street among the tarr men to look the price of tar; and so by water to White-hall, thinking to speak with Sir G. Carteret; but he lying in the City all night and meeting with Mr. Cutler the Merchant, I with him in his coach into the City to Sir G. Carteret; but missing him there, he and I walked to find him at Sir Tho Allens in Breadstreete, where not finding him, he and I walked toward our office, he discoursing well of the business of the Navy and perticularly of the victualling, in which he was once I perceive concerned. And

1. Lacy, who specialised in dialect roles, played Teague in this play, Sir Robert Howard's most popular comedy, now at the TR, Drury Lane. Teague was a more convincing character than any previous stage Irishman partly because Howard had modelled him on his own Irish servant: see F. R. Scott in *MLR*, 42/314+. *The Committee* was first acted in 1662 and published in *Four new plays* (1665). (A).

2. Viscountess Fauconberg; third daughter and seventh child of Oliver Cromwell.

3. An oval mask, at this time commonly worn by women at the theatre; at the end of the century, out of fashion and the mark of the prostitute.

he and I parted, and I to the office and there had a difference with Sir W. Batten about Mr. Bowyers tarr; which I am resolved to cross, though he sent me last night, as a bribe, a barrell of Sturgeon; which it may be I shall send back, for I will not have the King abused so abominably in the price of what we buy by Sir W. Batten's corruption and underhand dealing. So from the office by water, Mr. Wayth[1] with me, to the Parliament-house; and there I spoke and told*ª* Sir G. Carteret all, with which he is well pleased and doth recall his willingness, yesterday it seems, to Sir W. Batten, that we should buy a great Quantity of tarr, being abused by him.

Thence with Mr. Wayth, after drinking a cup of ale at the Swan, talking of the corruptions of the Navy, by water; I landed him at White-fryers, and I to the Exchange and so home to dinner, where I find my wife's brother; and thence after dinner by water to the Royall Theatre, where I am resolved to bid farewell, as shall appear by my oaths tomorrow, against all plays, either at public houses or Court, till Christmas be over.[2]

Here we saw *The Faithfull Shepheardesse*, a most simple thing and yet much thronged after and often shown; but it is only for the Scenes sake, which is very fine endeed, and worth seeing.*ᵇ* [3] But I quite out of opinion with any of their actings but Lacy's, compared with the other house.[4]

Thence to see Mrs. Hunt, which we did and were much made of; and in our way saw my Lady Castlemayne, who I fear is not so handsome as I have taken her for, and now she begins to decay something. This is my wife's opinion also, for which I am sorry. Thence by coach with a mad coachman that drove like mad, and down byeways through bucklersbury*ᶜ* home, everybody through the street cursing him, being ready to run over them. So home. ⟨And after writing letters by the post at*ᵈ* my office, home to supper and bed.⟩

a MS. 'took'   *b* blot below symbol
c l.h. repl. l.h. 'loathbury'   *d* repl. 'home to'

---

1. Paymaster to the Navy Treasurer.
2. Pepys kept these oaths. (A).
3. A pastoral play by Fletcher, first acted in 1608, and published in 1629; now at the TR, Drury Lane. This is the first record of a post-Restoration performance. Painted scenery was still such a novelty in public theatres that it constituted an attraction in itself. (A).
4. I.e. with the Duke of York's Company at the LIF. (A).

Yesterday, upon conference with the King in the Banquetting-house, the parliament did agree with much ado, it being carried but by 42 voices, that they would supply him with a sum of money; but what and how is not yet known, but expected to be done with great disputes the next week.[1] But if done at all, it's well.

14. ⟨*Lords day.*⟩ Lay long in bed; and so up and to church. Then to dinner, and Tom dined with me, who I think grows a very thriving man, as he himself tells me.

He tells me that his man John hath got a wife, and for that he entends to part with him,[2] which I am sorry for. And then that Mr. Armiger comes to be a constant lodger at his house, and he says hath money in his purse and will be a good paymaister, but I do much doubt it.[3]

He being gone, I up; and sending my people to church, my wife and I did even our reckonings and have a great deal of serious talk, wherein I took occasion to give her hints of the necessity of our saving all we can. I do see great cause every day to curse the time that ever I did give way to the taking of a woman for her, though I could never have had a better, and also the letting of her learn to dance; by both which her mind is so devilishly taken off of her business and minding her occasions, and besides, hath got such an opinion in her of my being jealous, that it is never to be removed I fear, nor hardly my trouble that attends it; but I must have patience.

I did give her 40s to carry into the country tomorrow with her, whereof 15s is to go for the coach hire for her and Ashwell, there being 20 paid here already in earnest.

In the evening our discourse turned to great content and love, and I hope that after a little forgetting our late differences, and

1. The King had asked for an extra supply and the Commons had agreed by a majority of 48, not 42: *CJ*, viii. 501. The result was the grant of four subsidies (15 Car. II c. 9): see below, p. 250 & n. 3.

2. John had probably been apprenticed to him, and lived in. He may have been the John Herbert who appears in Tom's papers as witness to a signature in April 1664: Rawl. A 182, f. 330r.

3. Both Armigers (father and son) owed considerable sums (£74 altogether) to Tom Pepys on his death: Rawl., loc. cit., f. 302r. They were relatives.

being a while absent one from another, we shall come to agree as well as ever.

So to Sir W. Penn to visit him; and finding him alone, sent for my wife, who is in her riding-suit, to see him; which she hath not done these many months I think. By and by in comes Sir J. Mennes and Sir W. Batten, and so we sat talking; among other things, Sir J. Mennes brought many fine expressions of Chaucer, which he dotes on mightily, and without doubt is a very fine poet.[1]

Sir W. Penn continues lame of the gout, that he cannot rise from his chair;[2] and so after staying an hour with him, we went home and to supper, and so to prayers and bed.

15. Up betimes; and anon my wife rose and did give me her keys and put other things in order, and herself, against her going this morning into the country. I was forced to go to Thames-street and strike up a bargaine for some tarr, to prevent being abused therein by Hill, who was with me this morning and is mightily surprized that I should tell him what I can have the same tarr with his for. Thence home; but finding my wife gone, I took coach and after her to her Inne; where I am troubled to see her forced to sit in the back of the coach, though pleased to see her company, none but women and one parson. She, I find, is troubled [not] at all and I seemed to make a promise to get a horse and ride after them; and so kissing her often and Ashwell once, I bid them Adieu; and so home by coach and thence by water to Deptford to the Trinity-house, where I came a little late but I found them reading their charter; which they did like fools, only reading here and there a bit, whereas they ought to

1. Chaucer's reputation stood high at this time, and Mennes had published imitations of him: *Musarum Deliciae* (1655), pp. 85+. Pepys later made a small collection of Chaucerian MSS; his collation of them with the edition of 1602 may be found inserted at the back of his copy: PL 2365. He also came to possess an engraved portrait of the poet: PL 2973, p. 393. Cf. below, 21 November 1666. For Pepys's share in Dryden's version of the 'Poure Persoun' (*The character of a good parson . . .* in *Fables, ancient and modern*, 1700), see *Letters*, pp. 280–1.

2. For his gout chair, see below, ix. 215 & n. 3.

do it all, every word;[1] and then proceeded to the Eleccion of a Maister, which was Sir W. Batten, without any controll; who made a heavy, short speech to them, moving them to give thanks to the late Maister[2] for his pains, which he said was very great, and giving them thanks for their choice of him, wherein he would serve them to the best of his power. Then to the choice of their Assistants and Wardens, and so rose. I might have received 2s-6d as a younger Brother, but I directed one of the servants of the house to receive it and keep it.[3]

Thence to church, where Dr Britton preached a sermon full of words against the Nonconformists; but no great matter in it, nor proper for the day at all. His text was, "With one minde and one mouth give glory to God, the father of our Lord Jesus Christ."[4]

That done, by water, I in the barge with the Maister, to the Trinity-house at London, where, among others, I find my Lord Sandwich and Craven[5] and my Cosen Rogr Pepys and Sir Wm Wheeler. Anon we sat down to dinner; which was very great, as they always have.[6] Great variety of talk. Mr. Prin, among many, had a pretty tale of one that brought in a bill in Parliament for the impowering him to dispose his land to such[a] children as he should have that should bear the name of his wife – it was in Queen Elizabeth's time. One replied that there are many Species of creatures where the Male gives the denominacion to both Sexes, as men and Woodcockes, but not above one where the female doth, and that is a goose.

Both at and after dinner we had great discourses of the nature and power of Spirits and whether they can animate dead bodies; in all which, as of the general appearing of spirits, my Lord Sandwich is very scepticall. He says the greatest warrants that

a repl. 'all'

1. This being Trinity Day on which they elected their officers. The charter was that of 27 November 1660.

2. Sir John Mennes.

3. The Younger Brethren received this amount annually in lieu of entertainment.

4. A loose recollection of Rom., xv. 6.

5. Lord Craven was elected an Elder Brother this day.

6. Cf. above, iii. 116, n. 1.

ever he had to believe any, is the present appearing of the Devil in Wiltshire, much of late talked of, who beats a drum up and down; there is books of it, and they say very true.[1] But my Lord observes that though he doth answer to any*a* tune that you will play to him upon another drum, yet one tune he tried to play and could not; which makes him suspect the whole, and I think it is a good argument.

Sometimes they talked of handsome women; and Sir J. Mennes saying that there was no beauty like what he sees in the country-markets, and especially at Bury,[2] in which I will agree with him that there is a prettiest woman I ever saw – my Lord replied: "Why, Sir John, what do you think of your neighbour's wife?" looking upon me, "do not you think that he hath a great beauty to his wife? Upon my word he hath" – which I was not a little proud of.

Thence by Barge along with my Lord to Blacke fryers, where he landed; and I thence walked home, where vexed to find my boy (whom I boxed at his coming for it) and Will abroad, though he was but upon tower-hill a very little while.

My head akeing with the healths I was forced to drink today, I sent for the barber; and he having done, I up to my wife's closet and there played on my viallin a good while; and without supper, anon to bed – sad for want of my wife, whom I love with all my heart, though of late she hath given me some troubled thoughts.

a   small red blot above symbol

---

1. These phenomena had been occurring in the house of John Mompesson at Tidworth, Wilts., for the past two years, and had recently become famous. For the pamphlet literature, see E. H. Goddard, *Wilts. Bibliog.*, pp. 240–1. Both the King and the Queen sent agents to investigate, but nothing happened while they were there. Mompesson in the end admitted it was all a trick. Pepys later read the story in Glanvill's version on 25 December 1667. Accounts of the incident are in *Merc.*

Pub., 23 April 1663, pp. 253–6; H. S. & I. M. L. Redgrove, *Joseph Glanvill and psychical research in 17th cent.*, ch. vi. Addison's play, *The Drummer, or The haunted house* (1716), was founded on it. Both the diary and his later writings show that Pepys's interest in such things was real and lasting, for all his scepticism: e.g. *Tangier Papers*, pp. 10, 15; *Priv. Corr.*, i. 240+ etc.

2. Bury   St   Edmunds,   Suff. Mennes had inherited estates in that region from his brother: *DNB*.

16. Up, but not so early as I entend now, and to my office, where doing business all the morning. At noon by desire dined with Sir W. Batten, who tells me that the House hath voted the supply entended for the King shall be by Subsidy.[1] After dinner, with Sir J. Mennes to see some pictures at Brewers,[2] said to be of good hands but I do not much like them. So I to the office and thence to Stacys the*a* Tarr merchant, whose servant, with whom I agreed yesterday for some tarr, doth by combinacion with Bowyer and Hill fall from our agreement; which vexes us all at the office, even Sir W. Batten himself, who was so earnest for it. So to the office, where we sat all the afternoon till night; and then to Sir W. Penn, who continues ill; and so home to bed about 10 a-clock.

17. Up before 4 a-clock, which is the hour I entend now [to] rise at – and to my office a while. And with great pleasure I fall to my business again. Anon went with money to my Tarr merchant to pay for the Tarr, which he refuses to sell me; but now the Maister is come home and so he speaks very civilly, and I believe we shall have it with peace. I brought back my money to my office; and thence to White-hall and in the garden spoke to my Lord Sandwich, who is in his gold buttoned suit, as the mode is, and looks nobly. Captain Ferrers, I see, is come home from ⟨France⟩; I only spoke one word to him, my Lord being there; he tells me the young gentlemen[3] are well there. So my Lord went to my Lord Albemarles to dinner; and I by water home and dined alone and at the office (after half an hour's Viallin practice after dinner) till late at night, and so home and to bed.

This day I sent my Cosen Edwd. Pepys his lady, at my cozen Turners, a piece of venison given me yesterday, and Madam Turner I sent for a dozen bottles of hers to fill with wine for her.

This day I met with Pierce the Serjeant, who tells me that the King hath made peace between Mr. Edwd Mountagu and his

a MS. 'is'

---

1. *CJ*, viii. 503; cf. above, p. 183 & n. 1.
2. William Brewer, of St Matthew's, Friday St, who had been in charge of the painting work at the Navy Office.
3. Sandwich's two eldest sons. For their stay in France, see above, ii. 114, n.1.

father, my Lord Mountagu, and that all is well again; at which, for the family's sake, I am very glad, but do not think it will hold long.[1]

18. Up by 4 a-clock and to my office, where all the morning writing out in my Navy Collections the Ordinary Estimate of the Navy, and did it neatly.[2] Then dined at home alone, my mind pleased with business but sad for the absence of my wife. After dinner, half an hour at my viallin and then all the afternoon setting at the office late; and so home and to bed. This morning Mr. Cutler[3] came and sat in my closet half an hour with me; his discourse very excellent, being a wise man, and I do perceive by him as well as many others that my diligence is taken notice of in the world, for which I bless God and hope to continue doing so.

Before I went into my house this night, I called at Sir W. Batten; where finding some great ladies at table at supper with him and his Lady, I retreated and went home, though they called to me again and again and afterward sent for me; so I went, and who should it be but Sir Fr. Clerke[4] and his Lady and another proper lady at supper there, and great cheer; where I stayed till 11 a-clock at night, and so home and to bed.

19. Lay till 6 a-clock; then up and to my office, where all the morning, and at noon to the Exchange; and coming home, I met Mr. Creede and took him back and he dined with me; and by and by came Mr. Moore, whom I supplied with 30*l.* And then abroad with them by water to Lambeth, expecting to have seen the Archbishop lie in state;[5] but it seems he is not laid out yet. And so over to White-hall, and at the privy Seale Office examined the books and found the grant of the encrease of salary to the

---

1. Pepys was right: see below, v. 244. According to Clarendon (*Life*, ii. 444), Lord Mountagu had objected to his son's accepting office in the household of the Queen, and had refused to pay him any allowance. Edward's undated letter of apology to his father (HMC, *Montagu*, p. 167) may possibly be ascribed to this period.

2. The estimates ran from 24 June. For the 'Navy Collections', see above, p. 11 & n. 1. Some details of these sums are in *CTB*, i. 555.

3. William Cutler, merchant.

4. Gentleman of the Privy Chamber to the King, and Batten's colleague as M.P. for Rochester.

5. See above, p. 173 & n. 2.

principall-officers in the year 1639, 300*l* among the Controller, Surveyor and Clerke of the Shipps.[1] Thence to Wilkinsons, after a good walk in the parke; where we met on horsebacke Captain Ferrers, who tells us that the King of France is well again[2] and that he saw him train his guards, all brave men, at Paris; and that when he goes to his mistress, Madame La Valiere, a pretty little woman now with child by him, he goes with his guards with him publicly and his trumpets and Kettle*a* drums with him, who stay before the house while he is with her; and yet he says that for all this, the Queene doth not know of it, for that nobody dares to tell her – but that I dare not believe. Thence,*b* I say, to Wilkinsons, where we had bespoke a dish of pease; where we eate them very merrily, and there being with us the little Gentleman, a friend of Captain Ferrers that was with my wife and I at a play a little while ago, we went thence to the Renish winehouse, where he called for a red Renish wine called *Bleakard*, a pretty wine, and not mixt as they say.[3]

Here Mr. Moore showed us the French manner when a health is drunk, to bow to him that drunk to you, and then apply yourself to him whose lady's health is drunk, and then to the person that you drink to; which I never knew before, but it seems is now the fashion.

Thence by water home and to bed – having played out of my chamber-window on my pipe before I went to bed – and making Will read a part of a Latin chapter,[4] in which I perceive in a little while he will be pretty ready, if he spends but a little pains in it.

20. Up and to my office, where all the morning; and dined at home, Mr. Deane with me of Woolwich, and he and I all the afternoon down by water and in a timber yard, measuring of

a MS. 'kettles'   *b* followed by small red blot

1. Cf. *CSPD 1638–9*, p. 592; secretary's warrant (22 March 1639) for the issue of a privy seal awarding increases of £120 p.a. to the Comptroller, £100 to the Surveyor and £80 to the Clerk of the Ships (the old form of the title of Pepys's office).

2. Cf. above, p. 156 & n. 2.

3. I.e. not red and white wine mixed. ? *Ahrbleichart*, a light red wine. Ferrer's friend may have been a German: above, p. 179 & n. 2.

4. Probably from the Paris Vulgate of 1618 (PL 2726); or possibly from one of the other two Latin Testaments in the PL (1277, 2429). But the latter have texts in English and Greek respectively, as well as the Latin, and, to judge by Pepys's shelfmarks, were not so likely to have been acquired by 1663.

timber, which I now understand thoroughly and shall be able in a little time to do the King great service.

Home in the evening, and to my office, where despatched business and so home. And after Wills reading a little in the Latin Testament, to bed.

21. *Lords day.* Up betimes and fell to reading my Latin grammer,¹ which I perceive I have great need of, having lately found it by my calling Will to the reading of a Chapter in Latin; and I am resolved to go through it.

After being trimmed, I by water to White-hall and so over the parke, it raining hard, to Mr. Coventrys chamber – where I spent two hours, talking with him about businesses of the Navy and how by his absence things are like to go with us; and with good content from my being with him, he carried me by coach and set me down at White-hall, and thence to rights home by water.

He showed me a list which he hath prepared for the parliament's viewe if the business of his selling of offices should be brought to further hearing, wherein he reckons up, as I remember, 236ᵃ offices of ships which have been disposed of without his taking one farthing.² This, of his own accord, he opened his Cabinettᵇ on purpose to show me; meaning, I suppose, that I should discourse abroad of it and vindicate him therein; which I shall with all my power do.

At home, being wet, shifting my band and things and then to dinner; and after dinner went up and tried a little upon my Tryangle,* which I understand fully and with a little use I believe could bring myself to do something.³

So to church and slept all the sermon, the Scott, to whose voice I am not to be reconciled, preaching.⁴

a repl. '136'   *b* l.h. repl. s.h. 'c'-

1. Probably one of William Lily's; possibly his *A short introduction of grammar . . . of the Latine tongue* (1662; PL 886); an edition which Pepys's catalogue ('Appendix Classica', p. 76) attributes to his old schoolmaster, John Langley.

2. An undated list containing 287 names is in Longleat, Coventry MSS 101, ff. 241-2. See below, p. 331. For the bill in parliament, see above, p. 156, n. 4.

3. For Pepys's interest in keyboard instruments, see below, ix. 127, 149. (E).

4. 'A simple bawling young Scott' (above, p. 96); cf. above, p. 12, n. 1.

Thence with Sir J. Mennes (who, poor man, had forgot that he carried me the other day[1] to the painter's to see some pictures which he hath since bought and are brought home) to his lodgings to see some rare pieces, he calls them, of great maisters of paynting; so I said nothing that he had shown me them already but commended them, and I think they are endeed good enough.

Thence to see Sir W. Penn,[a] who continues ill of the gout still. Here we stayed a good while; and then I to my office and read my vowes[2] seriously and with content; and so home to supper, to prayers, and to bed.

22. Up betimes and to my office, reading over all our letters of the office that we have writ since I came into the Navy – whereby to bring the whole series of matters into my memory and to enter in my manuscript[3] some of them that are needful and of general influence. By and by with Sir Wm. Batten by coach to Westminster, where all along I find the shops evening with the sides of the houses, even in the broadest streets; which will make the City very much better then it was.[4]

I walked in the hall from one man to another. Hear that the House is still divided about the manner of levying the Subsidys which they entend to give the King, both as to the manner, the time, and the number.[5]

It seems the House doth consent to send to the King to desire that he would be graciously pleased to let them know who it was that did inform him of what words Sir Rd. Temple should say, which were to this purpose: that if the King would side with him or be guided by him and his party, that he should not lack

a repl. 'Sir W. B.

---

1. On 16 June.
2. Cf. above, p. 182.
3. The 'Navy manuscript': above, p. 11 & n. 1.
4. See above, p. 77 & n. 3.

5. Cf. above, p. 183 & n. 1, p. 187. Clarendon's government often gave an uncertain lead on the vital matter of parliamentary supply.

money. But without knowing who told it, they do not think fit to call him to any account for it.[1]

Thence with Creed and bought a Lobster, and then to an ale-house; where the maid of the house is a confident merry lass and, if modest, is very pleasant to the customers that come thither. Here we eat it, and thence to walk in the parke a good while – the Duke being gone a-hunting; and by and by came in and shifted himself, he having in his hunting, rather then go[a] about, light and led his horse through a River up to his breast, and came so home; and when we were come, which was by and by, we went into to him; and being ready, he retired with us and we had a long discourse with him; but Mr. Creeds accounts[2] stick still, through the perverse ignorance of Sir G. Carteret, which I can[not] safely control as I would.

Thence to the park again and there walked up and down an hour or two till night with Creede, talking; who is so knowing and a man of that reason, that I cannot but love his company, though I do not love the man, because he is too wise to be made a friend of and acts all by interest and policy – but is a man fit to learn of. So to White-hall and by water to the Temple; and calling at my brother's and several places, but to no purpose, I came home; and meeting Strutt the purser, he tells me for a secret that he was told by Field that he hath a judgment against me in the Exchequer for 400*l*; so I went to Sir W. Batten, and

a repl. 'g' smudged

---

1. Temple was M.P. for Bucking-ham, and a leader of the Duke of Buckingham's connection. The House was extremely jealous of any attempt to manage it at this period, as an affront to its independence. A report had been made to the King that Temple 'was sorry his Majesty was offended with him that he could not go along with them that had undertaken his Business in the House of Commons: But, if his Majesty would take his Advice, and interest him and his Friends, he would under-take his Business should be effected, and Revenue settled, better than he could desire if the Counties did not hinder it': *CJ*, viii. 502. The King's complaint against Temple had been reported to the House on the 13th by Secretary Coventry, and the vote to which Pepys refers had passed on the 20th. The King had said that Temple's message had been com-municated to him by a 'person of Quality': on the 26th he revealed that his informant was Bristol: ib., pp. 502, 507, 511. For the im-mediate sequel, see below, p. 207 & n. 2. Temple's memorandum (c. 1668) on parliamentary 'undertaking' is printed by Clayton Roberts in *Hunt. Lib. Quart.*, 20/140+.

2. See below, p. 198, n. 1.

taking Mr. Batten his son the counsellor with me by coach, I went to Clerke our Sollicitor, who tells me there can be no such thing;[1] and after conferring with them two together, who are resolved to look well after that business, I returned home and to my office, setting down this day's passages; and having a letter that all is well in the country, I went home to supper; then a Latin Chapter* of Will and to bed.

23. Up by 4 a-clock and^a so to my office. But before I went out, calling, as I have of late done, for my boy's Copy-book, I find that he hath not done his taske, and so I beat him and then went up to fetch my ropes end; but before I got down the boy was gone; I searched the cellar with a Candle, and from top to bottom could not find him high nor low. So to the office; and after an hour or two, by water to the Temple to my Cosen Roger, who I perceive is a deadly high man in the parliament business, and against the Court – showing me how they have computed that the King hath spent, at least hath received, about four Millions of money since he came in.[2]

And in Sir J. Winters case, in which I spoke to him, he is so high that he says he deserves to be hanged,[3] and all the high words he could^b give; which I was sorry to see, though I am confident he means well.

Thence by water home and to the Change. And by and by comes the King and the Queenes by in great state, and the streets full of people. I stood in Mr.   Balcone. They dine all at

a accidental stroke above symbol   *b* MS. 'would'

1. Clerke was right; for this case, see above, iii. 23 & n. 2.
2. The figure was probably mentioned in the debates on the subsidy, 22-3 June. A committee of the Commons had reported on the real and potential value of the King's sources of revenue on 4 June: *CJ*, viii. 498. According to Prof. C. D. Chandaman (*Engl. public revenue, 1660–88* (1973), pp. 207, 332–3), the King had received just under £4 m. by Michaelmas 1663.
3. The grant of timber made to

Winter in July 1662 was bitterly resented by the commoners of the Forest of Dean: above, iii. 112 & n. 2. On 22 May 1663 a sub-committee of the Commons had criticised the terms of the grants made to him: *CJ*, viii. 489-90. See Milward, p. 187, for renewed criticisms in February 1668, when a bill to preserve the timber and protect commoners' rights was passed. Winter was a Catholic and unpopular with critics of the court such as Roger Pepys.

my Lord Mayors[1] – but what he doth for victuals or room for them, I know not.

So home to dinner alone; and there I find that my boy had got out of doors, and came in for his hat and band and so is gone away to his brother. But I do*a* resolve even to let him go for good and all.[2]

So I by and by to the office, and there had a great fray with Sir W. Batten and Sir J. Mennes, who, like an old dotard, is led by the nose by him. It was in Captain Cockes business of hemp, wherein the King is absolutely abused;[3] but I was for peace sake contented to be quiet and to sign to his bill, but in my manner so as to justify myself. And so all was well – but to see what a knave*b* Sir W. Batten is makes my heart ake. So late at my office and then home to supper – and to bed, my man Will not being well.

24. Up before 4 a-clock, and so to my lute an hour and more and then by water, drinking my morning draught alone in an alehouse in Thames-streete, to the Temple; and there, after a little discourse with my cousin Roger about some business, away by water to St. James and there an hour's private discourse with Mr. Coventry – where he told me one thing to my great joy, that in the business of Captain Cockes hemp, disputed before him the other day (Mr. Coventry absent), the Duke did himself tell him since, that Mr. Pepys and he did stand up and carry it against the rest that were there, Sir G. Carteret and Sir W. Batten, which doth please me much, to see that the Duke doth take notice of me.

We did talk highly of Sir W. Batten's corruption, which Mr. Coventry did very kindly say that it might be only his heaviness and unaptness for business that he doth things without advice and rashly and to gratify people that do eat and drink and play

a MS. 'am do'   *b* s.h. repl. l.h. 'knave'

---

1. Sir John Robinson.
2. Wayneman Birch was dismissed on 7 July: below, p. 220.
3. Possibly this was the question of payment for the 500 tons contracted for in 1662: see above, p. 49 & n. 1. Or possibly the abuse was in the

matter of its quality: Commissioner Pett wrote to Pepys on 29 June that if Cocke's Russia hemp were mixed with Riga and used for ground tackle and cables 'then farewell security to the ships in harbour': *CSPD 1663–4*, p. 186.

with him. And that now and then he observes that he signs bills only in anger and fury, to be rid of them.[a]

Speaking of Sir G. Carteret, of whom I perceive he speaks but slightly, and diminishing of him in his services for the King in Jersey, that he was well rewarded and had good lands and rents and other profits from the King all the time he was there[1] – and that it was alway his humour to have things done his way, he brought an Example, how he would not let the Castle[2] there be victualled for more then a month, that so he might keep it at his beck, though the people of the town did offer to supply it more often themselfs – which, when one did propose to the King, Sir George Carteret being by, "Oh," says Sir G, "Let me know who they are that would do it; I would with all my heart hug them." "Aye, by God," says the Commander that spoke of it, "that is it that they are afeared of, that you would hug them," meaning that he would not endure them.

Another thing he told me: how the Duke of Yorke did give Sir G. Carteret and the Island his profits as Admirall, and other things, toward the building of a peere there.[3] But it was never laid out, nor like to be. So it falling out that a lady being brought to bed, the Duke was to be desired to be one of the godfathers. And it being objected that that would not be proper, there being no peere of the land to be joyned with him – the lady replied, "Why, let him choose; and if he will not be a godfather without a peere, let him even stay till he hath made a peere of his own."

He tells me too, that he hath lately been observed to tack about at Court and to endeavour to strike in with the persons that are against the Chancellor; but this he says of him, that he doth not say or do anything to the prejudice of the Chauncellor. But he told me that the Chancellor was rising again and that of late Sir G. Carteret's business and imployment hath not been so full as it used to be while the Chancellor stood up.

a MS. 'men'

1. Carteret had been Governor from 1643 until Jersey was surrendered to Parliament in 1651. Clarendon (Carteret's guest there, 1646–8) accused Jermyn, the Governor, rather than Carteret, of self-interest: *Hist.*, v. 64–5, 261. The grants referred to above included that of New Jersey in America.

2. Castle Elizabeth, St Helier's.

3. At St Aubin's: S. E. Hoskins, *Charles II in Channel Is.*, ii. 298, 385.

From that, we discoursed of the evil of putting out men of experience in business, as the Chancellor; and from that, to speak of the condition of the King's party at present; who, as the papists, though otherwise fine persons, yet being by law kept for these four score years out of imployment, they are now wholly uncapable of business; and so the Cavalers for 20 years – who, says he, for the most part have either given themselfs over to look after country and family business, and those the best of them, and the rest to debauchery &c.; and that was it that hath made him high against the late bill brought into the House for the making all men incapable of imployment that had served against the King:¹ "Why," says he, "in the sea-service it is impossible to do anything without them, there being not more then three men of the whole King's side that are fit to command almost;" and those were Captain Allen, Smith and Beech – and it may be Holmes and Utber and Batts might do something.²

I desired him to tell me if he thought that I did speak anything that I do against Sir W. Batten or Sir J. Mennes out of ill-will or design.   He told me quite the contrary, and that there was reason enough.   After a good deal of good and fine discourse, I took leave; and so to my Lord Sandwich's house, where I met my Lord and there did discourse of our office businesses and how the Duke doth show me kindness, though I have endeavoured to displease more or less of my fellow-officers, all but Mr. Coventry and Pett, but it matters not. "Yes," says my Lord, "Sir J. Mennes, who is great with the Chancellor;" I told him the Chancellor I have thought was declining; and however, that the esteem he³ hath among them is nothing but for a jester or a ballat-maker; at which my Lord laughs and asks me whether I believe he ever could do that well.

Thence with Mr. Creed up and down to an ordinary; and the King's-head being full, went to the other over against it, a pretty man that keeps it, and good and much meat, better then the other; but the company and room so small that he must

---

1. See above, p. 125 & n. 1.

2. Cf. the Duke of York's similar views: above, iii. 122; and the Duchess of Albemarle's: below, vii. 10.

3. Mennes. He had published, as part author, two books of poems (*Wits Recreations* ... , 1640, and *Musarum Deliciae* ..., 1655), and probably wrote others. His verses were witty and coarse, and proved popular.

break, and there wants the pleasure that the other house hath in its company.

Here, however, dined an old Courtier that is now so – who did bring many*ᵃ* examples and arguments to prove that seldom any man that brings anything to Court gets anything, but rather the contrary; for knowing that they have wherewith to live, will not enslave themselfs to the attendance and flattery and fawning condition of a Courtier; whereas another, that brings nothing and will be contented to cog and lie and flatter every man and woman that hath any enterest with the persons that are great in favour and can cheat the King, as nothing is to be got without offending God and the King there, he for the most part and he alone saves anything.

Thence to St. James's parke and there walked two or three hours, talking of the difference between Sir G. Carteret and Mr Creede about his accounts, and how to obviate him; but I find Creede a deadly cunning fellow, and one that never doth anything openly but hath intrigues in all he doth or says.

Thence by water home to see all well; and thence down to Greenewich and there walked into a pretty common guarden and there played with him at nine-pins, for some drink and to make the fellows drink that set up the pins; and so home again, being very cold and taking a very great cold, being today the first time in my tabby doublet this year.

Home; and after a small supper, Creede and I to bed.

This day I observed the house (which I took to be the new tennis Court) newly built next my Lord's lodging to be fallen down, by the badness of the foundation or slight working;[1] which my Cosen Roger and his discontent party cries out upon, as an example how the King's work is done – which I am sorry to see him and others so apt to think ill of things. It hath beaten down a good deal of my Lord's lodgings and had liked to have killed Mrs. Sarah, she being but newly gone out of it.

25. Up, both of us, pretty earely; and to my chamber, where

a repl. 'good'

---

1. See *Comp.*: 'Whitehall Palace'. The court was rebuilt by 28 December: below, p. 435.

he and I did draw up a[a] letter to Sir G. Carteret in excuse and preparation for Creede, against we meet before the Duke upon his accounts[1] – which I drew up and it proved very well. But I am pleased to see with what secret cunning and variety of artifice this Creede hath carried on his business, even unknown to me, which he is now forced by an accident to communicate to me – as, the taking up all the papers of moment, which led to the clearing of his accounts, unobserved out of the Controllers hand; which he now makes great use of, knowing that the Controller hath not wherewith to betray him. About this all the morning; only, Mr. Bland came to me about some business of his and told me the news, which holds to be true, that the Portugues did let in the Spaniard by a plot; and they being in the midst of the country and we believing that they would have taken the whole country, they did all rise and kill the whole body, near 8000 men; and Don John of Austria, having two horses killed under him, was forced with one man to fly away.[2]

Sir G Carteret at the office (after dinner and Creed being gone; for, both now and yesterday, I was afeared to have him seen by Sir G. Carteret with me, for fear that he should encrease his doubt that I am of a plot with Creed in the business of his accounts) did tell us that up[on] Tuesday last, being with my Lord Treasurer, he showed him a letter from Portugall,[3] speaking [of] the advance of the Spaniards into their country and yet that the Portugues were never more courageous then now. For by an old Prophecy from France,[4] sent thither some years, though not many, since from the French King, it is foretold that the Spaniards

a l.h. repl. s.h. 'an'

---

1. John Creed had spent over £4660 on stores etc. as Deputy-Treasurer of Sandwich's fleet in the Mediterranean, 1661-2: PRO, Adm. 20/4, p. 254. The Navy Treasurer made some difficulties before passing the accounts: below, pp. 216, 219.

2. This was the battle of Ameixial, fought on 29 May/8 June 1663. Don Juan, bastard son of Philip IV of Spain, and commander of the Spaniards, fled to Badajoz. The best accounts of the action in English are the reports from the Portuguese side, of Schomberg, their commander, and of Col. James Apsley, who led the English auxiliaries: HMC, *Heathcote*, pp. 107-8, 115+. Cf. also HMC, *Portland*, iii. 274; [John Colbatch], *An account of the court of Portugal* (1700), pt ii. 126-52.

3. Untraced.

4. Untraced. It does not appear to be among those attributed to Nostradamus.

should come into their country and in such a vally they should be all killed, and then their country should be wholly delivered from the Spaniards.   This was on Tuesday last.*a*

And yesterday came the very first news that in this very valley they had thus routed and killed the Spainards – which is very strange, but true.

So late at the office and then home to supper and to bed.

This noon I received a letter from the country from my wife, wherein she seems much pleased with the country; God continue it that she may have pleasure while she is there.

She, by my Lady's advice, desires a new petticoate of the new silk-striped stuffs, very pretty.   So I went to paternoster-row presently and bought her one, with Mr. Creeds help; a very fine rich one, the best I did see there and much better then she desires or expects.   And sent it by Creed to Unthanke to be made against tomorrow to send by the carrier, thinking it had been but Wednesdy today, but I found myself mistaken; and also, the taylor being out of the way, it could not be done, but the stuff was sent me back at night by Creede, to dispose of some other way to make; but now I shall keep it to next week.

26.   Up betimes; and Mr. Moore coming to see me, he and I discoursed of going to Oxford this commencement, Mr. Nath. Crew being proctor and Mr. Childe commencing Doctor of Musique this year[1] – which I have a great mind to do; and if I can, will order my matters so that I may do it.

By and by he and I to the Temple, it raining hard; but my Cosen Roger being gone*b* out, he and I walked a good while among*c* the Temple trees, discoursing of my getting my Lord to let me have some security upon his estate, for 100 per annum for two lives, my own and my wife, for my money;[2] but upon

a l.h. repl. s.h. 'next'   *b* MS. 'got'   *c* repl. 'in'

---

1. Rain prevented their going: below, p. 221.   Nathaniel Crew (son of Lord Crew and later Bishop of Durham) was a fellow of Lincoln College.   William Child's doctoral exercise (an anthem) was performed at St Mary's: J. Pulver, *Biog. Dict.*, p. 99.   The 'commencement' (Pepys uses the Cambridge word for the Oxford 'Act') was the ceremony at which full degrees (those of master and doctor) were conferred.

2. A loan of £500 originally made by Pepys to Sandwich in 1661: above, ii. 61 & nn. 4,5; below, p. 286.

second thoughts, Mr. Moore tells me it is very likely my Lord will think that I beg something and may take it ill, and so we resolved not to move it there but to look for it somewhere else.

Here, it raining hard, he and I walked into the King's Bench court, where I never was before, and there stayed an hour almost, till it had done raining (which is a sad season,*a* that it is said there hath not been one fair day these three months, and I think it is true);[1] and then by water to Westminster, and at the Parliament door I spoke with Rogr Pepys. The House is upon the King's answer to their message about Temple, which is that my Lord of Bristoll did tell him that Temple did say those words;[2] so the House are resolved upon sending some of their members to him to know the truth and to demand satisfaction if it be not true.

Thence by water home; and after a little while getting me ready, Sir W. Batten, Sir J. Mennes, my Lady Batten and I by coach to Bednall-green to Sir W Riders to dinner – where a fine place, good lady, mother and*b* their daughter Mrs. Middleton, a fine woman.[3] A noble dinner and a fine merry walk with the ladies alone after dinner in the garden, which is very pleasant. The greatest Quantity of Strawberrys I ever saw, and good. Then a collacion and great mirth, Sir J. Mennes reading a book of scolding[4] very prettily.

This very house[5] was built by the blinde beggar of Bednall greene, so much talked of and sang in ballats;[6] but they say it was only some of the outhouses of it. We drank great store of wine and a beer glass at last, which made me almost sick.

At table, discoursing of thunder and lightning, they told many

a MS. 'session'   *b* symbol blotted

---

1. Dr D. J. Schove writes: 'This was the wettest summer of the 1660s.'

2. See above, p. 192 & n. 1.

3. Elizabeth, wife of Richard Myddelton of Crutched Friars.

4. Possibly burlesques: Mennes is said to have been one of the earliest English writers in this style. A. F. B. Clark, *Boileau in Engl.*, p. 327.

5. Kirby Castle, or Bethnal Green House; a large, mainly Elizabethan mansion: Stow, *Survey* (ed. Strype, 1720), bk iv. 48.

6. Cf. T. Percy, *Reliques* (1765), ii. 155+. The beggar (whose memory was still kept alive in Bethnal Green) was supposedly Henry, son of Simon de Montfort, rescued after the battle of Evesham (1265) by a baron's daughter.

stories of their own knowledge at table; of their masts being shivered from top to bottom, and sometimes only within and the outside whole. But among the rest, Sir*ᵃ* Wm. Rider did tell a story of his own knowledge, that a Genoese Gally in Legorne roade was struck by thunder so as the mast was broke a-pieces and the shackle upon one of the slaves was melted clear off of his leg, without hurting his leg. Sir Wm went on board the vessel and would have contributed toward the release of the slave whom Heaven had thus set free, but he could not compass it and so he was brought to his fetters again.

In the evening home; and I a little to my Tryangle* and so to bed.

27. Up by 4 a-clock and a little to my office. Then comes by agreement Sir Wm. Warren; and he and I from ship to ship to see Deales of all sorts,[1] whereby I have encreased my knowledge and with great pleasure. Then to his yard and house, where I stayed two hours or more, discoursing of the expense of the navy and the corruption of Sir W. Batten and his man Wood, that he brings or would bring to sell all that is to be sold to*ᵇ* the Navy.[2]

Then home to the office, where we sat a little. And at noon home to dinner alone; and thence, it raining hard, by water to the Temple and so to Lyncolns Inne, and there walked up and down to see the new garden which they are making, and will be very pretty;[3] and so to walk under the Chappell[4] by agreement, whither Mr. Clerke our Sollicitor came to me; and he fetched Mr. Long, our Atturny in the Exchequer in the business against Field, and I directed him to come to the best and speediest composition he could, which he will do.[5] So home on foot, calling

a repl. ? 'that'   *b* MS. 'by'

1. For the varieties of timber, see above, iii. 118 & n. 3; 119 & n. 2.

2. In the matter of timber supplies, Pepys and Warren were later to be accused in the parliamentary enquiry of 1669 of the offence here attributed to Batten and William Wood: PL 2554, n.p.

3. See the Benchers' orders (27 November 1662) for the 'modellinge of the Garden and Walkes', the felling of trees and the 'perfectinge of the plattforme' etc.: *Records Lincoln's Inn; The Black Books, 1660–1775*, iii. 23–4.

4. In the undercroft, on ground level.

5. Field in the end brought an action: below, p. 394; cf. above, iii. 23 & n. 2.

at my brother's and elsewhere upon businesses; and so home to
my office and there wrote letters to my father and wife; and so
home to bed – taking three pills overnight.

28. *Lords day.* Early in the morning my last night's physic
worked and did give me a good stool; and then I rose and had
three or four stools and walked up and down my chamber.
Then up my maid rose and made me a posset; and by and by
comes Mr. Creede and he and I spent all the morning discoursing,
against tomorrow before the Duke, the business of his peeces-of-
eight – in which the Treasurer makes so many Querys.[1]
At noon, my physic having done working, I went down to
dinner.   And then he and I up again and spent the most of the
afternoon reading in Cicero and other books and good discourse,
and then he went away; and then came my brother Tom to see
me – telling me how the Joyces do make themselfs fine clothes
against Mary is brought to bed.   He being gone, I went to cast
up my monthly accounts; and to my great trouble, I find myself
7*l*. worse then I was the last month,[2] but I confess it is by my
reckoning beforehand a great many things; yet however, I am
troubled to see that I can hardly promise myself to lay up much
from month's end to month's end, about 4 or 5*l* at most, one
month with another, without some extraordinary gettings.   But
I must and I hope I shall continue to have a care of my own
expenses.
So to the reading my vowes seriously, and then to supper.
This evening there came my boy's Brother to see for him; and
tells me he knows not where he is, himself being[a] out of towne
this week, and is very sorry that he is gone; and so am I, but he
shall come no more.   So to prayers and to bed.

29.   Up betimes and to my office; and by and by to the
Temple and there appointed to meet in the evening about my
business.   And thence I walked home; and up and down the
streets is cried mightily the great victory got by the Portugalls
against the Spaniards, where 10000 slain, 3 or 4000 taken prisoners,
with all the artillery, baggage, money, &c., and Don John of

a repl. ? 'beth'

───────────────

1. Cf. above, p. 132.   2. See above, p. 166.

Austria forced to fly with a man or two with him[1] – which is very great news.

Thence home and at my office all the morning, and so dined at home; and then by water to St. James, but no meeting, today being holy-day;[2] but met Mr. Creed in the park, and after a walk or two, discoursing his business, I took leave of him in Westminster-hall, whither we walked; and then came again to the hall and fell in talk with Mrs. Lane and after great talk that she never went abroad with any man as she used heretofore to do, I with one word got her to go with me and to meet me at the further Rhenish wine-house[3] – where I did give her a Lobster and do so towse her and feel her all over, making her believe how fair and good a skin she had; and endeed, she hath a very white thigh and leg, but monstrous fat. When weary, I did give over, and somebody having seen some of our dalliance, called aloud in the street, "Sir! why do you kiss the gentlewoman so?" and flung a stone at the window – which vexed me – but I believe they could not see my towsing her; and so we broke up and went out the back way, without being observed I think; and so she towards the hall and I to White-hall, where taking water, I to the temple and thence with my Cosen Roger and Mr. Goldsborough to Gray's-Inne to his counsel, one Mr. Rawworth, a very fine man. Where, it being the Question whether I as Executor should give a warrant to Golsborough in my reconveying her estate[4] back again, the morgage being performed against all acts of the Testator but only my own – my Cosen said he never heard it asked before, and the other that it was always asked and he never heard it denied or scrupled before – so great a distance was there in their opinions, enough to make a man forswear ever having to do with the law. So they agreed to refer it to Serjeant Maynard. And so we broke up, and I by water home from the Temple and there to Sir W. Batten and

---

1. *Kingd. Intell.*, 29 June, had just appeared, with news of the battle (and details roughly the same as these) at pp. 409+.

2. St Peter's Day: possibly the Duke put off the meeting because it clashed with a chapel service. Cf. below, ix. 251.

3. Probably Prior's Rhenish wine house. (R).

4. Mrs Goldsborough's. This dispute was inherited with Robert Pepys's estate, of which Pepys was executor: above, ii. 195 & n. 3; iii. 232 & n. 1.

eat with him, he and his lady and Sir J. Mennes having been below* today upon the East India men that are come in;¹ but never tell me so, but that they have been at Woolwich and Deptford and done great deal of business.   God help them.   So home and up to my lute long; and then after a little Latin chapter* with Will, to bed.   But I have used of late, since my wife went, to make a bad use of my fancy with whatever woman I have a mind to – which I am ashamed of and shall endeavour to do so no more.   And so to sleep.

30.   Up betimes.   Yesterday and today, the sun rising very bright and glorious; and yet yesterday, as it hath been these two months and more, was a foul day the most part of the day.

By and by, [by] water to White-hall and there to my Lord's lodgings by appointment; whither Mr. Creede comes to me, having been at Chelsey this morning to fetch my Lord to St. James's.   So he and I to the parke, where we understand that the King and Duke are gone out betimes this morning on board the East India ships lately come in, and so our meeting appointed is lost.   But he and I walked at the further end of the park, not to be observed; whither by and by comes my Lord Sandwich and he and we walked two hours and more in the park, and then in White-hall gallery and lastly in White-hall garden, discoursing of Mr. Creedes accounts and how to answer the Treasurer's objections.   I find that the business is 500 deep, the advantage of Creede;² and why my Lord and I should be concerned to pro-mote his profit, with so much dishonour and trouble to us, I know not; but however, we shall do what we can – though he deserves it not, for there is nothing even to his own advantage that can be got out of him but by mere force.   So full of policy he is in the smallest matters, that I perceive him to be made up of nothing but design.   I left him here, being in my mind vexed at the trouble that this business gets me and the distance that it makes between Sir G. Carteret and myself, which I ought to avoyd.   Thence by water home and to dinner.   And

1. The ships which had gone out in April 1662 to take possession of Bombay, newly acquired as part of the Queen's dowry.

2. See above, p. 198, n. 1.   Creed hoped to get £500 from a foreign-exchange transaction.

afterward to the office and there sat till evening; and then I by[a] water to Deptford to see Sir W. Penn, who lies ill at Captain Rooths but in a way to be well again; this weather this day being[b] the only fair day we have had these three or four months. Among other discourse, I did tell him plainly some of my thoughts concerning Sir W. Batten and the office in general, upon design for him to understand that I do mind things and will not balk to take notice of them, that when he comes to be well again he may know how to look upon me.

Thence homeward walked, and in my way met Creede coming to meet me; and then turned back and walk a while, and so to boat and home by water – I being not very forward to talk of his business; and he by design the same, to see how I would speak of [it], but I did not but in general terms; and so after supper with general discourse, to bed and sleep.

Thus, by God's blessing, end this book of two years. Being in all points in good health, and a good way to thrive and do well. Some money I do and can lay up, but not much; being worth now above 700*l*, besides goods of all Sorts. My wife in the country with Ashwell her woman, with my father. Myself at home with W. Hewre and my cook-maid Hannah, my boy Waynman being lately run away from me.

In my office, my repute and understanding good, especially with the Duke and Mr. Coventry. Only, the rest of the officers do rather envy then love me, I standing in most of their lights, especially Sir W. Batten, whose cheats I do daily oppose, to his great trouble, though he appears mighty kind and willing to keep friendship with mee,[c] while Sir J. Mennes, like a dotard, is led by the nose by him. My wife and I (by my late jealousy, for which I am truly to be blamed) have not that fondness between us which we used and ought to have, and I fear will be lost hereafter if I do not take some course to oblige her and yet preserve my authority. Public matters are in an ill condition – parliament sitting and raising[d] four subsidys for the King, which is but a little, considering his wants; and yet that parted withal with great hardness – they being offended to see so much money go, and no debts of the public paid, but all swallowed by a luxurious Court[e] – which the King, it is believed and hoped, will retrench in a little

---

        a   repl. 'out'   *b*   MS. 'being and being'
   c   l.h. repl. s.h. 'him'   *d*   repl. 'raised'   *e*   repl. 'course'

time, when he comes to see the utmost of the Revenue which shall be settled on him – he expecting to have his 1200000*l* made good to him, which is not*ᵃ* yet done by above 150000*l*, as he himself reports to the House.¹

My differences with my uncle Tho. at a good quiett,² blessed be God, and other matters.

The town full of the great overthrow lately given to the Spaniard by the portugall, they being advanced into the very middle of Portugall.

The weather wett for two or three months together, beyond belief; almost not one fair day coming between till this day, which hath been a very pleasant [day], and the first pleasant this summer.

The charge of the Navy entended to be limited to 200000*l* per annum, the ordinary charge of it, and that to be settled upon the Customes.³

The King yet greatly taken up with Madam Castlemayne and Mrs. Stewart – which God of Heaven put an end to.

Myself very studious to learn what I can of all things necessary for my place as an officer of the Navy – reading lately what concerns measuring of timber and knowledge of the tides.

I have of late spent much time with Creede, being led to it by his business of his accounts; but I find him a fellow of those designs or reaches, that there is no degree of true friendship to be made with him, and therefore I must cast him off, though he be a very understanding man and one that much may be learned of as to cunning* and judging of other men. Besides, too, I do perceive more and more that my time of pleasure and idlenesse of any sort must be flung off, to attend the getting of some money and the keeping of my family in order, which I fear by my wife's liberty may be otherwise lost.*ᵇ*

a l.h. repl. l.h. 'y'-
b Here end the entries in the second volume of the MS. Seventeen blank pages follow.

---

1. £1,200,000 was the over-optimistic estimate of the yield of the revenues granted to the King in 1660, and the deficit of over £150,000 had been reported to the Commons on 4 June 1663: *CJ*, viii. 498. As a result, four subsidies had been granted and measures taken to improve the collection of other sources of revenue. Cf. below, v. 69 & n. 2.

2. See above, p. 42 & n. 3.

3. See above, p. 152 & n. 3.

JULY. 1663./

1. This morning it rained so hard (though it was fair yester-day, and we thereupon in hopes of having some fair weather, which we have wanted these three months) that it wakened Creed (who lay with me last night) and me; and so we up and fell to discourse of the business of his accounts now under dispute, in which I have taken much trouble upon myself and raised a distance between Sir G. Carteret and myself which troubles me. But I hope we have this morning light of an Expedient that will right all – that is, will answer their Quærys and yet save Creede the 500*l* which he did purpose to make of the exchange abroad of the peeces-of-eight which he disbursed.[1] Being ready, he and I by water to White-hall; where I left him before we came into the Court, for fear I should be seen by Sir G. Carteret with him, which of late I have been forced to avoid to remove suspicion.

I to St. James's and there discoursed a while with Mr. Coventry, between whom and myself there is very good understanding and friendship.

And so to Westminster-hall; and being in the parliament Lobby, I there saw my Lord of Bristoll come to the Commons House to give his answer to their Quæstion – about some words he should tell the King that were spoke by Sir Rd. Temple, a member of their House.[2] A chair was set at the bar of the House for him, which he used but little – but made a Harangue of half an hour bareheaded, the House covered.

His speech being done, he came out and drew into a little room till the House had concluded of an answer to his speech – which they staying long upon, I went away; and by and by out comes Sir W. Batten and he told me – that his Lordshipp had made a long and a Comedian*-like speech, and delivered with such action as were not becoming his Lordshipp. He confesses he did tell

1. See above, p. 198, n. 1.
2. See above, p. 192 & n. 1. Bristol's speech (of which Pepys's account is a fair summary) is in Tanner 47, ff. 17–19; printed in *Parl. Hist.*, iv. 270–6. Temple was removed from the commission of the peace and his deputy-lieutenancy in August: *Hunt. Lib. Quart.*, 4/55.

the King such a thing of Sir Rd. Temple, but that upon his Honour they were not spoke by Sir Rd., he having taken a liberty of enlarging to the King upon the discourse which had been between Sir Rd. and himself lately; and so took upon himself the whole blame and desired their pardon, it being not to do any wrong to their fellow-member, but out of zeal to the King.

He told them, among many other things, that as to his Religion, he was a Roman Catholique, but such a one as thought no man to have right to the crown of England but the Prince that hath it. And such a one as, if the King should desire his counsel as*a* to his own, he would not advise him to another Religion then the old true reformed religion of this country, it being the properest of this kingdom as it now stands.

And concluded with a submission to what the House shall do with him; saying that whatever they shall do, says he, "thanks be to God, this head, this heart, and this sword (pointing to them all) will find me a being in any place in Europe."[1]

The House hath hereupon voted clearly Sir Rd. Temple to be free from the imputation of saying those words. But when Sir W. Batten came out, had not concluded what to say to my Lord, it being urged that to own any satisfaccion as to my Lord from his speech would be to lay some fault upon the King for the message he should, upon no better accounts, send to the impeaching of one of their members.

Walking out, I hear that the House of Lords are offended that my Lord Digby[2] should come to this House and make a speech there without leave first asked of the House of Lords. I hear also of another difficulty now upon [him] is that my Lord of Sunderland (whom I do not know) was so near to the marriage of his daughter as that the wedding-clothes were made, and portion and everything agreed on and ready; and the other day he goes away, nobody yet knows whither, sending her the next morning a release of his right or claim to her – and advice

a MS. 'at'

---

1. 'I will goe into some forreigne parts, where I trust this sword, this head and this heart, shall make mee live as formerly with some lustre to myselfe and honour to my nation': Tanner 47, f. 17r.
2. Bristol.

to his friends not to enquire into the reason of this doing, for he hath enough for it[1] – but that he gives them liberty to say and think what they will of him; so they do not demand the reason of his leaving her, being resolved never to have her – but the reason desires and resolves not to give.

Thence by water with Sir W. Batten to T[r]inity-house, there to dine with him, which we did; and after dinner we fell in talking, Sir J. Mennes and Mr. Batten[2] and I – Mr. Batten telling us of a late triall of Sir Charles Sydly the other day, before my Lord Chief Justice Foster and the whole Bench – for his debauchery a little while since at Oxford Kates;[3] coming in open day into the Balcone and showed his nakedness – acting all the postures of lust and buggery that could be imagined, and abusing of scripture and, as it were, from thence preaching a Mountebanke sermon from that pulpitt, saying that there he hath to sell such a pouder as should make all the cunts in town run after him – a thousand people standing underneath to see and hear him.

And that being done, he took a glass of wine and washed his prick in it and then drank it off; and then took another and drank the King's health.

It seems my Lord and the rest of the Judges did all of them round give him a most high reproofe – my Lord Chief Justice saying that it was for him and such wicked wretches as he was that God's anger and judgments hung over us – calling him "Sirrah" many times. It's said[a] they have bound him to his good

a repl. 'is'

1. Lady Anne Digby, second daughter of Bristol, was now 17 years old. Sunderland took flight to the Continent for the next eighteen months. Cf. de Cominges to de Lionne, London, 2/12 July 1663: '[Sunderland] se retira le soir que l'on devoit l'espouser et donna ordre à un de ses amis de rompre le mariage. Ce procédé surprit toute la cour et le Roy mesme s'en est moqué et l'a blasmé au dernier point': PRO, PRO 31/3/112, f. 69r. But the marriage did in the end take place, on 9 June 1665.

2. William, elder son of Sir William; a barrister of Lincoln's Inn.

3. A well-known cook's house at the sign of the Cock in Bow St, Covent Garden. The affair is recounted in Wood, *L. & T.*, i. 476–7. There it is stated that Sedley was fined £500 for riot. Dr Johnson repeats the story (from Wood) in his 'Life of Dorset': *Lives of Engl. poets* (ed. Birkbeck Hill), i. 303–4. For another frolic of Buckhurst's and Sedley's, see below, ix. 355–6.

behaviour (there being no law against him for it) in 5000*l*. It
being told that my Lord Buckhurst was there, my Lord asked
whether it was that Buckhurst that was lately tried for robbery;[1]
and when answered "Yes," he asked whether[a] he had so soon
forgot his deliverance at that time, and that it would have more
become him to have been at his prayers, begging God's forgiveness, then now running into such courses again.

Upon this discourse, Sir J. Mennes and Mr. Batten both say that
buggery is now almost grown as common among our gallants as
in Italy, and that the very pages of the town begin to complain of
their masters for it.   But blessed be God, I do not to this day
know what is the meaning of this sin, nor which is the agent nor
which the patient.   Thence home; and my clarkes being gone by
my leave to see the East India ships that are lately come home, I
stayed all alone within my office all the afternoon.   This day
I hear at dinner that Don John of Austria, since his flight out of
Portugall, is dead of his wounds.   So there is a great man gone,
and a great dispute like to be ended for[b] the crown of Spayne,
if the King should have died [be]fore him.[2]   I received this morning a letter from my wife, brought by John Goods to town –
wherein I find a sad falling-out between my wife and my father
and sister and Ashwell, upon my writing to my father to advise
pall not[c] to keep Ashwell from her mistress or making any difference between them.   Which pall telling to Ashwell and she
speaking some words that her mistress heard, caused great
difference among them all, which I am sorry from my heart to
hear of and I fear will breed ill-blood not to be laid again – so that
I fear my wife and I may have some falling-out about it, or at

a repl. 'him'   *b* repl. 'between'   *c* l.h. repl. s.h. 'to'

---

1. *Recte* manslaughter. See above,
iii. 34 & n. 2.

2. The story was untrue; Don
Juan lived until 1679. Pepys's information probably came from a
letter he received from John Pitts
(Lisbon, 7 June, o.s.): *CSPD 1663–4*,
p. 165. Don Juan had not in fact
been wounded at Ameixial (q.v.
above, p. 198 & n. 2), though he had
been forced to dismount and had lost
most of his bodyguard. For some years

(1646–61) he had been the only male
heir of Philip IV, and the birth of the
Infante Charles in 1661 had failed to
extinguish his ambition to succeed
(though illegitimate) to his father's
throne, for his half-brother was sickly
and not expected to live long. The
Infante, however, succeeded his father
in 1665 as Charles II, and Don Juan,
after some resistance to the Council of
Regency, made his submission in
June 1669.

least my father and I; but I shall endeavour to salve up all as well as I can, or send for her out of the country before the time entended – which I would be loath to do.

In the evening by water to my Cosen Roger Pepys's chamber, where he was not come; but I found Dr. John[1] newly come to town, and is well again after his sickness; but Lord, what a simple man he is as to any public matters of state, and talks so sillily.   And his Brother, Dr Tom, what the matter is I know not, but he hath taken (as my father told me a good while since) such displeasure, that he hardly would touch his*a* hat to me, and I as little to him.

By and by comes Roger and he told us the whole passage of my Lord Digby today, much as I have said here above; only, that he did say that he would draw his sword against the Pope himself, if he should offer anything against his Majesty and the good of these nations.   And that he never was the man that did either look for a Cardinall's cap for himself or anybody else, meaning Abbot Mountagu;[2] and the House upon the whole did vote Sir Rd. Temple innocent.   And that my Lord Digby hath cleared the honour of his Majesty, Sir Rd. Temples, and given perfect satisfaction of his own respects to the House.[3]

Thence to my brother's; and being vexed with his not minding my father's business here in getting his Landskips done, I went away in an anger and walked home; and so up to my lute and then to bed.

a   repl. 'is'

---

1. John Pepys, Fellow of Trinity Hall, Cambridge, younger brother of Roger; civil lawyer.

2. From the articles of impeachment which Bristol now drew up against Clarendon, it is clear that the reference here is to Ludovick Stuart, Lord d'Aubigny, not Mountagu. (See below, p. 224 & n. 2.) In November 1665 d'Aubigny was nominated cardinal but died almost immediately. Bristol's words on 1 July were: 'I am no Negotiator . . . of Cardinal's caps for his

majesty's subjects' domestics.' Both d'Aubigny and Mountagu were Household officers (the former of the Queen, the latter of the Queen Mother). For Mountagu's unpopularity at this time see C. H. Hartmann, *The King my brother*, p. 271.

3. The Commons combined a vote accepting Bristol's account with a vote giving Temple leave to petition the King's favour. *CJ*, viii. 515; *CSPD 1663-4*, p. 190.

2. Up betimes to my office – and there all the morning doing business. At noon to the Change – and there met with several people; among others, Captain Cox, and with him to a Coffee* and drank with him and some other merchants. Good discourse. Thence home and to dinner; and after a little alone at my vial, to the office, where we sat all the afternoon; and so rose at the evening and then home to supper and to bed – after a little Musique; my mind being troubled with the thoughts of the difference between my wife and my father in the country.

Walking in the garden this evening with Sir G. Carteret and Sir J. Mennes – Sir G. Carteret told us with great contempt how like a stage-player my Lord Digby spoke yesterday – pointing to his head as my Lord did and saying, "First, for his head," says Sir G. Carteret, "I know that a calfes head would have done better by half. For his heart and his sword, I have nothing to say to them." He told us that for certain his head cost the late King his, for it was he that broke off the treaty at Uxbrige.[1] He told us also how great a man he was raised from a private gentleman in France by Monsieur Grandmont, and afterward by the Cardinall,[2] who raised him to be a Lieutenant-Generall and then higher, and intrusted by the Cardinall, when he was banished out of France, with great matters, and recommended by him to the Queene[3] as a man to be trusted and ruled by. Yet when he came to have some power over the Queene, he begun to dissuade her from her opinion of the Cardinall; which she said nothing to till the Cardinall was returned, and then she told him of it; who told my Lord Digby, "*Et bien, Monsieur, vous estes un fort bon amy donc.*" But presently put him out of all; and then he was, from a certainty of coming in two or three years' time to be

1. Bristol (then Digby) had been Secretary of State at the time of the negotiations at Uxbridge with Parliament in January–February 1645, but there is no foundation for this explanation of their failure. He was not one of the commissioners who conducted them; Parliament had made it a condition of the negotiations that he should not be. Clarendon, *Hist.*, iii. 465; Rushworth, *Hist. Coll.* (1721), v. 805.

2. I.e. by Antoine, Duc de Gramont, and by Cardinal Mazarin. The latter had him made a lieutenant-general in August 1651. In 1656 he commanded the French army in Italy: Clarendon, op. cit., vi. 48.

3. Anne d'Autriche, widow of Louis XIII, and Queen Mother of France. Mazarin was in exile at Brühl in Cologne, February–December 1651, and at Bouillon, August 1652–February 1653.

Mareschall of France (to which all strangers, even protestants and those as often as French themselfs, are capable of coming, though it be one of the greatest places in France),[1] he was driven to go out of France into Flanders; but there was not trusted, nor received any kindness from the Prince of Conde,[2] as one to whom also he had been false, as he had been to the Cardinall and Grandmont. In fine, he told us how he is a man of excellent parts, but of no great faith nor judgment; and one very easy to get up to great heighth of preferment, but never able to hold it.

So in and to my Musique; and then comes Mr Creede to me, giving me an account of his accounts, how he hath now settled them fit for perusal the most strict; at which I am glad. And so he and I to bed together.

3. Up; and he home and I with Sir J. Mennes and Sir W. Batten by coach to Westminster to St. James, thinking to meet Sir G. Carteret and to attend the Duke; but he not coming, we broke up; and so I to Westminster-hall, and there meeting with Mr. Moore, he tells me great news; that my Lady Castlemayne is fallen from Court and this morning retired.[3] He gives me no account of the reason of it, but that it is so; for which I am sorry, and yet if the King doth it to leave off not only her but all other mistresses, I should be heartily glad of it, that he may fall to look after business. I hear my Lord Digby is condemned at Court for his speech. And that my Lord Chancellor grows great again. Thence with Mr. Creede, whom I called at his Chamber, over the water to Lambeth; but could not, it being morning, get to see

1. The marshals of France (whose number – now about 12 – was not fixed) were the highest-ranking officers of the French army after the suppression of the office of constable in 1627. They included Germans and Scandinavians, and Schomberg (cr. marshal 1675) was the greatest of the foreign Protestants who served in this capacity in the 17th century. See the lists in *Le nouveau estat de la France* (1661), p. 103; L. André, *Michel le Tellier*, p. 122.

2. Condé, leader of the 'Princes'

Fronde', had fled to the Spanish Netherlands in 1653 and taken service there, returning to France in 1659. Digby had been banished there in August 1656. Clarendon's account suggests that in the Spanish service Digby had some influence, although he was not trusted: *Hist.*, vi. 49+.

3. Her fall was attributed in the French despatches (25 June) to the rise of Frances Stuart: Ruvigny to Louis XIV, 15/25 June; PRO, PRO 31/3/112, f. 31r. But it was only temporary: below, p. 238 & n. 2.

the Archbishops hearse.[1] And so he and I walked over the fields to Southworke and there parted; and I spent half an hour in Mary Overy's church, where are fine Monuments, of great antiquity I believe, and hath been a fine church.[2] Thence to the Change; and meeting Sir J. Mennes there, he and I walked to look upon Backwell's design of making another ally from his shop through over against the Exchange-door; which will be very noble and quite put down the other two.[3]

So home to dinner, and then to the office and entered in my Manuscript-book[4] the victualler's contract. And then over the water and walked to see Sir W. Penn and sat with him a while;[5] and so home late and to my viall; so up comes Creede again to me and stays all night, tomorrow morning being a hearing before the Duke. So to bed, full of discourse of his business.

4. Up by 4 a-clock and sent him to get matters ready. And I to my office, looking over papers and mending my Manuscript by scraping out the blots and other things; which is now a very fine book.

1. Juxon had died on 4 June; his body had been embalmed and after lying in state was taken to Oxford for burial in St John's College chapel on 9 July.

2. The priory church of St Mary Overie had become the parish church of St Saviour at the Reformation. For the monuments, see R. Comm. Hist. Mon.: *London*, v (*E. London*), pp. 58–66. Since 1905 it has been the cathedral of Southwark diocese.

3. On 30 December 1668 Backwell obtained from the Fire Court the award of a lease for 45 years from 29 September 1668 of the site of a house and shop described six years earlier as at the s. end of 'the new alley called Exchange Alley next Lumbard Streete in the parish of Saint Mary Woolnoth'. Though its frontage on Lombard St was only 26 ft, it was 60 ft deep and in a key position, as is clear from its (presumably rack) rental of £140 p.a. when in the divided tenures of the goldsmiths Charles Everard and Joseph Hornby: BL, Add. 5086 (59). See below, ix. 517 & n. 1. The 'other two' alleys were alleys only in name, being narrow passages from Cornhill to Lombard St, running on either side of Exchange Alley. The westernmost, Pope's Head Alley, later Swan and Hoop Passage, was renewed after the Fire. The easternmost seems to have lost its exit on to Cornhill, becoming a leg of Exchange Alley. In the rebuilding, Backwell's foresight was rewarded, Exchange Alley being described as 'a Place of very considerable Concourse of Merchants, Seafaring Men and other Traders': Stow, *Survey* (ed. Strype, 1720), ii. 149. (R).

4. See above, p. 11 & n. 1.

5. Penn lay ill at Deptford.

So to St. James by water with Sir J. Mennes and Sir W. Batten, I giving occasion to a wager about the tide, that it did flow through bridge; by which Sir W. Batten won 5s of Sir J. Mennes.

At St. James we stayed while the Duke made himself ready; and among other things, Sir Allen Apsly showed the Duke the Lisbon Gazette in Spanish, where the late victory is set down perticularly, and to the great honour of the English, beyond measure.[1] They have since taken back Evora, which was lost to the Spaniard, the English making the assault and not lost more then three men.[2]

Here I learned that the English foot are highly esteemed all over the world; but the horse not so much, which yet we count among ourselfs the best – but they abroad have had no great knowledge of our horse it seems.[3]

The Duke being ready, we retired with him and there fell upon Mr. Creedes business,[4] where the Treasurer did like a mad coxcomb, without reason or method, run over a great many things against the account, and so did Sir J. Mennes and Sir W. Batten; which the Duke himself and Mr. Coventry and my

---

1. The battle of Ameixial: see above, p. 198 & n. 2. Sir Allen Apsley was the father of Col. James Apsley, who commanded the English troops. The Lisbon gazette's account was printed as *Relacion de la famosa y memorable vitoria* ... (Lisbon, 1663; BM 9195. c. 25, no. 3). The Portuguese usually printed news of importance in both Portuguese and Spanish. The English infantry had acquitted themselves remarkably well by a disciplined charge uphill against the enemy's right wing. The Portuguese commanders, according to James Apsley's account (HMC, *Heathcote*, pp. 101+), were so surprised to see the redcoats march in unbroken formation up the hill, without firing a shot, until they came within push of pike, that they believed their allies to be about to surrender to the Spaniards. 'But when they saw their thick firing and good success ... they called us comrades and good Chris-

tians.' The English ambassador made much of the fact that the action was fought on Charles II's birthday (op. cit., pp. 100–1). See also *Kingd. Intell.*, 6 July, p. 433.

2. Évora, capital city of the province of Alentejo, had fallen to the Spaniards in May, and was now (12/22 June) retaken by the Portuguese and their allies under Schomberg, an English force of 200 musketeers under Maj. John Belasyse making the vital assault at midnight on the fort of St Anthony. One captain and three soldiers were killed: HMC, *Heathcote*, p. 116.

3. At the battle of Ameixial the English cavalry had not played any decisive part. English military repute at this time rested chiefly on the victory won by Cromwell's infantry over the Spaniards at the battle of the Dunes in June 1658.

4. See above, p. 198, n. 1.

Lord Barkely and myself did remove; and Creede being called
in, did answer all with great method and excellently to the purpose (myself I am a little conscious did not speak so well as I
purposed and do think I use to do; that is, not so intelligibly and
perswasively as I well hoped I should); not that what I said was not
well taken, and did carry the business with what was urged and
answered by Creede and Mr. Coventry – till the Duke himself
did declare that he was satisfied, and my Lord Barkely offered to
lay 100*l* that the King could receive no wrong in the account.
And the two last knights held their tongues; or at least, by not
understanding it, did say what made for Mr. Creede; and so Sir
G. Carteret was left alone, but yet persisted to say that the
account was not good, but full of corruption and foul dealing.
And so we broke up, to his shame, but I do fear to the loss of his
friendship to me a good while, which I am heartily troubled for.

Thence with Creede to the King's-head ordinary; but coming
late, dined at the second table very well for 12*d.*; and a pretty
gentleman in our company who confirms my Lady Castlemaynes
being gone from Court, but knows not the reason.[1]   He told us
of one wipe the Queene a little while ago did give her, when she
came in and found the Queene under the dresser's hands and had
been so long – "I wonder your Majesty," says she, "can have the
patience to sit so long a-dressing:" "Oh," says the Queene, "I have
so much reason to use patience, that I can very well bear with it."
He thinks that it may be the Queene hath commanded her to
retire, though that is not likely.

Thence with Creede to hire a coach to carry us to Hide parke,
today there being a general muster of the King's Guards,[a] horse
and foot;[2] but they demand so high, that I spying Mr. Cutler
the merchant, did take notice of him; and he going into his
coach and telling me that he was going to show a couple of
Swedish strangers the Muster, I asked and went along with him.

Where a goodly sight to see so many fine horse and officers,
and the King, Duke and others come by a-horseback, and the
two Queens in the Queen-Mother's coach (my Lady Castlemayne

a   l.h. superimposed upon s.h. 'garden'

1. See below, p. 230 & n. 1.
2. A review;   Evelyn has an
account. J. Ashton, *Hyde Park*,
(pp. 132+), has notices of reviews
held in the park at this time.   Cf. also
Monconys, ii. 19.

not being there); and after long being there, I light and walked
to the place where the King, Duke, &c. did stand to see the horse
and foot march by and discharge their guns, to show a French
Marquesse[1] (for whom this muster was caused) the goodness of
our firemen; which endeed was very good, though not without a
slip now and then (and one broadside close to our coach we had
going out of the park, even to that neerenesse as to be ready to
burn our hairs); yet methought all these gay men are not the
soldiers that must do the King's business, it being such as these
that lost the old King all he had and were beat[a] by the most
ordinary fellows that could be.

    Thence with much ado out of the park; and I lighted and
through St. James down the waterside over to Lambeth to see the
Archbishopps corps (who is to be carried away to Oxford on
Monday); but came too late and so walked over the fields and
bridge home (calling by the way at old Georges,[2] but find that
he is dead) and there wrote several letters; and so home to
supper and to bed.

    This day in the Dukes chamber, there being a Roman story in
the hangings and upon the standards written these four letters,
S P Q R, Sir G. Carteret came to me to know what the meaning
of those four letters were – which ignorance is not to be borne
in a Privy-Counsellor methinks, that a schoolboy should be whipt
for not knowing.[3]

    5. *Lords day.* Lay, being weary and not very well last night,
long asleep. Anon, about 7 a-clock the maid calls me, telling
me that my Lady Batten had sent twice to invite me to go with
them to Walthamstowe today – Mrs. Martha being married
already this morning to Mr. Castle at this parish church.[4] I could

a MS. 'bead'

---

1. The French ambassador, Comte
de Cominges.
    2. ? the Sun tavern; cf. above,
i. 229.
    3. Was his command of his own
language any better? Cf. Marvell:
'*Carteret* the rich did the Accomptants
guide,/And in ill *English* all the

World defy'd.': *Last Instructions*,
ll. 203–4. He had received very little
formal education, and had spent
much of his boyhood at sea.
    4. At St Olave's, Hart St: *Harl.
Soc. Reg.*, 46/276. For this marriage,
see above, p. 177 & n. 3.

not rise soon enough to go with them; but got myself ready and
so to Games's, where I got a horse and rode thither very pleasantly;
only, coming to make water, I find a stopping, which makes me
fearful of my old pain.

Being come thither, I was well received and had two pair of
gloves, as the rest, and walked up and down with my Lady in the
garden; she mighty kind to me and I have the way to please her.

A good dinner and merry, but methinks none of the kindness
nor bridall respect between the bridegroom and bride that was
between my wife and I – but as persons that marry purely for
convenience.

After dinner to church by coach, and there (my Lady, Mrs.
Turner, Mrs. Lemon and I only) we, in spite to one another, kept
one another awake; and sometimes I read in my book of Latin
plays[1] which I took in my pocket, thinking to have walked it.

An[a] old doting parson[2] preached. So home again; and by
and by up and homewards, calling in our way (Sir J. Mennes
and I only) at Mr. Battens[3] (who with his lady and child went in
another coach by us), which is a very pretty house and himself
in all things, within and without, very ingenious; and I find a
very fine study and good books.

So set out, Sir J. Mennes and I in his coach together, talking all
the way of Chymistry, wherein he doth know something;[4] at
least, seems so to me that cannot correct him – Mr. Battens man
riding my horse; and so home and to my office a while to read
my vowes. Then home to prayers and to bed.

6. Up pretty early and to my office, where all the morning
writing out a list of the King's ships in my Navy collections,[5]
with great pleasure. At noon Creed comes to me, who tells
me how well he hath sped with Sir G. Carteret after all our

a MS. 'and'

---

1. PL 217; a duodecimo containing Edmund Stubbe's *Fraus Honesta*
(1632); Abraham Cowley's *Naufra-
gium Joculare* (1638); and Matthew
Gwinne's *Nero* (1639).
2. The Vicar, Dr Edward Sparkes,
was in his fifties; possibly this was a
visiting preacher.

3. William Batten, barrister; son
of Pepys's colleague.
4. For Mennes's interest in science,
see e.g. below, p. 334.
5. See above, p. 11 & n. 1.

trouble; that he had his[a] tallies up and all the kind words possible from him – which I believe is out of an apprehension what a fool he hath made of himself hitherto in making so great a stop therein.   But I find, and so my Lord Sandwich may, that Sir G. Carteret had a design to do him a disgrace if he could possibly; otherwise he would never have carried the business so far after that manner, but would first have consulted my Lord and given him advice what to do therein for his own honour, which he thought endangered.   Creede dined with me and then walked a while, and so away and I to my office at my morning's work till dark night, and so with good content home – to supper – a little Musique, and then to bed.

7.   Up by 4 a-clock and to my office, and there continued all the morning upon my Navy book, to my great content.   At noon down by barge with Sir J. Mennes (who is going to Chatham) to Woolwich, in our way eating of some venison pasty in the barge, I having neither eat nor drank today, which fills me full of wind.   Here also, in Mr. Petts garden I eat some (and the first cherries I have eat this year) off the tree where the King himself had been gathering some this morning.

Thence walked alone (only, part of the Way Deane walked with me, complaining of many abuses in the yard) to Greenwich, and so by water to Deptford, where I find Mr. Coventry and with him up and down all the stores – to the great trouble of the officers; and by his help I am resolved to fall hard to work again, as I used to do.

So thence he and I by water, talking of many things; and I see he puts his trust most upon me in the Navy and talks (as there is reason) slightly of the two old knights.   And I should be glad by any drudgery to see the King's stores and service looked to as they ought, but I fear I shall never understand half the mis-carriages and tricks that the King suffers by.[1]

He tells me what Mr. Pett did today: that my Lord Bristoll told the King that he will impeach the Chancellor of high treason;[2] but I find that my Lord Bristoll hath undone himself

a l.h. repl. s.h. 'them'

1. On this day the Navy Board ordered the Master-Attendant at Deptford to certify the quality of bewpers: NMM, SER 129, n.p.
2. See below, p. 223.

already in everybody's opinion, and now he endeavours to raise dust to put out other men's eys as well as his own.   But I hope it will not take – in consideration merely that it is hard for a prince to spare an experienced old officer, be he never so corrupt; though I hope this man is not so, as some report him to be.

He tells me that Don John is yet alive and not killed, as was said, in the great victory against the Spaniards in Portugall of late.[1]

So home and late at my office.   Thence home and to my musique.   This night, Mr. Turners house [of office] being to be emptied out of my cellar, and therefore I think to sit up a little longer then ordinary.

This afternoon, coming from the waterside with Mr. Coventry, I spied my boy upon Tower-hill, playing with the rest of the boys; so I sent W. Griffen to take him and he did bring him to me; and so I said nothing to him, but caused him to be stripped (for he was run away with his best suit); and so putting on his other, I sent him going, without saying one word more to him – though I am troubled for the rogue, though he doth not deserve it.

Being*a* come home, I find my stomach not well, for want of eating today my dinner as I should do, and so am become full of wind; I called late for some victuals and so to bed, leaving the men below in the cellar emptying the turds up through Mr. Turner's own house; and so, with more content, to bed late.

8.   Being weary and going to bed late last night, I slept till 7 a-clock, it raining mighty hard, and so did every minute of the day after, sadly – that I know not what will become of the corn this year, we having had but two fair days these many months.

Up and to my office, where all the morning busy.   And then at noon home to dinner alone, upon a good dish of eeles given me by Michell the Bewpers-man.[2]   And then to my viall a little. And then down into the cellar, and up and down with Mr. Turner to see where his vault for turds may be made bigger, or another made him; which I think may well be.   And so to my office, where very busy all day setting things in order, my contract books, and preparing things against the next sitting.   In

a repl. 'coming'

---

1. See above, p. 198, n. 2.
2. John Mitchell, flagmaker, was in the midst of a dispute with the Navy

Board about a bill: above, p. 73 & n. 2.

the evening I received letters out of the country; among others, from my wife, who methinks writes so coldly that I am much troubled at it and I fear shall have much ado to bring her to her old good temper.

So home to supper and music, which is all the pleasure I have of late given myself or is fit I should others, spending too much time and money.

Going in, I stepped to Sir W. Batten and there stayed and talked with him, my Lady being in the country, and sent for some lobsters; and Mrs. Turner came in and did bring us an Umble-pie*a* hot out of her oven, extraordinary good, and afterward some spirits of her making (in which she hath great judgment), very good; and so home, merry with this night's refreshment.

9. Up; making water this morning (which I do every morn-ing as soon as I am awake) with greater plenty and freedom then I used to do, which I think I may impute to last night drinking of Elder=spiritts. Abroad, it raining hard, by water to Black-Fryers, and there went into a little alehouse and stayed while I sent to the Wardrobe; but Mr. Moore was gone out. Here I kissed three or four times the maid of the house, which is a pretty girl but very modest. And God forgive me, had a mind to something more. Thence to my lawyer's up and down to the Six Clerks' Office, where I find my bill against Tom Trice dismissed; which troubles me, it being through my neglect and will put me to charges.[1] So to Mr. Phillips and discoursed with him about finding me out somebody that will let me have for money an annuity of about 100*l* per annum for two lifes.[2] So home and there put up my riding things against the evening, in case Mr. Moore should continue his mind to go to Oxford;[3] which I have little mind to do, the weather continuing so bad and the waters high. Dined at home; and Mr. Moore in the afternoon

a MS. 'by'

1. For this Chancery case, see above, ii. 215 & n. 1; below, p. 351, n. 2. On this day Pepys swore an affidavit alleging that the defendant had not given proper notice to the plaintiffs, and deposing that he had further witnesses in Huntingdonshire to examine: Whitear, p. 160.

2. No further trace of this pro-posal has been found. Cf. above, pp. 199–200.

3. See above, p. 199 & n. 1.

comes to me and concludes not to go.   Sir W. Batten and I sot a little this afternoon at the office; and then I by water to Deptford and there mustered the yard, purposely (God forgive me) to find out Bagwell, a carpenter whose wife is a pretty woman, that I might have some occasion of knowing him and forcing her to come to the office again – which I did so luckily, that going thence, he and his wife did of themselfs meet me in the way, to thank me for my old kindness; but I spoke little to her, but shall give occasion for her coming to me.[1]   Her husband went along with me to show me Sir W. Penn's lodging;[2]   which I knew before, but only to have a time of speaking to him and sounding him.   So left, and I went in to Sir W. Penn, who continues ill still, and worse I think then before.   He tells me my Lady Castlemayne was at Court, for all this talk, this week; which I am glad to hear, but it seems the King is stranger then ordinary to her.

Thence walked home as I use to do; and to bed presently, having taken great cold in my feet by walking in the dirt this day in thin shoes, or some other way – so that I begun to be in pain; and with warm clothes made myself better by morning, but yet in pain.

10.   Up late, and by water to Westminster-hall, where I met Pierce the Chyrurgeon, who tells me that for certain the King is grown colder to my Lady Castlemaine then ordinary, and that he believes he begins to love the Queene and doth make much of her, more then he used to do.   Up to the Lobby, and there sent out for Mr. Coventry and Sir W. Batten.   And told them, if they thought convenient, I would go to Chatham today, Sir J. Mennes being already there at a pay, and I could do such and such businesses there; which they*a* thought well of, and so I went home and prepared myself to go after dinner (with Sir W. Batten).

Sir W. Batten and Mr. Coventry tell me that my Lord Bristoll

a repl. 'he'

---

1. Mrs Bagwell was to be Pepys's mistress, 1664–7. Her husband appears to have been William, ship's carpenter, whose father, Owen Bag-well, was now foreman-shipwright at Deptford yard. Pepys's 'old kind-ness' has not been traced.

2. See above, p. 214, n. 5.

hath this day impeached my Lord Chancellor in the House of Lords of high treason: the chief of the articles are these:[1]

1. That he should be the occasion of the peace made with Holland lately, upon such disadvantageous terms;[2] and that he was bribed to it.
2. That Dunkirke was also sold by his advice chiefly, so much to the damage of England.[3]
3. That he had 6000*l* given him for the drawing-up or promoting of the Irish declaracion lately, concerning the division of the lands there.[4]
4. He did carry on the design of the Portugall match, so much to the prejudice of the crown of England, notwithstanding that he knew that the Queene is not capable of bearing children.[5]
5. That the Dukes marrying of his daughter was a practice of

1. This summary bears little relation to the articles of impeachment, in which Pepys's items numbered 1, 3, 5 and 6 do not appear at all: see *LJ*, xi. 555+.
2. The commercial treaty of September 1662.
3. A charge later revived in the final attack on Clarendon; below, viii. 485. His was the primary, though not the sole, responsibility. See Sandwich's statement: below, vii. 55 & n. 4. Clarendon's account (*Life*, ii. 242+) puts the responsibility in the first place on the Treasurer, secondly, on the service authorities (Albemarle and Sandwich), and only thirdly on himself. But it seems that it was he who opened the negotiations and who in the end overrode the hesitations of the negotiating committee. See C. L. Grose in *AHR*, 39/1+; L. Lemaire, *Le rachat de Dunkerque: documents inédits*; Feiling, pp. 59–60. The public took the simplest view possible and blamed Clarendon: cf. below, vi. 39.

4. Apart from the original declaration on this subject (30 November 1660), there had been four others issued since October 1662: Steele (*Ireland*), nos 670, 691, 697, 705. In its final form Bristol's accusation alleged malversation of revenue. Clarendon had received a grant of £20,000 from the Irish Exchequer in April 1662. Both he and his friend Ormond (Lord-Lieutenant) were the particular enemies of Bristol, Bennet and Lady Castlemaine. T. Carte, *Ormond*, iv. 32+, 152; Lister, ii. 463+; ib., iii. 246, 478+.
5. Pepys's account is mistaken. Bristol accused Clarendon of not having insisted on an official Anglican marriage service. It was the rumour-mongers who accused him of arranging a barren marriage in order to improve the chances of his son-in-law's succeeding to the throne: cf. Reresby, *Memoirs* (ed. Browning), pp. 41, 204; Ailesbury, *Memoirs*, i. 7; Wood, *L. & T.*, i. 440.

his, thereby to raise his family; and that it was done by indirect courses.

6. That the breaking-off of the match with Parma (in which he[1] was imployed at the very time when the match with Portugall was made up here, which he took as*a* a great Slurr to him, and so it was; and that, endeed, is the chief occasion of all this fewde).

7. That he hath endeavoured to bring in popery and wrote to the Pope for a cap for a subject of the King of Englands (my Lord Aubigny);[2] and some say that he lays it to the Chancellor that a good protestant Secretary (Sir Edwd Nicholas) was laid aside, and a papist, Sir H. Bennet, put in his room – which is very strange, when the last of these two is his[3] own creature and such an enemy accounted to the Chancellor that they never did nor do agree, and all the world did judge the Chancellor to be falling from the time that Sir H. Bennet was brought in. Besides, my Lord Bristoll being a Catholique himself, all this is very strange.

These are the main of the Articles. Upon which, the Lord Chancellor desired that the noble Lord that brought in these articles would sign to them with his hand; which my Lord Bristol did presently. Then the House did order that the Judges should, against Monday next, bring in their opinion whether these Articles are treason or no; and next, they would know whether

a repl. 'to'

---

1. Bristol. He had been foremost among the champions of a marriage with one of the two princesses of Parma, Maria Maddalena and Caterina, sisters of the reigning Duke. It was while he was in Italy making arrangements for the match, in April 1661, that Charles concluded the treaty with Portugal and recalled him. *CSPVen. 1659–61*, pp. 243–93, passim.

2. Cf. above, p. 211, n. 2. Clarendon knew and approved of the attempt to secure the appointment, but of any attempt 'to bring in popery' (a standard charge against a political enemy in impeachment cases) he was of course innocent. For the obscure matter of negotiations with Rome at this time, see D. Ogg, *Engl. in reign of Charles II*, i. 202–3.

3. Bristol's. Bennet was not a Papist: but see above, p. 47, n. 1. For his appointment, see above, iii. 226 & n. 2.

they were brought in regulerly or no, without leave of the Lords' House.[1]

After dinner I took boat (H. Russell)[2] and down to Gravesend in good time; and thence with a guide, post to Chatham, where I find Sir J. Mennes and Mr Wayth[a] walking in the garden; whom I told all this day's news, which I left the town full of, and it is great news and will certainly be in the consequence of it.

By and by to supper; and after long discourse, Sir J. Mennes and I, he saw me to my chamber – which not pleasing me, I sent word so to Mrs. Bradford[3] that I should be crowded into such a hole, while the Clerkes and boarders of her own take up the best rooms. However, I lay there and slept well.

11.[b] Up earely, and to the Docke and with the Storekeeper and other officers all the morning, from one office to another. At noon to the Hill-house in Comissioner Petts coach; and after paying the guardships, to dinner; and after dinner down to the Docke by coach, it raining hard, to see the *Prince* Lanched, which hath lain in the Docke in repairing these three years.[4] I went into her and was lanched in her. Thence by boat ashore, it raining and wet, to Mr. Barrows,[5] where Sir J. Mennes and Comissioner Pett; we stayed long eating sweetmeats and drinking, and looking over some antiquitys of Mr. Barrows; among others, an old manuscript Almanacke that I believe was made for some Monastery, in parchment; which I could spend much time upon to understand. Here was a pretty young lady, a niece of Barrows, which I took much pleasure to look on.

Thence by Barge to St. Mary Creeke, where Comissioner Pett (doubtful of the growing greatness of Portsmouth by the finding of those Creekes there)[6] doth design a Wett Docke at no

---

a repl. 'Comissioner Pett'   *b* repl. '10'

---

1. *LJ*, xi. 557. See below, p. 231, n. 2.
2. Waterman to the Navy Office.
3. Housekeeper of Hill House, where the Principal Officers stayed on their visits to Chatham.
4. Pepys had had much correspondence with Commissioner Pett about the progress of the repairs and the date of the launch: *CSPD 1663–4*, p. 168 etc. Twenty horses had been required to carry her rudder across the yard: ib., p. 184.
5. Storekeeper.
6. On 30 June the Board had ordered these creeks to be used for 4th-, 5th- and 6th-rate ships: NMM, SER 129, n.p.

great charge, and yet no little one; he thinks towards 10000*l*.
And that place endeed is likely to be a very fit place when the
King hath money to do it with.[1]

Thence I, it raining as hard as it could powre down, home to
the Hill-house and anon to supper; and after supper Sir J. Mennes
and I had great discourse with Captain Cox and Mr. Hempson[2]
about business of the yard, and perticularly of pursers accounts
with Hempson, who is a cunning knave in that poynt.

So late to bed; and Mr. Wayth being gone, I lay above in the
Treasurers bed – and slept well.

About 1 or 2 in the morning, the Curtains of my bed being
drawn waked me, and I saw a man stand there by the inside of my
bed, calling me "French dogg" twenty times, one after another;
and I starting, as if I would get out of bed, he fell a-laughing as
hard as he could drive – still calling me "French dog", and laid
his hand on my shoulder. At last, whether I said anything or no
I cannot tell, but I perceived the man, after he had looked wistely
upon me too and*a* found that I did not answer him to the names
that he called me by, which was Salmon[3] (Sir G. Carterets clerk)
and Robert Maddox, another of the clerks, he put off his hat of a
suddaine*b* and forebore laughing, and asked who I was – saying,
"Are you Mr. Pepys?" I told him "Yes" and now, being
come a little better to myself, found him to be Tom Willson
(Sir W. Batten's clerk); and fearing he might be in some melancholly fit, I was at a loss what to do or say. At last I asked him
what he meant: he desired my pardon for that he was mistaken,
for he thought verily (not knowing of my coming to lie there)

a repl. 'to'   *b* smudge over word

---

1. Various estimates for a wet dock
on the Medway at Chatham (to hold
24 2nd-rates) had been made in 1662,
but were about double the cost of
Pett's proposed improvements at St
Mary's Creek, which was a mile or
so to the north. See Bodl., MS. Eng.
hist. *c.* 311, p. 101; *CSPD 1661–2*,
p. 517; *CSPD Add. 1660–85*,
p. 79; Longleat, Coventry MSS

98, f. 100*r*. The project was revived in the 1670s and in 1681–2, and
was successfully resisted by Pepys on
the ground that the ships would be
exposed to enemy attack: *Letters*,
pp. 133, 137; Rawl. A 460; Bryant,
ii. 375 etc.

2. Master-Attendant and Clerk of
the Survey respectively.

3. Solomon Soulemont.

that it had been Salmon the Frenchman, with whom he entended to have made some sport. So I made nothing of it, but bid him good-night; and I after a little pause to sleep again – being well pleased that it ended no worse – and being a little the better pleased with it because it was the Surveyors clerke, which will make sport when I come to tell Sir W. Batten of it, it being a report that old Edgeborough,[1] the former Surveyor who died here, doth now and then walk.

12. *Lords day.* Up; and meeting Tom Willson, he asked my pardon again; which I easily did give him, telling him only that it was well I was not a woman with child, for it might have made me miscarry.

With Sir J. Mennes to church, where an indifferent good sermon. Here I saw Mrs. Becky Allen, who hath been married and is this day Churched, after her bearing a child. She is grown tall but looks very white and thin. And I can find no occasion while I am here to come to have her company, which I desire and expected in my coming; but only, coming out of the church, I kissed her and her sister and mother-in-law.

So to dinner, Sir J. Mennes, Comissioner Pett and I, &c.; and after dinner walked in the garden, it being a very fine day, the best we have had this great while, if not this whole summer.

To church again; and after that walked through the Rope-ground to the Docke, and there over and over the Docke and grounds about it and storehouses &c. with the officers of the yard; and then to Comissioner Petts and had a good Sullybub and other good things, and merry. Comissioner[a] Pett showed me alone his bodys as a Secrett[2] (which I find afterward, by discourse with Sir J. Mennes, that he had shown them him) wherein he seems to suppose great mystery in the nature of Lynes to be hid, but I do not understand it at all.

Thence walked to the Hill-house, being myself much dissatis-fyed, and more then I thought I should have been, with Com-issioner Pett, being by what I saw since I came hither, convinced

a repl. 'so'

1. Kenrick Edisbury: for his ghost, see above, ii. 68. For Pepys's disbelief in ghosts, see above, p. 186 & n. 1.

2. Shipwrights usually kept secret their sectional drawings ('bodys') of ships. See G. P. B. Naish in C. Singer *et al.*, *Hist. Technol.*, iii. 489.

that he is not able to exercise that command in the yard over the officers that he ought to do, or somebody else, if ever the service be well looked after there.

Sat up long with Sir J. Mennes talking, and he speaking his mind in slighting of the Comissioner, for which I wish there was not so much reason. For I do see he is but a man of words, though endeed he is the ablest man that we have to do service, if he would or durst. Sir J. Mennes being gone to bed, I took Mr. Whitfield, one of the Clerkes, and walked to the Docke about 11 at night and there got a boat and a crew and rowed down to the Guardshipps, it being a most pleasant Mooneshine evening that ever I saw almost. The Guardshipps were very ready to hale us, being no doubt commanded thereto by their Captain, who remembers how I surprized them the last time I was here;[1] however, I found him ashore, but the ship in pretty good order and the armes well fixed, charged, and primed. Thence to the *Souverayne*, where I find no officers aboard, no armes fixed, nor any powder to prime their few guns which were charged, without bullet though.

So to the *London*, where neither officer nor anybody awake; I boarded her and might have done what I would, and at last could[a] find but three little boys.

And so spent the whole night in visiting all the ships; in which I found, for the most part, ne'er an officer aboard nor any men so much as awake; which I was grieved to[b] find, especially so soon after a great Larum, as Comissioner Pett brought us word that he provided against and put all in a posture of defence but a week ago – all which I am resolve[d] to represent to the Duke.

13. So it being high day, I put in to shore, and to bed for two hours just; and so up again and with the Storekeeper and Clerk[c] of the Ropeyard up and down the Docke and Ropehouse. And by and by mustered the yard and instructed the Clerk of the Cheque in my new way of Call=booke;[2] and that and other things done, to the Hill-house and there we eat something; and so by barge to Rochester and there took Coach (hired for our passage to London) (and Mrs. Allen the clerke of the Ropeyard's wife with

a   MS. 'would'   b   repl. 'to' misplaced on line
c   l.h. repl. s.h. 'b'-

1. On 4 August 1662.   2. See above, iii. 234 & n. 2.

us, desiring her passage); and it being a most pleasant and warm day, we got by 4 a-clock home – in our way, she telling us in what condition Becky Allen is married, against all expectation; a fellow that proves to be a coxcombe and worth little, if anything at all, and yet are entered into a way of living above their condition that will ruin them presently;* for which, for the lady's sake I am much troubled.[1]

Home; I find all well there and after dressing myself, I walked to the Temple and there from my Cosen Roger hear that the Judges have this day brought in their answer to the Lords: that the Articles against my Lord Chancellor are not Treason; and tomorrow they are to bring in their arguments to the House for the same.[2]

This day also, the King did send by my Lord Chamberlin to the Lords to tell them from [him] that the most of the articles against my Lord Chancellor he himself knew to be false.[3] Thence by water to White-hall; and so walked to St. James's but missed Mr. Coventry.

I met the Queene-Mother walking in the pell Mell, led by my Lord St. Albans. And finding many coaches at the gate, I find upon enquiry that the Dutchesse is brought to bed of a boy.[4]

And hearing that the King and Queene are rode abroad with the Ladies of Honour to the parke, and seeing a great croude of gallants staying here to see their return, I also stayed, walking up and down; and among others, spying a man like Mr. Pembleton (though I have little reason to think it should be he, speaking and discoursing long with my Lord D'Aubigne); yet Lord, how my blood did rise in my face and I fall into a sweat from my old Jealousy and hate, which I pray God remove from me.

By and by, the King and Queene, who looked in this dress, a white laced waistcoat and a crimson short petty-coate and her hair

---

1. Rebecca Allen, then about 18, had in August 1662 married Henry Jowles of Chatham, aged about 24. Her sister had married rather better – her husband later this year succeeded his father-in-law as Clerk of the Rope-yard at Chatham.

2. *LJ*, xi. 559.

3. Ib., loc. cit.; the King's message also made it clear that the charges were a 'libel against his Person and Government' and that he would in due course take proceedings against their author.

4. James Stuart, second son of the Duke and Duchess of York; born at St James's Palace, 11 July; cr. Duke of Cambridge, 1664; d. 1667.

dressed *a la negligence*, mighty pretty; and the King rode hand in hand with her.   Here was also my Lady Castlemayne rode among the rest of the ladies, but the King took methought no notice of her; nor when they light did anybody press (as she seemed to expect, and stayed for it) to take her down, but was taken down by her own gentleman.   She looked mighty out of humour, and had a Yellow plume in her hat (which all took notice of) and yet is very handsome – but very melancholy; nor did anybody speak*ᵃ* to her or she so much as smile or speak to anybody.   I fallowed them up into White-hall and into the Queenes presence, where all the ladies walked, talking and fidling with their hats and feathers, and changing and trying one another's, but on another's heads, and laughing.   But it was the finest sight to me, considering their great beautys and dress, that ever I did see in all my life.   But above all, Mrs. Steward in this dresse, with her hat cocked and a red plume, with her sweet eye, little Roman nose, and excellent *Taille*, is now the greatest beauty I ever saw I think in my life; and if ever woman can, doth exceed my Lady Castlemayne; at least, in this dresse.   Nor do I wonder if the King changes, which I verily believe is the reason of his coldness to my Lady Castlemayne.[1]

Here late with much ado I left to look upon them and went away; and by water in a boat with other strange company, there being no other to be had, and out of him into a sculler half to the Bridge and so home; and to Sir W. Batten, where I stayed telling him and Sir J. Mennes and Mrs. Turner, with great mirth, my being frighted at Chatham by Young Edgeborough;[2] and so home to supper and to bed – before I sleep, fancying myself to sport with Mrs. Steward with great pleasure.

14.   Up a little late, last night recoverying my sleepiness for the night before, which was lost; and so to my office to put papers

a   MS. 'spoke'

---

1. Cf. de Cominges to Louis XIV, London, 25 June/5 July 1663: 'Il y ait eu depuis peu, grande querelle entre les dames jusques là que le Roy menaça la dame ou il soupe tous les soirs [Castlemaine], de ne metre jamais le pied chez elle, si la Demoiselle [Stewart] n'y estoit': PRO, PRO 31/3/112, f. 55*v*.

2. *Recte* Willson: above, p. 226.

and things to right and making up my Journall from Wednesday last to this day.

All the morning at my office doing of business; at noon Mr. Hunt came to me and he and I to the Exchange and a Coffee-house and drank there; and thence to my house to dinner, whither my uncle Thomas came and he tells me that he is going down to Wisbich, there to try what he can recover of my uncle Day's estate.[1] And seems to have good arguments for what he doth go about, in which I wish him good speed. I made him almost foxed, the poor man having but a weak head and not used I believe nowadays to drink much wine. So after dinner, they being gone, I to the office, where we sat all the afternoon; and I late there at my office and so home to bed.

This day I hear the Judges, according to order yesterday, did bring into the Lords' House their reasons of their judgment in the business between my Lord Bristoll and the Chancellor; and the Lords do concur with the Judges that the Articles are not treason, nor regularly brought into the House; and so voted that a committee should be chosen to examine them, but nothing to be done therein till the next sitting of this parliament (which is like to be adjourned in a day or two); and in the meantime the two Lords to remain without prejudice done to either of them.[2]

15. Up and all the morning at the office; among other things, with Cooper the Purveyor, whose dullnesse in his proceeding in his work I was vexed at, and find that though he understands, it may be, as much as other men that profess skill in timber, yet I perceive that many things they do by roate, and very dully.

Thence home to dinner, whither Captain Grove came and dined with me, he going into the country today; among other discourse, he told me of discourse very much to my honour, both as to my care and ability, happening at the Duke of Albe-marle's table the other day, both from the Duke and the Duchesse themselfs; and how I paid so much a year to him whose place it

---

1. John Day of Leverington, Cambs., had died in 1649; both Thomas Pepys and William Wight brought proceedings. See Whitear, pp. 137–8; VCH, *Cambs.*, iv. 241, n. 41.

2. According to the judges' view, reported in the Lords on 13 July, no charge of high treason could be brought by one peer against another without the previous consent of the House: *LJ*, xi. 559.

was of right.[1]   And that Mr. Coventry did report thus of me –
which was greatly to my content, knowing how against their
minds I was brought into the Navy.[2]

Thence by water to Westminster and there spent a good deal
of time walking in the Hall, which is going to be repaired.   And
God forgive me, had a mind to have got Mrs. Lane abroad – or
fallen in with any woman else in that hot[a] humour.   But it so
happened she could not go out, nor I meet with anybody else;
and so I walked homeward, and in my way did many and great
businesses of my owne at the Temple among my lawyers and
others, to my great content – thanking God that I did not fall
into any company to occasion the spending of time and money.
To supper and then to a little viall and to bed, sporting in my
fancy with the Queen.

16.   Up and despatched things into the country – to my
father's – and two Keggs of Sturgeon and a dozen bottles of wine
to Cambrige for my Cosen Rogr. Pepys, which I gave him.   By
and by down by water on several Deale ships and stayed upon
a Stage in one place, seeing Calkers sheathing of a ship.[3]   Then
at Wapping to my carvers about my viall-head.   So home, and
thence to my viall-maker's in Bishopsgate-street; his name
is Wise, who is a pretty fellow at it.   Thence to the Exchange
and so home to dinner.   And then to my office, where a full
board and busy all the afternoon; and among other things, made
a great contract with Sir W. Warren for 40000 deales Swinsound,
at 3*l*. 17s. per cent.[4]   In the morning, before I went on the
water, I was at Thamestreet about some pitch; and there meeting Anthony Joyce, I took him and Mr. Stacy the Tarr merchant

a MS. 'haughty'

---

1. For the annuity which Pepys
paid to Thomas Barlow, see above,
i. 202 & n. 1.

2. Cf. above, i. 183–4.

3. The sheathing (to prevent
damage by ship-worms) usually
consisted of nailing below the water-
line 'elm board half an inch thick over
layers of Stockholm tar and hair of
equal thickness': G. P. B. Naish in
C. Singer *et al.*, *Hist. Technol.*, iii.

481. Experiments with lead sheathing were made later in the reign, but
the only effective device (copper-
bottoming) was not introduced until
the later 18th century.

4. The first draft of this contract, in
Pepys's hand (23 July) is in PRO,
SP 29/77, no. 42. Svinesund deals
were from Norway: see above, ii.
118, n. 3.

to the tavern – where Stacy told me many old stories of my Lady Battens former poor condition, and how her former husband*a* [1] broke, and how she came to her estate.

At night, after office done, I went to Sir W. Batten, where my Lady and I [had] some high words about emptying our houses of office; where I did tell her my mind and at last agreed that it should be done through my office, and so all well. So home to bed.

17. Up; and after doing some business at my office, Creede came to me and I took him to my viall makers; and there I heard the famous Mr. Stefkins[2] play admirably well, and yet I find it as it is alway, I over-expected. I took him to the Taverne and find him a temperate sober man, at least he seems so to me. I commit the direction of my viall to him.

Thence to the Change and so home, Creede and I to dinner. And after dinner Sir W. Warren came to me and he and I in my closett about his last night's contract; and from thence to discourse of measuring of timber, wherein I made him see that I could understand that matter well, and did both learn of and teach him something.*b* Creede being gone, through my staying talking with him so long, I went alone by water down to Redriffe; and so to see and sit and talk with Sir W Pen;[3] where I did speak very plainly concerning my thoughts of Sir G. Carteret and Sir J. Mennes – so as it may cost me some trouble if he should tell them again; but he said as much or more to me concerning them both – which I may remember if ever it should come forth; and yet nothing but what is true and my real opinion of them: that they neither do understand at this day Creedes accounts[4] nor do deserve to be imployed in their places without better care, but that the King had better give them greater salaries to stand still and do nothing.

Thence coming home, I was saluted by Bagwell and his wife (the woman I have a kindness for) and they would have me into

a MS. 'hand band'   *b* repl. 'self'

1. Woodstock (Christian name unknown); see *Comp.*: 'Batten, Sir William'.
2. One of the German violists of that name: see *Comp.* (E).
3. See above, p. 214, n. 5.
4. See above, p. 198, n. 1.

their little house; which I was willing enough to, and did salute his wife. They had got wine for me and I perceive live prettily; and I believe the woman a virtuous modest woman.

Her husband*ᵃ* walked through to Redriffe with me, telling me things that I asked of in the yard; and so by water home, it being likely to rain again tonight, which God forbid. To supper and to bed.

18. Up and to my office, where all the morning. And Sir J. Mennes and I did a little, and but a little, business at the office. So I eate a bit of victuals at home and so abroad to several places, as my booksellers; and then to Thomson the instrument maker's to bespeak a Ruler for my pocket for Timber &c., which I believe he will do to my mind. So to the Temple, Wardrobe, and lastly to Westminster-hall – where I expected some bands made me by Mrs. Lane; and while she went to the starchers for them, I stayed at Mrs. Howletts, who with her husband*ᵇ* were abroad, and only their daughter (which I call my wife)¹ was in the shop; and I took occasion to buy a pair of gloves to talk to her, and I find her a pretty-spoken girl and will prove a mighty handsome wench – I could love her very well.

By and by Mrs. Lane comes; and my bands not being done, she and I parted and met at the Crowne in the palace-yard, where we eat (a chicken I sent for) and drank and were mighty merry, and I had my full liberty of towsing her and doing what I would but the last thing of all; for I felt as much as I would and made her feel my thing also, and put the end of it to her breast and by and by to her very belly – of which I am heartily ashamed. But I do resolve never to do more so.

But Lord, to see what a mind she hath to a husband and how she showed me her hands to tell her her fortune, and everything that she asked ended always, whom and when she was to marry; and I pleased her so well, saying as I know she would have me; and then she would say she had been with all the Artists in town and they alway told her the same things – as that she should live long and rich, and have a good husband but few children,

a MS. 'hand [s.h.]-band [l.h.]'　　　*b* repl. 'hand band'

---

1. See below, p. 242.

and a great fit of sickness, and twenty other things, which she says she hath alway been told by others.

Here I stayed late before my bands were done, and then they came; and so I by water to the Temple and thence walked home, all in a sweat with my tumbling of her and walking; and so a little supper and to bed – fearful of having taken cold.

19. *Lords day.* Lay very long in pleasant dreams till church-time, and so up; and it being foul weather, so that I cannot walk as I entended to meet my Cosen Roger at Tho. Pepys's house (whither he rode last night) to Hatcham[1] – I went to church, where a sober Doctor made a good sermon. So home to dinner alone. And then to read a little and so to church again, where the Scott made a ordinary sermon; and so home to my office and there read over my vowes, and encreased them by a vow against all strong drink till November next, of any sort or Quantity; by which I shall try how I can forbear it. God send it may not prejudice my health, and then I care not. Then I fell to read over a silly play, writ by a person of Honour (which is, I find, as much as to say a coxcomb) called *Love a la mode*.[2]

And that being ended – home and played on my lute and sung psalms till bedtime; then to prayers and to bed.

20. Up and to my office; and then walked to Woolwich, reading Bacon's *faber Fortune*,[3] which the oftener I read the more I admire. There found Captain Cocke, and up and down to many places to look after matters; and so walked back again with him to his house and there dined very finely. With much ado, obtained an excuse from drinking of wine, and did only taste a drop of Sacke which he had for his lady; who is, he fears, a little consumptive and her beauty begins to want its colour. It was Malago sack,[4] which he says is certainly 30 year old. I tasted a drop and it was excellent wine, like a spirit rather then wine.

1. Near Deptford. Thomas Pepys of Westminster ('the Executor'), Pepys's cousin, had recently moved to Hatcham from Covent Garden.

2. A comedy by 'T.S.' – probably Thomas Southland. It was acted by amateurs and published in 1663. PL 1075(11). (A).

3. See above, ii. 102, n. 1.

4. On 20 January 1662 Pepys had had his hogshead of sherry filled up with malaga.

Thence by water to the office; and taking some papers, by water to White-hall and St. James's; but there being no meeting with the Duke today, I returned by water and down to Greenwich to look after some blocks that I saw a load carried off by a cart*a* from Woolwich, the King's yard.[1] But I could not find them and so returned; and being heartily weary, I made haste to bed. And being in bed, made Will read and conster three or four Latin verses in the bible and chid him for forgetting his grammer. So to sleep; and slept ill all the night, being so very weary, and feavourish with it. And so lay long in the ⟪21.⟫ morning, till I heard people knock at my door; and I took it to be about 8 a-clock (but afterward found myself a little mistaken) and so I rose and ranted at Will and the maid and swore I could find my heart to kick them downstairs, which the mayde mumbled at mightily. It was my brother, who stayed and talked with me; his chief business being about his going about to build his house new at the top, which will be a great charge for him and above his judgment.[2]

By and by comes Mr. Deane of Woolwich with his draught of a Ship and the Bend and main Lynes in the body of a ship, very finely, and which doth please me mightily and so am resolved to study hard and learn of him to understand a body;[3] and I find him a very pretty fellow in it and rational,[4] but a little conceited – but that's no matter to me. At noon, by my Lady Battens desire, I went over the water to Mr. Castles, who brings his wife[5] home

a l.h. repl. l.h. 'carryed'

---

1. It was alleged that most of the houses in Chatham were built of chips purloined from the dockyard: J. Hollond, *Discourses* (ed. Tanner), p. 151 & n.

2. Tom had on 14 June told Pepys of his thriving condition. The house was the one in Salisbury Court in which Pepys had been born. Tom was given permission at the end of July to 'lay and frame his timber' in the churchyard in order to 'new build part of his house that lies neere the churchyard door': GL, 6554/1, f. 253r; Whitear, pp. 100–1. The work was completed by 19 October, when Pepys admired the results. Whether much rebuilding had been involved is doubtful: Tom rented the house, and he seems to have left no building debts at his death in the following year.

3. See above, p. 227, n. 2.

4. Sir William Petty in 1683 spoke of 'the benefit he received ... from Sir A. Deane's discourse, beyond all that he ever met with from the great builders of England with whom he has had conversation for forty years past': *Naval Minutes*, p. 211.

5. Martha, daughter of the Battens.

to his own house today; where I find a great many good old women, and my Lady, Sir W. Batten and Sir J. Mennes.

A good, handsome, plain dinner; and then walked in the garden, which is pleasant enough, more then I expected there. And so Sir J. Mennes, Sir W. Batten, and I by water to the office and there sat; and then I by water to the Temple about my law businesses;[1] and back again home and wrote letters to my father and wife about my desire that they should observe the feast at Brampton[2] and have my Lady and the family. And so home to supper and bed – my head akeing all this day from my last night's bad rest and yesterday's distempering myself with over-walking, and today knocking my head against a low door in Mr. Castles house.

This day the parliament kept a fast for the present unseasonable weather.[3]

22. Up; and by and by comes my uncle Tho., to whom I paid 10*l.* for his last half year's annuity – and did get his and his son's hand and seal for the confirming to us Piggotts morgage, which was forgot to be expressed in our late agreement with him, though entended.[4] And therefore they might have cavilled at it if they would.

Thence abroad, calling at several places upon small errands; among others, to my brother Toms barbers and had my hair cut while his boy played on the vyallin; a plain boy, but hath a very good genius and understands the book very well. But to see what a shift he made for a string of red silke was very pleasant. Thence to my Lord Crews; my Lord not being come home, I met and stayed below with Captain Ferrer, who was come to wait upon my Lady Jemimah to St. James's, she being one of the four

1. The Chancery suit against Tom Trice: q.v. above, ii. 215, n. 1. The latter filed an affidavit this day: Whitear, p. 160.

2. Cf. above, iii. 144 & n. 3.

3. Two services were held at St Margaret's: *CJ*, viii. 526.

4. See Thomas Pepys and his son to Pigott, 20 July, giving their con- sent (as heirs-at-law) to Pigott's proposal to sell land in order to pay the mortgage owed to the executors; witnessed by Hewer. Copies (in hands of Pepys and Hewer) in PL (unoff.), Freshfield MSS, nos 10, 11. Cf. *Comp.*: 'Pepys, Robert'. For the 'late agreement', see above, p. 42 & n. 2.

ladies that holds up the mantle at the christening this afternoon of the Dukes child, a boy.[1]

In discourse of the ladies at Court, Captain Ferrer tells me that my Lady Castlemayne is now as great again as ever[a] she was, and that her going away was only a fit of her own, upon some slighting words of the King's, so that she called for her coach at a Quarter of an hour's warning and went to Richmond;[2] and the King the next morning, under pretence of going a-hunting, went to see her and make friends, and never was a-hunting at all – after which she came back to Court and commands the King as much as ever, and hath and doth what she will.

No longer ago then last night there was a private entertainment made for the King and Queene at the Duke of Buckinghams, and she was not invited.   But being at my Lady Suffolkes her aunts (where my Lady Jemimah and my Lord Sandwich dined) yesterday, she was heard to say, "Well, much good may [it] do them, and for all that I will be as merry as they;" and so she went home and caused a great supper to be prepared; and after the King had been with the Queen at Wallingford-house, he came to my Lady Castlemayn's and was there all night, and my Lord Sandwich with him; which was the reason my Lord lay in town all night, which he hath not done a great while before.

He tells me he believes that as soon as the King can get a husband for Mrs. Steward, that however my Lady Castlemayne's nose will be out of Joynt, for that she comes to be in great esteem and is more handsome then she.

I find by his words that my Lord Sandwich finds some pleasure in the country where he now is, whether he means one of the daughters of the house or no, I know not; but hope the contrary, that he thinks he is very well pleased with staying there.[3]   But yet,

---

a repl. 'if'

---

1. See above, p. 229 & n. 4. 'The witnesses were the King and King of France with our two Queens, the last three by proxy': HMC, *Rawdon Hastings*, ii. 142. Of the eight children born to the Duke of York and his first wife, only two (later Queen Mary and Queen Anne) survived childhood.

2. Cf. above, iii. 139 & n. 2.   For her recent absence from court, see above, p. 213 & n. 3.   She gave birth to a boy (later 1st Duke of Grafton) in September.

3. He was at Chelsea, living with the Beckes.   For his affair with Betty Becke ('a woman of a very bad fame'), see below, pp. 270-1.

upon breaking up of the parliament (which the King by a message today says shall be on Monday next),[1] he resolves to go.

Ned Pickering the Coxcombe, notwithstanding all his hopes and my Lord's assistance (wherein I am sorry to hear my Lord hath much concerned himself) is defeated of the place he expected under the Queen.[2]

He came hither by and by and brought some Jewells for my Lady Jem to put on, with which and her other clothes she looks passing well.

I stayed and dined with my Lord Crew; who, whether he was not so well pleased with me as he used to be or that his head was full of business (as I believe it was), he hardly spoke one word to me all dinner-time, we dining alone, only young Jacke Crew, Sir Tho's son, with us.

After dinner, I bid him farewell. Sir Thomas, I hear, is gone this morning ill to bed, so I had no mind to see him.

Thence homeward; and in my way, first called at Wottons the shoe-maker who tells me the reason of Harris's going from Sir W. Davenant's house – that he grew very proud and demanded 20*l* for himself extraordinary there, [more] then Batterton or anybody else, upon every new play, and 10*l* upon every Revive – which, with other things, Sir W. Davenant would not give him; and so he swore he would never act there more – in expectation of being received in the other House; but the King will not suffer it, upon Sir W. Davenants desire that he would not; for then he might shut up house, and that is true.[3] He tells me that his going is at present a great loss to the house. And that he fears that he hath a stipend from the other House privately.

He tells me that the fellow grew very proud of late, the King and everybody else crying him up so high, and that above Baterton, he being a more ayery man, as he is endeed. But yet Baterton, he says, they all say doth act some parts that none but himself can do.

---

1. *CJ*, viii. 529.

2. In August 1664 he was appointed a Gentleman of the Privy Chamber in ordinary to the King.

3. Henry Harris was one of the leading actors in the Duke of York's Company, managed by Davenant. According to the letters patent issued to Davenant in 1662, an actor who withdrew from one of the two London companies could not be recruited by the other. Harris was popular and influential, and the Duke of York persuaded Davenant to accede to his demands: below, p. 347. (A).

Thence to my bookseller's and find my *Waggoners*[1] done – the very binding cost me 14*s* – but they are well done, and so with a porter home with them; and so by water to Ratcliffe and there went to speak with Cumberford the platt=maker. And there saw his manner of working, which is very fine and labourious. So down to Detford, reading Ben. Johnsons *Devil is an Asse.*[2] And so to see Sir W. Penn, who I find walking out of doors a little – but could not stand long;[3] but in a-doors and I with him and stayed a great while talking – I taking a liberty to tell him my thoughts in things of the office, that when he comes abroad again he may know what to think of me and to value me as he ought. Walked home, as I used to do. And being weary and after some discourse with Mr. Barrow,[4] who came to see and take his leave of me, he being tomorrow to set out toward the Isle of man – I went to bed.

This day I hear that the Moores have made some attaques upon the out workes of Tanger; but my Lord Tiviott, with the loss of about 200 men, did beat them off, and killed many of them.[5]

Tomorrow the King and Queene for certain go down to Tunbrige.[6] But the King comes back again against Monday, to raise the parliament.

1. The English translation of Lucas Janssen Wagenaer's *Spieghel der zeevaerdt*, published c. 1588 by Anthony Ashley as *The mariner's mirrour*. Pepys had the two parts bound together c. 1680: his copy survives as PL 2800, together with copies of the original Dutch version (Leyden, 1584) and the Latin (Amsterdam, 1591): PL 2798, 2799. It was a description – the most famous of its kind – of the sea-coasts of W. Europe, with charts. All such collections came to be known as 'Waggoners'. D. Gernez in *Mar. Mirr.*, 23/190+, 332+. Pepys has a long note on the English transl. in *Naval Minutes*, pp. 347–50.

2. A comedy, acted in 1616, and published in 1631; PL 2645 (*Works*, 1692 ed.). (A).

3. See above, p. 214, n. 5.

4. Philip Barrow, Storekeeper o₁ Chatham yard, had quarrelled with his colleagues; see above, p. 149 & n. 2.

5. The Moors attacked the troops working on the fortifications during their dinner-hour on 14 June. '200' is presumably a slip for '20': see below, p. 301; Routh, p. 39.

6. According to the French ambassador, the Queen went to take the waters in the hope they would cure her sterility. The King probably went to be near Frances Stuart. They travelled on 25 July. Tunbridge Wells was at this time one of the most fashionable of the spas, and its waters were highly regarded, though 'the wits maintained that it was the gallants and not the waters that cured barrenness': R. Lennard (ed.), *Englishmen at rest and play*, p. 56. See op. cit., pp. 54+; M. Barton, *Tunbridge Wells*, pp. 137+.

23. Up and to my office; and thence, by information from Mr. Ackworth, I went down to Woolwich and mustered the three East India ships that lie there[1] – believing that there is great juggleing between the pursers and Clerk of the Cheque in cheating the King of the wages and victuals of men that do not give attendance. And I find very few on board.

So to the yard and there mustered the yard; and found many faults and discharged several fellows that were absent from their business.[2]

I stayed also, by Mr. Ackeworths desire, at dinner with him and his wife; and there was a simple fellow, a gentleman I believe of the Court, there, their kinsman, that made me I could have little discourse or begin acquaintance with Ackeworths wife; and so after dinner away with all haste home and there find Sir J. Mennes and Sir W. Batten at the office; and by Sir W. Batten's testimony and Sir G Carterets concurrence (*vide* memorandum= book of the office this day)[3] was forced to consent to a business of Captain Cockes timber, as bad as anything we have lately

1. The *Dunkirk*, *Leopard* and *Mary Rose*; E. Indiamen hired to the royal navy as part of the squadron which had sailed in 1662 to take possession of Bombay.

2. In August 1662 Pepys had similarly disciplined the Woolwich absentees: above, iii. 179, n. 2.

3. The office memoranda books have now disappeared. In October 1688 four were still extant but only two covered any of the diary period (January 1665–March 1667; June 1668–June 1673): BM, Add. 9303, f. 124*v*. Pepys kept two personal memoranda books which have survived. One (PRO, Adm. 106/ 3520) is entitled in Pepys's hand 'Conclusions and Memorandums occasionall', and in a clerk's hand 'Memorandums and Conclusions of the Navy Board from July 1660 to 21 May 1668'. It begins with a section in Pepys's hand covering July 1660 to 24 July 1662, and thereafter is entered in a variety of hands, the last entry being dated 18 June 1668. The second is his 'Navy White Book' (PL 2581:) q.v. below, v. 116, n. 1. It is usually impossible to identify with certainty the memoranda books mentioned in the diary: not only has the office series completely disappeared, but since he probably made notes of the same matter in several books, the mere discovery of a note in one of them is inconclusive. His book of 'Navy Collections' seems to have been a more systematic reference book with an index: see above, p. 11, n. 1.

disputed about – and all through Mr. Coventry's not being with us.[1]

So up, and to supper with Sir W. Batten upon a soused mullett, very good meat; and so home and to bed.

24. Up pretty earely (though of late I have been faulty by an hour or two every morning of what I should do) and by water to the Temple and there took leave of my Cosen Roger Pepys, who goes out of town today. So to Westminster-hall, and there at Mrs. Michells shopp sent for beer and sugar, and drank and made great cheer with it among her and Mrs. Howlett, her neighbour, and their daughters, especially Mrs. Howletts daughter Betty, which is a pretty girl and one I have long called wife; being, I formerly thought, like my own wife. After this good neighbourhood, which I do to give them occasion of speaking well and commending me in some company that now and then I know comes to their shops – I went to the Six Clerks Office and there had a Writt[2] for Tom Trice and paid 20s for it to Wilkinson; and so up and down to many places; among others, to my viall=makers and there saw the head, which now pleases me mightily. And so home and being sent for presently to Mr. Blands, where Mr. Povey, Gauden and I were invited to dinner – which we had very finely, and great plenty but for drink, though many and good; I drunk nothing but small beer and water, which I drunk so much that I wish it may not do me hurt.[3]

They have a kinswoman they call daughter in the house, a short, ugly, red-haired slut that plays upon the virginalls and sings, but after such a country manner, I was weary of it but yet could not but commend it. So by and by after dinner comes Monsieur Gotier,[4] who is beginning to teach her; but Lord, what a drolle fellow it is, to make her hold open her mouth and telling this and that so drolly, would make a man burst; but himself I perceive sings very well.

1. Cocke was trying to sell to the Board 300 loads of Eastland plank which they did not want, and had appealed to Coventry to confirm his statement that the timber was contracted for in 1661: PRO, SP 46/136, no. 81; *CSPD 1663–4*, p. 214.

Pepys made a note of the matter in PRO, Adm. 106/3520, f. 14r.
2. See below, pp. 346–7, 351, 384–5.
3. Cf. above, iii. 47.
4. Identity uncertain; the name of a large family of 16th- and 17th-century lutenists. See *Comp.* (E).

Anon we sat down again to a Collacion of cheesecakes, tarts, custards*a* and such-like, very handsome; and so up and away home, where I at my office a while, till disturbed by Mr. Hill of Cambrige,[1] with whom I walked in the garden a while; and thence home and in my dining-room walked, talking of several matters of state till 11 at night – giving him a glass of wine.

I was not unwilling to hear him talk; though he is full of words, yet a man of large conversation, especially among the presbyters and Independents. He tells me that certainly, let the Bishops alone and they will ruin themselfs, and he is confident that the King's declaracion about two years since[2] will be the foundation of the settlement of the Church some time or other – for the King will find it hard to banish all those that will appear nonconformists upon this act that is coming out against them.[3]

He being gone, I to bed.

25. Up and to my office, setting papers in order for these two or three days in which I have been hindered a little. Then having intended this day to go to Bansted Downes to see a famous race,[4] I sent Will to get himself ready to go with me and I also by and by home and put on my riding suit; and being ready, came to the office to Sir J. Mennes and Sir W. Batten and did a little of course* at the office this morning; and so by boate to White-hall, where I hear that the Race is put off because the Lords do sit in parliament today. However, having appointed Mr. Creed to come to me to Fox hall, I went over

a accidental line above symbol

1. Joseph Hill, late Fellow of Magdalene, ejected from his fellowship for nonconformity, 1662. (In 1653 he had admonished Pepys for drunkenness: above, i. 67, n. 5.)
2. The declaration of 25 October 1660, proposing a scheme of reconciliation between Anglicans and Presbyterians. See above, i. 278 & n. 2.
3. This was the abortive bill of 1663 against conventicles, which the Commons were now pressing the Lords to pass in view of the near approach of the end of session: *CJ*, viii. 531–2. Transportation was to be the penalty for owners of premises on which conventicles were held if they refused to pay a fine of £10 and publicly recant: Carte 81, ff. 240–1. Most Puritans, unlike Hill, were cast into gloom by the prospect, but the bill was not passed in this session for lack of time. Hill himself emigrated when the bill became law in 1664, and spent the remaining 43 years of his life as a Presbyterian pastor in Holland.
4. For horse-races at Banstead (on Epsom Downs), see above, p. 160 & n. 5. This day (St James's Day) was often kept as a holiday in London.

thither. And after some debate, he and I resolve to go to Clapham to Mr. Gaudens, who had sent his coach to this place for me, because I was to have my horse of him to go to the race. So I went thither by coach, and my Will by horse with me. Mr. Creede, he went over back again to Westminster to fetch his horse. When I came to Mr. Gaudens, our first thing was to show me his house which is almost built, wherein he and his family lives.¹ I find the house very regular and finely contrived, and the gardens and offices about it as convenient and as full of good variety as ever I saw in my life. It is true he hath been censured for laying out so much money; but he tells me that he built it for his brother, who is since dead (the Bishopp); who, when he should come to be Bishop of Winchester, which he was promised, to which Bishopricke at present there is no house, he did entend to dwell here.² Besides, with the good husbandry in making his bricks and other things, I do not think it costs him so much money as people think and discourse.

By and by to dinner, and just as we were setting down, in comes Mr. Creede. I saluted his³ lady and the young ladies, he having many pretty children, and his sister, the Bishop's widow, who was, it seems, Sir W Russells daughter, the Treasurer of the Navy⁴ – who, by her discourse at dinner, I find to be a very well-bred and a woman of excellent discourse –

1. This was a house which Pepys later came to know well, since it was bought after Denis Gauden's death in 1688 by William Hewer. A frequent guest there, Pepys lived in it continuously from c. June 1701, and died there in 1703. Evelyn (26 May 1703) described it as 'a very noble House & sweete place'. It was on the n. side of Clapham Common and was pulled down in the 1750s: PL (unoff.), Jackson MSS 20(3).

2. Dr John Gauden (brother of Denis Gauden, the navy victualler), Bishop of Exeter since 1660, was translated to Worcester in June 1662. He died in the following September, from chagrin (it was said) at not getting Winchester: John Toland, *Amyntor* (1669), pp. 90–1. Winchester House, Southwark (close by the foot of London Bridge), had been sold by Parliament in 1649, and though now restored to the bishop was let out to tenants in 1662. George Morley (Bishop of Winchester, 1662–84) replaced it by a house (Winchester House) at Chelsea. The 17th-century diocese of Winchester extended to the s. bank of the Thames at Southwark. VCH, *Surrey*, ii. 14; ib., iv. 146–8; LCC, *Survey of London* (*Bankside*), 22/45+; HMC, *Rep.*, 11/2/16–17.

3. Denis Gauden's.

4. Sir William Russell was Treasurer of the Navy, 1618–27, 1630–34, and in 1642; and joint-Treasurer with Vane, 1639–41.

even so much as to have my attencion all dinner with much more pleasure then I did give to Creede, whose discourse was mighty merry in inveighing against Mr. Gaudens[a] victuals that they had at sea the last voyage; which he prosecuted till methought the women begun to take it seriously.

After dinner, by Mr. Gaudens motion, we got Mrs. Gauden and her sister to sing to a viall, on which Mr. Gaudens eldest son (a pretty man, but a simple one methinks)[1] played – but very poorly and the Musique bad, but yet I commended it. Only, I do find that the ladies have been taught to sing and do sing well now, but that the viall puts them out. I took the viall and played some things from one of their books, Lyra-lessons, which they seemed to like well.[2]

Thus we passed an hour or two after dinner, and towards the evening we bade them Adieu and took horse, being resolved that instead of the race which fails us, we would go to Epsum; so we set out; and being gone a little way, I sent home Will to look to the house, and Creed and I rid forward – the road being full of citizens going and coming toward Epsum – where, when we came, we could hear of no lodging, the town so full. But which was better, I went towards Ashted, my old place of pleasure, and there (by direction of one goodman Arthur, whom we met on the way) we went to Farmer Page's,[3] at which direction he and I made good sport, and there we got a lodging in a little hole we could not stand upright in, upon a low truckle-bed. But rather then go further to look, we stayed there. And while supper was getting ready, I took him to walk up and down behind my Cosen Pepys's house[4] that was, which I find comes [a] little short of what I took it to be when I was a little boy (as things use commonly to appear greater then then when one comes to be a man and know more); and so up and down in the Closes which I know so well methinks, and account it good fortune that I lie here, that I may have opportunity to renew my old walks. It seems there is one Mr. Rouse, they call him the Queens Tailor,

a repl. 'P'-

---

1. Samuel; unlike his two younger brothers, he was not made an executor of his father's will (1684).

2. The instrument would be a lyra-viol, or a bass viol 'tuned lyra-way'. Cf. above, i. 295, n. 4. (E).

3. William Page lived at what is now known as Ashtead Park Farm House.

4. A large house, once the home of John Pepys (d.?1652), secretary to Lord Chief Justice Coke.

that lives there now.   So to our lodging to supper; and among
other meat, had a brave dish of creame, the best I ever eat in my
life – and with which we pleased ourselfs much.   And by and
by to bed, where with much ado, yet good sport, we made shift
to lie, but with little ease.   And a little Spaniell by us, which
ath fallowed us all the way – a pretty dog, and we believe that
fallows my horse and doth belong to Mrs. Gauden, which*a* we
therefore are very careful of.

26. *Lords day.*   Up and to the Wells,[1] where great store of
Citizens; which was the greatest part of the company, though
there were some others of better Quality.   I met many that I
knew; and we drunk each of us two pots and so walked away –
it being very pleasant to see how everybody turns up his tail,
here one and there another, in a bush, and the women in their
Quarters the like.[2]   Thence I walked Creede to Mr. Minnes's
house,[3] which hath now a good way made to it, and finely
walled round; and thence to Durdans and walked round it and
within the Court yard and to the bowling-green, where I have
seen so much mirth in my time; but now no family in it (my Lord
Barkely, whose it is, being with his family at London);[4] and so

a   repl. 'at'

1. The waters had been discovered
in 1618, and Epsom (providing good
air as well as medicinal waters) was
now the most considerable spa in
England, reaching the height of its
popularity c. 1690–1715: J. Toland,
A new description of Epsom (1711) in
Misc. Works (1747), ii. 61+ ; [Anon.],
Some particulars of Epsom (1825); Celia
Fiennes, *Journeys* (ed. Morris), pp.
337–8; F. L. Clark in *Surrey Arch.
Coll.*, 57/1+. It was predominantly
a Londoners' spa. There was, until
1706, only one well. View by W.
Schellinks (June 1662), in *Drawings of
Engl. in 17th cent.* (ed. P. H. Hulton),
ii. pl. 21.
2. The downs were mercifully
close to the purgative waters. For
ribald commentaries, see Sir John
Mennes's poem, 'To a friend upon

a journey to Epsam Well', in *Musarum
Deliciae* (1656); and *Flos Ingenii ...
being an exact description of Epsom ...*
(1674). Schellinks's drawings (see
above, n. 1) define the separate places
of retirement for men and women on
the open downs.
3. Woodcote House, the property
of George Mynne, whose daughter
had married John Evelyn's brother,
Richard: Evelyn, ii. 542 & n. 3.
4. The gardens at Durdans were
judged by Evelyn to be among the
best in England: Evelyn to Sir
Thomas Browne, 28 January 1658, in
Browne, *Works* (ed. Keynes), vi.
305. The Berkeleys had a town
house in St John's St, Clerkenwell:
John Smyth, *Lives of Berkeleys* (ed.
Maclean), ii. 428.

up and down by Minnes's wood, with great pleasure viewing my old walks and where Mrs. Hely and I did use to walk and talk, with whom I had the first sentiments of love and pleasure in woman's company, discourse and taking her by the hand – she being a pretty woman.

So I led him to Ashted church (by the place where Peter, my cosens man, went blindfold*a* and found a certain place we chose for him upon a wager) where we had a dull Doctor, one Downe, worse then I think ever Parson King was (of whom we made so much scorn);[1] and after sermon home and stayed while our dinner, a couple of large Chickens, were dressed and a good mess of Creame – which anon we had with good content.   And after dinner (we taking no notice of other lodgers in the house, though there was one that I knew, and knew and spoke to me, one Mr. Rider a merchant) he and I to walk; and I led him to the pretty little wood behind my Cosen's house, into which we got at last by clambering and our little dog with us; but when we were in among the Hazletrees and bushes, Lord, what a course did we run for an hour together, losing ourselfs; and endeed, I despaired I should ever come to any path, but still from thicket to thicket – a thing I could hardly have believed a man could have been lost so long in so small a room. At last, I found out a delicate* walk in the middle that goes quite through the wood; and then went out of the wood and hallowed Mr. Creede and made him hunt me from place to place; and at last went in and called him into my fine walk – the little dog still hunting with us through the wood.   In this walk, being all bewildred and weary and sweating, Creed, he lay down upon the ground; which I did a little but durst not long, but walked from him in the fine green walk, which is half a mile long, there reading my vowes as I used to on Sundays.

And after that was done, and going and lying by Creede an hour, he and I rose and went to our lodging and paid our reckoning; and so mounted, either to go toward London home or to find out a new lodging.   And so rode through Epsum the whole town over, seeing the various companies that were there walking; which was very pleasant to see how they are there without knowing almost what to do, but only in the morning to drink

a l.h. repl. l.h. 'bil'-

1. Dr Elkanah Downes, a York-shireman, had become Vicar in succession to William King, ejected for nonconformity in 1662.

waters. But Lord, to see how many I met there of Citizens that I could not have thought to have seen there, or that they had ever had it in their heads or purses to go down thither.

We rode out of the town through Yowell, beyond Nonesuch-house[1] a mile; and there our little dog, as he used to do, fell a-running after a flock of sheep feeding on the common, till he was out of sight; and then endeavoured to come back again and went to the last gate that he parted with us at and there the poor thing mistakes our Scent; instead of coming forward, he hunts us backward, and runs as hard as he could drive back toward Nonesuch – Creed and I after him; and being by many told of his going that way and the haste he[a] made, we rode still and pursued him through Yowell, and there we lost any further informacion of him. However, we went as far as Epsum almost; and hearing nothing of him, we went back to Yowell and there was told that he did pass through the town. We rode back to Nonsuch to see whether he might be gone back again; but hearing nothing, we with great trouble and discontent for the loss of our dog came back once more to Yowell and there set up our horses and selfs for all night, imploying people to look for the dog in the town; but can hear nothing of him.

However, we gave order for supper, and while that was dressing, walked out through Nonesuch parke to the house, and there viewed as much as we could of the outside, and looked through the great gates and find a noble Court; and altogether, believe it to have been a very noble house. And a delicate* park about it, where just now ⟨there⟩ was a Doe killed for the King to carry up to Court.

So walked back again; and by and by, our supper being ready, a good leg of mutton boiled – we supped and to bed – upon two good beds in the same room – wherein we slept most excellently all night.

27. Up in the morning about 7 a-clock; and after a little study, resolved of riding to the Wells to look for our dog; which we did, but could hear nothing. But it being much a warmer day then yesterday, there was great store of gallant company, more then then to my greater pleasure. There was

a repl. 'we'

---

1. Nonsuch, a royal palace near Ewell ('Yowell').

at a distance, under one of the trees on the common, a company got together that sung; I, at that distance, and so all the rest, being a quarter of a mile off, took them for the waytes; so I rid up to them and find them only voices – some Citizens, met by chance, that sing four or five parts excellently. I have not been more pleased with a snapp of Musique, considering the circumstances of the time and place, in all my life anything so pleasant.

We drank each of us three cups; and so after riding up to the horsemen upon the Hill where they were making of matches to run – we went away and to Yowell, where we find our Breakefast, the remains of our supper last night hasht. And by and by, after the smith had set on two new shoos to Creedes horse – we mounted; and with little discourse, I being intent upon getting home in time, we rode hard home, observing Mr. Gaudens house but not calling there (it being too late for me to stay, and wanting their dog too); the house stands very finely and hath a graceful view to the highway. Set up their horse at Fox hall, and I by water (observing the King's barge attending his going to the House this day) home, it being about one a-clock. So got myself ready and shifting myself; and so by water to Westminster and there came, most luckily, to the Lords House as the House of Comons were going into the Lords' House, and there I crowded in along with the Speaker – and got to stand close behind him – where he made his speech[1] to the King (who sat with his crown on and robes, and so all the Lords in their robes, a fine sight); wherein he told his Majesty what they have done this parliment, and now offered for his Royall consent. The greatest matters were a Bill for the Lord's Day (which it seems the Lords have lost and so cannot be passed, at which the Commons are displeased)[2]–the bills against Conventicles and papists (but it seems the Lords have not passed them); and giving his Majesty four entire Subsidys; which last, with about twenty smaller acts, were

---

1. The Speaker was Sir Edward Turnor, M.P. for Hertford; his speech is in *LJ*, xi. 578–9. Pepys had no right to attend the ceremony, from which the public were supposedly barred.

2. It had disappeared from the table of the House that morning:

LJ, xi. 577. For this and similar incidents, see C. E. Fryer in *EHR*, 32/103+ (where Pepys's report is ignored). For legislation about Sunday observance, see W. B. Whitaker, *Sunday in Tudor and Stuart times*. An act to similar purpose was passed in 1677.

passed with this form: the Clerk of the House reads the title of the bill and then looks at the end and there finds (writ by the King I suppose) *Le Roy le veult*, and that he reads.[1] And to others he reads, *Soit faict comme vous desirez*.[2] And to the Subsidys, as well that for the Comons, I mean the Layety, as for the Clergy, the King writes, *Le Roy remerciant les Seigneurs, &c., Prelats, &c., accepte leur benevolences*.[3]

The Speakers speech was far from any Oratory, but was as plain (though good matter) as anything could be and void of elocution.

After the bills passed, the King, sitting in his throne with his speech writ in a paper which he held in his lap and scarce looked off of it, I thought, all the time he made his speech to them[4] – giving them thanks for[a] their subsidys, of which, had he not need, he would not have asked or received them – and that need not from extravagancys of his, he was sure, in anything; but the disorders of the times compelling him to be at greater charge then he hoped for the future, ⟨by their care⟩ in their country, he should be. And that for his family expenses and others, he would labour however to retrench in many things convenient, and would have all others to do so too.

He desired that nothing of old faults should be remembred, or severity for the same used to any in the country, it being his desire to have all forgot as well as forgiven. But however, to use all care in suppressing any tumults, &c.; assuring them that the restless spirits of his and their adversarys have great expectations of something to be done this summer.

a MS. 'from'

1. This was the form of assent to public bills which were not grants of money. There were 12 on this occasion: *LJ*, xi. 578–9. The words were in fact both written and read by the Clerk of the Parliaments; it was the Clerk of the Crown in Chancery who read their titles.

2. Correctly, '*Soit fait come il est désiré*': the form of assent to private bills, of which there were now 12.

3. Correctly, '*Le Roy, remerciant ses bons subjects* [or '*ses Prelats*'] *accepte leur benevolence, et ainsi le veult*'. This

was the last occasion on which subsidies were levied. They were badly out-of-date and were now replaced by land-taxes assessed on the Cromwellian model.

4. *LJ*, xi. 579–80. Cf. Charles's reputed remark (on an unknown occasion): 'I have asked them so often and for so much money that I am ashamed to look them in the face': (Jonathan Richardson, jun., *Richardsoniana . . .*, 1776, pp. 89–90). But he was always a poor public speaker: cf. below, v. 112.

And promised that though the acts about Conventicles and papists were not ripe for passing this sessions, yet he would take care of himself that neither of them should in this inte[r]vall be encouraged to the endangering of the peace. And that at their next meeting he would himself prepare two bills for them concerning them.

So he concluded, that for the better proceeding of Justice, he did think fit to make this a Sessions, and doth prorogue them to the 16th. of March next.

His speech was very plain, nothing at all of spirit in it, nor spoke with any; but rather on the contrary, imperfectly, repeating many times his words, though he read all – which I was sorry to see, it having not been hard for him to have got all the speech without booke.

So they all went away, the King out of the House at the upper end – he being by and by to go to Tunbrige to the Queene.

And I in the painted-chamber spoke with my Lord Sandwich while he was putting off his Robes – who tells me he will now hasten down into the country, as soon as he can get some money settled on the Wardrobe.

Here meeting Creede,*a* he and I down to the hall; and I having at Michells shop writ a little letter to*b* Mr. Gauden to go with his horse, and excusing my not taking leave or so much as askeing after the old lady, the Widdow,[1] when we came away the other day from them – he and I over the water to Fox-hall and there sent away the horse with my letter. And then to the new Spring garden, walking up and down; but things being dear and little attendance to be had, we went away, leaving much brave company there. And so to a less house hard by, where we liked very well their Codlin tarts (having not time, as we entended, to stay the getting ready of a dish of peese); and there came to us an idle boy to show us some tumbling tricks, which he did very well and the greatest bending of his body that ever I observed in my life.

Thence by water to White-hall and walked over the parke to St. James's; but missed Mr. Coventry, he not being within. And so out again, and there the Duke was coming along the Pell

<hr>

a l.h. repl. s.h. 'Cr'-   *b* l.h. repl. s.h. ? 'about'

1. The widow of Bishop Gauden: above, p. 244 & n. 2.

mell.   It being a little darkeish, I stayed not to take notice of him, but we went directly back again.   And in our walk over the parke, one of the Dukes footmen came running behind us and came looking just in our faces to see who we were, and went back again.   What his meaning is I know not, but was fearful that I might not go fur enough with my hat off, though methinks that should not be it;   besides, there was others covered nearer then myself was, but only it was my fear.

So to White-hall and by water to the Bridge;   and so home to bed – weary and well pleased with my Journy in all respects. Only, it cost me about 20*s*.; but it was for my health and I hope will prove so.   Only, I do find by my riding a little swelling to arise just by my Anus.   I had the same the last time I rode, and then it fell again;   and now it is up again about the bigness of the bagg of a Silke worme.   Makes me fearful of a Rupture, but I will speak to Mr. Hollyard about it, and I am glad to find it now, that I may prevent it before it goes too far.

28.   Up, after sleeping very well;   and so to my office, setting down the Journall of this last three days.   And so settled to business again – I hope with greater chearefullnesse and successe by this refreshment.

At the office all the morning;   and at noon I went to Wises about my viall that is a-doing;   and so home to dinner and then to the office, where we sat all the afternoon till night – and I late at it after the office was risen.   Late, came my Jane and her brother Will to entreat for my taking of the boy again, but I will not hear her, though I could yet be glad to do anything for her sake to the boy;   but receive him again I will not nor give him anything.   She would have me send him to sea;   which if I could I would do, but there is no ships going out.   The poor girl cried all the time she was with me and could not go from me, staying about two hours with me till 10 or 11 a-clock at night, expecting that she might obtain something of me;   but receive him I will not.   So the poor girl was fain to go away, crying and saying little.   So from thence home;   where my house of office was emptying, and I find they will do it with much more cleanness then*a* I expected.   I went up and down among them a good while;   but knowing that Mr. Coventry was to call me

a   repl. 'that'

in the morning, I went to bed and left them to look after the people. So to bed.

29. Up about 6 a-clock and find the people to have just done; and Hannah not gone to bed yet, but was making clean of the yard and Kitchin – Will newly gone to bed. So I to my office.

And having given some orders to Tom Hater, to whom I gave leave for his recreation to go down to Portsmouth this pay,[1] I went down to Wapping to Sir W Warren and there stayed an hour or two, discoursing of some of his goods and then things in general relating to this office, &c; and so home and there going to Sir W. Batten (having no stomach to dine at home, it being yet hardly clean of last night's turds); and there I dined with my Lady and her daughter and son, Castle – and mighty fond she is and I kind to her. But Lord, how freely and plainly she rails against Comissioner Pett, calling him rogue and wondering that the King keeps such a fellow in the Navy.[2]

Thence by and by and down; walked to see Sir W. Penn at Deptford, reading by the way a most ridiculous play, a new one call[ed] *The Politician cheated*.[3] After a little sitting with him, I walked to the yard a little and so home again (my Will with ⟨me⟩, whom I bid to stay at the yard for me) and so to bed.

This morning my brother Tom was with me and we had some discourse again concerning his country mistress – but I believe the most that is fit for us to condescend to will not content her friends.*[4]

30. Up and to the office to get businesses ready for our sitting, this being the first day of altering of it from afternoons during the Parliament sitting to the forenoons again.[5]

By and by Mr. Coventry only came (Sir J. Mennes and Sir W. Batten being gone this morning to Portsmouth to pay some ships and the yards there); and after doing a little business, he

1. The dockyards were paid quarterly.
2. Cf. above, pp. 53-4.
3. A comedy by Alexander Green, published in 1663, but never acted; not in the PL. Penn was convalescing at Deptford: above, p. 214, n. 5. (A).

4. Negotiations for a marriage-treaty had broken down in the previous autumn: above, iii. 232-3.
5. Since 1661 the Board had similarly adjusted its times of meeting.

and I down to Woolwich and there up and down the yard; and by and by came Sir G. Carteret and we all looked into matters; and then by water back to Deptford, where we dined with him at his house. A very good dinner and mightily tempted with wines of all sorts and brave french Syder, but I drunk none.

But that which is a great wonder, I find his little daughter Betty, that was in hanging-sleeves but a month or two ago and is a very little young child, married;[1] and to whom but to young Scott, son to Madam Catharin Scott that was so long in law and at whose trial I was with her husband – he pleading that it was unlawfully got, and would not own it – she, it seems, being brought to bed of it, if not got by somebody else, at Oxford. But it seems a little before his death he did owne the child and hath left him his estate – not long since.[2]   So Sir G. Carteret hath struck up of a sudden a match with him for his little daughter. He hath about 2000*l* per annum; and it seems hath by this means overreached Sir H Bennet, who did endeavour to get this gentleman for a sister of his; but Sir G. Carteret I say hath over-reached him.

By this means, Sir G. Carteret hath married two daughters this year, both very well.[3]

After dinner into Deptford yard; but our bellies being full, we could do no great business and so parted. And Mr. Coventry and I to White-hall by water, where we also parted, and I to several places about business; and so calling for my five books

1. Elizabeth Carteret died unmarried. This was Carolina (born 9 November 1649 and therefore not yet 14) who had married Thomas Scott of Scot's Hall, Kent, aged 20.

2. Edward Scott of Scot's Hall had married Catherine, daughter of Lord Goring (later Earl of Norwich), c. 1632, but had lived with his wife for only about two years. In the civil war he had served in the parliamentary army, while she had lived at Oxford, where she was suspected of adultery with Rupert. Both at Oxford and elsewhere she had had children whom her husband had disowned. He brought an action for separation in the ecclesiastical courts, and she an action for alimony in Chancery, but Pepys was probably a witness to some part of the parliamentary proceedings in the case which followed the husband's petition to Parliament in December 1656. The divorce was never obtained and Edward Scott, who died in May 1663, acknowledged Thomas Scott as his son and heir. T. Burton, *Diary* (1828), i. 204–6, 334–7; Evelyn, 19 July 1663; James R. Scott, *Memorials of family of Scott of Scot's Hall*, pp. 231+; ib., App., pp. xxxiv–xli.

3. The other marriage was that of Anne to Sir Nicholas Slan(n)ing, Bt, of Maristow, Devon.

of the Variorum print,[1] bound according[a] to my common binding instead of the other, which is more gaudy,[2] I went home.

The town talke this day is of nothing but the great foot race
run this day on Bansted downes, between Lee, the Duke of
Richmonds[b] footman,[3] and a Tyler, a famous runner. And Lee
hath beat him – though the King and Duke of Yorke, and all
men almost, did bet three or four to one upon the Tyler's head.

31. Up earely to my accounts this month; and I find myself
worth clear 730*l* – the most I ever had yet; which contents me,
though I encrease but very little.

Thence to my office doing business; and at noon to my viall=
makers, who hath begun it, and hath a good appearance. And so
to the Exchange, where I met Dr. Pierce, who tells me of his
good luck to get to be groom of the privy Chamber to the Queene;
and without my Lord Sandwiches help, but only by his good
fortune, meeting a man that hath let him have his right for a small
matter, about 60*l*; for which he can every day have 400*l*. But
he tells me that my Lord hath lost much honour in standing so
long and so much for that coxcomb Pickering, and at last not
carry it for him but hath his name struck out by the King and
Queen themselfs after he had been in ever since the Queenes

a repl. 'at'   *b* repl. 'Yorke's'

---

1. Not identified with certainty
Brian Walton's polyglot Bible (*Biblica
sacra polyglotta*, 1657; PL 2948–53) is
in six volumes and is bound in red
morocco. But 'five' may be a slip;
and the binding may have been
renewed. The sections are headed
'*Variæ Lectiones*'.

2. Mr H. M. Nixon writes:
'Pepys's "common binding" is a
brown calf, not sprinkled or marbled;
the spine has raised bands and the
panels of the spine are outlined with a
three-line gilt fillet. There is a blind
two-line border round the covers,
near the edges, and a small fleuron,
also in blind, at each corner. The
"more gaudy" binding is in marbled
brown calf. The covers have a gilt
two-line border, near the edges, and
a centre panel formed by a three-line
fillet, with gilt corner fleurons.' See
Mr Nixon's analysis of the binding
styles in the PL in the forthcoming
official *Catalogue*.

3. For athletic footmen, see above,
i. 218, n. 1.

coming.[1] But he tells me he believes that either Sir H. Bennet,
my Lady Castlemayne, or Sir Ch. Barkely had received some
money for that place; and so the King could not disappoint them,
but was forced to put out this fool rather then a better man.
And I am sorry to hear what he tells me, that Sir Ch. Barkely hath
still such power over the King as to be able to fetch him from the
Council-table to my Lady Castlemayne when he pleases.

He tells me also, as a friend, the great Injury that he thinks I
do myself by being so Severe in the yards,[2] and contracting the ill
will of the whole Navy for those offices singly upon myself.
Now I discharge a good conscience therein, and I tell him that no
man can (nor doth he say any say it) charge me with doing wrong,
but rather do as many good, offices as any man.   They think, he
says, that I have a mind to beget a good name with the King and
Duke, who he tells me do not consider any such thing; but I
shall have as good thanks to let all alone and do as the rest.
But I believe the contrary; and yet I told him I never go to the
Duke alone, as others do, to talk of anything of my many services
that I do.   However, I will make use of his counsel and take some
Course to prevent having the single ill will of the office.

Before I went to the office, I went to the Coffee-house where
Sir J Cutler and Mr. Grant came.   And there Mr. Grant showed
me letters of Sir Wm. Pettys, wherein he says that his vessel
which he hath built upon two Keeles (a modell whereof, built
for the King, he showed me) hath this month won a wager of
50*l* in sailing between Dublin and Holyhead with the pacquett-
boat, the best ship or vessel the King hath there; and he offers
to lay with any vessel in the world.[3] It is about 30 Ton in
burden and carries 30 men with good accomodacion – (as much

1. This was Edward (Ned) Pickering, Sandwich's brother-in-law. His
office in the Queen's Household has
not been identified. In 1664 he
obtained a post in the King's Household. His elder brother, Sir Gilbert,
had been Lord Chamberlain to the
Cromwellian court.
2. Cf. above, p. 241 & n. 2.
3. Cf. Petty's letter from Dublin
(8 July) in S. P. and S. J. Rigaud
(eds), *Corresp. of scientific men* (1841–

62), i. 101+. The race had occurred
on 20 July. Petty retained to the end
a fanatical faith in his ship. He built
four prototypes of which this is
Invention II. See Marquess of Lans-
downe (ed.), *The Double-Bottom, or
twin-hulled ship of Sir William Petty*
(Oxf., Roxburghe Club, 1921), esp.
illust. 3. For Pepys's interest in the
design, see ibid., p. 141–3; *Naval
Minutes*, p. 23 & n. 5.

more as any ship of her burden) and so shall carry any vessel of this figure more men, with better accommodation by half, then any other ship. This carries also ten guns of about five Tons weight.

In their coming back from Holyhead, they started together; and this vessel came to Dublin by 5 at night and the pacquet-boat not before 8 the next morning; and when they came they did believe that this vessel had been drownded or at least behind, not thinking she could have lived in that sea.

Strange things are told of this vessel, and he concludes his letter with this posicion, "I only affirme that the perfection of Sayling lies in my principle; Finde it out who can."

Thence home, in my way meeting Mr. Rawlinson, who tells me that my uncle Wight is off of his hampshire purchase[1] and likes less of the Wights, and would have me to be kind and study to please him; which I am resolved to do.

Being at home, he sent for me to dinner to meet Mr. Moore; so I went thither and dined well; but it was strange for me to refuse, and yet I did without any reluctancy, to drink wine in a taverne where nothing else almost was drunk, and that excellent good.

Thence with Mr. Moore to the Wardrobe and there sat while my Lord was private with Mr. Townsend about his accounts an hour or two – we reading of a merry book against the Presbyters called *Cabbala*, extraordinary witty.[2]

Thence walked home and to my office, setting papers of all sorts and writing letters and putting myself into a condition to go to Chatham with Mr. Coventry tomorrow. So at almost 12 a-clock and my eyes tired with seeing to write, I went home and to bed – ending the month with pretty good content of mind. My wife in the country – and myself in good esteem and likely by pains to become considerable I think, with God's blessing upon my diligence.[a]

a followed by one blank page

1. See above, iii. 295.
2. *Cabala, or An impartial account of the non-conformists' private design ...* (1663); attributed to Sir John Birkenhead; reprinted in *Somers Tracts* (ed. Scott), vii. 567+; not in the PL.

AUGUST.

1. Up betimes and got me ready; and so to the office and put things in order for my going. By and by comes Sir G. Carteret and he and I did some business; and then Mr. Coventry sending for me, he staying in the boate, I got myself presently ready and down to him; and he and I by water to Gravesend (his man Lambert with us) and there eat a bit; and so mounted, I upon one of his horses which met him there – a brave proud horse – all the way talking of businesses of the office and other matters to good purpose.

Being come to Chatham, we put off our boots and so walked to the yard, where we met Comissioner Pett and there walked up and down, looking and inquiring into many businesses. And in the evening went to the Comissioner's and there in his upper Arbor sat and talked; and there pressed upon the Comissioner to take upon him a power to correct and suspend officers that do not their duty and other things; which he unwillingly answered he would, if we would owne him in it. But being gone thence, Mr. Coventry and I did discourse about him and conclude that he is not able to do the good in that yard that he might and can and it may be will do in another – what with his old faults and the relations that he hath to most people that act there.[1] After an hour or two's discourse at the Hill-house before going to bed – I saw him to his and he me to my chamber, he lying in the Treasurers and I in the Controllers chambers.

2. *Lords day.* Up; and after the barber had done, he and I walked to the Docke and so on board the *Mathias*, where Comissioner Pett and he and I and a good many of the officers and others of the yard did hear an excellent sermon of Mr. Hudson's upon "All is yours and you are God's"[2] – a most ready, learned, and good sermon, such as I have not heard a good while nor ever thought he could have preached.

1. The Petts, a prolific family, had held posts in Chatham dockyard since Elizabeth's time. Criticism of their nepotism was not new: cf. A. W. Johns in *Mar. Mirr.*, 12/438.

Commissioner Peter Pett was not now moved from his post.
2. A loose recollection of 1 Cor., iii. 22–3. Michael Hudson had been chaplain to the dockyard since 1660.

We took him with us to the Hill-house, and there we dined – and an officer or two with us. So after*ᵃ* dinner the company withdrew; and we three to private discourse and laid the matters of the yard home again to the Comissioner. And discoursed largely of several matters.

Thence to the parish church – and there heard a poor sermon, with a great deal of false Greek in it, upon these words, "You are my friend, if you do those things which I command you."[1]

Thence to the Docke and by water to view St. Mary Creeke, but do not find it so proper for a wett docke[2] as we would have it, it being uneven ground and hard in the bottom, and no great depth of water in many places.

Returned and walked from the Docke home – Mr. Coventry and I very much troubled to see how backward Comissioner Pett is to tell any of the faults of the officers and to see nothing in better condition here for his being here then they are in other yards where there is none.[3] After some discourse, to bed. But I sat up an hour after Mr. Coventry was gone to read my vowes – it raining a wonderful hard showre about 11 at night for an hour together. So to bed.

3. Up, both of us, very betimes; and to the yard and saw the men called over, and chose some to be discharged. Then to the rope-houses*ᵇ* and viewed them all and made an experiment which was the stronger, English or Riga hemp. The latter proved the stronger, but the other is very good and much better we believe then any but Riga.[4]

We did many other things this morning, and I caused the Timber measurer to measure some timber, where I found much

<hr/>

a repl. 'to'   *b* repl. 'yard and'

<hr/>

1. A loose recollection of John, xv. 14.

2. See above, p. 226 & n. 1.

3. Chatham (largest of the yards) was the only one with a resident commissioner until Thomas Middleton was appointed to Portsmouth in 1664.

4. English hemp was made from crops grown both in England and Ireland. An act of 1665 (17–18 Car. II c. 9) made hemp-growing compulsory in Ireland, and several unsuccessful attempts to require this of English landowners were made later: *CJ*, viii. 633; Grey, iv. 160. Cf. Sir W. Petty, *Econ. Writings* (ed. Hull), p. 596. But Eastland (especially Riga) hemp was always reckoned the best: see above, iii. 142 & n. 3.

fault and with reason; which we took public notice of and did give them admonition for the time to come.

At noon Mr. Pett did give us a very great dinner, too big in all conscience – so that most of it was left untouched.

Here was Collonell Newman, and several other gentlemen of the country and officers of the yard. After dinner they withdrew, and Comissioner*a* Pett, Mr. Coventry and I sat close to our business all the afternoon in his parler, and there run through much business and answered several people. And then in the evening walked in the garden, where we conjured him to look after the yard, and for the time to come, that he would take the whole faults and ill management of the yard upon himself, he having full power and our concurrence to suspend or do anything else that he thinks fit to keep people and officers to their duty.¹

He having made good promises, though I fear his performance, we parted (though I spoke so freely that he could have been angry) good friends, and in some hopes that matters will be the better for the time to come. So walked to the hill-house (which we did view, and the yard about it, and do think to put it off as soon as we can conveniently);² and there made ourselfs ready and mounted and rode to Gravesend (my riding Coate not being to be found, and I fear it is stole), on our way being overtaken by Captain Browne that serves the office of the Ordnance at Chatham.³ All the way, though he was a rogue and served the late times all along, yet he kept us in discourse of the many services that he did for many of the King's party, Lords and Dukes; and among others, he recovered a dog that was stolne from Mr. Cary (now keeper of the buck-hounds to the King) and preserved several horses of the Duke of Richmonds; and his best stone-horse, he was forced to put out his eyes and keep him for a Stallion, to preserve ⟨him⟩ from being carried away.

a   l.h. repl. l.h. 'S'-

1. On 21 August the Duke of York ordered certain measures of economy in the ordinary establishment at Chatham, and reminded the Commissioner of his power to discharge unworthy officers: *Mem. (naval)*, pp. 89–93.
2. The house was rented from the Bishop of Rochester. The Board in fact retained it.
3. Capt. John Browne, Deputy-Storekeeper (under his father, Maj. John Browne) of the Ordnance. They belonged to a leading family of gunfounders.

But he begun at last, upon my enquiry, to tell us how (he having been heretofore Clerk of the Rope=yard) the day's work of the Ropemakers became settled, which pleased me very well.

Being come to our Inn, Mr. Coventry and I sat*a* and talked till 9 or 10 a-clock, and then to bed.

4. We were called up about 4 a-clock; and being ready, went and took a Gravesend boat, and to London by 9 a-clock – by the way talking of several businesses of the navy. So to the office, where Sir Wm. Pen (the first time that he hath been with us a great while, he having been long sick) met us, and there we sat all the morning.

My Brother John, I finde, came to town to my house, as I sent for him, on Saturday last. So at noon home and dined with him; and after dinner and the barber been with me, I walked out with him to my viall-maker's – and other places; and then left him and I by water to Blackburys and there talked with him about some Masts (and by the way he tells me that Paul's is now going to be repaired in good earnest);[1] and so with him to his guarden close by his house, where I eat some peaches and apricotes; a very pretty place. So over the water to Westminster hall; and not finding Mrs. Lane, with whom I purposed to be merry, I went to Jervas's and took him and his wife over the water to their mother Palmers (the woman that speaks in the belly and with whom I had two or three year ago so good sport with Mr. Mallard),[2] thinking, because I had heard that she is a woman of that sort, that I might

a smudge below symbol

---

1. On 18 April 1663 commissioners had been appointed to collect money and supervise the work; on 27 July they had ordered a survey of the building to be made by Sir John Denham, John Webb and Edward Marshall. Wren later made a survey and drew up plans: *Pub. Wren Soc.*, xiii. 13–14. The building had been in bad repair since the fire of 1561; attempts at renovation begun under Charles I had been interrupted by the civil war, during which further

damage was done; by now the central tower was in danger and the s. transept in ruins. About £3600 was now subscribed and spent (mostly in repairs to Inigo Jones's portico) before the fire of 1666 completely gutted the building. Sir W. Dugdale, *Hist. St Paul's* (1818), pp. 109+; *Pub. Wren Soc.*, vols i and xiii; Jane Lang, *Rebuilding St Paul's*.

2. The incident is not recorded in the diary.

there have light upon some lady of pleasure (for which God forgive me); but blessed be God, there was none nor anything that pleased me – but a poor little house which she hath set out as fine as she can.   And for her singing which she pretends to, is only some old bawdy songs, and those sung abominably; only, she pretends to be able to sing both bass and treble; which she doth, something like but not like what I thought formerly and expected now.   Nor doth her speaking in her belly take me now as it did then, but it may be that is because I know it and see her mouth when she speaks, which should not be.

After I had spent a shilling there in wine, I took boat with Jervas and his wife and set them at Westminster; and it being late, forbore Mrs. Lane and went by water to the Old Swan by a boat; where I had good sport with one of the young men[1] about his travells as far as Fox-hall – in mockery; which yet the fellow answered me most prettily and traveller-like in, to my very good mirth.   So home and with my brother eat a bit of bread and cheese; and so to bed, he with me.

This day I received a letter from my wife which troubles me mightily; wherein she tells me how Ashwell did give her the lie to her teeth.   And that thereupon my wife giving her a box on the eare, the other struck her again, and a deal of stir; which troubles me.   And that my Lady hath been told by my father or mother something of my wife's carriage; which all together vexes me and I fear I shall find a trouble of my wife when she comes home, to get down her head again; but if Ashwell goes, I am resolved to have no more – but to live poorly and low again for a good while, and save money and keep my wife within bounds – if I can; or else I shall bid Adieu to all content in the world.   So to bed, my mind somewhat disturbed at this; but yet I shall take care, by prudence, to avoid the ill consequences which I fear, things not being gone too far yet and this heighth that my wife is come to being occasioned from my own folly in giving her too much head heretofore, for the year past.

5.   All the morning at the office; whither Deane of Woolwich came to me and discoursed of the body of ships, which I am now

---

1. Watermen. The Old Swan was the river jetty of that name.

going about to understand. And then I took him to the Coffee-house, where he was very earnest against Mr. Grant's report in favour of Sir W Petty's vessel,[1] even to some passion on both sides almost.

So to the Exchange, and thence home to dinner with my brother. And in the afternoon to Westminster-hall and there found Mrs. Lane; and by and by, by agreement, we met at the parliament-stairs (in my [way] down to the boat, who should meet us but my Lady Jemimah, who saw me lead her but said nothing to me of her, though I stayed to speak to her to see whether she would take notice of it or no) and off to Stangate; and so to the Kingshead at Lambeth marsh and had variety of meats and drink; came to xs. But I did so towse her and handled her; but could get nothing more from her, though I was very near it. But as wanton and bucksome as she is, she dares not adventure upon that business – in which I very much commend and like her.

Stayed pretty late, and so over with her by water; and being in a great sweat with my towsing of her, I durst not go home by water, but took coach. And at home, my brother and I fell upon Des Cartes, and I perceive he hath studied him well[2] and I cannot find but he hath minded his book and doth love it.

This evening came a letter about business from Mr. Coventry,

1. The report was made at the Royal Society's meeting of 29 July: Birch, i. 287. For Petty's ship, see above, p. 256 & n. 3.
2. The *Discours de la méthode* and the *Géométrie* were now studied at Cambridge. Henry More of Christ's (John Pepys's college) defended Descartes against charges of atheism and strongly urged universities to encourage the study of his works as the best means of knowing the 'Mechanical powers of Matter'. See esp. *The immortality of the soul* (Preface, p. 13) in *A coll. of several philosophical writings* (1662). Cf. also his correspondence in M. H. Nicholson (ed.), *Conway Letters*, passim. Newton read the *Géométrie* in 1661 at Trinity, according to his diary (qu. W. W. Rouse Ball, *Hist. Trin. Coll.*, p. 77). See also R. North, *Life of . . . John North* (1744), pp. 261, 265–6. Cf. J. B. Mullinger, *Cambridge characteristics in 17th cent.*, pp. 108–22; M. H. Curtis, *Oxford and Cambridge, 1558–1642*, p. 387 & n. The introduction of Descartes's work marked the beginning of the decline of Aristotelian science in Cambridge.

and with it a Silver pen he promised me, to carry inke in; which is very necessary.[1] So to prayers and to bed.

6. Up; and was angry with my maid Hannah for keeping the house no better, it being more dirty nowadays then ever it was while my whole family was together.

So to my office, whither Mr. Coventry came and Sir W. Penn, and we sat all the morning. This day Mr. Coventry borrowed of[a] me my Manuscript of the Navy.[2]

At noon I to the Change; and meeting with Sir W Warren, to a Coffee-house and there finished a contract with him for the office, and so parted.[3] And I to my Cosen Mary Joyces at a Gossiping, where much company and good Cheere. There was the King's falconer[4] that lives by Pauls and his wife, a ugly pusse but brought him money. He speaking of the strength of hawkes, which will strike a fowle to the ground with that force that shall

---

a   repl. 'lent'

---

1. Cf. Coventry to Pepys, 5 August: 'I send you herewith the pen I promised you without the ceremony of making a new case for it, which would require time, and might whett your appetite (by the expectation) beyond the fare . . .': PRO, Adm. 106/8, f. 90r. Pens which carried their own ink had been made in Paris for some years. Cf. Journal du voyage de deux jeunes hollandais à Paris en 1656–1658 (ed. A.-P. Faugère, Paris, 1899), at 11 July 1657: 'Nous fusmes voir un homme qui a treuvé une merveilleuse invention pour escrire commodement. Il fait des plumes d'argent où il met de l'encre qui ne sèche point, et sans en prendre on peut escrire de suite une demy main de papier. . . . Il les vend 10 francs, et 12 francs à ceux qu'il sçait avoir fort envie d'en avoir'. Cf. the 'Fountain Inkhorns, or Fountain Pens' which Matthew Henry adduced when commenting on the 'seven pipes to

the seven lamps' in Zachariah, ch. iv: Exposition of prophetical books of the Old Testament (1712). Pepys's pen does not appear to have been a success: below, vi. 312. (But he took a 'silver pen' with him to Tangier in 1683–4: Rawl. C 859B, f. 152v.) Parisian goldsmiths and jewellers continued to experiment with metal pens, and what appears to be the direct ancestor of the modern fountain-pen was invented by Coulon de Thévenot (d. 1814) and advertised in the Moniteur in 1790. See Larousse de l'industrie . . . (ed. L. Guillet et al., 1935 ed.), p. 1019; S. T. McCloy, French inventions of 18th cent., p. 130. Fanny Burney used a 'fountain pen' occasionally: Diary (1854 ed.), v. 39.
2. See above, p. 11, n. 1.
3. See below, p. 304 & n. 1.
4. Thirty-four falconers were employed by the King at this time: Bull. Inst. Hist. Res., 19/21-2.

make the fowl rebound a great way from [the] ground, which no force of man or art can do. But it was very pleasant to hear what reasons he and another, one Ballard,[1] a rich man of the same company of Leathersellers of which the Joyces are, did give for this. Ballards wife, a pretty and*a* a very well-bred woman, I took occasion to kiss several times, and she to carve, drink and show me great respect. After dinner, to talk and laugh. I drank no wine, but sent for some water, the beer not being good. A fidler was sent for; and there one Mrs. Lurkin, a neighbour, a good and merry poor woman, but a very tall woman, did dance and show such tricks that made us all merry. But above all, a daughter of Mr. Brumfield's, black but well-shaped and modest, did dance very well, which pleased me mightily; and I begun the *Duchesse*[2] with her, but could not do it; but however, I came off well enough and made mighty much of her, kissing and leading her home with her Cosen Anthony and Kate Joyce (Kate being very handsome and well, that is, handsomely dressed today, and I grew mighty kind and familiar with her and kissed her soundly, which she takes very well). To their house and there I left them – having in our way, though 9 a-clock at night, carried them into a puppet-play in Lincolnes Inn fields; where there was the Story of Holofernes[3] and other clockwork, well done.

There was at this house today, Mr. Lawrence, who did give the name, it seems, to my Cosen Joyces child, Samuel; who is a very civil gentleman and his wife a pretty woman – who with Kate Joyce were stewards of the feast today, and a double share, cost for a man and a woman, came to 16*s*., which I also would pay, though they would not by any means have had me. So I walked home, very well contented with this afternoon's work, I thinking it convenient to keep in with the Joyces against a bad day, if I should have occasion to make use of them. So I walked home; and after a letter to my wife by the post, and my father – I home to supper; and after a little talk with my brother, to bed.

a repl. ? 'to' or 'tro'

---

1. ? Stephen Ballow (d. 1674).
2. See above, p. 141 & n. 1. (E).
3. A biblical play for puppets entitled *Judith and Holofernes*. It was probably represented by mechanical figures similar to the German clockwork scenes and characters which Pepys saw at Bartholomew Fair on the following 4 September. For these clockwork figures, see the illustrated account in A. Chapuis and E. Droz, *Automata*. (A).

7.[a] Up and to my office a little, and then to Browns for my Measuring Rule, which is made, and is certainly the best and the most commodious for carrying in one's pocket and most useful that ever was made, and myself have the honour of being as it were the inventor of this form of it.[1] Here I stayed discoursing an hour with him, and then home. And thither came Dr. Fairbrother to me and we walked a while together in the garden and then abroad into the City, and then we parted for a while and I to my Viall, which I find done and once varnished, and it will please me very well – when it is quite varnisht.

Thence home and to study my new Rule till my head aked cruelly. So by and by to dinner and the Doctor and Mr. Creed came to me.

The Doctors discourse, which (though he be a very good-natured man) is but simple, was some sport to me and Creede, though my head akeing, I took no great pleasure in it.

We parted after dinner, and I walked to Deptford and there found Sir W. Penn; and I fell to measuring of some plank that was serving into the yard; which the people took notice of and the measurer himself was amuzed* at, for I did it much more ready then he.[2] And I believe Sir W. Penn would be glad I could have done less, or he more.

By and by he went away, and I stayed walking up and down, discoursing with the officers of the yard of several things; and so walked back again, and on my way young Bagwell and his wife waylayd me to desire my favour about getting him a better ship; which I shall pretend to be willing to do for them, but my mind is to know his wife a little better.

They being parted, I went with Cadbury the mast-maker to view a parcel of good masts which I think it were good to buy and resolve to speak to the board about it.

So home; and my brother John and I up, and I to my Musique

a repl. '6'

---

1. See above, p. 180 & n. 1.
2. Pepys notes this incident in NWB, p. 3: 'Question what may be drawn from the King's Timber Measurer ⟨Mr. Fletcher⟩ at Deptford being trusted by the merchant Capt.

Cocke in measuring his East-country plank, which I see him do, and so did Sir W. Pen, whom by chance I met there in the yard last summer while he lay there for his health.'

and then to discourse with him; and I find him not so thorough
a philosopher, at least in Aristotle, as I took him for, he not being
able to tell me the definicion of fire nor which of the four Qualitys
belonged to each of the four elements.[1]

So to prayers and to bed. Among other things, being much
satisfyed in my new Rule.

8.[a] Up and to my office, whither I sent for Browne the Mathematical Instrument=maker, who now brought me a ruler for
measuring timber and other things, so well done and in all things
to my mind, that I do set up my rest upon it that I cannot have a
better, nor any man else have so good for this purpose, this being
of my own ordering. By and by we sat all the morning despatching of business; and then at noon rise and I with Mr. Coventry
down to the waterside, talking; wherein I see so much goodness
and endeavours of doing the King service that I do more and
more admire him. It being the greatest trouble to man, he says,
in the world, to see not only in the Navy, but in the greatest
matters of State, where he can lay his finger upon the soare
(meaning this man's faults,[b] and this man's office the fault lies in),
and yet dare or can not remedy matters.

Thence to the Exchange about several businesses, and so home
to dinner; and in the afternoon took my brother John and Will
down to Woolwich by water; and after being there a good
while and eating of fruit in Sheldens garden, we begun our walk
back again – I asking many things in physiques of my brother
John, to which he gives me so bad or no answer at all; as, in the
Regions of the ayre he told me that he knew of no such thing, for
he never read Aristotle's philosophy, and Des Cartes owns no
such thing; which vexed me to hear him say.[2] But I shall call

a repl. '7'   *b* repl. 'off'-

1. The four elements were earth,
water, fire and air, and their qualities,
respectively, dryness, moisture, heat
and cold.

2. In *Principia Philosophiae* (1644)
Descartes had suggested that space
was a single plenum of particles
arranged in vortices. This contra-
dicted Aristotle's theory of a series of
concentric spheres. Strictly speak-

ing, the air was held to be only one of
these spheres – that between earth and
moon – but the phrase was used
loosely: cf. J. Howell, *Epist. Ho-
Elianae* (ed. Jacobs), ii. 443. For the
spread of Descartes's influence, see
above, p. 263 & n. 2. Pepys retained
only one work of Aristotle: *Ars
Rhetoricae* (1606); PL 576 (1).

him to task and see what it is that he hath studied since his going to the university.

It was late before we could get from Greenwich to London by water, the tide being against us and almost past; so that to save time and to be clear of Anchors, I landed at Wapping, and so walked home weary enough, walking over the stones.

This night Sir W. Batten and Sir J. Mennes returned from Portsmouth, but I did not go see them.

9.[a] *Lords day.* Up; and leaving my brother John to go somewhither else, I to church and heard Mr. Mills (who is lately returned out of the country, and it seems was fetched in by many of the parishioners with great state) preach upon the Authority of the Ministers, upon these words: "Wee are therefore Embassadors of Christ."[1] Wherein, among other high expressions, he said that such a learned man used to say that if a minister of the word and an Angell should meet him together, he would salute the Minister first – which methought was a little too high. This day I begun to make use of the Silver pen (Mr. Coventry did give mee[b]) in writing of this sermon, taking only the heads of it in Latin; which I shall I think continue to do.[2] So home and at my office, reading my vowes; and so to Sir W. Batten to dinner, being invited and sent for and being willing to hear how they left things at Portsmouth; which I find but ill enough. And are mightily for a Commissioner to be at seat there, to keep the yard in Order.[3]

Thence in the afternoon with my Lady Batten, leading her through the streets by the hand to St. Dunstans church, hard by us (where by Mrs. Russells means we were set well); and heard an excellent sermon of one Mr. Gifford, the parson there – upon "Remember Lot's wife."[4] So from thence walked back to Mrs.

a repl. '8'   *b* l.h. repl. s.h. 'him'

---

1. A loose recollection of 2 Corinth., v. 20.

2. None of these sermon-notes appears to survive.

3. As at Chatham. The post was ater created and Col. Thomas Middleton appointed to it in November 1664. For Portsmouth's growing importance, see above, p. 226 & n. 1.

4. Luke, xvii. 32. The church was St Dunstan-in-the-East, of which George Gifford was Rector. Elizabeth, widow of Robert Russell, had carried on her husband's business as ship's-chandler since his death in 1663.

Russells and there drank and sat talking a great while – among other things, talking of young Daws that married the great fortune, who it seems hath*a* a Barronet's patent given him and is now Sir Tho. Dawes[1] – and a very fine-bred man they say he is. Thence home; and my brother being abroad, I walked to my uncle Wights and there stayed, though with little pleasure, and supped – there being the husband of Mrs. Anne Wight, who it seems is lately married to one Mr. Bently, a Norwich factor.

Home and stayed up a good while, examining Will in his Latin bible and my brother along with him in his Greeke. And so to prayers and to bed.

This afternoon I was amuzed* at the tune set to the psalm by the clerke of the parish; and thought at first that he was out, but I find him to be a good songster, and the parish could sing it very well and was a good tune. But I wonder that there should be a tune in the psalms that I never heard of.

10.*b* Up, though not so earely this summer as I did all the last, for which I am sorry; and though late, am resolved to get up betimes before the season of rising be quite past. To my office to fit myself to wait on the Duke this day.

By and by, by water to White-hall and so to St. James's and anon called into the Duke's chamber; and being dressed, we were all as usual taken*c* in with him and discoursed of our matters. And that being done, he walked and I in the company with him to White-hall; and there he took barge for Woolwich, and I up to the Comittee of Tanger, where my Lord Sandwich, my Lord Peterborough (whom I have not seen before since his coming back), Sir W Compton, and Mr. Povy – our discourse about supplying my Lord Tiviott[2] with money; wherein I am sorry to see, though they do not care for him, yet they are willing to let him for civility and compliment only, to let him have money, almost without expecting any account of it. But by this means, he being such a cunning fellow as he is, the King is

a repl. 'is'   *b* repl. '9'   *c* repl. 'were'

1. *Recte* Sir John Dawes: for his marriage, see above, p. 122 & n. 1. His baronet's patent was dated 1 June 1663.

2. Governor of Tangier; Peterborough was his predecessor.

like to pay dear for our Courtiers ceremony.   Thence by coach
with my Lords Peterborough and Sandwich to my Lord Peterborough's house;[1] and there, after an hour's looking over some
fine books of the Italian buildings with fine cuts, and also my
Lord Peterborough's bowes and arrows, of which he is a great
lover,[a] we sat down to dinner, my Lady coming down to
dinner also, and there being Mr. Williamson that belongs to
Sir H. Bennett, whom I find a pretty understanding and accom-
plisht man but a little conceited.[2]

After dinner I took leave and went to Greatorex's,[3] whom I
found in his garden and set him to work upon my Ruler, to
ingrave an Almanacke and other things upon the brasses of it –
which a little before night he did, but the latter part he slubberd
over, that I must[b] get him to do it over better or else I shall not
fancy my Rule.   Which is such a folly that I am come to now,
that whereas before my delight was in multitude of books and
spending money in that and buying alway of other things, now
that I am become a better husband and have left off buying, now
my delight is in the neatness of everything, and so cannot be
pleased with anything unless it be very neat;   which is a strange
folly.

Hither came W. Howe about business;   and he and I had a
great deal of discourse about my Lord Sandwich, and I find by
him that my Lord doth dote upon one of the daughters of Mrs.
      [4] where he lies, so that he spends his time and money
upon her.   He tells me she is a woman of a very bad fame and
very impudent, and hath told my Lord so.   Yet for all that, my
Lord doth spend all his evenings with her, though he be at Court
in the daytime.   And that the world doth take notice of it.
And that Pickering is only there as a blinde, that the world may
think that my Lord spends his time with him when he doth

a MS. 'loved'   *b* accidental thin stroke above symbol

---

1. Banbury House, Long Acre.
2. Cf. above, p. 35 & n. 3.
Joseph Williamson was Bennet's
chief man of business and secretary
(i.e. the equivalent of the modern
permanent under-secretary of state);
Keeper of the King's Library; Latin

Secretary; and head of the State
Paper office. He later became Secretary of State, 1674–8.
    3. The instrument maker on the
s. side of the Strand.
    4. Supply 'Becke', of Chelsea.

worse. And that hence it is that my Lord hath no more mind
to go into the country then he hath. in fine, I perceive my
Lord is dabling with this wench, for which I am sorry; though I
do not wonder at it, being a man amorous enough and now
begins to allow himself the liberty that he sees everybody else at
Court takes.

Here I am told that my Lord Bristoll is either fled or conceals
himself, having been sent for to the King – it is believed to be
sent to the tower,[1] but he is gone out of the way.

Yesterday, I am told also that Sir J: Lentall, in Southworke,
did apprehend about 100 Quakers and other such people, and
hath sent some of them to the gaole at Kingston, its being now
the time of the Assizes.[2]

Thence home and examined a piece of Latin of Will's with my
brother, and so to prayers and to bed.

This evening I have a letter from my father that says that my
wife will come to town this week, at which I wonder she should
come without my knowing more of it. But I find they have
lived very ill together since she went, and I must use all the
brains I have to bring her to any good when she doth come
home, which I fear will be hard to do, and do much disquiet me
the thoughts of it.

11.[a] Up and to my office; whither by and by my brother Tom
came and I did soundly rattle him for his neglecting to see and
please the Joyces, as he hath of late done. I confess I do fear that
he doth not understand his business nor will do any good at his
trade, though he tells me that he doth please everybody and that
he gets monies. But I shall not believe it till I see a state of his
accounts, which I have ordered him to bring me before he sees
me any more.

a repl. '10'

---

1. This was in consequence of his attack on Clarendon: see above, p. 223. A proclamation for his arrest was issued a fortnight later: below, p. 298.
2. The arrests were made under the terms of a proclamation of 27 July, and in fear of the rising which later broke out, chiefly in Yorkshire and Northumberland, in the autumn (the Derwentdale Plot). Sir John Lenthall (brother of Speaker Lenthall) was Marshal of King's Bench Prison, and a very active J.P.

We met and sat at the office all the morning.   And at noon, I to the Change, where I met Dr. Pierce;[1] who tells me that the King comes to town this day from Tunbrige to stay a day or two, and then fetch the Queen from thence – who he says is grown a very debonnaire lady and now hugs him and meets him galloping upon the road, and all the actions of a fond and pleasant lady that can be.   That he believes [he] hath a chat now and then of Mrs. Stewart, but that there is no great danger of her, she being only a innocent, young, raw girl; but my Lady Castlemayne, who rules the King in matters of state and doth what she list with him, he believes is now falling quite out of favour.   After the Queen is come back, she goes to the Bath and so to Oxford, where great entertainments are making for her.

This day I am told also that my Lord Bristoll had warrants issued out against him, to have carried him to the Tower; but he is fled away or hides himself – so much the Chancellor hath got the better of him.[2]

Upon the Change, my brother and Will brings me word that Madam Turner would come and dine with me today.   So I hasted home and found her and Mrs. Morrice there (The and Joyce being gone into the country), which is the reason of the mother's rambling.   I got a dinner for them; and after dinner my uncle Thom. and aunt Bell came and saw me and I made them almost foxed with wine, till they were very kind (but I did not carry them up to my ladies), so they went away; and so my two ladies and I in Mrs. Turners coach to Mr. Povys, who being not within, we went in and there showed Mrs. Turner his perspective and volary and the fine things that he is building of now,[3] which is a most neat thing.   Thence to the Temple and by water to Westminster; and there Morrice and I went to Sir R. Long's to have fetched a Neece of his, but she was not within; and so we went to boat again and then down to the bridge and there tried to find a sister of Mrs. Morrices, but she was not within neither, and so we went through bridge and I carried them on board the King's pleasure-boat[4] – all the way reading in a book of Receipts

1. Surgeon to the Duke of York.
2. See below, p. 298 & n. 4.
3. Povey's house was in Lincoln's Inn Fields. For the perspective, see above, p. 18 & n. 1.   The volary was a large bird-cage in which the birds could fly about.
4. The *Mary*.

of making fine meats and sweetmeats;[1] among others, one "To make my own sweet water" – which made us good sport.

So I landed them at Greenwich; and there to a garden and gave them fruit and wine, and so to boat again; and finally, in the cool of the evening, to Lyon Kee; the tide against us and so landed and walked to the bridge and there took a Coach by chance passing by; and so I saw them home and there eat some cold venison with them and drunk and bid them good-night, having been mighty merry with them; and I think it is not amisse to preserve, though it cost me a little, such a friend as Mrs. Turner.

So home and to bed, my head running upon what to do tomorrow to fit things against my wife's coming – as, to buy a bedsteade, because my brother John is here and I have now no more beds then are used.

12. Up, and a little to my office to put down my yesterday's[a] Journall; and so abroad to buy a bedstead and do other things.

So home again; and having put up the bedstead and done other things in order to my wife's coming, I went out to several places and to Mrs. Turners, she inviting me last night, and there dined – with her and Madam Morrice and a stranger; we were very merry and had a fine dinner. And thence I took leave and to White-hall, where my Lords Sandwich, Peterborough and others made a Tanger committee. Spent the afternoon in reading and ordering, with a great deal of alteration and yet methinks never a whit the better, of a letter drawn by Creed to my Lord Rutherford – the Lords being against anything that looked to be rough, though it was in matter of money and accounts, wherein their courtship may cost the King dear. Only, I do see by them that speaking in matters distasteful to him that we write to, it is best to do it in the plainest and without ambages[b] or reasoning, but only say matter of fact and leave the party to collect your meaning.

Thence by water to my brother's and there I hear my wife is

a repl. 'last'   *b* l.h. repl. l.h. 'aba'-

1. The book has not been identi-fied: many such were published. Pepys did not make a collection of cookery books in his library.

come and gone home, and my father is come to town also, at which I wondered. But I discern it is to give my brother advice about his building,[1] and it may be to pacify me about the differences that have been between my wife and him and my mother at her late being with them – though by and by, he coming to Mr. Holdens (where I was buying a hat), he took no notice to me of anything. I walked with him a little while and left him to lie at that end of the town, and I home – where methinks I find my wife strange, not knowing, I believe, in what temper she could expect me to be in; but I fell to kind words and so we were very kind; only, she could not forbear telling me how she had been used by them and her maid Ashwell in the country; but I find it will be best not to examine it, for I doubt she's in*a* fault too, and therefore I seek to put it off from my hearing; and so to bed and there enjoyed her with great content. And so to sleep.

13. Lay long in bed with my wife, talking of family matters. And so up and to the office, where we sat all the morning. And then home to dinner; and after dinner my wife and I to talk again about getting of a couple of good maids and to part with Ashwell; which troubles me for her father's sake, though I shall be glad to have that charge taken away of keeping a woman. Thence a little to the office and so abroad with my wife – by water to White-hall; and there at my Lord's lodgings met my Lady Jemimah, with whom we stayed a good while. Thence to Mrs. Hunts, where I left my wife; and I to walk a little in St. James's parke (while Mrs. Harper might come home, with whom we came to speak about her kinswoman, Jane Gentleman, to come and live with us as a chamber mayde) and there met with Mr. Hoole, my old acquaintance of Magdalen, and walked with him an hour in the park, discoursing chiefly of Sir Samll. Morland, whose lady is gone into France.[2] It seems he buys ground and a farme in the country, and lays out money upon building and God knows what, so that most of the money he sold his pension of 500*l* per annum for to Sir Arth. Slingsby is

a repl. 'is'

1. See above, p. 236, n. 2.
2. Both William Hoole (Howell) and Morland had been Fellows of

Magdalene. The latter had been Pepys's tutor. His wife came from Normandy.

believed is gone.[1] It seems he hath very great promises from
the King; and Hoole hath seen some of the Kings[a] letters under
his own hand to Morland, promising him great things (and
among others, the order of the guarter, as Sir Samuel says);[2]
but his lady thought it below her to ask anything at the King's
first coming, believing the King would do it of himself; when,
as Hoole doth really think, if he had asked to be Secretary of
State at the King's first coming, he might have had it.   And the
other day, at her going into France, she did speak largely to the
King herself how her husband hath failed of what his Majesty
had promised and she was sure entended him; and the King did
promise still, as he is a King and a gentleman, to be as good as his
word in a little time, to a tittle.   But I never believe it.

Here in the park I met with Mr.[b] Coventry; where he sent for
a letter he had newly writ to me, wherein he had enclosed one
from Comissioner Pett, complaining of his being defeated in his
attempt to suspend two pursers;[3] wherein the manner of his doing
it and complaint of our seeing him, contrary to our promises the
other day, deserted, did make us laugh mightily; and was good
sport to think how awkerdly he goes about a thing that he hath
no courage of his own nor mind to do.   Mr. Coventry answered
it very handsomely, but I perceive Pett hath left off his correspond-
ing with me any more.

a MS. 'things'   *b* l.h. repl. 'S'-

-----

1. In 1660 Morland had been given
a baronetcy, a place in the Privy
Chamber and a pension for his services to the King during the Interregnum, when he passed on information gained from his employment in
Secretary Thurloe's office. His im-
providence was notorious: in a short
account he wrote of his life in 1689 (in
a letter to Tenison) he complains of
these 'reports of . . . excessive prodi-
galities': Lambeth Palace MSS 931,
no. 1.   But the stories appear to have
been justified. In the same letter
Morland says that he was at this
period in debt, and forced to sell his

pension below its value. Slingsby,
he relates, was said to have bought
it for Lady Green with the King's
money. He denies having had any
real estate. Cf. below, v. 330.

2. Morland repeats this claim in his
letter to Tenison: Lambeth Palace
MSS, loc. cit. But he was never
appointed to the order.

3. Coventry to Pepys, 13 August:
'I send you enclosed Mr Pett's to me
and my answer, I feare his heart mis-
gives him, and hee seekes a cause':
PRO, Adm. 106/8, f. 98r. The en-
closures have disappeared. Cf.
above, p. 258.

Thence to fetch my wife from Mrs. Hunts, where now he[1] was come in and we eat and drunk; and so away (their child being at home; a very lively, but not pretty at all) by water to Mrs. Turners and there made a short visitt, and so home by coach. And after supper, to prayers and to bed. And before going to bed, Ashwell begun to make her complaint and by her I do perceive that she hath received most base usage from my wife; which my wife sillily denyes, but it is impossible the wench could invent words and matter so perticularly, against which my wife hath nothing to say but flatly to deny, which I am sorry to see, and blows to have passed and high words, even at Hinchingbrooke-house among my Lady's people, of which I am mightily ashamed.

I said nothing to either of them, but let them talk – till she was gone and left us abed; and then I told my wife my mind with great sobriety and grief. And so to sleep.

14.   Awake, and to chide my wife again; and I find that my wife hath got too great head to be brought down soon. Nor is it possible with any convenience to keep Ashwell longer, my wife is so set and concerned, as she was in Sarah, to make her appear a Lyer in every small thing, that we shall have no peace while she stays. So I up and to my office, doing several businesses in my study; and so home to dinner – the time having outslipped me and my stomach, it being past 2 a-clock. And yet before we could sit down to dinner, Mrs. Harper and her cousin Jane came, and we treated and discoursed long about her coming to my wife for a chamber-maid; and I think she will do well. So they went away, expecting notice when she shall come; and so we set down to dinner at 4 a-clock almost, and then I walked forth to my brother's; where I found my father, who is discontented and hath no mind to come to my house, but would have begun some of the differences between my wife and him. But I desired to hear none of them, but am sorry at my folly in forcing it and theirs in not telling me of it at the beginning; and therefore am resolved to make the best of a bad market and to bring my wife to herself again as soon and as well as I can. So we parted very kindly, and he will dine with me tomorrow or next day. Thence walked home, doing several errands by the way. And at home, took my wife to visit Sir W. Penn, who is

1. Her husband.

still very lame; and after an hour with him went home and supped, and with great content to bed.

15. Lay pretty long in bed, being a little troubled with some pain got by wind and cold; and so up with good peace of mind, hoping that my wife will mind her house and servants. And so to the office; and being too soon to sit, walked to my viall, which is well-nigh done and I believe I may have it home to my mind next week. So back to my office and there we sat all the morning and very busy, I till 2 a-clock before I could go to dinner again.

After dinner walked forth to my Instrument-maker and there had my Rule he made me last, now so perfected that I think in all points I shall never need or desire a better, or think that any man yet had one so good in all the several points of it for my use.

So by water down to Deptford, taking into my boat with me Mr. Palmer, one whom I knew and his wife when I was first married, being an acquaintance of my wife's and her friends, lodging at Charing-cross during our differences.[1] He joyed me in my condition; and himself it seems is forced to fallow the law in a common ordinary way, but seems to live well and is a sober man enough by his discourse. He landed with me at Deptford, where he saw by the officers' respect to me a piece of my command, and took notice of it; though God knows, I hope I shall not be elated with that, but rather desire to be known for serving the King well and doing my duty.

He gone, I walked up and down the yard a while, discoursing with the officers; and so by water home, meditating on my new Rule with great pleasure. So to my office, and there by candle light doing business. And so home to supper and to bed.

16. *Lords day.* Up and with my wife to church; and finding her desirous to go to church, I did suspect her meeting of Pembleton; but he was not there, and so I thought my jealousy in vain

---

1. This and the equally laconic reference at 13 August 1661 appear to be the only evidence that Pepys and his wife temporarily separated in the early years of their marriage. Cf. above, ii. 153 & n. 3.

and writ the sermon with great quiet.[1]   And home to dinner,
very pleasant; only, some angry words my wife could not forbear to give Ashwell.   And after dinner to church again; and
there looking up and down, I find Pembleton to stand in the
Isle against us, he coming too late to get a pew – which, Lord,
into what a sweat did it put me.   I do not think my wife did see
him, which did a little satisfy me.   But it makes me mad to see
of what a jealous temper[a] I am, I cannot help it; though let
him do what he can, I do not see, as I am going to reduce my
family, what hurt he can do me, there being no more occasion
now for my wife to learn of him.

Here preached a confident young coxcombe.   So home, and I
stayed a while with Sir J. Mennes at Mrs. Turners, hearing his
parrat talk, laugh, and cry, which it doth to admiration.   So home
and with my wife to see Sir W. Penn; and thence to my uncle
Wight, and took them at supper and sat down – where methinks
my uncle is much more kind then he used to be, both to me now
and, my father tells me, to him also; which I am glad of.

After supper home, it being extraordinary dark; but by
chance a lanthorn came by and so we hired it to light us home;
otherwise, were we no sooner within doors – but a great showre
fell, that had daubed us cruelly if we had not been within, it
being as dark as pitch.

So to prayers and to bed.

17.   Up; and then fell into discourse, my wife and I, to Ashwell; and much against my Will, I am fain to express a willing-
ness to Ashwell that she should go from us; and yet in my mind
I am glad of it, to ease me of the charge.   So she is to go to her
father this day.   And leaving my wife and her talking highly,
I went away by coach with Sir J. Mennes and Sir W. Batten to
St. James and there attended of course* the Duke.   And so to
White-hall, where I met Mr. Moore and he tells me with great
sorrow of my Lord's being debauched, he fears, by this woman at
Chelsy; which I am troubled at and resolve to speak to him of it
if I can seasonably.

a   repl. 'man'

1. Pepys had decided on the pre-   heads in Latin: above, p. 268.
vious Sunday to write the sermon-

Thence home, where I dined with my wife alone; and after dinner comes our old maid Susan to look for a Gorgett that she says she hath lost by leaving it here;*a* and by many circumstances, it being clear to me that Hannah, our present cook-maid, not only hath it but had it on upon her neck when Susan came in, and shifted it off presently upon her coming in, I did charge her so home with it (having a mind to have her gone from us), that in a huff she told us she would be gone tonight if I would pay her her wages; which I was glad and my wife of, and so fetched her her wages; and though I am doubtful that she may convey some things away with her clothes, my wife searching them, yet we are glad of her being so gone. And so she went away in a quarter of an houre's time – being much amused* at this, to have never a maid but Ashwell, that we do not entend*a* to keep, nor a boy; and my wife and I being left for an hour, till my brother came in, alone in the house, I grew very melancholy; and so my brother being come in, I went forth – to Mrs. Holden, to whom I formerly spoke about a girle to come to me instead of a boy, and the like I did to Mrs. Standing and also to my brother Tom, whom I found at an alehouse in popinjay ally, drinking. And I standing with him at the gate of the ally, Ashwell comes by, and so I left Tom and went almost home with her, talking of her going away. I find that she is willing to go and told her (though behind my back my wife hath told her that it was more my desire than hers that she should go, which was not well) that seeing my wife and she could not agree, I did choose rather, was she my sister, have her gone; it would be better for us and for her too. To which she willing agreed, and will not tell me anything but that she doth believe that my wife would have somebody there that might not be so liable to give me informacion of things as she takes her to be. But however, I must labour to prevent all that.

I parted with her near home, agreeing to take no notice of my coming*b* along with her, and so by and by came home after her.

Where I find a sad distracted house, which troubles me. However, to supper and prayers and to bed. And while we were getting to bed, my wife begin to discourse to her and plainly asked whether she had got a place or no; and the other answered that she could go, if we would, to one of our own office, to

a repl. 'is'   *b* repl. 'keep'   *c* repl. 'brothers' which we agreed, if she would. She thereupon said no; she would not go to any place but where she might teach children, because of keeping herself in use of what things she had learned, which she doth not here or will there, but only dressing – by which I perceive the wench is cunning, but one very fit for such a place, and accomplished to be woman to any lady in the land. So quietly to sleep – it being a cold night.

But till my house is settled, I do not see that I can mind my business of the office, which grieves me to the heart. But I hope all will over in a little time, and I hope to the best. This day at Mrs. Holdens I find my new Low crowned beaver, according to the present fashion, made; and will be sent home tomorrow.

18. Up and to my office, where we sat all the morning. And at noon home and my father came and dined with me, Susan being come and helped my wife to dress dinner. After dinner my father and I talked about our country matters; and in fine, I find that he thinks 50*l.* per annum will go near to keep them all – which I am glad of. He having taken his leave of me and my wife, without any mention of the differences between them and my wife in the country – I went forth to several places about businesses, and so home again; and after supper to bed.

19. Up betimes; and my wife up and about the house, Susan beginning to show her drunken tricks and put us in mind of her old faults of folly and distractednesse,[1] which we had forgot, so that I became mightily troubled with her. This morning came my Joyners to new-lay my floores, and begun with the dining-room.

I out and saw my vyall again, and it is very well. And to Mr. Hollyard and took some pills of him, and a note under his hand to drink wine with my beere;[2] without which I was obliged by my private vowe to drink none a good while, and have strictly observed it.[3] And by my drinking of small-beer and not eating, I am so mightily troubled with wind that I know not what to do almost.

Thence to[a] White-hall and there met Mr. Moore and fell

a repl. 'homeward and there'

1. Cf. above, p. 154.
2. I.e. wine mixed with beer: see below, p. 343.
3. See above, p. 235: a vow against strong drink until November.

a-talking about my Lord's folly at Chelsey, and it was our discourse by water to London and to the great Coffee-house against
the Exchange, where we sat a good while talking; and I find that
my Lord is wholly given up to this wench, who it seems hath
been reputed a common Strumpett. I have little incouragement
from Mr. Moore to meddle with it, to tell my Lord – for fear it
may do him no good, but me hurt.

Thence homewards, taking leave of him, and met Tom Marsh
my old acquaintance at Westminster, who talks mightily of the
Honour of his place, being Clerke Assistant to the Clerk of the
House of Commons, but I take him to be a Coxcombe; and so
did give him half a pint of wine, but drunk none myself, and so
got shut of him. So home; and there find my wife almost mad
with Susan's tricks, so as she is forced to let her go and leave the
house all in dirt and the clothes all wet, and gets Goody Taylour[1]
to do that business for her till another comes. Here came Will
Howe, and he and I alone in my chamber, talking of my Lord;
who desires me, out of love to my Lord, to tell my Lord of the
matters we discoursed of, which tend so much to the ruin of his
estate; and so I resolved to take a good heart and do [it], whatever
comes of it. He gone, we sat down and eat a bit of dinner fetched
from the Cookes; and so up again, and I to my Joyners, who will
make my floores very handsome. By and by comes in Pembleton, which begun to make me sweat; but I did give him so little
countenance and declared at one word against dancing any more,
and[a] bid him a short (good be with you) myself; and so he took
as short a leave of my wife and so went away, I think without any
time of receiving any great satisfaction from my wife, or invitation
to come again.

To my office till it was dark, doing business; and so home by
candle-light to make up my accounts for my Lord and Mr.
Moore. By and by comes Mr. Moore to me and stayed a good
while with me, making up his accounts and mine; but we did
not come to any end therein for want of his papers, and so put it
off to another time.

He supped with me in all my dirt and disorder, and so went
away and we to bed.

a repl. 'that'

1. Wife of Matthew Taylor, Navy Office handyman.

I discoursed with him a great while about my speaking to my Lord of his business, and I apprehend from him that it is likely to prove perhaps of bad effect to me^a and no good to him; and therefore I shall even let it alone and let God do his Will, at least till my Lord is in the country; and then we shall see whether he resolves to come to Chelsy again or no, and so order the stopping of him therein if we can.

20. Up betimes and to my office (having first been angry with my brother John and in the heat of my sudden passion called him Asse and coxcomb, for which I am sorry, it being but for leaving the key of his chamber with a spring-lock within-side of the door) and there we sat all the morning; and at noon dined at home and there find a little girle, which she told my wife herself her name was Jinny; by which name we shall call her – I think a good likely girl and a parish-child of St. Brides, of honest parentage and recommended by the church-warden.

After dinner, among my Joyners laying my floores, which please me well; and so to my office, and we sat this afternoon upon an extraordinary business of the victualling.

In the evening came Comissioner Pett, who fell foul on mee^b for my carriage to him at Chatham; wherein, after protestation of my love and good meaning to him, he was quiet. But I doubt he will not be able to do the service there that any other man of his ability would.

Home^c in the evening; my viall (and Lute, new-strung, being brought home too) was brought home and I ⟨would have⟩ paid Mr. Hunt for it; but^d he did not come along with it him-self; which I expected and was angry for it, so much it is against my nature to owe anything to anybody. ⟨This evening the girl that was brought me today for so good a one, being cleansed of lice this day by^e my wife and good new clothes put on her back, she run away from Goody Taylour that was showing her the way to the bakehouse, and we heard no more of her.⟩^f

So to supper and to bed.

21. Up betimes and among my Joyners; and to my office, where the Joyners are also laying mouldings in the inside of my closet.

a	repl. 'him'	*b*	l.h. repl. s.h. 'me'
c	repl. ? 'he'	*d*	repl. 'and it cost me'
e	MS. 'by and'	*f*	addition crowded into bottom of page

Then abroad and by water to White-hall, and there got Sir G. Carteret to sign me my last Quarter's bills for[a] my wages. And meeting with Mr. Creede, he told me how my Lord Tiviott hath received another attaque from Guyland at Tanger, with 10000 men; and at last, as is said, is come, after a personal treaty with him, to a good understanding and peace with him.[1]

Thence to my brother's and there told him how my girle hath served us which he sent me, and directed him to get my clothes again and get the girl whipped.

So to other places by the way about small businesses, and so home; and after looking over all my workmen, I went by water and land to Detford and there found by appointment Sir W. Batten, but he was got to Mr. Waiths to dinner; where I dined with him, a good dinner – and good discourse; and his wife, I believe, a good woman. We fell in discourse of Captain Cocke and how his lady hath lost all her fine Linnen almost; but besides that,[b] they say she gives out that she hath 3000*l* worth of linen, which we all laugh at; and Sir W. Batten (who I perceive is not so fond of the Captain as he used to be; and less of her, from her slight receiving of him and his lady, it seems, once) told me how he should say that he saw he must spend 700*l* per annum, get it how he could – which was a high speech; and by all men's discourse, his estate not good enough to spend so much.

After dinner altered our design to go to Woolwich, and put it off to tomorrow morning; and so went all to Greenwich (Mrs. Waith excepted; who went thither but not ⟨to the same house⟩ with us, but to her father's that lives there) to the Musique-house,[2] where we had paltry musique till the Maister Organist came (whom by discourse I afterward knew, having imployed him for my Lord Sandwich to prick out something, his name Arundell) and he did give me a fine voluntary or two. And so home by water. And at home I find my girl that run away, brought by a beadle of St. Brides parish, and stripped her and

a repl. 'to'   *b* l.h. repl. overlong symbol

---

1. Creed greatly exaggerated the Moors' numbers. The treaty was a six months' truce arranged on 31 August: below, p. 304; Routh, p. 41.

2. ? the King's Head: see below, vi. 242 & n. 4. For organs in taverns, see above, ii. 116, n. 1; P. A. Scholes, *Puritans and music*, p. 244. (E).

sent her away;[1] and a new one came, of Griffings helping too, which I think will prove a pretty girl – her name, Susan. And so to supper, after having this evening paid Mr. Hunt 3*l* for my viall (besides the Carving, which I paid this day 10*s* for to the Carver); and he tells me that I may without flattery say I have as good a Theorbo, viall and viallin as is in England. So to bed.[a]

22. Up by 4 a-clock to go with Sir W. Batten to Woolwich, and Sir J. Mennes; which we did, though not before 6 or 7 by their lying a-bed. Our business was to survey the new wharfe building there, in order to the giving more to him that doth it, Mr. Randall, then contracted for;[2] but I see no reason for it, though it be well done, yet not better then contracted to be.

Here we eat and drunk at the Clerk of the Cheques;[3] and in taking water at the Tower-gate, we drank a cup of strong water, which I did out of pure conscience to my health; and I think is not excepted by my oaths, but it is a thing I shall not do again, hoping to have no such occasion. After breakfast there, Mr. Castle and I walked to[b] Greenwich and in our way met some Gypsys who would needs tell me my fortune, and I suffered one of them – who told me many things common, as others do, but bid me beware of a John and a Thomas, for they did seek to do me hurt. And that somebody should be with me this day sennit to borrow money of me, but I should lend them none.[4] She got ninepence of me; and so I left them, and to Greenwich and so to Deptford, where the two Knights were come; and thence home by water, where I find my closet done at my office to my mind and work gone well on at home. And Ashwell gone abroad to her father, my wife having spoken plainly to her. After dinner

a last three sentences crowded into bottom of page
b repl. 'in'

1. Cf. St Bride's churchwardens' accounts: 'August 21st 1663. To Smith the Staffman when hee found the Girle which ranne away . . . 000.00.06d': GL, MS. 6552/1.
2. On 15 June Edward Rundells (house carpenter at Deptford yard) had sent in his bill for framing and pitching the new wharf, and had charged more than his contract allowed for: *CSPD 1663-4*, p. 171. He made a habit of under-estimating, and Pepys distrusted him: ib., *1664-5*, pp. 381-2.
3. William Sheldon's.
4. See below, p. 296.

to my office, getting my closet made clean and setting some
papers in order; and so in the evening home – and to bed.

This day Sir W. Batten tells me that Mr. Newburne (of whom
the nick-word came up among us for "Arise Tom Newburne")
is dead of eating Cowcoumbers, of which the other day I heard
another, I think Sir Nich. Crisps son.[1]

23. *Lords day.* Up and to church without my wife, she being
all dirty, as my house is. God forgive me, I looked about to see
if I could spy Pembleton; but could not, which did please me
not a little. Home to dinner, and then to walk up and down in
my house with my wife, discoursing of our family matters; and
I hope, after all my troubles of mind and jealousy, we shall live
happily still. To church again; and so home to my wife and
with her read *Iter boreale*, a poem made just at the King's coming
home but I never read it before, and now like it pretty well
but not so as it was cried up.[2] So to supper; no pleasure or discourse with Ashwell, with whom for her neglect and unconcern-
ment to do anything in this time of dirt and trouble in the
house, but gadding abroad as she hath been all this afternoon, I
know not whither.[a] After supper to prayers and to bed, having
been, by a sudden letter coming to me from Mr. Coventry, been
with Sir W. Penn to discourse with him about sending 500 soldiers
into Ireland.[3] I doubt matters do not go very right there. So[b]

24. Up very early, and my Joyners came to work. I to Mr
Moore and from him came back home again and drew up an
account to my Lord; and that being done, met him at my Lord

a sentence incomplete in MS.
b ? the beginning of the next day's entry

---

1. Probably his son Ellis. New-
borne appears to have been a solicitor
in the Old Jewry: Richard Smyth,
Obituary, p. 58. Evelyn refers to the
belief that cucumbers were poisonous
as a common superstition: *Acetaria*
(1699), pp. 22, 77.

2. Several poems of this title were
published in 1660 to celebrate

Monck's march from Scotland. This
is probably by Robert Wild: repr.
Poems on affairs of state . . . 1660–1714,
vol. i (*1660–1678*; ed. G. deF. Lord),
pp. 3+. None survives in the PL.

3. Cf. *CSP Ireland 1663–5*, p. 202;
CSPD 1663–4, pp. 255, 267, 288.
For the news of plots in Ireland, see
above, p. 168 & n. 2.

Sandwiches, where I was a good while alone with my Lord; and I perceive he confides in me and loves me as he use to do – and tells me his condition, which is now very well; all I fear is that he will not live within compass, for I am told this morning of strange dotages of his upon that slut at Chelsy, even in the presence of his daughter my Lady Jem and Mrs. Ferrers, who took notice of it.

There came to him this morning his prints of the River Tagus and the City of Lisbon, which he measured with his own hand and printed by command of the King. My Lord pleases himself with it, but methinks it ought to have been better done then by Iching. Besides, I put him upon having some took off upon white Sattin – which he ordered presently.[1]

I offered my Lord my accounts and did give him up his old bond for 500*l*. and took a new one of him for 700*l*.;[2] which I am, by lending him more money, to make up – and am glad of it.

My Lord would have had me dined with him, but I had a mind to go home to my workmen, and so took a kind good-bye of him; and so with Creede to St. James, and missing Mr. Coventry, walked to the New Exchange and there drunk some Whey; and so I by water home. And find my closet at my office made very clean and neat, to my mind mightily. And home to dinner, and then to my office to brush my books and put them and my papers in order again. And all the afternoon, till late at night, doing business there; and so home to supper and then to work in my chamber, making matters of this day's accounts clear in my books, they being a little extraordinary; and so being very late, I put myself to bed,[3] the rest being long ago gone.

1. There is a sketch, with a scale of miles, of the mouth of the Tagus in Sandwich's journal: Mapperton MSS, Journal, i. 388–9. ('The rest of my observations of the river of Lisbone,' he wrote, 'are perfected and printed by my Copper Plate at the Kinges Command.') Another drawing by him of the Tangier roads (November 1661) is in BM, King's Maps, CXVII 77. Sandwich's sketch may have been the basis of Dirk Stoop's very rare etching 'The River Tagus and Citty of Lisbona' (c. 16⅞ × 28⅝ ins.); see E. Dutuit, *Manuel de l'amateur d'estampes*, iii. 325 (27 *bis*), decorated with the English royal arms and those of Sandwich. An impression in the BM (Sheepshanks Coll., vol. 23) is printed on white satin. Pepys's criticism of the etching ('Iching') technique for such a subject is justified: an engraved plate would probably have produced a firmer and more durable line. (OM).

2. See above, p. 199; ii. 61 & n. 5.
3. A duty normally performed by a servant.

25. Up very earely and removed the things out of my chamber into the dining-room, it being to be new-floored this day. So the workmen being*ᵃ* come and falling to work there, I to the office and thence down to Lymehouse to Phin Petts about Masts. And so back to the office, where we sat; and being rose and Mr. Coventry being gone, taking his leave for that he is to go to the Bath with the Duke tomorrow, I to the Change and there spoke with several persons, and lastly with Sir W Warren and with him to a Coffee-house and there sat two hours, talking of office business and Mr. Woods knavery, which I verily believe.[1] And lastly, he tells me that he hears that Captain Cocke is like to become a principal-officer, either a Controller or Surveyor; at which I am not sorry, so either of the other[2] may be gone. And I think it probable enough that it may be so.

So home at 2 a-clock and there I find Ashwell gone; and her wages come to 50s and my wife, by a mistake from me, did give her 20s. more. But I am glad that she is gone and that charge saved.

After dinner, among my Joyners and with them till dark night and this night they made an end of all; and so having paid them 40s for their six days' work,[3] I am glad they have ended and are gone, for I am weary, and my wife too, of their dirt.

My [wife] growing peevish at night, being weary, and I a little vexed to see that she doth not retain things in her memory that belong to the house, as she ought and I myself do, I went out in a little seeming discontent to the office; and after being there a while, home to supper and to bed.

Tomorrow they say the King and Duke sets out for the Bath.

This noon, going to the Exchange, I met a fine fellow with Trumpets before him in Leadenhall-street, and upon enquiry I find that he is the Clerk of the City market, and three or four

a repl. 'become'

---

1. William Wood (timber merchant) was distrusted by Pepys: cf. above, p. 201. He was now tendering for a contract in competition with Warren: below, p. 304, n. 1.
2. I.e. Mennes or Batten. Cocke

never joined the Board. It was held to be undesirable to appoint merchants: cf. below, v. 324, 326 & nn.
3. See below, p. 293 & n. 1.

men carried each of them a Arrow of a pound weight in their hands. It seems this Lord Mayor[1] begins again an old Custome, that upon the three first days of Bartolomew fayre – the first, there is a match of wrestling, which was done, and the Lord Mayor there and Aldermen in Moore-fields yesterday. Today, Shooting; and tomorrow, Hunting. And this officer of course* is to perform this ceremony of riding through the city, I think to proclaim or challenge any to shoot. It seems the people of the Faire cry out upon it as a great hindrance to them.[2]

26. Up; and after doing something in order to the putting of my house in order now the Joynery is done, I went by water to White-hall, where the court full of wagons and horses, the King and Court going this day out toward the Bath; and I to St. James's, where I spent an hour or more, talking of many things to my great content with Mr. Coventry in his chamber, he being ready to set forth too with the Duke today. And so left him; and I meeting Mr. Gauden, with him to our office, and in Sir W. Penn's chamber did discourse, by a meeting on purpose with Mr. Waith, about the victualling business, and came to some issue in it.

So home to dinner, and Mr. Moore came and dined with me; and after dinner I paid him some money, which evened all reckonings between him and me to this day; and for my Lord also I paid him some money, so that now my Lord owes me, for which I have his bond, just 700*l*.

After long discourse with him of[a] the fitness of his giving me a receipt for this money, which I for my security think necessary, and he otherwise doth not think so, at last, after being a little angry, and I resolving not to let go my money without it, he did give me one.

Thence I took him, and he and I took a pleasant walk to Dept-

a MS. 'whom' or 'om'

1. Sir John Robinson.
2. The city had allowed these customs to lapse during the Interregnum. The men of the fair quarrelled with the Mayor over the dues payable for their stalls, and also objected to the city's view that the fair should open with the mayoral proclamation late on the 23rd rather than at midnight on the 22nd, and that the fair should last for three days instead of fourteen. See H. Morley, *Mem. Bartholomew Fair.*

ford and back again, I doing much business there. He went home and I home also, in-a-doors to supper, being very glad to see my house begin to look like itself again; hoping, after this is over, not to be in any dirt a great while again – but it is very handsome, and will be more when the floors come to be of one colour.

So, weary to bed.

Pleased this day to see Captain Hickes come to me with a list of all the officers of Deptford yard; wherein he, being a high old Cavalier, doth give me an account of every one of them, to their reproach in all respects; and discovers many of their knaveries[1] and tells me, and so I thank God I hear everywhere, that my name is up for a good husband for the King, and a good man, for which I bless God, and that he did this by perticular direction of Mr. Coventry.

27. Up, after much pleasant talk with my wife and a little that vexes me, for I see that she is confirmed in it that all that I do is by design, and that my very keeping of the house in dirt, and the doing of this and anything else in the house, is but to find her imployment to keep her within and from minding of her pleasure in – which, though I am sorry to see she minds it, is true enough in a great degree.

To my office; and there we sat and despatched much business. Home and dined with my wife well; and then up and made clean my closet of books and had my chamber a third time made very clean, so that it is now in a very fine condition.

Thence down to see some good plank in the River with Sir W. Batten. And back again, it being a very cold day and a cold winde. Home again; and after seeing Sir W. Penn, to my office and there till late doing of business – being mightily incouraged by everybody that I meet withal upon the Change and everywhere else, that I am taken notice of for a man that doth the King's business wholly and well – for which the Lord be praised, for I know no honour I desire more.

Home to supper, where I find my house very clean from top to

1. Cf. *CSPD 1663-4*, p. 249: a letter from William Hickes to Pepys, 22 August, reporting embezzlement of the King's stores.

bottom again, to my great content.   I find a *feacho*[1] (as he calls it) of fine Sugar and a Case[a] of Orange flower water come from Mr. Cocke of Lisbon – the fruits of my last year's service to him; which I did in great justice to the man, a perfect stranger.[2]   He sends it me, desiring that I would not let Sir J. Mennes know it, from whom he expected to have found that service done which he had from me, from whom he could expect nothing, and the other failed him, and would have done, I am sure, to this day had not I brought it to some end.[3]

After supper to bed.

28.   At the office betimes (it being cold all night and this morning, and a very great frost they say abroad; which is much, having had no summer at all almost); where we sat, and in the afternoon also, about settling the Establishment of the number[b] of men borne on ships, &c., till the evening; and after that, in my closet till late, and quite tired with business, home to supper and to bed.

29.   Up betimes and settled some necessary papers relating to my security in the accounts which I lately passed with my Lord Sandwich; then to the office and there all the morning sitting. So home to dinner and then abroad with my wife by water to Westminster; and there left her at my Lord's lodgings, talking with Mrs. Harper about her kinswoman's coming to my wife next week.   And I to Jervas the barbers and there was trimmed and did deliver back a periwigg which be brought me by my desire the other day to show me, having some thoughts, though no great desire or resolution yet, to wear one.   And so I put it off for a while.[4]

Thence to my wife, and calling at both the Exchanges, buying stockings for her and myself; and also at Leaden-hall,[5] where she and I, it being candle-light, bought meat for tomorrow, having

a l.h. repl. s.h. 'ch'-   *b* repl. 'namber'

---

1. *Fecho* (Port.); a small case.

2. Capt. Robert Cocke, navy victualling agent at Lisbon, had been busy of late supplying the Mediterranean fleets and the Tangier soldiers: *CSPD 1663–4*, passim.   His accounts were now under examination by the Board: below, p. 325 & n. 1.

3. Robert Cocke's correspondence with Mennes about his accounts is referred to in HMC, *Heathcote*, pp. 70, 79.

4. He bought two later: below, p. 358 & n. 1.

5. The market.

ne'er a maid to do it; and I myself bought, while my wife was gone to another shop, a leg of beef, a good one, for sixpence, and my wife says is worth my money. So walked home, with a woman carrying our things, and had a very pleasant walk from White-hall home. So to my office and there despatched some business; and so home to supper and to bed.

We called at Toms as we came by, and there saw his new building,[1] which will be very convenient. But I am mightily displeased at a letter he sent me last night to borrow 20*l* more of me; and yet gives me no account, as I have long desired, how matters stand with him in the world.[2] I am troubled also to see how, contrary to my expectation, my brother ⟨John⟩ neither is the schollar nor minds his studies as I thought he would have done – but loiters away his time, so that I must send him soon to Cambrige again.

30. *Lords day.* Lay long, then up; and Will being ill of the tooth-ake, I stayed at home and made up my accounts; which to my great content arise to 750*l* clear Creditor, the most I have had yet. Dined alone with my wife, my brother dining abroad at my uncle Wights I think. To church, I alone, in the afternoon; and there saw Pembleton come in and look up, which put me into a sweat, and seeing not my wife there, went out again. But Lord – how I was afeared that he might, seeing me at church, go home to my wife; so much it is out of my power to preserve myself from jealousy*a* – and so sot impatient all the sermon. Home and find all well and no sign of anybody being there, and so with great content playing and dallying with my wife; and so to my office, doing a little business there among my papers, and home to my wife to talk – supper and bed.

31. Up and at my office all the morning, where Sir W. Batten and Sir J. Mennes did pay the short-allowance money to the East

a s.h. repl. l.h. 'Jealousy' written over another l.h. word (-'ment') now illegible.

1. See above, p. 236 & n. 2.   year Tom owed Pepys £87: Rawl.
2. At his death in the following   A 182, f. 301*r*.

India companies,[1] and by the assistance of the City-Marshall and his men did lay hold of two or three of the chief of the companies that were in the mutiny the other day and sent them to prison.[2] I home to dinner; and my wife after dinner going with my brother to see a play, I to my office, where very late doing business; and so home to supper and to bed.

This noon came Jane Gentleman to serve my wife as her chambermaid; I wish she may prove well;[3] she is only thick of hearing, which may be a trouble, but we know not yet, nor is it always so much as at other times.

So ends this month, with my mind pretty well in quiet, and in good disposition of health since my drinking at home of a little wine with my beer; but nowhere else do I drink any wine at all. My house in a way to be clean again, the Joyners and all having done; but only we lack a Cooke-maid and Jane our chambermaid is but new come to us this day.

The King and Queene and the Court at the Bath. My Lord Sandwich in the country,[4] newly gone, with my doubts concerning him having been debauched by a slut at his lodgings at Chelsy. My brother John with me, but not to[a] my great content, because I do not see him mind his study or give me so good account thereof as I expected.

My Brother ⟨Tom⟩ embarqued in building, and I fear in no good condition for it, for he sent to me to borrow more money, which I shall not lend him.

Myself in good condition in the office, and I hope in a good way of saving of money at home.[b]

a repl. 'my'   *b* followed by one blank page

---

1. For the payment, see PRO, Adm. 20/4, p. 539. These E. Indiamen had taken part in Marlborough's Bombay voyage (q.v. above, p. 139) and for a time their crews had been supplied with only four-fifths of their rations: see authorities at n. 2 below. Short-allowance ('pinch-gut') money was the usual form of compensation.

2. On the 27th Mennes had been attacked 'in or near' Fenchurch St by some of the sailors discontented with their pay. The Privy Council ordered the Principal Officers to use their authority as magistrates, and required the Lord Mayor to lend his assistance. See PRO, PC 2/56, p. 532; Adm. 2/1745, n.p. With these arrests, Pepys reported to Coventry that 'all's well againe'; NMM, LBK/8, pp. 68–9. For the Principal Officers' magisterial authority, see above, p. 82, n. 1.

3. She stayed until March 1664.

4. At Hinchingbrooke: below, pp. 307–8.

SEPTEMBER.

1. Up pretty betimes; and after a little at my Viall, to my office, where we sat all the morning, and I got my bill, among others, for my carved work, which I expected to have paid for myself, signed at the table, and hoped to get the money back again – though if the rest had not got it paid by the King, I never entended nor did desire to have him to pay for my vanity.[1]

At noon to the Exchange, where among many merchants about provision for the navy; and so home to dinner, where I met Mr. Hunt, his wife and child, and dined with us very merry. And after dinner I to my office with Captain Hickes, who brought my wife some shells, very pretty.[2] He gives me great informacion against the officers and men at Deptford; I find him a talking fellow, but believe much of what he says is true.

In the evening, my brother John coming to me to complain that my wife seems to be discontented at his being here and shows him great disrespect; so I took and walked with him in the garden and discoursed long with him about my affairs, and how imprudent it is for my father and mother and him to take exceptions without great cause at my wife, considering how much it concerns them to keep her their friend, and for my peace; not that I would ever be led by her to forget or desert them in the main, but yet she deserves to be pleased and complied with a little, considering the manner of life that I keep her to and how convenient it were for me to have Brampton for her to be sent to when I have a mind or occasion to go abroad to Portsmouth or elsewhere about pleasure or business, when it will not be safe for

1. The bill for carved work at Pepys's lodgings submitted this day to the Treasurer amounted to £21 15s. 4d.: PRO, Adm. 20/4, p. 238. His colleagues' bills are probably those for £55 spent on the Navy Office in July: ib., loc. cit. Cf. also the other bills, ib., pp. 227, 358. Pepys had paid 40s. to joiners on 25 August (above, p. 287). Penn seems to have been the first to propose to get the work paid for by the King: above, p. 68.

2. On 9 September Hickes wrote to Pepys from Deptford promising to 'plunder abroad for more rarities' and to share them with Pepys's wife: *CSPD 1663-4*, p. 269.

me to leave her alone. So directed him how to behave himself to her, and gave him other counsel; and so to my office, where late, and then home to supper and to bed.

2. Up betimes and to my office; and thence with Sir J. Mennes by coach to White-hall, where met us Sir W. Batten; and there stayed by the council-chamber till the Lords called us in, being appointed four days ago to attend them with an account of the Ryott among the Seamen the other day, which Sir J. Mennes did as like a coxcombe as ever I saw any man speak in my life; and so we were dismissed, they making nothing almost of the matter.[1] We stayed long without, till by and by my Lord Mayor comes, who also was commanded to be there; and he having, we not being within with him, an[a] Admonicion from the Lords to take better care of preserving the peace, we joyned with him; and the Lords having commanded Sir J. Mennes to prosecute the fellows for a Ryott, we rode along with my Lord Mayor in his coach to the Sessions-house in the Old Bayly, where the Sessions are now sitting. Here I heard two[b] or three ordinary tryalls; among others, one (which they say is very common nowadays; and therefore in my now taking of maids, I resolve to look to have somebody to answer for them)[2] woman that went and was endicted by four names for entering herself a cook-maid to a gentleman that prosecuted her there, and after three days run away with a silver tankard, a porringer of silver, and a couple of spoons. And being now found, is found guilty and likely will be hanged.[3]

By and by up to dinner with my Lord Mayor and the Aldermen; and a very great dinner and most excellent venison, but it almost made me sick by not daring to drink wine. After dinner

a   l.h. repl. s.h. 'a'
b   page heading corrected from 'August' to 'September.'

---

1. A committee meeting; not reported in the Privy Council Register. For the riot, see above, p. 292 & n. 2.

2. Cf. above, p. 79 & n. 1.

3. She was Anne Pettis, alias Petwer, alias Reade, alias Cade; indicted for stealing goods to the value of £5 12s. of Richard Bridges. Sentenced to be hanged, she was reprieved by the court after judgment: LRO, Sessions Minute Book and File, s.d. For the Old Bailey court at this period, see *London Sessions records, 1605–85* (ed. H. Bowler), Introduction. A later observer's comments are in Z. C. von Uffenbach, *London in 1710* (ed. Quarrell and Mare), pp. 124–5.

into a withdrawing-room and there we talked, among other things, of the Lord Mayor's sword; they tell me this sword, they believe, is at least a hundred or two hundred years old; and another that he hath, which is called the Black Sword, which the Lord Mayor wears when he mournes but properly is their Lenten sword to wear upon Good Friday and other Lent days, is older*a* then that.[1] Thence, I leaving Sir J. Mennes to look after his inditement drawing up, I home by water and there find my wife mightily pleased with a present of shells, fine shells, given her by Captain Hickes; and so she and I up to look them over, and endeed they are very pleasant ones. By and by in comes Mr. Lewellin, lately come from Ireland, to see me. He tells me how the English interest falls mightily there, the Irish party being too great; so that most of the old Rebells are found Innocent and their lands, which were forfeited and bought or given to the English, are restored to them; which gives great discontent there among the English.[2]

He being gone, I to my office, where late putting things in order; and so home to supper and to bed. Going through the City, my Lord Mayor told me how the piller set up by Exeter-house is only to show where the pipes of Water run to the City.[3] And observed that this city is as well watered as any city in the world, and that the bringing the water to the City hath cost it, first and last, above 300000*l*; but by the new building, and the building of St. James's by my Lord St. Albans, which he is now about (and which the City stomach I perceive highly, but dare not

a repl. 'ol'- badly formed

1. See Llewellyn Jewitt and W. H. St John Hope, *Corporation plate and insignia of cities and towns of Engl. and Wales*, ii. 100–11.
2. Peter Llewellyn was an old friend of Pepys; in 1660 an under-clerk of the English Council of State; now in the service of the Earl of Anglesey, Vice-Treasurer of Ireland. He is here referring to the work of the commission appointed under the act for the settling of land disputes in Ireland. The 'old Rebells' are those of 1641.
3. At this date water was supplied to the city mainly from the London Bridge waterworks begun in 1580 and worked by tidal waterwheels; by the New River Company, established under James I, with its reservoirs by Sadler's Wells; and by the much more ancient works constructed at various dates by the city corporation, of which the most important drew from the Tyburn. The great increase of buildings between Temple Bar and Piccadilly made necessary this marking of the line of the water-pipes. (R).

oppose it), were it now to be done, it would*a* not be done for a
million of money.¹

3. Up betimes, and for an hour at my viall, before my people
rise. Then up and to the office a while, and then to Sir W.
Batten, who is going this day for pleasure down to the Downes.
I eat a breakfast with them, and at my Lady's desire with them
by coach to Greenwich, where I went aboard with them on the
Charlotte=Yacht. The wind very fresh, and I believe they will be
all sick enough – besides that she is mighty troublesome on the
water. Methinks she makes over-much of her husband's Ward,
young Mr. Griffin, as if she expected some service from him when
he comes to it, being a pretty young boy.

I left them under sail, and I to Deptford; and after a word or
two with Sir J. Mennes, walked to Redriffe and so home. In
my way, it coming into my head, overtaking of a beggar or two
on the way that looked like Gypsys, it came into my head what
the Gypsys eight or nine days ago² had foretold, that somebody
that day sennit should be with me to borrow money, but I
should lend none; and looking, when I came to my office, upon
my Journall, that my Brother John had brought a letter that day
from my Brother Tom to borrow 20*l* more of me, which had
vexed me so, that I had sent the letter to my father into the
country, to acquaint ʼhim of it and how little he is beforehand that
he is still forced to borrow. But it pleased me mightily to see
how, contrary to my expectation, having so lately lent him 20*l*,³
and believe that he had money by him to spare, and that after
some days not thinking of it, I should look back*b* and find what
the Gypsy had told me to be so true.

After dinner at home, I to my office and there till late doing
business, being very well pleased with Mr. Cutlers coming to me
about some business; and among other things, tells me that he

a repl. 'will'   *b* repl. 'find'

---

1. See *Comp.*: 'St James's Fields'.
The city corporation was consistently
opposed to new buildings, and
especially to new markets, one of
which in defiance of the city's
chartered monopoly thereof was
shrewdly included in St Albans's
plans. (R).
2. See above, p. 284.
3. See above, iii. 103.

values me as a man of business, which he accounts the best virtuoso;[1] and I know his thinking me so, and speaking where he comes, may be of good use to me.

Home to supper and to bed.

4. Up betimes, and an hour at my viall; and then abroad by water to White-hall and to Westminster-hall and there bought the first news-books of Lestrange's writing, he beginning this week; and makes methink but a simple beginning.[2] Then to speak to Mrs. Lane, who seems desirous to have me come to see her and to have her company as I had a little while ago, which methinks, if she were very modest, considering how I tumbled and tossed her, she should not.

Thence to Mrs. Harpers and sent for Creed; and there Mrs. Harper sent for a maid for me to come to live with my wife; I like the maid's looks well enough and I believe may do well, she looking very modestly and speaking so too.[3] I directed her to speak with my wife. And so Creed and I away to Mr. Povys; and he not being at home, walked to Lincolnes Inn walks, which they are making very fine. And about one o'clock went back to Povys; and by and by in comes he, and so we sat down to dinner, and his lady[4] whom I never saw before (a handsome old woman that brought him money, that makes him do as he does); and so we had plenty of meat and drink (though I drunk no wine, though mightily urged to it) and in the exact manner that

1. In contemporary usage 'virtuoso' was the fashionable word for the accomplished *savant*, the man of learned parts. The 'man of business' was the practical administrator. William Cutler was a prosperous merchant.

2. The production of government newspapers was now taken over by Roger L'Estrange from Henry Muddiman. *The Intelligencer* appeared on Mondays, beginning on 31 August, and *The Newes* on Thursdays, beginning on 3 September. The titles were new. The first number of *The Intelligencer* (to which Pepys presumably refers) was published at ½*d*.

and contained little more than a prospectus about the danger of publishing any news at all, and a few random items of foreign intelligence. There was only one small piece of home news. It ran till 29 January 1666. Pepys preserved in his library an almost complete run both of these papers and of their immediate predecessors: PL 1743-7 (4 vols; 1 January 1660-1 January 1666).

3. Pepys never names this girl: she fell ill, and left on the 10th.

4. Mary, widow of John Agard, of King's Bromley, Staffs. Povey had married her in 1657.

I never saw in my life anywhere – and he the most full and satisfied in it that man can be in this world with anything.

After dinner down to see his new cellars which he hath made so fine, with so noble an arch and such contrivances for his barrels and bottles, and in a room next to it such a Grotto and fountayne, which in summer will be so pleasant as nothing in the world can be almost.

But to see how he himself doth pride himself too much in it, and commend and expect to have all admired, though indeed everything doth highly deserve it, is a little troublesome.

Thence Creed and I away, and by his importunity away by coach to Bartholomew fayre,[1] where I had no mind to go without my wife; and therefore rode through the fair without lighting and away home, leaving him there. And at home made my wife get herself presently ready, and so carried her by coach to the fair and showed her the Munkys dancing on the ropes; which was strange, but such dirty sport that I was not pleased with it. There was also a horse with hoofes like Rams hornes – a goose with four feet – and a cock with three. Thence to another place and saw some German clocke-works,[2] the Salutacion of the Virgin Mary and several Scripture stories; but above all, there was at last represented the Sea, with Neptune, Venus, mermaids, and Cupid[3] on a Dolphin, the sea rolling; so well done, that had it been in a gaudy manner and placed[a] at a good distance, it had been admirable.

Thence home by coach with my wife, and I a while to the office; and so to supper and to bed. This day I read a proclamacion for calling in and commanding everybody to apprehend my Lord Bristoll.[4]

5. Up betimes and to my vyall awhile; and so to the office and there sat, and busy all the morning. So at noon to the exchange; and so home to dinner, where I met Creed, who dined with me; and after dinner mightily importuned by Captain

<hr>

a MS. 'place and'

1. See above, ii. 166, n. 2.
2. Cf. above, p. 265 & n. 3. (A).
3. *Recte* Arion: the semi-mythical Greek poet who, after being thrown overboard by sailors coveting his wealth, was carried ashore by a dolphin which he had charmed by his songs.
4. Dated 25 August; Steele, no. 3386. See above, p. 271 & n. 1.

Hickes, who came to tell my wife the names and story of all the shells, which was a pretty present which he made her the other day.

He being gone, Creed, my wife, and I to Cornhill and after many tryalls bought my wife a Chinke; that is, a paynted Indian Callico for to line her new Study, which is very pretty.[1]

So home with her, and then I away (Creed being gone) to Captain Minors upon Tower hill; and there, abating only some impertinences of his, I did inform myself well in things relating to the East Indys, both of the country and the disappointment the King met with the last voyage by the Knavery of the Portugall ViceRoy, and the inconsiderablenesse of the place of Bombaim if we had had it.[2] But above all things, it seems strange to me that matters should not be understood before they went out; and also that such a thing as this, which was expected to be one of the best parts of the Queens portion, should not be better understood; it being, if we had it, but a poor place and not really so was as described to our King in the draught of it, but a poor little Island; whereas they made the King and Lord Chancellor and the other learned men about the King believe that that and other Islands which are near it were all one piece; and so the draught was drawn and presented to the King, and believed by the King and expected to prove so when our men came thither;[3] but it is quite otherwise.

Thence to my office; and after several letters writ – home to supper and to bed – and took a pill. I hear this day that Sir W. Batten was fain to put ashore at Quinbrough with my Lady, who hath been so sick shee[a] swears never to go to sea again. But it happens well that Holmes is come home into the Downes, where he will meet my Lady and it may[b] be do her more good then she looked for. He brings news of the peace between Tanger and the Moores,[4] but the perticulars I know not; he is come but yesterday.

a l.h. repl. s.h. ? 'as he'   *b* MS. 'made'

1. For the use of chintz and other fabrics for this purpose, see *Comp.*: 'Furniture etc.'. Cf. also above, i. 256, n. 1.

2. For Bombay, see above, p. 139 & n. 2. Richard Minors had commanded the *Leopard* on this ex-pedition. He and the Portuguese Governor had quarrelled violently: *Journ. Indian Hist.*, 1/445.

3. This is confirmed by the evidence in W. Foster, *Engl. factories in India 1661–4*, pp. 126, 134.

4. See above, p. 283 & n. 1.

6. *Lords day.* My pill I took last night worked very well, and I lay long in bed and sweat to get away the Itching, all about my body from head to foot, which is beginning again as it did the last winter; and I find after I am up that it is abated. I stayed at home all day and my wife also; whom, God forgive me, I stayed along with me for fear of her seeing of Pembleton. But she and I enjoyed one another all day long with great pleasure, contriving about my wife's closet and the red chamber, whither we entend to go up, she and I, to lie.

We dined alone – and supped also at night, my brother John with us; and so to prayers and to bed.

7. Up pretty betimes and a while to my vyall; and then abroad to several places to buy things for the furnishing my house and my wife's closet. And then met my uncle Thomas by appointment, and he and I to the Prærogative Office in Paternoster Row[1] and there searched and found my Uncle Day's will and read it over and advised upon it, and his wife's after him.[2] And though my aunt Perkins's testimony is very good, yet I fear, the estate being great, and the rest that are able to inform us in matters are all possessed of more or less of the estate, it will be hard for us ever to do anything; nor will I adventure anything till I see what part will be given to us by my uncle Tho. of all that is gained. But I had another end, of putting my uncle into some doubts, that so I might keep him from going yet into the country, that he may be there against the Court[3] at his own charge; and so I left him and his son at a loss what to do till I see them again. And so I to my Lord Crews, thinking to have dined there, but it was too late and so back and called at my brother's and Mrs. Holdens about several businesses; and went all alone to the black spread Eagle in Bride lane and there had a

1. More accurately, in Ivy Lane, Paternoster Row; the archiepiscopal court in which wills were proved and administrations granted. (R).

2. The wills of John Day of Leverington, Cambs., gent. (proved 1649) and of his widow Beatrice (proved 1651); now in PCC, Fairfax, 181, and Grey, 82; summaries in Whitear, pp. 137–9. They were childless, and most of the estate (consisting of land in Leverington, Wisbech and Newton) had passed to Beatrice Day's nephews, Robert and John Twells. For Pepys's interest in it, see below, pp. 311–12.

3. The manorial court of Brampton, which had jurisdiction over this copyhold estate.

chop of veale and some bread, cheese and beer, cost me a shilling to my dinner; and so through fleete ally, God forgive me, out of an itch to look upon the sluts there; against which, when I saw them, my stomach turned; and so to Bartholomew-fayre, where I met with Mr. Pickering and he and I to see the Monkys at the Duch house, which is fur beyond the other that my wife and I saw the other day, and thence to see the dancing on the ropes, which was very poor and tedious.

But he and I fell in discourse about my Lord Sandwich; he tells me how he is sorry for my Lord at his being at Chelsy, and that his but seeming so to my Lord, without speaking one word, hath put him clear out of my Lord's favour, so as that he was fain to leave him before he went into the country, for that he was put to eat with his servants. But I could not fish from him (though I know it) what was the matter; but am very sorry to see that my Lord hath thus much forgot his honour, but am resolved not to meddle with it.

The play being done, I stole from him and hied home, buying several things at the Ironmongers: dogs, tongs, and Shovells for my wife's closet and the rest of my house – and so home. And thence to my office a while, and so home to supper and to bed. By my letters from Tanger today, I hear that it grows very strong by land, and the Molle goes on. They have lately killed 200 of the Moores, and lost about 40 or 50.[1] I am mightily afeared of laying out too much money in goods upon my house; but it is not money flung away, though I reckon nothing money but what it is in bank till I have a good sum beforehand in the world.

8. Up and to my vyall a while; and then to my office, one Phillips having brought me a draught of the *Katharin* Yacht, prettily well done for the common way of doing it.[2] At the

---

1. This was the action of 14 June (q.v. above, p. 240 & n. 5); estimates of the casualties varied greatly. For the battle and for the progress of the fortifications under Teviot's vigorous lead, see Routh, pp. 39+.

2. The bearer (? and artist) was possibly Philip Phillips, 'a diligent youth' employed as a labourer by Christopher Pett. The yacht had been built at Deptford for the King. The drawing has not been traced; a sketch by the elder van de Velde (c. 1673), now in the Boymans Museum, Rotterdam, is reproduced in *Mar. Mirr.*, 5/115-16.

office all the morning, making up our last half-year's account to
my Lord Treasurer, which comes to 160000*l* or thereabouts,
the proper expense of this half-year;[1] only, with an addition of
13000*l* for the threepences[2] due of the last account*ᵃ* to the Treasurer
for his disbursements and 1100*l* for this half-year's; so that in
three years and half, his threepences come to 14100*l*. Dined
at home with my wife, it being washing day; we had a good pie,
baked of a leg of mutton. And then to my office and then
abroad; and among other places, to Moxon's and there bought a
payre of Globes, cost me 3*l*. 10*s*[3] – with which I am well pleased,
I buying them principally for my wife, who hath a mind to
understand them – and I shall take pleasure to teach her. But
here I saw his great Window in his dining-room, where there is the
two Terrestriell Hemispheres, so painted as I never saw in my life,
and nobly done and to good purpose – done by his own hand.
Thence home to my office and there at business late. And
then to supper, home and to bed – my people sitting up longer
then ordinary before they had done their washing.

9. Up by break-a-day and then to my Vyall a while, and so
to Sir W Warren's*ᵇ* by agreement; and after talking and eating
something with him, he and I down by water to Woolwich
and there I did several businesses and had good discourse. And
thence walked to Greenwich; in my way, a little boy overtook
us with a fine cup turned out of Lignum vitæ,[4] which the poor
child confessed was made in the King's yard by his father, a
turner there, and that he doth often do it, and that I might have

a s.h. repl. l.h. ? 'Br'-   *b* repl. 'Sir WP'

1. The half-year's expense was £167,215 (25 March–30 September). The Lord Treasurer protested strongly because the Board had agreed to keep within the limit of £200,000 a year: *CTB*, i. 555; above, iii. 297; iv. 152; below, p. 305 & nn. Details in PRO, Adm. 106/3520, f. 15r; Pepys to Coventry, 12 September: LBK/8, pp. 74–5.
2. Poundage allowed to the Navy Treasurer.
3. I.e. a terrestrial and a celestial globe. Joseph Moxon had at first made globes to be used with his translation of Blaeu's *Institutio astronomica de usu globorum & sphaerarum caelestium ac terrestrium*: but he had published his own textbook (*A tutor to astronomie and geographie*) in 1659. The early editions were based on the cosmology of Tycho Brahe. See Eva G. R. Taylor, *Mathematical practitioners*, p. 93. C. F. Bryant, iii. 224.
4. This hard and heavy W. Indian wood (much in demand for drinking vessels) was used for ship's pulleys and blocks.

one and God knows what; which I shall examine. Thence to Sir W. Warren again and there draw up a contract for Masts which he is to sell us.[1] And so home to dinner, finding my poor wife busy.

I after dinner to the office, and then to White-hall to Sir G Carterets, but did not speak with him; and so to Westminster-hall, God forgive me, thinking to meet Mrs. Lane, but she was not there; but here I met with Ned Pickering, with whom I walked three or four hours till evening, he telling me the whole business of my Lord's folly with this Mrs. Becke at Chelsy, of all which I am ashamed to see my Lord so grossly play the beast and fool, to the flinging off of all Honour, friends, servants and every thing and person that is good, and only will have his private lust undisturbed with this common whore – his sitting up, night after night alone, suffering nobody to come to them, and all the day too – casting off Pickering, basely reproaching him with his small estate, which yet is a good one; and other poor courses to obtain privacy beneath his Honour – with his carrying her abroad and playing on his lute under her window, and forty other poor sordid things; which I am grieved to hear, but believe it to no purpose for me to meddle with it; but let him go on till God Almighty and his own conscience and thoughts of his Lady and family do it. So after long discourse, to my full satisfaction but great trouble, I home by water and at my office late; and so to supper to my poor wife, and so to bed – being troubled to think that I shall be forced to go to Brampton the next*a* Court, next week.

10. Up betimes and to my office. And then sat all the morning, making a great contract with Sir W. Warren for 3000*l* worth of Masts; but good God, to see what a man might do were I a knave – the whole business, from beginning to the end, being done by me out of the office, and signed to by them upon but once reading of it to them, without the least care or consultation either of quality, price, number, or need of them, only in general that it was good to have a store. But I hope my pains

a repl. 'very'

---

1. See below, p. 304 & n. 1.

was such as the King hath the best bargain of Masts hath been bought these 27 years in this office.[1]

Dined at home and then to my office again, many people about business with me. And then stepped a little abroad about business to the Wardrobe, but missed Mr. Moore, and elsewhere. And in my way met Mr. Moore, who tells me of the good peace that is made at Tanger with the Moores, but to continue but from six months to six months.[2] And that the Molle is laid out and likely to be done with great ease and successe. ⟨We to have a Quantity of ground for our cattle about the towne to our use.⟩[a][3]

To my office late, and then home to supper after writing letters, and to bed.

This day our cook-mayde (we having no luck in maids nowadays), which was likely to prove a good servant, though none of the best cooks, fell sick and is gone to her friend, having been with me but four days.

11.[b] This morning, about 2 or 3 a-clock, knocked up in our backyard; and rising to the window, being moonshine, I find it was the Constable and his watch, who had found our backyard door open and so came in to see what the matter was. So I desired them to shut the door and bid them good-night. And so to bed again. And at 6 a-clock up and a while to my vyall, and then to the office, where all the morning upon the victuallers account and then with him to dinner to the Dolphin, where I eat well but drunk no wine neither, which keeps me in such good order that I am mightily pleased with myself for it. Hither Mr. Moore came to me, and he and I home and advised about business; and so after an hour's examining the state of the Navy debts lately cast up, I took coach to Sir Ph. Warwickes; but finding Sir G. Carteret there, I did not go in, but directly home again,

a addition crowded in between paragraphs   *b* repl. '9'

---

1. Pepys's papers about this contract, with a note of a 5–7% advantage of Warren's tender (6 August) over that of Wood, are in PRO, SP 29/80, no. 47 (incomplete summary in *CSPD 1663–4*, p. 270); Adm. 106/3520, f. 14*v*; NWB, pp. 5–6. Cf. below, p. 421 & n. 3; B. Pool,

Navy Board contracts, 1660–1832, pp. 26–7.

2. See above, p. 283 & n. 1.

3. The cattle were kept in newly enclosed pastures protected by an outer wall of fortifications: Routh, p. 38.

it raining hard – having first of all been with Creed and Mrs.
Harper about a cook-maid, and am like to have one from Creede's
lodging. In my way home visited my Lord Crew and Sir Tho,
thinking they*a* might have enquired by the by of me, touching my
Lord's matters at Chelsey, but they said nothing; and so after
some slight common talk, I bid them good-night.

At home to my office; and after a while doing business, home
to supper – and bed.

12. Up betimes; and by water to White-hall and thence to
Sir Ph. Warwickes;[1] and there had half an hour's private discourse with him and did give him some good satisfaccion in our
Navy matters, and he also me, as to the money paid and due to
the Navy – so as he makes me assured, by perticulars, that Sir
G. Carteret is paid within 80000*l*, every farthing, that we to this
day, nay to Michaelmas-day next, have demanded; and that I am
sure is above*b* 50000*l* more then truly our expense hath been –
whatever is become of the money.[2]

Home, with great content that I have thus begun an acquaintance with him, who is a great man and a man of as much business
as any man in England – which I will endeavour to deserve and
keep.

Thence by water to my office, where all the morning; and so
to the Change at noon and there by appointment met and bring
home my uncle Tho, who resolves to go with me to Brampton
on Monday next – I wish he may hold his mind. I do not tell
him, and yet he believes that there is a Court to be, that he is to
do some business for us there. The truth is, I do find him a
much more cunning fellow then I ever took him for; nay, in
his very drink he hath his wits about him.

I took him home to dinner; and after dinner he begun, after a
glass a wine or two, to exclaim against Sir G Carteret and his

a l.h. repl. s.h. 'they' badly formed   *b* repl. 'about'

---

1. Secretary to the Lord Treasurer.
2. These figures do not accord
with those given in Pepys's letter
to Coventry: below, p. 306, n. 2.
It is there stated that Carteret and
Mennes had given an inflated figure

(£277,000) to the Lord Treasurer,
which Pepys had with difficulty succeeded in reducing to £136,000, a
sum still a little high, in his view. Cf.
above, p. 302 & n. 1.

family in Jersey,¹ bidding me to have a care of him, and how high, proud, false and politique a fellow he is – and how low he hath been under his command in the Island.

After dinner and long discourse he went away, to meet on Monday morning, and I to my office and thence by water to White-hall and Westminster-hall about several businesses; and so home and to my office, writing a laborious letter about our last account to my Lord Treasurer,² which took me till one a-clock in the morning, *Lords day*. So that Griffin was fain to carry it to Westminster to go by express, and my other letters of import to my father and elsewhere could not go at all.

⟪13.⟫

To bed between one and two, and slept till 8 and lay talking till 9 with great pleasure with my wife; so up and put my clothes in order against tomorrow's Journy; and then at noon to dinner, and all the afternoon almost, playing and discoursing with my wife with great content; and then to my office, there to put papers in order against my going; and by and by comes my Uncle Wight to bid us to dinner tomorrow to a hanch of venison I sent them yesterday, given me by Mr. Povey, but I cannot go – but my wife will.

Then into the garden to read my weekly vowes. And then home; where at supper, saying to my wife in ordinary fondness, "Well, shall*a* you and I never travell together again?" – she took me up and offered and desired to go along with me. I, thinking by that means to have her safe from harm's way at*b* home here, was willing enough to feign; and after some difficulties made, did send about for a horse and other things, and so I think she will go. So, in a hurry getting myself and her things ready, to bed.

14. Up betimes, and my wife's mind and mine holds for her going. So she to get her ready, and I abroad to do the like for

a repl. 'you'   *b* repl. 'out'

---

1. Thomas Pepys had married a Jersey woman, Marie Syvret. Carteret had been Governor of the island, 1643–51, and came himself of a Jersey family. Cf. Coventry's stories about Carteret's government: above, p. 195.

2. Pepys to Coventry, 12 September: copy (in Hayter's hand), NMM, LBK/8, pp. 74–5; printed incompletely in *Further Corr.*, pp. 5–6.

myself, and so home; and after setting everything at my office and at home in order, by coach to Bishop-gate – it being a very promising fair day. There at the Dolphin we met my uncle Tho. (and his son-in-Law,[1] which seems a very sober man) and Mr. Moore. So Mr. Moore and my wife set out before, and my uncle and I stayed for his son Thomas, who by a sudden resolution is preparing to go with us, which makes me fear something of mischief which they design to do us. He staying a great while, the old man and I before and about eight mile off his son comes after us, and about six mile further we overtake Mr. Moore and my wife (which makes me mightily consider what a great deal of ground is lost in a little time, when it is to be got up again by another; that is, to go his own ground and the other's too); and so after a little bayte (I paying all the reckonings the whole Journy) at Ware,*a* to Buningford; where my wife, by drinking some cold beer, being hot herself, presently after lighting, begins to be sick and became so pale, and I alone with her in a great chamber there, that I thought she would have died; and so in great horror (and having a great trial of my true love and passion for her) called the maids and mistress of the house; and so with some strong water, and after a little vomitt, she came to be pretty well again; and so to bed, and I having put her to bed with great content – I called in my company and supped in the chamber by her; and being very merry in talk, supped and then parted, and I to bed and lay very well. This day my Cosen Tho dropped his hanger and [it] was lost.

15. Up pretty betimes and rode as far as Godmanchester (Mr. Moore having two falls, once in water and another in dirt) and there light and eat and drunk, being all of us very weary, but especially my uncle and wife. Thence to Brampton to my father's, and there found all well but not sensible how they ought to treat my*b* uncle and his son, at least till the Court bee over; which vexed me. But upon my counsel, they carried it fair to them; and so my father, Cosen Tho, and I up to Hinchingbrooke, where I find my Lord*c* and his company gone to

a repl. 'G'-   b repl. 'for'   c l.h. repl. l.h. 'Uncle'

---

1. Samuel de Santhune, weaver.

Boughton,[1] which vexed me.   But there I find my Lady and the young ladies; and there I alone with my Lady two hours, she carrying me through every part of the house and gardens, which are and will be mighty noble endeed.[2]   Here I saw Mrs. Betty Pickering, who is a very well-bred and comely lady, but very fat.   Thence, without so much as drinking, home with my father and Cosen (who stayed for me) home and to a good supper, after I had had an hour's talk with my*a* father abroad in the fields; wherein he begin to talk very highly of my promises to him, of giving him the profits of Sturtlow, as if it were nothing that I give him out of my purse, and that he would have me to give this also from myself to my brothers and sisters; I mean, Brampton and all I think.   I confess I was angry to hear him talk in that manner, and took him up roundly in it and advised him, if he could not live up[on] 50*l* per annum, which was another part of his discourse, that he would think to come and live at Toms again, where 50*l* per annum will be a good addition to Toms trade; and I think that must be done when all is done.   But my father spoke nothing more of it all the time I was in the country, though at that time he seemed to like it well enough.   I also spoke with Piggott, too, this evening before I went in to supper, and doubt that I shall meet with some knots in my business tomorrow before I can do it at the Court, but I shall do my best.

After supper my uncle and son to Stankes's to bed (which troubled me), all our father's beds being lent to Hinchingbrooke; and so my wife and I to bed – she very weary.

16.   Up betimes, and with my wife to Hinchingbrooke to see my Lady, she being to go to my Lord this morning; and there I left her.   And so back to the Court and heard Sir R. Bernards charges to the Courts Baron and Leete,[3] which took up till noon

a   l.h. repl. l.h. 'Pig'-

---

1. Near Kettering, Northants.; home of Sandwich's cousin, the 2nd Lord Mountagu of Boughton.
2. For the alterations now in progress, see above, i. 314 & n. 1.

3. These courts (civil and criminal respectively) were frequently held together, and in this case Bernard, as Steward (presiding judge) of both, gave the charges to the juries.

and was worth hearing; and after putting my business into some way, went home to my father's to dinner. And after dinner to the Court, where Sir Rob and his son came again by and by, and then to our business; and my father and I having given bond to him for the 21*l* Piggott owed him, my uncle Tho. did quietly*a* admit himself and surrender to us the lands first morgaged for our whole debt, and Sir Robts. added to it; which makes it up 209*l*, to be paid in six months.[1] But when I came to give him an account of more lands to be surrendered to us, wherein Piggott's wife was concerned and she there to give her consent, Sir Rob. would not hear of it, but begin to talk very high: that we were very cruel, and we had caution enough for our money, and he could not in conscience let the woman do it, and reproached my Uncle, both he and his son, with taking use upon use for this money. To all which I did give him such answers and spoke so well and kept him so to it, that all the Court was silent to hear us; and by report since, do confess they did never hear the like in that place. But he by a wile had got our bond; and I was content to have as much as I could, though I could not get all, and so took Piggott's surrender of them, without his wife, and by Sir Rob.'s own consent did tell the Court that if the money were not paid in the time and the Security prove not sufficient, I would conclude myself wronged by Sir Robt; which he granted I should do.

This kept us till night, but am heartily glad it ended so well on my uncles part, he doing that and Priors little house[2] very willingly. So the Court broke up, and my father and Mr. Sheply and I to Gorrums to drink; and then I left them and to the Bull,[3] where my uncle was to hear what he and the people said of our business, and hear nothing but what liked me very well; and so by and by home and to supper, and with my mind in pretty good quiet, to bed.

a   MS. 'quieting'

---

1. I.e. the original debt of £164 (above, ii. 137) plus interest: it was not settled until the autumn of 1664.
2. For its sale, see above, ii. 204 & n. 2.

3. More recently known as the Old Black Bull, an early 17th-century house on the s. side of the churchyard at Brampton: VCH, *Hunts.*, iii. 12.

17. Up; and my father being gone to bed ill last night, and continuing so this morning, I was forced to come to a new consideration, whether it was fit for to let my uncle and his son go to Wisbeech about my uncle Days estate[1] alone or no, and concluded it unfit and so resolved to go with them myself; and so leaving my wife there, I begun a journy with them; and with much ado through the Fens, along Dikes, where sometimes we were ready to have our horses sink to the belly, we got by night, with great deal of stir and hard riding, to Parsons drove,[2] a heathen place – where I found my uncle and aunt Perkins and their daughters, poor wretches, in a sad poor thatched cottage, like a poor barne or stable, peeling of Hemp[3] (in which I did give myself good content to see their manner of preparing of hemp) and in a poor condition of habitt; took them to our miserable Inne[4] and there, after long stay[a] and hearing of Franke their son, the miller, play upon his Treble[5] (as he calls it), with which he earnes part of his living, and singing of a country bawdy song, we set down to supper: the whole Crew and Frankes wife and children (a sad company, of which I was ashamed) supped with us. And after supper, I talking with my aunt about her report concerning my uncle Days Will and surrender, I find her in such different reports from what she writes and says to other people, and short of what I expected, that I fear little will be done of good in it. By and by news is brought us that one of our horses is stole out of the Stable; which proves my uncles, at which I was inwardly glad; I mean, that it was not mine. And at this we were at a great loss; and they doubting a person that lay at next door, a Londoner, some lawyer's clerk, we caused him to be secured in his bed and made care to be taken to seize the horse; and so, about 12 at night or more, to bed in a sad, cold, nasty chamber; only, the maid was indifferent handsome, and so I had a kiss or two of her, and I to bed. And a little after I was

a MS. 'stayed'

---

1. See above, p. 231 & n. 1.
2. Parson Drove, Isle of Ely, Cambs., five miles west of Wisbech; then in the parish of Leverington.
3. For English-grown hemp, see above, p. 259, n. 4.

4. The Swan, Parson Drove; still (1971) surviving.
5. Probably a treble viol. Cf. the 'two Trebles': above, 1, 114. (E).

asleep, they waked me to tell me that the horse was found, which was good news; and so to sleep till the morning – but was bit cruelly (and nobody else of our company, which I wonder at) by the gnatts.[1]

18. Up, and got our people together as soon as we could; and after eating a dish of cold Creame, which was my supper last night too, we took leave of our beggarly company, though they seem good people too, and over most sad Fenns (all the way observing the sad life that the people of that place (which if they be born there, they call the "Breedlings"[2] of the place) do live, sometimes rowing from one spot to another, and then wadeing) to Wisbeech, a pretty town and a fine church and library, where sundry very old Abbee manuscripts[3] – and a fine house, built on the church ground by[a] Secretary Thurlow, and a fine gallery built for him in the church, but now all in the Bishop of Elys hands.[4] After visiting the church &c., we out of the town by the help of a stranger, to find out one Blinkehorne a miller, of

a repl. 'they say'

1. Travellers commonly remarked on the fenland gnats – 'the humming Gnatts, which is all the Towne Musicke they have': Hammond, *Relation* [1634] in *Camden Misc.*, xvi. 90. Cf. also Evelyn, 22 July 1670. The agues or malarial fevers endemic in the fen country were carried by mosquitoes which bred in the marshes until the drainage of the fens in the 18th century: H. C. Darby, *Draining of fens*, p. 177.

2. Natives: Macaulay mistook the word for a proper name. *Hist. Engl.* (ed. Firth, 1914), iii. 1349.

3. The library (founded c. 1654, and housed in a room over the church porch) was one of a fairly large number of parochial libraries formed at about this time from private gifts and subscriptions. Thurloe (Cromwell's Secretary of State) had contributed 81 volumes; in 1718 there were 697: lists in HMC, *Rep.*, 9/293–4; *A catalogue of books in the library at Wisbech* (1718). The MSS (from Bury and Ramsey) included some from the 13th century. In the 19th century the collection was moved to the Town Hall and later to the Museum, where it now remains.

4. The town had built a gallery for Thurloe's use at the s. end of the church; it was taken down in 1856. Thurloe had bought the manor (originally belonging to the bishops of Ely) and c. 1658 had replaced the late 15th-century palace built by Bishop Morton by a house probably designed by Peter Mills: H. M. Colvin, *Dict. Engl. architects*, p. 391; illust. in VCH, *Cambs.*, iv. opp. p. 251. This had now reverted to the bishop, but later was let to tenants, and demolished in 1816. It stood in the grounds of the castle, not the church. [Anon.], *Hist. Wisbech* (Wisbech, 1833), p. 163.

whom we might inquire something of old Days disposal of his
estate and in whose hands it now is; and by great chance we met
him and brought him to our Inne to dinner; and instead of being
informed in his estate by this fellow, we find that he is the next
heire to the estate, which was matter of great sport to my Cosen
Tho and me, to see such a fellow prevent us in our hopes – he
being Days brother's daughter's son, whereas we are but his
sister's Sons and grandsons – so that after all, we were fain to
propose our matter to him and to get him to give us leave to
look after the business; and so he to have one third-part, and we
two the other two third-parts of what should be recovered of
the estate – which he consented to; and after some discourse and
paying the reckoning, we mounted again and rode (being very
merry at our defeate) to Chattres,[1] my uncle very weary; and
after supper and my telling of three stories to their good liking,
of Spiritts, we, all three in a chamber, went to bed.

19. Up pretty betimes; and after eating something, we set
out; and I (being willing thereto) went by a mistake with them
to St. Ives, and there, it being known that it was their nearer way
to London, I took leave of them there, they going straight to
London and I to Brampton; where I find my father ill in bed
still, and Madam Norbery (whom and her fair daughter and sister
I was ashamed to kiss, but did, my lip being sore with riding
in the winde and bit with the gnats)[a] lately come to[b] towne,[2]
come to see my father and mother; and they after a little stay
being gone, I told my father my successe.* And after dinner
my wife and I took horse and rode, with marvellous and the
first and only hour of pleasure that ever I had in this estate since
I had to do with it, to Brampton woods, and through the wood
rode and gathered nuts in my way; and then at Graffam to an
old woman's house to drink, where my wife used to go; and
being in all Circumstances highly pleased and in my wife's riding
and good company at this time, I rode and she showed me the
River behind my father's house, which is very pleasant; and so
saw her home, and I straight to Huntington; and there met Mr.
Sheply and to the Crowne (having sent home my horse by
Stankes) and there a barber came and trimmed me; and thence

a repl. 'gl'-   b l.h. repl. s.h. 'the'

1. Chatteris, Cambs.   2. Brampton.

walked to Hinchingbrooke, where my Lord and ladies all are just alighted.   And so I in among them and my Lord glad to see me, and the whole company; here I stayed and supped with them, and after a good stay talking, but yet observing my Lord not to be so mightily ingulphed in his pleasure in the country and company as I expected and hoped, I took leave of them; and after a walk in the Court-yard in the dark with W. Howe, who tells me that my Lord doth not enjoy himself and please himself as he used to do, but will haste up to London, and that he is resolve[d] to go to Chelsy again, which we are heartily grieved for and studious how to prevent if it be possible, I took horse, there being one appointed for me, and a groome to attend me, and so home, where my wife stayed up and sister for me.   And so to bed, troubled for what I hear of my Lord.

20.[a] *Lords day.*   Up; and finding my father somewhat better, walked to Huntington church; where in my Lord's pew (with the young ladies, by my Lord's own showing me the place), I stayed the sermon; and so to Hinchingbrooke, walking with Mr. Sheply and Dr King (whom they account a witty man here, as well as a good physician); and there my Lord took me with the rest of the company and singly demanded my opinion, in the walks in his garden, about the bringing of the Crooked wall on the Mount to a shape.   And so to dinner, there being Colloncll Williams[1] and much other company, and a noble dinner.   But having before got my Lord's warrant for travailyng today (there being a proclamacion read yesterday against it at Huntington, at which I am very glad),[2] I took leave, leaving them at dinner; and I walked alone to my father's and there, after a word or two to my father and mother, my wife and I mounted, and with my father's boy upon a horse I borrowed of Captain Ferrers, we rode to Bigglesworth by the help of a couple of countrymen that led us through the very long and dangerous waters (because of the diches[b] on each side) though it begin to be very dark.

a repl. '18'   *b* l.h. repl. s.h. 'ditched'

---

1. Henry Williams of Ramsey, Hunts.; a cousin of Oliver Cromwell who had changed his surname to Williams at the Restoration (cf. above, p. 83 & n. 1).

2. The proclamation for 'observa- tion of the Lord's Day' issued on 22 August (Steele, no. 3383) had to be read once a month for six months to every congregation. Cf. above, i. 206, n. 1.

And there we had a good breast of mutton roasted for us, and supped and to bed.

21.   Up very betimes, by break of day, and got my wife up, whom the thought of this day's long journy doth discourage; and after eating something and changing of a piece of gold to pay the reckoning, we mounted and through Baldwicke, where a fayre is kept today, and a great one for Cheese and other such commodities;[1] and so to Hatfield, it being most curious weather from the time we set out to our getting home.   And here we dined, having got hither at 12 a-clock.   And my wife being very weary, and believing that it would be hard to get her home tonight and a great charge to keep her longer abroad, I took the opportunity of a empty coach that was to go to London and left her to come in it to*a* London, for half-Crowne; and so I and the boy home as fast as we could drive, and it was even night before we got home, so that I account it very good fortune that we took this Course; being myself very weary, much more would my wife have been.   At home, find all very well and my house in good order.   To see Sir W. Penn, who is pretty well, and Sir J. Mennes, who is a little lame on one foot; and the rest gone to Chatham – *viz.* Sir G. Carteret and Sir W. Batten, who hath in my absence inveighed against my Contract the other day for Warrens masts,[2] in which he is a knave and I shall find matter of tryumph – but it vexes me a little.   So home.   And by and by comes my wife by coach well home; and having got a good fowle ready for supper against her coming, we eat heartily; and so with great content and ease to our own bed, there nothing appearing so to our content as to be at our*b* own home after being abroad awhile.

22.   I up, well refreshed after my Journy, and to my office and there set some things in order; and then Sir W Pen and I meet

a   repl. 'home'   *b*   MS. 'home'

---

1. For the fair at Baldock, Herts., see above, ii. 183 & n. 6.   The district was well known for its cheeses.

2. See above, p. 304 & n. 1.

and hold an office; and at noon home to dinner, and so by water with my wife to Westminster, she to see her father and mother; and we met again at my Lord's lodgings and thence by water home again, where at the door we met Sir W. Penn and his daughter, coming to visitt us. And after their visitt, I to my office; and after some discourse to my great satisfaction with Sir W Warren about our bargain of Masts, I wrote my letters by the post; and so home to supper and to bed.

This day my wife showed me bills printed, wherein her father, with Sir John Collidon and Sir Edwd. Ford, hath got a patent for curing of smoking chimnys.[1] I wish they may do good thereof – but fear it will prove but a poor project.

This day the King and Queene are to come to Oxford. I hear my Lady Castlemayne is for certain gone to Oxford to meet him, having lain within here at home this week or two, supposed to have miscarried; but for certain is as great in favour as heretofore; at least, Mrs. Sarah at my Lord's, who hears all from their own family, doth say so.[2]

Every day brings news of the Turkes advance into Germany, to the awakeing of all the Christian princes thereabouts, and

---

1. The patent was issued on 2 May 1663 and ran for 14 years: PRO, C 66/3040/11; printed in H. B. Wheatley, *S. Pepys and the world he lived in*, pp. 241+. It proposed to effect the cure by inserting 'tunnells' into the chimneys. I have not traced any copies of the printed bills. 'Sir John Collidon' is a mistake for Dr John Colladon, physician to the Queen. (Pepys is confusing him with Sir John Colleton, Bt, a London merchant.) Ford (who was not mentioned in the patent but may have joined the scheme later) was a royalist soldier and inventor who had been con-

cerned with other projects: below, p. 366 & n. 1. Alexandre St Michel, Elizabeth Pepys's father, often busied himself with such projects, never to any great profit.

2. On 20 September Lady Castlemaine had given birth to a son Henry (the second of her illegitimate sons by the King); cr. Duke of Grafton 1675; d. 1690. It was alleged that Charles admitted paternity only after some hesitation: Wood, *Fasti Oxon.* (ed. Bliss), ii. 270. Sarah (at Sandwich's lodgings in Whitehall) was a close neighbour of Lady Castlemaine in King St.

possessing himself of Hungary.¹   My present care is fitting my
wife's Closett and my house, and making her a velvet Coate and
me a new black cloth suit and coat and cloak, and evening my
reckonings as well as I can against Michaelmas day, hoping for
all that to have my ballance as great or greater then ever I had
yet.

23.   Up betimes and to my office, where setting down my
Journall while I was in the country to this day; and at noon by
water to my Lord Crews and there dined with him and Sir
Thomas, thinking to have them enquire something about my
Lord's going to Chelsy, or anything of that sort; but they did
not, nor seem to take the least notice of it; which is their discretion, though it might be better for my Lord, and them too, if
they did; that so, we might advise together for the best, which
cannot be while we seem ignorant one to another, and it is not
fit for me to begin the discourse.   Thence walked to several
places about business, and to Westminster-hall, thinking to meet
Mrs. Lane; which is my great vanity upon me at present, but I
must correct it.   She was not in the way.

So by water home and to my office; whither by and by came
my Brother John to me, who is to go to Cambrige tomorrow,
and I did give him a most Severe repremende for his bad account
he gives me of his studies.   This I did with great passion and
sharp words, which I was sorry to be forced to say, but that I
think it for his good; forswearing doing anything for him, and
that what I have yet and now do give him is against my heart
and will also be hereafter, till I do see him give me a better
account of his studies.   I was sorry to see him give me no
answer; but for aught I see, to hear me without great resentment

1. From June onwards a large Turkish army under Ahmed Kiuprili operating from Turkish territory in E. Hungary overran Transylvania and parts of W. Hungary. It now threatened Austria ('Germany'). The Diet at Ratisbon ordered prayers to be offered at midday every day for the protection of the Empire. This advance of the Turks – for the first time in a hundred years – made a profound impression on W. Europe. For reports at this time from Ratisbon, see *The Newes*, 17 September, p. 23. Even Hamburg and the Hanse Towns felt the alarm: ib., loc. cit.; HMC, *Ormonde*, n.s., iii. 84. Pepys (in common with the English news-papers of the time) gives a fair amount of attention to these events. The danger did not pass until the Turks' defeat at St Gotthard (W. Hungary) in August 1664.

and such as I should have had in his condition. But I have done my duty, let him do his; for I am resolved to be as good as my word. After two hours walking in the garden, till after it was dark, I ended with him; and to my office and there set some papers in order; and so to supper, I and my poor wife, who is mighty busy at home, fitting her closet. So to bed.

24. Up betimes; and after taking leave of my brother John, who went from me to my father's this day, I went forth by water to Sir Ph. Warwickes, where I was with him a pretty while; and in discourse he tells me and made it appear to me that the King cannot be in debt to the Navy at this time 5000*l*.; nay, it is my opinion that Sir G. Carteret doth owe the King money, and yet the whole Navy debt paid. Thence I parted, being doubtful of myself that I have not spoke with the gravity and weight that I ought to do in so great a business. But I rather hope it is my doubtfulness of myself and the haste which he was in, some very great personages waiting for him without while he was with me, that made him willing to be gone. To the office by water; where we sat, doing little now Mr. Coventry is not here, but only vex myself to see what a sort of coxcombs we are when he is not here to undertake such a business as we do. In the afternoon, telling my wife that I go to Deptford, I went by water to Westminster-hall; and there finding Mrs. Lane, took her over to Lambeth where we were lately, and there did what I would with her but only the main thing, which she would not consent to, for which God be praised; and yet I came so near, that I was provoked to spend. But trust in the Lord I shall never do so again while I live. After, being tired with her company, I landed her at White-hall and so home and at my office writing letters, till 12 at night almost; and then home to supper and bed and there find my poor wife hard at work, which grieved my heart to see that I should abuse so good a wretch, and that it is just with God to make her bad to me for my wronging of her; but I do resolve never to do the like again. So to bed.[a]

25. Lay pretty long in bed; and so to my office all the morning, till by and by, called out by Sir J. Mennes and Sir W. Batten, with them by water to Deptford, where it of a sudden

a This entry is in a fairly small hand throughout. There are three small blots at the bottom of the page.

did lighten, thunder, and rain, so as we could do nothing but stay in Davis's house; and by and by Sir J. Mennes and I home again by water and I home to dinner; and after dinner to the office and there till night all alone, none of my clerks being there, doing of business; and so home and to bed.

26. Up and to my office and there we sat till noon; and then I to the Exchange, but did little there; but meeting Mr. Rawlinson, he would need have me home to dinner; and Mr. Deane of Woolwich being with me, I took him with me and there we dined very well at his own dinner, only no invitation. But here I sat with little pleasure, considering my wife at home alone, and so I made what haste home I could and was forced to sit down again at dinner with her, being unwilling to neglect her by being known to dine abroad; my doing so being only to keep Deane from dining at home with me, being doubtful what I have to eat. So to the office and there till late at night; and so home to supper and bed, mightily pleased to find my wife so mindful of her house.

27. *Lords day.* Lay chatting with my wife a good while; then up and got me ready, and to church without my man William, whom I have not seen today, nor care; but could be glad to have him put himself far enough out of my favour that he may not wonder to have me put him away.[1] So home to dinner, being a little troubled to see Pembleton look into the church as he used to do, and my wife not being there, to go out again; but I do not discern in my wife the least memory of him.

Dined; and so to my office a little and then to church again, where a drowzy sermon; and so home to spend the evening with my poor wife – consulting about her closet, clothes, and other things. At night to supper, though with little comfort, I finding myself, both head and breast, in great pain; and which troubles me most, my right eare is almost deaf. It is a cold, which God Almighty in justice did give me while I sat lewdly sporting with Mrs. Lane the other day with the broken window in my neck.

---

1. Hewer appears to have been 'corrupting the maids by his idle talk and carriage': below, p. 358. Jane Birch in particular made complaints about him: below, p. 356. On 14 November he left for lodgings of his own and never returned to live in the Pepys household during the diary period. Good relations with his master were soon, however, resumed.

I went to bed with a posset, being very melancholy in consideration of the loss of my hearing.

28. Up, though with pain in my head, stomach, and eare,
and that deaf, so as in my way by coach to White-hall with
Sir J. Mennes, I called at Mr. Holliards, who did give me some
pills and tells me I shall have my hearing again and be well. So
to White-hall, where Sir J. Mennes and I did spend an hour in the
gallery looking upon the pictures,[1] in which he hath some judgment; and by and by the Comissioners for Tanger met, and
there my Lord Tiviott, together with Captain Cuttance, Captain
Evans, and Jonas Moore, sent to that purpose, did bring us a
brave draught of the Molle to be built there, and report that it is
likely to be the most considerable place the King of England hath
in the world; and so I am apt to think it will. After discourse
of this and of supplying the Guarrison with some more horse, we
rise; and Sir J. Mennes and I home again, finding the street about
our house full, Sir R. Ford beginning his Shrevalty today.[2] And
what with his and our houses being new-painted, the street begins
to look a great deal better then it did – and more gracefull.

Home and eat one bit of meat; and then by water with him
and Sir W. Batten to a sale of old provisions at Deptford; which
we did at Captain Boddilys house, to the value of 6 or 700*l.*;
but I am not satisfied with the method*a* used in this thing.[3]

Then home again by water; and after a little at my office and
visit Sir W. Penn, who is not very well again with his late pain,
home to supper, being hungry and my eare and cold not so bad
I think as it was. So to bed, taking one of my pills. News that
the King comes to town for certain on Thursday next from his
progress.[4]

29. Took two pills more in the morning and they worked all
day and I keeped the house. About noon dined; and then to
carry several heavy things with my wife up and down stairs in

a repl. 'moth'-

---

1. See below, p. 393, n. 1.

2. He lived in Seething Lane.

3. The sale was advertised on the
Exchange on 19 September: PRO,
Adm. 106/3520, f. 15*r*. William
Baddiley was Master-Attendant at
Deptford.

4. He had made a progress during
the past month to Bath, Bristol and
the West, and was returning via
Oxford.

order to our going to lie above and Will to come down to the Wardrobe.¹ And that put me into a violent sweat, so I had a fire made; and then being dry again, she and I to put up some paper pictures in the red chamber where we go to lie, very pretty – and the map of Paris.² Then in the evening, toward night, it fell to thunder, lighten, and rain so violently, that my house was all afloat and I in all the rain up to the gutters, and there dabled in the rain and wet half an hour, enough to have killed a man. That done, downstairs to dry myself again; and by and by came Mr. Symson³ to set up my wife's chimney-piece in her closet, which pleases me; and so that being done, I to supper and to bed, shifting myself from top to toe and doubtful of my doing myself hurt.

30. Rise very well, and my hearing pretty well again; and so to my office. By and by Mr. Holliard came, and at my house he searched my eare and I hope all will be well, though I do not yet hear so well as I used to do with my right eare.

So to my office till noon and then home to dinner. And in the afternoon by water to White-hall to the Tanger Committee, where my Lord Tiviott brought his accounts;⁴ which grieves me to see, that his accounts being to be examined by us, there is none of the great men at the Board that in compliment will except against anything in his accounts, and so none of the little persons dare do it: so the King is abused.

Thence home again by water with Sir W Rider, and so to my office, and there I sat late making up my month's accounts; and blessed be God, do find myself 760*l*. Creditor, notwithstanding that for clothes for myself and wife, and layings-out on her closet, I have spent this month 47*l*. So home, where I find our new cook-maid Elizabeth, whom my wife never saw at all, nor I but

1. See below, p. 336.

2. Possibly an early issue of the map by Jacques Gomboust. See below, vii. 379 & n. 2; ix. 286.

3. Thomas Simpson was the Master-Joiner of Deptford and Woolwich

dockyards who also made Pepys's first bookcases, the complete set of which now survives in the PL.

4. Summary in PRO, E 351/357.

once at a distance before; but recommended well by Mr. Creed, and I hope will prove well.[1]   So to supper – prayers, and bed.

This evening Mr. Coventry is come to St. James, but I did not go see him; and tomorrow, the King, Queene, Duke and his Lady, and the whole Court comes to town from their progresse. Myself and family well – only, my father sick in the country.

All the common talk for news is the Turkes advance in Hungary &c.[2]

1. The Pepyses came to be very fond of Bess, who stayed until 6 March 1665, being promoted upper-maid in 1664.

2. Cf. above, pp. 315–16 & n.

OCTOBER.

1. Up and betimes to my office, and then to sit; where Sir G. Carteret, Sir W. Batten, Sir W. Penn, Sir J. Mennes, W. Coventry, and myself, a fuller board then by the King's progress and the Dukes absence and the late pays and my absence hath been a great while.

Sat late, and then home to dinner. After dinner I by water to Deptford about a little business, and so back again ⟨buying a couple of good eales by the way⟩. And after writing by the post, home to see the painter at work late in my wife's closet; and so to supper and to bed – ⟨having been very merry with the painter late while he was doing his work⟩.*a*

This day the King and Court returned from their Progress.

2. Up betimes, and by water to St. James's and there visited Mr. Coventry as a compliment after his new coming to town; but had no great talk with him, he being full of business. So back by foot through London, doing several errands; and at the Change met with Mr. Cutler, and he and I to a Coffee-house and there discoursed; and he doth assure me that there is great likelihood of a war with Holland[1] – but I hope we shall be in good condition before it comes to break out. I like his company and will make much of his acquaintance.

So home to dinner with my wife, who is over head and ears in getting her house up; and so to the office and with Mr. Lewes late upon some of the old victuallers accounts;[2] and so home to

a addition crowded in between paragraphs

---

1. William Cutler, hemp merchant, may well have spoken the views of that section of the mercantile interest which favoured a war. The government undertook serious naval preparations only in the following spring. The English began hostilities with Holmes's raids on the Dutch colonies in W. Africa, and with attacks on Dutch commercial shipping which culminated in Allin's capture of the Smyrna fleet (December 1664). The English declaration of war came in March 1665.

2. An enquiry was being made into the question of paying for provisions ordered before 24 June 1660 but delivered afterwards: PRO, SP 46/136, no. 92*a*.

supper and to bed – ⟨up to our red chamber, where we purpose alway to lie⟩. This day I received a letter from Mr. Barlow with a Terella,[1] which I had hoped he had sent me but to my trouble I find it is to present from him to my Lord Sandwich;[a] but I will make a little use of it first, and then give it him.

3. Up, being well pleased with my new lodging and the convenience of having our maids and none else about us, Will lying below. So to the office, and there we sat, full of business all the morning. At noon I home to dinner and then abroad to buy a bell to hang by our chamber-door to call the maids. Then to the office and met Mr. Blackburne, who came to know the reason of his kinsman's (my Will) his being observed by his friends of late to droop much; I told him my great displeasure against him and the reasons of it, to his great trouble, yet satisfaction for my care over him and how everything I said was for the good of the fellow. And he will take time to examine the fellow about all and to desire my pleasure concerning him, which I told him was either that he should become a better servant or that we would not have him under my roof to be a trouble. He tells me in a few days he will come to me again and we shall agree what to do therein. I home and told my wife all, and am troubled to see that my servants and others should be the greatest trouble I have in the world, more then for myself. We then to set up our bell with a smith, very well; and then I late at the office. So home to supper and bed.

4. *Lords day.* Up and to church, my house being miserably

---

a name smudged

---

1. Correctly, 'terrella'; a spherical loadstone. This example is no longer in the possession of the Sandwich family.

overflowed with rain last night, which makes me almost mad.

《 *My great fitt of the Collique* 》[1]   At home to dinner with my wife, and so to talk and to church again; and so home and all the evening most pleasantly passed the time in good discourse of our fortune and family, till supper; and so to bed – in some pain below, through cold got.

5. Up with pain. And with Sir J. Mennes by coach to the Temple; and then I to my brother's and up and down on business; and so to the New Exchange and there met Creed, and he and I walked two or three hours, talking of many businesses, especially about Tanger and my Lord Tiviotts bringing of high accounts and yet, if they were higher, are like to pass without exception. And then of my Lord Sandwich sending a messenger to know whether the King entends to come to Newmarket[2] as is talked, that he may be ready to entertain him at Hinchingbrooke.

Thence home and dined, and my wife all day putting up her hangings in her closet; which she doth very prettily herself with her own hand, to my great content. So I to the office till night about several businesses. And then went and sat an hour or two with Sir W. Penn, talking very largely of Sir J. Mennes's

1. The entries for 5–13 October constitute one of the best-documented attacks of flatulence in history. Flatulence was fashionable then, as now, as an explanation of symptoms which it has nothing to do with. Burton gave over 50 remedies to 'expel' or 'resolve' wind or 'flatuous melancholy': *Anat. of melancholy* (ed. Shilleto), ii. 300–2. Pepys was particularly subject to it, and in 1677 when he wrote a survey of his health he put it second only to his eye-trouble. 'From the furthermost of my memory backward,' he then wrote, '(both before I [was] cutt [of] the stone and since) to this day I have been Subject upon all Cold, especially taken in my feet on an empty Stomach to have the same paines in my Bowels and Bladder and stoppage of Urine, and almost in the same

degree, as what the stone itselfe gave me. And this soe certaine, and orderly, that I never have a fitt thereof but I can assigne the time and occasion of it, as alsoe of its Cure, Namely; Soe Soone (and not before) as I can breake wind behind in a plentifull degree.... The preventions which I use ... are the keeping of my feet warme, and my Stomach full . : Rawl. A 185, f. 210r–v; printed Bryant, ii. 409–10.

2. For the preparations now made for the King's hunting at Newmarket, see *CSPD 1663–4*, pp. 245, 270. For the horse-racing there (spring and autumn meetings were established at about this time), see J. P. Hore, *Hist. Newmarket and annals of turf.* The King attended regularly from 1666 onwards. Cf. *Verney Mem.*, ii. 220–1, 316–17, 324; Magalotti, pp. 209–12.

simplicity and unsteadiness and Sir W. Batten's suspicious dealings, wherein I was open and he sufficiently, so that I do not care for his telling of tales, for he said as much; but whether that were so or no, I said nothing but what is my certain knowledge and belief concerning him. Thence home, and to bed in great pain.

6. Slept pretty well, and my ⟨wife⟩ waked to ring the bell to call up our maids to the washing about 4 a-clock and I was, and she, angry that our bell did not wake them sooner; but I will get a bigger bell. So we to sleep again till 8 a-clock; and then I up in some ease to the office, where we had a full board – where we examined Cocke's second account,[1] which Mr. Turner had drawn a bill directly to be paid the balance thereof, as Mr. Cocke demands; and Sir J. Mennes did boldly assert the truth of it and that he had examined it; when there is no such thing, but many vouchers upon examination missing;[2] and we saw reason to strike off several of his demands and to bring down his 5 per cent Comission to 3 per cent – so that we shall save the King some money which both the Controller and his clerk had absolutely given away. There was also two occasions more of difference at the table – the one being to make out a bill to Captain Smith for his salary abroad as commander-in-chief in the Streights. Sir J. Mennes did demand an encrease of salary for his being vice-admirall in the Downes, he having received but 40s without an encrease, when Sir J Lawson in the same voyage had 3l., and others have also had encrease;[3] only he, because he was an officer of the Board, was worse used then anybody else; and perticularly told Sir W. Batten that he was the opposer formerly of his having an encrease; which I did wonder to hear him so boldly lay it to him. So we husht up that dispute and offered, if he would, to examine precedents and report them, if there was anything to his advantage to be found, to the Duke.

1. For victuals supplied at Lisbon, where Robert Cocke was navy victualling agent.

2. For these disputed accounts, see HMC, *Heathcote*, pp. 33, 66–7, 70, 78–9. Mennes seems to have favoured Cocke because of his services to Rupert during the civil war.

3. £2 a day was the normal rate at this time for a vice-admiral: Tanner, *Pepys and navy*, p. 52. Mennes had been Commander-in-Chief in the Downs in the winter of 1661–2; Lawson in that of 1662–3.

The next was Mr. Chr. Pett and Deane were summoned to give an account of some Knees[1] which Pett reported bad, that were to be served in by Sir W Warren, we having contracted that none should be served but such as were to be approved of by our officers – so that if they were bad, they were to be blamed for receiving them. Thence we fell to talk of Warrens other goods, which Pett had said were generally bad; and falling to this contract again, I did say it was the most cautious and as good a contract as had been made here, and the only that had been in such terms. Sir J. Mennes told me angrily that Winters Timber, bought for 33*s* per loade, was as good and in the same terms; I told him that it was not so, but that he and Sir W. Batten were both abused, and I would prove it was as dear a bargain as had been made this half year – which occasioned high words between them and me, but I am able to prove it and will.[2] That also was so ended, and so to other business.

At noon, Lewellin coming to me, I took him and Deane, and there met my uncle Thomas and we dined together. But was vexed that it being washing-day, we had no meat dressed; but sent to the cook's and my people had so little wit to send in our meat from abroad in the cook's dishes, which were marked with the name of the Cooke upon them; by which, if they observed anything, they might know it was not my own dinner.

After dinner we broke up, and I by coach, setting down Luellin in Cheapside; and so to White-hall, where at the Committee of Tanger; but Lord, how I was troubled to see my Lord

---

1. Timbers cut from the intersection of large branches with the trunk, and used in shipbuilding to attach the beams supporting the decks to the ribs of the vessel. There were 'standing', 'hanging' and 'lodging' knees – all made from timbers whose grain ran with the shape required. See G. P. R. Naish in C. Singer *et al.*, *Hist. Technol.*, iii. 487 (fig. 301), 488; Ehrman, pp. 38–9. Illust. in R. G. Albion, *Forests and sea power*, opp. pp. 8, 9. They were obtained usually from hedgerow oaks. Because of their scarcity, contractors were often required to deliver a specified number of knees and other curved pieces ('compass-timber') with each load of straight timber. Anthony Deane for the same reason later substituted iron dogs: Bryant, ii. 54.

2. Cf. below, p. 381 & n. 2. Timber supplied from Essex by Thomas Winter had been reported on adversely by the Navy Board's purveyor, who referred to its 'visabull defects'. It had been contracted for on 2 June 1663. PRO, SP 46/136, no. 94.

Tiviotts accounts of 10000*l* passed in that manner and wish 1000 times I had not been there.

Thence rise with Sir G. Carteret, and to his lodgings and there discoursed of our frays at the table today, and perticularly of that of the contract and the contract of masts[1] the other day, declaring my fair dealing and so needing not any man's good report of it or word for it, and that I would make it so appear to him if he desired it; which he did, and I will do it.

Thence home by water in great pain, and at my office a while; and thence a little to Sir W. Penn, and so home to bed. And finding myself beginning to be troubled with wind, as I used to be, and with pain in making water, I took a couple of pills that I had by me of Mr. Hollyards.

7. They wrought in the morning and I did keep my bed; and my pain continued on me mightily, that I keeped within all day in great pain, and could break no wind nor have any stool after my physic had done working. So in the evening I took coach and to Mr. Hollyards, but he was not at home; and so home again. And whether the coach did me good or no I know not, but having a good fire in my chamber, I begun to break six or seven small and great farts; and so to bed and lay in good ease all night, and pissed pretty well in the morning, but no more wind came as it used to do plentifully, after it once begun, nor 《8.》 any inclination to stool. So, keeping myself warm, to the office; and at noon home to dinner, my pain coming again by breaking no wind nor having any stool; so to Mr. Hollyard and by his direction (he assuring me that it is nothing of the stone, but only my constitution being costive, and that and cold from without breeding and keeping the wind) I took some powder that he did give me in white wine and sat late up, till past 11 at night, with my wife in my chamber, till it had done working; which was so weakly that I could hardly tell whether it did work or no. My maids, being at this time in great dirt toward getting of all my house clean, and weary and having a great deal of work to do therein tomorrow and next day, were gone to bed before my wife and I, who also do lie in our room, more like beasts then Christians; but that it is only in order to

1. This latter was also with Warren: above, p. 315.

having of the house shortly in a cleaner, or rather very clean condition.

Some ease I had so long as this did keep my body loose, and I slept well.

9.   And did keep my bed most of this morning, my body I find being still bound and little wind, and so my pain returned again, though not so bad; but keeping my body with warm clothes very hot, I made shift to endure it; and at noon sent word to Mr. Hollyard of my condition – that I could neither have a natural stool nor break wind, and by that means still in pain and frequent offering to make water. So he sent me two bottles of drink and some Syrrop, one bottle to take now and the other tomorrow morning. So in the evening after Comissioner Pett, who came to visit me and was going to Chatham but methinks doth talk to me quite in another manner, doubtfully and shyly and like a stranger, to what he did heretofore[1] – after I saw he was gone, I did drink one of them, but it was a most loathsome draught; and did keep myself warm after it and had that afternoon still a stool or two,[a] but in no plenty nor any wind almost carried away; and so to bed. In no great pain, but do not think myself likely to be well till I have a freedom of stool and wind.

Most of this day and afternoon, my wife and I did spend together in setting things now up and in order in her closet, which endeed is and will be, when I can get her some more things to put in it, a very pleasant place; and is at present very pretty – and such as she, I hope, will find great content in.

So to bed.

10.   Up; and not in any good ease yet, but have pain in making water; and some course I see I must take, besides keeping myself warm, to make myself break wind and go freely to stool before I can be well – neither of which I can do yet, though I have drunk the other bottle of Mr. Hollyards against my stomach this morning.

a MS. 'no

---

1. Cf. above, p. 282.

I did however make shift to go to the office, where we sat; and there Sir J. Mennes and Sir W. Batten did advise me to take some Juniper water, and Sir W. Batten sent to his Lady for some for me, strong water made of Juniper. Whether that, or anything else of my draught this morning did it, I cannot tell, but I had a couple of stools forced after it and did break a fart or two; but whether I shall grow better upon it I cannot tell.

Dined at home at noon, my wife and house in the dirtiest pickle that ever she and it was in almost; but in order, I hope, this night to be very clean.

To the office all the afternoon upon victuallers business, and late at it; so after wrote by the post to my father, I home.

This evening Mr. Hollyard sends me an electuary to take, a wallnutt quantity of it, going to bed; which I did. Tis true, I slept well and rise in a little ease in the morning.

11. *Lords day.* And was mightily pleased to see my house clean and in good condition; but something coming into my wife's head and mine to be done more, about bringing the green bed into our chamber, which is handsomer then the*a* red one, though not of the colour of our hangings, my wife forebore to make herself clean today but continued in a sluttish condition till tomorrow – I after the old passe, all the day within doors, I finding myself neither to fart nor go to stool after one stool in the morning, the effect of my electuary last night. And the greatest of my pains I find to come by my straining to get something out backwards, which strains my yard and cods, so as to put me to a great and long pain after it, and my pain and frequent desire to make water; which I must therefore forbear.

For all this, I eat with a very good stomach, and as much as I use to do; and so I did this noon. And stayed at home, discoursing and doing things in my chamber, altering my chairs in my chamber and set them above in the red room, they being Turkey work; and so put their green Covers upon those that were above, not so handsome.

At night fell to reading in the *Church History* of Fullers, and perticularly Cranmers letter to Queen Elizabeth, which pleases

a   repl. 'another'

me mightily for his zeal, obedience and boldness in a cause of religion.[1]

After supper to bed as I use to be, in pain, without breaking wind and shitting.

12.   Up (though slept well and made some water in the morning [as] I used to do) and a little pain returned to me and some fears; but being forced to go to the Duke at St. James, I took coach, and in my way called on Mr. Hollyard and had his advice to take a glister.

At St. James's we attended the Duke all of us. And there, after my discourse, Mr. Coventry of his own accord begun to tell the Duke how he found that discourse abroad did run to his prejudice, about the fees that he took and how he sold places and other things; wherein he desired to appeal to his Highness whether he did anything more then what his predecessors did, and appealed to all us.   So Sir G. Carteret did answer that some fees were heretofore[a] taken, but what, he knew not; only, that selling of places never was nor ought to be countenanced.   So Mr. Coventry very hotly answered to Sir G. Carteret and appealed to himself whether he was not one of the first that put him upon looking after this taking of fees, and that he told him that Mr. Smith should say that he made 5000*l* that first year, and he believed he made 7000*l*.[2]   This Sir G. Carteret denied, and said that if he did say so, he told a lie; for he could not nor did know that ever he did make that profit of his place; but that he believes he might say 2500*l* the first year.   Mr. Coventry instanced in another thing perticularly, wherein Sir G. Carteret did advise with him about the selling of the Auditors place of the stores, when in the beginning there was an intention of creating such an

a smudge above symbol

---

1. A mistake: Cranmer died in 1556, and was in any case not remarkable for 'zeal, obedience and boldness'. Presumably Pepys is referring to the letter of Archbishop Grindal to Queen Elizabeth which Fuller prints in his *Church-History* (1655), ii. 123–30 (bk ix, sect. iv), and wrongly ascribes to 1580 (*recte* 20 December 1576: see *Harvard Theol. Rev.*, 38/71–3). Fuller's comment is: 'What could be written with more spirit, and less animosity? more humility and less dejection? I see a *Lambe* in his own, can be a *Lion*, in God, and his churches Cause.'

2. See above, p. 170 & n. 2.

office.[1] This he confessed but with some lessening of the tale Mr. Coventry told, it being only for a respect to my Lord Fitz-Harding.[2]

In fine, Mr. Coventry did put into the Duke's hand a list of above 250 places that he did give without receiving one farthing, so much as his ordinary fee for them, upon his life and oath.[3] And that since the Duke's establishment of fees,[4] he had never seed[a] one token more of no man. And that in his whole life he never conditioned or discoursed of any consideration from any commanders since he came to the Navy.

And afterward my Lord Barkely[5] merrily discoursing that he wished his profit greater then it was and that he did believe that he had got 50000*l* since he came in – Mr. Coventry did openly declare that his Lordshipp, or any of us, should have not only all he had got, but all he had in the world (and yet he did not come a beggar into the Navy, nor would yet be thought to speak in any contempt of his Royal Highness's bounty) and should have a year to consider of it too, for 25000*l*.

The Duke's answer was that he wished we all had made more profit then he had of our places, and that we had all of us got as much as one man below Stayres in the Court – which he presently

---

a Whether this represents a s.h. mistake (? for 'asked') or a conscious or unconscious vulgarism one can only guess.

---

1. This proposal was made at the time Sir Robert Slingsby was Comptroller (1660–1): see J. Hollond, *Discourses* (ed. Tanner), pp. 339–40. A third commissioner was appointed in 1671 to do the work: Ehrman, p. 182.
2. A favourite of the King; later Earl of Falmouth.
3. See above, p. 190.
4. Made in April 1661: above, p. 169,n. 3. In September 1664 Coven-try exchanged this arrangement for a fixed income (from fees) of £500 p.a.: NWB, p. 62. Cf. below, vii. 307 & n. 2.
5. Berkeley of Stratton, Navy Commissioner, Steward of the Household to the Duke of York, Governor of Galway and Lord President of Connaught; a critic of Coventry. For an example of his profits, see below, ix. 319 & n. 1.

named, and it was Sir George Lane.[1]   This being ended and the List left in the Duke's hand, we parted; and I with Sir G. Carteret, Sir J. Mennes and Sir W. Batten by coach to the Exchange, and there a while and so home; and whether it be the jogging, or by having of my mind more imployed (which I believe is a great matter) I know not, but I do now piss with much less pain and begin to be suddenly well; at least, better then I was.   So home and to dinner; and thence by coach to the Old Exchange and there cheapened some laces for my wife; and then to Mr.   , the great lace-man in Cheapside, and bought one cost me 4*l*., more by 20*s* then I entended;[2] but when I came to see them, I was resolved to buy one worth wearing with credit. And so to the New Exchange and there put it to making.   And so to my Lord's Lodgeings and left my wife; and so I to [the] Comittee of Tanger and then late home with my wife again by coach, beginning to be very well; and yet when I came home and went to try to shit,[a] the very little straining, which I thought was no strain at all at the present, did by and by bring me some pain for a good while.

Anon, about 8 a-clock, my wife did give me a Clyster which Mr. Hollyard directed, *viz*., A pinte of strong ale, four ounces of Sugar, and two ounces of butter.   It lay while I lay upon the bed above an hour, if not two.   And then, thinking it quite lost, I rose; and by and by it begun with my walking to work, and gave me three or four most excellent stools and carried away wind – put me into excellent ease; and taking my usual wallnutt quantity of Electuary at my going into bed, I had about two stools in the night – and pissed well.   Voided some wind.

13.   And so rose in the morning in perfect good ease, but only strain I put myself to to shit, more then I needed.   But continued

---

a On a small sheet pasted at this point into the MS., there are two prescriptions: see below, Appendix, p. 441.

---

1. Lane's avarice was notorious: see below, v. 73 & n. 6. He was, *inter alia*, secretary to Ormond, Lord-Lieutenant of Ireland and Lord Steward of the Household.

2. The lace (made into a 'point': below, p. 337) would be of gold- or silver-thread.

all the morning well; and in the afternoon had a natural easily and dry Stoole, the first I have had these five days or six, for ⟪*Rules for my health.*⟫ which God be praised; and so am likely to continue well, observing for the time to come, when any of this pain comes again:

1. To begin to keep myself warm as I can.
2. Strain as little as ever I can backwards, remembering that my pain will come by and by, though in the very straining I do not feel it.
3. Either by physic forward or by clyster backward, or both ways, to get an easy and plentiful going to stool and breaking of wind.
4. To begin to suspect my health immediately when I begin*a* to become costive and bound, and by all means to keep my body loose, and that to obtain presently after I find myself going to the contrary.

This morning at the office; and at noon with Creede to the Exchange, where much business. But Lord, how my heart, though I know not reason for it, begun to doubt myself after I saw Stint, Fields one=eyed solicitor; though I know not anything that they are doing or that they endeavour anything further against us in that business till the tearme.[1]

Home, and Creede with me to dinner; and after dinner John Cole my old friend[2] came to see and speak with me about a friend. I find him ingenious, but do more and more discern his City pedantry; but however, I will endeavour to have his company now and then, for that he knows much of the temper of the City and is able to acquaint therein as much as most young men – being of large acquaintance, and himself I think somewhat unsatisfied with the present state of things at Court and in the Church.

Then to the office and there busy till late; and so home to my wife, with some ease and pleasure that I hope to be able to fallow my business again; which, by God's leave, I am resolved to

a repl. 'become'

---

1. See below, p. 396.

2. A schoolfellow; now a London tradesman.

return to with more and more eagernesse. I find at Court that either the King is doubtful of some disturbance, or else would seem so (and I have reason to hope it is no worse), by his commanding all commanders of Castles &c. to repair to their charges[1] – and mustering the guards the other day himself; where he found reason to dislike their condition to my Lord Gerard, finding so many absent men or dead pays.

My Lady Castlemayne, I hear, is in as great favour as ever, and the King supped with her the very first night he came from Bath.

And last night and*a* the night before supped with her; when, there being a chine of beef to roast and the tide rising into their kitchen,[2] that it could not be roasted there, and the cook telling her of it, she answered: Zounds! she must set the house on fire but it should be roasted; so it was carried to Mrs. Sarahs husband's,[3] and there it was roasted.

So home to supper and to bed – being mightily pleased with all my house and my red chamber, where my wife and I entend constantly to lie, and the having of our dressing-room and maids close by us, without any interfering or trouble.[4]

14.   Up and to my office, where all the morning – and part of it Sir J. Mennes spent as he doth everything else, like a fool, reading the Anatomy of the body to me,[5] but so sillily as to the making of me understand anything that I was weary of him.   And so I toward the Change and met with Mr. Grant; and he and I to the Coffee-house, where I understand by him that Sir W. Petty and his vessel[6] are coming, and the King entends to go to Portsmouth to meet it.   Thence home; and after dinner my wife

a repl. 'and this night supped with him'

1. The alarm was caused by reports of an imminent rising in the North: below, p. 347 & n. 4; *CSPD 1663–4*, pp. 291+. Cf. PRO, PC 2/56, f. 296r.

2. Parts of Westminster were subject to floods: above, i. 93, n. 1.

3. Sarah (Sandwich's housekeeper) had married a cook.

4. The reference here is to Will Hewer: cf. above, p. 318 & n. 1.

5. For another example of Mennes's interest in science, see above, p. 218.

6. For his 'double-bottom' ship, see above, p. 256 & n. 3.

and I, by Mr. Rawlinsons conduct, to the Jewish Synagogue[1] – where the men and boys in their Vayles,[2] and the women behind a lettice out of sight; and some things stand up, which I believe is their Law, in a press,[3] to which all coming in do bow; and at the putting on their veils do say something, to which others that hear him do cry Amen, and the party doth kiss his veil. Their service all in a singing way, and in Hebrew. And anon their Laws, that they take out of the press, is carried by several men, four or five, several burthens in all, and they do relieve one another, or[a] whether it is that everyone desires to have the carrying of it, I cannot tell. Thus they carried [it] round, round about the room while such a service is singing. And in the end they had a prayer for the King, which they pronounced his name in Portugall; but the prayer, like the rest, in Hebrew. But Lord, to see the disorder, laughing, sporting, and no attention, but confusion in all their service, more like Brutes then people[b] knowing the true God, would make a man forswear ever seeing them more; and endeed, I never did see so much, or could have imagined there had been any religion in the whole world so absurdly performed as this.[4] Away thence, with my mind strangely disturbed with them, by coach, and set down my wife in Westminster-hall and I to White-hall, and there [the] Tanger Comittee met; but the Duke and the Affrica Comittee meeting in our room, Sir G. Carteret, Sir W Compton, Mr. Coventry, Sir W.[c] Rider, Cuttance, and myself met in another room, with chairs set in form but no table; and there we had very fine discourses of the

a MS. 'and or' *b* MS. 'place' *c* repl. 'R'

---

1. In Creechurch Lane: Sephardic Jews (mostly from Portugal) had worshipped there since 1657, the year after their *de facto* re-settlement in England. In 1664 visits by Gentiles were forbidden. Pepys's account is one of the few which have survived from the early days of the congregation. He needed tickets (or influence) to pass through the three doors guarding the entrance. He had attended this synagogue once before in 1659 'for observacion sake': Carte

73, f. 325r. See *Trans. Jew. Hist. Soc. Engl.*, 10/1+; Sir Henry Ellis (ed.), *Orig. Letters* (1825–46, ser. 2), iv. 3+ : J. Picciotto, *Sketches of Anglo-Jewish hist* (ed. Finestein), pp. 30+. Rawlinson was not a Jew.

2. Praying shawls.

3. The Ark, containing the Pentateuch.

4. This was a festival ('The Rejoicing for the Law') at which some latitude was traditionally allowed.

business of the fitness to keep Sally,[1] and also of the terms of our
King's paying the Portugues that deserted their houses at Tanger[2]
– which did much please me; and so to fetch my wife, and so to
the New Exchange about her things, and called at Tho: Pepys the
Turners and bought some things there; and so home to supper
and to bed – after I had been a good while with Sir W. Penn,
railing and speaking freely our minds against Sir W. Batten and
Sir J. Mennes; but no more then the folly of one and the knavery
of the other doth deserve.

15.   Up; I bless God, being now in pretty good condition,
but cannot come to make natural stools yet; and going to enjoy
my wife this morning, I had a very great pain in the end of my
yard when my yard was stiff, as if I strained some nerve or vein,
which was great pain to me.[3]
    So up and to the office, where we sat all the morning; and at
noon dined at home, my head full of business. And after stepping abroad to buy a thing or two – Compasses, and Snuffers for
my wife, I returned to my office, and there mighty busy till it was
late; and so home, well contented with the business that I had
done this afternoon, and so to supper and to bed.

16.   Up and to my office, where all the morning doing business; and at noon home to dinner, and then up to remove my
chest and clothes upstairs to my new Wardrobe,* that I may have
all my things above where I lie; and so by coach abroad with
my wife, leaving her at my Lord's till I went to the Tanger
Committee, where very good discourse concerning the Articles

1. Salli (Sallee), south of Tangier, stronghold of the Salli Rovers, the worst of all Moroccan pirates; an independent 'republic' now threatened both by Gayland and his Moorish rival, Ben Boukir, 'the Saint'. The English hoped to get control of it either through 'the Saint', or by direct conquest. See Routh, pp. 43–8.
2. The Portuguese traders who had migrated from Tangier on its transfer to England. This question of the amount of compensation due to them was not settled until 1684. Routh, p. 56.
3. Dr C. E. Newman writes: 'Pepys attributed all compatible symptoms to stone, but this is more likely to have been a not uncommon transient pain of no significance.'

of peace to be continued with Guyland;[1] and thence took up my wife and with her to her tailors, and then to the Exchange and to several places; and so home and to my office, where doing some business; and then home to supper and to bed.

17.   Up and to my office; and there we sat, a very full board, all the morning upon some accounts of Mr. Gauden's.   Here happened something concerning my Will; which Sir W. Batten would fain charge upon him, and I heard him mutter something against him of complaint for his often receiving of people's money to Sir G. Carteret, which displeased me much – but I will be even with him.

Thence to the Dolphin Taverne, and there Mr. Gauden did give us a great dinner.   Here we had some discourse of the Queenes being very sick, if not dead, the Duke and Duchesse of York being sent for betimes this morning to come to White-hall to her.[2]

So to my office and there late, doing business; and so home to supper, my house being got mighty clean, to my great content, from top to toe; and so to bed – myself beginning to be in good condition of health also; but only, my laying out so much money upon clothes for myself and wife and her closet troubles me.

18.   *Lords day.*   Up, and troubled at a distaste my wife took at a small thing that Jane did, and to see that she should be so vexed that I took part with Jane, wherein I had reason.   But by and by well again.   And so my wife, in her best gowne and new poynt that I bought her the other day, to church with me, where she hath not been these many weeks, and her maid Jane with her. I was troubled to see Pembleton there, but I thought it prudence

1. A six-months truce had been concluded with him on 21 July. Hostilities were to break out again in 1664, and no peace was concluded until 2 April 1666.

2. She had the spotted fever (q.v. above, ii. 131, n. 4), and had a dangerously high temperature for about three weeks. Cf. Sir H. Bennet to Burlington, 17 October: 'The condition of the Queen is much worse, and the Physicians give us but little hopes of her Recovery; by the next you will hear she is either in a fair way to it, or dead; tomorrow is a very critical day with her, God's will be done.   The King coming to see her the morning, she told him she willingly left all the World but him, which hath very much afflicted his Majesty ...': Thomas Brown, *Misc. Aulica* (1702), pp. 306–7.

to take notice myself first of it and show my wife him; and so
by little and little considering that it mattered not much his
being there, I grew less concerned; and so mattered it not much,
and the less when anon my wife showed me his wife, a pretty little
woman and well-dressed, with a good Jewell at her breast. The
Parson, Mr. Mills, I perceive, did not know whether to pray for
the Queen or no, and so said nothing about her; which makes
me fear she is dead. But enquiring of Sir J. Mennes, he told me
that he heard she was better last night.

So home to dinner and Tom came and dined with me; and
so anon to church again and there a simple coxcombe preached,
worse then the Scott.¹ And no Pembleton nor his wife there,
which pleased me not a little. And then home and spent most
of the evening at Sir W Pens; in complaisance seeing him,
though he deserves no respect from me.

This evening came my uncle Wight to speak with me about
my uncle Tho.'s business; and Mr. Moore came, four or five
days out of the country and not come to see me before, though I
desired by*a* two or three messengers that he would come to me
as soon as he came to town – which doth trouble me, to think
that he should so soon forget my kindness to him, which I am
afeared he doth. After walking a good while in the garden with
these, I went up again to Sir W. Penn and took my wife home;
and after supper, to prayers. And read very seriously my vowes,
which I am fearful of forgetting by my late great expenses – but
I hope in God I do not. And so to bed.

19. Waked with a very high winde, and said to my wife, "I
pray God I hear not of the death of any great person, this wind is
so high;" fearing that the Queene might be dead.²

So up; and going by coach with Sir W. Batten and Sir J.
Mennes to St. James, they tell me that Sir W: Compton, who it is
true had been a little sickly for a week or fortnight, but was very
well upon Friday at night last at the Tanger Committee with us,

a l.h. repl. '2'

---

1. For the Scot, see above, p. 12,
n. 1.
2. It was an old superstition that
a severe storm betokened the death
of some eminent person. Cf. above,
iii. 32 & n. 2.

was dead – died yesterday[1] – at which I was most exceedingly surprized; he being, and so all the world saying that he was, one of the worthyest men and best officers of State now in England; and so in my conscience he was – of the best temper, valour, abilities of mind, Integrity, birth, fine person, and diligence of any one man he hath left behind him in the three kingdoms; and yet not forty year old, or if so, that is all. I find the sober men of the Court troubled for him; and yet[a] not so as to hinder or lessen their mirth, talking, laughing, and eating, drinking and doing everything else, just as if there was no such thing – which is as good an Instance for me hereafter to judge of Death, both as to the unavoydablenesse, suddenness, and little effect of it upon the spirits of others, let a man be never so high or rich or good; but that all die alike, no more matter being made of the death of one then another; and that even to die well, the prise of it is not considerable in the world, compared[b] to the many in the world that know not nor make anything of it. Nay, perhaps to them (unless to one the like this poor gentleman, which is one of a thousand there, nobody speaking ill of him) that will speak ill of a man.

Coming to St. James's, I hear that the Queene did sleep five hours pretty well tonight, and that she waked and gargled her mouth, and to sleep again – but that her pulse beats fast, beating twenty to the King's or my Lady Suffolkes eleven – but not so strong as it was. It seems she was so ill as to be shaved and pigeons put to her feet,[2] and to have the Extreme unction given her by the priests, who were so long about it that the Doctors were angry.[3] The King, they all say, is most fondly disconsolate for her and weeps by her, which makes her weep; which one this day told

a l.h. repl. s.h. 'not'   *b* repl. 'either'

---

1. Compton, Master of the Ordnance, died at the age of 38.
2. This last was a medieval remedy used well into the 18th century, mainly for fevers, but also, as a last resort, for other illnesses.
3. Cf. de Cominges to de Lionne, London, c. 20/30 October 1663; 'La nuit de vendredi au samedi [16–17 October] la Reine pensa mourir – elle

recut la viatique, fit son testament, et se fit couper les cheveux, apres avoir donné ordre à ses affaires domestiques. Le Roi se jetta à ses genoux fondant en larmes; elle le console avec beaucoup de tranquillité et de douceur': qu. *Pepysiana*, p. 294. She also received the last rites on the morning of the 22nd: PRO, PRO 31/3/112, f. 384r.

me he reckons a good sign, for that it carries away some Rheume from the head.

This morning Captain Allen tells me how the famous Ned Mullins by a slight fall broke his leg at the Ancle, which festered and he had his*a* leg cut off on Saturday, but so ill done, notwithstanding all the great Chyrurgeons about the town at the doing of it, that they fear he will not live with it, which is very strange, besides the Torment he was put to with it.[1]

After being a little with the Duke and being invited to dinner to my Lord Barkelys, and so not knowing how to spend our time till noon, Sir W. Batten and I took Coach and to the Coffeehouse in Cornhill; where much talk about the Turkes proceedings and that the plague is got to Amsterdam, brought by a ship from Argier[2] – and it is also carried to Hambrough. The Duke says the King purposes to forbid any ⟨of their⟩ ships coming into the River.[3] The Duke also told us of several Christian Comanders, French, gone over to the Turkes to serve them.[4] And upon enquiry, I find that the King of France doth by this aspire to the Empire, and so to get the Crowne of Spayne also upon the death of the King, which is very probable it seems.[5]

a repl. 'it'

---

1. Edward Molins ('the ancientest surgeon of St Thomas's') had died by the 23rd: F. G. Parsons, *Hist. St Thomas's Hosp.*, ii. 95. Amputations (usually for gangrene) were done without anaesthesia, very quickly and with the co-operation of several strong men who pinioned the patient. Description of methods and illust. of instruments in J. Woodall, *The surgeon's mate* (1639), esp. pp. 390+; opp. p. 412.

2. Bubonic plague was endemic in N. Africa and the Near East. This outbreak in Holland was at its height in the summer of 1664. See J. Wagenaar, *Amsterdam* (1760–7), i. 605–6 (who also has the story about the ship from Algiers). For the (unconnected) outbreak in England in 1665, see below, esp. vi. 93, n. 2.

3. See below, p. 399 & n. 1.

4. Cf. the similar report in *The Newes*, 15 October, pp. 52–3. For the Turkish war, see above, p. 316, n. 1.

5. Philip IV of Spain was now ill, and died in 1665. His only son, aged two, was not expected to survive him. Louis XIV (who was both his nephew and his son-in-law) was already claiming parts of the Spanish Netherlands in negotiations with Spain in 1662, and was preparing at the same time to make further territorial claims. He never, however, pretended to the Spanish crown for himself. Nor did he aspire to become Emperor, but his association with the Turks (and in November his invasion of Italy) gave colour to the belief: cf. HMC, *Portland*, iii. 282.

Back to St. James and there dined with my Lord Barkely and his Lady; where Sir G. Carteret, Sir W. Batten and myself, with two Gentlemen more – my Lady and one of the Ladies of Honour to the Duchesse, no handsome woman but a most excellent hand. A fine French dinner;[1] and so we after dinner broke up, and I to Creedes new lodgings in Axe-yard, which I like very well. And so with him to White-hall and walked up and down in the gallerys with good discourse, and anon Mr. Coventry and Povy, sad for the loss of one of our number, we sat down as a Comittee for Tanger and did some business and so broke up, and I down with Mr. Coventry and in his chamber discoursed of businesses of the office and Sir J. Mennes and Sir W. Batten's carriage, which he most ingeniously tells me how they have carried themselfs to him, in forbearing to speak the other day to the Duke what they know they have so largely at other times said to him. And I told him what I am put to about the Bargaine for masts.[2] I perceive he thinks of it all and will remember it.

Thence took up my wife at Mrs. Harpers, where she and Jane was, and so called at the New Exchange for some things for her; and then at Toms went up and saw his house now it is finished;[3] and endeed it is very handsome, but he not within and so home and to my office; and then to supper and to bed.

20. Up and to the office, where we sat; and at noon Sir G. Carteret, Sir J. Mennes and I to dinner to my Lord Mayors,[4] being invited; where was the Farmers of the Customes,[5] my Lord Chancellors three Sons,[6] and other great and much company, and a very great noble dinner, as this Mayor is good for nothing else. No extraordinary discourse of anything, every man being intent upon his dinner, and myself willing to have drunk some wine to have warmed my belly; but I did for my oath sake[7] willingly refrain it, but am so well pleased and satisfied afterwards thereby, for it doth keep me always in so good a frame of mind that I

---

1. See below, vi. 112, n.1.
2. See above, p. 304 & n. 1.
3. See above, p. 236 & n. 2.
4. Sir John Robinson's.
5. Since September 1662 the farm had been leased by Sir Job Harby, Sir John Wolstenholme, Sir John Jacob, Sir Nicholas Crispe, Sir John Harrison and Sir John Shaw.
6. Henry (later Earl of Clarendon, d. 1709); Laurence (later Earl of Rochester, d. 1711) and Edward Hyde (d. 1665).
7. See above, p. 235.

hope I shall not ever leave this practice.   Thence home and took
my wife by coach to White-hall; and she set down at my
Lord's lodgings, I to a Comittee of Tanger, and thence with her
homeward; called at several places by the way – among others,
at Paul's churchyard; and while I was in Kirtons shop, a fellow
came to offer kindness or force to my wife in the coach.   But she
refusing, he went away, after the coachman had struck him and
he the coachman.   So I being called, went thither; and the
fellow coming out again of a shop, I did give him a good cuff
or two on the chops; and seeing him not oppose me, I did give
him another; at last, found him drunk, of which I was glad and
so left him and home; and so to my office a while and so home
to supper and to bed.*a*

This*b* evening at my Lord's lodgings, Mrs. Sarah, talking with
my wife and I how the Queene doth and how the King tends her,
being so ill, she tells us that the Queene's sickness is the spotted
fever;[1] that she was as full of the spots as a Leopard; which is
very strange that it should be no more known, but perhaps it is
not so.   And that the King doth seem to take it much to heart,
for that he hath wept before her; but for all that, that he hath
not missed one night since she was sick, of supping with my Lady
Castlemayne;[2] which I believe is true, for she says that her
husband hath dressed the suppers every night; and I confess I
saw him myself, coming through the street dressing of a great
supper tonight, which Sarah says is also for the King and her –
which is a very strange thing.

21.   Up; and by and by came my brother Tom to me, though
late (which doth vex me to the blood that I could never get him
to come time enough to me, though I have spoke a hundred
times; but he is very sluggish, and too negligent ever to do well

---

a last ten lines of text crowded into bottom of page   *b* repl. 'at'

---

1. See above, ii. 134, n. 4.
2. Cf. de Cominges to Louis XIV,
London, 25 October/5 November:
'Le Roi me paroist fort affligé. Il
souppa néantmoins hyer au soir chez

Madame de Castlemene, et eut ses
conversations ordinaires avec Made-
moiselle Stuard dont il est fort
amoureux': PRO, PRO 31/3/112,
f. 203r.

at his trade[a] I doubt); and having lately considered with my wife very much of the inconvenience of my going in no better plight, we did resolve of putting me into a better garbe; and among other things, to have a good velvet cloak, that is, of cloth lined with velvet, and other things modish, and a perruque;[1] and so I sent him and her out to buy me velvet; and I to the Exchange, and so to Trinity-house and there dined with Sir W. Batten, having some businesses to speak with him and Sir W. Rider. Thence, having my belly full, away on foot to my brother's all along Thames-street; and my belly being full of small beer, I did all alone, for health's sake, drink half a pint of Renish wine at the Stillyard, mixed with beere.

From my brother's with my wife to the Exchange to buy things for her and myself, I being in a humour of laying out money; but not prodigally, but only in Cloaths, which I every day see that I do suffer for want of. And so home; and after a little at my office, home to supper and to bed.

Memorandum: this morning one Mr. Commander, a Scrivener, came to me from Mr. Moore, with a deed of which Mr. Moore had told me that my Lord had made use of my name and that I was desired by my Lord to sign it. Remembering this very well, though understanding little of the perticulars, I[b] read it over, and find it concern Sir Robt. Bernards and Duckinford their interest in the manor of Brampton. So I did sign it, declaring to Mr. Comander that I am only concerned in having my name, at my Lord Sandwiches desire, use[d] therein; and so I sealed it up after I had signed and sealed the deed, and desired him to give it so sealed to Mr. Moore. I did also call at the Wardrobe this afternoon to have told Mr. Moore of it, but he was not within; but knowing Mr. Comander to have the esteem of a good and honest man with my Lord Crew, I did not doubt to entrust him with the deed after I had signed it.

This evening after I came home, I begun to enter my wife in Arithmetique, in order to her studying of the globes, and she takes it very well – and I hope with great pleasure I shall bring her to understand many fine things.

a l.h. repl. s.h. 'dr'-   *b* repl. 'it'

---

1. A periwig: see below, p. 358 & n. 1.

22. Up and to the office, where we sat till noon, and then I home to dinner; and after dinner, with my wife to her study and there read some more Arithmetique, which she takes with great ease and pleasure. This morning, hearing that the Queene grows worse again, I sent to stop the making of my velvett cloak, till I see whether she lives or dies.

So a little abroad about several businesses, and then home and to my office till night, and then home to supper. Teach my wife, and so to bed.

23. Up; and this morning comes Mr. Clerke and tells me that my Injunction against Trice[1] is dismissed again, which troubles me much – so I am to look after it in the afternoon. There comes also, by appointment, my uncle Thomas to receive the first payment of his daughter's money. But showing of me the originall of the deed by which his daughter gives her right to her legacy to him, and the copy of it attested by the Scrivener for me to keep by me – I did find some difference; and thereupon did look more into it, and at last did find the whole thing a forgery; yet he maintained it again and again, upon oath, that it had been signed and sealed by my Cosen Mary ever since before her marriage.[2] So I told him to his teeth he did like a knave,

1. See above, p. 221, n. 1.
2. Robert Pepys of Brampton (of whose estate Pepys was executor, with his father) had left £20 to his niece Mary, daughter of Thomas Pepys of London, payable on her parents' death. By the agreement made this year with Thomas Pepys (above, p. 42), the legacy had been increased to one of £50, of which £20 was to be paid on 8 August of this year, and the remainder on the same day of the following year. Thomas had, however, already advanced the original £20 to his daughter in the autumn of 1662 as part of her marriage portion. (Cf. above, p. 35 & n. 4.) The deed he now produced was dated 22 October 1662; her marriage had taken place on 12 November. Pepys retained both the deed and his note on it:

PL (unoff.), Freshfield MSS, no. 12. This note (mostly in shorthand) runs: 'My Uncle has offered that the scrivener and his daughter and himself would swear that this paper, now signed by her, was brought and signed before Marriage. That (upon my insisting that this was not that that he showed us upon the Change and promised me to copy true, and at first he said it was) it was a Duplicate of it word for word. That the true Originall is lost, and that this is taken out of the entry in the Scriveners book. *Memd.* False date: the Originall in November, this in October and that scracht.' Pepys had not objected to what appears to have been a similar forgery by Richard Pigott – a bond by which Pepys himself benefited: above, iii. 222.

and so he did; and went with him to the Scrivener at Bedlam[1] and there find how it came to pass – *viz.*, that he had lost, or pretends to have lost, the true Originall, and that so he was forced to take this Course. But a knave, at least a man that values not what he swears to, I perceive he is. But however, I am now the better able to see myself fully secured before I part with the money – for I find that his Son Charles hath right to this legacy till the first 100*l* of his daughter's portion be paid, he being bond[a] for it. So I put him upon getting both his sons to be bound for my security, and so left him; and so home and then abroad to my brother's, but find him abroad at the young Couple that was married yesterday,[2] and he one of the Bride's-men – a kinswoman (Brumfield) of the Joyces, married to an Upholster.

Thence walked to the Kings-head at Charing Cross and there dined; and hear that the Queene slept pretty well last night, but that her feaver continues upon her still. It seems she hath never a portuguese Doctor here.

Thence by appointment to the Six Clerks Office to meet Mr. Clerke, which I did; and there waited all the afternoon for Wilkinson my atturny, but he came not; and so, vexed and weary, we parted. I endeavoured, but in vain, to have found Dr. Williams, of whom I shall have use in Trices business, but I could not find him. So, weary, walked home. In my way bought a large Kitchin knife and half Dozen oyster knifes. Thence to Mr. Hollyard, who tells me that Mullins is dead of his leg cut off the other day, but most basely done.[3]

He tells me that there is no doubt but that all my Slyme doth come away in my water, and therefore no fear of the stone; but that my water being so slimy is a good sign. He would have me now and then to take a Glister, the same I did the other day, though I feel no pain; only to keep me loose. And instead of butter, which he would have to be salt butter, he would have

a ? 'bound'

1. Samuel Chidley, who also drew up Thomas Pepys's will, dated 2 February 1664. 'Bedlam' (Bethlehem) was the precinct, not the hospital, of that name.

2. Mary Bromfield and Philip Harman.

3. See above, p. 340 & n. 1.

me sometimes use two or three ounces of hony – and at other times, two or three ounces of Lyncett oyle.

Thence to Mr. Rawlinsons and saw some of my New bottles, made with my Crest upon them, filled with wine, about five or six dozen.[1]

So home and to my office a little; and then home to prepare myself against T. Trice, and also to draw a bond fit for my uncle and his sons to enter into before I pay them the money. That done, to bed.

24. Up and to the office, where busy all the morning about Mr. Gaudens account; and at noon to dinner with him at the Dolphin, where mighty merry by pleasant stories of Mr. Coventry's and Sir J. Mennes – which I have put down some of in my book of tales.[2]   Just as I was going out, my uncle Thomas came to me with a draft of a bond, for him and his sons to sign, to me about the payment of the 20*l* Legacy[3] – which I agreed to, but he would fain have had from me the copy of the deed which he had forged and did*a* bring me yesterday; but I would not give him it.   Says, "I perceive then, you will keep it to defame me with," and desired me not to speak of it, for he did it innocently.   Now, I confess I do not find any great hurt in the thing, but only to keep from me a sight of the true Originall deed; wherein perhaps there was something else that might*b* touch this business of the legacy, which he would keep from me – or it may be it is really lost as he says it is.   But then he need not have used such a sleight, but confessed it without danger.

Thence by coach*c* with Mr. Coventry to the Temple; and thence I to the Six Clerks Office and discoursed with my Atturny and Sollicitor; and he and I to Mr. Turner, who puts me in great

---

a repl. 'would'   *b* MS. 'my'   *c* repl. 'water'

---

1. For the use of wine-bottles, see above, p. 18, n. 2. Pepys's crest was a camel's head erased: for his arms, see above, iii. 50, n. 3. In this case the crest would probably be made in the form of a glass seal: cf. *Country Life*, 28 July 1960, p. 181.

2. Untraced.

3. The bond (24 October) is in PL (unoff.), Freshfield MSS, no. 13. Pepys was now secured from any action for the recovery of the £20 by Mary Pepys or her husband, and from any charge of having improperly paid a legacy not payable according to the will during the lives of her parents.

fear that I shall not get my bill retayned again[1] against Tom
Trice, which troubles me.

Thence, it being night, homewards; and called at Wotton's
and tried some shoes, but he had none to fit me. He tells me
that by the Duke of Yorkes persuasion, Harris is come again to
Sir W Davenant upon his terms that he demanded, which will
make him very high and proud.[2] Thence to another shop and
there bought me a pair of shoes. And so walked home and to
my office and despatch letters by the post; and so home to supper
and to bed – where, to my trouble, I find my wife begin to talk
of her being alone all day, which is nothing but her lack of
something to do; for while she was busy, she never or seldom
complained. She hath also a pain in the place which she used
to have swellings in; and that that troubles me is that we fear
that it is my matter that I give her that causes it, it never coming
but after my having been with her.

The Queene is in a good way of recovery; and Sir Frances
Pridgeon[3] hath got great Honour by it, it being all imputed to
his Cordiall, which in her dispaire did give her rest and brought
her to some hopes of recovery.

It seems, after the much talk of troubles and a plot, something
is found in the North; that a party was to rise, and some persons
that were to command it are found, as I find in a letter that
Mr. Coventry read today about it from those parts.[4]

25. *Lords day.* Up, and my wife and I to church; where it is
strange to see how by use and seeing Pembleton come with his
wife thither to church, I begin now to make no great matter of
it, which before was so terrible to me. Dined at home, my wife
and I alone, a good dinner; and so in the afternoon to church

1. See above, p. 221 & n. 1.
2. See above, p. 239 & n. 3. (A).
3. Prujean, her physician.
4. The Farnley Wood or Derwentdale Plot, largest and most
ambitious of the conspiracies of this
period. Inspired by puritan ex-
tremists of the W. Riding, it had
been in preparation since the spring.
The government had been in possession of many of the secrets for the

past ten weeks and made several
arrests. Nevertheless, on the appointed day, 12 October, a number of the
plotters rose at Farnley Wood, near
Leeds, but were swiftly suppressed.
See below, p. 391 & n. 1. Some of
the letters sent to the King and
government from 10 October onwards are in *CSPD 1663-4*, pp. 293-4
etc.; possibly Coventry read one of
those.

again, where*ᵃ* the Scott[1] preached and I slept most of the afternoon. So home and my wife and I together all the evening, discoursing; and then*ᵇ* after reading my vowes to myself, and my wife with her maids (who are mighty busy to get it despatched, because*ᶜ* of their mistress promise that when it is done they shall have leave all to go see their friends at Westminster, whither*ᵈ* my wife will carry them) preparing for their washing tomorrow, we hastened to supper and to bed.*ᵉ*

26. Waked about one a-clock in the morning to piss (having gone so soon over-night to bed) and then my wife, being waked, rung her bell and the maids rose and went to washing. We to sleep again till 7 a-clock, and then up; and I abroad to look out Dr Williams, but being gone out, I went to Westminster and there seeing my Lord Sandwich's footman, knew he was come to town; and so I went in and saw him, and received a kind salute from him but hear that my father is very ill still. Thence to Westminster-hall with Creed and spent the morning walking there; where, it being terme time, I met several persons and talked with them; among others, Dr Pierce, who tells me that the Queene is in a way to be pretty well again, but that her delirium in her head continues still, that she talks idle, not by fits, but alway; which in some lasts a week after so high a feaver, in some more, and in some for ever. That this morning she talked mightily that she was brought to bed, and that she wondered that she should be delivered without pain and without spueing or being sick, and that she was troubled that her boy was but an ugly boy. But the King being by, said, "No, it is a very pretty boy;" "Nay," says she, "if it be like you, it is a fine boy endeed, and would be very well pleased with it."

The other day she talked mightily of Sir H Woods lady's great belly; and if she should miscarry, he would never get another. And that she never saw such a man as this Sir H Wood

a repl. ? 'when'   *b* l.h. repl. s.h. 'after'   *c* repl. 'but'
d repl. 'where'   *e* smudge at bottom of page

1. See above, p. 12, n. 1.

in her life.[1] And seeing of Dr. Prigeon, she said, "Nay, Doctor, you need not scratch your head, there is hair little enough already in that place."

But methinks it was not handsome for the weaknesses of princes to be talked of thus.

Thence Creed and I to the Kings-head Ordinary, where much and very good company; among others, one very talking man, but a Scholler, that would needs put in his discourse and philosophy upon every occasion; and though he did well enough, yet his readiness to speak spoilt all. Here they say that the Turkes go on apace, and that my Lord Castlehaven is going to raise 10000 men here to go against him.[2] That the King of France doth offer to assist the Empire, upon condition that he may be their Generallissimo and the Dolphin chosen King of the Romans.[3] And it is said that the King of France doth occasion this difference among the Christian Princes of the Empire, which gives the Turke such advantages.[4] They say also that the King of Spayne is making all imaginable force against Portugall again.[5]

1. Sir Henry Wood was Clerk of the Board of Green Cloth; Evelyn (17 November 1651) called him 'that odd person'. He was now 66. His wife Mary was one of the four dressers to the Queen.

2. Castlehaven (an impoverished Irish soldier) was full of such schemes but there appears to be no trace of this one. In 1662 he had twice volunteered to help Venice against the Turks, and in May 1665 he had offered himself as commander of the English troops in the Spanish–Portuguese war: *CSPVen. 1661–4*, pp. 127–9 etc.; *CSP Ireland 1663–5*, p. 86; Castlehaven, *Review* (1684), App. pp. 19–20. Cf. also below, viii. 246.

3. It does not appear that Louis XIV made his help conditional, beyond insisting on sending troops as a member of the League of the Rhine, whose army was distinct from that of the Emperor: B. Auerbach, *La France et le Saint-Empire*, p. 99. The 'Dolphin' was the Dauphin.

4. The Diet (assembled in January) had, ever since the Turks' attack in May, been discussing the ways and means of resistance. Only the Confederation of the Rhine (a league of west German princes under French patronage) had acted. The other princes hung back, reluctant to present the Emperor with an army which might be used to reinforce imperial authority and which would certainly be used mainly for the defence of the Habsburg hereditary lands. Leopold went to Ratisbon on 15/25 October to make a personal appeal to the Diet, but there was no agreement on a plan to raise money and troops until February 1664. Auerbach, op. cit., pp. 96–8.

5. Spain, in preparation for the next year's campaign (in the war of 1640–68), was recruiting troops in the Netherlands: *CSPD 1663–4*, p. 234.

Thence Creed and I to one or two Periwegg shops about the Temple (having been very much displeased with one that we saw, a head of greazy and old woman's haire, at Jervas's in the morning); and there I think I shall fit myself of one very handsomely made.

Thence by coach, my mind being troubled for not meeting with Dr Williams, to St. Catharines to look at a Duch shop or two for some good handsome maps; but met none, and so back to Cornhill to Moxons; but it*a* being dark, we stayed not to see any; then to coaches again; and presently spying Sir W. Batten, I light and took him in, and to the Globe in Fleetstreete by appointment; where by and by he and I with our Sollicitor to Sir Edw. Turner about Fields business[1] and so back to the globe; and thither I sent for Dr. Williams, and he is willing to swear in my behalf against T. Trice, *viz.*, that at T. Trice's desire we have met to treat about our business.

Thence (I drinking no wine) after an hour's stay Sir W. Batten and another, and he drinking, we home by coach; and so to my office to set down my Journall; and then home to supper and to bed – my washing being in a good condition, over.

I did give Dr. Williams 20s tonight, but it was after he had answered me well to what I had to ask him about this business; and it was only what I had long ago in my petty-bag book allotted for him, besides the bill of near 4l which I paid him a good while since by my Brother Tom, for phisique for my wife – without any consideration to this business that he is to do for me, as God shall save me.

Among the rest, talking of the Emperour at table today, one young gentleman, a pretty man and it seems a parliament-man, did say that he was a sot; for he minded nothing of the government, but was led by the Jesuites.[2] Several at table took him up – some for saying that he was a sot in being led by the Jesuites [who] are the best counsel he can take. Another commander, a Scottish Collonell, who I believed had served under him, that he was a man that had thus long kept out the Turke till now, and did

a repl. 'there'

---

1. See below, p. 396 & n. 3.
2. This exaggerates Leopold I's

neglect of business, though not his dependence on the Jesuits.

many other great things. And lastly, Mr. Progers, one of our
Courtiers, who told him that it was not a thing to be said of any
Soveraigne prince, be his weaknesses what they will, to be called
a Sott, which methinks was very prettily said.

27. Up; and my uncle Tho. and his Scrivener bringing me a
bond and Affidavit to my mind, I paid him his 20*l* for his
daughter's Legacy, and 5*l*. more for a Quarter's Annuity, in the
manner expressed in each acquittance;[1] to which I must be referred on any future occasion, and to the Bond and Affidavit.

Thence to the office and there sat till noon, and then home to
dinner; and after dinner (it being a foule house today among my
maids, making up their clothes) abroad, with my Will with me,
by coach to Dr. Williams; with him to the Six Clerks Office, and
there, by advice of his acquaintance, I find that my case, through
my neglect and the neglect of my lawyers, is come to be very
bad, so as that it will be very hard to get my bill retayned again.[2]
However, I got him to sign and swear an affidavit that there was
treaties between T. Trice and me, with as[a] much advantage as I
could for me; but I will say that for him, he was most exact,
as ever I saw man in my life, word by word what it was that he
swore to; and though, God forgive me, I could have been almost
naturally willing to have let him ignorantly have sworn to something that was not of itself very certain, either ayc or no, yet
out of his own conscience and care he altered the words himself,
so as to make them very safe for him to swear. This I carrying
to my Clerke Wilkinson and telling him how I heard matters to
stand with me, he, like a conceited fellow, made nothing of it
but advised me to offer Trices clerks the cost of the dismission,
viz., 46*s* 8*d*.; which I did, but they would not take it without his
Client. Immediately thereupon we parted, and met T Trice
coming into the room; and he came to me and served me with a
Suppena for these very costs, so I paid it him; but Lord, to see
his resolucion, and endeed discretion, in the wording of his receipt,
he would have it most express, to my greatest disadvantage that

a l.h. repl. s.h. 'so'

1. See above, p. 346 & n. 3. The
annuity was payable to the father.
2. For the bill, see above, p. 221,
n. 1; for the dispute, see above, ii.
215 & n. 1. Trice had obtained the
£200 which was at issue; it was the
interest on it and the legal costs which
now remained in dispute.

could be; yet so as I could not deny to give it him – that being paid my Clerke; and then his beginning to ask why we could not think, being friends, of referring it or stating it first ourselfs, and then put it to some good lawyer to judge in it. From one word to more, we were resolved to try; and to that end, to step to the Popes-head*a* taverne. And there, he and his clerk and Atturny, and I and my clerk, and sent for Mr. Smallwood and by and by comes Mr. Clerke my Sollicitour; and after I had privately discoursed with my men and seen how doubtfully they talked, and what future certain charge and trouble it would be, with a doubtful victory, I resolved to condescend very low. And after some talk all together, Trice and I retired, and he came to 150*l* the lowest and I bid him 80*l*. So broke off and then went to our company; and they putting us to a second private discourse, at last I was contented to give him 100*l*, he to spend 40*s* of it among this good company that was with us. So we went to our company, both seeming well pleased that we were come to an end; and endeed I am, in the respects abovesaid, though it be a great sum for us to part with.

I am to pay him by giving him leave to buy about 40*l* worth of piggots land, and to strike off so much of Piggotts debt;[1] and the other to give him bond to pay him in 12 months after, without Interest.[2] Only, giving him a power to buy more land of Piggott and paying him that way, as he did for the other, which I am well enough contented with – or at least, to take the land at that price and give him the money. This last I did not tell him, but I shall order it so.

Having agreed upon tomorrow come sennit for the spending of the 40*s* at Mr. Rawlinson's, we parted; and I set T Trice down in Pauls churchyard, and I by coach home and to my office and there set down this day's passages; and so home to supper and to bed.

Mr. Coventry tells me today*b* that the Queene had a very good night last night; but yet it is strange that still she raves and talks of little more then of her having of children, and fancies now that she hath three children and that the girle is very like the King. And this morning, about 5 a-clock, waked (the

1. See above, p. 309 & n. 1.   2. See below, p. 384 & n. 4.

Physician feeling her pulse,*ª* thinking to be better able to judge,
she being still and asleep, waked her) and the first word she said
was, "How do the children?"

28. Up and at my*ᵇ* office all the morning; and at noon Mr.
Creed came to me and dined with me; and after dinner Captain
Murford came to me and he and I discoursed highly upon his
breach of contract with us.¹ After that, Mr. Creed and I abroad,
I doing several errands; and with him at last to the great Coffee-
house and there, after some common discourse, we parted and
I home, paying what I owed at the Miter in my way; and at
home, Sympson the Joyner coming, he set up my press for my
cloaks and other small things; and so to my office a little, and to
supper and to bed.

This morning Mr. Blackeburne came to me; and telling me
what complaints Will made of the usage he had from my wife
and other discouragements, and I seeing him, instead of advising,
rather favouring his kinsman, I told him freely my mind, but
friendlily; and so we have concluded to have him have a lodging
elsewhere, and that I will spare him 15*l* of his salary; and if I
do not need to keep another, 20*l*.*ᶜ*²

29. Up, it being *my Lord Mayors Day*,³ Sir Anthony Bateman.

This morning was brought home my new velvet cloak; that is,
lined with velvet, a good cloth the outside – the first that ever I
had in my life, and I pray God it may not be too soon now that I
begin to wear it. I had it this day brought home, thinking to

a symbol smudged   *b* l.h. repl. s.h. 'the'
c paragraph crowded into bottom of page

1. William Murford, timber merchant, had contracted for plank to be
delivered at Chatham. In the spring
he had explained to Commissioner
Pett that 'had not the person he contracted with most notoriously played
the jack with him, it would have been
performed long since': *CSPD 1663-
4*, p. 128. Cf. ib., pp. 275, 282;
CSPD Add. 1660-85, p. 84.

2. For Hewer's disagreements with
the household, see above, p. 318 &
n. 1. He lodged from November
onwards (in some style) with William
Mercer, merchant, of St Olave's
parish: below, vii. 152. He became
the means of introducing Mary
Mercer to the Pepys household: below,
v. 255-6. His salary was £30 p.a.
3. By the Old Style.

have worn it to dinner; but I thought it would be better to go without it because of the Crowde, and so I did not wear it.

We met a little at the office; and then home again and got me ready to go forth – my wife being gone forth by my consent before, to see her father and mother, and taken her cook-maid and little girl to westminster with her for them to see their friends.

This morning, in dressing myself and wanting a band, I found all my bands that were newly made clean, so ill-smoothed that I crumpled them and flung them all on the ground and was angry with Jane, which made the poor girl mighty sad, so that I were troubled for it afterwards.

At noon I went forth, and by coach to Guild-Hall (by the way calling to shit at Mr. Rawlinsons) and there was admitted; and meeting with Mr. Proby (Sir R Ford's son) and Lieutenant-Collonell Baron, a City commander,[1] we went up and down to see the tables; where under every salt there was a Bill of fare, and at the end of the table the persons proper for that table. Many were the tables, but none in the Hall but the Mayors and the Lords of the privy Councell that had napkins or knives – which was very strange.[2] We went into the Buttry and there stayed and talked, and then into the hall again; and there wine was offered and they drunk, I only drinking some Hypocras, which doth not break my vowe,[3] it being, to the best of my present judgment, only a mixed compound drink, and not any wine – if I am mistaken, God forgive me; but I hope and do think I am not.

By and by met with Creed; and we with the others went within the several Courts and there saw the tables prepared for the ladies and Judges and Bishops – all great sign of a great dinner to come. By and by, about one a-clock, before the Lord Mayor came, came into the hall, from the room where they were first

1. Probably Benjamin Baron, an officer in the city militia.

2. At this time hand-basins and napkins had not yet been displaced by forks. Sorbière, in 1664, found that at the best English tables the meat was served in the lump, each guest carving his own portion, and wiping his hands on a napkin after dipping them in a basin, both forks and ewers being almost unknown: *Relation d'un voyage en Angleterre* (Cologne, 1667), pp. 106–7. On the occasion Pepys here describes some guests may have brought their own knives, but Pepys was presumably provided with one.

3. It had only two more days to run: above, p. 235.

led into, the Lord Chancellor (Archbishopp before him), with
the Lords of the Council and other Bishopps, and they to dinner.
Anon comes the Lord Mayor, who went up to the Lords and
then to the other tables to bid wellcome; and so all to dinner.
I set near Proby, Baron, and Creed at the Merchant Strangers
table – where ten good dishes to a messe, with plenty of wine of
all sorts, of which I drunk none; but it was very unpleasing that
we had no napkins nor change of trenchers, and drunk out of
earthen pitchers and wooden dishes.[1]

It happened that, after the Lords had half dined, came the
French Embassador up to the Lords' table, where he was to have
sat; but finding the table set, he would not sit down nor dine
with the Lord Mayor, who was not yet come, nor have a table to
himself, which was offered; but in a discontent went away again.[2]

After I[a] had dined, I and Creed rose and went up and down
the house, and up to the ladies room and there stayed gazing
upon them. But though there were many and fine, both young
and old, yet I could not discern one handsome face there, which
was very strange. Nor did I find the lady that young Dawes
married[3] so pretty as I took her for, I having here an opportunity
of looking much upon her very near.

I expected Musique, but there was none; but only trumpets

a repl. 'dinner'

---

1. A great deal of city plate had
been melted down during the Civil
War.

2. De Cominges, the ambassador,
recounts the incident in his despatch
to Louis XIV of 31 October/9
November 1663: PRO, PRO 31/3/
112, ff. 208+; printed in J. J. Jusserand, *French Ambassador*, p. 221.
The principal table was set, and
around it the Lord Chancellor and
other ministers were sitting. 'Je
marché droict a eux, a dessein de leur
faire une raillerie de leur bon appétit,
mais je les trouvé si froids, et si
interdits, que je jugé a propos de
me retirer, le Chancelier, et tous les
assistans s'estant pas seulement levés,

pour me recevoir, à la reserve de
Benet, qui me dit quelque chose à
quoy je respondis avec mespris.' In
a letter to Ormond of 3 November,
Anglesey gives an explanation.
Only two of the Privy Council knew
of the ambassador's coming; it was
after three o'clock; the Council had
decided to dine before the Lord
Mayor's arrival: HMC, *Ormonde*,
n.s., iii. 101–2. On the following
day the Lord Mayor visited de
Cominges and apologised: Jusserand,
pp. 76+; *Pepysiana*, pp. 297–8. On
the next Lord Mayor's Day, in 1664,
full honours were done to de Cominges: *Pepysiana*, p. 303.

3. The heiress: see above, pp. 121-2.

and drums, which displeased me.   The dinner, it seems, is made
by the Mayor and two Sheriffs for the time being, the Lord
Mayor paying one half and they the other – and the whole,
Proby says, is reckoned to come to about 7 or 800*l* at most.

Being wearied with looking upon a company of ugly women,
Creed and I went away; and took coach and through Cheapside
and there saw the pageants,¹ which were very silly.   And thence
to the Temple; where meeting Greatorex, he and we to the
Hercules pillers, there to show me the manner of his going about
a great work of drayning of Fenns,² which I desired much to
know; but it did not appear very satisfactory to me as he discoursed it, and I doubt he will fail in it.

Thence I by coach home and there find my wife come home;
and by and by came my Brother Tom, with whom I was very
angry for not sending me a bill with my things, so as that I
think never to have more work done by him if ever he serves
me so again.   And so I told him.

The consideration of laying out 32*l*. 12*s*. 00*d* this month
in his very work this month troubles me also – and one thing
more; that is to say, that Will having been at home all this day
I doubt is the occasion that Jane hath spoke to her mistress tonight
that she sees she cannot please us and will look out to provide
herself elsewhere; which doth trouble both of us, and we wonder
also at her; but yet, when the rogue is gone, I do not fear but the
wench will do well.

To the office a little to set down my Journall; and so home late
to supper and to bed.

The Queene mends apace they say; but yet talks idle still.

30.   Lay long in bed with my wife; and then up and a while
to my office and so to the Change; and so [home] again, and
there I find my wife in a great passion with her maids.   I upstairs
to set some things in order in our chamber and Wardrobe; and

---

1. Described in John Tatham,
Londinum Triumphans (1663), pp. 17–
18; they greeted the Lord Mayor on
his way from Guildhall to his house in
Mincing Lane.

2. Nothing appears to be known
of any work by Greatorex in fen
drainage.   In July 1663 the draining

of the Bedford Level had been entrusted to a newly appointed corporation (15 Car. II c. 17), and Greatorex
may have been consulted by them, or
may have offered his advice.   He had
in 1660 devised a machine for raising
water: above, i. 264 & n. 1.

so to dinner upon a good dish of stewed beef and then up again about my business. Then by coach with my wife to the New Exchange and there bought and paid for several things; and then back, calling at my periwegg-makers,[1] and there showed my wife the periwig made for me, and she likes it very well; and so to my brother's and to buy a pair of boddice for her; and so home and to my office late; and then home to my wife, purposing to go on to a new lesson in Arithmetique with her; so to supper and to bed. The Queene mends apace, but her head still light.

My mind very heavy, thinking of my great layings-out lately and what they must be still for clothes; but I hope it is in order to getting of something the more by it, for I perceive how I have hitherto suffered for lack of going as becomes my place.

After a little discourse with my wife upon Arithmetique – to bed.

31. Up and to the office, where we sat all the morning; and at noon home to dinner, where Creed came and dined with me. And after dinner he and I upstairs, and I showed him my velvet cloak and other things of clothes that I have lately bought, which he likes very well; and I took his opinion as to some things of clothes which I purpose to wear, being resolved to go a little handsomer then I have hitherto.

Then to the office, where busy till night; and then to prepare my monthly account, about which I stayed till 10 or 11 a-clock at night; and to my great sorrow, find myself 43*l* worse then I was the last month; which was then 760*l* and now it is but 717*l*.[2] But it hath chiefly arisen from my layings-out in clothes for myself[a] and wife – *viz.*, for her, about 12*l*; and for myself, 55*l* or thereabouts – having made myself a velvet cloak, two new cloth-suits, black, plain both – a new shag-gown, trimmed with gold buttons and twists; and a new hat, and silk top[s] for my[b] legs, and many other things, being resolved henceforward to go

a MS. 'my lord'   *b* repl. 'myself'

1. See below, p. 358.   2. Cf. above, p. 320.

like myself. And also two periwigs, one whereof costs me 3*l* and the other 40*s*.[1] I have wore neither yet, but will begin next week, God willing. So that I hope I shall not now need to lay out more money a great while, I having laid out in clothes for myself and wife, and for her closet and other things without, these two months (this and the last), besides household expenses of victuals &c., above 110*l*. But I hope I shall with more comfort labour to get more, and with better successe then when, for want of clothes, I was forced to sneak like a beggar. Having done this, I went home; and after supper to bed, my mind being eased in knowing my condition, though troubled to think that I have been forced to spend so much.

Thus I end this month, worth 717*l*[a] or thereabouts, with a good deal of good goods more then I had and a great deal of new and good clothes.

My greatest trouble and my wife's, is our family; mighty out of order by this fellow Wills corrupting the maids by his idle talk and carriage; which we are going to remove by hastening him out of the house, which his uncle Blackeburne is upon doing. And I am to give him 20*l* per annum towards his maintenance.

The Queen continues light-headed, but in hopes to recover.

The Plague is much in Amsterdam, and we in fears of it here – which God defend.

The Turke goes on mightily in the Emperors dominions, and the princes cannot agree among themselfs how to go against him.

Myself in pretty good health now, after being ill this month for a week together. But cannot yet come to shit well, being so costive, that for this month almost, I have not had a good natural stool; but to this hour am forced to take physic every night, which brings me neither but one stool, and that in the morning as soon as I am up – all the rest of the day very costive.

My father hath been very ill in the country, but I hope better again now.

a MS. '117*l*'

---

1. Periwigs had been worn in the 1650s, but only by old men; they had now come into fashion in the previous spring: cf. above, p. 130; Cunnington, pp. 73, 163-4.

I am lately come to a conclusion with Tom Trice to pay him 100*l*; which is a great deal of money, but I hope it will save a great deal more.

But thus everything lessens what I have and am like to have; and therefore I must look about me to get something more then just my salary, or else I may resolve to live well and die a beggar.[a]

[a]   followed by one blank page

NOVEMBER.

1. *Lords day.* This morning my brother's man brought me a new black bays waistcoat faced with silk, which I put on – from this day laying by half-shirts for this winter. He brought me also my new gowne of purple Shagg, trimmed with gold, very handsome. He also brought me, as a gift from my brother, a velvet hat, very fine to ride in and the fashion, which pleases me very well; to which end I believe he sent it me, for he knew I had lately been angry with him.

Up and to church with my wife; and at noon dined at home alone – a good calf's head boiled and dumplings, an excellent dinner methought it was.

Then to church again; whither Sir W Pen came, the first time he hath been at church these several months, he having been sick all the while.

Home and to my office, where I taught my wife some part of Substraction and then fell myself to set some papers of my last night's accounts in order, and so to supper home. And after supper, another bout at Arithmetique with my wife, and then to my office again and made an end of my papers; and so home to prayers, and then to read my vowes and to bed.

2. Up and by coach to White-hall; and there in the long matted-gallery I find Sir G. Carteret, Sir J. Mennes, and Sir W. Batten; and by and by comes the King to walk there, with three or four with him; and as soon as he saw us, "Oh," says he, "here is the Navy Office," and there walked twenty turns the length of the gallery – talking methought but ordinary talk. By and by came the Duke, and he walked and at last went into the Duke's lodgings. The King stayed so long that we could not discourse with the Duke, and so we parted. I heard the Duke say that he was going to wear a perriwigg; and they say the King also will.[1] I never till this day observed that the King is mighty gray.[2]

1. The Duke first wore one on 15 February 1664, and Pepys first saw the King in one on the following 18 April.

2. He was now 33.

Thence, meeting with Creed, walked with him to Westminster-hall; and thence by coach took up Mrs. Hunt and carried her towards my house, and we light at the Change and sent her to my house. Creed and I to the Coffee-house and then to the Change; and so home and carried a barrel of oysters with us, and so to dinner; and after a good dinner, left Mrs. Hunt and my wife making Marmalett of Quinces, and Creed and I to my periwig-makers; but it being dark, concluded of nothing, and so Creed went away and I with Sir W. Penn (who spied me in the street) in his coach home.

There[a] find them busy still, and I up to my vyall. Anon, the comfiture being well done, my wife and I took Mrs. Hunt at almost 9 at night by coach and carried Mrs. Hunt home, and did give her a box of Sugar and a hanch of Venison, given me by Mapleden the other day.[1] We did not light, but saw her within doors and straight home – where after supper, there happening some discourse where my wife thought she had taken Jane in a lie, she told me of it mighty Tryumphantly; but I not seeing reason to conclude it a lie, was vexed and my wife and I to very high words came; and I up to my chamber and she by and by fallowed me up and to very bad words from her to me, calling me perfidious and a man of no conscience, whatever I pretend to, and I know not what – which troubled me mightily; and though I would allow something to her passion, yet I saw again and again that she spoke but somewhat of what she had in her heart. But I tempered myself very well; so as that though we went to bed with discontent, she yielded to me and begun to be fond; so that being willing myself to peace, we did before we sleep become very good friends, it being past 12 a-clock. And so with good hearts and joy, to rest.

3. Up and to the office, where busy all the morning; and at noon to the Coffee-house and there heard a long and most passionate discourse between two Doctors of Physique (of which one

a Here six pages, covering 2–8 November, were misheaded 'October' and later corrected.

---

1. Gervase Maplesden was a landowner and timber merchant of Shorne, Kent. The gift may have been connected with disputes about his contracts: *CSPD 1661–2*, p. 426; ib., *1663–4*, p. 257. Payments to him were authorized by the Navy Treasury on 11 October and 11 November: PRO, Adm. 20/4, p. 285.

was Dr. Allen, whom I knew at Cambrige)[1] and a Couple of Apothecarys; these maintaining Chymistry against their Galenicall physic;[2] and the truth is, one of the Apothecaries, whom they charged most, did speak very prettily; that is, his language and sense good, though perhaps he might not be so knowing a physician as to offer to contest with them. At last they came to some cooler term and broke up. I home; and there Mr. Moore, coming by my appointment, dined with me; and after dinner came Mr. Goldsbrough and we discoursed about the business of his mother,[3] but could come to no agreement in it but parted dissatisfied. By and by comes Chapman the periwigmaker, and [upon] my liking it, without more ado I went up and there he cut off my haire; which went a little to my heart at present to part with it, but it being over and my periwig on, I paid him 3*l* for it; and away went he with my own hair to make up another of; and I by and by, after I had caused all my maids to look upon it and they conclude it to become me, though Jane was mightily troubled for my parting with my own hair and so was Besse – I went abroad to the Coffee-house; and coming back, went to Sir W. Penn and there sat with him and Captain Cocke till late at night, Cocke talking of some of the Roman history very well, he having a good memory. Sir W. Penn[a] observed mightily and discoursed much upon my cutting off my hair, as he doth of everything that concerns me; but it is over, and so I perceive, after a day or two, it will be no great matter.

a   repl. 'Sir WB'

---

1. Thomas Allen; Fellow of Caius, 1651–60; later physician to the Bethlehem Hospital.
2. This refers to the contemporary controversy between orthodox physicians, who used mainly Galenical (i.e. vegetable) medicines, and the followers of Paracelsus and Van Helmont, the 'iatrochemists' who advocated chemical medicines and disapproved of other aspects of Galen's teaching. The apothecaries naturally defended their art of dispensing vegetable preparations. The iatrochemists, however, did no better than the orthodox in the plague of 1665, and it was about then that they were forced to abandon their proposal to establish an 'anti-college' in opposition to the College of Physicians. See Sir George Clark, *Hist. Roy. Coll. Physicians*, i. 322–6. Lord Crew and Mennes were among the allies of the innovators: ib., pp. 63–4.
3. She owed mortgage payments to the estate of Robert Pepys of Brampton: above, iii. 232 & n. 1; iv. 203 & n. 4.

Home, and there I find my wife and her girl Susan fallen out, and she had struck her and the girl run to Griffen's; but they not receiving nor encouraging of her, I sent for her home and there she fell on her knees and begged pardon; and so I made peace between her mistress and her and so all well again; and a pretty girl she will be, if she doth not get too much head.

To supper and then a little to my viall, and afterward with my wife to her Arithmetique, and so to bed.

4. Up and to my office, showing myself to Sir W. Batten and Sir J. Mennes, and no great matter made of my periwig, as I was afeared there would. Among other things, there came to me this morning Shales of Portsmouth by my order, and I begun to discourse with him about the arreares of stores belonging to the Victualling-Office there; and by his discourse, I am in some hopes that if I can get a grant from the King of such a part of all I discover, I may chance to find a*a* way to get something by the by, which doth greatly please me the very thoughts of. Home to dinner and very pleasant with my wife, who is this day also herself making of Marmalett of Quince, which she now doth very well herself. I left her at it, and by coach I to the New Exchange and several places to buy and bring home things; among others, a case I bought of the Trunke-makers for my periwigg; and so home and to my office late. And among other things, wrote a letter to Wills uncle to hasten his removal from me; and so home to supper and to bed. This morning Captain Cocke did give me a good account of the Guinny trade. The Queene is in a great way to recovery. ⟨This noon came John Angier to me in a pickle; I was sad to see him desiring my good word for him to go a trooper to Tanger, but I did school him and sent him away with good advice but no present encouragement.[1] Presently after, I had a letter from his poor father[2] at

a repl. 'me'

---

1. Angier ('a very rogue': below, p. 439) was a relative from Cambridge. At the end of the year Pepys sent him to sea: below, loc. cit.

He appears to have died at Lisbon in 1664: below, v. 291.
2. Also John.

Cambrige; who is broke it seems, and desires me to get him a protection or a place of employment; but, poor man, I doubt I can help him, but will endeavour it.*ᵃ*⟩

5. Lay long in bed. Then up, called by Captain Cocke about business of a contract of his for some Tarr;¹ and so to the office and then to Sir W. Penn with him and there talked; and he being gone, came Sir W Warren and discoursed about our business with Field;² and at noon, by agreement to the Miter to dinner, upon T. Trice's 40s to be spent upon our late agreement.³ Here was a very poor dinner and great company – all our lawyers on both sides and several friends of his and some of mine, brought by him, *viz*, Mr. Moore, Uncle Wight, Dr Williams, and my Cosen Angier that lives here in town – who after dinner carried me aside and showed me a letter from his poor brother at Cambrige to me, of the same contents with that yesterday to me, desiring help from me.

Here I was among a sorry company, without any content or pleasure; and at the last, the reckoning coming to above 40s by 15s, he would have me pay the 10s and he would pay the 5s – which was so poor, that I was ashamed of it, and did it only to save contending with him. There, after agreeing a day for him and I to meet and seal our agreement, I parted and home; and at the office, by agreement, came Mr. Shales, and there he and I discourse till late the business of his helping me in the discovery of some arreares of provisions and stores due to the stores at Portsmouth, out of which I may chance to get some*ᵇ* money and save the King some too; and therefore I shall endeavour to do the fellow some right in other things here, to his advantage, between Mr. Gauden and him.

He gone, my wife and I to her Arithmetique, in which she pleases me well; and so to the office, there set down my Journall, and so home to supper and to bed – a little troubled to see how my

a addition crowded into bottom of page   *b* repl. 'pay'

---

1. Contradictory reports on his tar were sent from Woolwich ropeyard on 2 and 5 November: *CSPD 1663–4*, pp. 324, 327.

2. See below, p. 396.
3. See Trice's promise: above, p. 352.

family is out of order by Wills being there, and also to hear that Jane doth not please my wife as I expected and could have wished.

6. This morning, waking, my wife was mighty earnest with me to persuade me that she should prove with child since last night – which if it be, let it come and welcome. Up to my office, whither Comissioner Pett came, newly come out of the country, and he and I walked together in the garden, talking of business a great while. And I perceive that by our countenancing of him, he doth begin to pluck up his head and will do good things I hope in the yard.[1] Thence, he being gone, to my office and there despatched many people. And at noon to the Change to the Coffee-house; and among other things, heard Sir John Cutler say that of his own experience in time of thunder, so many barrels of beer as have a piece of Iron laid upon them[2] will not be stirred, and the others will. Thence to the Change and there discoursed with many people, and I hope to settle again to my business and revive my report of fallowing of business, which by my being taken off for a while by sickness and laying out of money hath slackened for a little while.

Home; and there find Mrs. Hunt, who dined very merry, good woman, with us. After dinner came in Captain Grove, and he and I alone to talk of many things; and among*a* many other, of the Fishery,[3] in which he gives me such hopes, that being at this time full of projects how to get a little money honestly, of which some of them I trust in God will take, I resolved this afternoon to go and consult my Lord Sandwich about it; and so, being to carry home Mrs. Hunt, I took her and my wife by coach and set them at Axeyard, and I to my Lord's and thither sent for Creed and discoursed with him about it; and he and I to White-hall, where Sir G. Carteret and my Lord met me very fortunately; and wondered first to see me in my perruque, and I am glad it is over. And then, Sir G. Carteret being gone, I took my Lord aside, who doth give me the best

a repl. 'above'

---

1. Cf. above, p. 259.
2. This was a common practice in Kent, Herefordshire 'and other parts': John Aubrey, *Miscellanies* (1696), p. III.

3. See above, iii. 268, n. 3. Grove was employed as a shipping agent by the Tangier committee.

advice he can; and telling me how there are some projectors, by name Sir Edwd Ford, who would have the making of Farthings, and out of that give so much to the King for the maintenance of the Fishery;[1] but my Lord doth not like that, but would have it go as they offered the last year; and so upon my desire, he promises me when it is seasonable to bring me into the commission with others, if any of them take. And I perceive he and Mr. Coventry are resolved to fallow it hard.

Thence, after walking a good while in the long gallery, home to my Lord's lodgings, my Lord telling me how my father did desire him to speak to me about my giving of my sister something; which doth vex me, to see that he should trouble my Lord in it; but however, it is a good occasion for me to tell my Lord my condition, and so I was glad of it. After that, we begun to talk of the Court; and he tells me how Mr. Edw. Mountagu begins to show respect to him again, after his endeavouring to bespatter him all was possible[2] – but he is resolved never to admit him into his friendship again. He tells me how he and Sir H Bennett, the Duke of Buckingham and his Duchesse, was of a committee with somebody else for the getting of Mrs. Stuart for the King. But that she proves a cunning slut, and is advised at Somerset-house ⟨by the Queen-Mother⟩ and by her mother; and so all the plot is spoilt and the whole committee broke – Mr. Mountagu and the Duke of Buckingham fallen a-pieces – the Duchesse going to a nunnery; and so Mountagu begins to enter friendship with my Lord and to attend the Chancellor, whom he had deserted. My Lord tells me that Mr.

1. Sir Edward Ford(e), soldier and inventor, published his proposals in *Experimented proposals how the King may have money to pay and maintain his fleets with ease to his people* (1666); reprinted in *Harl. Misc.* (1808–13), iv. 195–6. The papers in this matter are calendared in HMC, *Rep.*, 6/App., pp. 330-1. Cf. also *CSPClar.*, v. 360. Ford proposed to make farthings from Swedish copper, claiming that his method made counterfeits impossible. The Fishery Company, led by the Duke of York, supported the project: so, too, did the Queen

Mother. A meeting in December 1664 (attended by Pepys) once more approved it. But there was some dispute about the payment to the King (Ford offered 6s. 8d. in the pound), and the officials of the Mint were from the beginning hostile. The plan was revived in 1667-8, again without effect: *CSPD 1666–7*, p. 439; J. R. Elder, *Royal fish. companies*, pp. 102, 105. Ford was allowed to issue Irish farthings, but died before the scheme could take effect.

2. For this quarrel, see esp. above, pp. 46-7.

Mountagu, among other things, did endeavour to represent him to the Chancellor's sons as one that did desert their father in the business of my Lord of Bristoll;[1] which is most false, being the only man that hath several times*a* dined with him when no soul hath come to him, and went with him that very day home when the Earle impeached him in the Parliament-house, and hath refused ever to pay a visit to my Lord of Bristoll, not so much as in return to a visit of his – so that the Chancellor and my Lord are well known and trusted one by another. But yet my Lord blames the Chancellor for desiring to have it put off to the next session of Parliament, contrary to my Lord Treasurers advice, to whom he swore he would not do it. And perhaps my Lord Chancellor, for aught I see by my Lord's discourse, may suffer by it when the Parliament comes to sit.

My Lord tells me that he observes the Duke of Yorke to fallow and understand business very well, and is mightily improved thereby. Here, Mr. Pagett coming in, I left*b* my Lord and him; and thence I called my wife and her maid Jane, and by coach home; and to my office, where late writing some*c* things against tomorrow, and so home to supper and to bed.

This morning Mr. Blackeburne came to me to let me know that he had got a lodging very commodious for his Kinsman,*d* [2] and so he is ready at my pleasure to go when I would bid him; and so I told him that I would in a day or two send to speak with him, and he and I would talk and advise Will what to do – of which I am very glad.

7. Up and to the office, where we sat all the morning; and Sir W. Penn and I had a word or two, where by opposing him in not being willing to excuse a mulct put upon the*e* purser of the *James*, absent from duty, he says by his business and order, he was mighty angry and went out of the office like an Asse discontented – at which I am never a whit sorry; I would not have [him] think that I dare not oppose him where I see reason and cause for it.

Home to dinner; and then by coach abroad about several

a repl. 'dine'   *b* MS. 'lent' or 'lef' badly formed
c repl. 'letters'   *d* l.h. repl. s.h. 'son'   *e* repl. 'a'

---

1. The abortive impeachment of Clarendon: see above, pp. 223–4.   2. Will Hewer, Pepys's clerk, Robert Blackborne's nephew.

businesses to several places. Among others, to Westminster-hall; where seeing Howlett's daughter going out of the other end of the hall, I fallowed her; if I could, to have offered talk to her and dallied with her a little, but I could not overtake her.

Then calling at Unthankes[1] for something of my wife's not done, a pretty little gentlewoman, a lodger there, came out to tell me that it was not yet done – which though it vexed me, yet I took opportunity of taking her by the hand over the boot,[2] and so found matters to talk a little the longer to her; but I was ready to laugh at myself to see how my anger could not operate, my disappointment coming to me by such a messenger. Thence to Doctors Commons and there consulted Dr Turner about some differences we have with the officers of the East India ships, about goods brought by them without[a] paying freight which we demand of them.[3]

So home to my office and there late writing letters; and so home to supper and to bed – having got a scurvy cold by lying cold in my head the last night.

This day Captain Taylor brought me a piece of plate, a little small state dish, he expecting that I should get him some allowance for demorage of his ship *William*,[4] kept long at Tanger – which I shall, and may justly do.

8. *Lords day.* Up; and it being late, to church without my

------

a   l.h. repl. s.h. 'from'

------

1. John Unthank, tailor.

2. The boot of the coach.

3. This dispute concerned the Bombay expedition of April 1662–June 1663. The ships belonged to the King, but were manned and victualled by the company, which had undertaken to load cargo on the return voyage and pay the usual freightage. This was to be deducted from the company's bill for victualling etc., and brought into account in the subsequent settlement for customs duties. The Navy Board alleged that the company broke the contract and deprived the government of its expectation of about £10,000 for

freightage by sending the ships back empty; the company alleged that the officers of the royal ships had illegally engaged in private trade on their own account. See below, v. 26, 76; CSPD 1663–4, p. 278; *Cal. court mins E. India Co. 1660–3* (ed. E. B. Sainsbury), pp. xxxii–iii, xxxix; ib., 1664–7, p. iii; PRO, Adm. 2/1733, pp. 91, 94; PRO, SP 46/18, 19, 19a.

4. The *William and Mary* (owned by Capt. John Taylor), which had been detained on its way back from Aleppo by a dispute about fees payable to the Levant Company: CSPD 1663–4, pp. 107, 273; see below, p. 414 & n. 1.

wife; and there I saw Pembleton come into the church and bring his wife with him, a good comely plain woman. And by and by my wife came after me all alone, which I was a little vexed at. I found that my coming in a perriwigg did not prove so strange to the world as I was afeared it would, for I thought that all the church would presently have cast their eye all upon me – but I found no such thing. Here an ordinary lazy sermon of Mr. Mills, and then home to dinner and there Tom came and dined with us; and after dinner, to talk about a new black cloth-suit that I have a-making; and so at church-time I to church again – where the Scott preached, and I slept most of the time. Thence home and I spent most of the evening upon Fullers *Church History* and Barcklys *Argenis*;[1] and so after supper to prayers and to bed, a little ill, fearing my pain coming back again, myself continuing as costive as ever and my physic ended; but I had sent a porter today for more and it was brought me before I went to bed; and so with pretty good content to bed.

9. Up, and find myself very well; and so by coach to White-hall and there met all my fellow-officers; and so to the Duke, where, when we came into his closet, he told us that Mr. Pepys was so altered with his new perriwigg that he did not know him. So to our discourse; and among and above other things, we were taken up in talking upon Sir J. Lawsons coming home – he being come to Portsmouth; and Captain Berkely is come to town with a letter from the *Duana* of Algier to the King, wherein they do demand again the searching of our ships and taking out of strangers and their goods; and that what English ships are taken without the Dukes pass, they will detain (though it be flat contrary to the words of the peace)[2] as prize, till they do hear from our King, which they advise him may be speedy. And this they did the very next day, after they had received with great joy the Grand Segnors confirmation of the peace from

1. John Barclay's *Argenis*: see above, i. 231 & n. 1. For Fuller's *Church History*, see above, i. 57 & n. 1.
2. The peace recently concluded by Lawson: see above, iii. 89 & n. 1. This had severely limited the right of search granted them by a treaty of 1660, but the new agreement was now repudiated by the Algerines immediately after it had been confirmed by their overlords, the Turkish government in Constantinople.

Constantinople, by Captain Berkely[1] – so that there is no command nor certainty to be had of these people. The King is resolved to send his[a] answer by a fleet of ships; and it is thought best and speediest to send these very ships that are now come home, five sail of good ships, back again, after cleaning, victualling and paying them.[2] But it is a pleasant thing to think how their Bassha, Shavan Aga, did tear his hair to see the soldiers order things thus; for (just like his late predecessor) when they see the evil of war with England, then for certain they complain to the Grand Segnor of him and cut his head off.[3] This he is sure of, and knows as certain.

Thence to Westminster-hall, where I met with Mr. Pierce the surgeon; and among other things, he asked me seriously whether I knew anything of my Lord's being out of Favour with the King. And told me that for certain the King doth take mighty notice of my Lord's living obscurely in a corner, not[b] like himself and becoming the honour that he is come to. I was sorry to hear; and the truth is, from my Lord's discourse among his people (which I am told) of the uncertainty of princes favours and his melancholy keeping from Court, I am doubtful of some such thing; but I seemed wholly strange to ⟨him in⟩[c] it, but will make my use of it.

a repl. 'is'   *b* repl. 'with'   *c* repl. 'his'

---

1. Winchilsea, ambassador to Turkey, had sent his secretary Paul Rycaut to Algiers with the Sultan's ratification. The meeting of the Divan (12 September) at which this perfidious decision was taken is described in Rycaut's letter to Winchilsea (10–13 September) in HMC, *Finch*, i. 276–7. Algiers was the most populous and dangerous of the pirate states on the Barbary coast. Distrust of the Algerines was as strong with the Turks as with the western powers.

2. See below, p. 415 & n. 1. They sailed under Thomas Allin, who forced the Algerines to accept terms similar to those they now rejected: see below, v. 332 & n. 3.

3. In 1659 the presidency of the Divan was taken from the pashas and given to elected aghas or military officers. All five holding office in 1659–71 were murdered – Sha 'ban ('Shavan Aga') himself in 1664. His predecessor Ramadhan had been cut to pieces in August 1661 in a revolt of the Janissaries. Rycaut, like Berkeley, also blames the soldiers (and sea-captains) for the rejection of the treaty. Both had a financial interest in licensed privateering. See HMC, *Finch*, pp. 266, 273, 276–7, 282, 284; G. N. Clark, *War and society in 17th cent.*, pp. 109–10, 119–20.

He told me also how loose the Court is, nobody looking after business but every man his lust and gain; and how the King is now become besotted upon Mrs. Steward, that he gets into corners and will be with her half an hour together, kissing her to the observation of all the world; and she now stays by herself and expects it, as my Lady Castlemayne did use to do; to whom the King, he says, is still kind, so as now and then he goes to have a chat with her as he believes, but with no such fondness as he used to do. But yet it is thought that this new wench is so subtle, that she lets him not do anything more then is safe to her. But yet his doting is so great that Pierce tells me it is verily thought, that if the Queen had died, he would have married her.[1]

The Duke of Monmouth is to have part of the Cockepitt new built for lodgings for him; and they say to be made Captain of the Guards in the room of my Lord Gerard.[2]

Having thus talked with him, there comes into the hall Creed and Ned Pickering; and after a turn or two with them, it being noon, I walked with them two to the Kings-head ordinary and there we dined; little discourse but what was common, only that the Duke of Yorke is a very desperate huntsman.[3] But I was ashamed of Pickering, who could not forbear having up my Lord Sandwich now and then, in the most paltry matters, abominably.[4]

Thence I took leave of them; and so having taken up something at my wife's tailors, I home by coach and there to my office, whither Shales came and I had much discourse with him about the business of the victualling; and thence in the evening to the Coffee-house and there sat, till by and by, by appointment, Will brought me word that his uncle Blackeburne was ready to speak with me. So I went down to him, and he and I to a taverne hard by; and there I begun to speak to Will friendlily, advising him how to carry himself now he is going from under my roof, without any reflections upon the occasion from whence his re-

1. The French ambassador reported (1 November) roughly to the same effect: J. J. Jusserand, *French Ambassador*, p. 88. There were similar rumours in 1667.

2. He did not replace Lord Gerard as captain of the Lifeguard until 1668.

3. Cf. the story reported of him above, p. 192.

4. For Pickering's recent quarrel with Sandwich, see above, p. 303. It was Pickering who told Pepys about Sandwich's affair with Betty Becke.

moval arose.¹   This his uncle seconded; and after laying down to
him his duty to me and what I expect of him, in a discourse of
about quarter of an hour or more, we agreed upon his going this
week, toward the latter of the week, and dismissed him.   And
Mr. Blackeburne and I fell to talk of many things; wherein I did
speak so freely to him in many things agreeing with his sense,
that he was very open to me in*ᵃ* all things.

First, in that of Religion, he makes it great matter of prudence
for the King and Council to suffer liberty of conscience.   And
imputes the loss of Hungary to the Turke from the Emperors
denying them this liberty of their religion.²

He says that many pious Ministers of the word of God – some
thousands of them, do now beg their bread.³   And told me how
highly the present Clergy carry themselfs everywhere, so as that
they are hated and laughed at by everybody; among other
things, for their excommunicacions, which they send upon the
least occasions almost that can be.⁴   And I am convinced in my
judgment, not only from his discourse but my thoughts in
general, that the present clergy will never heartily go down with
the generality of the commons of England; they have been so
used to liberty and freedom, and they are so acquainted with the
pride and debauchery of the present clergy.   He did give me many
stories of the affronts which the clergy receive in all places of
England from the Gentlemen and ordinary persons of the parish.⁵

He doth tell me what the City thinks of Generall Monke, as of
a most perfidious man, that hath betrayed everybody, and the

a l.h. repl. s.h. 'and'

---

1. Cf. above, p. 318 & n. 1.
2. See above, pp. 315–16. The Hungarian Protestants had been backward in the defence of their country. Blackborne (secretary to the Admiralty Committee under the Protectorate) was a Puritan.
3. An exaggeration. Approximately 1760 had been extruded since the Restoration, and not many were reduced to beggary: A. G. Matthews, *Calamy Revised*, pp. xii–xiii.
4. Excommunication was used as a means of enforcing the orders of church courts – e.g. to punish nonappearance. Its use for these purposes had long been an offence to Puritans. After 1689 it was employed much less frequently, and in 1813 was abolished except as a spiritual censure.
5. Both Blackborne and Pepys were prejudiced: cf. above, iii. 135 & n. 2. For anti-clericalism generally, see P. H. Hardacre, *Royalists during Puritan Revolution*, p. 163.

King also; who, as he thinks and his party, and so I have heard other good friends of the King say, it might have been better for the King to have had his hands a little bound for the present, then to be forced to bring such a crew of poor people about him, and be liable to satisfy the demands of every one of them.[1]

He told me that to his knowledge, being present at every meeting at the Treaty at the Isle of Wight, that the old King did confess himself overruled and convinced in his judgment against the Bishops, and would have suffered and did agree to exclude the service out of the churches; nay, his own chappell;[2] and that he did alway say that this he did not by force, for that he would never abate one inch by any vyolence; but what he did was out of his reason and judgment. He tells me that the King, by name, with all his dignities, is prayed for by them that they call Fanatiques, as heartily and powerfully as in any of the other churches that are thought better. And that let the King think what he will, it is them that must help him in the day of Warr – for, as they are the most, so generally they are the most substantiall sort of people, and the soberest.[3] And did desire me to observe it to my Lord Sandwich, among other things, that of all the old army now, you cannot see a man begging about the street. But what? You shall have this Captain turned a shoemaker; the lieutenant, a Baker; this, a brewer; that, a haberdasher; this common soldier, a porter; and every man in his apron and frock, &c., as if they

---

1. Blackborne's argument was that if the King at his restoration had accepted limitations on his power – as the Presbyterians wanted but others (including Monck) successfully opposed – he would have been protected from such importunities. Almost exactly the same advice was given to Charles by a cavalier (Sir William Killigrew) in a letter of 8 April 1660: Thurloe, *State Papers*, vii. 889. For the demands made by the poor cavaliers, see below, vi. 329–30 & n.; P. H. Hardacre, *Royalists*, p. 147.
   2. In the negotiations conducted with commissioners of Parliament in Newport Town Hall in September–October 1648 (just before his trial), Charles I agreed to the establishment of Presbyterianism for three years, and of a limited form of episcopacy thereafter. He made this concession only to gain time to allow a plot for his escape to mature: he never at any time agreed to accept Presbyterianism himself or to suffer it in his own chapel.
   3. Protestant dissenters were in fact a minority – how large a minority is not exactly known. But they included many rich merchants.

never had done anything else – whereas the other[1] go with their belts and swords, swearing and cursing and stealing – running into people's houses, by force oftentimes, to carry away something. And this is the difference between the temper of one and the other; and concludes (and I think with some reason) that the spirits of the old Parliament-soldier[s] are so quiet and contented with God's providences, that the King is safer from any evil meant him by them, a thousand times more then from his own discontented Cavalier[s].

And then to the public management of business: it is done, as he observes, so loosely and so carelessly, that the kingdom can never be happy with it, every man looking after himself and his own lust and luxury; among other things, he instanced in the business of mony; he doth believe that half of what the Parliament gives the King is not so much as gathered. And to that purpose, he told me how the Bellamys (who had some of the Northern counties assigned[a] them for their debt for the petty-warrant victualling) have often complained to him that they[b] cannot get it collected, for that nobody minds; or if they do, they won't pay it in[2] – whereas (which is a very remarkable thing) he hath been told by some of the Treasurers at warr here of late, to whom the most of the 120000*l* monthly was paid, that for most months the payments were gathered so duly, that they seldom had so

---

a l.h. repl. s.h. ? 'assigned'　　　　*b* l.h. repl. s.h. ? 'after'

---

1. The cavaliers. Cf. the case of Col. Turner: below, v. 11 & n. 1. But there were many impostors masquerading as royalist ex-officers. 'A ruffler ever goes under the pretence of a maimed soldier: if he strolls the country he lets not a gentleman's house escape, having a catalogue of them all along as he goeth for his more convenient calling upon them: he carrieth in his pocket (for the help of his memory) a list of the old commanders in the late civil wars which were noted royalists ...': [R. Head], *The canting academy* (1673), pp. 65–6, qu. P. H. Hardacre, *Royalists*, pp. 164–5.

2. Thomas and Robert Bellamy (who appear to have been related to Pepys through the Trices) had unpaid bills for petty-warrant (locally bought) victuals supplied in Chatham and London going back to 1658 and amounting to at least £6,000: *CSPD 1660–1*, p. 186; ib., *1663–4*, p. 156; PRO, Adm. 106/3520, ff. 13*r*–14*v*. In partial settlement they had been awarded sub-commissionerships in the Excise when it was put out to farm in September 1662 (*CSPD 1663–4*, p. 624; *CTB*, i. 398), but the bills were still unpaid much later: below, vi. 111. The excise was at this time farmed by counties.

much, or more then 40s or the like short in the whole colleccion.¹
Whereas now, the very Commissioners for Assessements and other
public payments are such persons, and those that they choose in
the countries so like themselfs, that from top to bottom, that there
is [not] a man careful of anything; or if he be, he is not Solvent;
that what between the beggar and the knave, the King is abused
the best part of all his revenue.

From thence we begun to talk of the Navy, and perticularly of
Sir W Pen – of whose rise to be a general I had a mind to be
informed. He told me he was alway a conceited man and one
that would put the best side outward, but that it was his pretence
of sanctity that brought him*ᵃ* into play.² Lawson and Portman
and the Fifth-monarchy men, among whom he was a great brother,
importuned that he might be general; and it was pleasant to see
how Blackburn himself did act it; how when the Comissioners
of the Admiralty would enquire of the Captains and Admiralls
of such and such men, how they would with a sithe and casting
up the eye say, "Such a man fears the Lord" – or, "I hope such a
man hath the Spirit of God," and such things as that. But he
tells me that there was a cruel Articling against Pen after one
fight, for cowardice in putting himself within a Coyle of Cables,
of which he had much ado to acquit himself; and by great friends
did it, not without remains of guilt, but that his Brethren had a
mind to pass it by and Sir H. Vane did*ᵇ* advise him to search his
heart and see whether this fault or a greater sin was not the

a repl. 'his into'   *b* repl. 'till'

---

1. The monthly assessments levied
by the revolutionary governments
(1645–60) were fixed (until 1654) at
£120,000 a month, and were paid to
the Treasurers-at-War instead of
going through the usual course of
Exchequer. Pepys preserved among
his papers a summary in his own hand
of some of these accounts (1645–51)

given to him by Carteret, which
support Blackborne's statement:
Rawl. A 195a, f. 243r. Cf. M. P.
Ashley, *Fin. and comm. policy under
Crom. Prot.*, p. 79.
2. Penn was unpopular with
Commonwealth men like Blackborne because of his correspondence
with the royalists after 1656.

occasion of this so great tryall.[1] And he tells me that what Pen gives out about Cromwells sending and entreating him to go to Jamaica is very false; he knows the contrary; besides, the Protector never was a man that needed to send for any man, especially such a one as he, twice. He tells me that the business of Jamaica did miscarry absolutely by his pride; and that when he was in the tower, he would cry like a child[2] – this he says of his own personal knowledge. And lastly, tells me that just upon the turne, when Moncke was come from the North to the City and did begin to think of bringing in the King, Pen was then turned Quaker; this he is most certain of.[3] He tells me that Lawson was never counted anything but only a seaman, and a stout man but a false man; and that now he appears the greatest hypocrite in the world – and Pen the same. He tells me that it is much talked of, that the King entends to legitimate the Duke of Monmouth;[4] and that he hath not, nor his friends of his persuasion, had any hopes of getting their consciences at liberty but by God[a] Almighty's turning of the King's heart, which they expect; and are resolved to live and die in quiet hopes of it, but never to repine or act anything more then by prayers towards it. And

a repl. 'the'

---

1. This incident allegedly occurred in the battle off the Kentish Knock (28 September 1652) when Penn was Vice-Admiral under Blake. His ship had struck the sands during the encounter. See his own account in Penn, i. 446–8. Pepys made a note on 2 February 1664 of the same story as recounted by Hempson, Clerk of the Survey at Chatham, who said that Penn was 'articled against . . . for cowardice, for not coming into the fight, and that he was very melancholly a great while upon it, and doubted of ever being employed again; but Sir H. Vane, being of his own religion, kept him in': NWB, p. 11. There is a reference to his hiding in a cable in Marvell's *Second advice to a painter*, l. 87.

2. The expedition of 1655 under Penn and Venables to the W. Indies

had been repulsed at Hispaniola, but had gone on to take Jamaica. On their return both commanders were imprisoned for a short while and never afterwards employed under the Protectorate. Penn was not responsible for the failure of the soldiers' attack on Hispaniola – in which Venables had command – but may have been guilty of favouring the sailors over the soldiers in the matter of supplies: S. R. Gardiner, *Hist. Commonwealth* (1903 ed.), iv. 144–5.

3. Penn had attended Quaker meetings in Cork in 1657: W. Penn, jun., *My Irish journal* (ed. Grubb), p. 13. He was said to be an Anabaptist by one of his critics (Hempson): NWB, p. 11. But he objected to his son's Quakerism, and died an Anglican.

4. See above, iii. 238 & n. 4.

that not only himself, but all of them have and are willing at any time to take the oaths of Allegiance and Supremacy.

Thus far, and upon many more things, we had discoursed, when some persons in a room hard by begun to sing[a] in three parts very finely, and to play upon a Flagilette so pleasantly, that my discourse afterward was but troublesome and I could not attend it; and so anon considering of a sudden the time a-night, we find it 11 a-clock, which I thought it had not been by two hours, but we were close in talk; and so we rise, he having drunk some wine and I some beer and sugar, and so by a fair moon-shine home and to bed. My wife troubled with tooth-ake.

Mr. Black[b]urne observed further to me some certain notice that he had of the present plot so much talked of; that he was told by Mr. Rushworth how one Captain Oates, a great discoverer, did imploy several to bring and seduce others into a plot; and that one of his agents met with one that would not listen to him nor conceal what he had offered him, but so detected the trapan.[1] This, he says, is most true.

He also, among other instances how the King is served,[b] did much insist upon the cowardize and corruption of the King's Guards and Militia; which to be sure will fail the King, as they have done already,[2] when there will be occasion for them.

10. Up and to the office, where we sat till noon; and then to the Exchange, where spoke with several and had my head casting about how to get a penny, and I hope I shall. And then home, and there Mr. Moore by appointment dined with me; and after dinner, all the afternoon till night drawing a bond and release

a MS. 'sung'   b MS. 'several'

---

1. Thomas Oates, of Morley, Yorks., was one of the ringleaders of the Derwentdale Plot and had led the rising at Farnley Wood on 12 October: cf. above, p. 347 & n. 4. Finding that only 30 men had gathered, he sent them home. Suspicion that he, like others of the leaders, was an *agent provocateur* was widespread (cf. *CSPD 1663-4*, p. 326), but seems to have been unjustified: Reresby, *Memoirs* (ed. Browning), p. 47. See *CSPD 1663-4*, p. 326, for a letter from York of 3 November from which Rushworth may have derived the story; and ib., *1661-2*, pp. 537-8, for the use of informers.

2. In Venner's rising, January 1661: cf. above, ii. 9.

against tomorrow, for T. Trice and I to come to a conclusion; in which I proceed with great fear and Jealousy, knowing him to be a rogue and one that I fear hath at this time got too great a hank over me by the neglect of my lawyers.

But among other things, I am come to an end with Mr. Moore for a 32*l* a good while lying in my hand of my Lord Privy Seales,[1] which he for the odd 7*l*. doth give me a Bond to secure me against, and so I get 25*l* clear.

Then he being gone, to the office and there late, setting down yesterday's remarkable discourses; and so home to supper late, and to bed.

The Queene, I hear, is now very well again, and that she hath bespoke herself a new gown.

11. Up and to my office all the morning; and at noon to the Coffee-house, where with Dr. Allen some good discourse about physic and Chymistry.[2]   And among other things, I telling him what Dribble the German Doctor do offer, of an Instrument to sink ships,[3] he tells me that which is more strange: that something made of gold, which they call in Chymistry *Aurum Fulminans*; a grain, I think he said, of it put into a silver spoon and fired, will give a blow like a musquett and strike a hole through the spoon downward, without the least force upward;[4] and this he can make a cheaper experiment of, he says, with Iron prepared.

Thence to the Change; and then being put off of a meeting with T. Trice, he not coming, I home to dinner; and after dinner, by coach with my wife to my periwigg-maker's for my second periwig, but it is not done; and so calling at a place or two, home. And there to my office and there taught my wife a new lesson in Arithmetique, and so sent her home; and then I to several businesses, and so home to supper and to bed – being mightily troubled with a cold in my stomach and head, with a great pain by coughing.

1. Both Moore and Pepys had served as Sandwich's deputies in the Privy Seal Office. For their sharing of fees, see above, i. 238 & n. 4.
2. Cf. above, p. 362 & n. 2.
3. See above, iii. 46 & n. 1.
4. For experiments with gold fulminate at this time, see Birch, i. 455. It was not until the early 19th century that fulminates were first used successfully as detonators in firearms: *DNB*, 'Forsyth, A. J.' Cf. also C. Singer *et al.*, *Hist. Technol.*, iii. 355 & n. 1.

12. Lay long in bed; endeed too long, divers people and the officers at the office staying for me – my Cosen Tho. Pepys the Executor being below; and I went to him and stated reckonings about our debt to him for his payments of money to my uncle Tho. heretofore by the Captains[1] order. I did not pay him, but will soon do it if I can.

To the office and there all the morning; where Sir W. Penn, like a coxcomb, was so ready to cross me in a motion I made unawares, for the entering a man at Chatham into the works – wherein I was vexed to see his spleen, but glad to understand it and that it was in no greater a matter, I being not at all concerned here.

To the Change and did several businesses there; and so home with Mr. Moore to dinner – my wife having dined with Mr. Hollyard with her today, he being come to advise about her hollow sore place below in her privities.

After dinner, Mr. Moore and I discoursing of my Lord's negligence in attendance at Court and the discourse the world makes of it, with the too great reason that I believe there is for it, I resolved and took coach to his lodgings, thinking to speak with my Lord about it without more ado. Here I met Mr. How, and he and I largely about it and he very soberly acquainted me how things are with my Lord. That my Lord doth not do anything like himself, but follows his folly and spends his time either at Cards at Court with the ladies, when he is there at all, or else at Chelsy with that slut, to his great disgrace. And endeed, I do see and believe that my Lord doth apprehend that he doth grow less, too, at Court.

Anon my Lord doth come in and I begun to fall in discourse with him; but my heart did misgive me that my Lord would not take it well, and then found him not in a humour to talk; and so after a few ordinary words, my Lord not talking in that manner as he uses to do, I took leave and spent some time with W. Howe again; and told him how I could not do what I had so great a mind and resolution to do, but that I thought it would be as well to do it in writing; which he approves of, and so I took leave of him and by coach home, my mind being full of it and in pain concerning it. So to my office, busy very late, the

1. Capt. Robert Pepys of Brampton.

nights running on faster then one thinks.   And so home to supper and to bed.

13.   Up and at my office, busy all the morning with Comissioner Pett.   At noon, I to the Exchange; and meeting Shales, he and I to the Coffee-house and there talked of our victualling matters, which I fear will come to little.   However, I will go on and carry it as far as I can.

So home to dinner, where I expected Comissioner Pett; and had a good dinner, but he came not.   After dinner came my Perriwigg-maker and brings me a second perriwigg, made of my own hair; which comes to 21s. and 6d. more*a* then the worth of my own hair – so that they both come to 4l.1s-6d, which he sayth*b* will serve me two years – but I fear it.

He being gone, I to my*c* office and put on my new Shagg purple gown with gold buttons and loop lace – I being a little fearful of taking cold and of pain coming upon me.   Here I stayed, making an end of a troublesome letter, but to my advantage against Sir W. Batten, giving Sir G. Carteret an account of our late great contract with Sir W. Warren for masts;[1] wherein I am sure I did the King 600l service.

That done, home to my wife to take a Clyster; which I did and it wrought very well and brought away a great deal of wind, which I perceive is all that doth trouble me.   After that, about 9*d* or 10 a-clock, to supper in my wife's chamber, and then about 12 to bed.

14.   Up and to the office, where we sat; and after we had almost done, Sir W. Batten desired to have the room cleared; and there he did acquaint the Board how he was obliged to answer to something lately said which did reflect upon the

a repl. 'there'   *b* l.h. repl. s.h. 'thinks'   *c* repl. 'the'
               d repl. 'I'

1. For the contract, see above, p. 304 & n. 1.   A copy of the letter and its covering note (14 and 15 November: in Pepys's hand) is in NMM, LBK/8, pp. 84–7; printed (except for the note) in *Further Corr.*, pp. 6–10.   It is a long, closely argued statement and a good example of Pepys's best business style.

Comptroller and him; and to that purpose told how the bargain of Winter's timber did not prove so bad as I had reported to the Board it would.[1] After he had done, I cleared the matter: that I did not mention the business as a thing designed by me against them, but was led to it by Sir J. Mennes; and that I said nothing but what I was told by Mayers the purveyor, as much as by Deane upon [whom] they laid all the fault – which I must confess did and doth still trouble me, for they report him to be a fellow not fit to be imployed, when in my conscience he deserves better then any officer in the yard.[2] I thought it not convenient to vindicate him much now, but time will serve when I will do it; and I am bound to do it. I offered to proceed to examine and prove what I said if they please; but Mr. Coventry most discreetly advised not, it being to no purpose – and that he did believe that what I said did not, by my manner of speaking it, proceed from any design of reproaching them. And so it ended – but my great trouble is for poor Deane.

At noon home and dined with my wife. And after dinner Will told me, if I pleased, he was ready to remove his things; and so, before my wife, I did give him good counsel, and that*a* his going should not abate my kindness for him if he carried himself well, and so bid God bless him and left him to remove his things, the poor lad weeping. But I am apt to think matters will be the better for it, both for him and us.[3]

So to the office and there late, busy. In the evening Mr. Moore came to tell me that he had no opportunity of speaking his mind to my Lord yesterday, and so I am resolved to write to him very suddenly.

So after my business done, I home – I having stayed till 12

a repl. 'so

1. Cf. above, p. 326 & n. 2.
2. In a note (19 June 1664) on Batten's part in this dispute (NWB, p. 49), Pepys wrote that whereas Anthony Deane had always been well spoken of by Batten, 'so soon as he saw me to favour him [Deane], and that he did inform me of the truth in the business of Hornechurch timber, he could never endure him, but presently he and Sir J. Mennes cried out that he was a useless officer, that there was no need of such an office, and what do we do with him, and I know not what.'
3. Cf. above, p. 318 & n. 1.

a-clock at night almost, making an end of a letter to Sir G Carteret about the late contract for Masts;[1] wherein I have done myself right, and no wrong to Sir W. Batten.

This night I think is the first that I have lain without ever a man in my house besides myself since I came to keep any – Will being this night gone to his lodgings. And by the way, I hear today that my boy Waynman hath behaved himself so with Mr. Davis, that they have got him put into a Berbados ship to be sent away;[2] and though he sends to me to get a release for him, I will not, out of love to the boy; for I doubt to keep him here were to bring him to the gallows.

15. *Lords day.* Lay very long in bed with my wife. And then up and to my office, there to copy fair my letter to Sir G. Carteret; which I did, and by and by, most opportunely a footman of his came to me about other business and so I sent it him by his own servant. I wish good luck with it. At noon home to dinner, my wife not being up, she lying to expect Mr. Hollyard the surgeon. So I dined by myself; and in the afternoon to my office again and there drew up a letter to*ª* my Lord,[3] stating to him what the world talks concerning him, and leaving it to him; and myself to be thought of by him as he pleases, but I have done but my duty in it. I wait Mr. Moores coming for his advice about sending it. So home to supper to my wife, myself finding myself, by cold got last night, beginning to have some pain; which grieves me much in my mind, to see to what a weakness I am come.*ᵇ* This day being our Queenes birthday, the guns of the tower went all off. And in the evening the Lord Mayor sent from church to church to order the constables to cause bonefires to be made in every street – which methinks is a poor thing to be forced to be commanded.

a repl. 'of'   *b* followed by two blank pages

---

1. The same letter that he reports having 'made an end of' on the previous evening: above, p. 380 & n. 1.

2. As an indentured servant.

3. Dated 17 November; printed below, pp. 387–8.

After a good supper with my wife, and hearing on the maids read in the Bible, we to prayers and to bed.

16. Up; and being ready, then abroad by coach to Whitehall and there with the Duke, where Mr. Coventry did a second time go to vindicate himself[1] against reports and prove, by many testimonies that he brought, that he did nothing but what had been done by the Lord Admiralls Secretarys heretofore, though he doth not approve of it; nor, since he had any rule from the Duke, hath he exceeded what he is there directed to take. And the thing I think is very clear, that they always did take, and that now he doth take less then ever they did heretofore.

Thence away, and Sir G. Carteret did call me to him and discourse with me about my letter yesterday; and did seem to take it unkindly that I should doubt of his satisfaccion in the bargain of masts; and did promise me that hereafter, whatever he doth hear to my prejudice, he would tell me before he would believe it; and that this was only Sir W. Batten's report in this business, which he says he did ever approve of; in which I know he lies.

Thence to my Lord's lodgings, thinking to find Mr. Moore, in order to the sending away my letter of reproof to my Lord, but I do not find him; but contrary, do find my Lord come to Court; which I am glad to hear and should be more glad to hear that he doth fallow his business, that I may not have occasion to venture upon his good nature by such provocacion as my letter will be to him.

So by coach home to the Exchange, where I talked about several businesses with several people; and so home to dinner with my wife; and then in the afternoon to my office and there late; and in the evening Mr. Hollyard came, and he and I about our great work to look upon my wife's malady in her secrets; which he did, and it seems her great conflux of humours heretofore, that did use to swell there, did in breaking leave a hallow; which hath since gone in further and further, till now it is near three inches deep; but as God will have it, it doth not run into the bodyward, but keeps to the outside of the skin, and so he

1. In the matter of selling places and taking fees: see esp. above, pp. 330–1.

must be forced to cut it open all along;[1] and which my heart I doubt will not serve for me to see done, and yet she will not have anybody else to see it done; no, not her own maids; and therefore I must do it, poor wretch, for her. Tomorrow night he is to do it.

He being gone, I to my office again a little while; and so home to supper and to bed.

17. Up, and while I am dressing myself, Mr. Deane of Woolwich came to me and I did tell him what had happened to him last Saturday in the office; but did encourage him to make no matter of it, for that I did not fear but he would in a little time be master of his enemies as much as they think to maister him. And so he did tell me many instances of the abominable dealings of Mr. Pett of Woolwich[2] toward him. So we broke up, and I to the office, where we sat all the forenoon doing several businesses; and at noon I to the Change, where Mr. Moore came to me, and by and by T. Trice and my uncle Wight; and so we off to a taverne (the New Exchange tavern over against the Change, where I never was before, and I find my old playfellow Ben Stanly master of it) and thence to a Scrivener to draw up a bond; and to another tavern (the Kingshead)[3] we went; and calling on my Cosen Angier at the India-house there, we eat a bit of pork from a Cookes together; and after dinner did seal the bond,[4] and I did take up the old bond of my uncles to my aunt.[5] And here T. Trice, before them, doth own all matters in difference between us is clear as to this business, and that he will in six days give me it, under the hand of his atturney, that there is no judgment against the bond which may give me any future trouble – and also a copy of the letters of his

---

1. The trouble has been diagnosed as an abscess in the vulva, which had developed into an ischio-rectal abscess, and later became a fistula: *Occ. papers Pepys Club*, i. 90. It was usual for surgeons, rather than physicians, to deal with all such external conditions.

2. Christopher Pett, Master-Shipwright of Deptford and Woolwich yards, to whom Anthony Deane was assistant.

3. There were two of this name near the Exchange, one in Sweeting's Rents, the other in St Benet Fink. (R).

4. For its terms, see above, p. 352. For Pepys's copy, see Sotheby's *Cat.*, 30 November 1970, no. 223 (3).

5. Robert Pepys's bond; the subject of the Chancery proceedings just ended: see above, pp. 351-2. The bond has survived: see *Mar. Mirr.*, 19/215. Copy in Whitear, p. 166.

Administracion to Godfry,[1] as much of it as concerns me to have.

All this being done, toward night we broke up; and so I home, and with Mr. Moore to my office and there I read to him the letter I have writ to send to my Lord, to give him an account how the world, both City and Court, doth talk of him and his living as he doth there, in such a poor and bad house, so much to his disgrace – which Mr. Moore doth conclude so well drawn, that he would not have me by any means to neglect sending it; assuring me, in the best of his judgment, that it cannot but endear me to my Lord, instead of what I fear, of getting his offence; and did offer to take the same words and send them, as from him with his hand, to him – which I am not unwilling should come (if they are at all fit to go) from anybody but myself. And so he being gone, I did take a copy of it to keep by me in short-hand,[2] and sealed them up to send tomorrow by my Will. So home, Mr. Hollyard being come to my wife. And there, she being in bed, he and I alone to look again upon her parts, and there he doth find that though it would not be much pain, yet she is so fearful, and the thing will be somewhat painful in the tending, which I shall not be able to look after but must require a nurse and people about her; so that upon second thoughts, he believes that a fomentacion will do as well; and though it will be troublesome, yet no pain, and what her maid will be able to do without knowing directly what it is for, but only that it may be for the piles – for though it be nothing but what is very honest, yet my wife is loath to give occasion of discourse concerning it.

《*Physique*》   By this, my mind and my wife's is much eased; for I confess I should have been troubled to have had my wife cut before my face – I could not have borne to have seen it. I had great discourse with him about my disease. He tells me again that I must eat in a morning some loosening grewell; and at night, roasted apples. That I must drink now and then ale with my wine, and eat bread and butter and honcy – and rye bread if I can endure it, it being loosening. I must also take once

---

1. For this copy, see Sotheby's *Cat.*, 30 November 1970, no. 223 (2). Thomas Trice was administrator of the estate of Richard Godfrey of Broughton with whom Robert Pepys had made the bond which had oc-

casioned the dispute: Whitear, p. 154.

2. The original letter has not been traced. For the copy, see below, pp. 387–8.

a week a glister of his last prescription; only, honey now and then instead of butter – which things I am now resolved to apply myself to. He being gone, I to my office again to a little business; and then home to supper and to bed – being in a little pain by drinking of cold small beer today, and being in a cold room at the Taverne I believe.

18. Up; and after being ready and done a little business at the office, I and Mr. Hater by water to Redriffe; and so walked to Deptford (where I have not been a very great while) and there paid off the *Milford*[1] in very good order; and all respect showed me in the office, as much as there used to be to any of the rest or the whole board. That done, at noon I took Captain Terne[2] and there coming in by chance Captain Berkely, him also to dinner with me to the Globe. Captain Berkely, who was lately come from Algier, did give us a good account of the place, and how the Bassha there doth live like a prisoner, being at the mercy of the soldiers and officers, so that there is nothing but a great confusion there.

After dinner came Sir Wm Batten, and I left him to pay off another ship and I walked home again, reading of a little book of new poems[a] of Cowly's, given me by his brother.[3] Abraham doth lie, it seems, very sick still; but like to recover.[4]

At my office till late; and then came Mr. Hollyard, so full of discourse and Latin that I think he hath got a cup, but I do not know; but full of talk he is, in defence of Calvin and Luther. He begun this night the fomentacion to my wife, and I hope it will do well with her. He gone, I to the office again a little, and so to bed.

This morning I sent Will with my great letter of reproof to my Lord Sandwich, who did give it into his own hand.[b]

a l.h. repl. s.h. 'p'-
b A copy is here inserted as a loose sheet gummed onto the upper edge of the page.

---

1. £1043 for eight months' service: PRO, Adm. 20/4, p. 528.
2. Of the *Milford*.
3. The book was Abraham Cowley's *Verses lately written upon several occasions*; licensed 20 August 1663: *Trans. Stat. Reg.*, ii. 327. (An unauthorised edition had appeared earlier in the year in Dublin: *Poems*,

ed. Waller, p. 461.) Pepys retained in his library the fourth edition of the *Works* (1674; PL 2428). Cowley's brother Thomas was Clerk of the Cheque at Deptford.
4. For his illness, see Evelyn, 2 January 1664; A. H. Nethercot, *Cowley*, p. 243. He died in 1667.

My Lord.

I do verily hope that neither the manner nor matter of this advice will be condemned by your Lordshipp, when for my defence in the first I shall allege my double attempt (since your return from Hinchingbrooke) of doing it personally, in both of which your Lordships occasions, no doubtfulness of mine prevented me.[1] And that being now fearful of a sudden summons to Portsmouth for the discharge of some ships there, I judge it very unbecoming the duty which (every bit of bread I eat tells me) I owe to your Lordshipp to expose the safety of your Honour to the uncertainty of my return. For the matter (my Lord), it is such as could I in any measure think safe to conceal from, or likely to be discovered to you by any other hand, I should not have dared so far to own what from my heart I believe is false, as to make myself but the relater of others discourse. But, Sir, your Lordships honour being such as I ought to value it to be, and finding both in City and Court that discourses pass to your prejudice,[a] too generally for mine or any man's controlling but your Lordships, I shall (my Lord), without the least greatening or lessening the matter, do my duty in laying it shortly before you.

People of all conditions (my Lord) raise matter of wonder from your Lordships so little appearance at Court – some concluding thence your[b] disfavour there. To which purpose I have had Questions asked me; and endeavouring to put off such insinuacions by asserting the contrary, they have replied that your Lordships living so beneath your Quality, out of the way and declining of Court attendance, hath been more then once discoursed about[c] the King.

Others (my Lord), when the chief Ministers of State, and those most active of the Council have been reckoned up (wherein your Lordship never use to want an eminent place), have said, touching your Lordshipp, that now your turn was served and the King had given you a good estate, you left him to stand or fall as he

---

a l.h. repl. s.h. ? 'ch'-   *b* MS. 'their'   *c* repl. 'of'

---

1. The diary records only one such occasion, when his heart misgave him: above, p. 379. But Moore's attempt to speak to Sandwich (above, p. 381) may have been a preliminary to another approach from Pepys.

would.   And, perticularly in that of the Navy, have enlarged upon your letting fall all service there.

Another sort (and those the most) insist[a] upon the bad report of the house wherein your Lordship (now observed in perfect health again) continues to sojourne.   And by name have charged one of the daughters for a common Courtizan, alleging both places and persons where and with whom she hath been too well known. And how much her wantonness occasions (though unjustly) scandal to your Lordship; and that as well to gratifying of some enemies as to[b] the wounding of more friends, I am not able to tell.

Lastly (my Lord), I find a general coldness in all persons towards your Lordship; such as, from my first dependence on you, I never yet knew.   Wherein I shall not offer to interpose any thoughts or advice of mine, well knowing your Lordship needs not any.   But, with a most faithful assurance that no person nor papers under Heaven is privy to what I here write, besides myself and this,[1] which I shall be careful to have put into your own hands, I rest confident of your Lordships just construction of my dutiful intents herein, and in all humility take leave.

May it please your Lordship,

Nov. 17. 1663./   Your Lordships most obedient servant,
                                                              S.P./

Memorandum.   The letter beforegoing was sent sealed up, and enclosed in this that fallows.

My Lord.

If this finds your Lordshipp either not alone or not at leisure, I beg the suspending your opening of the enclosed till you shall be both – (the matter very well bearing such a delay) and in all humility remain.

May it please your Lordshipp

Nov. 17. 1663./   Your Lordships most obedient servant,
                                                              S.P./

My servant hath my directions to put this into your Lordships own hand, but not to stay for any answer.

a   l.h. repl. s.h. 'inst'   b   repl. 'well'

---

1. But Pepys had confided the   on 17 November.
secret to his diary, and had told Moore

I pray God give a blessing to it. But I confess I am afeared what the consequence may be to me of good or bad, which is according to the ingenuity that he doth receive it with. However, I am satisfied that it will do him good – and that he needs it.

19. Up, and to the office, where (Sir J. Mennes and Sir W. Batten being gone this morning to Portsmouth) the rest of us met, and rose at noon. So I to the Change, where little business, and so home to dinner; and being at dinner, came Creede in and dined with us; and after dinner, Mr. Gentleman, my Jane's father, to see us and her. After a little stay with them, I was sent for by Sir G. Carteret by agreement, and so left them; and to him and with him by coach to my Lord Treasurer, to discourse with him about Mr. Gauden's having of money and to offer to him whether it would not be necessary, Mr. Gaudens credit being so low as it is, to take security of him if he demands any great sum, such as 20000*l*, which now ought to be paid him upon his next year's declaration – which is a sad thing, that being reduced to this by us, we should be the first to doubt his credit; but so it is. However, it will be managed with great tenderness to him.[1] My Lord Treasurer we found in his bed-chamber, being laid up of the goute; I find him a very ready man and certainly a brave servant to the King, he spoke so quick and sensibly of the King's charge. Nothing displeased me in him but his long nails, which he lets grow upon a pretty thick white short hand, that it troubled me to see them.

Thence with Sir G. Carteret by coach, and he set me down at the New Exchange. In our way he told me there is no such thing likely yet as a Dutch war, neither they nor we being in condition for it, though it will come certainly to that in some time, our interests lying the same way, that is to say in trade. But not yet.[2]

Thence to the Temple and there visited my cousin Rogr. Pepys and his brother Dr. John; a couple, methinks, of very ordinary men. And thence to speak Mr. Moore, and met him by the way; who tells me, to my great content, that he

1. A privy seal for the payment of just over £8400 to Gauden was issued on 23 November, but the money was not paid until the following March.

Gauden was owed c. £30,500 altogether for the year's sea-victuals. *CTB*, i. 592.

2. Cf. above, p. 322 & n. 1.

believes my letter to my Lord Sandwich hath wrought well upon him, and that he will look after himself and his business upon it, for he begins already to do so. But I dare not conclude anything till I see him, which shall be tomorrow morning, that I may be out of my pain to know how he takes of me.

He and I to the Coffee-house and there drank and talked a little; and so I home, and after a little at my office, home to supper and to bed – not knowing how to avoid hopes from Mr. Moores words tonight, and yet I am fearful of the worst.[a]

20. Up, and as soon as I could to my Lord Sandwiches lodgings; but he was gone out before, and so I am defeated of my expectation of being eased one way or other in the business of my Lord; but I up to Mr. Howe (who I saw this day the first time in a periwig, which becomes him very well) and discoursed with him; he tells me that my Lord is of a sudden much changed, and he doth believe that he doth take my letter well: however, we do both bless God that it hath so good an effect upon him. Thence I home again, calling at the Wardrobe; where I found my Lord, but so busy with Mr. Townsend, making up accounts there, that I was unwilling to trouble him and so went away. By and by to the Exchange, and there met by agreement Mr. Howe and took him with a barrel of oysters home to dinner, where we were very merry; and endeed, I observe him to be a very hopeful young man, but only a little conceited.

After dinner I took him and my wife; and setting her in Covent-garden at her mother's, he and I to my Lord's. And thence I with Mr. Moore to White-hall; and there, the King and Council being close and I thinking it an improper place to meet my Lord first upon that business, I took coach, and calling my wife, went home – setting Mr. Moore down by the way. And having been late at the office alone, looking over some plats of the Northerne Seas, the White Seas and Archangell River,[1] I went home; and after supper to bed.

My wife tells me that she and her brother have had a great falling-out tonight, he taking upon him to challenge great obligation upon her, and taxing her for not being so as she

a blot at bottom of page

---

1. The Board was worried about a hemp ship overdue from those parts: below, p. 394.

ought to her friends, and that she can do more with me then she pretends, and I know not what; but God be thanked, she cannot.

A great talk there is today of a Crush between some of the phanatiques up in arms and the King's men in the North;[1] but whether true or no, I know not yet.

21. At the office all the morning; and at noon I receive a letter from Mr. Creed with a token, *viz.*, a very noble parti-coloured Indian gowne for my wife. The letter is oddly writ, over-prizing his present and little owning any past service of mine, but that this was his genuine respects and I know not what. I confess I had expectations of a better account from him of my service about his accounts,[2] and so gave his boy 12*d* and sent it back again. And after having been at the pay of a ship this afternoon at the Treasury, I went by coach to Ludgate; and by pricing several there, I guess this gowne may be worth about 12 or 15*l*. But however, I expect at least 50*l* of him. So in the evening I wrote him a letter telling him clearly my mind, a copy of which I keep, and his letter;[3] and so I resolve to have no more such correspondence as I used to have, but will have satisfaction of him as I do expect.

So to write my letters; and after all done, I went home to supper and to bed – my mind being pretty well at ease from my letter to Creed, and more for my receipt this afternoon of 17*l* at the Treasury, for the 17*l* paid a year since to the Carver for his work at my house,[4] which I did entend to have paid myself; but finding others to do it, I thought it not amisse to gett it too – but I am afeared that we may hear of it to our greater prejudices hereafter.

22. *Lords day.* Up pretty early; and having last night be-spoke a coach, which failed me this morning, I walked as far as the Temple and there took coach and to my Lord's lodgings; whom I find ready to go to chappell. But coming, he begin

1. The Farnley Wood rising in Yorkshire: see above, p. 347 & n. 4; H. Gee in *Trans. R. Hist. Soc.* (ser. 3), 11/125+; J. Walker in *Yorks. Arch. Journ.*, 31/348+.
2. See above, p. 198 & n. 1. For the payments to Creed, see PRO, Adm. 20/4, pp. 254, 260, 263, 267.
3. Both untraced.
4. PRO, Adm. 20/4, p. 238; cf. above, iii. 140, 225; above, p. 293 & n. 1.

with a very serious countenance to tell me that he had received my late letter; wherein, first he took notice of my care of him and his honour and did give me thanks for that part of it where I say that from my heart I believe the contrary of what I do there relate to be the discourse of others. But since I entended it not a reproach, but matter of information and for him to make a judgment of it for his practice, it was necessary for me to tell him the persons of whom I have gathered the several perticulars which I there insist on. I would have made excuses in it; but seeing him so earnest in it, I found myself forced to it; and so did tell him Mr. Pierce the surgeon in that of his low living being discoursed of at Court – a maid-servant that I kept that lived at Chelsy school;[1] and also Mr. Pickering, about the report touching the young woman; and also Mr. Hunt in axe-yard, near whom she lodged. I told him the whole City doth discourse concerning his neglect of business; and so I many times asserting my dutiful intention in all this, and he owning his accepting of it as such. That that troubled me most in perticular is that he did there assert the civility of the people of the house and the young gentlewoman, for whose reproach he was sorry. His saying that he was resolved how to live; and that though he was taking a house, meaning to live in another manner, yet it was not to please any people or to stop report, but to please himself (though this I do believe he might say that he might not seem to me to be so much wrought upon by what I have writ); and lastly and most of all, when I spoke of the tenderness that I have used in declaring this to him, there being nobody privy to it, he told me that I must give him leave to except one. I told him that possibly somebody might know of some thoughts of mine, I having borrowed some intelligence in this matter from them, but nobody could say they knew of the thing itself when I writ.[2] This, I confess however, doth trouble me, for that he seemed to speak it as a quick retort; and it must sure be Will Howe, who did not see anything of what I writ, though I told him indeed that I would write; but in this I think there is no great hurt.

I find him, though he cannot but own his opinion of my good intentions, and so he did again and again profess it, that he is

1. Mary Ashwell.   2. But Pepys had read the letter to Moore: above, p. 385.

troubled in his mind at it; and I confess I think I may have done myself an injury for his good; which, were it to do again and that I believed he would take it no better, I think I should sit quietly, without taking any notice of it – for I doubt there is no medium between his taking it very well and very ill.

I could not forbear weeping before him at the latter end; which since I am ashamed of, though I cannot see what he can take it to proceed from but my tenderness and good will to him.

After this discourse was ended, he begun to talk very cheerfully of other things, and I walked with him to White-hall and we discoursed of the pictures in the gallery;[1] which, it may be, he might do out of policy, that the boy might not see any strangeness in him; but I rather think that his mind*a* was somewhat eased, and hope that he will be to me as he was before. But however, I doubt not but when he sees that I fallow my business and become an honour to him, and not to be like to need him or to be a burden to him, and rather able to serve him then to need him, and if he doth continue to fallow business and so come to his right wits again, I do not doubt but he will then consider my faithfulness to him – and esteem me as he ought.

At Chappell I had room in the Privy Seale pew with other gentlemen, and there heard Dr. Killigrew[2] preach; but my mind was so, I know not whether troubled or only full of thoughts of what had passed between my Lord and me, that I could not mind it nor can at this hour remember three words; the Anthemne was good after sermon, being the 51 psalme – made for five voices by one of Captain Cookes boys, a pretty boy – and they say

a   MS. 'man'

---

1. Probably the Long Matted Gallery or the Privy Gallery. In the time of Charles I these two galleries had housed many of his most important possessions, and they seem to have been reconstituted as far as possible after the Restoration: MS. inventory of Charles II's pictures, in the office of the Surveyor of The Queen's Pictures, items 1–81, 93–156. (OM).

2. Henry Killigrew, chaplain to the King, Almoner to the Duke of York, and Master of the Savoy.

there are four or five of them that can do as much.¹ And here I first perceived that the King is a little Musicall, and kept good time with his hand all along the Anthem.²

Up into the gallery after sermon, and there I met Creed; we saluted one another but spoke but not one word of what had passed yesterday between us; but told me he was forced to go to such a place to dinner and so we parted.

Here I met Mr. Povy, who tells me how Tanger had like to have been betrayed, and that one of the King's officers is come, to whom 8000 pieces-of-eight were offered for his part.³

Thence I to the Kings-head ordinary and there dined; good and much company and a good dinner; most of their discourse was about hunting, in a dialect* I understand very little.

Thence by coach to our own church; and there, my mind being yet unsettled, I could mind nothing; and after sermon home and there told my wife what had passed; and thence to my office, where doing business only to keep my mind imployed till late; and so home to supper, to prayers and to bed.

23. Up and to Alderman Backewells, where Sir W Rider by appointment met us to consult about the insuring of our Hemp-ship from Archangell,⁴ in which we are all much concerned by my Lord Treasurers command. That being put in a way, I went to Mr. Beacham, one of our Jury, to confer with him about our business with Field at our trial tomorrow. And thence to

1. The composer was probably Pelham Humfrey, now aged about 16, whose anthem 'Have mercy upon me, O God' is found (in whole or in part) in BM, Add. 17784, 17840, 33235; Harl. 7338; Ch. Ch. Oxford, MS. 621; Fitzwilliam, Cambridge, MS. 117; St Michael's Coll. Tenbury, MSS 310, 1029, 1034; W. Boyce, *Cathedral Music* (1760–73), ii. 235. John Blow, Thomas Tudway, William Turner and Michael Wise also composed anthems. (E).

2. 'It was, and is yet a mode among the *Monseurs*, always to act the musick, which habit the King had got,

and never in his life could endure any that he could not act by keeping the time': North (ed. Wilson), p. 299. Cf. also ib. (ed. Andrews), p. 27; ib. (ed. Rimbault), pp. 103–4; BM, Add. 32532, f. 11v. (E).

3. Spain and the Moors had recently plotted to drive the English out of Tangier: no doubt this money was provided by Spain. Spies abounded and the air was thick with rumours and alarms until the end of the year, but it all came to nothing. See Routh, pp. 49+.

4. See above, p. 175 & n. 5.

St. Paul's churchyard and there bespoke Rushworths *collections*[1] and Scobells *acts of the Long Parliament*, &c.;[2] which I will make the King pay for as to the office, and so I do not break my vowe at all.

Back to the Coffee-house and then to the Change, where Sir W Rider and I did bid 15 per cent; and nobody will take it under 20 per cent, and the lowest was 15 per cent premio and 15 more to be abated in case of loss; which we did not think fit without order to give.[3] And so we parted, and I home to a speedy, though too good a dinner to eat alone; *viz*, a good goose and a rare piece of roast beef. Thence to the Temple; but being there too soon and meeting Mr. Moore, I took him up and to my Lord Treasurers and thence to Sir Ph. Warwickes, where I found him and did desire his advice; who left me to do what I thought fit in this business of the insurance. And so back again to the Temple, all the way telling Mr. Moore what had passed between my Lord and me yesterday; and endeed, my fears do grow that my Lord will not reform as I hoped he would nor have the ingenuity to take my advice as he ought, kindly. But however, I am satisfied that the one person whom he said he would take leave to except is not Mr. Moore; and so W Howe, I am sure, could tell him nothing of my letter that ever he saw it.

Here Moore and I parted; and I up to the Speaker's chamber and there met Mr. Coventry by appointment, to discourse about Fields business. And thence, we parting, I homewards[a] and called at the Coffee-house, and there by great accident hear that a letter is come that our ship is safe come to Newcastle: with this news I went, like an asse, presently to Alderman Backewell and told him of it; and he and I went to the Affrican-house in Broadstreete to have spoke with Sir W Rider to tell him of it, but missed him. Now, what an opportunity had I to have

a repl. 'home'

---

1. John Rushworth, *Historical Collections* (1659; PL 2386); a book of documents on English political affairs, 1618–29. Pepys later bought the other seven volumes of the set (covering 1618–49), published 1680–1701: PL 2387–93.

2. Henry Scobell, *Collection of acts and ordinances . . . made in the parlia-*ment . . . [*1640–1658*], (1657–8; PL 2520).

3. The war-time rate of insurance ('both against Sea and Enemy') for cargo of Baltic ships in 1665 was c. 7%: Brouncker and Pepys to Coventry, 14 December 1665; BL, Add. 28084, f. 8r.

concealed this, and seemed to have made an insurance and got 100*l*, with the least trouble and danger in the whole world.   This troubles me, to think I should be so overseen.

So back again with Alderman Backewell, talking of the new money; which he says will never be counterfeited, he believes,[1] but it is deadly inconvenient for telling, it is so thick and the edges are made to turn up.

I find him as full of business and, to speak the truth, he is a very painful man and ever was, and nowadays is well paid for it.

So home and to my office, doing business late in order to the getting a little money; and so home to supper and to bed.

24.   Up and to the office, where we sat all the morning.   And at noon to the Change, where everybody joyed me in our Hemp-ship's coming safe.   And it seems one man, Middleburgh, did give 20 per cent in gold last night, three or four minutes before the news came of her being safe.

Thence with Mr. Deane home and dined; and after dinner and a great deal of discourse of the business of Woolwich yard, we opened his draught*a* of a ship which he hath made for me; and endeed, it is a most excellent one and that that I hope will be of good use to me as soon as I get a little time – and much endebted I am to the poor man.

Toward night, I by coach to White-hall to the Tanger Com-mittee; and there spoke with my Lord and he seems mighty kind to me, but I will try him tomorrow by a visitt, to see whether he holds it or no.   Then home by coach again and to my office, where late with Captain Miners about the East India business.[2]

So home to supper and to bed – being troubled to find myself so bound as I am, notwithstanding all the physic that I take.

This day, our Tryall was with Field; and I hear that they have given him 20*l* damage more[3] – which is a strange thing, but yet not so much as formerly nor as I was afeared of.

a repl. 'pla'-

---

1. The new coins minted in 1662-3 had milled edges: see above, iii. 265 & n. 2.
2. See above, p. 368, n. 3.

3. Field had already obtained damages and costs against Pepys in the previous year: above, iii. 23 & n. 2.

25. Up; and to Sir G. Carteret's house and with him by coach to White-hall. He uses me mighty well, to my great joy, and in our discourse took occasion to tell me that as I did desire of him the other day, so he desires of me the same favour; that we may tell one another at any time anything that passes among*ᵃ* us at the office or elsewhere wherein we are either dissatisfied one with another; and that I should find him in all things as kind and ready to serve me as my own brother. This methought was very sudden and extraordinary, and doth please me mightily and I am resolved by no means ever to lose him again if I can.[1] ⟨He told me that he did still observe my care for the King's service in my office.⟩*ᵇ*

He set me down in Fleet-street; and thence I by another coach to my Lord Sandwichs and there I did present him Mr. Barlow's Terella,[2] with which he was very much pleased and he did show me great kindness; and by other discourse, I have reason to think that he is not at all, as I feared he would be, discontented against me, more then the trouble that the thing will work upon him. I left him in good humour; and I to White-hall to the Duke of Yorke and Mr. Coventry and there advised about insuring the Hempship at 1 and ½ per cent, notwithstanding her being come to Newcastle – and I do hope that in all my three places[3] which are my hopes and supports, I may not now fear anything; but with care, which through the Lord's blessing I will never more neglect, I don't doubt but to keep myself up with them all – for in the Duke and Mr. Coventry – my Lord Sandwich and Sir G Carteret, I place my greatest hopes. And it pleased me yesterday that Mr. Coventry in the coach (he carrying me to the Exchange at noon from the office) did, speaking of Sir W. Batten, say that though there was a difference between them, yet he could imbrace any good motion of Sir W. Batten's to the King's advantage, as well as of Mr. Pepys's or any friend he had. And when I talked that I would go about doing some-

a repl. 'by'   *b* addition crowded in between paragraphs

---

1. For their recent dispute (over Creed's accounts), see above, pp. 215–16.
2. See above, p. 323 & n. 1.
3. His work in the Navy Office, the Tangier committee and Sandwich's household. (He had reckoned himself clear of his work at the Privy Seal on 17 August 1662.)

thing of the Controllers work when I had time, and that I thought the Controller would not take it ill, he wittily replied that there was nothing in the world so hateful as a dog in a manger.

Back by coach to the Exchange; there spoke with Sir W Rider about insuring – and spoke with several other persons about business, and shall become pretty well-known quickly.

Thence home to dinner with my poor wife; and with great joy to my office and there all the afternoon about business; and among others, Mr. Bland came to me and had good discourse, and he hath chose me a referree for him in a business.[1] And anon, in the evening, comes Sir W. Warren, and he and I had admirable discourse. He advised me in things I desired about Bummary[2] and other ways of putting out money; as, in parts of ships, how dangerous they are.

And lastly fell to talk of the Duch management of the Navy; and I think will help me to some accounts of things of the Dutch Admiralty which I am mighty desirous to know.

He seemed to have been mighty privy with my Lord Albemarle in things before this great turn, and to the King's dealings with him and others for some years before; but I doubt all was not very true.[3] However, his discourse is very useful in general, though he would seem a little more then ordinary in this.

Late at night home to supper and to bed. My mind in good ease, all but my health – of which I am not a little doubtful.

26. Up and to the office, where we sat all the morning; and at noon I to the Change and there met with Mr. Cutler the merchant, who would needs have me home to his house by the Dutch church; and there in an old but good house with his wife and mother, a couple of plain old women, I dined; a good plain dinner, and his discourse after dinner with me upon matters of the navy victualling, very good and worth my hearing. And so home to my office in the afternoon, with my mind full of business; and there at it late, and so home to supper to my poor wife and to bed – myself being in a little pain in one of my

1. A dispute about freightage: see below, p. 404 & n. 2.
2. Bottomry; a form of mortgage: see below, p. 401, n. 3.

3. Albemarle had not been in touch with the King until immediately before the Restoration.

testicles, by a stroke I did give it in pulling up my breeches yesterday over-eagerly; but I will lay nothing to it till I see whether it will cease of [it]self*ᵃ* or no.

The plague, it seems, grows more and more at Amsterdam.¹ And we are going upon making of all ships coming from thence and Hambrough, or any other infected places, to perform their Quarantine (for 30 days as Sir Rd. Browne expressed it in the order of the Council, contrary to the import of the word; though in the general acceptation, it signifies now the thing, not the time spent in doing it) in Holehaven – a thing never done by us before.²

27. Up and to my office, where busy with great delight all the morning; and at noon to the Change, and so home to dinner with my poor wife and with great content to my office again, and there hard at work upon stating the accounts of the freight due to the King from the East India Company³ till late at night; and so home to supper and to bed. My wife mightily pleased with my late discourse of getting a trip over to Calis or some other port of France the next summer, in one of the Yachts; and I believe I shall do it.⁴ And it makes good sport that my maid Jane dares not go and Besse is wild to go and is mad for joy – but yet will be willing to stay if Jane hath a mind, which is the best temper in this and all other things that ever I knew in my life.

28. Up and at the office; sat all the morning and at noon by Mr. Coventrys coach to the Change; and after a little while there, where I met with Mr. Pierce the surgeon, who tells me for good news that my Lord Sandwich is resolved to go no

a repl. symbol rendered illegible

---

1. See above, p. 340, n. 2. About 400 were now dying weekly: *CSPClar.*, v. 342, 348.

2. On 11 November the Council ordered the Admiral to have two small ships stationed as low in the river as possible to enquire of all incoming vessels whether they came from the infected places. If they did, they were either to turn back to sea or to stay in quarantine in Hole (Holl, Holy) Haven, a creek on the s.-e.

coast of Essex: PRO, PC 2/56, f. 311r-*v*. For certain other ships and goods, the period was forty days: ib., f. 300*v*. Hamburg was the port from which Bohemian timber was shipped.

3. See above, p. 292 & n. 1.

4. Pepys and his wife did not go to France until 1669; in September-October visiting Holland, Flanders and Paris: *Priv. Corr.*, ii. 242.

more to Chelsy, and told me he believed that I had been giving
my Lord some counsel, which I neither denied nor affirmed but
seemed glad with him that he went thither no more. And so
I home to dinner, and thence abroad to Pauls churchyard and
there looked upon the second part of *Hudibras*;[1] which I buy
not but borrow to read, to see if it be as good as the first, which
the world cries so mightily up; though it hath not a good liking
in me, though I had tried by twice or three times reading to
bring myself to think it witty. Back again home; and to my
office and there late doing businesses, and so home to supper and
to bed. I have been told it two or three times, but today for
certain I am told how in Holland publicly they have pictured
our King with reproach. One way is with his pockets turned
the wrong side outward, hanging out empty – another, with two
courtiers picking of his pocket – and a third, leading of two ladies,
while others abuse him – which amounts to great contempt.[2]

29. *Lords day.* This morning I put on my best black cloth-
suit trimmed with Scarlett ribbon, very neat, with my cloak
lined with Velvett and a new Beaver, which altogether is very
noble, with my black silk knit canons I bought a month ago.[3]

I to church alone, my wife not going; and there I find my
Lady Batten in a velvet gowne, which vexed me that she should
be in it before my wife, or that I am able to put her into one;
but what cannot be, cannot be. However, when I came home
I told my wife of it; and to see my weakness, I could on the
sudden have found my heart to have offered her one, but second
thoughts put it by; and endeed, it would undo me to think of
doing as Sir W. Batten and his Lady do, who hath a good estate
besides his office.[4] A good dinner we had of *bœuf a la mode*,

1. Licensed on 5 November 1663,
and bearing the date of the following year (as books appearing at the
end of the year usually did): *Trans.
Stat. Reg.*, ii. 332. Pepys bought it
on 10 December. For his initial
dislike of the first part, see above, p.
35 & n. 2.

2. No such cartoons have been
traced in the published catalogues of
Dutch political cartoons, or in the

despatches of the English envoy at
The Hague. For the Dutch use of
political cartoons, see M. D. George,
Engl. polit. caricature, i. 48+; C. R.
Boxer in *Hist. Today*, 16/621.

3. Above, p. 357.

4. Lands at Easton St George's,
Som., inherited from his father, and a
house and property at Walthamstow,
Essex. (R).

but not dressed so well as my wife used to do it. So after dinner I to the French church; but that being too far begun, I came back to St. Dunstans by us,[1] and heard a good sermon and so home. And to my office all the evening, making up my accounts of this month; and blessed be God, I have got up my crumb again to 770*l*, the most that ever I had yet, and good clothes a great many besides; which is a great mercy of God to me.

So home to supper and to bed.

30. Was called up by a messenger from Sir W. Penn to go with him by coach to White-hall. So I got up and went with him; and by the way he begun to observe to me some unkind dealing of mine to him a week or two since[2] at the table, like a coxcomb; which I answered him pretty freely, that I could not think myself to owe any man that service, to do this or that because they would have it so (it was about taking of a mulct upon a purser for not keeping guard at Chatham when I was there);[a] so he talked and I talked and let fall the discourse, without giving or receiving any great satisfaction. And so to other discourse, but I shall know him still for a false knave. At White-hall, the Duke we met in the matted gallery, and there he discoursed with us; and by and by my Lord Sandwich came and stood by and talked. But it being St. Andrew's and a Collar-day, he went to Chappell and we parted from him; and Sir W. Penn and I back again and I light at the Change, and to the Coffee-house; where I heard the best story of a cheat entended by a Maister of a ship, who had borrowed twice his[b] money upon Bottomaryne,[3] and as much more insured upon his ship and goods as they were worth, and then would have cast her away upon the coast of France and there left her, refusing any pilott which was offered him; and so the Governor of the place took her and sent her over hither to find any Owner; and so the ship is come safe, and goods and all – not all worth 500*l*, and he had

a followed by 'last' struck out   *b* MS. 'as'

---

1. St Dunstan-in-the-East, on St Dunstan's Hill, below Eastcheap.
2. On 7 November: above, p. 367.
3. Bottomry, a method of borrow-ing money by pledging the ship. The master could do it as owner's agent: W. Burney, *Dict. of marine* (1815).

one way or other taken 3000*l*. The cause is to be tried tomorrow at Guildhall, where I entend to be.

Thence home to dinner – and then with my wife to her Arithmetique. In the evening came W. Howe to see me, who tells me that my Lord hath been angry three or four days with him, would not speak to him; at last did, and charged him with having spoken to me about what he had observed concerning his Lordshipp – which W. Howe denying stoutly, he was well at ease; and continues very quiet and is removing from Chelsy as fast as he can; but methinks both by my Lord's looks upon me today (or it may be it is only my doubtfulness) and by W. Howe's discourse, my Lord is not very well pleased; nor, it may be, will be a good while – which vexes me, but I hope all will over in time, or else I am but ill rewarded for my good service.

Anon, he and I to the Temple and there parted; and I to my Cosen Roger Pepys, whom I met going to his chamber; he was in haste, and to go out of town tomorrow. He tells me of a letter from my father, which he will keep to read to me at his coming to town again; I perceive it is about my father's jealousy concerning my wife's doing ill-offices with me against him, only from the differences they had when she was there; which he very unwisely continues to have and trouble himself and friends about to speak to me in – as, my Lord Sandwich, Mr. Moore and my Cosen Roger, which vexes me; but I must impute it to his age and care for my mother and Pall, and so let it go.

After little discourse with him, I took coach and home, calling upon my booksellers for two books, Rushworths and Scobells *colleccions*[1] – I shall make the King pay for them. The first I spent at my office some time to read and it is an excellent book. So home and spent the evening with my wife in Arithmetique; and so to supper and to bed.

⟨I end this month with my mind in good condition for anything else, by my unhappy adventuring to disoblige my Lord by doing him service in representing to him the discourse of the world concerning him and his affairs.⟩*a*

a addition crowded into bottom of page

---

1. See above, p. 395 & nn.

DECEMBER./

1. Up and to the office, where we sat all the morning. At noon, I home to dinner with my poor wife, with whom nowadays I enjoy great pleasure in her company and learning of Arithmetique.

After dinner I to Guildhall to hear a trial at King's Bench before Lord Chief Justice Hide, the same I mention in my yesterday's journall. Where everything was proved, how money was so taken up upon Bottomary and Insurance, and the ship left by the Maister and Seamen upon rocks, which, when the sea fell at the Ebb, she must perish. The Maister was offered help, and he did give the pilotts 20 *sols* to drink to bid them go about their business, saying that the rocks were old but his ship was new. And that she was repaired for 6*l* and less, all the damage that she received, and is now brought by one sent over on purpose by the Insurers, into the Thames – with her cargo, vessels of tallow daubed over with butter, instead of all butter – the whole not worth above 500*l*, ship and all, and they had took up, as appeared, above 2400*l*.[a] He had given his men money to content them. And yet for all this, he did bring some of them to swear that it was very stormy weather and did all they could to save her, and that she was seven feete deep water in hold, and were fain to cut her main and foremast. That the Maister was the last man that went out, and they were fain to force out when she was ready to sink and her rudder broke off; and she was drawn into the Harbour after they were gone, as a wrack all broke[b] and goods lost, that could not be carried out again without new building, and many other things so contrary as is not imaginable more. There was all the great counsel in the kingdom in the case; but after one wittnesse or two for the plaintiff, it was cried down as a most notorious cheat; and so the Jury, without going out, found it for the plaintiff. But it was pleasant to see what mad sort of testimonys the seamen did give, and could not be got to speak in order; and then their terms such as the Judge could not understand; and to hear how sillily the Counsel and Judge would speak as to the terms necessary in the matter would make one laugh. And

a repl. '1400*l*'   *b* repl. 'broken'

403

above all, a Frenchman that was forced to speak in French, and took an english oath he did not understand and had an interpreter sworn to tell us what he said, which was the best testimony of all. So home, well satisfied with this afternoon's work, purposing to spend an afternoon or two every term so; and so to my office a while and then home to supper – arithmetique with my wife, and to bed.

《I heard other causes, and saw the course of pleading by being at this trial, and heard and learned two things. One is that every man hath a right of passage in, but not a title to, any highway. The next, that the Judge would not suffer Mr. Crow, who hath fined for Alderman,[1] to be called so, but only "Maister," and did eight or nine times fret at it and stop every man that called him so.》

2. My wife troubled all last night with the tooth-ake, and this morning.

I up and to my office, where busy; and so home to dinner with my wife, who is better of her teeth then she was. And in the afternoon by agreement called on by Mr. Bland, and with him to the Ship, a neighbour tavern, and there met his Antagonist Mr. Custos and his referee Mr. Clerke, a merchant also, and begun the dispute about the freight of a ship hired by Mr. Bland to carry provisions to Tanger, and the freight is now demanded; whereas, he says that the goods were some spoiled, some not delivered; and upon the whole, demands 1300*l* of the other. And their minds are both so high, their demands so distant, and their words so many and hot against one another, that I fear we shall bring it to nothing. But however, I am glad to see myself so capable of understanding the business as I find I do, and shall endeavour to do Mr. Bland all the just service I can therein.[2]

Here we were in a bad room, which vexed me most; but we meet at another house next. So at noon I home and to my office till 9 a-clock; and so home to my wife to keep her company, Arithmetique, then to supper and to bed – she being well of her teeth again.

1. William Crow, elected in October 1659, was discharged in April 1660 on payment of a fine of £420.

2. Pepys had agreed on 25 November to act as arbiter in this dispute. For its settlement, see below, v. 36.

3. Up*ª* and to the office, where all the forenoon; and then (by Mr. Coventry's coach) to the Change; and so home to dinner, very pleasant, with my poor wife. Somebody from Portsmouth, I know not who, hath this day sent me a Runlett of Tent. So to my*ᵇ* office all the afternoon, where much business till late at night; and so home to my wife and then to supper and to bed.

This day Sir G Carteret did tell us at the table that the navy (excepting what is due to the yards upon the Quarter now going on, and what few bills he hath not heard of) is quite out of debt[1] – which is extraordinary good news; and upon the Change, to hear how our Creditt goes*ᶜ* as good as any merchant's upon the Change is a joyful thing*ᵈ* to consider; which God continue. I am sure the King will have the benefit of it – as well as we some peace and Creditt.

4th.*ᵉ* Up pretty betimes; that is, about 7 a-clock, it being now dark then. And so got me ready with my clothes, breeches and warm stockings, and by water with Henry Russell,[2] cold and wet and windy, to Woolwich to a hemp ship there; and stayed looking upon it and giving direction as to the getting it ashore, and so back again, very cold; and at home, without going on shore anywhere, about 12 a-clock, being fearful of taking cold. And so dined at home – and shifted myself, and so all the afternoon at my office till night, and then home to keep my poor wife company; and so to supper and to bed.

5. Up, and to the office, where we sat all the morning; and then with the whole Board, *viz.*, Sir J. Mennes, Sir W. Batten, and myself, along with Captain Allen home to dinner where he lives, hard by in Marke lane; where we had a very good plain dinner and good welcome – in a pretty little house, but so smoky that it was troublesome to us all, till they put out that fire and made one of charcoale.

I was much pleased with this dinner for the many excellent

---

a MS. 'at'   *b* repl. 'the'   *c* repl. 'good'   *d* repl. 'thing'   *e* repl. '6'

---

1. He exaggerated: see *CSPD Add. 1660–85*, p. xvii; Tedder, pp. 45–7. In November 1660 the navy debt had stood at over £1¼m. Cf. above, i. 226 & n. 4.

2. Waterman to the Navy Office.

stories told by Mr.*a* Coventry; which I have put down in my book of tales,[1] and so shall not mention them here.

We stayed till night, and then Mr. Coventry away; and by and by I home to my office till 9 or 10 at night, and so home to supper and to bed – after some talk and Arithmetique with my poor wife, with whom nowadays I live with great content, out of all trouble of mind by jealousy (for which God forgive me), or any other distraction more then my fear of my Lord Sandwiches displeasure.

6. *Lords day.* Lay long in bed; and then up and to church alone (which is the greatest trouble that I have, by not having a man or boy to wait on me) and so home to dinner; my wife, it being a cold day and it begin to snow (the first snow we have seen this year), kept her bed till after dinner. And I below by myself looking over my arithmetique books and Timber Rule.[2]

So my wife rise anon, and she and I all the afternoon at Arithmetique; and she is come to do Addicion, Substraccion and Multiplicacion very well[3] – and so I purpose not to trouble her yet with Division, but to begin with the globes to her now.

At night came Captain Grove to discourse with me about Fields business and of other matters. And so he being gone, I to my*b* office and spent an hour or two reading Rushworth;[4] and so to supper home, and to prayers and bed – finding myself by cold to have some pain begin with me, which God defend should encrease.

7. Up betimes; and it being a frosty morning, walked on foot to White-hall, but not without some fears of my pain coming. At White-hall I hear and find that there was the last night the greatest Tide that ever was remembered in England to have been in this River – all White-hall having been drowned – of which there was great discourse.[5]

Anon we all met, and up with the Duke and did our business;

a repl. 'Sir'　　　*b* l.h. repl. s.h. 'the'

---

1. Untraced.
2. See above, p. 84 & n. 2.
3. The lessons had begun on 21 October.
4. See above, p. 395, n. 1.
5. A high spring tide had coincided

with a northerly gale in the North Sea. Rugge (ii, f. 81*r*) reports that £100,000 worth of damage was caused. For floods in Westminster, see above, i. 93, n. 1.

and by and by my*a* Lord of Sandwich came in, but*b* whether it
be my doubt or no I cannot tell, but I do not find that he made
any sign of kindness or respect to me, which troubles me more
then anything in the world. After done there, Sir W. Batten
and Captain Allen and I by coach to the Temple, where I light,
they going home; and endeed, it being only my trouble of
mind to try whether I could meet with my Lord Sandwich and
try him, to see how he will receive me, I took coach and back
again to White-hall; but there could not find him. But here I
met Dr Clerke and did tell him my story of my health; how my
pain comes to me nowadays. He did write something for me,
which I shall take when there is occasion.[1] I then fell*c* to other
discourse, of Dr. Knapp; who tells me he is the King's Physician
and is become a Sollicitor for places for people – and I am mightily
troubled with him.[2] He[3] tells me he is the most impudent fellow
in the world, that gives himself out to be the King's Physician,
but is not so – but is cast out of the Court – from whence*d* I may
learn what impudence there is in the world, and how a man may
be deceived in persons.

Anon the King and Duke and Duchesse came to dinner in the
Vane=roome, where I never saw them before; but it seems, since
the tables are down, he dines there altogether.[4]

The Queene is pretty well,[5] and goes out of her chamber to her
little chapel in the house. The King of France,*e* they say, is hiring
of 60 sail of ships of the Dutch, but it is not said for what design.[6]

a l.h. repl. s.h. 'the'
c repl. 'fall' or 'full' badly formed
b l.h. repl. s.h. 'and'
d repl. 'his'   *e* l.h. 'e' above name

1. See below, p. 441.
2. On 2 December John Knapp, 'dr. medecinae', had written to his 'honoured friend Mr Peeps' reminding him of an alleged promise to have one George Gouye [? Gouge] appointed surgeon in a frigate: BL, Add. 38849, f. 40r.
3. Clarke.
4. In August public dining days (q.v. above, i. 299 & n. 2) had been discontinued, to save money: Evelyn, iii. 360-1 & n.; HMC, *Ormonde*, n.s., iii. 76.

5. For her illness, see above, p. 337 & n. 2.
6. There is no mention of his hiring ships in the printed correspondence of d'Estrades, French ambassador in Holland. But Louis bought warships from the Dutch (17 altogether by 1666) to strengthen a naval force which amounted to only c. 20 ships of the line in 1661. See Downing to Clarendon, 18 December 1663: Bodl., Clar. 107, ff. 45+; C. Bourel de la Roncière, *Hist. marine française*, v. 374+. For similar rumours, see below, p. 418.

By and by, not hoping to see my Lord, I went to the Kingshead ordinary, where a good dinner but no discourse almost; and after dinner, by coach home and find my wife this cold day just got out of bed; and after a little good talk with her, to my office and there spent my*a* time till late.

Sir W Warren two or three hours with me, talking of trade and other very good discourse – which did please me very well; and so after some reading in Rushworth, home to supper and to bed.

8. Lay long in bed, and then up and to the office, where we sat all the morning; and among other things, my Lord Barkely called in Question his clerk, Mr. Davis, for something which Sir W. Batten and I did tell him yesterday, but I endeavoured to make the least of it, and so all was put up.

At noon to the Change; and among other businesses, did discourse with Captain Taylor, and I think I shall safely get 20*l* by his ships freight at present, besides what it may be I may get hereafter.[1]

So home to dinner, and thence by coach to White-hall, where a great while walked with my Lord Tiviott, who I find a most careful, thoughtful, and cunning man, as I also ever took him to be.   He is this day bringing in an account, where he makes the King debtor to him 10000*l* already on the garrison of Tanger account.   But yet demands not ready money to pay it, but offers such ways of paying it out*b* of the sale of old decayed provisions as will enrich him finely.

Anon came my Lord Sandwich, and then we fell*c* to our business at the Comittee, about my Lord Tiviotts accounts – wherein I took occasion to speak now and then, so as my Lord Sandwich did well seem to like of it; and after we were up, did bid me good-night in a tone that methinks he is not so displeased with me as I did doubt he is; however, I will take a course to know whether he be or no.

The Committee done, I took coach; and home to my office and there late, and so to supper at home and to bed – being

a repl. 'the'   *b* repl. 'as'   *c* repl. 'sat'

----

1. See above, p. 52, n. 1.

doubtful of my pain, through the very cold weather which we have; but I will take all the care I can to prevent it.

9. Lay very long in bed today, for fear of my pain; and then rise and went to stool (after my wife's way, who by all means would have me sit long and upright) very well; and being ready, to the office – from whence I was called by and by to my wife, she not being well.   So to her, and find her in great pain of those. So by and by to my office again, and then abroad to look out a Cradle to burn Charcoale in in my office and I found one to my mind in Newgate-market; and so meeting Foly's[1] man in the street, I spoke to him to serve it in to the office for the King. So home to dinner; and after talk with my wife, she in bed and pain all day, I to my office most of the evening, and then home to my wife. ⟨This day Mrs. Russell did give my wife a very fine St. George in Alabaster, which will set out my wife's closet mightily.⟩*a*
This evening in the office, after I had wrote my day's passages, there came to me my Cosen Angier of Cambridge, poor man,*b* making his moan; and obtained of me that I would send his son to sea as a Reformado, which I will take care to do.   But to see how apt every man is to forget friendship in time of adversity – how glad was I when he was gone, for fear he should aske me to be bond for him, or to borrow money of me.

10.   Up, pretty well, the weather being become pretty warm again.   And to the office, where we sat all the morning; and I confess, having received so lately a token from Mrs. Russell, I did find myself concerned for our not buying some tallow of her (which she bought on purpose yesterday most unadvisedly, to her great loss, upon confidence of putting it off to us*c*); so hard it is for a man not to be warped against his duty and maister's interest that receives any bribe or present, though not as a bribe, from anybody else.   But she must be contented, and I, to do her a good turn when I can without wrong to the King's service.

a addition crowded into bottom of page   *b* MS. 'woman'
c repl. 'is to'

---

1. Robert Foley, ironmonger to the navy.

Then home to dinner ⟨(and did drink a glass of wine and beer, the more for joy that this is the shortest day in the year,[1] which is a pleasant consideration)⟩*a* with my wife; she in bed but pretty well. And having a messenger from my brother that he is not well nor stirs out of door, I went forth to see him. And found him below; he hath not been well, but is not ill. I found him taking order for the distribution of Mrs. Ramsy's coles, a thing my father for many years did, and now he after him;[2] which I was glad to see – as also to hear that Mr. Wheately begins to look after him; I hope it is about his daughter.[3]

Thence to St. Paul's churchyard to my booksellers; and having gained this day in the office, by my stationer's bill to the King, about 40*s* or 3*l.*, I did here sit two or three hours, calling for twenty books to lay this money out upon; and found myself at a great loss where to choose, and do see how my nature would gladly returne to the laying out of money in this trade. I could not tell whether to lay out my money for books of pleasure, as plays, which my nature was most earnest in; but at last, after seeing Chaucer – Dugdales *History of Pauls*, Stow's *London*, Gesner, *History of Trent*, besides Shakespeare, Johnson, and Beaumonts plays,[4] I at last chose Dr. Fuller's *worthys, the Cabbala or collections of Letters of State* – and a little book, *Delices de Hollande*, with another little book or two, all of good use or serious

a addition crowded in between paragraphs over caret

---

1. By the Old Style: see above, vol. i, p. clii.

2. Mrs Ramsey was a parishioner of St Bride's, Fleet St, who had left the sum of 6*s.* a year for 30 years to be spent on seacoals for distribution to poor housekeepers of the parish by two feoffees of whom John Pepys had been for some time the sole survivor. See GL, MS. 6554/1, ff. 219*r*, 231*r*; Whitear, pp. 90–1.

3. See above, ii. 159 & n. 2.

4. All of these Pepys later bought and kept except for the Gesner (*Liber quatuor de conciliis, quorum unus generalem tractationem, alter historicam narrationem omnium conciliorum, posteriores duos refutationem duorum librorum Roberti Bellarmini continent*, Wittemberg, 1st edition, 1600–1, by Salomon Gesner, d. 1606, Lutheran theologian). For the Chaucer and the Shakespeare, see below, v. 198, 199 & nn. The rest are: Sir W. Dugdale, *Hist. of St Paul's Cathedral* (1658; PL 2444); John Stow, *Survey of London* (1633; PL 2476); Jonson, *Works* (1692; PL 2645); and Beaumont and Fletcher, *Fifty comedies and tragedies* (1679; PL 2623).

pleasure; and *Hudibras*, both parts,[1] the book now in greatest
Fashion for drollery, though I cannot, I confess, see enough where
the wit lies. My mind being thus settled, I went by link home;
and so to my office and to read in Rushworth;[2] and so home to
supper and to bed.

Calling at Wotton my shoemaker's today, he tells me that
Sir H. Wright[3] is dying. And that Harris is come to the Dukes
house again;[4] and of a rare play to be acted this week of Sir Wm.
Davenant's, the story of Henry the 8th with all his wifes.[5]

11. Up, and abroad toward the Wardrobe; and going out,
Mr. Clerke met me to tell me that Field hath a writ against me
in this last business, of 30*l.* 10*s.*;[6] and that he believes he will get
an Execucion against me this morning. And though he told me
it could not be well before noon and that he would stop it at the
Sheriffes, yet it is hard to believe with what fear I did walk, and
how I did doubt at every man I saw, and do start at the hearing of
one man coffe behind my neck. I to the Wardrobe and there
missed Mr. Moore. So to Mr. Holden's and evened all reckonings there for hats. And then walked to Paul's churchyard; and
after a little at my booksellers and bought at a shop Cardinall

a repl. 'Ex'-

---

1. All the four books named are
still in the PL, the last two in later
editions. Thomas Fuller, *The history
of the worthies of England* (1662; PL
2438); *Cabala, sive scrinia sacra,
Mysteries of state and government in
letters of . . . the reigns of King Henry
the Eighth, Q. Elizabeth, K. James,
and K. Charles* (1663; PL 2261); [J.
N. de Parival], *Les délices de la
Hollande* (Amsterdam, ed. 1678; PL
147); and Butler's *Hudibras* (3 pts,
1689; PL 889, cf. above, p. 35 &
n. 2).

2. See above, p. 395, n. 1.

3. Sandwich's brother-in-law; he
had made his will on 24 October, and
died on 5 February 1664.

4. Henry Harris had been suc-

cessful in his demands for extra payment: see above, p. 239 & n. 3.
(A).

5. Davenant now revived Shakespeare's *Henry VIII* at the LIF.
There is no evidence of Davenant's
having altered this history play. It
was first acted in 1613 and published
in 1623. Downes (p. 24) describes the
revival as a great success and records
that Betterton played the part of
Henry VIII, 'he being instructed in it
by Sir *William* [Davenant], who had it
from Old Mr *Lowen*, that had his
Instructions from Mr Shakespeare
himself. . . .' Harris appeared as
Wolsey, Mrs Betterton as Queen
Katharine. (A).

6. See above, p. 396 & n. 3.

Mazarins will in French,[1] I to the Coffee-house[a] and there, among others, had good discourse with an Iron=merchant, who tells me the great evil of discouraging our natural manufacture of England in that commodity by suffering the Swede to bring in three times more then ever they did, and our own Ironworkes be lost – as almost half of them, he says, are already.[2]　Then I

《*Eastland storys.*》 went and sat by Mr. Harrington and some East Country merchants; and talking of the country about Quinsborough[3] and thereabouts – he told us[b] himself that for fish, none there, the poorest body, will buy a dead fish; but must be alive, unless[c] it be in winter; and then they told us the manner of putting[d] their nets into the water through holes made in the thicke Ice; they will spread a net[e] of half a mile long, and he hath known a 130 and 170 barrells of fish taken at one draught. And then the people comes with Sledges upon the Ice, with snow at the Bottome, and lay the fish in and cover them with snow, and so carry them to market.　And he hath seen when the said fish have been frozen in the sled, so as that he hath taken a fish and broke a-pieces, so hard it hath been; and yet the[f] same fishes, taken out of the snow and brought into a hot room, will be alive and leap up and down.　Swallow often are brought up in

a l.h. repl. l.h. 'Ex'-　　*b* repl. 'me'　　*c* repl. 'but must be'
d repl. 'casting'　　　*e* MS. 'ned'　　*f* repl. 'some of'

---

1. Probably *Le testament du defunt Cardinal Jul. Mazarini, duc de Nivernois, premier ministre du roi de France* (Cologne, 1663); not in the PL. Bogus wills of Mazarin had been published long before his death (1661) as part of the press campaign against him: C. Moreau, *Bibliog. des mazarinades*, iii, nos 3766–7.

2. An exaggeration: see *Econ. Hist. Rev.* (ser. 2), 11/144+. Despite local difficulties, especially in the Wealden ironfield, domestic production increased steadily from 1660 onwards. But the importation of Swedish ore, produced by cheap labour, alarmed English ironmasters. For a petition against it in 1664, see E. Straker, *Wealden Iron*, pp. 62–3. Cf. also *CSPD 1668–9*, p. 140. The Navy Office was one of the importers: PL 2874, pp. 408+. Cf. Pepys's notes on the relative qualities of English, Swedish and Spanish iron (22 March 1664) in NWB, p. 31.

3. Königsberg, E. Prussia. William Harrington was an Eastland merchant; a neighbour of Pepys and a younger brother of James Harrington, the republican writer. The 'Eastland' or 'East Country' was the Baltic region, principal source for England of timber and naval stores, which were shipped from Baltic and N. German ports by the Eastland Company.

their nets out of the mudd from under water, hanging together
to some twigg or other, dead in ropes; and brought to the fire,
will come to life.[1] Fowl killed in December (Alderman Barker
said) he did buy; and putting into the box under his sled, did
forget to take them out to eate till Aprill next, and they then
were found there and were, through the frost, as sweet and fresh
and eat as well as at first killed. Young Beares are there; their
flesh sold in market as ordinarily as beef here, and is excellent
sweet meat. They tell us that Beares there do never hurt anybody, but fly away from you unless you pursue and set upon
them – but Wolves do much mischief. Mr. Harrington told us
how they do to get so much[a] honey as they send abroad. They
make hallow a great Firr tree, leaving only a small slitt down
straight in one place; and this they close up again, only leave a
little hole and there the Bees go in and fill the bodies of these
trees as full of wax and honey as they can hold; and the inhabitants at their times go and open that slit and take what they
please, without killing the bees, and so let them live there still
and make more. Firr trees are always planted close together,
because of keeping one another from[b] the violence of the windes;
and when a fellet is made, they leave here and there a grown
tree to preserve the young ones coming up. The great entertainment and sport of the Duke of Corland and the princes thereabouts is hunting; which is not with dogs as we, but he appoints
such a day and summons all the country-people as to a *Campagnia*;
and by several companies gives every one their circuit, and they
agree upon a place where the Toyle is to be set; and so, making
fires every company as they go, they drive all the wild beast –
whether bears – wolfe, foxes, Swine, and stags and rowes, into the

a MS. 'much as'   *b* repl. 'for'

---

1. Cf. the similar story in Samuel
Purchas, *Hakluytus posthumus or Purchas his pilgrimes* (1906 ed.), xiii. 452;
and also *Philos. Trans.*, i. 344+. The
migration of swallows was difficult to
establish, and down to the end of the
18th century most experts in W.
Europe (including Gilbert White)
held the view that in autumn they
became torpid and hibernated. In
the Baltic and N. Europe the usual
learned, as well as popular, opinion
(e.g. of Olaus Magnus in the 16th and
Linnaeus in the 18th century) was
that they hibernated under water, in
much the way as Pepys's informant
describes. See White, *Nat. hist. Sel-
borne* (ed. Nicholson), pp. 42+, 230
etc.; J. Rennie, *Bird Miscell.* (1847),
ch. xii.

Toyle; and there the great men have their stands in such and such places and shoot at what they have a mind to, and that is their hunting. They are not very populous there, by reason that people marry women seldom till they are towards or above 30; and men 30 or 40, or more oftentimes, year old.

Against a public hunting, the Duke sends that no wolfes be killed by the people; and whatever harm they do, the Duke makes[a] it good to the person that suffers it – as Mr. Harrington instanced in a house where he lodged, where a wolfe broke into a hog-stye and bit three or four great pieces off of the back of the hog before the house could come to help it (it crying, and that did give notice to the people of the house); and the man of the house told him that there was three or four wolfs thereabouts that did them great hurt; but it was no matter, for the Duke was to make it good to him, otherwise he could kill them.

Thence home and upstairs, my wife keeping her bed, and had a very good dinner; and after dinner to my office and there till late busy. Among other things, Captain Taylor came to me about his bill for freight;[1] and besides that I find him contented that I have the 30l. I got, he doth offer me to give me 6l. to take the getting of the bill paid upon me; which I am ready to do, but I am loath to have it said that I ever did it. However, I will do him that service, to get it paid if I can and stand to his courtesy what he will give me.

Late to supper home; and to my great joy, I have by my wife's good advice almost brought myself, by going often and leisurely to the stool, that I am come almost to have my natural course of stool as well as ever, which I pray God continue to me.

12. Up and to the office, where all the morning; and among other things, got Sir G. Carteret to put his letters to Captain Taylor's bill, by which I am in hopes to get 5l – which joys my heart. We had this morning a great dispute between Mr.

a repl. symbol rendered illegible

---

1. A bill for carrying goods to Tangier in the *William and Mary* (£278 15s.) with charges for demurrage for 46 days (£73 17s.). Warrants for payment were issued from the Navy Treasury on 28 November: PRO, Adm. 20/5, p. 52. See above, pp. 52, 368; below, p. 423 & nn.

Gauden, victualler of the Navy, and Sir J Lawson and the rest of the Commanders going out against Argier,[1] about their fish and keeping of Lent; which Mr. Gauden so much insists upon to have it observed, as being the only thing that makes up the loss of his dear bargain all the rest of the year.[2]

At noon went home; and there I find that one Abrahall, who strikes in for the serving of the King with Ship=chandlery ware, hath sent my wife a Japan gowne; which pleases her very[a] well and me also, it coming very opportune – but[b] I know not how to carry myself to him, I being already obliged so far to Mrs. Russell – so that I am in both their pays.

To the Exchange, where I had sent Luellin word I would come to him; and thence brought him home to dinner with me. He tells me that W. Symons's wife is dead,[3] for which I am sorry, she being a good woman; and tells me an odde story of her saying before her death, being in good sense, that there stood her uncle Scobell.

Then he begin to tell me that Mr. Deering had been with him to desire him[c] to speak to me that if I would get him off with those goods upon his hands, he would give me 50 peeces. And further, that if I would stand his friend, to help him to the benefitt of his patent as the King's merchant, he could spare me 200*l* per annum out of his profits.[4] I was glad to hear both of these; but answered him no further then that as I would not by anything be bribed to be unjust in my dealings, so I was not so squeemish as not to take people's acknowledgment where I have the good fortune by my pains to do them good and just offices. And so I would not come to be at an agreement with him, but I would labour to do him this service, and to expect his considera-

---

a symbol smudged   *b* l.h. repl. s.h. 'and'   *c* repl. 'me'

---

1. The fleet sailed in January, with orders to attack Algiers. A new agreement was imposed on the authorities there in October 1664.

2. The fleet would buy fresh fish locally.

3. Both Llewellyn and Symons had been colleagues of Pepys at the Exchequer. The former was now clerk to Edward Dering, merchant.

4. Dering had in August 1660 been appointed 'King's merchant' for the purchase of naval material in the Baltic. The office, dating from days when trade was much smaller, was now obsolescent, and carried fewer privileges. Dering had had a surplus of deals to dispose of since the autumn: *CSPD 1663–4*, pp. 320, 373, 453.

tion thereof afterward, as he thought fit.   So I expect to hear more of it.

I did make very much of Luellin, in hopes to have some good by this business; and after he was gone, I to my office doing business; and in the evening received some money from^a Mr. Moore and so went and settled accounts in my books between him and me; and I do hope at Christmas not only to find myself as rich or more then ever I was yet, but also my accounts in less compass, fewer reckonings, either of debts or moneys due to me, then ever I have seen for some years.   And endeed do so, the goodness of God bringing me from better to a better expectation and hopes of doing well.   This day I heard my Lord Berkely tell Sir G Carteret^b that he hath letters from France that the King hath unduked twelve Dukes,[1] only to show his power and to crush his Nobility, whom he said he did see had heretofore laboured to cross him.   And this my Lord Barkely did mightily magnify, as a sign of a brave and vigorous mind, that what he sees^c fit to be done he dares do.

At night, after business done at my office – home to supper and to bed.

I have forgot to set down a very remarkable passage: that Lewellen being gone and I going into the office and it begin to be dark, I found nobody there, my clerks being at a burial^d of a child of W Griffins;[2] and so I spent a little time till they came, walking in the garden; and in the meantime, while I was walking, Mrs.^e Pen's pretty maid came by my side and went into the office; but finding nobody there, I went in to her, being glad of the occasion; she told me, as she was going out again, that there was nobody there and that she came for a sheet of paper; so I told her I would supply her, and left her in the office and went into my office and opened my garden door, thinking to have got

a repl. 'of'   *b* repl. 'the Duke'   *c* repl. 'his'
d repl. 'christening'   *e* repl. 'I saw'

1. A mistake. But since 1661 an enquiry had been proceeding into false titles of nobility (assumed in order to evade taxes), and several orders had been issued which culminated in September 1664 in a royal edict revoking all titles granted since

1634: L. Chérin, *Abrégé chronologique d'édits ... concernant le fait de la noblesse* (Paris, 1788), pp. 134, 141.

2. William, son of William Griffin, doorkeeper to the Navy Office, was buried this day in the churchyard of St Olave's.

her in and there to have caressed her; and seeming looking for paper, I told her this was as^a near a way for her; but she told me she had left the door open and so did not come to me; so I carried her some paper and kissed her, leading her by the hand to the garden door and there let her go. But Lord, to see how much I was put out of order by this surprizal, and how much I could have subjected my mind to have treated* and been fond with this wench, and how afterward I was troubled to think what if she should tell this, and whether I had spoke or done anything that might be unfit for her to tell. But I think there was nothing more passed then just what I here write.

13. *Lords day.* Up, and made me ready for church; but my wife and I had a difference about her old folly, that she would fasten lies upon her maids, and now upon Jane; which I did not see enough to confirm me in it, and so would not consent to her.

To church; where after sermon, home and to my office^b before dinner, reading my vowes; and so home to dinner, where Tom came to me and he and I dined together, my wife not rising all day. And after dinner I made even accounts with him – and spent all the afternoon in my chamber, talking of many things with him – about Wheatelys daughter for a wife for him. And then about the Joyces and their father Fenner, how they are sometimes all honey one with another and then all turd, and a strange rude life there is among them.

In the evening, he gone, I to my office to read Rushworth upon the charge and answer of the Duke of Buckingham,¹ which is very fine; and then to do a little business against tomorrow; and so home to supper to my wife, and then to bed.

14. Up by candlelight, which I do not use to do, though it be very late, that is to say almost 8 a-clock; and out by coach to White-hall, where we all met, and to the Duke – where I heard a large discourse between one that goes over an Agent from the King to Legorne and thereabouts to remove the inconveniences

a s.h. repl ? l.h. 'cl'-   *b* repl. 'house'

---

1. The 1st Duke. The articles of his impeachment in 1626, with his   answer, are in Rushworth, *Hist. Coll.*, i. 303+, 376+.

his ships are put to by denial of pratique – which is a thing that is nowadays made use of only as a cheat, for a man may buy a bill of health for a piece-of-eight, and my enemy may agree with the *Intendent* of the *Santé*, for ten pieces-of-eight or so, that he shall not give me a bill of health, and so spoil me in my design, whatever it be.   This the King will not endure, and so resolves either to have it removed or to keep all ships from coming in or going out there, so long as his ships are stayed for want hereof.¹

Then my Lord Sandwich being there, we all went into the Duke's closet and did our business.   But among other things, Lord, what an account did Sir J. Mennes and Sir W. Batten make of the pulling down and burning of the head of the *Charles*, where Cromwell was placed with people under his horse, and Peter, as the Duke called him, praying to him.²   And Sir J. Mennes would needs infer the temper of the people from their joy at the doing of this and their building a Jibbett for the hanging of his head up – when, God knows, it is even the flinging away of 100*l* out of the King's purse to the building of another – which it seems must be a Neptune.

Thence I through White-hall, only to see what was doing; but meeting none that I knew, I went through the garden to my Lord Sandwiches lodging, where I found my Lord got before me (which I did not entend or expect) and was there trying Some*ᵃ*

a   repl. 'a'

---

1. For some time Leghorn had been much used by English ships in the Mediterranean for victualling and other purposes.   It remained important in that connection until Gilbraltar was taken in 1704, and was specially important when relations with Spain were strained.   It was the Spaniards who now seem to have put about the story that English ships carried plague from Tangier and should be denied facilities: *CSPVen.* 1661–4, pp. 192–3, 199, 210.   The agent was probably either Thomas Clutterbuck (resident navy agent at Leghorn) or Francis Williamson, cousin of Joseph

Williamson, Secretary Bennet's man of business (cf. PRO, SP 98/4, f. 276).

2. The *Royal Charles* (then the *Naseby*) had been built in 1655, and was now at Chatham.   The figure-head is described by Evelyn (9 April 1655): 'In the *Prow* was *Oliver* on horseback trampling 6 nations under foote, a *Scott, Irishman, Dutch, French, Spaniard* & *English* as was easily made out by their several habits: A *Fame* held a laurell over his insulting head, & the word *God with us.*' The Duke's reference was probably to Hugh Peters, the best-known of the Protector's court preachers.

musique which he entends for an Anthemne of three parts;[1] I
know not whether for the King's Chappell or no – but he seems
mighty intent upon it.   But it did trouble me to hear him swear
"Before God" and other oaths, as he did now and then without
an occasion, which methought did so ill become him – and I
hope will be a caution for me, it being so ill a thing in him.[2]

The Musique being done, without showing me any good or ill
countenance, he did give me his hat and so Adieu, and went down
to his coach without saying anything to me.   He being gone,
I and W Howe talked a good while.   He tells me that my Lord,
it is true, for a while after my letter was displeased, and did show
many slightings of me when he had occasion of mentioning me
to his Lordshipp, but that now my Lord is in good temper, and
he doth believe will show me as much respect as ever – and
would have me not to refrain to come to him.   This news, I
confess, did much trouble me; but when I did hear how he
is come to himself and hath wholly left Chelsy and that slut, and
that I see he doth fallow his business and becomes in better repute
then before, I am rejoiced to see it, though it doth cost me some
disfavour for a time; for if not his good nature and ingenuity,
yet I believe his memory will not bear it alway in his mind.   But
it is my comfort that this is the thing, after so many years good
service, that hath made him my enemy.

Thence to the Kings-head ordinary and there dined among a
company of fine gentlemen; some of them discoursed of the King
of France's greatness, and how he is come to make the Princes
of blood to take place of all Forraine Embassadors; which it seems
is granted by them of Venice and other States, and expected from
my Lord Hollis our King's Embassador there; and that either upon
that score or something else, he hath not ⟨had⟩ his Entry yet
in Paris, but hath received several affronts; and among others, his
harnesse Cutt and his gentlemen of his*a* horse killed, which will

a repl. 'the'

---

1. Untraced. See below, p. 428.   2. Cf. Pepys's dislike of his wife's
(E).   swearing: above, p. 150.

breed bad blood if true.[1] They say also that he hath hired three
score ships of Holland and 40 of the Swede, but nobody knows
what to do. But some great designs he hath on foot against
the next year.[2]

Thence by coach home and to my office, where I spent all the
evening till night with Captain Taylor, discoursing about keeping
of Masts;[3] and when he was gone, with Sir W. Warren, who did
also give me excellent discourse about the same thing, which I
have committed to paper.[4] And then fell to other talke, of his
being at Chatham lately; and there, discoursing of his Masts,
Comissioner Pett did let fall several scurvy words concerning my
pretending to know masts as well as anybody – which I know
proceeds ever since I told him I could measure a piece of timber
as well as anybody imployed by the King.[5] But however, I
shall remember him for a black sheep again a good while, with
all his fair words to me, and perhaps may let him know that my
ignorance does the King as much good as all his knowledge;
which would do more, it is true, if it were well used.

Then we fell to talk of Sir J. Mennes and Sir W. Batten burning
of Olivers head while he was there; which was done with so
muchinsulting*and folly as I never heard of, and had the trayned-
band of Rochester to come to the solemnity – when, when all

1. It was untrue: Holles has no
reference in his despatches to any such
incident. He had arrived in Paris
on 9/19 August but, because of these
disputes, did not make his public
entry and have his first formal
audience until the following March:
below, v. 60 & n. 1. Louis XIV was
now claiming royal rights for all
princes of the French blood royal –
precedence over ambassadors on all
public occasions, the right to be
visited in audience, etc. These pre-
tensions were allowed by the Spanish
ambassador, but not, contrary to
Pepys's information, by the Venetian.
The latter, like the English, resisted
them: see, e.g., Holles's amusing
account of the Venetian ambassador's
asserting his right to a *fauteuil* (1/11
March 1664; PRO, SP 78/118, ff.

93–4); and cf. ib., f. 230r; *CSPVen.
1661–4*, pp. 260, 281. Secretary Bennet and Charles II seem to have taken
a less rigid view than Holles: PRO,
SP 78/117, f. 161r; C. H. Hartmann,
The King my brother, pp. 84–90.

2. For the rumour about the ships,
see above, p. 407 & n. 4. The
French were threatening both Italy
and Flanders (cf. Downing to Clarendon, 11/21 December: Bodl., Clar.
MSS 107, ff. 33+), but the outbreak
of the Anglo-Dutch war in 1664
delayed Louis' plans, and his troops
did not move against the Spanish
Netherlands until the spring of 1667.

3. For mast-docks, see below, v.
15 & n. 1.

4. Untraced.

5. Cf. above, pp. 259–60.

comes to all, Comissioner Pett says it never was made for him. But it troubles me the King should suffer 100*l* loss in his purse to make a new one, after it was forgot whose head it was or any words spoke of it.

He being gone, and I mightily pleased with his discourse, by which I alway learn something, I to read a little in Rushworth;[1] and so home to supper to my wife, it having been washing day, and so to bed – my mind, I confess, a little troubled for my Lord Sandwiches displeasure.   But God will give me patience to bear, since it rises from so good an occasion.

15.   Before I was up, my brother's Man came to tell me that my Cosen Edwd. Pepys was dead – died at Mrs. Turner's; for which my wife and I are very sorry, and the more for that his wife was the only handsome woman of our name.[2]

So up and to the office, where the greatest business was Sir J. Mennes and Sir W. Batten against me for Sir W Warrens contract for masts; to which I may go to my Memorandum booke[3] to see what passed.   But came off with conquest, and my Lord Barkely[a] and Mr. Coventry well convinced that we are well used.

So home to dinner; and thither came to me Mr. Mount and Luellin, I think almost foxed, and there dined with me; and very merry as I could be, my mind being troubled to see things so ordered at the board – though with no disparagement to me at all.

At dinner comes a messenger from the Counter,[4] with an Execucion against me for the 30*l*. *x*s given the last verdict to Field. The man's name is Thomas, of the Poultry Counter.   I sent Griffin with him to the Dolphin, where Sir W. Batten was at

a   repl. 'Sir J. Mennes'

---

1. See above, p. 395, n. 1.
2. Edward Pepys (of Brooms-thorpe, Norf.), brother of Jane Turner, had died on the 14th at the age of 46 and was buried at Tattersett, Norf.   His wife was Elizabeth, daughter of John Walpole of Broomsthorpe.

3. This was later copied into another memorandum-book: NWB, pp. 5–6 ('a great dispute about the signing of Sir W. W.'s bill for his masts delivered lately at Chatham'). For these books, see above, p. 241, n. 3;   below, v. 116 & n. 1;   for the contract, see above, p. 304 & n. 1. Mennes and Batten had supported the competing tender from William Wood.

4. A city prison.   For the case, see above, pp. 396, 411 & nn.

dinner; and he being satisfied that I should pay the money, I did cause the money to be paid him, and Griffin to tell it out to him in the office. He offered to go along with me^a to Sir R. Ford; but I thought it not necessary, but let him go with it; he also telling me that there is never any receipt for it given – but I have good witness of the payment of it.

They being gone, Luellin having again told me by myself that Deering is content^b to give me 50l if I can sell his^c Deales for him to the King, not that I did ever offer to take it or bid Luellin bargain for me with him, but did tacitely seem to be willing to do him what service I could in it, and expect his thanks what he thought good.

Then to White-hall^d by coach, by the way overtaking Mr. Moore and took him into the coach to me; and there he could tell me nothing of my Lord, how he stands as to his thoughts or respect to me; but concludes that though at present he may be angry, yet he will come to be pleased again with me no doubt – and says that he doth mind his business well and keeps at Court.

So to White-hall and there by order find some of the Commissioners of Tanger met, and my Lord Sandwich among the rest; to whom I bowed, but he showed me very little if any countenance at all, which troubles me mightily.

Having soon done there, I took up Mr. Moore again and set him down at Pauls; by the way he proposed to me of a way of profit which perhaps may shortly be made by money by Fines* upon houses at the Wardrobe; but how I did not understand but left it to another discourse.

So homeward, calling upon Mr. Fen by Sir G. Carteret's desire; and did there show him the Bill of Captain Taylors whereby I hope to get something justly.

Home and to my office, and there very late with Sir W Warren upon very serious discourse, telling him how matters passed today. And in the close, he and I did fall to talk very openly of the business of this office, and (if I was not a little too open to tell him my interest, which is my fault) he did give me most admirable advice, and such as doth speak him a most able and worthy man, and understanding seven times more then ever I thought to be

---

a repl. 'him' *b* repl. 'to give' *c* repl. 'the'
    d repl. 'my office'

in him. He did perticularly run over every one of the officers
and Comanders, and showed me how I had reason to mistrust
every one of them, either for their falseness or their over-great
power, being too high to fasten a real friendship in. And did
give me a common but a most excellent [saying] to observe in all
my life; he did give it in rhyme, but the sense was this: that a
man should treat every friend in his discourse and opening of his
mind to him as of one that may hereafter be his foe.[1] He did
also advise me how I should take occasion to make known to the
world my care and the pains that I take in my business; and above
all, to be sure to get a thorough knowledge in my imployment,
and to that add all the Interest at Court that I can – which I hope
I shall do.

He stayed talking with me till almost 12 at night, and so good-
night, being sorry to part with him and more sorry that he should
have as far as Wapping to walk tonight.[a] So I to my Journall
and so home – to supper and to bed.

16. Up; and with my head and heart full of my business, I
to my office and there all the morning – where among other
things, to my great content Captain Taylor brought me 40*l*,
the greater part of which I shall gain to myself, after much care
and pains, out of his bill of freight, as I have at large set down in
my book of Memorandums.[2]

At noon to the Change, and there met with Mr. Wood by
design and got out of him, to my advantage, a confession which
I shall make good use of against Sir W. Batten – *vide* my book of

a repl. 'over'

1. One of the 'Proverbs of Alfred'
(cf. B. J. Whiting, *Proverbs* etc.,
Camb. Mass. 1968, F 635); in current
use within living memory. I owe
this ref. to J. Wilson.
2. For this transaction, see above,
p. 414, n. 1. Pepys later entered the

details into NWB, pp. 3–4. The
bill had 'an addition for myself under
the name of demurrage, of 30*l*'. He
added: 'I have not herein done the
King the least wrong, nor the man,'
but for safety's sake he kept a careful
record of how the deceit was worked.

Memorandums[1] touching the contract of masts of Sir W Warrens,[a] about which I have had so much trouble.

So home to dinner and then to the Star tavern hard by to our arbitracion of Mr. Blands business;[2] and at it a great while, but I find no order like to be kept in our enquiry, and Mr. Clerke the other arbitrator, one so far from being fit (though able as to his trade of a merchant) to enquire and to take pains in searching out the truth on both sides, that we parted without doing anything, nor do I believe we shall at all even attain to anything in it.

Then home, and till 12 at night making up my accounts, with great account of this day's receipt of Captain Taylor's money and some money reimbursed me which I have laid out on Fields business. So home, with my mind in pretty good quiet, and to supper and to bed.

17. Up and to the office, where we sat all the morning. At noon home to my poor wife and dined; and then by coach abroad to Mrs. Turner's, where I have not been many a day. And there I find her and her sister Dike, very sad for the death of their Brother.[3] After a little common expression of sorrow, Mrs. Turner told me that the trouble she would put me to was to consult about getting an Achievement prepared (Scucheons were done already)[4] to set over the door. So I did go out to Mr. Smith's,[5] where my brother tells me the scutcheons are made. But he not being within, I went to the Temple and there spent

a repl. 'Sir WB'

1. A note of this confession was later copied into NWB, p. 6. Pepys first called on a friend, Capt. David Lambert, and gave him 'in his eare direction to stand close by and hear what passed between Mr. Wood and I'. He then tricked Wood (by giving him the impression that a sale might still be arranged) into stating that it was Pepys who had opposed his original tender and that the reason was that the masts were too old. 'But it is a pretty consideration, that hence Wood will go to W. Batten and tell him how I seem willing to buy his masts, and what Sir W. Batten will do therein – for either he must now contradict himself by offering to buy these, when he says we have too many already, or else he must, sore against his will, be contented to have Woods lie still upon his hands.'
2. See above, p. 404 & n. 2.
3. See above, p. 421, n. 2.
4. The achievement or hatchment was a diamond-shaped board bearing the arms; the escutcheons were armorial shields, hung over the windows and later fixed on the hearse.
5. John Smith, herald painter, of Fleet St.

my time in a bookseller's shop, reading in a book of some Embassages into Moscovia, &c.,[1] where was very good reading. And then to Mrs. Turners and thither came Smith to me, with whom I did agree for 4*l* to make a handsome one, ell[2] square within the frame.   After he was gone, I sat an hour talking of the suddenness of his death, within seven days, and how by little and little death came upon him, he nor they thinking it would come to that.   He died after a day's raveing, through lightness in his head for want of sleep.   His lady did not know of his sickness.   Nor do they hear yet how she takes it.

Thence home, taking some books by the way in Paul's churchyard, by coach and to my office, where late doing business; and so home to supper and to bed.

18.   Up, and after being ready and done several businesses with people, I took water (taking a dram of the bottle at the waterside) with a gally, the first that ever I had yet; and down to Woolwich, calling at Ham Creeke, where I met Mr. Deane and had a great deal of talk with him about businesses; and so to the Ropeyard and Docke, discoursing several things; and so back again and did the like at Deptford; and I find that it is absolute necessary for me to do thus once a week at least, all the year round, which will do me great good.   And so home with great ease and content, especially out of the content which I met with in a book I bought yesterday; being a discourse of the state of Rome under the present Pope, Alexander the 7th[3] – it being a very excellent piece.   After eating something at home, then to my office, where till night about business to despatch.   Among other people came Mr. Primate the Leather-sale[4] in Fleet-street to see me, he says, coming this way.   And he tells me that he is upon a proposal to the King, whereby, by a law already in being, he

---

1. Probably Adam Olearius, *The voyages and travels of the ambassadors from the Duke of Holstein, to the Great Duke of Muscovy, and the King of Persia* [in 1633–9], trans. by John Davies, 1662; PL 2161 (1).

2. 45 ins.

3. Angelo Corraro, *Rome exactly described ... in two curious discourses* (trans. J[ohn] B[ulteel]; licensed 30 September and 9 November 1663, but dated 1664; PL 383; an account of the characters and political inclinations of the Pope and Cardinals in 1661, in the form of reports by a Venetian ambassador.

4. *Recte* 'seller'.

will supply the King, without wrong to any man or charge to
the people in general, so much as it is now, above 200000*l* per
annum, and God knows what; and that the King doth like the
proposal and hath directed that the Duke of Monmouth, with
their consent, be made privy and go along with him and his
fellow-proposers in that business.¹   God knows what it is; for I
neither can guess nor believe there is any such thing in his head.
At night made an end of the discourse I read this morning, and
so home to supper and to bed.

19.   Up and to the office, where we sat all the morning and I
laboured hard at Deerings business of his deals, more then I
would if I did not think to get something, though I do verily
believe that I did but what is to the King's advantage in it.   And
yet, God knows, the expectation of profit will have its force and
make a man the more earnest.   Dined at home; and then with
Mr. Bland to another meeting upon his Arbitracion; and seeing
we were likely to do no good, I even put them upon it and they
chose Sir W Rider alone to end the matter, and so I am rid of it.
Thence by coach to my shoemaker's and paid all there, and gave
something to the boy's box against Christmas; and then to Mrs.
Turners, whom I find busy with Sir W. Turner about advising
upon going down to Norfolke with the Corps.   And I find him
in talk a sober, considering man.   So home to my office late;
and then home to supper and to bed.   My head full of business,
but pretty good content.*a*

20.   *Lords day.*   Up and alone to church, where a common
sermon of Mr. Mills; and so home to dinner in our parlour, my
wife being clean, and the first time we have dined here a great
while together.   And in the afternoon went to church with me
also, and there begin to take her place above Mrs. Pen, which
heretofore, out of a humour,*b* she was wont to give her as an
affront to my Lady Batten.   After a dull sermon of the Scotchman,

a last seven lines of text crowded into bottom of page   *b* MS. 'humuor'

1. This may be the scheme for the
recovery of prize money which
appears in Monmouth's name in an
undated petition of about this time:
PRO, SP 29/89, no. 47; summary in
CSPD 1663–4, p. 419. Nothing
came of it.

home; and there I find my brother Tom and my two Cosens
Scotts, he and she – the first time they were ever here. And by
and by in comes my uncle Wight and Mr. Norbury, and they
sat with us a while drinking of wine, of which I did give them
plenty. But they two would not stay supper, but the other two
did; and we were as merry as I could be with people that I do
wish well to but know not what discourse either to give them or
find from them. We showed them our house from top to
bottom, and had a good turkey roasted for our supper, and store
of wine. And after supper sent them home on foot; and so we
to prayers and to bed.

21. Up betimes, my wife having a mind to have gone abroad
with me but I had not, because of troubling me; and so left her,
though against my will, to go to see her father and mother by
herself. And I straight to my Lord Sandwiches; and there I had
a pretty kind salute from my Lord and went*a* on to the Duke's,
where my fellow officers by and by came, and so in with him to
his closet and did our business; and so broke up and I with
Sir W. Batten by coach to Salsbury-Court and there spoke with
Clerke our Sollicitor about Fields business; and so parted, and I
to Mrs. Turners and there saw the Achievement well set up; and
it is well done. Thence I on foot to Charing-cross to the
ordinary and there dined, meeting Mr. Gauden and Creed.
Here, variety of talk, but to no great purpose. After dinner
won a wager, of a pair of gloves of a Crowne, of Mr. Gauden
upon some words in his contract for victualling.

There parted in the street with them, and I to my Lord's;
but he not being within, took Coach, and being directed by
sight of bills upon the walls, did go to Shooe lane to see a Cocke-
fighting at a new pit there – a sport I was never at in my life.[1]
But Lord, to see the strange variety of people, from Parliament-

a MS. 'waited'

---

1. Shoe Lane had been famous for
its cockpit years before this. Pepys
may have visited a new, or a revival of an old one. In Charles
Cotton's *Compleat Gamester* (1674,
p. 206) cock-fighting is described as
'a sport ... full of delight and
pleasure'. Pepys has added in the
margin of his copy: 'and of Barba-
rity': PL 714.

man (by name Wildes,[1] that was Deputy-governor of the Tower
when Robinson was Lord Mayor) to the poorest prentices, bakers,
brewers, butchers, draymen, and what not; and all these[a] fellows
one with another in swearing, cursing, and betting. I soon had
enough of it; and yet I would not but have seen it once, it being
strange to observe the nature of those poor creatures, how they
will fight till they drop down dead upon the table and strike
after they are ready to give up the ghost – not offering to run
away when they are weary or wounded past doing further.
Whereas, where a Dunghill brood comes, he will, after a sharp
stroke that pricks him, run off the stage, and then they wring
off his neck without more ado. Whereas the other they preserve, though their eyes be both out, for breed only of a true cock
of the game.

   Sometimes, a cock that hath had ten to one against him will
by chance give an unlucky blow will strike the other stark-dead
in a moment, that he never stirs more. But the common rule is,
that though a cock[b] neither run nor dies, yet if any man will bet
10*l* to a Crowne and nobody take the bett, the game is given over,
and not sooner. One thing more it is strange to see, how people
of this poor rank, that look as if they had not bread to put in
their mouths, shall bet 3 or 4*l* at one bet and lose it, and yet bet
as much the next battell, as they call every make of two cocks –
so that one of them will lose[c] 10 or 20*l* at a meeting.

   Thence, having enough of it, by coach to my Lord Sandwiches;
where I find him within with Captain Cooke and his boys,
Dr. Childe, Mr. Mage, and Mallard, playing and singing over
my Lord's Anthemne which he hath made to sing in the King's
Chappell.[2] My Lord saluted me kindly and took me into the
withdrawing-room to hear it at a distance; and endeed, it sounds
very finely and is a good thing, I believe, to be made by him –
and they all commend it. And after that was done, Captain
Cooke and his two boys did sing some Italian songs, which I
must in a word say I think was fully the best Musique that I
ever[d] yet heard in all my life – and it was to me a very great
pleasure to hear them.

a MS. 'this'   *b* repl. 'god'   *c* MS. 'look'   *d* repl. 'never'

---

   1. George Weld (Wild), M.P. for   2. See above, p. 417, n. 1. (E).
Much Wenlock, Salop.

After all Musique ended and my Lord going to White-hall, I*a* went along with him and made a desire for to have his coach to go along with my Cosen Edwd. Pepys's hearse through the City on Wednesday next – which he granted me presently, though he cannot yet come to speak*b* to me in the familiar style that he did use to do, nor can I expect it; but I was the willinger of this occasion to see whether he would deny me or no, which he would, I believe, had he been at open defyance* against me.

Being not a little pleased with all this, though I yet see my Lord is not right yet, I thanked his Lordshipp and parted with him in White-hall. And I back to my Lord's, and there took up W. Howe in a coach and carried him as far as the Half-Moone and there set him down – by the way talking of my Lord, who is come another and a better man then he was lately, and God be praised for it; and he says that I shall find my Lord as he used to be*c* to me – of which I have good hopes; but I shall beware of him, I mean W. Howe, how I trust him; for I perceive he is not so discreet as I took him for, for he hath told Captain Ferrers (as Mr. Moore tells me) of my letter to my Lord; which troubles me, for fear my Lord should think that I might have told him.

So called with my coach at my wife's brother's lodging, but she was gone newly in a coach homewards; and so I drove hard and overtook her at Templebarr, and there paid off mine and went home with her in her coach. She tells me how there is a sad house among her friends. Her brother's wife proves very unquiet, and so her mother is gone back to be with her husband and leaves the young couple to themselfs; and great trouble, and I fear great want, will be among them; I pray keep me from being troubled with them.

At home to put on my gowne; and to my office and there set down this day's Journall; and by*d* and by comes Mrs. Owen, Captain Allens daughter, and causes me to stay while the papers relating to her husband's place,[1] bought of his father,* be copied out, because of her going by this morning's tide home to Chatham – which vexes me, but there is no help for it. I home to

a MS. 'and' *b* repl. 'spoke' *c* repl. 'me' *d* repl. 'then

---

1. The clerkship of the ropeyard, Chatham.

supper*a* while a young [man] that she brought with her did copy
out the things, and then I to the office again and despatched her.
And so home to bed.

22.   Up, and there comes my she-Cosen Angier of Cambrige
to me to speak about her son.   But though I love them and have
reason so to do, yet Lord, to consider how cold I am to speak to
her, for fear of giving her too much hopes of expecting either
money or anything else from me besides my care of her son.
I let her go without drinking, though that was against my will,
being forced to hasten to the office – where we sat all the morning; and at noon I to Sir R Fords, where Sir Rd. Browne (a dull,
but it seems upon action a hot man); and he and I met upon
setting a price upon the freight of a barge sent to France to the
Duchesse of Orleans.¹   And here by discourse I find them greatly
cry out against the choice of Sir John Cutler to be Treasurer for
Pauls, upon condition that he gives 1500*l* towards it; and it seems
he did give it upon condition that he might be Treasurer for that
work² – which they say will be worth three times as much
money – and talk as if his being chosen to that office will make
people backward to give; but I think him as likely a man as
either of them, or better.

The business being done, we parted, Sir Rd: Ford never inviting
me to dine with him at all, and I was not sorry for it.

Home and dined – and had a letter from W How that my
Lord hath ordered his coach and six horses for me tomorrow –
which pleases me mightily, to think that my Lord should do so
much, hoping thereby that his anger is a little over.

After dinner abroad by coach with my wife to Westminster;
and set her at Mrs. Hunts – while I about my business – having
in our way met with Captain Ferrers luckily, to speak to him

a   symbol smudged

1. On 15 December passes had
been granted for Sir Richard Ford
and one horse, and also for twelve
horses sent for the use of the Duchess
(Charles II's sister): *CSPD 1663–4*, p.
374.   Sir Richard Browne was Clerk
of the Privy Council, and had been

the King's resident in France during
the exile.

2. The scheme for the repair of St
Paul's cathedral, inaugurated by the
royal proclamation of 18 April 1663:
see above, p. 261 & n. 1.

about my coach¹ – who was going in all haste whither I perceive the King and Duke and all the Court was going, to the Duke's playhouse to see *Henery the 8th* acted, which is said to be an Admirable play.ᵃ² But Lord, to see how near I was to have broken my oath³ or run the hazard of 20s loss, so much my nature was hot to have gone thither, but I did not go; but having spoke with W How also, and known how my Lord did do this kindly, as I would have it, I did go to Westminster-hall and there met Hawly and walked a great while with him; among other discourse, encouraging him to pursue his love to Mrs. Lane, while God knows I had a roguish meaning in it.

Thence calling my wife, home by coach, calling at several places and to my office, where late; and so home to supper and to bed.

This day I hear for certain that my Lady Castlemayne is turned papist,⁴ which the Queen for all doth not much like, knowing that she doth it not for conscience sake.

I heard today of a great fray lately, between Sir H. Finch's coachman, who struck with hisᵇ whip a coachman of the King's, to the loss of one of his eyes; at which the people of the Exchange seeming to laugh and makeᶜ sport with some words of contempt to him, my Lord Chamberlin did come from the King to shut up the Change; and by the help of a Justice did it. But upon petition to the King it was opened again.⁵

a repl. 'part' *b* MS. 'him' or 'is'
c repl. symbol rendered illegible

1. Robert Ferrer was Sandwich's Master of the Horse.
2. See above, p. 411 & n. 5. (A).
3. His oath not to see plays until after Christmas: above, p. 182. (A).
4. The French ambassador reported this news on 31 December, adding that Charles had refused to intervene to dissuade her: 'pour l'âme des Dames, il ne s'en mêlait point': J. J. Jusserand, *French Ambassador*, p. 224. Stillingfleet is said to have commented: 'If the Church of Rome has got by her no more than the Church of England has lost, the Matter is not much': J. Oldmixon, *Hist. Engl. during reigns of Stuarts* (1730), ii. 577. In 1673 she was deprived of her post as Lady of the Bedchamber because of her Catholicism.
5. The incident occurred on 3 December, in front of the door of the New Exchange in the Strand. The Queen was in the royal coach at the time. According to Rugge (ii, ff. 81v–82r), the Exchange was shut over the weekend of 5–7 December. When, with the help of some of its shopkeepers, the offending coachman was discovered, it was re-opened.

23. Up betimes, and my wife; and being in as mourning a dress as we could at present, without cost, put ourselfs into, we by Sir W. Penn's coach to Mrs. Turners at Salsbury-Court, where I find my Lord's coach and six horses. We stayed till almost 11 a-clock, and much company came. And anon, the corps being put into the Herse and the scutcheons set upon it, we all took coach; and I and my wife and Auditor Beale[1] in my Lord Sandwiches coach and went next to Mrs. Turners mourning-coach. And so through all the City and Shoredich; I believe about twenty coaches, and four or five with six and four horses.

Being come thither, I made up to the mourners; and bidding them a good journy, I took leave and back again; and setting my wife into a hackney out of Bishopsgate-street, I sent her home, and I to the Change and Auditor Beale about his business.

Did much business at the Change,[a] and so home to dinner; and then to my office and there late doing business also, to my great content to see God bless me in my place; and opening honest ways, I hope to get a little money to lay up and yet to live handsomely. So to supper and to bed – my wife having strange fits of the tooth ach; sometimes on this, and by and by on that side of her mouth; which is not common.

24. Up betimes; and though it was a most foggy morning and cold, yet with a gally down to Eriffe, several times being at a loss whither we went. There I mustered two ships of the King's, lent by him to the Guiny-Company, which are manned better then ours at far less wages.[2] Thence on board two of the King's; one of them the *Leopard*,[3] Captain Beech, who I find an able and serious man. He received me civilly, and his wife was there, a very well-bred and knowing woman – born at Antwerp, but speaks as good English as myself, and an ingenious woman.

a repl. 'chance'

---

1. Bartholomew Beale, Auditor of the Imprests in the Exchequer, a relative of the Pepyses.

2. The *Sophia* and the *Welcome*: Pepys has a note in NWB, p. 35. Most of the men served at 17s. and 16s. a month, as against 24s. in the royal navy. For the record of the muster of the *Sophia*, 24 December, with notes of wages (in Hewer's hand with endorsement by Pepys), see PRO, SP 29/86, no. 49.

3. About to convoy a fleet of merchantmen to the Mediterranean and the Levant: Duke of York, *Mem.* (*naval*), pp. 87–9.

Here was also Sir G Carteret's son,[1] who I find a pretty, but very talking man; but good humour.

Thence back again, entertaining myself upon my sliding-rule[2] with great content; and called at Woolwich, where Mr. Chr. Pett, having an opportunity of being alone, did tell me his mind about several things he thought I was offended with him in,[3] and told me of my kindness to his Assistant;[4] I did give him such an answer as I thought was fit, and left him well satisfied – he offering to do me all the service, either by draughts or modells, that I should desire. Thence straight home, being very cold but yet well, I thank God. And at home find my wife making mince-pies; and by and by comes in Captain Ferrers to see us and among other talk, tells us of the goodness of the new play of *Henry the 8th*,[5] which makes me think long till my time is out; but I hope before I go, I shall set myself such a stint as I may not forget myself, as I have hitherto done till I was forced for these   months last past wholly to forbid myself the seeing of one.[6]

He gone, I to my office and there late, writing and reading; and so home to bed.

25. *Christmas.* Lay long, talking pleasantly with my wife; but among other things, she begin, I know not whether by design or chance, to enquire what she should do if I should[a] by an accident die; to which I did give her some slight answer, but shall make good use of it to bring myself to some settlement for her sake, by making a Will as soon as I can.[7]

Up, and to church, where Mr. Mills made an ordinary sermon; and so home and dined with great pleasure with my wife; and all the afternoon, first looking out at window and seeing the boys playing at many several sports in our back-yard by Sir W Pens, which minded me of my own former times; and then I begin to read to my wife upon the globes, with great pleasure

a repl. 'died'

---

1. Benjamin, a lieutenant in 1662.
2. See above, p. 84 & n. 2.
3. Cf. above, p. 326.
4. Anthony Deane, shipwright: for Pepys's kindness, see above, p. 384.

5. The recent revival of Shakespeare's history play: above, p. 411. (A).
6. See above, p. 182. (A).
7. For this will, see below, v. 20 & n. 2.

and to good purpose, for it will be pleasant to her and to me to have her understand those things.

In the evening to the office, where I stayed late reading Rush-worth,[1] which is a most excellent collection of the beginning of the late quarrels in this kingdom. And so home to supper and to bed with good content of mind.

26.   Up; and walked forth first to the Minerys to Brown's,[2] and there with great pleasure saw and bespoke several Instruments – and so to Cornhill to Mr. Cades, and there went up into his warehouse to look for a map or two; and there finding great plenty of good pictures, God forgive me how my mind run upon them. And bought a little one for my wife's closet presently, and concluded presently of buying 10*l* worth, upon condition he would give me the buying of them.[3]   Now, it is true I did still within me resolve to make the King one way or other pay for them, though I saved it to him another way; yet I find myself too forward to fix upon that expense, and came away with a resolution of buying them; but do hope that I shall not upon second thoughts do it without a way made out, before I buy them to myself,[a] how to do [it] without charge to my main stock.   Thence to the Coffee-house; and sat long in good discourse with some gentlemen concerning the Roman Empire.   So home and find Mr. Hollyard there; and he stayed and dined with us, we having a pheasant to dinner.   He gone, I all the afternoon with my wife to Cards.   And God forgive me, to see how the very discourse of plays, which I shall be at[b] liberty to see after New Year's day next, doth set my mind upon them, that I must be forced to stint myself very strictly before I begin, or else I fear I shall spoil all.

In the evening came my aunt Wights kinswoman to see how my wife doth, with a compliment from my aunt, which I take kindly as it is unusual for her to do it – but I do perceive my uncle is very kind to me of late.[4]

a repl. 'of'   *b* repl. 'but'

---

1. See above, p. 395, n. 1.
2. John Brown(e), of the Minories, maker of mathematical instruments.
3. Sc. provided he would reserve them: see below, v. 41.
4. Uncle Wight appears to have

been overfond of Mrs Pepys: see the remarkable proposition he made to her on 11 May 1664. The kins-woman here mentioned was possibly the 'cousin Mary' of 1 April 1666.

So to my office, writing letters, and then to read and make an end of Rushworth;[1] which I did, and do say that it is a book the best worth reading for a man of my condition, or any man that hopes to come to any public condition in the world, that I do know.

So home to supper and to bed.

27. Up and to church alone; and so home to dinner with my wife, very pleasant, and pleased with one another's company and in our general enjoyment one of another, better we think then most other couples do. So after dinner to the French church, but came too late; and so back to our own church, where I slept all the sermon, the Scott preaching; and so home, and in the evening Sir J. Mennes and I met at Sir W. Penn about ordering some business of the Navy; and so I home to supper – discourse – prayers and bed.

28. Up and by coach to my Lord's lodgings, but he was gone abroad – so I lost my pains; but however, walking through White-hall I heard the King was gone to play at Tennis, so I down to the new Tennis Court[2] and saw him and Sir Arthur Slingsby play against my Lord of Suffolke and my Lord Chesterfield. The King beat three and lost two sets: they all, and he perticularly, playing well I thought. Thence went and spoke with the Duke of Albemarle about his wood at Newhall.[3] But I find him a heavy dull man, methinks, by his answers to me. Thence to the Kings-head ordinary and there dined; and found Creed there, but we met and dined and parted without anything more ⟨then⟩ "How do you?" After dinner straight on foot to Mr. Hollyards and there paid him 3*l* in full for his physic and work to my wife about her evill below; but whether it is cured for ever or no I cannot tell, but he says it will never come to anything, though it may be it may ooze now and then a little. So home, and find my wife gone out with Will (whom she sent for as she doth nowadays upon occasion) to have a tooth drawn,

1. See above, p. 395, n. 2.
2. In Whitehall Palace. For the King's love of tennis, see, e.g., below, viii. 418-19.
3. The timber at New Hall, Essex, belonging to Albemarle, was about to be surveyed for purchase by the Navy Board: *CSPD 1663-4*, pp. 447, 464, 570.

she having it seems been in great pain all day; and at night came home with it drawn, and pretty well. This evening I had a Stove brought me to the office to try it; but it being an old one, it smokes as much as if there was nothing but a hearth, as I had before; but it may be your new ones do not, and therefore I must enquire further. So at night home to supper and to bed.

The Duchesse of York is fallen sick of the meazles.

29. Up and to the office, where all the morning sitting. And at noon to the Change, and there I found and brought home Mr. Pierce the surgeon to dinner – where I find also Mr. Luellin and Mount – and merry at dinner – but their discourse so free about claps and other foul discourse that I was weary of them. But after dinner Luellin took me up with him to my chamber, and there he told me how Deering did entend to be as good as his word, to give me 50*l.* for the service I did him;[1] though not so great as he expected and I entended. But I told him that I would not sell my liberty to any man. If he would give me anything by another's hand, I would endeavour to deserve it, but I will never give him himself thanks for it, nor*a* acknowledge the receiving of any – which he told me was reasonable. I did also tell him that neither this nor anything should make me to do anything that should not be for the King's service besides. So we parted, and I left them three at home with my wife going to Cards; and I to my office and there stayed late.

Sir W. Penn came like a cunning rogue to sit and talk with me about office business, and freely about the Controllers business of the office; to which I did give him free answers and let him make the best of them. But I know him to be a knave, and do say nothing that I fear to have said again.

Anon came Sir W. Warren; and after talking of his business of the Masts and helping me to understand some foul dealing in the business of Woods,[2] we fell to other talk; and perticularly, to speak of some means how to part this great familiarity between Sir W. Batten and Sir J. Mennes; and it is easy to do by any good friend of Sir J. Mennes, to whom it will be a good service, and he thinks that Sir J Denham will be a proper man for it,

a MS. 'not'

---

1. In his contract for deals: see above, p. 422; below, v. 1. 　　2. See above, p. 304, n. 1.

and so do I. So after other discourse, we parted and I home and to bed.

30. Up betimes and by coach to my Lord Sandwich; who I met going out, and he did ask me how his Cosen (my wife) did – the first time he hath done so since his being*ᵃ* offended; and in my conscience, he would be glad to be free with me again, but he knows not how to begin. So he went out; and I through the garden to Mr. Coventry, where I saw Mr. Chr. Pett bring him a Modell, and endeed it is a pretty one, for a New Year's gift – but I think the work not better done then mine.¹

With him by coach to London, with good and friendly discourse of business and against Sir Wm Batten – and his foul dealings. So leaving him at the Guiny-house,² I to the Coffee, whither came Mr. Grant and Sir Wm Petty, with whom I talked and so did many, almost all the house there, about his new Vessell;³ wherein he did give me much satisfaction in every point that I am almost confident she will prove an admirable invencion.

So home to dinner, after been upon the Change a while, and dined with my wife, who took physic today; and so to my office and there all the afternoon till late at night, about office business; and so to supper and to bed.

31. Up and to the office, where we sat all the morning. And among other things, Sir W. Warren came about some contract and there did at the open table, Sir W. Batten not being there, openly defy him and insisted how Sir W. Batten did endeavour to oppose him in everything that he offered. Sir W. Penn took him up for it like a counterfeit rogue, though I know he was as much pleased to hear him talk so as any man there. But upon his speaking, no more was said; but to the business. At noon we broke up, and I to the Change a while and so home again to dinner, my head akeing mightily with being overcharged with business. We had to dinner, my wife

a repl. 'come'

---

1. See above, ii. 121 & n. 5.
2. Africa House, near Throgmorton St. (R).

3. Petty's double-keeled ship: see above, p. 256 & n. 3.

and I, a fine Turkey and a mince-pie, and dined in state, poor wretch,* she and I; and have thus kept our Christmas together, all alone almost – having not once been out. But tomorrow my vowes are all out as to plays and wine; but I hope I shall not be long before I come to new ones, so much good, and God's blessing, I find to have attended them. Thence to the office and did several businesses and answered several[a] people; but my head akeing and it being my great night of accounts, I went forth, took coach, and to my brother's, but he was not within; and so I back again and sat an hour or two at the Coffee, hearing some simple discourse about Quakers being charmed by a string about their wrists.[1] And so home; and after a little while at my office, I home and supped; and so had a good fire in[b] my chamber and there sat till 4 a-clock in the morning, making up my accounts and writing this last Journall of the year. And first, I bless God I do, after a large expense, even this month by reason of Christmas and some payments to my father and other things extraordinary, find that I am worth in money, besides all my household stuff or anything of Brampton, above 800*l*; whereof, in my Lord Sandwiches hand, 700*l*., and the rest in my hand; so that there is not above 15*l* of all my estate in money at this minute out of my hands and my Lord's – for which the good God be pleased to give me a thankful heart and a mind careful to preserve this and encrease it.

I do live at my lodgings in the Navy Office – my family being, besides my wife and I, Jane Gentleman, Besse our excellent good-natured cook-maid, and Susan, a little girl – having neither man nor boy, nor like to have again a good while – living now in most perfect content and quiet and very frugally also. My health pretty good, but only that I have been much troubled with a costivenesse which I am labouring to get away, and have hopes of doing it. At the office I am well, though envied to the

a   symbol smudged   b   repl. 'at'

---

1. George Fox, founder of the Quakers, remarked that he was accused of hanging ribbons on people's arms to make them follow him: *Journal* (ed. Penney), i. 169. Similar accusations of witchcraft were often made at this time against most extreme Puritans.

devil by Sir W. Batten, who hates me to death but cannot hurt me. The rest either love, or at least do not show otherwise, though I know Sir W. Penn to be a false knave touching me, though he seems fair.

My father and mother well in the country; and at this time, the young ladies of Hinchingbrooke with them, their house having the small-pox in it.

The Queene, after a long and sore sickness, is become well again. And the King minds his mistresses a little too much, [as] if it pleased God. But I hope all things will go well, and in the Navy perticularly; wherein I shall do my duty, whatever comes of it.

The great talk is the designs of the King of France; whether against the Pope or King of Spain nobody knows; but a great and a most promising prince he is, and all the princes of Europe have their eye upon him. My wife's brother come to great unhappiness by the ill-disposition, my wife says, of his wife, and her poverty; which she now professes, after all her husband's pretence of a great portion. But I see none of them; at least, they come not to trouble me.

At present, I am concerned for my Cosen Angier of Cambrige, lately broke in his trade. And this day am sending his son John, a very rogue, to sea.

My brother Tom I know not what to think of, for I cannot hear whether he minds his business or no. And my brother John, at Cambrige with as little hopes of doing good there; for when he was here, he did give me great cause of dissatisfaction with his manner of life. Pall with my father, and God knows what she doth there or what will become of her, for I have not anything yet to spare her, and she grows now old[1] and must be disposed of one way or other.

The Duchesse of Yorke at this time sick of the Mezles, but is growing well again.

The Turkes very fur entered into Germany,[2] and all that part of the world at a loss what to expect from his proceedings.

Myself, blessed be God, in a good way and design and resolu-

1. She was 23.
2. In fact, into W. Hungary only: winter had prevented their advance into Austria itself.

tion of sticking to my business to get^a a little money, with doing the best service I can to the King also – which God continue.   So ends the old year.^b

a   MS. 'give'
b   The whole of this day's entry is written in a small hand.   A blank page follows.

APPENDIX

Two Medical Prescriptions[a][1]

Recipe   Sem: Millet[b] ʒij;[c] sem Carui ʒij.
Manna Calab: ℥iij   Salis prunel: ʒj

Dr Clerke.

boilt the[d] seeds at 2 qts. of posset[e] drink to 3 pints. Then dissolve the manna and salt and strain it. Drink it at 3 or 4 draughts in half an hour.[2]   *Turne over.*

Balsom of Sulphur, 3 or 4 Drops in a Spoonfull of the Syrrup of Coltsfoote not eating or drinking 2 houres before or after.
   The making of this Balsom:
2 3ds. of fine Oyle and 1 3*d.* of fine Brimstone, sett 13 or 14 houres upon the fire, Simpring till a thicke Stuffe lyes at the Bottome and the Balsom at the Topp.   Take this offten.

Sir Robt. Parkhurst for the Collique.

   a 'Recipe ... Clerke' is an apothecary's (?) hand; the next three lines (to 'hour') in Pepys's s.h., and the rest in his l.h.
   b word smudged
   c figure smudged
   d MS. 'them'
   e MS. 'pontet' (or 'petunt'). Carelessly written, like all this prescription.

----

   1. See above, p. 332 & note *a*.
   2. Dr C. E. Newman writes: 'This is a diuretic draught composed of various quantities, in drachms (ʒ), of millet seeds, caraway seeds, *Sal Prunellae* (potassium nitrate); and three ounces (℥) of Calabrian (or Sicilian) manna (dried sap of *Fraxinus ornus L.*).

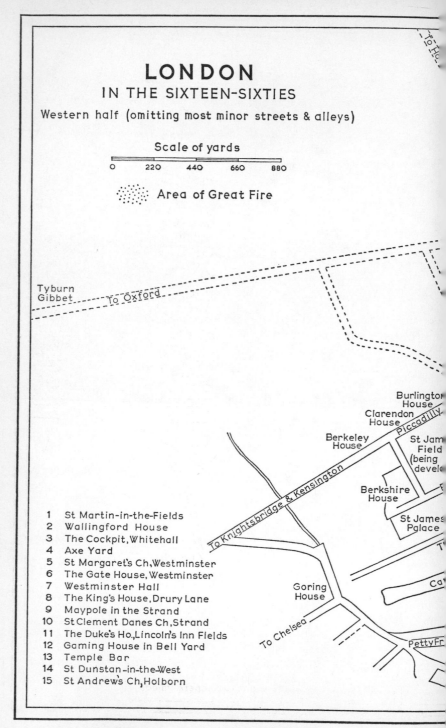

LONDON
IN THE SIXTEEN-SIXTIES
Western half (omitting most minor streets & alleys)

Scale of yards

0   220   440   660   880

Area of Great Fire

To Ho

Tyburn
Gibbet   To Oxford

Burlington
House
Clarendon
House   Piccadilly
Berkeley
House   St Jam
Field
(being
devel

Berkshire
House

St James
Palace

To Knightsbridge & Kensington

Goring
House

To Chelsea

Ca

PettyFr

1   St Martin-in-the-Fields
2   Wallingford House
3   The Cockpit, Whitehall
4   Axe Yard
5   St Margaret's Ch, Westminster
6   The Gate House, Westminster
7   Westminster Hall
8   The King's House, Drury Lane
9   Maypole in the Strand
10   St Clement Danes Ch, Strand
11   The Duke's Ho., Lincoln's Inn Fields
12   Gaming House in Bell Yard
13   Temple Bar
14   St Dunstan-in-the-West
15   St Andrew's Ch, Holborn

Map prepared by the late Professor T. F. Reddaway

FLEET RIVER

Southampton House

Gray's Inn

Hatton Garden

Leather Lane

Court Road

Southampton Market

Holborn

15

Chancery Lane

St-Giles-in-the-Fields

Lincoln's Inn

Portugal Row Fields

Fetter Lane

Drury Gt Queen St Lane

11

St Giles's Fields

12 14

Newport Ho.

Clare Market

Long Acre

Wich Street

13 Fleet Street

eicester Ho.

8

Bow Street

The 9 Strand

10

St Martins Lane

Covent Garden Exeter Ho.

Arundel House

Essex House

Temple & Church

Dorset House.

Bedford Ho.

Somerset House

Milford Stairs

Temple Stairs

Whitefriars Stairs

Mews

Savoy Palace

1

New Exchange

Worcester House

T H A M E S

arket

Charing Cross

York House

2

Tilt Yard

Whitehall Palace

Whitehall

R I V E R

Lambeth Marsh

King Street

3

Cannon Row

4

Westminster Stairs

Palace Yard

5 7

Stangate Stairs

ill St 6

Westminster Abbey

Old Palace Yard

To Lambeth Palace

LONDON
IN THE SIXTEEN-SIXTIES
Eastern half (omitting most minor streets & alleys)

Scale of yards

0   220   440   660   880

····· **Area of Great Fire**

16 Holborn Conduit
17 St Sepulchre's Ch.
18 Salisbury Court
19 St Bride's Church
20 Bridge in Bridewell
21 Christ Ch. Newgate
22 Newgate Market
23 Ludgate
24 St Martin's Ch.
25 The Wardrobe
26 Doctors' Commons
27 Goldsmiths' Hall
28 Barber Surgeons' Hall
29 St Giles, Cripplegate
30 Haberdashers' Hall
31 Guildhall
32 St Lawrence Jewry
33 St Mary le Bow
34 Dutch Ch. Austin Friars
35 Treasury Office, Navy
36 Gresham College
37 The Post Office, 1666
38 Stocks Market

39 The Great Coffee House
40 Royal Exchange
41 Cornhill Conduit
42 French Church
43 Merchant Taylors' Hall
44 Leadenhall Market
45 St Dionis Backchurch
46 The Mitre, Fenchurch St
47 St Katherine Cree
48 Clothworkers' Hall
49 St Olave's Ch. Hart St
50 Skinners' Hall, Dowgate Hill
51 St Lawrence Poultney
52 All Hallows the Great
53 All Hallows the Less
54 Fishmongers' Hall
55 St Magnus's Church
56 St Dunstan in the East
57 Trinity House
58 All Hallows, Barking
59 Navy Office
60 St Katherine's by the Tower
61 The Bear at the Bridge Foot
62 St Mary Overie (now Southwark Cath.)

Petticoat Lane
To Colchester
Whitechapel
Aldgate
Minories
Goodman's Fields
Victualling Office
The Tower
East Smithfield
To Ratcliff
60
Iron-Gate Stairs
THAMES
Pasture Grounds
Wapping Church
To Ratcliff & Limehouse
Sir William Warren's shipyard
To Deptford, Woolwich & Chatham
Rotherhithe Church

Map prepared by the late Professor T. F. Reddaway

SELECT LIST OF PERSONS

ADMIRAL, the: James, Duke of York, Lord High Admiral of England

ALBEMARLE, 1st Duke of (Lord Monke): Captain-General of the Kingdom

ARLINGTON, 1st Earl of (Sir Henry Bennet): Secretary of State

ASHLEY, 1st Baron (Sir Anthony Ashley Cooper, later 1st Earl of Shaftesbury): Chancellor of the Exchequer

ATTORNEY-GENERAL: Sir Geoffrey Palmer

BACKWELL, Edward: goldsmith-banker

BAGWELL, Mrs: Pepys's mistress; wife of ship's carpenter

BALTY: Balthasar St Michel; brother-in-law; minor naval official

BATTEN, Sir William: Surveyor of the Navy

BETTERTON (Baterton), Thomas: actor in the Duke's Company

BIRCH, Jane: maidservant

BOOKSELLER, my: Joseph Kirton (until the Fire)

BOWYER, my father: Robert Bowyer, senior Exchequer colleague

BRISTOL, 2nd Earl of: politician

BROUNCKER (Bruncker, Brunkard, Brunkerd), 2nd Viscount: Commissioner of the Navy

BUCKINGHAM, 2nd Duke of: politician

CARKESSE (Carcasse), James: clerk in the Ticket Office

CARTERET, Sir George: Treasurer of the Navy and Vice-Chamberlain of the King's Household

CASTLEMAINE, Barbara, Countess of: the King's mistress

CHANCELLOR, the: see 'Lord Chancellor'

CHILD, the: usually Edward, eldest son and heir of Sandwich

CHOLMLEY, Sir Hugh: courtier, engineer

COCKE, George: hemp merchant

COFFERER, the: William Ashburnham

COMPTROLLER (Controller), the: the Comptroller of the Navy (Sir Robert Slingsby, 1660–1; Sir John Mennes, 1661–71)

COVENTRY, Sir William: Secretary to the Lord High Admiral, 1660–7; Commissioner of the Navy (occasionally called 'Mr.' after knighted, 1665)

CREED, John: household and naval servant of Sandwich

CREW, 1st Baron: Sandwich's father-in-law; Presbyterian politician

CUTTANCE, Sir Roger: naval captain

DEANE, Anthony: shipwright

DEB: *see* 'Willet, Deborah'

DOWNING, Sir George: Exchequer official, Envoy-Extraordinary to the United Provinces, and secretary to the Treasury Commission

DUKE, the: usually James, Duke of York, the King's brother; occasionally George (Monck), Duke of Albemarle

DUKE OF YORK: *see* 'James, Duke of York'

EDWARD, Mr: Edward, eldest son and heir of Sandwich

EDWARDS, Tom: servant

EVELYN, John: friend, *savant*; Commissioner of Sick and Wounded

FENNER, Thomas (m. Katherine Kite, sister of Pepys's mother): uncle; ironmonger

FERRER(S), Capt. Robert: army captain; Sandwich's Master of Horse

FORD, Sir Richard: Spanish merchant

FOX, Sir Stephen: Paymaster of the Army

GAUDEN, Sir Denis: Navy victualler

GENERAL(S), the: Albemarle, Captain-General of the Kingdom, 1660–70; Prince Rupert and Albemarle, Generals-at-Sea in command of the Fleet, 1666

GIBSON, Richard: clerk to Pepys in the Navy Office

GWYN, Nell: actress (in the King's Company) and King's mistress

HARRIS, Henry: actor in the Duke's Company

HAYTER, Tom: clerk to Pepys in the Navy Office

HEWER, Will: clerk to Pepys in the Navy Office

HILL, Thomas: friend, musician, Portuguese merchant

HINCHINGBROOKE, Viscount (also 'Mr Edward', 'the child'): eldest son of Sandwich

HOLLIER (Holliard), Thomas: surgeon

HOLMES, Sir Robert: naval commander

HOWE, Will: household and naval servant of Sandwich

JAMES, DUKE OF YORK: the King's brother and heir presumptive (later James II); Lord High Admiral

JANE: usually Jane Birch, maidservant

JOYCE, Anthony (m. Kate Fenner, 1st cousin): innkeeper

JOYCE, William (m. Mary Fenner, 1st cousin): tallow-chandler

JUDGE-ADVOCATE, the: John Fowler, Judge-Advocate of the Fleet

KNIPP (Knepp), Mrs: actress in the King's Company

LADIES, the young/ the two/ the: often Sandwich's daughters

LAWSON, Sir John: naval commander

SELECT LIST OF PERSONS 449

LIEUTENANT OF THE TOWER: Sir John Robinson
L'IMPERTINENT, Mons.: [?Daniel] Butler, friend, ? clergyman
LORD CHAMBERLAIN: Edward Mountagu, 2nd Earl of Manchester; Sandwich's cousin
LORD CHANCELLOR: Edward Hyde, 1st Earl of Clarendon (often called Chancellor after his dismissal, 1667)
LORD KEEPER: Sir Orlando Bridgeman
LORD PRIVY SEAL: John Robartes, 2nd Baron Robartes (later 1st Earl of Radnor)
LORD TREASURER: Thomas Wriothesley, 4th Earl of Southampton
MARTIN, Betty (née Lane): Pepys's mistress; shopgirl
MENNES (Minnes), Sir John: Comptroller of the Navy
MERCER, Mary: maid to Mrs Pepys
MILL(E)S, Rev. Dr John: Rector of St Olave's, Hart St; Pepys's parish priest
MONCK (Monke), George (Lord): soldier. See 'Albemarle, 1st Duke of'
MONMOUTH, Duke of: illegitimate son of Charles II
MOORE, Henry: lawyer; officer of Sandwich's household
MY LADY: usually Jemima, wife of Sandwich
MY LORD: usually Sandwich
NELL, NELLY: usually Nell Gwyn
PALL: Paulina Pepys; sister (sometimes spelt 'pall')
PEARSE (Pierce), James: courtier, surgeon to Duke of York, and naval surgeon
PENN, Sir William: Commissioner of the Navy and naval commander (father of the Quaker leader)
PEPYS, Elizabeth (née St Michel): wife
PEPYS, John and Margaret: parents
PEPYS, John (unm.): brother; unbeneficed clergyman
PEPYS, Tom (unm.): brother; tailor
PEPYS, Paulina (m. John Jackson): sister
PEPYS, Capt. Robert: uncle, of Brampton, Hunts.
PEPYS, Roger: 1st cousin once removed; barrister and M.P.
PEPYS, Thomas: uncle, of St Alphege's, London
PETT, Peter: Commissioner of the Navy and shipwright
PICKERING, Mr (Ned): courtier, 1662-3; Sandwich's brother-in-law and servant
POVEY, Thomas: Treasurer of the Tangier Committee, 1663-5
PRINCE, the: usually Prince Rupert

QUEEN, the: (until May 1662) the Queen Mother, Henrietta-Maria, widow of Charles I; Catherine of Braganza, wife of Charles II (m. 21 May 1662)

RIDER, Sir William: merchant

ROBERT, Prince: Prince Rupert

RUPERT, Prince: 1st cousin of Charles II; naval commander

ST MICHEL, Alexandre and Dorothea: parents-in-law

ST MICHEL, Balthasar ('Balty'; m. Esther Watts): brother-in-law; minor naval official

SANDWICH, 1st Earl of: 1st cousin once removed, and patron; politician, naval commander and diplomat

SHIPLEY, Edward: steward of Sandwich's household

SIDNY, Mr: Sidney Mountagu, second son of Sandwich

SOLICITOR, the: the Solicitor-General, Sir Heneage Finch

SOUTHAMPTON, 4th Earl of: Lord Treasurer

SURVEYOR, the: the Surveyor of the Navy (Sir William Batten 1660–7; Col. Thomas Middleton, 1667–72)

TEDDEMAN, Sir Thomas: naval commander

THE: Theophila Turner

TREASURER, the: usually the Treasurer of the Navy (Sir George Carteret, 1660–7; 1st Earl of Anglesey, 1667–8); sometimes the Lord Treasurer of the Kingdom, the Earl of Southampton, 1660–7

TRICE, Tom: step-brother; civil lawyer

TURNER, John (m. Jane Pepys, distant cousin): barrister

TURNER, Betty and The[ophila]: daughters of John and Jane Turner

TURNER, Thomas: senior clerk in the Navy Office

VICE-CHAMBERLAIN, the: Sir George Carteret, Vice-Chamberlain of the King's Household and Treasurer of the Navy

VYNER, Sir Robert: goldsmith-banker

WARREN, Sir William: timber merchant

WARWICK, Sir Philip: Secretary to the Lord Treasurer

WIGHT, William: uncle (half-brother of Pepys's father); fishmonger

WILL: usually Will Hewer

WILLET, Deborah: maid to Mrs Pepys

WILLIAMS ('Sir Wms. both'): Sir William Batten and Sir William Penn, colleagues on the Navy Board

WREN, Matthew: Secretary to the Lord High Admiral, 1667–72

SELECT GLOSSARY

A Large Glossary will be found in the *Companion*. This Select Glossary is restricted to usages, many of them recurrent, which might puzzle the reader. It includes words and constructions which are now obsolete, archaic, slang or dialect; words which are used with meanings now obsolete or otherwise unfamiliar; and place names frequently recurrent or used in colloquial styles or in non-standard forms. Words explained in footnotes are not normally included. The definitions given here are minimal: meanings now familiar and contemporary meanings not implied in the text are not noted, and many items are explained more fully in *Companion* articles and in the Large Glossary. A few foreign words are included. The spellings are taken from those used in the text: they do not, for brevity's sake, include all variants.

ABLE: wealthy
ABROAD: away, out of doors
ACCENT (of speech): the accentuation and the rising and falling of speech in pronunciation
ACCOUNTANT: official accountable for expenditure etc.
ACHIEVEMENT: hatchment, representation of heraldic arms
ACTION: acting, performance
ACTOR: male or female theatrical performer
ADDES: adze
ADMIRAL SHIP: flagship carrying admiral
ADMIRATION; ADMIRE: wonder, alarm; to wonder at
ADVENTURER: investor, speculator
ADVICE: consideration
AFFECT: to be fond of, to be concerned
AFFECTION: attention
AGROUND: helpless
AIR: generic term for all gases
ALL MY CAKE WILL BE DOE: all my plans will miscarry
ALPHABET: index, alphabetical list
AMBAGE: deceit, deviousness

AMUSED, AMUZED: bemused, astonished
ANCIENT: elderly, senior
ANGEL: gold coin worth *c.* 10*s.*
ANGELIQUE: small archlute
ANNOY: molest, hurt
ANOTHER GATE'S BUSINESS: different altogether
ANSWERABLE: similar, conformably
ANTIC, ANTIQUE: fantastic
APERN: apron
APPRENSION: apprehension
APPROVE OF: criticise
AQUA FORTIS (FARTIS): nitric acid
ARTICLE: to indict
ARTIST: workman, craftsman, technician, practitioner
ASTED: Ashtead, Surrey
AYERY: airy, sprightly, stylish

BAGNARD: bagnio, prison, lock-up
BAILEY, BAYLY: bailiff
BAIT, BAYTE: refreshment on journey (for horses or travellers). *Also* v.
BALDWICK: Baldock, Herts.
BALLET: ballad, broadside

451

BAND: neckband

BANDORE: musical instrument resembling guitar

BANQUET: course of fruits, sweets and wine; slight repast

BANQUET-, BANQUETING-HOUSE: summer-house

BARBE (s.): Arab (Barbary) horse

BARBE (v.): to shave

BARN ELMS: riverside area near Barnes, Surrey

BARRECADOS (naval): fenders

BASE, BASS: bass viol; thorough-bass

BASTE HIS COAT: to beat, chastise

BAVINS: kindling wood, brushwood

BAYLY: see 'Bailey'

BAYT(E): see 'Bait'

BEARD: facial hair, moustache

BEFOREHAND, to get: to have money in hand

BEHALF: to behave

BEHINDHAND: insolvent

BELL: to throb

BELOW: downstream from London Bridge

BELOW STAIRS: part of the Royal Household governed by Lord Steward

BEST HAND, at the: the best bargain

BEVER: beaver, fur hat

BEWPERS: bunting, fabric used for flags

BEZAN, BIZAN (Du. *bezaan*): small yacht

BIGGLESWORTH: Biggleswade, Beds.

BILL: (legal) warrant, writ; bill of exchange; Bill of Mortality (weekly list of burials; *see* iii. 225, n. 2)

BILLANDER (Du. *bijlander*): bilander, small two-masted merchantman

BIRD'S EYE: spotted fabric

BIZAN: see 'Bezan'

BLACK (adj.): brunette, dark in hair or complexion

BLACK(E)WALL: dock on n. shore of Thames below Greenwich used by E. Indiamen

BLANCH (of coins): to silver

BLIND: out of the way, private, obscure

BLOAT HERRING: bloater

BLUR: innuendo; charge

BOATE: boot or luggage compartment on side of coach

BODYS: foundations, basic rules; structure; (of ship) sectional drawings

BOLTHEAD: globular glass vessel with long straight neck

BOMBAIM: Bombay

BORDER: *toupée*

BOTARGO: dried fish-roe

BOTTOMARYNE, BOTTUMARY, BUMMARY: mortgage on ship

BOWPOTT: flower pot

BRAINFORD: Brentford, Mdx.

BRAMPTON: village near Huntingdon in which Pepys inherited property

BRANSLE: branle, brawl, group dance in duple measure

BRAVE (adj.): fine, enjoyable

BRAVE (v.): to threaten, challenge

BREAK BULK: to remove part of cargo

BREDHEMSON, BRIGHTHEMSON: Brighton, Sussex

BRIDEWELL-BIRD: jailbird

BRIDGE: usually London Bridge; also jetty, landing stairs

BRIEF: collection authorised by Lord Chancellor for charity

BRIG, BRIGANTINE: small vessel equipped both for sailing and rowing

BRIGHTHEMSON: see 'Bredhemson'

BRISTOL MILK: sweet sherry

BROTHER: brother-in-law; colleague

BRUMLY: Bromley, Kent

BRUSH (s.): graze

BUBO: tumour

BULLEN: Boulogne

BULLET: cannon-ball

BUMMARY: see 'Bottomaryne'

BURNTWOOD: Brentwood, Essex

BURY (of money): pour in, salt away, invest

BUSSE: two- or three-masted fishing boat

CABALL: inner group of ministers; knot
CABARETT (Fr. *cabaret*): tavern
CALES: Cadiz
CALICE, CALLIS: Calais
CALL: to call on/for; to drive
CAMELOTT, CAMLET, CAMLOTT: robust, ribbed cloth made of wool or goat hair
CANAILLE, CHANNEL, KENNEL: drainage gutter (in street); canal (in St James's Park)
CANCRE: canker, ulcer, sore
CANNING ST: Cannon St
CANONS: boot-hose tops
CANTON (heraldic): small division of shield
CAPER (ship): privateer
CARBONADO: to grill, broil
CARESSE: to make much of
CARRY (a person): to conduct, escort
CAST OF OFFICE: taste of quality
CATAPLASM: poultice
CATCH: round song; (ship) ketch
CATT-CALL: whistle
CAUDLE: thin gruel made with wine
CELLAR: box for bottles
CERE CLOTH: cloth impregnated with wax and medicaments
CESTORNE: cistern
CHAFE: heat, anger
CHALDRON: 1½ tons (London measure)
CHAMBER: small piece of ordnance for firing salutes
CHANGE, the: the Royal (Old) Exchange
CHANGELING: idiot
CHANNELL: *see* 'Canaille'
CHANNELL ROW: Cannon Row, Westminster
CHAPEL, the: usually the Chapel Whitehall Palace
CHAPTER: usually of Bible
CHARACTER: code, cipher; verbal portrait

CHEAP (s.): bargain
CHEAPEN: to ask the price of, bargain
CHEQUER, the: usually the Exchequer
CHEST, the: the Chatham Chest, the pension fund for seamen
CHILD, with: eager, anxious
CHIMNEY/CHIMNEY-PIECE: structure over and around fireplace
CHIMNEY-PIECE: picture over fireplace
CHINA-ALE: ale flavoured with china root
CHOQUE: a choke, an obstruction
CHOUSE: to swindle, trick
CHURCH: after July 1660, usually St Olave's, Hart St
CLAP: gonorrhoea
CLERK OF THE CHEQUE: principal clerical officer of a dockyard
CLOATH (of meat): skin
CLOSE: shutter; (of music) cadence
CLOUTERLY: clumsily
CLOWNE: countryman, clodhopper
CLUB (s.): share of expenses, meeting at which expenses are shared   *Also* v.
CLYSTER, GLISTER, GLYSTER: enema
COACH: captain's state-room in large ship
COCK ALE: ale mixed with minced chicken
COCKPIT(T), the: usually the theatre in the Cockpit buildings, Whitehall Palace; the buildings themselves
COD: small bag; testicle
CODLIN TART: apple (codling) tart
COFFEE: coffee-house
COG: to cheat, banter, wheedle
COLEWORTS: cabbage
COLLAR DAY: day on which knights of chivalric orders wore insignia at court
COLLECT: to deduce
COLLIER: coal merchant; coal ship
COLLOPS: fried bacon
COLLY-FEAST: feast of collies (cullies, good companions) at which each pays his share

COMEDIAN: actor
COMEDY: play
COMFITURE (Fr. *confiture*): jam, marmalade
COMMEN, COMMON GUARDEN: Covent Garden
COMMONLY: together
COMPASS TIMBER: curved timber
COMPLEXION: aspect
COMPOSE: to put music to words. *Also* Composition
CONCEIT (s.): idea, notion
CONCLUDE: to include
CONDITION (s.): disposition; social position, state of wealth
CONDITION (v.): to make conditions
CONDITIONED: having a (specified) disposition or social position
CONGEE: bow at parting
CONJURE: to plead with
CONJUROR: wizard who operates by conjuration of spirits
CONSIDERABLE: worthy of consideration
CONSTER: to construe, translate
CONSUMPTION: (any) wasting disease. *Also* 'Consumptive'
CONTENT, by/in: by agreement, without examination, at a rough guess
CONVENIENCE: advantage
CONVENIENT: morally proper
CONVERSATION: demeanour, behaviour; acquaintance, society
COOLE: cowl
CORANT(O): dance involving a running or gliding step
COSEN, COUSIN: almost any collateral relative
COUNT: reckon, estimate, value
COUNTENANCE: recognition, acknowledgement
COUNTRY: county, district
COURSE, in: in sequence
COURSE, of: as usual
COURT BARON: manorial court (civil)
COURT-DISH: dish with a cut from every meat
COURT LEET: local criminal court

COUSIN: *see* 'Cosen'
COY: disdainful; quiet
COYING: stroking, caressing
CRADLE: fire-basket
CRAMBO: rhyming game
CRAZY: infirm
CREATURE (of persons): puppet, instrument
CRUSADO: Portuguese coin worth 3*s*.
CUDDY: room in a large ship in which the officers took their meals
CULLY: dupe; friend
CUNNING: knowledgeable; knowledge
CURIOUS: careful, painstaking, discriminating; fine, delicate
CURRANT: out and about
CUSTOMER: customs officer
CUT (v.): to carve meat
CUTT (s.): an engraving

DAUGHTER-IN-LAW: stepdaughter
DEAD COLOUR: preparatory layer of colour in a painting
DEAD PAYS: sailors or soldiers kept on pay roll after death
DEALS: sawn timber used for decks, etc.
DEDIMUS: writ empowering J.P.
DEFALK: to subtract
DEFEND: to prevent
DEFY (Fr.): to mistrust. *Also* Defyance
DELICATE: pleasant
DELINQUENT: active royalist in Civil War and Interregnum
DEMORAGE: demurrage, compensation from the freighter due to a shipowner for delaying vessel beyond time specified in charter-party
DEPEND: to wait, hang
DEVISE: to decide; discern
DIALECT: jargon
DIALL, double horizontal: instrument telling hour of day
DIRECTION: supervision of making; arrangement
DISCOVER: to disclose, reveal

DISCREET: discerning, judicious
DISGUST: to dislike
DISPENSE: outgoings
DISTASTE (s.): difference, quarrel, offence. *Also* v.
DISTINCT: discerning, discriminating
DISTRINGAS: writ of distraint
DOATE: to nod off to sleep
DOCTOR: clergyman, don
DOE: dough. *See* 'All my cake ...'
DOGGED: determined
DOLLER: *see* 'Rix Doller'
DORTOIRE: dorter, monastic dormitory
DOTY: darling
DOWNS, the: roadstead off Deal, Kent
DOXY: whore, mistress
DRAM: timber from Drammen, Norway
DRAWER: tapster, barman
DRESS: to cook, prepare food
DROLL: comic song
DROLLING, **DROLLY**: comical, comically
DRUDGER: dredger, container for sweetmeats
DRUGGERMAN: dragoman, interpreter
DRY BEATEN: beaten without drawing blood
DRY MONEY: hard cash
DUANA: divan, council
DUCCATON: ducatoon, large silver coin of the Netherlands worth 5s. 9d.
DUCKET(T): ducat, foreign gold coin worth 9s.
DUKE'S [PLAY] HOUSE, the: playhouse in Lincoln's Inn Fields used by the Duke of York's Company from June 1660 until 9 November 1671; often called 'the Opera'. Also known as the Lincoln's Inn Fields Theatre (LIF)
DULL: limp, spiritless

EARTH: earthenware
EASILY AND EASILY: more and more slowly

EAST INDIES: the territory covered by the E. India Company, including the modern sub-continent of India
EAST COUNTRY, EASTLAND: the territory (Scandinavia and Baltic area) covered by the Eastland Company
EFFEMINACY: love of women
ELECTUARY: medicinal salve with a honey base
EMERODS: haemorrhoids
ENTENDIMIENTO (Sp.): understanding
ENTER (of horse): to break in
ENTERTAIN: to retain, employ
EPICURE: glutton
ERIFFE: Erith, Kent
ESPINETTE(S): spinet, small harpsichord
ESSAY: to assay
EVEN (adv.): surely
EVEN (of accounts): to balance
EVEN (of the diary): to bring up to date
EXCEPT: to accept
EXPECT: to see, await

FACTION: the government's parliamentary critics
FACTIOUS: able to command a following
FACTOR: mercantile agent
FACTORY: trading station
FAIN: to be forced; to like
FAIRING: small present (as from a fair)
FALCHON: falchion, curved sword
FAMILY: household (including servants)
FANCY (music): fantasia
FANFARROON: fanfaron, braggart
FARANDINE, FARRINDIN: *see* 'Ferrandin'
FASHION (of metal, furniture): design, fashioning
FAT: vat
FATHER: father-in-law (similarly with 'mother' etc.)
FELLET (of trees): a cutting, felling
FELLOW COMMONER: undergraduate

paying high fees and enjoying privileges

FENCE: defence

FERRANDIN, FARRINDIN, FARANDINE: cloth of silk mixed with wool or hair

FIDDLE: viol; violin

FINE (s.): payment for lease

FINE FOR OFFICE (v.): to avoid office by payment of fine

FIRESHIP: ship filled with combustibles used to ram and set fire to enemy

FITS OF THE MOTHER: hysterics

FLAG, FLAGGMAN: flag officer

FLAGEOLET: end-blown, six-holed instrument

FLESHED: relentless, proud

FLOOD: rising tide

FLUXED (of the pox): salivated

FLYING ARMY/FLEET: small mobile force

FOND, FONDNESS: foolish; folly

FOND: fund

FORCE OUT: to escape

FORSOOTH: to speak ceremoniously

FORTY: many, scores of

FOXED: intoxicated

FOX HALL: Vauxhall (pleasure gardens)

FOY: departure feast or gift

FREQUENT: to busy oneself

FRIENDS: parents, relatives

FROST-BITE: to invigorate by exposure to cold

FULL: anxious

FULL MOUTH, with: eagerly; openly, loudly

GALL: harass

GALLIOTT: small swift galley

GALLOPER, the: shoal off Essex coast

GAMBO: Gambia, W. Africa

GAMMER: old woman

GENERAL-AT-SEA: naval commander (a post, not a rank)

GENIUS: inborn character, natural ability; mood

GENT: graceful, polite

GENTILELY: obligingly

GEORGE: jewel forming part of insignia of Order of Garter

GERMANY: territory of the Holy Roman Empire

GET UP ONE'S CRUMB: to improve one's status

GET WITHOUT BOOK: to memorise

GHOSTLY: holy, spiritual

GIBB-CAT: tom-cat

GILDER, GUILDER: Dutch money of account worth 2s.

GIMP: twisted thread of material with wire or cord running through it

GITTERNE: musical instrument of the guitar family

GLASS: telescope

GLEEKE: three-handed card game

GLISTER, GLYSTER: *see* 'Clyster'

GLOSSE, by a fine: by a plausible pretext

GO TO ONE'S NAKED BED: to go to bed without night-clothes

GO(O)D BWYE: God be with ye, goodbye

GODLYMAN: Godalming, Surrey

GOODFELLOW: convivial person, good timer

GOODMAN, GOODWIFE (Goody): used of men and women of humble station

GOOD-SPEAKER: one who speaks well of others

GORGET: neckerchief for women

GOSSIP (v.): to act as godparent, to attend a new mother; to chatter. *Also* s.

GOVERNMENT: office or function of governor

GRACIOUS-STREET(E): Gracechurch St

GRAIN (? of gold): sum of money

GRAVE: to engrave

GREEN (of meat): uncured

GRESHAM COLLEGE: meeting-place of Royal Society; the Society itself
GRIEF: bodily pain
GRUDGEING, GRUTCHING: trifling complaint, grumble
GUEST: nominee; friend; stranger
GUIDE: postboy
GUILDER: *see* 'Gilder'
GUN: cannon, salute
GUNDALO, GUNDILOW: gondola
GUNFLEET, the: shoal off Essex coast

HACKNEY: hack, workhorse, drudge
HAIR, against the: against the grain
HALF-A-PIECE: gold coin worth *c.* 10*s.*
HALF-SHIRT: sham shirt front
HALFE-WAY-HOUSE: Rotherhithe tavern halfway between London Bridge and Deptford
HALL, the: usually Westminster Hall
HAND: cuff
HANDSEL: to try out, use for first time
HAND-TO-FIST: hastily
HANDYCAPP: handicap, a card game
HANG IN THE HEDGE: to be delayed
HANGER: loop holding a sword; small sword
HANGING JACK: turnspit for roasting meat
HANK: hold, grip
HAPPILY: haply, perchance
HARE: to harry, rebuke
HARPSICHON, HARPSICHORD: keyboard instrument of one or two manuals, with strings plucked by quills or leather jacks, and with stops which vary the tone
HARSLET: haslet, pigmeat (esp. offal)
HAT-PIECE: protective metal skull cap
HAVE A GOOD COAT OF [HIS] FLEECE: to have a good share
HAVE A HAND: to have leisure, freedom
HAVE A MONTH'S MIND: to have a great desire
HAWSE, thwart their: across their bows
HEAD-PIECE: helmet

HEART: courage
HEAVE AT: to oppose
HECTOR: street-bully, swashbuckler
HERBALL: botanical encyclopaedia; *hortus siccus* (book of dried and pressed plants)
HERE (Du. *heer*): Lord
HIGH: arrogant, proud, high-handed
HINCHINGBROOKE: Sandwich's house near Huntingdon
HOMAGE: jury of presentment at a manorial court
HONEST (of a woman): virtuous
HOOKS, off the: out of humour
HOPE, the: reach of Thames downstream from Tilbury
HOPEFUL: promising
HOUSE: playhouse; parliament; (royal) household or palace building
HOUSE OF OFFICE: latrine
HOY: small passenger and cargo vessel, fore-and-aft rigged
HOYSE: to hoist
HUMOUR (s.): mood; character, characteristic; good or ill temper
HUMOUR (v.): to set words suitably to music
HUSBAND: one who gets good/bad value for money; supervisor, steward
HYPOCRAS: hippocras, red or white wine (flavoured)

ILL-TEMPERED: out of sorts, ill-adjusted (to weather etc.; cf. 'Temper')
IMPERTINENCE: irrelevance, garrulity, folly. *Also* 'Impertinent'
IMPOSTUME: abscess
IMPREST: money paid in advance by government to public servant
INDIAN GOWN: loose gown of glazed cotton
INGENIOUS, INGENUOUS: clever, intelligent
INGENUITY: wit, intelligence; freedom
INGENUOUS: *see* 'Ingenious'

INSIPID: stupid, dull

INSTITUCIONS: instructions

INSTRUMENT: agent, clerk

INSULT: to exult over

INTELLIGENCE: information

INTRATUR: warrant authorising payment by Exchequer

IRISIPULUS: erysipelas

IRONMONGER: often a large-scale merchant, not necessarily a retailer

JACK(E): flag used as signal or mark of distinction; rogue, knave. *See also* 'Hanging Jack'

JACKANAPES COAT: monkey jacket, sailor's short close-fitting jacket

JACOB(US): gold sovereign coined under James I

JAPAN: lacquer, lacquered

JARR, JARRING: quarrel

JEALOUS: fearful, suspicious, mistrustful. *Also* Jealousy

JERK(E): captious remark

JES(S)IMY: jasmine

JEW'S TRUMP: Jew's harp

JOCKY: horse-dealer

JOLE (of fish): jowl, a cut consisting of the head and shoulders. *See also* 'Pole'

JOYNT-STOOL: stout stool held together by joints

JULIPP: julep, a sweet drink made from syrup

JUMBLE: to take for an airing

JUMP WITH: to agree, harmonise

JUNK (naval): old rope

JURATE (of Cinque Ports): jurat, alderman

JUSTE-AU-CORPS: close-fitting long coat

KATCH: (ship) ketch

KEEP A QUARTER: to make a disturbance

KENNEL: *see* 'Canaille'

KERCHER: kerchief, head-covering

KETCH (s.): catch, song in canon

KETCH (v.): to catch

KING'S [PLAY] HOUSE, the: playhouse in Vere St, Clare Market, Lincoln's Inn Fields, used by the King's Company from 8 November 1660 until 7 May 1663; the playhouse in Bridges St, Drury Lane, used by the same company from 7 May 1663 until the fire of 25 January 1672. Also known as the Theatre Royal (TR)

KITLIN: kitling, kitten, cub

KNEES: timbers of naturally angular shape used in ship-building

KNOT (s.): flower bed; difficulty; clique, band

KNOT (v.): to join, band together

KNOWN: famous

LACE: usually braid made with gold- or silver-thread

LAMB'S-WOOL: hot ale with apples and spice

LAMP-GLASS: magnifying lens used to concentrate lamp-light

LAST: load, measure of tar

LASTOFFE: Lowestoft, Suff.

LATITUDINARIAN: liberal Anglican

LAVER: basin of a fountain

LEADS: flat space on roof top, sometimes boarded over

LEAN: to lie down

LEARN: to teach

LEAVE: to end

LECTURE: weekday religious service consisting mostly of a sermon

LESSON: piece of music

LETTERS OF MART: letters of marque

LEVETT: reveille, reveille music

LIBEL(L): leaflet, broadside; (in legal proceedings) written charge

LIE UPON: to press, insist

LIFE: life interest

LIFE, for my: on my life

LIGHT: window

LIGNUM VITAE: hard W. Indian wood with medicinal qualities, often used for drinking vessels

LIMB: to limn, paint
LIME (of dogs): to mate
LINK(E): torch
LINNING: linen
LIPPOCK: Liphook, Hants.
LIST: pleasure, desire
LOCK: waterway between arches of bridge
LOMBRE: *see* 'Ombre'
LONDON: the city of London (to be distinguished from Westminster)
LOOK: to look at/for
LOOK AFTER: to have eyes on
LUMBERSTREETE: Lombard St
LUTE: pear-shaped instrument with six courses of gut strings and a turned-back peg-box; made in various sizes, the larger instruments having additional bass strings
LUTESTRING: lustring, a glossy silk
LYRA-VIALL: small bass viol tuned for playing chords

MAD: whimsical, wild, extravagant
MADAM(E): prefix used mainly of widows, elderly/foreign ladies
MAIN (adj.): strong, bulky
MAIN (s.): chief purpose or object
MAISTER: expert; professional; sailing master
MAKE (s.): (of fighting cocks) match, pair of opponents
MAKE (v.): to do; to copulate
MAKE LEGS: to bow, curtsey
MAKE SURE TO: to plight troth
MALLOWS: St Malo
MAN OF BUSINESS: executive agent, administrator
MANAGED-HORSE (cf. Fr. *manège*): horse trained in riding school
MANDAMUS: royal mandate under seal
MARGARET, MARGETTS: Margate, Kent
MARGENTING: putting margin-lines on paper
MARK: 13s. 4d.
MARMOTTE (Fr., term of affection): young girl

MARROWBONE: Marylebone, Mdx
MASTY: burly
MATCH: tinderbox and wick
MATHEMATICIAN: mathematical instrument-maker
MEAT: food
MEDIUM: mean, average
METHEGLIN: strong mead flavoured with herbs
MINCHIN-LANE: Mincing Lane
MINE: mien
MINIKIN: treble string of a viol
MISTRESS (MRS.): prefix used of unmarried girls and women as well as of young married women
MISTRESS: sweetheart
MITHRYDATE: drug used as an antidote
MODEST (of woman): virtuous
MOHER (Sp. *mujer*): woman, wife
MOIS, MOYS: menstrual periods
MOLD, MOLDE, MOLLE (archit.): mole
MOLEST: to annoy
MOND: orb (royal jewel in form of globe)
MONTEERE, MOUNTEERE: riding cap; close-fitting hood
MOPED: bemused
MORECLACK(E): Mortlake, Surrey
MORENA (Sp.): brunette
MORNING DRAUGHT: drink (sometimes with snack) usually taken mid-morning
MOTHER-IN-LAW: stepmother (similarly with 'father-in-law' etc.)
MOTT: sighting line in an optical tube
MOUNTEERE: *see* 'Monteere'
MOYRE: moire, watered silk
MUM: strong spiced ale
MURLACE: Morlaix, Brittany
MUSCADINE, MUSCATT: muscatel wine
MUSIC: band, choir, performers
MUSTY: peevish

NAKED BED: *see* 'Go to one's n.b.'
NARROWLY: anxiously, carefully
NAUGHT, NOUGHT: worthless, bad in condition or quality, sexually wicked

NAVY: Navy Office
NAVY OFFICERS: Principal Officers of the Navy – i.e. the Comptroller, Treasurer, Surveyor, Clerk of the Acts, together with a variable number of Commissioners; members of the Navy Board. Cf. 'Sea-Officers'
NEARLY: deeply
NEAT (adj.): handsome
NEAT(s.): ox, cattle
NEITHER MEDDLE NOR MAKE: to have nothing to do with
NEWSBOOK: newspaper (weekly, octavo)
NIBBLE AT: to bite at
NICOTIQUES: narcotics, medicines
NIGHTGOWN(E): dressing gown
NOISE: group of musical instruments playing together
NORE, the: anchorage in mouth of Thames
NORTHDOWNE ALE: Margate ale
NOSE: to insult, affront
NOTE: thing deserving of note, note of credit
NOTORIOUS: famous, well-known
NOUGHT: see 'Naught'

OBNOXIOUS: liable to
OBSERVABLE (adj.): noteworthy, notorious
OBSERVABLE (s.): thing or matter worthy of observation
OF: to have
OFFICE DAY: day on which a meeting of the Navy Board was held
OFFICERS OF THE NAVY: see 'Navy Officers'
OLEO (Sp. *olla*): stew
OMBRE (Sp. *hombre*): card game
ONLY: main, principal, best
OPEN: unsettled
OPERA: spectacular entertainment (involving use of painted scenery and stage machinery), often with music

OPERA, the: the theatre in Lincoln's Inn Fields. *See* 'Duke's House, the'
OPINIASTRE, OPINIASTREMENT (Fr.): stubborn, stubbornly
OPPONE: to oppose, hinder
ORDER: to put in order; to punish
ORDINARY (adj.): established
ORDINARY (s.): eating place serving fixed-price meals; peace-time establishment (of navy, dockyard, etc.)
OUTPORTS: ports other than London
OVERSEEN: omitted, neglected; guilty of oversight
OWE: to own

PADRON (?Sp., ?It. *patrone*): master
PAGEANT: decorated symbolic float in procession
PAINFUL: painstaking
PAIR OF OARS: large river-boat rowed by two watermen, each using a pair of oars. Cf. 'Scull'
PAIR (OF ORGANS/VIRGINALS): a single instrument
PALACE: New Palace Yard
PALER: parlour
PANNYARD: pannier, basket
PARAGON: heavy rich cloth, partly of mohair
PARALLELOGRAM: pantograph
PARCEL: share, part; isolated group
PARK, the: normally St James's Park (Hyde Park is usually named)
PARTY: charter-party
PASQUIL: a lampoon
PASSION: feeling, mood
PASSIONATE: touching, affecting
PATTEN: overshoe
PAY: to berate, beat
PAY A COAT: to beat, chastise
PAYSAN (Fr.): country style
PAY SAUCE: to pay dearly
PENDANCES, PENDENTS: lockets; earrings
PERPLEX: to vex

PESLEMESLE: pell-mell, early form of croquet

PETTY BAG: petty cash

PHILOSOPHY: natural science

PHYSIC: laxative, purge

PHYSICALLY: without sheets, uncovered

PICK: pique

PICK A HOLE IN A COAT: to pick a quarrel, complain

PICKAROON (Sp. *picarón*): pirate, privateer

PIECE: gold coin worth *c*. 20*s*.

PIECE (PEECE) OF EIGHT: Spanish silver coin worth 4*s*. 6*d*.

PIGEON: coward

PINK(E): small broad-beamed ship; poniard, pointed weapon

PINNER: coif with two long flaps; fill-in above low *décolletage*

PIPE: measure of wine (c. 120 galls.)

PIPE (musical): flageolet, after 16 Apr. 1668 usually a recorder, specified as such

PISTOLE: French gold coin worth 16*s*.

PLACKET: petticoat

PLAT(T): plate, plan, chart, map; arrangement; level; [flower] plot

PLATERER: one who works silver plate

PLAY (v.): to play for stakes

PLEASANT: comical

POINT, POYNT: piece of lace

POINT DE GESNE: Genoa lace

POLE: head; head-and-shoulder (of fish); poll tax

POLICY: government; cunning; self-interest

POLLARD: cut-back, stunted tree

POMPOUS: ceremonious, dignified

POOR JACK: dried salt fish

POOR WRETCH: poor dear

POSSET: drink made of hot milk, spices, and wine (or beer)

POST (v.): to expose, pillory

POST WARRANT: authority to employ posthorses

POSY: verse or phrase engraved on inside of ring

POWDERED (of meat): salted

PRACTICE: trick

PRAGMATIC, PRAGMATICAL: interfering, conceited, dogmatic

PRATIQUE: ship's licence for port facilities given on presentation of clean bill of health

PRESBYTER JOHN: puritan parson

PRESENT (s.): shot, volley

PRESENT, PRESENTLY: immediate, immediately

PRESS BED: bed folding into or built inside a cupboard

PREST MONEY (milit., naval): earnest money paid in advance

PRETTY (of men): fine, elegant, foppish

PREVENT: to anticipate

PRICK: to write out music; to list

PRICK OUT: to strike out, delete

PRINCE: ruler

PRINCIPLES (of music): natural ability, rudimentary knowledge

PRISE, PRIZE: worth, value, price

PRIVATE: small, secret, quiet

PRIZE FIGHT: fencing match fought for money

PROPRIETY: property, ownership

PROTEST (a bill): to record non-payment; represent bill after non-payment

PROUD (of animals): on heat

PROVOKE: to urge

PULL A CROW: to quarrel

PURCHASE: advantage; profit; booty

PURELY: excellently

PURL(E): hot spiced beer

PUSS: ill-favoured woman

PUT OFF: to sell, dispose of, marry off

PYONEER: pioneer (ditch digger, labourer)

QU: cue

QUARREFOUR: crossroads

QUARTERAGE: any salary or sum paid quarterly

QUARTRE: position in dancing or fencing

QUEST HOUSE: house used for inquests, parish meetings

QUINBROUGH: Queenborough, Kent

QUINSBOROUGH: Königsberg, E. Prussia

RACE: to rase, destroy

RAKE-SHAMED: disreputable, disgraceful

RARE: fine, splendid

RATE: to berate, scold

RATTLE: to scold

RATTOON: rattan cane

READY: quick, accomplished

REAKE: trick

RECEBI: writ of receipt issued by Chancery

RECITATIVO (*stilo r.*): the earliest type of recitative singing

RECONCILE: to settle a dispute, to determine the truth

RECORDER: family of end-blown, eight-holed instruments (descant, treble, tenor, bass)

RECOVER: to reconcile

RECOVERY (legal): process for re-establishment of ownership

REDRIFFE: Rotherhithe, Surrey

REFERRING: indebted, beholden to

REFORM: to disband

REFORMADO: naval/military officer serving without commission

REFRESH (of a sword): to sharpen

RELIGIOUS: monk, nun

REPLICACION (legal): replication, plaintiff's answer to defendant's plea

RESEMBLE: to represent, figure

RESENT: to receive

RESPECT: to mean, refer to

RESPECTFUL: respectable

REST: wrest, tuning key

RETAIN (a writ): to maintain a court action from term to term

REVOLUTION: sudden change (not necessarily violent)

RHODOMONTADO: boast, brag

RIDE POST: to travel by posthorse, to ride fast

RIGHT-HAND MAN: soldier on whom drill manoeuvres turn

RIGHTS, to: immediately, directly

RIS (v.): rose

RISE: origin

RIX DOLLER: Dutch or N. German silver coin (*Rijksdaalder, Reichsthaler*) worth c. 4s. 9d.

ROCKE: distaff

ROMANTIQUE: having the characteristics of a tale (romance)

ROUNDHOUSE: uppermost cabin in stern of ship

ROYALL THEATRE, the: *see* 'Theatre, the'

RUB(B): check, stop, obstacle

RUFFIAN: pimp, rogue

RUMP: remnant of the Long Parliament

RUMPER: member or supporter of the Rump

RUNLETT: cask

RUNNING: temporary

SACK: white wine from Spain or Canaries

SALT: salt-cellar

SALT-EELE: rope's end used for punishment

SALVE UP: to smooth over

SALVO: excuse, explanation

SARCENET: thin taffeta, fine silk cloth

SASSE (Du. *sas*): sluice, lock

SAVE: to be in time for

SAY: fine woollen cloth

SCALE (of music): key; gamut

SCALLOP: scalloped lace collar

SCALLOP-WHISK: *see* 'Whiske'

SCAPE (s.): adventure

SCAPE (v.): to escape

SCARE-FIRE: sudden conflagration

SCHOOL: to scold, rebuke

SCHUIT (Du.): canal boat, barge

SCONCE: bracket, candlestick

SCOTOSCOPE: spy-glass for use in dark

SCOWRE: to beat, punish

SCREW: key, screw-bolt

SCRUPLE: to dispute

SCULL, SCULLER: small river-boat rowed by a single waterman using one pair of oars. Cf. 'Pair of oars'

SEA-CARD: chart

SEA-COAL: coal carried by sea

SEA-OFFICERS: commissioned officers of the navy. Cf. 'Navy Officers'

SECOND MOURNING: half-mourning

SEEL (of a ship): to lurch

SEEM: to pretend

SENNIT: sevennight, a week

SENSIBLY: perceptibly, painfully

SERPENT: variety of firework

SERVANT: suitor, lover

SET: sit

SET UP/OFF ONE'S REST: to be certain, to be content, to make an end, to make one's whole aim

SEWER: stream, ditch

SHAG(G): worsted or silk cloth with a velvet nap on one side

SHEATH (of a ship): to encase the hull as a protection against worm

SHIFT (s.): trial; dressing room

SHIFT (v.): to change clothes; to dodge a round in paying for drinks (or to get rid of the effects of drink)

SHOEMAKER'S STOCKS: new shoes

SHOVE AT: to apply one's energies to

SHROUD: shrewd, astute

SHUFFLEBOARD: shovelboard, shove-ha'penny

SHUTS: shutters

SILLABUB, SULLYBUB, SYLLABUB: sweetened milk mixed with wine

SIMPLE: foolish

SIT: to hold a meeting

SIT CLOSE: to hold a meeting from which clerks are excluded

SITHE: sigh

SKELLUM: rascal, thief

SLENDERLY: slightingly

SLICE: flat plate

SLIGHT, SLIGHTLY: contemptuous; slightingly, without ceremony

SLIP A CALF/FILLY: to abort

SLOP(P)S: seamen's ready-made clothes

SLUG(G): slow heavy boat; rough metal projectile

SLUT (not always opprobrious): drudge, wench

SMALL (of drink): light

SNAP(P) (s.): bite, snack, small meal; attack

SNAP (v.): to ambush, cut down/out/off

SNUFF: to speak scornfully

SNUFFE, take/go in: to take offence

SOKER: old hand; pal; toper

SOLD(E)BAY: Solebay, off Southwold, Suff.

SOL(L)ICITOR: agent; one who solicits business

SON: son-in-law (similarly with daughter etc.)

SON-IN-LAW: stepson

SOUND: fish-bladder

SOUND, the: strictly the navigable passage between Denmark and Sweden where tolls were levied, but more generally (and usually in Pepys) the Baltic

SPARROWGRASS: asparagus

SPEAK BROAD: to speak fully, frankly

SPECIALITY: bond under seal

SPECIES (optical): image

SPEED: to succeed

SPIKET: spigot, tap, faucet

SPILT, SPOILT: ruined

SPINET: single-manual wing-shaped keyboard instrument with harpsichord action

SPOIL: to deflower; injure

SPOTS: patches (cosmetic)

SPRANKLE: sparkling remark, *bon mot*

SPUDD: trenching tool

STAIRS: landing stage

STAND IN: to cost

STANDING WATER: between tides

STANDISH: stand for ink, pens, etc.

STATE-DISH: richly decorated dish; dish with a round lid or canopy

STATESMAN: Commonwealth's-man

STATIONER: bookseller (often also publisher)

STEEPLE: tower

STEMPEECE: timber of ship's bow

STICK: blockhead

STILLYARD, the: the Steelyard

STIR(R): commotion

STOMACH: courage, pride; appetite

STOMACHFULLY: proudly

STONE-HORSE: stallion

STOUND: astonishment

STOUT: brave, courageous

STOWAGE: storage, payment for storage

STRAIGHTS, STREIGHTS, the: strictly the Straits of Gibraltar; more usually the Mediterranean

STRANG: strong

STRANGERS: foreigners

STRIKE (nautical): to lower the top-sail in salute; (of Exchequer tallies) to make, cut

STRONG WATER: distilled spirits

SUBSIDY MAN: man of substance (liable to pay subsidy-tax)

SUCCESS(E): outcome (good or bad)

SUDDENLY: in a short while

SULLYBUB: see 'Sillabub'

SUPERNUMERARY: seaman extra to ship's complement

SURLY: imperious, lordly

SWINE-POX: chicken-pox

SWOUND: to swoon, faint

SYLLABUB: see 'Sillabub'

SYMPHONY: instrumental introduction, interlude etc., in a vocal composition

TAB(B)Y: watered silk

TABLE: legend attached to a picture

TABLE BOOK: memorandum book

TABLES: board games

TAILLE, TALLE (Fr. taille): figure, shape (of person)

TAKE EGGS FOR MONEY: to cut one's losses, to accept something worthless

TAKE A CRAP: to defecate

TAKE OUT: to learn; perform

TAKE POST: to ride hired posthorses

TAKING (s.): condition

TALE: reckoning, number

TALL: fine, elegant

TALLE: see 'Taille'

TALLY: notched wooden stick used by the Exchequer in accounting

TAMKIN: tampion, wooden gun plug

TANSY, TANZY: egg pudding flavoured with tansy

TARGETT: shield

TARPAULIN: 'tar', a sea-bred captain as opposed to a gentleman-captain

TAXOR: financial official of university

TEAR: to rant

TELL: to count

TEMPER (s.): moderation; temperament, mood; physical condition

TEMPER (v.): to moderate, control

TENDER: chary of

TENT: roll of absorbent material used for wounds; (Sp. tinto) red wine

TERCE, TIERCE: measure of wine (42 galls.; one-third of a pipe)

TERELLA: terrella, spherical magnet, terrestrial globe containing magnet

TERM(E)S: menstrual periods

THEATRE, the: before May 1663 usually Theatre Royal, Vere St; afterwards usually Theatre Royal, Drury Lane (TR)

THEM: see 'Those'

THEORBO: large double-necked tenor lute

THOSE: menstrual periods

THRUSH: inflammation of throat and mouth

TICKELED: annoyed, irritated

TICKET(T): seaman's pay-ticket

TIERCE: see 'Terce'

TILT: awning over river-boat

TIMBER: wood for the skeleton of a ship (as distinct from plank or deals used for the decks, cabins, gun-platforms etc.)

TIRE: tier

TOKEN, by the same: so, then, and

TONGUE: reputation, fame

TOPS: turnovers of stockings

TOUCHED: annoyed

TOUR, the: coach parade of *beau monde* in Hyde Park

TOUSE: to tousle/tumble a woman

TOWN(E): manor

TOY: small gift

TOYLE: foil, net into which game is driven

TRADE: manufacture, industry

TRANSIRE: warrant allowing goods through customs

TRAPAN, TREPAN: (surg.) to perforate skull; cheat, trick, trap, inveigle

TREASURY, the: the Navy Treasury or the national Treasury

TREAT: to handle (literally)

TREAT, TREATY: negotiate, negotiation

TREBLE: treble viol

TREPAN: see 'Trapan'

TRIANGLE, TRYANGLE: triangular virginals

TRILL(O): vocal ornament consisting of the accelerated repetition of the same note

TRIM: to shave

TRUCKLE/TRUNDLE-BED: low bed on castors which could be put under main bed

TRYANGLE: see 'Triangle'

TRY A PULL: to have a go

TUITION: guardianship

TUNE: pitch

TURK, the: used of all denizens of the Turkish Empire, but usually here of the Berbers of the N. African coast, especially Algiers

TURKEY WORK: red tapestry in Turkish style

TURKY-STONE: turquoise

TUTTLE FIELDS: Tothill Fields

TWIST: strong thread

UGLY: unpleasant, offensive

UMBLES (of deer): edible entrails, giblets

UNBESPEAK: cancel, countermand

UNCOUTH: out of sorts or order, uneasy, at a loss

UNDERSTAND: to conduct oneself properly; (s.) understanding

UNDERTAKER: contractor; parliamentary manager

UNHAPPY, UNHAPPILY: unlucky; unluckily

UNREADY: undressed

UNTRUSS: to undo one's breeches, defecate

UPPER BENCH: name given in Interregnum to King's Bench

USE: usury, interest

USE UPON USE: compound interest

VAPOURISH: pretentious, foolish

VAUNT: to vend, sell

VENETIAN CAP: peaked cap as worn by Venetian Doge

VESTS: robes, vestments

VIALL, VIOL: family of fretted, bowed instruments with six gut strings; the bowing hand is held beneath the bow and the instrument held on or between the knees; now mostly superseded by violin family

VIRGINALS: rectangular English keyboard instrument resembling spinet; usually in case without legs

VIRTUOSO: man of wide learning

WAISTCOAT, WASTECOATE: warm undergarment

WAIT, WAYT (at court etc.): to serve a turn of duty (usually a month) as an official

WARDROBE, the: the office of the

King's Great Wardrobe, of which
Lord Sandwich was Keeper; the
building at Puddle Wharf contain-
ing the office; a cloak room,
dressing room
WARM: comfortable, well-off
WASSAIL, WASSELL: entertainment
(e.g. a play)
WASTCOATE: *see* 'Waistcoat'
WASTECLOATH: cloth hung on ship as
decoration between quarter-deck
and forecastle
WATCH: clock
WATER: strong water, spirits
WAY, in/out of the: accessible/in-
accessible; in a suitable/unsuitable
condition
WAYTES: waits; municipal musicians
WEATHER-GLASS(E): thermometer (or,
less likely, barometer)
WEIGH (of ships): to raise
WELLING: Welwyn, Herts.
WESTERN BARGEMAN (BARGEE): bargee
serving western reaches of Thames
WESTMINSTER: the area around
Whitehall and the Abbey; not the
modern city of Westminster

WHISKE: woman's neckerchief
WHITE-HALL: royal palace, largely
burnt down in 1698
WHITSTER: bleacher, launderer
WIGG: wig, cake, bun
WILDE: wile
WIND (s.): wine
WIND LIKE A CHICKEN: to wind round
one's little finger
WINDFUCKER: talkative braggart
WIPE: sarcasm, insult
WISTELY: with close attention
WITTY: clever, intelligent
WONDER: to marvel at
WOODMONGER: fuel merchant
WORD: utterance, phrase
WOREMOODE: wormwood
WORK: needlework. *Also* v.
WRETCH: *see* 'Poor wretch'

YARD: penis
YARE: ready, skilful
YILDHALL: Guildhall
YOWELL: Ewell, Surrey

ELAINE PAGELS

BEYOND BELIEF

Elaine Pagels earned a B.A. in history and an M.A. in classical studies at Stanford, and holds a Ph.D. from Harvard University. She is the author of *Adam, Eve, and the Serpent*; *The Origin of Satan*; and *The Gnostic Gospels*, which won the National Book Critics Circle Award and the National Book Award. She is currently the Harrington Spear Paine Professor of Religion at Princeton University, and she lives in Princeton, New Jersey, with her husband and children.

BEYOND BELIEF

ELAINE PAGELS

BEYOND
BELIEF

THE SECRET GOSPEL
OF THOMAS

VINTAGE BOOKS

A DIVISION OF RANDOM HOUSE, INC.

NEW YORK

FIRST VINTAGE BOOKS EDITION, MAY 2004

The Library of Congress has cataloged the Random House edition as follows:
Pagels, Elaine H.
Beyond belief : the secret Gospel of Thomas / Elaine Pagels.
p. cm.
Includes bibliographical references and index.
1. Gospel of Thomas (Coptic Gospel)–Criticism, interpretation, etc.
2. Bible. N.T. John–Criticism, interpretation, etc.
3. Christianity–Essence, genius, nature. I. Title.
BS2860.T52 P34   2003   229'.8–dc21   2002036840

Vintage ISBN: 0-375-70316-0

Author photograph © Jerry Bauer
Book design by J. K. Lambert

www.vintagebooks.com

Printed in the United States of America
10 9 8 7 6 5 4 3 2 1

FOR KENT

with love

There is an invisible world out there, and we are living in it.

BILL VIOLA, VIDEO ARTIST

CONTENTS

BEYOND BELIEF

tototot

FROM THE FEAST OF AGAPE
TO THE NICENE CREED

On a bright Sunday morning in February, shivering in a T-shirt and running shorts, I stepped into the vaulted stone vestibule of the Church of the Heavenly Rest in New York to catch my breath and warm up. Since I had not been in church for a long time, I was startled by my response to the worship in progress—the soaring harmonies of the choir singing with the congregation; and the priest, a woman in bright gold and white vestments, proclaiming the prayers in a clear, resonant voice. As I stood watching, a thought came to me: Here is a family that knows how to face death.

That morning I had gone for an early morning run while my husband and two-and-a-half-year-old son were still sleeping. The previous night I had been sleepless with fear and worry.

Two days before, a team of doctors at Babies Hospital, Columbia Presbyterian Medical Center, had performed a routine checkup on our son, Mark, a year and six months after his successful open-heart surgery. The physicians were shocked to find evidence of a rare lung disease. Disbelieving the results, they tested further for six hours before they finally called us in to say that Mark had pulmonary hypertension, an invariably fatal disease, they told us. How much time? I asked. "We don't know; a few months, a few years."

The following day, a team of doctors urged us to authorize a lung biopsy, a painful and invasive procedure. How could this help? It couldn't, they explained; but the procedure would let them see how far the disease had progressed. Mark was already exhausted by the previous day's ordeal. Holding him, I felt that if more masked strangers poked needles into him in an operating room, he might lose heart—literally—and die. We refused the biopsy, gathered Mark's blanket, clothes, and Peter Rabbit, and carried him home.

Standing in the back of that church, I recognized, uncomfortably, that I needed to be there. Here was a place to weep without imposing tears upon a child; and here was a heterogeneous community that had gathered to sing, to celebrate, to acknowledge common needs, and to deal with what we cannot control or imagine. Yet the celebration in progress spoke of hope; perhaps that is what made the presence of death bearable. Before that time, I could only ward off what I had heard and felt the day before.

I returned often to that church, not looking for faith but because, in the presence of that worship and the people gathered there—and in a smaller group that met on weekdays in the church basement for mutual encouragement—my defenses fell away, exposing storms of grief and hope. In that church I gathered new energy, and resolved, over and over, to face whatever awaited us as constructively as possible for Mark, and for the rest of us.

When people would say to me, "Your faith must be of great help to you," I would wonder, What do they mean? What is faith? Certainly not simple assent to the set of beliefs that worshipers in that church recited every week ("We believe in one God, the Father, the Almighty, maker of heaven and earth . . .")—traditional statements that sounded strange to me, like barely intelligible signals from the surface, heard at the bottom of the sea. Such statements seemed to me then to have little to do with whatever transactions we were making with one another, with ourselves, and—so it was said—with invisible beings. I was acutely aware that we met there driven by need and desire; yet sometimes I dared hope that such communion has the potential to transform us.

I am a historian of religion, and so, as I visited that church, I wondered when and how being a Christian became virtually synonymous with accepting a certain set of beliefs. From historical reading, I knew that Christianity had survived brutal persecution and flourished for generations—even centuries—*before* Christians formulated what they believed into creeds. The origins of this transition from scattered groups to a unified community have left few traces. Although the apostle Paul, about twenty years after Jesus' death, stated "the gospel," which, he says, "I too received" ("that Christ died for our sins according to the Scriptures; that he was buried, and that he was raised on the third day"),[1] it may have been more than a hundred years

later that some Christians, perhaps in Rome, attempted to consolidate their group against the demands of a fellow Christian
named Marcion, whom they regarded as a false teacher, by
introducing formal statements of belief into worship.[2] But only
in the *fourth* century, after the Roman emperor Constantine
himself converted to the new faith—or at least decriminalized
it—did Christian bishops, at the emperor's command, convene
in the city of Nicaea, on the Turkish coast, to agree upon a
common statement of beliefs—the so-called Nicene Creed, which
defines the faith for many Christians to this day.

Yet I know from my own encounters with people in that
church, both upstairs and down, believers, agnostics, and
seekers—as well as people who don't belong to any church—
that what matters in religious experience involves much more
than what we believe (or what we do not believe). What *is*
Christianity, and what is religion, I wondered, and why do so
many of us still find it compelling, whether or not we belong to
a church, and despite difficulties we may have with particular
beliefs or practices? What is it about Christian tradition that we
love—and what is it that we *cannot* love?

From the beginning, what attracted outsiders who walked
into a gathering of Christians, as I did on that February morning, was the presence of a group joined by spiritual power into
an extended family. Many must have come as I had, in distress;
and some came without money. In Rome, the sick who fre-
quented the temples of Asclepius, the Greek god of healing, expected to pay when they consulted his priests about herbs,
exercise, baths, and medicine. These priests also arranged for
visitors to spend nights sleeping in the temple precincts, where
the god was said to visit his suppliants in dreams. Similarly,

those who sought to enter into the mysteries of the Egyptian goddess Isis, seeking her protection and blessings in this life, and eternal life beyond the grave, were charged considerable initiation fees and spent more to buy the ritual clothing, offerings, and equipment.

Irenaeus, the leader of an important Christian group in provincial Gaul in the second century, wrote that many newcomers came to Christian meeting places hoping for miracles, and some found them: "We heal the sick by laying hands on them, and drive out demons," the destructive energies that cause mental instability and emotional anguish. Christians took no money, yet Irenaeus acknowledged no limits to what the spirit could do: "We even raise the dead, many of whom are still alive among us, and completely healthy."[3]

Even without a miracle, those in need could find immediate practical help almost anywhere in the empire, whose great cities—Alexandria in Egypt, Antioch, Carthage, and Rome itself—were then, as now, crowded with people from throughout the known world. Inhabitants of the vast shantytowns that surrounded these cities often tried to survive by begging, prostitution, and stealing. Yet Tertullian, a Christian spokesman of the second century, writes that, unlike members of other clubs and societies that collected dues and fees to pay for feasts, members of the Christian "family" contributed money voluntarily to a common fund to support orphans abandoned in the streets and garbage dumps. Christian groups also brought food, medicines, and companionship to prisoners forced to work in mines, banished to prison islands, or held in jail. Some Christians even bought coffins and dug graves to bury the poor and criminals, whose corpses otherwise would lie unburied beyond the city

walls. Like Irenaeus, the African convert Tertullian emphasizes
that among Christians

> there is no buying and selling of any kind in what belongs
> to God. On a certain day, each one, if he likes, puts in a
> small gift, but only if he wants to do so, and only if he be
> able, for there is no compulsion; everything is voluntary.[4]

Such generosity, which ordinarily could be expected only
from one's own family, attracted crowds of newcomers to Christian groups, despite the risks. The sociologist Rodney Stark notes
that, shortly before Irenaeus wrote, a plague had ravaged cities
and towns throughout the Roman empire, from Asia Minor
though Italy and Gaul.[5] The usual response to someone suffering from inflamed skin and pustules, whether a family member
or not, was to run, since nearly everyone infected died in agony.
Some epidemiologists estimate that the plague killed a third to
a half of the imperial population. Doctors could not, of course,
treat the disease, and they too fled the deadly virus. Galen, the
most famous physician of his age, who attended the family of
Emperor Marcus Aurelius, survived what people later called
Galen's plague by escaping to a country estate until it was over.

But some Christians were convinced that God's power was
with them to heal or alleviate suffering. They shocked their
pagan neighbors by staying to care for the sick and dying, believing that, if they themselves should die, they had the power
to overcome death. Even Galen was impressed:

> [For] the people called Christians . . . contempt of death is
> obvious to us every day, and also their self-control in

sexual matters. . . . They also include people who, in self-
discipline . . . in matters of food and drink, and in their
keen pursuit of justice, have attained a level not inferior to
that of genuine philosophers.[6]

Why did Christians act in such extraordinary ways? They would
say that their strength came from their encounter with divine
power—but it was a power wholly unlike that of the gods
whose temples crowded the city streets, and whose images
adorned the theaters and public baths. Jupiter and Diana, Isis
and Mithras, required their worshipers to offer devotion, pour-
ing out wine, making sacrifices, and contributing money to the
priests at their temples. Such gods were understood to act, like
human beings, out of self-interest. But Jews and Christians believed that their God, who created humankind, actually *loved*
the human race, and evoked love in return. Jesus succinctly
summarized Jewish teaching when he said, "You shall love the
Lord your God with all your heart, mind, and soul; and you
shall love your neighbor as yourself."[7] What God requires is
that human beings love one another and offer help—even, or
especially, to the neediest.

Such convictions became the practical basis of a radical new
social structure. Rodney Stark suggests that we read the following passage from Matthew's gospel "as if for the very first time,"
in order to feel the power of this new morality as Jesus' early
followers and their pagan neighbors must have felt it:[8]

For I was hungry and you gave me food, I was thirsty and
you gave me drink. I was a stranger and you welcomed
me, I was naked and you clothed me, I was sick and you

visited me, I was in prison and you came to me. . . . Truly,
I say to you, as you did it to one of the least of these my
brethren, you did it to me.[9]

These precepts could hardly have been universally practiced,
yet Tertullian says that members of what he calls the "peculiar
Christian society" practiced them often enough to attract public
notice: "What marks us in the eyes of our enemies is our practice of lovingkindness: 'Only look,' they say, 'look how they love
one another!' "[10]

Tertullian also says that outsiders ridiculed Christians "because we call each other brother and sister." Yet when he writes
his *Defence of the Christians*, he adds that members of "God's
family" also believed that the human family as a whole is inter-
related. Thus, he says, "we are *your* brothers and sisters as well,
by the law of our common mother, nature," although, he con-
cedes,

perhaps it is more appropriate to call *brother* and *sister*
those who have come to know God as their father, and
who, from the same womb of a common ignorance, have
agonized into the clear light of truth.[11]

The agonizing birth process he refers to is *baptism*, for to join
God's family one had to die—symbolically—and become a new
person. The apostle Paul had said that whoever is plunged into
the baptismal waters and submerged, as in the waters of death,
dies to his or her former self.[12] For many Christians this was a
wrenching event that severed all familiar bonds, including, of

course, those with the families of their birth. Tertullian describes how non–Christian families rejected those who joined this illicit sect:

> The husband . . . casts the wife out of his house; the father . . . disinherits the son; the master commands the slave to depart from his presence: it is a huge offence for anyone to be reformed by this hated name [Christian].[13]

Why a "huge offence"? Because in the eyes of their relatives, converts were joining a cult of criminals—a choice that could be suicidal for the convert, and disastrous for the family left behind. The Roman senator Tacitus, who despised Christians for their superstitions, probably would have agreed that Tertullian reflected public opinion when he said that, for outsiders, conversion made the initiate "an enemy of the public good; of the gods; of public morals," of all that patriotic and religious Romans held sacred.[14] Tertullian knew what had happened during the summer of 202 in his own African city, Carthage, where a twenty–two–year–old aristocrat named Vibia Perpetua, recently married and the mother of an infant son, resolved to undergo baptism along with four other young people, at least two of them slaves. When the magistrate asked whether she was a Christian, she said she was. She was arrested, imprisoned, and sentenced to be torn apart by beasts in the public arena—a death sentence ordinarily reserved for slaves—along with her fellow converts.

Perpetua recorded in her diary what happened when her patrician, gray–haired father arrived at the prison:

While we were under arrest, my father, out of love for me, was trying to persuade me and shake my resolution. "Father," I said, "do you see this vessel, or waterpot, or whatever it is?" "Yes, I do," he said. "Could it be called by any other name than what it is?" I asked; and he said, "No." "Well, so too, I cannot be called anything other than what I am, *Christian*."[15]

Because she was repudiating her family name, Perpetua wrote, "my father was so angry . . . that he started towards me as though he would tear out my eyes; but he left it at that, and departed."[16] A few days later, hoping that his daughter might be given a hearing, Perpetua says, "My father arrived from the city, exhausted with worry, and came to see me to try to persuade me. 'Daughter,' " he said, understandably desperate,

have pity . . . on me, your father, if I deserve to be called your father; if I have loved you more than all your brothers. . . . Do not abandon me to people's scorn. Think of your brothers; think of your mother and your aunt; think of your child, who will not be able to live without you. Give up your pride! You will destroy all of us! None of us will ever be able to speak freely again if anything happens to you.[17]

Perpetua wrote, "My father spoke this way out of love for me, kissing my hands and throwing himself down before me. With tears in his eyes . . . he left me in great sorrow."[18]

Then, on the day when the governor interrogated the prisoners, her father arrived carrying her infant son and continued to plead with her, she says, until the governor "ordered him to be thrown to the ground and beaten with a rod. I felt sorry for father, just as if I myself had been beaten; I grieved for his misery in old age."[19] But Perpetua believed that she now belonged to God's family and maintained her detachment. On the birthday of Emperor Geta, she walked calmly from prison into the amphitheater "as one beloved of God . . . putting down everyone's stare by her own intense gaze,"[20] to die with her new relatives, who included her slave Felicitas as her sister and Revocatus, also a slave, as her brother.

To join the "peculiar Christian society," then, a candidate had to repudiate his or her family, along with its values and practices. Justin Martyr, called "the philosopher," baptized in Rome around the year 140, says that he had come to see himself as one who had been "brought up in bad habits and evil customs"[21] to accept distorted values and worship demons as gods. He tells how he and others had given up promiscuity, magic, greed, wealth, and racial hatred:

> We, out of every tribe of people . . . who used to take pleasure in promiscuity, now embrace chastity alone; we, who once had recourse to magic, dedicate ourselves to the good God; we, who valued above everything else acquiring wealth and possessions, now bring what we have into a common fund, and share with everyone in need; we who hated and killed other people, and refused to live with people of another tribe because of their different customs, now live intimately with them.[22]

Every initiate, Justin adds, who "has been convinced, and agreed to our teaching," would pledge to live as a person transformed.

Having changed his or her mind (which is the meaning of the Latin word *paenitentia*) about the past, the candidate could undergo the baptismal "bath" that cleanses away its pollution. The initiate, often shivering beside a river, undressed and went underwater, to emerge wet and naked, "born again." And just as any Roman newborn would first be presented to the father to accept—or reject—before it could be embraced as a member of the family, so the newly baptized would be presented before "God, the Father of all." Now the initiate, no longer called, as before, by his or her paternal name, would hear the initiator pronouncing the name of the "Father of all," of Jesus Christ, and of the holy spirit. Then, clothed in new garments, the reborn Christian would be fed a mixture of milk and honey, the food of newborn infants, and be brought in to greet "those we call brothers and sisters" with a kiss. Now members of the assembled community would invite the newcomer to share bread and wine in the *eucharist* (literally, "thanksgiving"), the sacred family meal. Justin says that believers call baptism "*illumination,* because all who receive it are illuminated in their understanding."[23] These simple, everyday acts—taking off old clothes, bathing, putting on new clothes, then sharing bread and wine—took on, for Jesus' followers, powerful meanings.

As I began sometimes to participate in church services after decades of absence, I experienced the power of worship in new ways. I had grown up nominally Protestant, and thought of ritual as empty form, but now I saw how it could join people of diverse cultures and viewpoints into a single community, and focus and renew their energies. But, apart from these effects, what do such acts mean, and what does it mean to join such a community? These questions are not easy to answer. Many people have tried to impute a single, definitive meaning shared by all "early Christians"; but first-century evidence—much of it from the New Testament—tells a different story.[24] Various groups interpreted baptism in quite different ways; and those who ate bread and drank wine together to celebrate "the Lord's supper" often could not confine the meaning of their worship to any single interpretation.

One of the earliest sources, for example, the Teaching of the Twelve Apostles to the Gentiles, shows that members of certain early groups of Jesus' followers did not think of themselves as *Christians*—as we think of *Christians*—as separate from *Jews*, but as God's people—by which some apparently meant Jews who revered Jesus as the great interpreter of God's law, the Torah. Written in Syria about ten years *before* the New Testament gospels of Matthew and Luke,[25] this writing, known as the Didache (Greek for "teaching"), opens with a succinct summary of God's law, along with a *negative* version of the so-called golden rule: "The Way of Life is this: First, you shall love the God who made you, and your neighbor as yourself; and whatever you do not want to have done to you, do not do to another."[26] The Didache quotes other sayings that Matthew and Luke, writing perhaps about ten years later, will also attribute to Jesus:

> Bless those who curse you; pray for your enemies . . . love those who hate you. . . . If anyone smites you on the right cheek, turn to him the other also. . . . Give to everyone who asks you, and do not refuse

—although its editor adds a prudent warning *not* included in the New Testament: "Let your money sweat in your hands until you know to whom you are giving."[27]

Thus the Didache sets forth what the "way of life" demands, mingling the Ten Commandments with sayings best known to Christians from Jesus' Sermon on the Mount. Like many other pious Jews, the author amplifies these sayings with moral warnings similar to those his contemporaries directed against what they regarded as the everyday crimes of pagan culture, including sex with children, often slave boys, abortion, and killing newborns:

> You shall not kill; you shall not commit adultery; you shall not have sexual intercourse with boys . . . you shall not practice magic; you shall not murder the child in the womb, nor kill newborns . . . you shall not turn away the destitute.[28]

Then, after warning them not to follow the "way of death"— the way especially of the "advocates of the rich," who "turn away the poor and oppress those who suffer, and judge the poor unjustly"—the author, like Jesus in the Gospel of Matthew, urges his hearers to "be perfect." But, *unlike* Matthew, the Didache explains that "being perfect" suggests "bearing the whole yoke of the Lord"—that is, obeying the whole divine law.[29] Also, unlike Matthew, this anonymous follower of Jesus adds, more practically, "If you cannot [be perfect], do what you can."

The historian Jonathan Draper suggests that one early version of the Didache reveals a group of Jesus' followers who were still participating in the life of the Jewish community in their home city in Syria. When members of this group baptized new-comers, they understood baptism as their fellow Jews did then, and still do today: as a "bath" that purifies outsiders—that is, Gentiles—who seek admission to God's people, Israel. The point of this early and influential manual, Draper shows, is to demon-strate how non-Jews may become part of God's people; that is, to offer, just as the title promises, "the teaching of the twelve apostles *to the Gentiles*."[30] The Didache provides these Gentiles an exposition of the "way of life" set forth in the Hebrew Scriptures as Jesus interpreted it, and then shows how Gentiles willing to follow that "way" may be baptized, so that they, too, can share in the blessings of God's coming kingdom.

Finally, the Didache tells how the initiate, who fasts and prays before being baptized, would have learned how sharing in this simple meal of bread and wine links the human family gathered for worship with "God, our Father," and with "Jesus, [his] servant" (or his "child," as the Greek term *pais* may be trans-lated). And by "breaking bread" together, his people celebrate the way God has brought together people who once were scat-tered, and has joined them as one:

> As this broken bread was scattered upon the mountains but was brought together and became one loaf, so let your people be gathered together from the ends of the earth into thy kingdom.[31]

Those speaking this prayer in unison ended by calling—in an ancient Aramaic phrase some Christians invoke to this day—for the imminent coming of the Lord: "Let grace come, and let this world pass away. . . . *Maran atha!* [Our Lord, come!] Amen."[32] According to Draper's analysis, these are Jews who revere Jesus as "God's servant" and believe that his coming signals Israel's restoration at the end of time.

But other early followers of Jesus, like the majority ever since, saw the sacred meal in a much stranger—even macabre—way: as eating human flesh and drinking human blood. Only twenty years after Jesus' death, Paul declared that Jesus himself commanded his followers to do this. Paul, like the gospels of Mark, Matthew, and Luke, tells how, on the night Jesus was betrayed,

> while [the disciples] were eating, [Jesus] took bread, and after blessing it he broke it, gave it to them, and said, "Take: this is my body." Then he took a cup, and after giving thanks he gave it to them, and all of them drank from it, and he said to them, "This is my blood."[33]

Tertullian satirizes the reaction of outsiders to this practice: "We are accused of observing a sacred ritual in which we kill a little child and eat it."[34] He writes,

> No doubt [the Christian] would say, "You must get a child still very young, who does not know what it means to die, and can smile under your knife; and bread to collect the gushing blood. . . . Come, plunge your knife into the infant. . . . Or, if that is someone else's job, simply stand before a human being dying before it has really lived. . . . Take the fresh young blood, saturate your bread with it, and eat freely."[35]

Despite his sarcasm, Tertullian cannot dispel the shocking fact that the Christian "mystery" invites initiates to eat human flesh—even if only symbolically. Pagans might be repelled by the practice of instructing newcomers to drink wine as human blood, but devout Jews, whose very definition of *kosher* (pure) food requires that it be drained of all blood, would be especially disgusted.[36]

But, in their own time, many Jews and Gentiles might have recognized the eucharist as typical of ancient cult worship. Justin Martyr the philosopher worried that pagans would dismiss these rituals with contempt and charge that Christians were simply copying what worshipers in the so-called mystery religions did every day in their exotic cults. Justin admits that the priests who presided over the various temples of "devils"—the gods of Greece, Rome, Egypt, and Asia Minor—often asked their initiates to perform "washings" like baptism, and that priests of the Persian sun god Mithras and the Greek Dionysus "command[ed] the same things to be done" as Jesus allegedly did—even "eating the flesh and drinking the blood" of their god in their sacred meals.[37] But Justin insists that these supposed similarities are actually *imitations* of Christian worship inspired by demons who hope to "deceive and seduce the human race"[38] into thinking that the Christian cult is no different from the mystery cults. Justin might have worried more had he foreseen that, from the fourth century on, Christians would celebrate a new festival—the birthday of Jesus—on December 25, the birthday of the sun god Mithras, around the time of the winter solstice, when the waning sun is reborn as the days grow longer.

Yet the followers of Jesus invoked the mystery cults less than

Jewish tradition as they struggled with a practical—and painful—problem. If Jesus was God's messiah, why did he die such a hideous death? This question troubled Paul himself, who, like many others, wrestled to reconcile the crucifixion with his belief in Jesus' divine mission. In the decades after his death, some followers of Jesus in Jerusalem invoked religious tradition to suggest that, just as animal sacrifices were offered in the Temple, so Jesus had died as a sacrificial offering. And just as those who brought goats, sheep, or bulls to sacrifice afterward feasted on the slain carcasses, so, some suggested, those who benefit from this *human* sacrifice might appropriate its benefits by symbolically "eating" the sacrificial victim. By placing the drama of Jesus' death at the center of their sacred meal, his followers transformed what others would see as total catastrophe—what Paul calls "scandal"[39]—into religious paradox: in the depths of human defeat they claimed to find the victory of God.[40]

Seen this way, Jesus' capture, torture, and death were not, they insisted, simply disastrous. These events had not devastated their hopes, as someone might think who heard what happened from the disciple who concluded ruefully that "we had hoped that he was the one to deliver Israel."[41] Mark insists that Jesus was not captured because his followers lacked the strength to fight for him, after one of them fought with his sword and wounded a member of the arresting party but was routed and fled like the rest. Rather, Mark says, Jesus moved deliberately toward his dreadful death because he recognized that it was somehow "necessary"[42]—but necessary for what?

Mark repeats what some of Jesus' followers in Jerusalem had begun to say—that Jesus foresaw his own death, and voluntarily offered himself as a sacrifice. Giving his disciples bread, he

told them to "take, eat; this is my body."[43] Mark says that after
he had given his disciples wine to drink, he told them, "This is
my blood . . . poured out for many."[44] Matthew invokes the
theme of sacrificial atonement, adding to Mark's account that
Jesus' blood is "poured out for many, *for the forgiveness of sins.*"[45]
Mark and Paul include as well, in different ways, the image of
sacrificial blood ratifying a covenant. Mark looks back to the
covenant of Moses, recalling how Moses threw the blood of sacrificial oxen upon the people, saying, "Behold, the *blood of the
covenant* which the Lord has made with you."[46] So now, Mark
suggests, Jesus anticipates shedding what he calls *"my blood of the
covenant."*[47] But Paul, instead of looking back to the Mosaic covenant, looks forward to the *new*—and better—covenant prophesied by Jeremiah:

> Behold, the days are coming, says the Lord, when I will
> make a *new covenant* with the house of Israel. . . . *Not like the
> covenant which I made with their fathers.* . . . I will put my law
> within them, and I will write it upon their hearts; and I
> will be their God, and they shall be my people . . . and
> they shall all know me . . . and I will remember their sin
> no more.[48]

Thus Paul depicts Jesus offering wine to his disciples with the
words "This cup is the new covenant in my blood."[49]

We do not know for sure whether Jesus actually said these
words. Some historians believe that he must have said something like them; others believe that as his followers struggled to
come to terms with what had happened, and began to reenact
Jesus' "last supper," they formulated these enormously powerful

words. In any case, Jewish tradition suggested a wealth of associations with sacrifice that Paul, Mark, Matthew, and Luke incorporated into various versions of the story.[50] In the process, as we have seen, the sacred meal took on not a single meaning but clusters of meanings that became increasingly rich and complex. Justin tells us what second-century Christians actually did, in various groups he visited as he traveled from Asia Minor to Rome (c. 150 C.E.):

> All those who live in the city or the country gather together in one place on the day of the sun, and the memoirs of the apostles or the writings of the prophets are read. . . . Then we all rise together and pray, and then . . . bread and wine and water are brought[51]

to be shared as Jesus commanded. Christians to this day, including those who do not center their worship on communion, know that how they interpret Jesus' death—whether as sacrifice, and what kind of sacrifice—has much to do with how they understand their faith.

Seen as sacrifice, the meal could suggest not only forgiveness and a new relationship with God but also, like Passover, divine deliverance. Thus Paul recalls how the Passover lamb was slaughtered before the feast and invites his hearers to "the Lord's supper," proclaiming that "Christ, our Passover [lamb], has been sacrificed for us; therefore, let us celebrate the feast."[52] Mark actually writes the Passover feast into the narrative, declaring that Jesus' last supper with his disciples *was* a Passover feast—one that Jesus had carefully, even miraculously, directed his disci-

ples to prepare.[53] Luke and Matthew each expand Mark's version of the story, Luke adding that after the disciples

> prepared the Passover, when the time came, he sat at table,
> and his apostles with him, and he said to them, *"With
> [great] desire I have desired to eat this Passover with you* before I
> suffer; for I tell you, no longer shall I eat it until it is ful-
> filled in the kingdom of God."[54]

According to Luke and Paul, Jesus not only blessed the bread
and wine but also told his followers to "do this in remembrance
of me."[55] Thus they imply that, just as Passover recalls how God
delivered Israel through Moses, so those who celebrate *this*
Passover are to recall simultaneously how God is now deliver-
ing his people through Jesus.

The author of the Gospel of John gives a *different* chronology
for Jesus' last days, though John, as much as—or even more
than—Paul and Luke, nevertheless intends to connect Jesus'
death with Passover. However, John writes that *"before* the feast
of Passover"[56] Jesus shared a meal with his disciples for the last
time, a meal that obviously could not have celebrated Passover.
John says that, at that final meal, Jesus washed his disciples'
feet—an act which millions of Christians, from Roman Catholic
and Orthodox to Baptist or Mormon—have turned into *another*
sacrament. But John does *not* tell the story of the last supper
that, from the accounts of Paul, Mark, Luke, and Matthew, has
shaped Christian worship ever since. Instead, John says that
Jesus was arrested on the *previous* night—Thursday—and brought
to trial the following morning.

Because John believed that Jesus *became* the Passover lamb, he says that at "about noon, on the day of preparing the Passover"[57]—Friday, the time prescribed for preparing the Passover lamb—Jesus was sentenced to death, tortured, and crucified. Every detail of John's version of Jesus' death dramatizes his conviction that Jesus himself *became* the sacrificial lamb.[58] Thus, to show that Jesus, like the sacrificial Passover lamb, actually died before sunset on the evening of the first day of Passover, John says that a Roman soldier thrust a spear into Jesus' side to make sure that he was dead. At that moment, John says, "out of his side came blood and water,"[59] a physiological observation which also shows how Jesus' sacrifice provides the wine mixed with water that his followers would ritually drink as "his blood."[60] John adds that when the soldiers saw that Jesus was dead, they refrained from breaking his legs, and then he quotes from Exodus that, when preparing the Passover lamb, "you shall not break a bone of [it]."[61] For John, these instructions have become prophecies; thus, he declares, "not a single bone of [Jesus'] body was broken."[62]

Although John omits the story of the last supper itself, he does say that Jesus told his followers to eat his flesh and drink his blood—a suggestion that, he says, offended "the Jews," including many of Jesus' own disciples:

> Jesus said, "I am the living bread which comes down from heaven . . . whoever eats of this bread will live forever; and the bread which I shall give for the life of the world is my flesh."
>
> The Jews then disputed among themselves, saying, "How can this man give us his flesh to eat?"

So Jesus said to them, "Truly, truly I say to you, unless you eat the flesh of the Son of Man and drink his blood, you have no life in you. . . . For my flesh is truly food, and my blood is truly drink."

Many of his disciples, when they heard it, said, "This is a hard saying; who can listen to it?"[63]

Yet despite the weirdness of such images—and perhaps because of it—every version of this last supper in the New Testament, whether by Paul, Mark, Matthew, or Luke, interprets it as a kind of death-feast, but one that looks forward in hope. So Paul declares that "whenever you eat this bread and drink the cup, *you proclaim the Lord's death, until he comes.*"[64]

Many Christians *preferred* these powerful images, apparently, to the more innocuous interpretation found, for example, in Didache; for later generations chose to include in the New Testament the versions of the story that tell of eating flesh and drinking blood, dying and coming back to life. Yet during the centuries in which crucifixion remained an immediate and hideous threat, Jesus' followers did not paint a cross—much less a crucifix—on the walls of the catacombs in Rome as a symbol of hope. Instead, they depicted Jesus as one who, delivered from destruction, now delivers others: like Daniel freed from the lions' den, Jonah released from the belly of the whale, or Lazarus, his shroud unwinding, walking out of his grave. The Apocalypse of Peter, one of the so-called gnostic gospels discovered at Nag Hammadi in Upper Egypt in 1945, goes further, depicting Jesus "glad and laughing on the cross,"[65] a radiant being of light; and, as we shall see, the Acts of John, another "heretical" source, depicts Jesus celebrating the eucharist by leading his disciples as they chant and dance together a mystical hymn, the "Round Dance of the Cross."[66]

Within decades of his death, then, the story of Jesus became for his followers what the Exodus story had become for many generations of Jews: not simply a narrative of past events but a story through which they could interpret their own struggles, their victories, their sufferings, and their hopes. As Jesus and his disciples had traditionally gathered every year to act out the Exodus story at Passover, so his followers, after his death, gathered at Easter to act out the crucial moments of Jesus' story. As Mark tells the story of Jesus, then, he simultaneously offers the script, so to speak, for the drama that his followers are to live out. For just as Mark opens his gospel by telling of Jesus' baptism, so, as we have seen, every newcomer's experience would begin as each is baptized, plunged into water to be "born again" into God's family. And as Mark's account concludes with what happened on "the night Jesus was betrayed," so those who were baptized would gather every week to act out, in their sacred meal, what he said and did that night.

This correspondence helps account, no doubt, for the fact that Mark's gospel—the simplest version of the story later amplified by Matthew and Luke—became the basis for the New Testament gospel canon. Just as Exodus serves as the story line for the Passover ritual, so the story Mark tells came to serve as the story line for the Christian rituals of baptism and the sacred meal.[67] Receiving baptism and gathering every week—or even every day—to share the "Lord's supper," those who participate weave the story of Jesus' life, death, and resurrection into their own lives.[68]

This, then, is what I dimly recognized as I stood in the doorway of the Church of the Heavenly Rest. The drama being played out there "spoke to my condition," as it has to that of millions of people throughout the ages, because it simultaneously acknowledges the reality of fear, grief, and death while—paradoxically—nurturing hope. Four years later, when our son, then six years old, suddenly died, the Church of the Heavenly Rest offered some shelter, along with words and music, when family and friends gathered to bridge an abyss that had seemed impassable.

Such gatherings can also communicate joy—celebrating birth, marriage, or simply, as Paul said, "communion";[69] such worship refracts a spectrum of meaning as varied as the experience of those who participate. Those repenting acts of violence they have done, for example, might find hope for release and forgiveness, while those who have suffered harm might take comfort in the conviction that their sufferings are known to—even shared by—God. Perhaps most often believers experience the shared meal as "communion" with one another and with God; thus when Paul speaks of the "body of Christ," he often means the collective "body" of believers—the union of all who, he says, were "baptized into *one body*, Jews or Greeks, slaves and free, and all were made to drink from one spirit."[70]

Yet, since the fourth century, most churches have required those who would join such communion to profess a complex set of beliefs about God and Jesus—beliefs formulated by fourth-century bishops into the ancient Christian creeds. Some, of course, have no difficulty doing so. Many others, myself included, have had to reflect on what the creeds mean, as well as on what we believe (what does it mean to say that Jesus is the "only Son of God, eternally begotten of the Father," or that "we believe in one holy catholic and apostolic Church"?). Anyone with an ear for poetry can hear this creed as a sonorous tone poem in praise of God and Jesus. Certainly, as a historian, I can recognize how these creeds came to be part of tradition, and can appreciate how Constantine, the first Christian emperor, became convinced that making—and enforcing—such creeds helped to unify and standardize rival groups and leaders during the turmoil of the fourth century. Yet how do such demands for belief look today, in light of what we now know about the origins of the Christian movement?

As we have seen, for nearly three hundred years before these creeds were written, diverse Christian groups had welcomed newcomers in various ways. Groups represented by the Didache required those who would join them to embrace the "way of life" taught by Moses and by Jesus, "God's child." Justin Martyr the philosopher, now regarded as one of the "fathers of the church," cared about belief, of course—above all, that the pagan gods were false, and that one should acknowledge only the one true God, along with "Jesus Christ, his son"—but what mattered most was to share—and practice—the values of "God's people." So, Justin says, "we baptize those" who not only accept Jesus' teaching but *undertake to be able to live accordingly.*[71] What sustained many Christians, even more than belief, were stories—above all, shared stories of Jesus' birth and baptism, and his teachings, his death, and his resurrection. Furthermore, the astonishing discovery of the gnostic gospels—a cache of ancient secret gospels and other revelations attributed to Jesus and his disciples—has revealed a much wider range of Christian groups than we had ever known before.[72] Although later denounced by certain leaders as "heretics," many of these Christians saw themselves as not so much *believers* as *seekers,* people who "seek for God."

The Church of the Heavenly Rest helped me to realize much that I love about religious tradition, and Christianity in particular—including how powerfully these may affect us, and perhaps even transform us. At the same time, I was also exploring in my academic work the history of Christianity in the light of the Nag Hammadi discoveries, and this research helped clarify what I cannot love: the tendency to identify Christianity with a single, authorized set of beliefs—however these actually vary from church to church—coupled with the conviction that Christian belief alone offers access to God.

Now that scholars have begun to place the sources discovered at Nag Hammadi, like newly discovered pieces of a complex puzzle, next to what we have long known from tradition, we find that these remarkable texts, only now becoming widely known, are transforming what we know as Christianity.[73] As we shall see in the following chapters, we are now beginning to understand these "gospels" much better than we did when I first wrote about them twenty years ago. Let us start by taking a fresh look at the most familiar of all Christian sources—the gospels of the New Testament—in the perspective offered by one of the *other* Christian gospels composed in the first century and discovered at Nag Hammadi, the Gospel of Thomas. As we shall soon see, those who later enshrined the Gospel of John within the New Testament and denounced Thomas's gospel as "heresy" decisively shaped—and inevitably limited—what would become Western Christianity.

CHAPTER TWO

tototot

GOSPELS IN CONFLICT:
JOHN AND THOMAS

I have always read the Gospel of John with fascination, and
often with devotion. When I was fourteen, and had joined an
evangelical Christian church, I found in the enthusiastic and
committed gatherings and in John's gospel, which my fellow
Christians treasured, what I then craved—the assurance of belonging to the right group, the true "flock" that alone belonged
to God. Like many people, I regarded John as the most spiritual
of the four gospels, for in John, Jesus is not only a man but a
mysterious, superhuman presence, and he tells his disciples to
"love one another."[1] At the time, I did not dwell on disturbing
undercurrents—that John alternates his assurance of God's gracious love for those who "believe" with warnings that everyone
who "does not believe is condemned already"[2] to eternal death.
Nor did I reflect on those scenes in which John says that Jesus

spoke of his own people ("the Jews") as if they were alien to him and the devil's offspring.[3]

Before long, however, I learned what inclusion cost: the leaders of the church I attended directed their charges not to associate with outsiders, except to convert them. Then, after a close friend was killed in an automobile accident at the age of sixteen, my fellow evangelicals commiserated but declared that, since he was Jewish and not "born again," he was eternally damned. Distressed and disagreeing with their interpretation—and finding no room for discussion—I realized that I was no longer at home in their world and left that church. When I entered college, I decided to learn Greek in order to read the New Testament in its original language, hoping to discover the source of its power. Reading these terse, stark stories in Greek, I experienced the gospels in a new way, often turning the page to see what happened next, as if I had never read them before. Reading Greek also introduced me firsthand to the poems of Homer, the plays of Sophocles and Aeschylus, Pindar's hymns, and Sappho's invocations; and I began to see that many of these "pagan" writings are also religious literature, but of a different religious sensibility.

After college I studied dance at the Martha Graham School in New York. I loved dance but still wondered what it was about Christianity that I had found so compelling and at the same time so frustrating. I decided to look for the "real Christianity"—believing, as Christians traditionally have, that I might find it by immersing myself in the earliest Christian sources, composed soon after Jesus and his disciples had wandered in Galilee. When I entered the Harvard doctoral program, I was astonished to hear from the other students that Professors Helmut Koester and George MacRae, who taught the early history of Christianity, had file cabinets filled with "gospels" and "apocrypha" written during the first centuries, many of them secret writings of which I'd never heard. These writings, containing sayings, rituals, and dialogues attributed to Jesus and his disciples, were found in 1945 among a cache of texts from the beginning of the Christian era, unearthed near Nag Hammadi in Upper Egypt.[4] When my fellow students and I investigated these sources, we found that they revealed diversity within the Christian movement that later, "official" versions of Christian history had suppressed so effectively that only now, in the Harvard graduate school, did we hear about them. So we asked who wrote these alternative gospels, and when. And how do these relate to—and differ from—the gospels and other writings familiar from the New Testament?

These discoveries challenged us not only intellectually but—in my case at least—spiritually. I had come to respect the work of "church fathers" such as Irenaeus, bishop of Lyons (c. 180), who had denounced such secret writings as "an abyss of madness, and blasphemy against Christ."[5] Therefore I expected these recently discovered texts to be garbled, pretentious, and trivial. Instead I was surprised to find in some of them unexpected spiritual power—in sayings such as this from the Gospel of Thomas, translated by Professor MacRae: "Jesus said: 'If you bring forth what is within you, what you bring forth will save you. If you do not bring forth what is within you, what you do not bring forth will destroy you.' "[6] The strength of this saying is that it does not tell us what to believe but challenges us to discover what lies hidden within ourselves; and, with a shock of recognition, I realized that this perspective seemed to me self-evidently true.

In 1979 I published *The Gnostic Gospels*, a preliminary exploration of the impact of the Nag Hammadi discoveries. Now,
about twenty years later, many scholars say that these texts may
not be "gnostic"—since many of us are asking what that perplexing term means. Insofar as *gnostic* refers to one who "knows,"
that is, who seeks experiential insight, it may characterize many
of these sources accurately enough; but more often the "church
fathers" used the term derisively to refer to those they dismissed
as people claiming to "know it all." One thoughtful scholar, Michael Williams, suggests that we should no longer use the term,
and another, Karen King, demonstrates its many connotations.[7]
Nevertheless, I intended that book to raise certain questions:
Why had the church decided that these texts were "heretical"
and that only the canonical gospels were "orthodox"? Who made
those decisions, and under what conditions? As my colleagues
and I looked for answers, I began to understand the political
concerns that shaped the early Christian movement.

Thanks to research undertaken since that time and shared by
many scholars throughout the world, what that book attempted to offer as a kind of rough, charcoal sketch of the history of Christianity now can be seen as if under an electron
microscope—yielding considerably more clarity, detail, and accuracy. What I focus on in this book is how certain Christian
leaders from the second century through the fourth came to reject many other sources of revelation and construct instead the
New Testament gospel canon of Matthew, Mark, Luke, and John
along with the "canon of truth," which became the nucleus of
the later creeds that have defined Christianity to this day.

As I worked with many other scholars to edit and annotate
these Nag Hammadi texts, we found that this research gradually

clarified—and complicated—our understanding of the origins of Christianity. For instead of discovering the purer, simpler "early Christianity" that many of us had been looking for, we found ourselves in the midst of a more diverse and complicated world than any of us could have imagined. For example, many scholars are now convinced that the New Testament Gospel of John, probably written at the end of the first century, emerged from an intense debate over who Jesus was—or is.[8] To my surprise, having spent many months comparing the Gospel of John with the Gospel of Thomas, which may have been written at about the same time, I have now come to see that John's gospel was written in the heat of controversy, to defend certain views of Jesus and to oppose others.

This research has helped clarify not only what John's gospel is *for* but what it is *against.* John says explicitly that he writes "so that you may *believe, and believing, may have life* in [Jesus'] name."[9] What John opposed, as we shall see, includes what the Gospel of Thomas teaches—that God's light shines not only in Jesus but, potentially at least, in everyone. Thomas's gospel encourages the hearer not so much to *believe in Jesus,* as John requires, as to *seek to know God* through one's own, divinely given capacity, since all are created in the image of God. For Christians in later generations, the Gospel of John helped provide a foundation for a unified church, which Thomas, with its emphasis on each person's search for God, did not.

I have also learned after years of study that, although John's gospel is written with great simplicity and power, its meaning is by no means obvious. Even its first generation of readers (c. 90 to 130 C.E.) disagreed about whether John was a true gospel or a false one—and whether it should be part of the New Testament.[10] John's defenders among early Christians revered it as the "*logos* gospel"—the gospel of the divine word or reason (*logos*, in Greek)—and derided those who opposed it as "irrational" (*alogos*, lacking reason). Its detractors, by contrast, were quick to point out that John's narrative differs significantly from those of Matthew, Mark, and Luke. As I compared John with these other gospels, I saw that at certain points this is true, and that some of these differences are much more than variations on a theme.

At crucial moments in its account, for example, John's gospel directly contradicts the combined testimony of the other New Testament gospels. We have seen already that John differs in its version of Jesus' final days; moreover, while Mark, Matthew, and Luke agree that disrupting merchants doing business in the Temple was Jesus' *last* public act, John makes it his *first* act. The three other gospels all say that what finally drove the chief priest and his allies to arrest Jesus was this attack on the money changers, when Jesus in Jerusalem

> entered the temple and began to drive out those who were selling and those who were buying in the temple, and he overturned the tables of the moneychangers and the seats of those who sold doves, and he would not allow anyone to carry anything through the temple.[11]

Mark says of this shocking incident that "when the chief priests and scribes heard of it, they kept looking for a way to kill him,"[12] and Matthew and Luke agree with Mark that the temple authorities had Jesus arrested shortly afterward.

But John places this climactic act at the *beginning* of his story, to suggest that Jesus' whole mission was to purify and transform the worship of God. John also increases the violence of the scene by adding that Jesus "knotted a whip out of small cords" and "drove them all out of the Temple."[13] Unlike the other gospel writers, John mentions no immediate repercussions for this act, probably because, had Jesus been arrested at this point, he would have had no story to tell. To account for Jesus' arrest, John inserts at the end of his narrative a startling story that occurs in none of the other gospels: how Jesus raised his friend Lazarus from the dead, which so alarmed the Jewish authorities that they determined to kill Jesus, and, he adds, the chief priests even "planned to put Lazarus to death as well."[14]

John intends his story of the raising of Lazarus, like his version of the "cleansing of the Temple," to point to deeper meanings. As John tells it, the chief priests had Jesus arrested not because they regarded him as a troublemaker who caused a disturbance in the Temple but because they secretly recognized and feared his power—power that could even raise the dead. John pictures Caiaphas, the high priest, arguing before the Jewish council that "if we let him go on like this, *everyone will believe in him*, and the Romans will come and destroy our holy place and our nation."[15] According to John, such opposition was by no means a matter of the past; even in his own time, about sixty years after Jesus' death, those who opposed Jesus and his followers still feared that "everyone will believe in him." Thus, while John diverges from the other gospels in what he says and how he says it, the brilliant Egyptian teacher named Origen, who lived in the early third century and became one of John's earliest defenders, argues that "although he does not always tell the truth *literally*, he always tells the truth *spiritually*."[16] Origen writes that John's author had constructed a deceptively simple narrative, which, like fine architecture, bears enormous weight.

John's gospel differs from Matthew, Mark, and Luke in a second—and far more significant—way, for John suggests that Jesus is not merely God's human servant but God himself revealed in human form. John says that "the Jews" sought to kill Jesus, accusing him of "making yourself God."[17] But John believed that Jesus actually *is* God in human form; thus he tells how the disciple Thomas finally recognized Jesus when he encountered him risen from the dead and exclaimed, "My Lord and my God!"[18] In one of the earliest commentaries on John (c. 240 C.E.), Origen makes a point of saying that, while the other gospels describe Jesus as *human*, "none of them clearly spoke of his *divinity*, as John does."[19]

But don't the other gospels also say that Jesus is God? Don't Matthew and Mark, for example, call Jesus "son of God," and doesn't this mean that Jesus is virtually—almost *genetically*—the same as God? Like most people who grow up familiar with Christian tradition, I assumed that all the gospels say the same thing or, at most, offer variations on a single theme. Because Matthew, Mark, and Luke share a similar perspective, scholars call these gospels synoptic (literally, "seeing together"). Only in graduate school, when I investigated each gospel, so far as possible, in its historical context, did I see how radical is John's claim that Jesus is God manifest in human form.

Although Mark and the other evangelists use titles that Christians today often take as indicating Jesus' divinity, such as "son of

God" and "messiah," in Mark's own time these titles designated *human* roles.[20] The Christians who translated these titles into English fifteen centuries later believed they showed that Jesus was uniquely related to God, and so they capitalized them—a linguistic convention that does not occur in Greek. But Mark's contemporaries would most likely have seen Jesus as a *man*—although one gifted, as Mark says, with the power of the holy spirit, and divinely appointed to rule in the coming kingdom of God.

Yet as we shall see, after the gospels of Mark, Matthew, and Luke were joined with John's gospel and Paul's letters to become the "New Testament"—a process that took place over some two hundred years (c. 160 to 360 C.E.)—most Christians came to read these earlier gospels through John's lens, and thus to find in all of them evidence of John's conviction that Jesus is "Lord and God."[21] The gospels discovered in 1945 in Upper Egypt, however, offer different perspectives. For if Matthew, Mark, and Luke had been joined with the Gospel of Thomas instead of with John, for example, or had *both* John and Thomas been included in the New Testament canon, Christians probably would have read the first three gospels quite differently. The gospels of Thomas and John speak for different groups of Jesus' followers engaged in discussion, even argument, toward the end of the first century. What they debated is this: Who is Jesus, and what is the "good news" (in Greek *euangellion*, "gospel") about him?

The Gospel of Thomas contains teaching venerated by "Thomas Christians," apparently an early group that, like those devoted to Luke, Matthew, and John, thrived during the first century. What astonished scholars when they first read Thomas, in the 1940s, was that, although it contains many sayings of Jesus that Luke and Matthew also include in their gospels, it contains *other* sayings that apparently derive from a tradition different from that of the synoptic gospels.[22] Although we do not know where the Gospel of Thomas was written, many scholars, noting names associated with Syria, think that it originated there. The Acts of Thomas (c. 200 C.E.), probably written in Syriac, claims that Thomas himself evangelized India,[23] and to this day there are Thomas Christians in India who call Thomas the founder of their faith. Although Mark, Matthew, and Luke mention him among "the twelve" apostles, Thomas is not a proper name but means "twin" in Aramaic, the language that Jesus would have spoken. As Professor Helmut Koester shows, although this disciple was called by his Aramaic nickname, the gospel itself explains that his given name was Judas (but, his admirers specify, "not Iscariot"). Since this disciple was known by the name of Thomas, both the Gospel of Thomas and the Gospel of John also translate Thomas into Greek, explaining to their Greek readers that this disciple is "the one called 'Didymus,'" the Greek term for "twin."[24]

As we shall see, John probably knew what the Gospel of Thomas taught—if not its actual text. Many of the teachings in the Gospel of John that differ from those in Matthew and Luke sound much like sayings in the Gospel of Thomas: in fact, what first impressed scholars who compared these two gospels is how similar they are. Both John and Thomas, for example, apparently assume that the reader already knows the basic story Mark and the others tell, and each claims to go beyond that story and reveal what Jesus taught his disciples in private. When, for example, John tells what happened on the night that Judas betrayed Jesus, he inserts into his account nearly *five chapters* of teaching unique to his gospel—the so-called farewell discourses of John 13 through 18, which consist of intimate dialogue between the disciples and Jesus, as well as a great deal of monologue. Similarly, the Gospel of Thomas, as we noted, claims to offer "secret sayings, which the living Jesus spoke," and adds that "Didymus Judas Thomas wrote them down."[25]

John and Thomas give similar accounts of what Jesus taught privately. Unlike Matthew, Mark, and Luke, who say that Jesus warned of the coming "end of time," both John and Thomas say that he directed his disciples instead toward the beginning of time—to the creation account of Genesis 1—and identify Jesus with the divine light that came into being "in the beginning."[26] Thomas and John both say that this primordial light connects Jesus with the entire universe, since, as John says, "all things were made through the word [logos; or, the light]."[27] Professor Koester has noted such similarities in detail, and concludes that these two authors drew upon common sources.[28] While Mark, Matthew, and Luke identify Jesus as God's human agent, John and Thomas characterize him instead as God's own light in human form.

Yet, despite these similarities, the authors of John and Thomas take Jesus' private teaching in sharply different directions. For John, identifying Jesus with the light that came into being "in the beginning" is what makes him unique—God's "only begotten son." John calls him the "light of all humanity,"[29] and believes that Jesus alone brings divine light to a world otherwise sunk into darkness. John says that we can experience God only through the divine light embodied in Jesus. But certain passages in Thomas's gospel draw a quite different conclusion: that the divine light Jesus embodied is shared by humanity, since we are all made "in the image of God."[30] Thus Thomas expresses what would become a central theme of Jewish—and later Christian—mysticism a thousand years later: that the "image of God" is hidden within everyone, although most people remain unaware of its presence.

What might have been complementary interpretations of God's presence on earth became, instead, rival ones; for by claiming that Jesus alone embodies the divine light, John challenges Thomas's claim that this light may be present in everyone. John's views, of course, prevailed, and have shaped Christian thought ever since. For after John's teaching was collected along with three other gospels into the New Testament, his view of Jesus came to dominate and even to define what we *mean* by Christian teaching. Some Christians who championed the "fourfold gospel"[31]—Matthew, Mark, Luke, and John—of the New Testament denounced the kind of teaching found in the Gospel of Thomas (along with many other writings that they called "secret and illegitimate")[32] and called upon believers to cast out such teaching as *heresy*. How this happened, and what it means for the history of Christian tradition, is what this work will explore.

To appreciate the tremendous leap that John—and Thomas—took, let us recall how the gospels of Mark, Matthew, and Luke characterize Jesus. The earliest of these gospels, Mark, written about forty years after Jesus' death (c. 70 C.E.), presents, as its central mystery, the question of who Jesus is. Mark tells how Jesus' disciples discussed—and discovered—the secret of his identity:

And Jesus went on with his disciples to the villages of Caesarea Philippi; and on the way he asked his disciples,

"Who do people say that I am?" And they told him, "John the Baptist; and others say, Elijah; and others, one of the prophets." And he asked them, "But who do you say that I am?" Peter answered him, "You are the messiah."[33]

Then Mark immediately shows how Peter, although rightly seeing Jesus as God's *messiah*, literally "anointed one"—the man designated to be Israel's future king—does not understand what is going to happen. When Jesus explains that he must suffer and die, Peter protests in shock, since he expects God's "anointed one" not to die but to be crowned and enthroned in Jerusalem.

At the desolate scene of the crucifixion, Mark tells how Jesus cried out that God had abandoned him, uttered a final, inarticulate cry, and died; yet a Roman centurion who watched him die declared, "Truly, this man was a son of God."[34] Although to a non-Jew like the centurion, "son of God" might have indicated a divine being, Jesus' earliest followers, like Mark, were Jewish and understood that "son of God," like "messiah," designated Israel's human king. During Israel's ancient coronation ceremonies, the future king was anointed with oil to show God's favor while a chorus singing one of the ceremonial psalms proclaimed that when the king is crowned he becomes God's representative, his human "son."[35] Thus when Mark opens his gospel saying that "this is the gospel of Jesus, the *messiah*, the *son of God*,"[36] he is announcing that God has chosen Jesus to be the future king of Israel. Since Mark writes in Greek, he translates the Hebrew term *messiah* as *christos* ("anointed one" in Greek), which later becomes, in English, "Jesus [the] christ."

In Mark, Jesus also characterizes himself as "son of man," the meaning of which is ambiguous. Often in the Hebrew Bible, "son of man" means nothing more than "human being" (in Hebrew, *ben adam* means "son of Adam"). The prophet Ezekiel, for example, says that the Lord repeatedly addressed him as "son of man," often translated "mortal";[37] thus when Mark's Jesus calls himself "son of man," he too may simply mean "human being." Yet Mark's contemporaries who were familiar with the Hebrew Bible may also have recognized "son of man" as referring to the mysterious person whom the prophet Daniel saw in a vision appearing before God's throne to be invested with power:

> I saw in the night visions, and behold, coming with the clouds of heaven was one like a *son of man*, and he came to the Ancient of Days and was presented before him. And to him was given dominion and glory, and kingdom, so that all peoples, nations, and languages should serve him . . . an everlasting dominion, which shall not pass away.[38]

Mark says that when the high priest interrogated Jesus at his trial, and asked, "Are you the messiah, the son of God?" Jesus answered, "I am; and you will see the son of man . . . 'coming with the clouds of heaven.' "[39] According to Mark, then, Jesus not only claimed the royal titles of Israel's king ("messiah," "son of God") but actually quoted Daniel's vision to suggest that he—or perhaps someone else whose coming he foresaw—was the "son of man" whom the prophet saw appearing before God's throne in heaven. Matthew and Luke follow Mark in describing Jesus both as a future king ("messiah," "son of God") and as a mortal invested with divine power ("son of man").

None of these titles, however, explains precisely who Jesus is. Instead, the gospel writers invoke a cluster of traditional terms to express their radical conviction that Jesus of Nazareth was a man raised to unique—even supernatural—status. Luke suggests, however, that it was only after Jesus' death that God, in an unprecedented act of favor, restored him to life, and thus *promoted* Jesus, so to speak, not only to "messiah" but also to "Lord"—a name that Jewish tradition ordinarily reserves strictly for the divine Lord himself. According to Luke's account, written ten to twenty years after Mark's, Peter dares announce to the "men of Jerusalem" that Jesus alone, of the entire human race, returned alive after death, and that this proves that "God *has made him both Lord and messiah*—this Jesus whom you crucified."[40]

Yet John, who wrote about a decade after Luke, opens his gospel with a poem which suggests that Jesus is not human at all but the divine, eternal Word of God in human *form* ("in the beginning was the word, and the word was with God, and the word was God").[41] The author whom we call John probably knew that he was not the first—and certainly not the only— Christian to believe that Jesus was somehow divine. Some fifty years earlier, the apostle Paul, probably quoting an early hymn, had said of Jesus that

> although *he was in the form of God, he did not count equality with God as a thing to be grasped*, but emptied himself, *taking the form of a servant, being found in the likeness of a human being.*[42]

Unlike Luke, who depicts Jesus as a man raised to divine status, John, as does the hymn Paul quotes, pictures him instead as a divine being who descended to earth—temporarily—to take on human *form*. Elsewhere, Paul declares that it is the holy spirit who inspires those who believe that "Jesus is Lord!"[43] Sixty years later, one of Paul's admirers, the Syrian bishop Ignatius of Antioch, anticipating his impending martyrdom, wrote that he passionately longed to "imitate the suffering of my God"[44]—that is, of Jesus. So Pliny, the Roman governor of Bithynia in Asia Minor, probably was right when, after investigating suspicious persons in his province, he wrote to the emperor Trajan (c. 115) that these Christians "sing a hymn to Jesus as to a god"[45]—perhaps it was the same hymn that Paul knew.

This is why some historians, having compared the Gospel of Mark (written 68 to 70 C.E.) with the gospels of Matthew and Luke (c. 80 to 90), and then with that of John (c. 90 to 100), have thought that John's gospel represents a transition from a lower to a higher Christology—an increasingly elevated view of Jesus. These historians point out that such views developed from the first century on and culminated in phrases like those enshrined in the Nicene Creed, which proclaim Jesus to be "God from God, Light from Light, true God from true God."

Yet Christian teaching about Jesus does not follow a simple evolutionary pattern. Although John's formulations have virtually defined orthodox Christian doctrine for nearly two thousand years, they were not universally accepted in his own time. And while the claims of Jesus' divinity by Paul and John surpass those of Mark, Luke, and Matthew, Thomas's gospel, written perhaps around the same time as John's, takes similar language to mean something quite different. Because the Gospel of Thomas diverges from the more familiar pattern found in John, let us look at it first.

We should note that, although I am using here the traditional names, Thomas and John, and the traditional term *author,* no one knows who actually wrote either gospel. Some scholars have observed that whoever assembled the sayings that constitute the Gospel of Thomas may have been less an author than a compiler—or several compilers—who, rather than *composing* these sayings, simply *collected* traditional sayings and wrote them down.[46] In Thomas's gospel, then, as in John, Matthew, and Luke, we sometimes find sayings that seem to contradict each other. For example, both John and Thomas include some sayings suggesting that those who come to know God are very few—a chosen few. Such sayings echo traditional teaching about divine election, and teach that God chooses those who are able to know him;[47] while the cluster of sayings I take as the key to interpreting Thomas suggest instead that everyone, in creation, receives an innate capacity to know God. We know almost nothing about the person we call Thomas, except that, like the evangelists who wrote the gospels of the New Testament, he wrote in the name of a disciple, apparently intending to convey "the gospel" as this disciple taught it. As we noted, then, Thomas apparently assumes that his hearers are already familiar with Mark's story of how Peter discovered the secret of Jesus' identity, that "you are the messiah." When Matthew repeats this story, he adds that Jesus blessed Peter for the accuracy of his recognition: "Blessed are you, Simon Bar Jonas; it was not a human being who revealed this to you, but my Father in heaven."[48]

Thomas tells the same story differently. According to Thomas, when Jesus asks, "Who am I?" he receives not one but three responses from various disciples. Peter first gives, in effect, the same answer as he does in the gospels of Mark and Matthew: "You are like a *righteous messenger,*" a phrase that may interpret the Hebrew term *messiah* ("anointed one") for the Greek-speaking audience whom Thomas addresses. The disciple Matthew answers next: "You are like a *wise philosopher*"—a phrase perhaps intended to convey the Hebrew term *rabbi* ("teacher") in language any Gentile could understand. (This disciple is the one traditionally believed to have written the Gospel of Matthew, which, more than any other, depicts Jesus as a rabbi.) But when a third disciple, Thomas himself, answers Jesus' question, his response confounds the other two: "Master, my mouth is wholly incapable of saying whom you are like." Jesus replies, "I am not your master, because you have drunk, and have become drunk from the same stream which I measured out."[49] Jesus does not deny what Peter and Matthew have said but implies that their answers represent inferior levels of understanding. Then he takes Thomas aside and reveals to him alone three sayings so secret that they cannot be written down, even in this gospel filled with "secret sayings":

> Jesus took Thomas and withdrew, and told him three things. When Thomas returned to his companions, they asked him, "What did Jesus say to you?" Thomas said, "If I tell you even one of the things which he told me, you will pick up stones and throw them at me; and a fire will come out of the stones and burn you up."[50]

Though Thomas does not reveal here what these "secret words" are for which the others might stone him to death for blasphemy, he does imply that these secrets reveal more about Jesus and his message than *either* Peter or Matthew understands.

What then is the gospel—the "good news"—according to

Thomas, and how does it differ from what is told in the synoptic gospels of Mark, Matthew, and Luke? Mark opens his gospel when Jesus announces "the good news of the kingdom of God," and Mark tells how Jesus, baptized by John, sees "the heavens torn apart" and God's spirit descending upon him.[51] Immediately afterward, having been driven by God's spirit into the wilderness to contend against Satan, Jesus returns triumphantly to announce his first, urgent message: "The kingdom of God is coming near: repent, and believe in the gospel."[52] According to Mark, Jesus teaches that this kingdom will come during the lifetime of his disciples: "There are some of you standing here who will not taste death until you see the kingdom of God come in power!"[53] Later, in Jerusalem, where his disciples admire the gleaming walls of the great Temple, Jesus asks, "Do you see these great stones? Not one stone will be left here upon another; all will be torn down."[54]

Hearing Jesus announce the coming kingdom of God—an earth-shattering event that is about to transform the world—Peter, James, John, and Andrew ask privately when these things will happen. Jesus does not name the day but tells them the "signs of the times" that will signal its approach. He predicts that "wars and rumors of wars," earthquakes, and famine will initiate "the birth pangs of the messiah," and warns his followers to expect to be "beaten in synagogues," arraigned before "governors and kings," betrayed by family members, and "hated by all." Still worse: the great Temple in Jerusalem will be desecrated and ruined, floods of refugees will flee the city—"such suffering as has not been from the beginning of creation . . . until now, and no, never will be."[55] Still later, Mark says, Jesus predicted that "the sun will be darkened, and the moon will not give light; stars will fall from heaven" as people see in the sky supernatural events foreseen by the prophet Daniel, who told of the " 'Son of man coming in the clouds' with great power and glory."[56] Solemnly Jesus warns his disciples that "truly, I tell you, this generation will not pass away until all these things have taken place"; above all, he warns, "Keep awake."[57]

But according to both the Gospel of Thomas and the Gospel of John, Jesus reveals that the kingdom of God, which many believers, including Mark, expect in the future, not only is "coming" but is already here—an immediate and continuing spiritual reality. According to John, Jesus announces that the Day of Judgment, which the prophets call "the day of the Lord," "is coming, *and is now*,"[58] and adds that the "resurrection of the dead" also may happen now. For when Jesus consoles his friends Mary and Martha on the death of their brother Lazarus and asks whether they believe he will rise from the dead, Martha repeats the hope of the pious, saying, "I know that he will rise in the resurrection on the last day."[59] But in John, Jesus astonishes everyone as he immediately proceeds to raise Lazarus, four days dead, calling him forth alive from his grave. Thus the great transformation expected at the end of time can—and does—happen here and now.

According to the Gospel of Thomas, the "living Jesus" himself challenges those who mistake the kingdom of God for an otherworldly place or a future event:

> Jesus said, "If those who lead you say to you, 'Look, the kingdom is in the sky,' then the birds of the sky will get there before you. . . . If they say to you, 'It is in the sea,' then the fish will get there before you."[60]

Here Thomas's Jesus ridicules certain unnamed leaders—perhaps even Peter himself, or his disciple Mark; for it is in Mark that the troubled disciples ask Jesus what to look for as "signs of the end," and Jesus takes them seriously, warning of ominous events to come, and concludes by admonishing them to "watch."[61] But Thomas claims that Jesus spoke differently in secret:

His disciples said to him, "When will the resurrection of the dead come, and when will the new world come?" He said to them, "What you look forward to has already come, but you do not recognize it."[62]

When they ask again, "When will the kingdom come?" Thomas's Jesus says,

"It will not come by waiting for it. It will not be a matter of saying, 'Here it is,' or 'There it is.' Rather, the kingdom of the Father is spread out upon the earth, and people do not see it."[63]

The Gospel of Luke includes passages suggesting that other believers agree with Thomas that the kingdom of God is somehow present here and now; in fact, Luke offers an alternate version of the same saying:

Being asked by the Pharisees when the kingdom of God was coming, [Jesus] answered them, "The kingdom of God is not coming with signs that can be observed, nor will they say, 'Look, here it is!' or 'There it is!,' for the kingdom of God is within you."[64]

Some have taken the phrase "within you" to mean that the kingdom is among the disciples so long as Jesus is with them, while others take it to mean that the kingdom of God is embodied not only in Jesus but in everyone. The New Revised Standard Version of the Bible adopts the first sense—that Jesus alone embodies the kingdom of God. But a century ago, in a book called *The Kingdom of God Is Within You*, Leo Tolstoy urged Christians to give up coercion and violence in order to realize God's kingdom here and now. Thomas Merton, the twentieth-century writer and Trappist monk, agreed with Tolstoy but interpreted the kingdom of God mystically rather than practically.[65]

In certain passages, then, the Gospel of Thomas interprets the kingdom of God as Tolstoy and Merton would do nearly two thousand years later. The Gospel of Mary Magdalene, also discovered in Egypt, but in 1896, about fifty years before the Nag Hammadi find, echoes this theme: Jesus tells his disciples, "Let no one lead you astray, saying, 'Lo, here!' or 'Lo, there!' For the Son of Man is within you. Follow after him!"[66] Yet after including his version of this saying at one point in his gospel, Luke retreats from this position and concludes his account with the kind of apocalyptic warnings found in Mark: the Son of Man is not a divine presence in all of us but a terrifying judge who is coming to summon everyone to the day of wrath that, Luke's Jesus warns, may

> catch you unexpectedly, like a trap; for it will come upon all who live upon the face of the whole earth. Be alert at all times, and pray that you may have the strength to escape all these things that will happen, and to stand before the Son of Man.[67]

The Gospels of Thomas and John, however, speak for those who understand Jesus' message quite differently. Both say that, instead of warning his disciples about the *end of time*, Jesus points them toward the *beginning*. John opens with the famous prologue describing the beginning of the universe, when "the word was with God, and the word was God."[68] John is referring, of course, to the opening verses of Genesis: "in the beginning" there was a vast, formless void, darkness, and "the abyss," or deep water, and "a wind [or spirit] from God swept over the face of the waters."[69] Yet before there were sun, moon, or stars, there was, first of all, light: "And God said, 'Let there be light,' and there was light."[70] Thus John identifies Jesus not only with the *word* that God spoke but also with the divine *light* that it called into being—what he calls "the true light that enlightens everyone, coming into the world."[71]

Thomas's Jesus also challenges those who persist in asking him about the "end time": "Have you found the beginning, then, that you look to the end?" Here, too, he directs them to go back to the beginning, "for whoever takes his place in the beginning will know the end, and will not taste death"[72]—that is, will be restored to the luminous state of creation before the fall. Thomas, like John, identifies Jesus with the light that existed before the dawn of creation. According to Thomas, Jesus says that this primordial light not only brought the entire universe into being but still shines through everything we see and touch. For this primordial light is not simply impersonal energy but a being that speaks with a human voice—with *Jesus'* voice:

Jesus said, "I am the light which is before all things. It is I who am all things. From me all things came forth, and to me all things extend. Split a piece of wood, and I am there; lift up the stone, and you will find me."[73]

Yet, despite similarities between John's and Thomas's versions of Jesus' secret teaching, when we look more closely, we begin to see that John's understanding of Jesus' "way" is diametrically opposed to Thomas's on the practical and crucial question: How can we find that light? Let us look first at the Gospel of Thomas.

Thomas's gospel offers only cryptic clues—not answers—to those who seek the way to God. Thomas's "living Jesus" challenges his hearers to find the way for themselves: "Jesus said, 'Whoever finds the interpretation of these words will not taste death,' "[74] and he warns the disciples that the search will disturb and astonish them: "Jesus said, 'Let the one who seeks not stop seeking until he finds. When he finds, he will become troubled; when he becomes troubled, he will be astonished and will rule over all things."[75] Thus here again Jesus encourages those who seek by telling them that they already have the internal resources they need to find what they are looking for: "Jesus said, 'If you bring forth what is within you, what you bring forth will save you. If you do not bring forth what is within you, what you do not bring forth will destroy you.' "[76]

Yet the "disciples [still] questioned him," Thomas writes, "saying, 'Do you want us to fast? How should we pray? Should we give alms? What diet should we observe?' "[77] In Matthew and Luke, Jesus responds to such questions with practical, straightforward answers. For example, he instructs them that "when you give alms, do not let your left hand know what your right hand is doing, so that your alms may be done in secret."[78] When you fast, "put oil on your head, and wash your face."[79] And "when you pray, pray like this, [saying], 'Our Father, who art in heaven. . . .' "[80] In Thomas, Jesus gives no such instructions. Instead, when his disciples ask him what to do—how to pray, what to eat, whether to fast or give money, he answers only with another *koan*: "Do not tell lies, and do not do what you hate; for all things are plain in the sight of heaven."[81] In other words, the capacity to discover the truth is within you. When the disciples still demand that Jesus "tell us who you are, so that we may believe in you," he again deflects the question and directs them to see for themselves: "He said to them, 'You read the face of the sky and the earth, but you have not recognized the one who stands before you, and you do not know how to read this present moment.' "[82] Plotinus, an Alexandrian philosopher baffled and apparently irritated by such sayings, complained that "they are always saying to us, 'Look to God!' But they do not tell us *where* or *how* to look."[83]

Yet Thomas's Jesus offers some clues. After dismissing those who expect the future coming of the kingdom of God, as countless Christians have always done and still do, Thomas's Jesus declares that

the Kingdom is inside you, and outside you. When you come to know yourselves, then you will be known, and you will see that it is you who are the children of the living Father. But if you will not know yourselves, you dwell in poverty, and it is you who *are* that poverty.[84]

This cryptic saying raises a further question: *How* can we know ourselves? According to Thomas, Jesus declares that we must find out first where we came from, and go back and take our place "in the beginning." Then he says something even stranger: "Blessed is the one who came into being before he came into being."[85] But how can one go back before one's own birth—or even before human creation? What *was* there before human creation—even before the creation of the universe?

According to Genesis, "in the beginning" there was, first of all, the primordial light. For Thomas this means that in creating "*adam* [humankind] in his image," as Genesis 1:26 says, God created us in the image of the primordial light. Like many other readers of Genesis, then and now, Thomas suggests that what appeared in the primordial light was "a human being, very marvelous," a being of radiant light, the prototype of the human Adam, whom God created on the sixth day. This "light Adam," although human in form, is simultaneously, in some mysterious way, also divine.[86] Thus Jesus suggests here that we have spiritual resources within us precisely because we were made "in the image of God." Irenaeus, the Christian bishop of Lyons (c. 180), warns his flock to despise "heretics" who speak like this, and who "call humankind [*anthropos*] the God of all things, also calling him *light*, and *blessed*, and *eternal*."[87] But, as we noted, what Irenaeus here dismisses as heretical later became a central theme of Jewish mystical tradition—that the "image of God" is hidden within each of us, secretly linking God and all humankind.[88]

Thus Thomas's Jesus tells his disciples that not only *he* comes forth from divine light but so do we all:

If they say to you, "Where did you come from?" say to them, "*We came from the light, the place where the light came into being by itself,* and was revealed through their image." If they say to you, "Who are you?" say, "We are its children, the chosen of the living father."[89]

According to Thomas, Jesus rebukes those who seek access to God elsewhere, even—perhaps especially—those who seek it by trying to "follow Jesus" himself. When certain disciples plead with Jesus to "show us the place where *you* are, since it is necessary for us to seek it," he does not bother to answer so misguided a question and redirects the disciples away from themselves toward the light hidden within each person: "There is light within a person of light, and it lights up the whole universe. If it does not shine, there is darkness."[90] In other words, one either discovers the light within that illuminates "the whole universe" or lives in darkness, within and without.

But discovering the divine light within is more than a matter of being told that it is there, for such vision shatters one's identity: "When you see your likeness [in a mirror] you are pleased; but when you see your images, which have come into being before you, how much will you have to bear!"[91] Instead of self-gratification, one finds the terror of annihilation. The poet Rainer Maria Rilke gives a similar warning about encountering the divine, for "every angel is terrifying." Giving oneself over to such an encounter, he says, involves terror, as if such an angel

> would come more fiercely to interrogate you,
> and rush to seize you blazing like a star,
> and bend you as if trying to create you,
> and break you open, out of who you are.[92]

What "breaks [us] open, out of who [we] are," shatters the ways in which we ordinarily identify ourselves, by gender, name, ethnic origin, social status. So, Thomas adds, "Jesus said, 'Let the one who seeks not stop seeking until he finds. When he finds, he will become troubled. When he becomes troubled, he will be astonished.'"[93]

Finally Jesus reveals to Thomas that "whoever drinks from my mouth will become as I am, and I myself will become that person, and the mysteries shall be revealed to him."[94] This, I believe, is the symbolic meaning of attributing this gospel to Thomas, whose name means "twin." By encountering the "living Jesus," as Thomas suggests, one may come to recognize oneself and Jesus as, so to speak, identical twins. In the Book of Thomas the Contender, another ancient book belonging to Syrian Thomas tradition discovered at Nag Hammadi, "the living Jesus" addresses Thomas (and, by implication, the reader) as follows:

> Since you are my twin and my true companion, examine yourself, and learn who you are. . . . Since you will be called my [twin], . . . although you do not understand it yet . . . you will be called "the one who knows himself." For whoever has not known himself knows nothing, but whoever has known himself has simultaneously come to know the depth of all things.[95]

I was amazed when I went back to the Gospel of John after reading Thomas, for Thomas and John clearly draw upon similar language and images, and both, apparently, begin with similar "secret teaching." But John takes this teaching to mean something so different from Thomas that I wondered whether John could have written his gospel to refute what Thomas teaches. For months I investigated this possibility, and explored the work of other scholars who also have compared these sources, and I was finally convinced that this is what happened. As the scholar Gregory Riley points out, John—and only John—presents a challenging and critical portrait of the disciple he calls "Thomas, the one called Didymus,"[96] and, as Riley suggests, it is John who invented the character we call *Doubting* Thomas, perhaps as a way of caricaturing those who revered a teacher—and a version of Jesus' teaching—that he regarded as faithless and false. The writer called John may have met Thomas Christians among people he knew in his own city—and may have worried that their teaching would spread to Christian groups elsewhere. John probably knew that certain Jewish groups—as well as many pagans who read and admired Genesis 1—also taught that the "image of God" was within humankind; in any case, John decided to write his own gospel insisting that it is Jesus—and only Jesus—who embodies God's word, and therefore speaks with divine authority.

Who, then, wrote the Gospel of John? Although we cannot answer this question with certainty, the text itself provides some clues. The author we call John was probably a Jewish follower of Jesus who, various scholars suggest, may have lived in Ephesus or in Antioch, the capital of Syria, and probably wrote toward the end of the first century (c. 90 to 100 C.E.).[97] Some scholars suggest that, as a young man, before mid-century, he may have been attracted to the circle gathered around John the Baptist, as was Jesus of Nazareth, who also came to hear John preach, and received baptism from him in the Jordan River, which the Baptist John promised would prepare people for the coming day of divine judgment. At some point—perhaps after King Herod beheaded the Baptist—this other John may have followed Jesus. His account shows his familiarity with Judaea and its local Jewish practices, and includes details which suggest that he traveled with Jesus and his other disciples during their last journey to Jerusalem, as he claims to have done.

The conclusion added by John to the gospel implies that after that time John lived so long that some of Jesus' followers hoped that the kingdom of God would come during his lifetime, and so that he would never die.[98] According to church tradition, John lived as an old man in Ephesus, revered as the spiritual leader of a circle of Jesus' followers—a passionate, articulate man, educated in Jewish tradition and by no means provincial. Like many other Jews of his time, John was influenced by Greek philosophic and religious ideas. But, if this surmise is true—which I regard as possible, although not likely—his old age must have been a stormy time, for he would have been excluded from his home synagogue and threatened by Roman persecution. Thus John contended not only against hostile outsiders but also with other Jews—including other groups of Jesus' followers.

From the second century to the present, most Christians have assumed that the author of this gospel was in fact the John who was the brother of James, whom Jesus saw mending nets with their father, Zebedee, and called to himself—one of those who "immediately left the boat and their father, and followed him."[99] In that case, John would be one of the group called "the twelve," headed by Peter. Yet the gospel itself (and its possibly added conclusion) declares that it was written by "the disciple whom Jesus loved." If John, the son of Zebedee, was that "beloved disciple," why does his name never appear in the gospel, and why does the gospel never mention either "the apostles" or "the twelve"? If the author had been one of them, why doesn't he say so? Why, while acknowledging Peter as a leader, does he simultaneously denigrate Peter's leadership in favor of the "beloved disciple" and claim that this—otherwise anonymous—disciple's greater authority ensures the truth of his gospel? Could a fisherman from Galilee have written the elegant, spare, philosophically sophisticated prose of this gospel?

Two generations of scholars have devoted hundreds of articles and monographs to such questions, and have proposed various solutions. Some suggest that the author was a different John, "John the elder," a follower of Jesus from Ephesus, whom Christians in later generations confused with John the apostle; others say that the disciple John was the witness whose authority stood behind the gospel but was not its actual author; still others believe that the author was an anonymous leader of a lesser-known circle of disciples, distinct from "the twelve."

Furthermore, while the author of this gospel accepts Peter's authority and his teaching, he also claims that the "beloved disciple" surpasses Peter. So while John pictures Peter as one of Jesus' first disciples, he does *not* repeat the story that Mark, Matthew, and Luke so prominently featured, in which Peter first recognized Jesus—the story that Mark, and many Christians to this day, take to mean that Peter was the disciples' leader, and the church's founder. Moreover, Matthew adds that Jesus promised Peter would succeed him as the founding "rock" upon which the future church would stand[100]—a statement many later took to mean that Peter stood first in the apostolic succession and was the spiritual ancestor of all subsequent popes. Matthew's gospel, like Mark's and Luke's, apparently reflects the view of the so-called Peter Christians—a group based in Rome. Yet all four gospels that eventually formed the New Testament either endorsed Peter's leadership—as Matthew, Mark, and Luke did— or at least grudgingly accepted it—as John did. From the mid-second century, this group, which called themselves catholic (literally, "universal"), remain the founders with whom Roman Catholic and most Protestant Christians identify.

But not all first-century Christians agreed that Jesus named Peter as his primary successor, or identified with that founding group. The gospel we call by John's name insists, on the contrary, that no one—not even Peter—knew Jesus as well as "the disciple whom Jesus loved,"[101] the mysterious, unnamed disciple who is usually assumed to be John himself. Though John acknowledges Peter's importance by featuring him often in his narrative, he always places him second to this "disciple, whom Jesus loved," who, he says, actually witnessed the events he records. For example, John tells how "the disciple whom Jesus loved" reclined next to Jesus at the last meal he shared with his disciples and dared ask him directly—as Peter did not—who would betray him.[102] John adds that even after Judas, and then Peter, betrayed Jesus and fled, the "disciple whom Jesus loved" remained with his mother beside his cross as the dying Jesus entrusted to him his mother's care. John also says that this disciple, who had seen Roman soldiers hasten the death of other crucified men by breaking their legs, saw a soldier pierce Jesus' body with a spear. Later, when Mary Magdalene told him that

Jesus' body had disappeared from the grave, he and Peter ran to see what had happened. Luke says that Peter outran all the rest, and was the first to realize that Jesus had risen; but John says that Peter and the beloved disciple "both ran, but the other disciple outran Peter and reached the tomb first," so that *he* was the first who "saw and believed."[103] When the risen Jesus appeared to his disciples by Lake Gennesaret, the "disciple whom Jesus loved" was the first to recognize him and "said to Peter, 'It is the Lord!'"[104]

Although the author of this gospel may not have been one of "the twelve," he does acknowledge Peter's leadership—but with qualifications. John's final chapter, perhaps added later, tells how Jesus himself ordered Peter to care for his flock ("Feed my sheep").[105] But John adds that Jesus reserved for his "beloved disciple" a special, mysterious role that he refused to explain to Peter. When Peter saw that disciple and asked, "Lord, what about this man?" Jesus answered only, "If it is my will that he should remain until I come, what is that to you? Follow me!"[106] Such stories may imply that John's teaching, including the "farewell discourses" which Jesus addressed to the disciples, entrusting "the beloved disciple" to write them down, is superior to Peter's. Such stories suggest rivalry—but not necessarily opposition— between the Peter Christians and those whom John assumes to be his audience, the so-called Johannine Christians, who regard "the disciple whom Jesus loved" as their spiritual mentor.

Such stories, and the differences they show among various leaders and groups, involve more than power struggles: they involve the substance of Christian faith. As the stories themselves show, at stake is the central question Who is Jesus, and what is the "gospel" (good news) about him? Not surprisingly, each group characterizes its own patron apostle as the one who best understands "the gospel." So, for example, even the "gnostic" Gospel of Mary, like many other gospels, tells how its primary apostle—in this case, Mary Magdalene—received direct revelation from "the Lord," and claims that Jesus authorized her to teach.[107]

What John writes about Peter and "the beloved disciple" suggests that while John accepted the teaching associated with Peter, and even wrote his own gospel "so that you might believe that Jesus is the messiah, the son of God,"[108] his own teaching went further. So, while he agrees with Peter—and Mark—that Jesus is God's messiah, John goes further, and also insists that Jesus is actually *"Lord and God."*[109]

John must have known that this conviction branded him a radical among his fellow Jews—and even, apparently, among many of Jesus' followers. The scholar Louis Martyn suggests that John himself, along with those in his circle who shared his belief, had been accused of blasphemy for "making [Jesus] God" and forcibly expelled from their home synagogue.[110] In his gospel, John dramatizes this situation by turning a miracle story of Jesus healing a blind man into a parable for their own situation.[111] Speaking for himself and his fellow believers, John protested that their only crime was that God had opened their eyes to the truth, while the rest of the congregation remained blind. Thus in John's version, when Jesus met a man born blind, he "spat on the ground, made mud with the saliva, and spread it on the man's eyes, and said to him, 'Go, and wash in the pool of Siloam.' Then he went and washed and came back able to see."[112] But what the man had come to "see" was Jesus' divine power, which others denied; so, John says, "the Jews had already agreed that anyone who confessed Jesus to be the Messiah would be put out of the synagogue."[113] Although the man's parents—and thus, John implies, an older generation—did not dare to acknowledge Jesus' power because, he says, they were afraid that "the Jews" would expel them, the man whose eyes were opened defied the synagogue leaders by confessing faith in Jesus ("Lord, I believe") and worshiping him.[114]

Thus John's account implicitly places Jesus—and his power to heal and change lives—into his own time. By showing the man born blind facing expulsion from the synagogue, this story echoes John's own experience and that of his fellow believers. They, too, having been "born blind," now, thanks to Jesus, are able to "see"—but at the cost of rejection by their own people. So John's followers are relieved and grateful to hear Jesus' harsh, ironic words at the end of the story: "For judgment I came into this world, so that those who do not see may see; and so that those who do see may become blind."[115] Jesus says that he alone offers salvation: "All who came before me are thieves and robbers. . . . I am the door; whoever enters through me shall be saved."[116] Thus John's Jesus consoles his circle of disciples that, although hated "by the world," they alone belong to God.

Spurred by rejection but determined to make converts, John challenges his fellow Jews, including many who, like himself, follow Jesus. For John believes that those who regard Jesus merely as a prophet, or a rabbi, or even the future king of Israel, while not wrong, nevertheless are blind to his full "glory." John himself proclaims a more radical vision—one that finally alienates him from other Jews, and even from other Jewish followers of Jesus. Not only is Jesus Israel's future king, and so messiah and son of God, but, John declares, he is "greater than Moses" and older than Abraham. When he pictures Jesus declaring to a hostile crowd that "before Abraham was, *I am*,"[117] John expects his readers to hear Jesus claiming for himself the divine name that God revealed to Moses ("tell them that *I am* has sent you");[118] thus Jesus is nothing less than God himself, manifest in human form.

John warns those who doubt him that Jesus, acting as divine judge, will condemn those who reject this "good news," even if they constitute the main body of the Jewish people, rather than the handful of the faithful who alone see the truth and proclaim it to a hostile and unbelieving world. According to John, "the Jews" regard Jesus himself (and thus his followers) as insane or demon-possessed. John warns that, just as they wanted to kill Jesus for "making himself God," they will hate and want to kill his followers for believing such blasphemy: "Whoever kills you will think he is doing service to God."[119] But John assures Jesus' followers that God judges very differently: "Whoever believes in him [Jesus] is not condemned; but whoever does not believe is condemned already, because he has not believed in the name of the only begotten Son of God."[120] For John, Jesus has become more than the messenger of the kingdom—and even more than its future king: Jesus *himself* has become the message.

How could anyone who heard John's message—or that of Mark, Thomas, or any of the others, for that matter—decide what to believe? Various Christian groups validated their teaching by declaring allegiance to a specific apostle or disciple and claiming him (and sometimes her, for some claim Mary as a disciple) as their spiritual founder. As early as 50 to 60 C.E., Paul had complained that members of different groups would say, for example, "I am from Paul," or "I am from Apollos,"[121] for those who wrote stories about various apostles—including John, as well as Peter, Matthew, Thomas, and Mary Magdalene—would often promote their groups' teachings by claiming that Jesus favored their patron apostle, so that, while John acknowledges Peter as a leader, he insists that "the beloved disciple" surpassed Peter in spiritual understanding. He is aware that other groups make similar claims for other disciples. He seems to know, for example, of Thomas Christians, who claim that *their* patron apostle, Thomas, understood more than Peter. Though John's gospel begins by seeming to agree with Thomas about God's presence in Jesus, by the end John tells three anecdotes about Thomas to show how wrong these Thomas Christians are.

John's gospel begins by recalling, as Thomas does, the opening of the first chapter of Genesis—saying that, since the beginning of time, divine light, "the light of all people," has shone forth:

> *In the beginning* [Gen. 1:1] was the word, and the word was with God, and the word was God . . . what came into being in him was life, and *the life was the light of all people.*"[122]

But John's next lines suggest that he intends not to complement but to *reject* Thomas's claim that we have direct access to God through the divine image within us, for John immediately adds—three times!—that the divine light did not penetrate the deep darkness into which the world has plunged. Though he agrees that, since the beginning of time, the divine light "shines into the darkness," he also declares that *"the darkness has not grasped it.*"[123] (Here the Greek verb *katalambanein*, which means "to seize," has a double meaning, as does the English verb "to grasp"). Moreover, he says that, although the divine light had come into the world, "and the world was made through it, *the world did not recognize it.*"[124] John then adds that even when that light "came unto its own, *its own*—God's people, Israel—*did not receive it.*"[125] Thus, because that divine light was not available to those "in the world," finally "the word became flesh and dwelt among us"[126] in the form of Jesus of Nazareth, so that some people now may declare triumphantly, as John does, "we saw his glory [the Greek term translates the Hebrew *kabod*, which means "shining," or "radiance"], the glory as of the only begotten son of the Father."[127] Thus the invisible God became visible and tangible in a unique moment of revelation. A letter later attributed to John declares that "we have seen [him] with our eyes, and we have touched [him] with our hands!"[128]

But to anyone who claims, as Thomas does, that we are (or may become) like Jesus, John emphatically says *no*: Jesus is unique or, as John loves to call him, *monogenes*—*"only begotten"* or "one of a kind"[129]—for he insists that God has only *one* son, and he is different from you and me. Though John goes further than the other three New Testament evangelists in saying that Jesus is not only a man raised to exalted status ("messiah," "son of God," or "son of man") but God himself in human form, and though he presumably agrees that human beings are made in God's image, as Genesis 1:26 teaches, he argues that human-kind has no innate capacity to know God. What John's gospel does—and has succeeded ever after in persuading the majority of Christians to do—is claim that only by believing in Jesus can we find divine truth.

Because this claim is John's primary concern, his Jesus does not offer ethical and apocalyptic teachings as he does in Mark, Matthew, and Luke; he delivers no "sermon on the mount," no parables teaching how to act, no predictions of the end of time. Instead, in John's gospel—and only in this gospel—Jesus continually proclaims his divine identity, speaking in what New Testament scholars call the "I am" sayings: "I am the way; I am the truth; I am the light; I am the vine; I am the water of life"— all metaphors for the divine source that alone fulfills our deepest needs. What John's Jesus *does* require of his disciples is that they believe: "You believe in God; believe also in me."[130] Then, speaking intimately to those who believe, he urges them to "love one another as I have loved you."[131] Jesus tells them that this strong sense of mutual support will sustain believers as together they face hatred and persecution from outsiders.[132]

Now we can see how John's message contrasts with that of Thomas. Thomas's Jesus directs each disciple to discover the light within ("within a person of light there is light");[133] but John's Jesus declares instead that "I am the light of the world" and that "whoever does not come to me walks in darkness."[134] In Thomas, Jesus reveals to the disciples that "you are from the kingdom, and to it you shall return" and teaches them to say for themselves that "we come from the light"; but John's Jesus speaks as the only one who comes "from above" and so has rightful priority over everyone else: *"You are from below; I am from above. . . . The one who comes from above is above all."*[135] Only Jesus is from God, and he alone offers access to God. John never tires of repeating that one must believe in Jesus, follow Jesus, obey Jesus, and confess him alone as God's *only* son. We are not his "twin," much less (even potentially) his equal; we must follow him, believe in him, and revere him as God in person: thus John's Jesus declares that *"you will die in your sins, unless you believe that I am he."*[136]

We are so different from Jesus, John says, that he is our only hope of salvation. Were Jesus like ourselves, he could not save and deliver a human race that is "dying in sin." What gives John hope is his conviction that Jesus descended into the world as an atonement sacrifice to save us from sin and from eternal damnation, and then rose—bodily—from the dead. As John tells it, the story of Jesus' baptism reaches its climax not, as in Mark, when Jesus announces the coming of God's kingdom, but when John the Baptist announces that Jesus has come: "Behold—the lamb of God, who takes away the sin of the world!"[137]

To draw near to God we must be "born again, of water and the spirit"[138]—reborn through faith in Jesus. The spiritual life received in baptism requires supernatural nourishment; so, John's Jesus declares,

> unless you eat the flesh of the Son of Man and drink his blood, you have no life in you. Those who eat my flesh and drink my blood have eternal life, and I will raise them up on the last day, for my flesh is true food, and my blood is true drink.[139]

Jesus offers access to eternal life, shared when those who believe join together to participate in the sacred meal of bread and wine that celebrates Jesus' death and resurrection.

Mark, Matthew, and Luke mention Thomas only as one of "the twelve." John singles him out as "the doubter"—the one who failed to understand who Jesus is, or what he is saying, and rejected the testimony of the other disciples. John then tells how the risen Jesus personally appeared to Thomas in order to rebuke him, and brought him to his knees. From this we might conclude, as most Christians have for nearly two millennia, that Thomas was a particularly obtuse and faithless disciple—though many of John's Christian contemporaries revered Thomas as an extraordinary apostle, entrusted with Jesus' "secret words." The scholar Gregory Riley suggests that John portrays Thomas this way for the practical—and polemical—purpose of deprecating Thomas Christians and their teaching.[140] According to John, Jesus praises those "who have not seen, and yet believed" without demanding proof, and rebukes Thomas as "faithless" because he seeks to verify the truth from his own experience.

John offers three anecdotes that impose upon Thomas the image—Doubting Thomas!—he will have ever afterward in the minds of most Christians. In the first, Thomas, hearing Jesus say that he is going toward Judaea to raise Lazarus from the dead, does not believe him, and "speaks the desperate words, 'Let us go, so that we may die with him.' "[141] Thus John pictures Thomas as one who listens to Jesus in disbelief, imagining that he is merely human, like everyone else.

In the second episode, Jesus, anticipating his death, urges his disciples to trust in God and in himself, and promises to "prepare a place for you," and to show them the way to God, since, as he says, "you know where I am going, and you know the way.' "[142] Thomas alone, of all the disciples, objects that he knows nothing of the kind: "Thomas said to him, '. . . We do not know where you are going. How can we know the way?' " In answer, John's Jesus proclaims to this ignorant and obtuse disciple what

I believe John wants to say to everyone who fails to understand how unique Jesus is: "Jesus said to [Thomas], 'I am the way, the truth, and the life; *no one comes to the Father, except through me.*' "[143]

In the third episode Jesus even returns after his death to rebuke Thomas. Luke specifies that, after the crucifixion, the risen Jesus appeared to "the eleven,"[144] and Matthew agrees that he appeared to "the eleven disciples"[145]—all but Judas Iscariot— and conferred the power of the holy spirit upon "the eleven." But John's account differs. John says instead that *"Thomas, called 'the twin'* . . . *was not with them when Jesus came."*[146]

According to John, the meeting Thomas missed was crucial; for after Jesus greeted the *ten* disciples with a blessing, he formally designated them his apostles: "As the Father has sent me, so I send you." Then he "breathed upon them" to convey the power of the holy spirit; and finally he delegated to them his authority to forgive sins, or to retain them.[147] The implication of the story is clear: Thomas, having missed this meeting, is not an apostle, has not received the holy spirit, and lacks the power to forgive sins, which the others received directly from the risen Christ. Furthermore, when they tell Thomas about their encounter with Jesus, he answers in the words that mark him forever—in John's characterization—as Doubting Thomas: "Unless I see the mark of the nails in his hands, and put my finger in the mark of the nails, and my hand in his side, *I will not believe.*" A week later, the risen Jesus reappears and, in this climactic scene, John's Jesus rebukes Thomas for lacking faith and tells him to believe: *"Do not be faithless, but believe."* Finally Thomas, overwhelmed, capitulates and stammers out the confession, "My Lord and my God!"[148]

For John, this scene is the coup de grâce: finally Thomas understands, and Jesus warns the rest of the chastened disciples: "Have you believed because you have seen? Blessed are those who have not seen, and yet believe."[149] Thus John warns all his readers that they *must* believe what they cannot verify for themselves—namely, the gospel message to which he declares himself a witness[150]—or face God's wrath. John may have felt some satisfaction writing this scene; for here he shows Thomas giving up his search for experiential truth—his "unbelief"—to confess what John sees as the truth of his gospel: the message would not be lost on Thomas Christians.

Addressing those who see Jesus differently, John urges his uncompromising conviction: belief in Jesus alone offers salvation. To those who heed, John promises great reward: forgiveness of sins, solidarity with God's people, and the power to overcome death. In place of Thomas's cryptic sayings, John offers a simple formula, revealed through the story of Jesus' life, death, and resurrection: "God loves you; believe, and be saved." John adds to his narrative scenes that Christians have loved and retold for millennia: the wedding at Cana; Nicodemus's nighttime encounter with Jesus; Jesus meeting a Samaritan woman at a well and asking her for water; Pilate asking his prisoner, "What is truth?"; the crucified Jesus telling his "beloved disciple" to care for his mother; the encounter with "Doubting Thomas," and Mary Magdalene mistaking the risen Jesus for the gardener.

John, of course, prevailed. Toward the end of the second century, as we shall see in the next chapter, the church leader Irenaeus, as well as certain Christians in Asia Minor and Rome, championed his gospel and declared that it bore the authority of "John the apostle, the son of Zebedee," whom Irenaeus, like

most Christians after him, identified with "the beloved disciple."[151] From that time to the present, Christians threatened
by persecution, or met with hostility or misunderstanding, often have found consolation in John's declaration that, although
hated by "the world," they are uniquely loved by God. And,
even apart from persecution, the boundaries John's gospel
draws between "the world" and those whom Jesus calls "his
own" have offered innumerable Christians a basis of group solidarity grounded in the assurance of salvation.

But the discovery of Thomas's gospel shows us that other
early Christians held quite different understandings of "the gospel." For what John rejects as religiously inadequate—the conviction that the divine dwells as "light" within all beings—is
much like the hidden "good news" that Thomas's gospel proclaims.[152] Many Christians today who read the Gospel of Thomas
assume at first that it is simply wrong, and deservedly called
heretical. Yet what Christians have disparagingly called gnostic
and heretical sometimes turn out to be forms of Christian teaching that are merely unfamiliar to us—unfamiliar precisely because of the active and successful opposition of Christians such
as John.

How, then, did John prevail? To answer this question, let us
look at the challenges that confronted the first generations of
his readers.

CHAPTER THREE

tototot

GOD'S WORD
OR HUMAN WORDS?

About a year after I had written *The Gnostic Gospels*, I was sitting at tea one brilliant October afternoon at the Zen Center in San Francisco, a guest of the Roshi, along with Brother David Steindl-Rast, a Benedictine monk. The Roshi, an American whose name is Richard Baker, told us how he, as a young man, had gone from Boston to Kyoto, where he entered a Buddhist monastery and became a disciple of the Zen master Shunryu Suzuki Roshi. "But"—he laughed—"had I known the Gospel of Thomas, I wouldn't have had to become a Buddhist!" Brother David, who that morning had offered to the Zen students a succinct and incisive exposition of the Apostles' Creed, shook his head. Thomas and some other unorthodox gospels, he acknowledged, may be Christian mystical writings, but, he insisted, they are essentially no different from what the church offers: "There's nothing in those texts that you can't find in the writings of the great mystics of the church, like Saint Teresa, or Saint John of the Cross."

I said that I did not agree. In the first place, Teresa of Avila and John of the Cross—to say nothing of Jacob Boehme, the German mystic of the seventeenth century, and others like him, who were condemned and excommunicated as heretics—were intensely aware that whatever "revelations" they confided to their monastic superiors would have to conform—or seem to conform—to orthodox teaching. Christian mystics, like their Jewish and Muslim counterparts, have always been careful not to identify themselves with God. But the Gospel of Thomas teaches that recognizing one's affinity with God is the key to the kingdom of God. The remarkable modern scholar Theodor Gaster, the thirteenth son of the chief rabbi of London, observed that Jewish mystics are careful to speak of *relationship* with God but not of *identification:* "The Jewish mystic can say, with Martin Buber, 'I *and* Thou,' but can never say 'I *am* Thou,' which is permissible in Hindi religious teaching, for example, as in the phrase, *tat thvam asi* [literally, "Thou art *that*"]."[1]

Orthodox Jews and Christians, of course, have never wholly denied affinity between God and ourselves. But their leaders have tended to discourage or, at least, to circumscribe the process through which people may seek God on their own. This may be why some people raised as Christians and Jews today are looking elsewhere to supplement what they have not found in Western tradition. Even Father Thomas Keating, the former abbot of St. Joseph's Abbey in Spencer, Massachusetts, who has been a Cistercian monk for over fifty years, has sought through dialogue with the Buddhist and other wisdom traditions, as well as with contemporary science, to deepen the ancient practice he calls Centering Prayer. Fr. Keating finds that certain elements of Buddhist meditative practice complement Christian tradition by offering other experiential ways to discover divine truth. Thomas Merton, the famous monk who wrote the best-seller of the 1940s *The Seven Storey Mountain*, a Trappist like Keating, had similarly investigated Buddhist tradition. Thus even some devoted Christians have found that the impulse to seek God overflows the banks of a single tradition.

But as we have seen, within a century of Jesus' death, some of his most loyal followers had determined to exclude a wide range of *Christian* sources, to say nothing of borrowing from other religious traditions, although, as we have also seen, this often happened. But why, and in what circumstances, did these early church leaders believe that this was necessary for the movement to survive? And why did those who proclaimed Jesus the "only begotten son of God," as the Gospel of John declares, dominate later tradition, while other Christian visions, like that of Thomas, which encourages disciples to recognize themselves, as well as Jesus, as "children of God," were suppressed?

Traditionally, Christian theologians have declared that "the Holy Spirit guides the church into all truth"—a statement often taken to mean that what has survived must be right. Some historians of religion have rationalized this conviction by implying that in Christian history, as in the history of science, weak, false ideas die off early, while the strong and valid ones survive. The late Raymond Brown, a prominent New Testament scholar and Roman Catholic Sulpician priest, stated this perspective baldly: What orthodox Christians rejected was only "the rubbish of the second century"—and, he added, "it's still rubbish."[2] But such polemics tell us nothing about how and why early church leaders laid down the fundamental principles of Christian teaching. To understand what happened we need to look at the specific challenges—and dangers—that confronted believers during the critical years around 100 to 200 C.E., and how those who became the architects of Christian tradition dealt with these challenges.

The African convert Tertullian, living in the port city of Carthage in North Africa about eighty years after the Gospels of John and Thomas were written, around the year 190 (or, as Tertullian and his contemporaries might have said, during the reign of Emperor Commodus), acknowledged that the Christian movement was attracting crowds of new members—and that outsiders were alarmed:

> The outcry is that the State is filled with Christians—that they are in the fields, in the cities, in the islands; and [outsiders] lament, as if for some calamity, that both men and women, of every age and condition, even high rank, are going over to profess Christian faith.[3]

Tertullian ridiculed the non-Christian majority for their wild suspicions and denounced the magistrates for believing them:

> [We are called] monsters of evil, and accused of practicing a sacred ritual in which we kill a little child and eat it; in which, after the feast, we practice incest, while the dogs, our pimps, overturn the lights and give us the shameless darkness to gratify our lusts. *This is what people constantly*

charge, yet you take no trouble to find out the truth. . . . Well, *you think the Christian is capable of every crime—an enemy of the gods, of the emperor, of the laws, of good morals, of all nature.*[4]

Tertullian was distressed that throughout the empire, from his native city in Africa to Italy, Spain, Egypt, and Asia Minor, and in the provinces from Germany to Gaul, Christians had become targets of sporadic outbreaks of violence. Roman magistrates often ignored these incidents and sometimes participated in them. In the city of Smyrna on the coast of Asia Minor, for example, crowds shouting "Get the atheists!" lynched the convert Germanicus and demanded—successfully—that the authorities arrest and immediately kill Polycarp, a prominent bishop.[5]

What outsiders saw depended considerably on which Christian groups they happened to encounter. Pliny, governor of Bithynia, in modern Turkey, trying to prevent groups from sheltering subversives, ordered his soldiers to arrest people accused as Christians. To gather information, his soldiers tortured two Christian women, both slaves, who revealed that members of this peculiar cult "met regularly before dawn on a certain day to sing a hymn to Christ as to a god." Though it had been rumored that they were eating human flesh and blood, Pliny found that they were actually eating only "ordinary, harmless food." He reported to the emperor Trajan that, although he found no evidence of actual crime, "I ordered them to be taken away and executed; for, whatever they admit to, I am convinced that their stubbornness and unshakable obstinacy should not go unpunished."[6] But twenty years later in Rome, Rusticus, the city prefect, interrogated a group of five Christians who looked to him less like members of a cult than like a philosophy seminar. Justin Martyr the philosopher, arraigned along with his students, admitted to the prefect that he met with like-minded believers in his Roman apartment "above the baths of Timothy" to discuss "Christian philosophy."[7] Nevertheless Rusticus, like Pliny, suspected treason. When Justin and his pupils refused his order to sacrifice to the gods, he had them beaten, then beheaded.

Thirty years after Justin's death, another philosopher, named Celsus, who detested Christians, wrote a book called *The True Word*, which exposed their movement and accused some of them of acting like wild-eyed devotees of foreign gods such as Attis and Cybele, possessed by spirits. Others, Celsus charged, practiced incantations and spells, like magicians; still others followed what many Greeks and Romans saw as the barbaric, Oriental customs of the Jews. Celsus reported, too, that on large estates throughout the countryside Christian woolworkers, cobblers, and washerwomen, people who, he said, "ordinarily are afraid to speak in the presence of their superiors," nevertheless gathered the gullible—slaves, children, and "stupid women"— from the great houses into their workshops to hear how Jesus worked miracles and, after he died, rose from the grave.[8] Among respectable citizens, Christians aroused the same suspicions of violence, promiscuity, and political extremism with which secretive cults are still regarded, especially by those who fear that their friends or relatives may be lured into them.

Despite the diverse forms of early Christianity—and perhaps because of them—the movement spread rapidly, so that by the end of the second century Christian groups were proliferating throughout the empire, despite attempts to stop them. Tertul-

lian boasted to outsiders that "the more we are mown down by
you, the more we multiply; the blood of Christians is seed!"[9] De-
fiant rhetoric, however, could not solve the problem that he and
other Christian leaders faced: How could they strengthen and
unify this enormously diverse and widespread movement, so it
could survive its enemies?

Tertullian's younger contemporary Irenaeus, often identified
as bishop of Lyons, himself had experienced the hostility Tertullian was talking about, first in his native town of Smyrna
(Izmir, in today's Turkey) and then in the rough provincial town
of Lyons, in Gaul (now France). Irenaeus also witnessed the frac-
tiousness that divided Christian groups. As a boy he had lived
in the household of his teacher Polycarp, the venerable bishop
of Smyrna, whom even his enemies called the teacher of Asia
Minor.[10] Although he knew that they were scattered in many
small groups throughout the world, Irenaeus shared Polycarp's
hope that Christians everywhere would come to see themselves
as members of a single church they called catholic, which means
"universal."[11] To unify this worldwide community, Polycarp urged
its members to reject all deviants. According to Irenaeus, Polycarp liked to tell how his own mentor, "John, the disciple of the
Lord"—the same person whom tradition reveres as the author
of the Gospel of John—once went to the public baths in Ephesus, but, seeing Cerinthus, whom he regarded as a heretic, John
"ran out of the bath house without bathing, exclaiming, 'Let
us flee, lest the bath house fall down; because Cerinthus, the
enemy of the truth, is inside.' " When Irenaeus repeated this
story, he added another to show how Polycarp himself treated
heretics. When the influential but controversial Christian teacher
Marcion confronted the bishop and asked him, "Do you rec-

ognize me?" Polycarp replied, "Yes, I recognize you—firstborn of Satan!"[12]

Irenaeus says that he tells these stories to show "the horror that the apostles and their disciples had against even speaking with those who corrupt the truth."[13] But his stories also show what troubled Irenaeus: that even two generations after the author of the Gospel of John qualified the claims of Peter Christians and confronted Thomas Christians, the movement remained contentious and divided. Polycarp himself denounced people who, he charged, "bear the [Christian] name with evil deceit"[14] because what they teach often differs from what he had learned from his own teachers. Irenaeus, in turn, believed that he practiced true Christianity, for he could link himself directly to the time of Jesus through Polycarp, who personally had heard Jesus' teaching from John himself, "the disciple of the Lord."[15] Convinced that this disciple wrote the Gospel of John, Irenaeus was among the first to champion this gospel and link it forever to Mark, Matthew, and Luke. His contemporary Tatian, a brilliant Syrian student of Justin Martyr the philosopher, killed by Rusticus, took a different approach: he tried to unify the various gospels by rewriting all of them into a single text.[16] Irenaeus left the texts intact but declared that only Matthew, Mark, Luke, and John *collectively*—and only these gospels *exclusively*—constitute the *whole* gospel, which he called the "four formed gospel."[17] Only these four gospels, Irenaeus believed, were written by eyewitnesses to events through which God has sent salvation to humankind.[18] This four gospel canon was to become a powerful weapon in Irenaeus's campaign to unify and consolidate the Christian movement during his lifetime, and it has remained a basis of orthodox teaching ever since.

While he supervised and taught his fellow believers in Smyrna, Polycarp sent one of his associates, Pothinus, to organize and unify a group of Greek-speaking Christians from the same region who had settled in the western hinterlands of Celtic Gaul. Later he sent his protégé, Irenaeus, then sixteen or seventeen years old, to work with Pothinus. In the winter of 167, however, when public hostility against Christians broke out in Smyrna, Roman police arrested Polycarp, whom they found hiding in a friend's country estate. Accused of atheism, and ordered by the governor to swear an oath to the emperor's *genius* (the spirit of his family), to curse Christ, and to say "Away with the atheists" (the Christians), Polycarp refused. Marched into the public stadium, the eighty-six-year-old bishop shook his fist at the hostile, noisy crowd and defiantly shouted, "Away with the atheists!" He was then stripped naked, bound to a stake, and burned alive.[19] Irenaeus, visiting in Rome at the time, says that on that very afternoon, of February 23, 167 C.E., he heard a voice "like a trumpet call" revealing to him what was happening to his beloved teacher. From accounts of eyewitnesses, he (or another of Polycarp's students) later wrote a moving report of his teacher's arrest, interrogation, and death.

Ten years later Irenaeus, perhaps still in his twenties, witnessed mob violence against Christians at first hand in Lyons, where he lived, and in the town of Vienne, some thirty miles away. Public officials had banned Christians, as polluted persons, from entering the baths and markets and, finally, from all public places protected by the city's gods. Then, when the provincial governor was away from the city, "the mob broke loose. Christians were hounded and attacked openly. They were treated as public enemies, assaulted, beaten, and stoned."[20] Bishop Pothinus, now in his nineties, was arrested and tortured, along with between thirty and fifty of the most outspoken members of his congregation. Many were taken to prison and strangled. Ten Christians changed their minds and recanted but were not released. Those who survived and still confessed to being Christians were sentenced to be tortured in public and torn apart by wild animals. When the governor returned and heard that some of the prisoners were Roman citizens, he wrote to Marcus Aurelius, the so-called philosopher emperor, to ask whether these should die in a public spectacle in the arena like the rest or be granted the citizens' usual privilege of a quicker, more private death—for example, by beheading.

We do not know what the emperor replied; but meanwhile those terrified Christians who managed to escape arrest marveled at how God's power energized the confessors. At their trial, for example, the young nobleman Vettius Epagathus dared to defend them before a hostile, shouting crowd. When the magistrate, apparently irritated by his objections, turned to him and asked, "Are you one of them too?" the sympathizer who wrote their story says that the holy spirit inspired him to say yes, and so to die with them.[21] God's spirit filled the least of them as well: some said that it was Christ himself who suffered in the slave girl Blandina, when she astonished everyone by withstanding the most agonizing torture; and others told how Christ triumphed in the suffering of the slave named Sanctus, and inspired Bishop Pothinus's unwavering courage until he expired. Many testified that they had experienced the power of the holy spirit as they prayed together in the dark, stinking prison of Lyons.

But when the imprisoned confessors heard from their visitors that in Rome *other* "spirit filled" Christians were being persecuted—and not by Roman magistrates but, worse, by their fellow Christians—they decided to intervene. Claiming the special authority that Christians accorded those who had given up their lives for Christ, they wrote a letter to the bishop of Rome, urging him to deal peaceably with those under attack, who had joined a revival movement called "the new prophecy." The prisoners asked Irenaeus, who had somehow escaped arrest, to travel to Rome to deliver their letter, and he agreed.

Irenaeus does not tell us his own attitude toward the new prophecy, but he probably knew that this movement of charismatic Christians had arisen about ten years before in rural towns of his native Asia Minor (present-day Turkey), when the prophets Montanus, Maximilla, and Priscilla, popularly called "the three," began traveling from one rural church to another, claiming to communicate directly with the holy spirit. Wherever they went, the three shared their visions, spoke in ecstasy, and urged others to fast and pray so that they too could receive visions and revelations. From Asia Minor the movement swept through churches all across the empire, to Africa, Rome, and Greece, and even to remote provinces like Gaul, arousing enthusiasm—and opposition.

Apollinarius, who became bishop of the Asian town of Hierapolis in 171 C.E., says that when he went to Ancyra (contemporary Ankara, in Turkey) "and saw that the church in that place was torn in two by this new movement," he opposed it, declaring that "it is not *prophecy*, as they call it, but, as I shall show, *false prophecy*."[22] Such opponents accused Montanus, Maximilla, and Priscilla of being opportunists, or even demon-possessed. In one town a Christian named Zotimus interrupted Maximilla while she was prophesying and tried to exorcise her, ordering her "demons" to leave, until her followers seized him and dragged him outside the church. Maximilla had received outpourings of the spirit and had left her husband to devote herself to prophecy. Speaking in an ecstatic trance, she declared, "Do not listen to me, but to Christ. . . . I am compelled, whether willing or not, to come to know God's *gnosis*."[23] Priscilla claimed that Christ had appeared to her in female form. Opponents accused both Maximilla and Priscilla of breaking their marriage vows, wearing expensive clothes, and making money by deceiving gullible people. After a group of bishops in Turkey finally excommunicated her, Maximilla protested: "I am driven away like the wolf from the sheep. I am no wolf; I am word, and spirit, and power!"[24]

When Irenaeus arrived in Rome, he found on every side groups and factions that challenged his own understanding of the gospel. The letter he brought may have helped persuade Bishop Eleutherus to refrain from censuring the new prophecy, but the movement was dividing Christians throughout Asia Minor as well as Rome. While many attacked its leaders as liars and frauds, others defended it—and those on both sides drew the Gospel of John into the controversy. Some members of the new prophecy claimed that the spirit's presence among them fulfilled what Jesus promised in John's gospel: "I will send you the advocate [*paraclete*], the spirit of truth, . . . [who] will guide you into all truth."[25] Angered by such argument, Gaius, a Christian leader in Rome, charged that the Gospel of John, along with that other controversial book of "spiritual prophecy," the Reve-

lation, was written not by "John, the disciple of the Lord," but by
his worst enemy, Cerinthus—the man whom Polycarp said John
had personally denounced as a heretic.[26] Not long afterward,
however, Tertullian, already famous as a champion of orthodoxy, himself joined the new prophecy and defended its members as genuinely spirit-filled Christians. Although to this day
Tertullian stands among the "fathers of the church," at the end
of his life he turned against what, at this point, he now began to
call "the church of a bunch of bishops."[27]

When Irenaeus met in Rome a childhood friend from Smyrna
named Florinus, who like himself as a young man had studied with Polycarp, he was shocked to learn that his friend
now had joined a group headed by Valentinus and Ptolemy—
sophisticated theologians who, nevertheless, like the new prophets, often relied on dreams and revelations.[28] Although they
called themselves spiritual Christians, Irenaeus regarded them
as dangerously deviant. Hoping to persuade his friend to re-
consider, Irenaeus wrote a letter to warn him that "these views,
Florinus, to put it mildly, are not sound; are not consonant with
the church, and involve their devotees in the worst impiety,
even heresy."[29] Irenaeus was distressed to learn that an increasing number of educated Christians were moving in the same
direction.

When he returned from Rome to Gaul, Irenaeus found his
own community devastated; some thirty people had been bru-
tally tortured and killed in the public arena on a day set aside
to entertain the townspeople with this spectacle. With Bishop
Pothinus dead, the remaining members of his group now looked
to Irenaeus for leadership. Aware of the danger, he nevertheless

agreed, determined to unify the survivors. But he saw that members of his own "flock" were splintered into various, often fractious groups—all of them claiming to be inspired by the holy spirit.

How could he sort out these conflicting claims and impose some kind of order? The task was enormous and perplexing. Irenaeus believed, certainly, that the holy spirit had initiated the Christian movement. From the time it began, a hundred and fifty years earlier, both Jesus and his followers claimed to have experienced outpourings of the holy spirit—dreams, visions, stories, sayings, ecstatic speech—many communicated orally, many others written down—reflecting the vitality and diversity of the movement. The New Testament gospels abound in visions, dreams, and revelations, like the one that Mark says initiated Jesus' public activity:

> In those days, Jesus came from Nazareth, and was baptized by John in the Jordan. And just as he was coming up out of the water, *he saw the heavens torn apart and the spirit descending like a dove upon him, and a voice came from heaven:* "You are my beloved son; with you I am well pleased."[30]

Luke adds to his version of this story an account of Jesus' birth, in which a vision precedes every event in the drama, from the moments the angel Gabriel appeared to the aging priest Zacharias and later to Mary, to the night when "an angel of the Lord" appeared to shepherds to tell them of Jesus' birth, terrifying them with a sudden radiance that lighted up the nighttime sky.[31]

But the visions and dreams that occurred during Jesus' lifetime were overshadowed by those the gospels say happened
after his death, when his grieving followers heard that "the Lord
actually has risen and has appeared to Simon [Peter]!"[32] Each
gospel indicates that Jesus' disciples received visions after his
death, a time that Luke says was especially charged with supernatural power. For Luke, this outpouring of dreams and visions
proved that God's spirit was present to Jesus' followers. This, he
says, is what the prophet Joel had predicted:

In the last days it will be, God declares, that I will pour out
my spirit upon all flesh, and your sons and your daughters shall prophesy, and your young men shall see visions,
and your old men shall dream dreams.[33]

Decades before Luke wrote, his mentor, Paul of Tarsus, then
unknown to Jesus' disciples—or known to them all too well as
an enemy and a spy—suddenly claimed that Jesus had personally appeared to him in a blazing light and chosen him as his
special representative. Henceforth Paul, who had never met
Jesus during his lifetime, called himself "an apostle of Jesus
Christ" (apostolos, in Greek, means "representative") and claimed
to rely on the spirit's direct guidance throughout his life.[34] Paul
wrote to Christians in Corinth that he had been "caught up into
Paradise," but said that what he had seen and heard there he
could never tell, since these were "things that no mortal is
allowed to speak."[35] Luke relates in the Acts of the Apostles,
which he wrote as a sequel to the gospel, that even after the
risen Jesus appeared personally to his astounded disciples and

then ascended into heaven forty days later, the spirit continued to flood his followers with *charismata*—power to heal, to exorcise, to prophesy, even to raise the dead.

Even a hundred years or so after Luke wrote these things, members of the new prophecy loved to recall what the Gospel of John says Jesus promised to his followers: "The holy spirit will guide you into all truth" and enable you "to do greater works than I do."[36] Then, as now, many Christians believed that the author of that gospel also wrote the Revelation, which describes astonishing visions the author says he received "in the spirit," that is, in an ecstatic state. The author of Revelation, whose name was John, says that, while imprisoned on the island of Patmos "because of God's word and the witness to Jesus," he was "caught up into heaven" and beheld the Lord enthroned in glory above a heavenly sea, glittering like crystal, and heard angels intoning the secrets of "what is to come."[37] Unlike Paul, however, John *did* write down what he said he saw and heard in heaven, and this is why his book is called Revelation.

Without visions and revelations, then, the Christian movement would not have begun. But who can tell the holy spirit when to stop—or, as Irenaeus's contemporaries might have said, who can say whether the holy spirit *has* stopped? And when so many people—some of them rivals or even antagonists—all claim to be divinely inspired, who knows who has the spirit and who does not? These questions concerned Irenaeus—and concern many Christians today. Some ask now, as many did then, whether people living *after* the time of the apostles still receive direct revelation. A growing number of charismatic Christians today believe that they do, and some, unlike Irenaeus, believe that the spirit may say different things to different people. Those who call themselves Pentecostalists, for example, identify with the apostles Luke describes in the New Testament Acts of the Apostles. Luke tells how the apostles, at the feast of Pentecost, experienced God's spirit streaming down upon them "like tongues of fire" and filling them with power.[38] Those early Christians who joined the new prophecy no doubt agreed. One anonymous member of the movement objected to "those who want to restrict the power of the one Spirit to seasons and times" and declared that, on the contrary, "we recognize and honor not only new prophecies but new visions as well."[39]

Yet their opponents, including Gaius in Rome, argued that genuine visions and revelations had ended with the close of the apostolic age. Gaius urged his fellow believers to reject any revelation received after that time—from the visions in the Revelation to those of the new prophets. For, Gaius argued, since "the number of the prophets and apostles is [now] complete,"[40] no one who lived after the apostolic age could receive revelation directly from Jesus himself. As for Luke's story of the day of Pentecost, those who agreed with Gaius could point out that in that same opening scene in Acts, Jesus' disciples communed directly with the risen Christ for *only forty days*. Luke says that after forty days, "as they were looking on, he was lifted up, and a cloud took him out of their sight,"[41] forever ending direct communication between the risen Jesus and his disciples.

Irenaeus himself tried to forge a middle ground. Unlike Gaius, he refused to draw a sharp line between the apostolic age and the present. After all, he himself had received revelation—for example, on the day of Polycarp's death. He had heard, too, that Polycarp, while hiding from the police, had dreamed that his pillow caught fire and prophesied that "I am to be burnt alive."[42] Irenaeus also heard from the martyrs in his own town, as well as from other Christians, that such things still happen:

> We hear many brothers and sisters in the church who have prophetic gifts, speaking through the spirit in all kinds of tongues, and bringing things hidden from human beings into clarity, and revealing the mysteries of God.[43]

So Irenaeus challenged those who suggested that miracle stories in the gospels were not to be taken literally, or that miracles no longer happen:

> Those who are truly his disciples actually do drive out demons. . . . Others foresee things that will happen; they see visions and speak prophecies . . . others, still, heal the sick by laying their hands upon them, and they are completely healthy. . . .
>
> Yes, and furthermore, as I have said, even the dead have been raised up, and they have remained alive among us for many years. What more should I say? It is not possible to tell how many gifts which the church throughout the world has received in the name of Jesus Christ, and uses every day to benefit the nations, neither deceiving anyone, nor taking any money.[44]

These miracles attracted crowds of newcomers to Christian groups, despite the danger. Those who receive healing, Irenaeus added, "often believe and join the church."[45]

Although Irenaeus stopped short of defending Maximilla,

Montanus, and Priscilla, or even mentioning the new prophets by name—if, indeed, he knew their names—he criticized their opponents for wrongly "disregarding both the gospel [of John] and the spirit of prophecy." He reminded his contemporaries that Paul, too, not only received visions and spoke prophecies but also "recognized men and women prophesying in the churches."[46]

But the immediate problem Irenaeus confronted in Lyons was not a lack of spiritual revelation but an overwhelming surplus. Perhaps he refrained from criticizing the new prophets because he thought the things they said when they spoke "in the spirit" did not deviate that much from the tradition he accepted. But *other* would-be prophets said and did things he thought were completely wrong, and Irenaeus judged them to be schismatics and frauds. The problem was how to discriminate: "How," he asked, "can we tell the difference between the word of God and mere human words?"[47]

What especially troubled Irenaeus was that "even in our own district of the Rhone valley," a prophet named Marcus was causing a stir among believers; he had attracted from Irenaeus's congregation

a great number of men and quite a few women . . . whom he [had] persuaded to join him, as one who possesses the greatest understanding and maturity, and who has received the highest power from the invisible and ineffable regions above.[48]

Although his account is hostile, and accuses Marcus of being an agent of Satan, Irenaeus offers a detailed picture of what this prophet did. Marcus not only received visions and spoke in prophecy himself but also encouraged others to do so. When someone asked Marcus to invoke the power of the spirit, Marcus would place his hands upon the person's head and offer prayer that echoed Jesus' words from the Gospel of Matthew ("Do not despise the little ones, for, I tell you, their angels continually see the face of my Father in heaven").[49] Marcus prayed for each initiate that "you may receive grace, since the Father of all sees your angel standing before him." Then he placed his hands upon the person's head and said, "Behold, grace has descended upon you; open your mouth, and prophesy." Then, Irenaeus says, the candidate would protest, having been instructed to do so, that "I have not at any time prophesied, nor do I know how to prophesy," in order to acknowledge that prophecy has nothing to do with natural human capacity but only with the gift of divine grace. Finally Marcus again would encourage the initiate to speak prophecy—often, Irenaeus says, a "foolish woman"—and at that point, he says indignantly,

> she, then, puffed up with vanity and elated by these words, and enormously excited in soul by expecting that she herself is about to prophesy, her heart beating wildly, reaches the necessary pitch of audacity, and, foolishly as well as brazenly, utters whatever nonsense happens to occur to her, such as one might expect from someone heated up by an empty spirit.[50]

Having received the spirit through this initiation, each member of Marcus's circle believed that he or she shared "the gift of prophecy." When they would gather to celebrate the sacred

meal, the eucharist, Irenaeus says that "all of them [were] accus-
tomed to cast lots." Thus they followed an ancient Israelite practice, which, as Luke says in Acts, Christians revived, of throwing
lots in order to invite the holy spirit to show, by the way the lots
fell, whom the spirit chose to offer that day's prophecy.[51]

As Irenaeus tells it—perhaps adding details for the sake of
sensation—Marcus claimed that divine truth had revealed itself
to him naked, "in feminine form, having descended upon him
from invisible and ineffable space, for the world could not have
borne [the truth] coming in masculine form."[52] According to
Irenaeus, Marcus said that she revealed herself through letters
and numbers, each part of her body adorned with one of the
twenty-four letters of the Greek alphabet; and she spoke the
mystical name "Christ Jesus."[53] The letters and numbers in which
Marcus received his vision reflected Jewish traditions known to
followers of his spiritual teacher, Valentinus, who claimed to be
initiated into Paul's secret wisdom teaching. Similar traditions
would flower, more than a thousand years later, among mystically inclined Jewish groups, who would call them *kabbalah*.

Although the Hebrew term simply means "tradition," *kabbalah* radically transforms tradition. The late Gershom Scholem,
professor of Jewish mysticism at the Hebrew University of Jerusalem, far more sympathetic to Marcus than Irenaeus was,
explained that those who take the path of *kabbalah* seek to know
God "not through dogmatic theology but through living experience and intuition."[54] Like other Jews, kabbalists interpret the
Scriptures; but in their hands the Scriptures become the language of spiritual exploration. Like kabbalists more than a thousand years later, Marcus asked, How can we speak of what is

ineffable? How can the invisible, incomprehensible God become manifest? Marcus's vision suggests that the whole alphabet— all of human speech—can become a mystical form of divine truth—a conviction that many kabbalists would share.

Like many others, Marcus was fascinated with Genesis, as he wondered what happened "in the beginning"—and even *before* the beginning—of the universe. And like the authors of Thomas and John, Marcus interpreted Genesis 1, and suggested that "when first the unbegotten, inconceivable father, who is neither male nor female, willed to bring forth . . . he opened his mouth and spoke the word" (*logos*).[55] Marcus explained that, as he envisioned this process, each separate letter that God spoke at first recognized neither its own nature nor that of the others, for "while every one of them is part of the whole, each one imagines its own sound to be the whole name" of the divine being. Yet, Marcus continued, "the restoration of all things will take place" only when this illusion of separateness is overcome, and "all these [elements], mingling into one sound, shall join unanimously" in the same song of praise.[56] For the universe itself came forth from "the glory of that sound of praise." Marcus believed that this is something everyone knows intuitively, and acknowledges from the first cry a newborn utters emerging from the womb to those moments of anguish when a person moans or cries out "in difficulty and distress . . . saying 'oh.' "[57] Such sounds, Marcus said, echo the divine name, which, he believed, people instinctively—even unconsciously—utter in the form of spontaneous prayer for divine help. And when people join their voices together in worship to chant "Amen" (Hebrew for "May it be so"), their unanimous voice anticipates how all that exists finally shall be restored into a single, harmonious whole.

Irenaeus says that he tried hard, at a friend's request, to investigate Marcus's teaching in order to expose him as an interloper and a fraud. For by attracting disciples, performing initiations, and offering special teachings to "spiritual" Christians, Marcus's activity threatened Irenaeus's effort to unify all Christians in the area into a homogenous church. Irenaeus charged that Marcus was a magician, "the herald of Antichrist"—a man whose made-up visions and pretense to spiritual power masked his true identity as Satan's own apostle.[58] He ridiculed Marcus's claims to investigate "the deep things of God" and mocked him for urging initiates to seek revelations of their own:

> While they say such things as these about the creation, every one of them generates something new every day, according to his ability; for no one is considered "mature" [or "initiated"] among them who does not develop some enormous lies.[59]

Irenaeus expresses dismay that many other teachers, too, within Christian communities, "introduce an indescribable number of secret and illegitimate writings, which they themselves have forged, to bewilder the minds of foolish people, who are ignorant of the true scriptures."[60] He quotes some of their writings, including part of a well-known and influential text called the Secret Book of John (discovered among the so-called gnostic gospels at Nag Hammadi in 1945), and he refers to many others, including a Gospel of Truth (perhaps the one discovered at Nag

Hammadi), which he attributes to Marcus's teacher, Valentinus, and even a Gospel of Judas. Irenaeus decided that stemming this flood of "secret writings" would be an essential first step toward limiting the proliferation of "revelations" that he suspected of being only delusional or, worse, demonically inspired.[61]

Yet the discoveries at Nag Hammadi show how widespread was the attempt "to seek God"—not only among those who wrote such "secret writings" but among the many more who read, copied, and revered them, including the Egyptian monks who treasured them in their monastery library even two hundred years after Irenaeus had denounced them. But in 367 c.e., Athanasius, the zealous bishop of Alexandria—an admirer of Irenaeus—issued an Easter letter in which he demanded that Egyptian monks destroy all such writings, except for those he specifically listed as "acceptable," even "canonical"—a list that constitutes virtually all of our present "New Testament."[62] But someone—perhaps monks at the monastery of St. Pachomius—gathered dozens of the books Athanasius wanted to burn, removed them from the monastery library, sealed them in a heavy, six-foot jar, and intending to hide them, buried them on a nearby hillside near Nag Hammadi. There an Egyptian villager named Muḥammad 'Alī stumbled upon them sixteen hundred years later.

Now that we can read for ourselves some of the writings that Irenaeus detested and Athanasius banned, we can see that many of them express the hope of receiving revelation, and encourage "those who seek for God." The author of the Secret Book of James, for example, *reinterprets* the opening scene we noted from the New Testament Acts, in which Luke tells how Jesus ascended into heaven and departed. The Secret Book, apparently written as a *sequel* to that scene, opens as James, Jesus' brother, offers to reveal in this book what happened *after* Jesus "departed from us while we gazed after him."⁶³ After that, he says,

> the twelve disciples were all sitting together and recalling what the Savior had said to each one of them, either secretly or openly, and putting it into books, and I was writing what is in my book.⁶⁴

But the Secret Book says that Jesus astonished his disciples by suddenly coming back—a year and a half after he had departed—and explained that he had not actually removed himself from his disciples:

> Lo, the Savior appeared. . . . And *five hundred and fifty days* since he had risen from the dead, we said to him, *"Have you departed and removed yourself from us?"* But Jesus said, *"No;* but I go to the place whence I came. If you wish to come with me, come!"⁶⁵

According to the Secret Book, Jesus then invited James and Peter to travel with him to heaven, perhaps in the kind of ecstatic trance that John of Patmos said he experienced before he wrote the book of Revelation. First Jesus separated them from the others and privately explained that they could join him not only after death but also here and now, by becoming "full of the spirit."⁶⁶ But instead of urging his disciples simply to *follow* him, here Jesus encourages them to *surpass* him. He explains that those who suffer and overcome the fear of death may "become better than I; make yourselves like the son of the Holy Spirit! Be zealous, and if possible, arrive [in heaven] even before I do."[67] As the Secret Book concludes, James tells how

> Peter and I gave thanks, and sent our hearts upward toward heaven. We heard with our ears, and saw with our eyes, the noise of war, trumpets blaring and a great turmoil. And when we had passed beyond that place, we sent our minds farther upwards, and saw with our eyes and heard with our ears . . . angels rejoicing, as we, too, rejoiced.[68]

Many other Christians who sought revelation—and may even have hoped to ascend into heaven during their lifetime—took Paul, naturally enough, as their patron apostle. The author of the Prayer of the Apostle Paul, discovered at Nag Hammadi, is one of many to recall what Paul wrote in his letter to Christians in Corinth about his own "visions and revelations of the Lord," especially the famous episode in which Paul says he was

> caught up into the third heaven—whether in the body or out of the body, I do not know; God knows. . . . I heard things that are not to be spoken, that no mortal is allowed to speak.[69]

The author of the Prayer of the Apostle Paul, then, takes Paul as the paradigm of "those who seek for God" and articulates the longing to enter into God's presence, as Paul had:

My redeemer, redeem me, for I am yours, one who has come forth from you. You are my mind; bring me forth. You are my treasure; open to me. You are my fulfillment; join me to you![70]

Finally, echoing what Paul writes in his first letter to the Corinthians, the prayer concludes, "Grant what no angel's eye has seen and what no ruling power's ear has heard, and what has not entered into the human heart . . . since I have faith and hope."[71]

Those who wrote, translated, and carefully copied works such as the Secret Book of James and the Prayer of the Apostle Paul may have known about techniques that certain Jewish groups used to induce a state of ecstasy and invoke visions. For example, one group of Jewish ascetics living in Egypt at the time of Jesus, called the Therapeutae, practiced a rigorous regimen of prayer, celibacy, fasting, and singing to prepare themselves to receive "the vision of God." Some of the Dead Sea Scrolls also offer prayers and rituals apparently intended to help the devout enter God's presence and join in worship with angels.[72]

We do not know precisely what was meant by "the vision of God." Different people probably conceived it differently. Some scholars take this phrase to mean that such people sought to experience God's presence through ecstatic trance.[73] Paul's account of his own ascent into Paradise suggests that this happened to him, although, as we noted, he claims that his vision occurred spontaneously and admits that "whether in the body or out of the body, I do not know; God knows."[74] Other scholars, however, point out that those who say they are seeking a vision of God may be referring to what happens in devotional practices and worship.[75] For to this day many Jews and Christians use mystical language in worship services every week—or even every day—at a culminating moment understood to unite the human congregation with the angels, as they join in singing what the prophet Isaiah says angels sing in heaven: "Holy, holy, holy; Lord God almighty; heaven and earth are full of your glory." Isaiah says that he heard this song when he himself received a vision and was taken into God's presence.[76]

Scholars of Jewish history and literature are also investigating an enormous wealth of mystical literature that flourished for about a thousand years preceding *kabbalah*. Some of these so-called *hekalot* texts focus upon the figure of Enoch, who, according to Genesis, "walked with God" and, without dying, was taken up into God's presence.[77] Even before the first century B.C.E., Enoch had become a paradigm for those seeking access to heavenly wisdom.[78] Other groups of Jews were devoted to the so-called Merkabah (chariot) literature, which thrived from the second century through the sixth. These writings emerged from Jewish teachers and their disciples who tried to act upon hints they found in the prophet Ezekiel's marvelous vision of God enthroned upon a chariot shining like fire, borne by winged cherubim, and praised by the angelic host.[79]

Some of those who described visions like the ones found in the Secret Book of James seem to imply that they themselves, like the prophets Isaiah and Ezekiel, received such visions. Some of the books discovered at Nag Hammadi offer specific techniques for invoking revelations; others suggest that such techniques did not always work. The Apocalypse of Peter, for example, tells how Peter saw people running toward him and his fellow apostles, threatening them with stones "as if they would kill us." Peter immediately appealed to the risen Jesus—probably in prayer—who told his terrified disciple to

> "put your hands over your eyes, and tell what you see." But when I had done it, I did not see anything. I said, "No one sees [this way]." Again he told me, "Do it again." And there came into me fear and joy, for I saw a new light, greater than the light of day.[80]

During a moment suspended in time, while Peter hears the crowd shouting, he is shocked to see a vision of Jesus being crucified. After he cries out in fear and anguish, Peter learns from the "living Jesus" that what is spiritual cannot die. Finally, an astonished Peter sees a vision of Jesus "glad and laughing on the cross . . . and he was filled with a holy spirit . . . and there was a great, ineffable light around them, and a multitude of ineffable and invisible angels blessing them."[81] The anonymous author of the Apocalypse of Peter says that this vision encouraged Peter to face his own death with equanimity, knowing that the spirit within him may overcome death, as those facing persecution in later generations might do as well.

But how are visions received, and which are divinely inspired? Practically speaking, who is to judge? This central—and perplexing—question is what Christians since ancient times have called the problem of discerning spirits: how to tell which apparent inspirations come from God, which from the power of evil, and which from an overheated imagination. Although most people at the time—Jews, pagans, and Christians alike—assumed that the divine reveals itself in dreams, many people then, as now, recognized that dreams may also express only wishes and hopes, and that some may lead to fatal delusions. We have seen that Irenaeus recognized God's power in certain prophets, healers, and teachers, perhaps especially in those whose teaching agreed with what many Christians accepted in common. In others, however, he saw Satan at work—for example, in the case of Marcus, whom he called "Satan's apostle" and accused of inventing visions in order to deceive his followers and to exploit them for sexual favors and money.

In the Gospel of Mary Magdalene, discovered in Egypt in 1896, the apostles Andrew and Peter raise the same questions that troubled Irenaeus—but this time we hear a response from the visionary's point of view. The Gospel of Mary dramatizes how certain group leaders—here represented by the apostles Peter and Andrew—sometimes attacked and denounced those who claimed to see visions. Although the opening is lost, what we have of the Gospel of Mary begins with a vision in which the risen Jesus tells his disciples, "The Son of Man is *within you*. Follow after him! Those who seek him will find him. Go, then, and preach the gospel of the kingdom." Yet most of the disciples, apparently at a loss to find the divine within themselves, "were grieved, and wept greatly," terrified that they would be killed as Jesus was. Then Mary stood up, spoke, and "turned their hearts to the good":

> Do not weep, and do not grieve nor be afraid, for his grace will be with you completely, and will protect you. But rather let us praise his greatness, for he has prepared us, and has turned us into human beings.[82]

Then Peter says to Mary: "Sister, we know that the Savior loved you more than the rest of women. Tell us the words of the Savior which you remember—which you know but we do not, nor have we heard them."[83] Peter apparently expects to hear things that Jesus had said at times when he himself was absent. But Mary startles Peter by saying that she knows not only what Peter did not happen to hear but also what Jesus *chose* not to tell him: "What is hidden from you I will tell you." So, she continues, "I saw the Lord today in a vision," and she says that she was so astonished that she immediately asked him how visions occur:

> "How does one who sees the vision see it—through the soul, or through the spirit?" The Savior answered and said, "One does not see through the soul, nor through the spirit, but the mind which is between the two: that is what sees the vision."[84]

After hearing that visions come through the *mind*, or *consciousness*, Mary turns her attention to what the vision shows her. At this crucial point the papyrus text is broken, and much is lost; what remains is a fragment in which, as in the Dialogue of the Savior, Jesus reveals what happens after death. He explains that the soul encounters "seven powers of wrath," which challenge it, saying, "Whence do you come, killer of humans, and where are you going, conqueror of space?" Through this vision, Jesus teaches the soul how to respond, so that it may overcome these hostile powers.

When Mary stops speaking, an argument breaks out:

When Mary had said this, she fell silent, since it was to this point that the Savior had spoken with her. But Andrew answered and said to the brethren, "Say what you will about what she has said. I, at least, do not believe that the Savior said this, for certainly these teachings are strange ideas."[85]

Andrew's brother Peter adds: "Did he really speak with a woman without our knowledge, and not openly? Are we supposed to turn and listen to *her*? Did he love her more than *us*?"

Then Mary wept, and said to Peter, "My brother Peter, what do you think? Do you think that I made this up myself in my heart, or that I am lying about the Savior?" Levi answered and said to Peter, "Peter, you have always been hot tempered. Now I see you contending against the woman as our enemies do. But if the Savior made her worthy, who are you, indeed, to reject her? Surely the Savior knows her very well. That is why he loved her more than us. Rather, let us be ashamed, and . . . preach the gospel."[86]

Thus the author of the Gospel of Mary differs from Irenaeus about how to distinguish genuine visions. For when Irenaeus confronted a prophet he mistrusted, like Marcus, he might well have said what Peter and Andrew said to Mary, accusing those who claimed to have received visions of having "strange ideas" or of "making them up."

Irenaeus may have realized as he wrestled with this problem that it was nothing new; some of Israel's ancient prophets had asked—and been asked—the same questions. When Jeremiah, for example, predicted that war with Babylonia (c. 580 B.C.E.) would end in Israel's defeat, prophets who had predicted victory accused him of false prophecy. Jeremiah protested that he spoke only what came "from the mouth of the Lord" and accused his opponents of speaking lies that came "from their own mouths." So, he wrote,

> The Lord himself said to me, "I have heard what the prophets have said . . . who say, 'I have dreamed, I have dreamed.' See, I am against the prophets, says the Lord, who use *their own tongues,* and say, 'Says the Lord.' See, I am against the prophets, says the Lord, who *use their own tongues and prophesy lying dreams,* says the Lord, and who tell them, and who lead my people astray by their lies and wickedness, when I did not send them, nor did I command them or speak to them. They are prophesying to you *a lying vision, worthless divination, and the deceit of their own minds.*"[87]

Thus Jeremiah dismisses as worthless whatever comes from the prophets' "own mouths," "their own dreams," and "their own minds." Irenaeus, who has Marcus in mind, agrees, and adds what he learned from his anonymous Christian mentor, whom he calls "that divine elder and preacher of the truth"—false prophecy, especially Marcus's, comes from Satan.

Irenaeus adopted from Israel's prophetic tradition a second way of distinguishing which prophecies come from God: the conviction that the truth of oracles is revealed by events that bear them out. When Babylonian armies defeated Israel, Jeremiah's followers, convinced that this event proved his divine inspiration, collected his prophecies—having discarded those of his opponents—and added them to the sacred collection that would become the Hebrew Bible.

Followers of Jesus of Nazareth had made similar claims, as Irenaeus well knew. The author of the Gospel of Matthew, for example, insists that David, Isaiah, and Jeremiah had predicted specific events that happened at the time of Jesus, five hundred to a thousand years after the prophecies were written; thus these events demonstrate a divine plan. Many scholars today, however, suggest that the correspondence between prophecy and event that Matthew describes shows that he sometimes tailored his narrative to fit the prophecies. Matthew found, for example, the following oracle in the writings of the prophet Zechariah:

> Rejoice greatly . . . O daughter of Jerusalem! Behold, your king comes to you; triumphant and victorious is he; humble, and *riding on a donkey, [and] on a colt, the foal of a donkey.*[88]

Matthew read this passage as a prediction of how Jesus entered Jerusalem at Passover, but apparently he did not notice that Zechariah repeated the final phrases only for poetic effect. Consequently he wrote in his gospel that, when Jesus was preparing to enter Jerusalem, he ordered his disciples to bring him *both* a donkey and a colt. So, Matthew wrote, "the disciples went and did as Jesus had directed them; they brought *the donkey and the colt,* and put their clothes *on them,* and he sat *on them.*"[89] (The gospels of Mark and Luke, by contrast, agree that Jesus entered Jerusalem riding not on *two* animals but on a single colt.) Matthew did not intend to mislead his readers; what probably motivated him to correlate prophecy with event in this way was his conviction that, since Jesus *was* the messiah, his coming *must* have fulfilled the ancient prophecies.

Yet from the first century to the present, "arguments from prophecy" have persuaded many people; apparently including Irenaeus's mentor, The philosopher Justin Martyr, who wrote that, as a young student seeking truth (c. 140 C.E.), he had become disillusioned with one philosophy teacher after another—first a Stoic, then a Peripatetic, a Pythagorean teacher, and a disciple of Plato. Finally he concluded that the human mind by itself was incapable of finding truth and asked in dismay, "Should anyone, then, employ a teacher? For how could anyone be helped, if there is no truth even in them?" Justin writes that one day, as he was walking along the shore and thinking about these questions, he met an old man who told him about the Hebrew prophets, and how their ancient oracles had been proven true by events that had happened when Jesus came. The old man explained that

> there existed, long before now, certain men more ancient than all those who are regarded as philosophers—men both righteous and beloved by God who spoke by the divine spirit, and foretold events which would take place, and are now taking place. They are called prophets. These alone both saw and proclaimed the truth . . . being filled with the holy spirit. They did not use [logical] demonstration in their writings, since they were witnesses to truth

beyond such demonstration . . . and those events which have happened and are happening now, compel you to assent to what they say.[90]

"After he had said these things," Justin said, "he went away . . . and I have not seen him since. But immediately a fire was kindled in my soul, and a love of the prophets, and of those people who are friends of Christ, possessed me."[91]

Justin met with a group of these people, and eventually received baptism in the name of the "holy spirit, who through the prophets foretold everything about Jesus," and who, he later wrote, illuminated his mind. Then, having become a "Christian philosopher," he offered to prove to a Jewish philosopher named Trypho that "we have not believed empty fables, or words without any foundation, but words filled with the spirit of God, and great with power, and flourishing with grace."[92] Although he says that Trypho's companions "laughed and shouted rudely" when they heard this, Justin offered what he believed was incontrovertible proof. He explained to Trypho, for example, that the prophet Isaiah had foretold that "a virgin shall conceive and bear a son"[93]—a miracle that Matthew says occurred nearly five hundred years later, when Mary gave birth to Jesus. Justin adds that other prophets, including David, Isaiah, and Zechariah, had predicted in detail Jesus' birth, his final entry into Jerusalem, the betrayal by Judas, and his crucifixion. Justin says that when he engaged Trypho in public debate, he carefully set forth correlations between specific prophecies and the events that he believed fulfilled them—correlations impossible to explain, he argued, apart from divinely inspired prophecy, and God's intervention in human history.

But those who criticize such "proof from prophecy" suggest that Christians like Justin argue fallaciously—for example, by mistaking a misleading translation for a miracle. The author of the Gospel of Matthew, for example, apparently reading Isaiah's prophecy in Greek translation, took it to mean that "a *virgin* [*parthenos* in Greek] shall conceive." Justin himself acknowledges that Jewish interpreters, arguing with Jesus' followers, pointed out that what the prophet had actually written in the original Hebrew was simply that "a *young woman* [*almah*] shall conceive and bear a son"—apparently predicting immediate events expected in the royal succession.[94]

Yet Justin and Irenaeus, like many Christians to this day, remained unconvinced by such arguments, and believed instead that ancient prophecies predicted Jesus' birth, death, and resurrection, and that their divine inspiration has been proven by actual events. Unbelievers often find these proofs far-fetched, but for believers they demonstrate God's "history of salvation." Justin staked his life on this conviction, and believed that he had given up philosophical speculation for truth as empirically verifiable as that of the scientist whose experiments turn out as predicted.

Since Irenaeus saw the proof from prophecy as one way to resolve the problem of how to tell which prophecies—and which revelations—come from God, he added certain writings of "the apostles" to those of "the prophets," since he, like Justin, believed that together these constitute indispensable witnesses to truth. Like other Christians of their time, Justin and Irenaeus, when they spoke of "the Scriptures," had in mind primarily the Hebrew Bible: what we call the New Testament had not yet been assembled. Their conviction that God's truth is revealed in the events of salvation history provides the essential link between the Hebrew Bible and what Justin called "the apostles' memoirs," which we know as the gospels of the New Testament.

It was Irenaeus, so far as we can tell, who became the principal architect of what we call the four gospel canon, the framework that includes in the New Testament collection the gospels of Matthew, Mark, Luke, and John. First Irenaeus denounces various Christian groups that settle on only one gospel, like the Ebionite Christians, who, he says, use only Matthew, or followers of Marcion, who use only Luke. Equally mistaken, Irenaeus continues, are those who invoke many gospels. Certain Christians, he says, declared that certain Christians "boast that they have more gospels than there really are . . . but really, they have no gospel which is not full of blasphemy."[95] Irenaeus resolved to hack down the forest of "apocryphal and illegitimate" writings—writings like the Secret Book of James and the Gospel of Mary—and leave only four "pillars" standing.[96] He boldly declared that "the gospel," which contains all truth, can be supported by only these four "pillars"—namely, the gospels attributed to Matthew, Mark, Luke, and John. To defend his choice, he declared that "it is not possible that there can be either more or fewer than four," for "just as there are four regions of the universe, and four principal winds," the church itself requires "only four pillars."[97] Furthermore, just as the prophet Ezekiel envisioned God's throne borne up by four living creatures, so the divine Word of God is supported by this "four formed gospel." (Following his lead, Christians in later generations took the faces of these four "living creatures"—the lion, the bull, the eagle, and the man—as symbols of the four evangelists.) What makes these gospels trustworthy, he claimed, is that their authors, who he believed included Jesus' disciples Matthew and John, actually *witnessed* the events they related; similarly, he added, Mark and Luke, being followers of Peter and Paul, wrote down only what they had heard from the apostles themselves.

Few New Testament scholars today would agree with Irenaeus; we do not know who actually wrote these gospels, any more than we know who wrote the gospels of Thomas or Mary; all we know is that all of these "gospels" are attributed to disciples of Jesus. Nevertheless, as the next chapters will show, Irenaeus not only welded the Gospel of John to the far more widely quoted gospels of Matthew and Luke but praised John as the greatest gospel. For Irenaeus, John was not the *fourth* gospel, as Christians call it today, but the *first* and *foremost* of the gospels, because he believed that John alone understood who Jesus really is—God in human form. What God revealed in that extraordinary moment when he "became flesh" trumped any revelations received by mere human beings—even prophets and apostles, let alone the rest of us.

Irenaeus could not, of course, stop people from seeking revelation of divine truth—nor, as we have seen, did he intend to do so. After all, religious traditions survive through time only as their adherents relive and reimagine them and, in the process, continually transform them. But, from his own time to the present, Irenaeus and his successors among church leaders did strive to compel all believers to subject themselves to the "fourfold gospel" and to what he called apostolic tradition. Henceforth all "revelations" endorsed by Christian leaders would have to agree with the gospels set forth in what would become the New Testament. Throughout the centuries, of course, these gospels have given rise to an extraordinary range of Christian art, music, poetry, theology, and legend. But even the church's most gifted saints, like Teresa of Avila and John of the Cross, would be careful not to transgress—much less transcend—these boundaries. To this day, many traditionally minded Christians continue to believe that whatever trespasses canonical guidelines must be "lies and wickedness" that come either from the evil of the human heart or from the devil.

Yet Irenaeus recognized that even banishing all "secret writings" and creating a canon of four gospel accounts could not, by itself, safeguard the Christian movement. What if some who read the "right" gospels read them in the wrong way—or in *many* wrong ways? What if Christians interpreted these same gospels to inspire—or, as the bishop might say, to spawn—new "heresies"? This is what happened in Irenaeus's congregation—and, as we shall see, he responded by working to construct what he called orthodox (literally, "straight-thinking") Christianity.

tototot

THE CANON OF TRUTH
AND THE TRIUMPH
OF JOHN

People engaged in spiritual exploration often are especially attracted to the Gospel of John; for, although written with great simplicity—and, apparently, to advocate faith—this gospel shines with paradox, mystery, and hints of deeper meaning. Thus T. S. Eliot, moved by its opening lines, wrote these in response:

> And the light shone in darkness and
> Against the Word the unstilled world still whirled
> About the center of the silent Word.[1]

Some four centuries before Eliot, another poet, the son of converted Jews, an intense young Spanish monk who would become a saint and mystic, chose John's name as his own, calling himself John of the Cross. Now, largely because of the Nag Hammadi discoveries, we can see that, nearly two thousand years ago, many of John's earliest readers also responded to this gospel in surprising and imaginative ways.

How did those Christians whom Irenaeus calls "evil interpreters" read John and the other Scriptures—and why did he oppose what they found there? Irenaeus warns that these people "have cast truth aside";[2] they introduce lies that entice and delude naïve believers, but to many people their obvious fictions actually seem true. Irenaeus says that the Christian poet and teacher Valentinus, his disciple Ptolemy, and others like them have invented all kinds of myths about what happened "in the beginning," and even *before* the beginning of the world, and how the unknown Source of all being, which these Christians sometimes call the primal Father and other times call Silence—since there are no words to describe this Source—first poured forth streams of divine energies, both masculine and feminine, whose dynamic interaction brought forth the universe. Some followers of Ptolemy go on to say that divine Wisdom came forth "in the beginning" and participated with God to bring forth the universe, as described in Genesis 1 through 3.

Irenaeus may not have known that such questions were widely discussed in certain Jewish circles among teachers and their disciples, who apparently influenced the questions that teachers like Valentinus and Ptolemy asked, as well as their interpretation of passages from Israel's Scriptures—especially Genesis, the Psalms, and the oracles of Isaiah and Proverbs.

We know little of Valentinus himself, since only a few fragments of his writing survive,[3] but he, too, wrote a poem reflecting on the mystery of how the visible universe emerges from the invisible Source, as Genesis 1:2 says, after "the spirit moved above the depth":

> All things I see suspended through spirit;
> All things borne along through spirit;
> Flesh depending on soul,
> Soul bound to air,
> Air depending on ether,
> From the depth, fruit brought forth,
> From the mother's womb, a child.[4]

At the same time, Valentinus and his disciples were among the first, perhaps a hundred years before the New Testament canon was established, to place these newer "apostolic" writings along with Genesis and the prophets, and to revere the authority of Jesus' sayings as equal to or even above that of Israel's Scriptures.[5] Ptolemy even wrote in a letter to Flora, an aristocratic Roman woman who studied with him, that Jesus' sayings offer "the *only* unerring way to comprehend reality."[6] In discussing divine mysteries, Irenaeus says that Ptolemy and members of his circle often cited passages from Paul's letters and the "sayings of the Lord" known to us from Matthew and Luke; but what they quoted repeatedly, "making the fullest possible use"[7] of it, was the Gospel of John—which was, in fact, their favorite. When Irenaeus decided to arm himself against these teachers by reading their commentaries and confronting their authors, he may have known that Heracleon, whom he calls Valentinus's "most respected" disciple, had written a famous *Commentary on John*—which is, so far as we know, the earliest commentary written on *any* New Testament book.[8]

When I first heard about Heracleon's commentary, I wondered: Why would anyone bother to write a *commentary* on a gospel written so clearly? And what would attract a *heretic* to a gospel that was to become the touchstone of orthodoxy? Later, after studying the newly discovered sources, I saw that, by putting my questions this way, I had unconsciously adopted Irenaeus's terminology and incorporated his viewpoint. For what he did, with remarkable success, was convince Christians that his reading of John's gospel—or any gospel, for that matter—was the only correct reading, and that his approach was the "canonical" scriptural interpretation. Irenaeus, as we shall see, insisted on what he called the "canon of truth" and rejected the kind of exegesis which he said was "current among Greek philosophers,"[9] such as certain Stoics who read Homer's poems allegorically, taking gods like Zeus and Hera to represent elements of the natural universe, and such as followers of Plato, who claimed to find in Homer's poems allusions to teachings such as the transmigration of the soul.[10] Irenaeus, alarmed by what Valentinus's disciples were doing, warns believers to beware of approaching their own sacred texts in such ways. On the contrary, he declares that, wherever possible, one must discern the obvious meaning; and whenever a certain passage seems ambiguous or difficult, one's understanding should be guided by those passages whose meaning seems clear.[11]

Heretics, Irenaeus warns, read wildly, concentrating on the enigmas, mysteries, and parables they find in the Scriptures, rather than on passages that seem plain; often they read incoherently, or in conflict with the obvious meaning of the text.[12] Although some write commentaries, many more respond to what they find in Genesis, in Isaiah's oracles, Paul's letters, the

Psalms, and the gospels by coming up with songs, poems, visions, and "revelations" of their own—even liturgical dance. As we shall see, the texts discovered at Nag Hammadi bear out Irenaeus's suspicions, as well as his conviction about what was at stake: what is spiritual truth, and how it may be discerned.

Let us look, then, at a few of these "wild readings" to see how the Gospel of John became a center of controversy. Despite its simplicity of style, few readers have found John's gospel easy to understand. Especially in the context of the synoptic gospels, even its earliest admirers noticed, for example, that it sometimes contradicts Matthew, Mark, and Luke. For example, as we noted, John begins with the story of Jesus attacking the money changers and merchants in the Temple, a scene whose violence John increases by adding that Jesus "knotted a whip out of small cords" and wielded it as he "drove them all out of the Temple, and the sheep and the oxen, and poured out the changers' money, and overthrew the tables."[13] The other gospels, as we have seen, all place this incident at the end of Jesus' life, when it must logically have happened, since this act, according to Matthew, Mark, and Luke, was what impelled the chief priests to have Jesus arrested and turned over to the Roman authorities to be killed. When Origen, the brilliant Egyptian "father of the church" (later accused of heresy himself), was asked about this, he explained, as we have seen, that although "John does not always tell the truth *literally*, he always tells the truth *spiritually*"[14]—that is, symbolically. Origen even suggests that the holy spirit inserted such contradictions into John's gospel in order to startle the reader into asking what they mean, and to show that these stories are not meant to be taken literally; he agreed with Valentinus and his disciples that the reader has to plunge beyond the shimmering surface of John's words—or those of any of "the scriptures"—to seek their hidden meanings.

Valentinus, a poet himself, loved the power of biblical images, especially John's. Though orthodox Christians later sought to destroy his teachings, the surviving fragments show that he took the story of the cleansing of the Temple, for example, as a parable showing how, when God shines into our hearts, he shatters and transforms what he finds there to make us fit dwellings for the holy spirit.[15] Another fragment suggests that Valentinus's own spiritual awakening occurred when he received a revelatory dream in which a newborn child appeared and said to him, "I am the *logos*"[16]—in John's language, the divine *word* revealed in human form.

Let us look at several examples of what Irenaeus calls "evil exegesis," and then consider what he finds objectionable. Irenaeus identifies Valentinus as the author of what he calls the Gospel of Truth, and if this is the same one discovered at Nag Hammadi, we now can see, for the first time, how Valentinus praised the "hidden mystery, Jesus the Christ."[17] Whether written by Valentinus or, more likely, by one of his followers, the Gospel of Truth depicts a world devoid of God as a nightmare, a world like the one Matthew Arnold described nearly two thousand years later:

> . . . the world, which seems
> to lie before us like a land of dreams,
> so various, so beautiful, so new,
> hath really neither joy, nor love, nor light, nor certitude, nor
>   peace, nor help for pain;
> and we are here as on a darkling plain

swept with confused alarms of struggle and flight
where ignorant armies clash by night.[18]

The Gospel of Truth, too, pictures human existence, apart from
God, as a nightmare, in which people feel

> as if . . . they were fleeing, or, without strength they come
> from having chased after others; or they are . . . striking
> blows, or . . . receiving blows themselves; or they have
> fallen from high places, or they take off into the air,
> though they do not even have wings; . . . or as if people
> were murdering them, though there is no one pursuing
> them, or they themselves are killing their neighbors, for
> they have been stained with their blood.[19]

But *unlike* Arnold, the author of this gospel believes that we
can awaken from horror to discover God's presence here and
now; and when we wake up, the terror recedes, for the divine
breath—the spirit—runs after us, "and, having extended a hand,
lift[s] [us] up to stand on [our] feet."[20] Thus, the Gospel of Truth
continues, echoing John's prologue, the "*word* of the Father, . . .
Jesus of the infinite sweetness . . . goes forth into all things, supporting all things," and finally restores all things to God, "bringing them back into the Father, and into the Mother."[21]

The Gospel of Truth also says that what we see in Jesus—or
God—depends on what we need to see, and what we are capable of seeing. For although the divine is "ineffable, unimagin-
able," our understanding is bound by words and images, which
can either limit or extend what we perceive. So, although God

is, of course, neither masculine nor feminine, when invoking the image of God the Father, this author also speaks of God the Mother. Moreover, while drawing upon images of Jesus familiar from the gospels of Matthew and Luke (the "good shepherd")[22] and from Paul, who speaks of wisdom's "hidden mystery,"[23] as well as from John ("the word of the Father"), this author offers other visions of Jesus as well. Acknowledging that believers commonly see Jesus "nailed to the cross" as an image recalling sacrificial death, this author suggests seeing him instead as "fruit on a tree"—none other than the "tree of knowledge" in Paradise.[24] But instead of destroying those who eat the fruit, as Adam was destroyed, *this* fruit, "Jesus the Christ," conveys *genuine* knowledge—not intellectual knowledge but the knowing of mutual recognition (a word related to the Greek term *gnosis*)—to those whom God "discovers . . . in himself, and they discover him in themselves."[25]

This gospel takes its name from the opening line: "The gospel of truth is joy, to those who receive from the Father the grace of knowing him,"[26] for it transforms our understanding of God and ourselves. Those who receive this gospel no longer "think of [God] as petty, nor harsh, nor wrathful"—not, that is, as some biblical stories portray him—"but as a being without evil," loving, full of tranquillity, gracious, and all-knowing.[27] The Gospel of Truth pictures the holy spirit as God's breath, and envisions the Father first breathing forth the entire universe of living beings ("his children are his fragrant breath"), then drawing all beings back into the embrace of their divine source.[28] Meanwhile, he urges those who "discover God in themselves, and themselves in God" to transform *gnosis* into action:

Speak the truth to those who seek it,
And speak of understanding to those who have
    committed sin through error;
Strengthen the feet of those who have stumbled;
Extend your hands to those who are sick;
Feed those who are hungry;
Give rest to those who are weary;
And raise up those who wish to rise.[29]

Those who care for others and do good "do the will of the Father."

A second example of what Irenaeus calls "evil interpretation"—the so-called Round Dance of the Cross—illustrates what he means by "heretics" who often add "their own inventions" to the gospels. The anonymous follower of Valentinus who wrote the Round Dance offers to fill in a scene missing from John's gospel, in which Jesus chanted and danced with his disciples "on the night he was betrayed."[30] The Round Dance author notes that John's gospel *leaves out* an account of the last supper in which Jesus tells his disciples to eat bread as his body and drink wine as his blood—that scene which Matthew, Luke, and Paul all regard as central, for it shows believers how to celebrate the "Lord's supper." But in John's account of that night, something quite different happened. After dinner, according to John, Jesus

got up from the table, took off his outer robe, and tied a cloth around himself. Then he poured water into a basin and began to wash the disciples' feet and to wipe them with the cloth that was tied around him.[31]

John means to say that this act is significant—even necessary—for anyone who wants to share communion with Jesus, for as he recounts it, when Peter protested that his teacher must not wash his feet like a slave, Jesus told him that "you do not now recognize what I am doing, but later you will understand," and added, "Unless I wash you, you have no share in me."[32] From ancient times to the present, many Christians have reenacted *this* scene as if it, like the last supper, offered directions for a ritual; so, on the Thursday before Easter, the pope of the Roman Catholic Church takes the role of Jesus and ritually washes the feet of his cardinals. Within the Church of Jesus Christ of Latter-day Saints, the church's president washes the feet of the Mormon "elders"; and to this day many other Christian groups—various Orthodox churches and many Protestant groups, including some Baptists and Pentecostalists—do likewise.

Whoever wrote the Round Dance of the Cross boldly revised John's account of that night by adding a different episode—apparently meant to be kept secret. In the Round Dance, which is found in the Acts of John, a second-century collection of stories and traditions inspired by John's gospel, John begins the story of Jesus' final night where the gospel account leaves off, and says that Jesus invited his disciples to dance and sing with him:

> Before he was arrested . . . he assembled us all, and said, "Before I am delivered to them, let us sing a hymn to the Father, and so go to meet what lies before us." So he told us to form a circle, holding one another's hands, and he himself stood in the middle and said, "Answer Amen to me."[33]

Then, as the disciples circled him, dancing, Jesus began to chant a hymn in words that echo the Gospel of John:

> "Glory to you, Father." And we, circling around him,
>   answered him, "Amen."
> "Glory to you, Logos; glory to you, Grace." "Amen."
> "Glory to you, Spirit; glory to you, Holy One. . . ." "Amen."
> "We praise you, Father; we thank you, Light, in whom
>   dwells no darkness." "Amen. . . ."
> "I am a light to you who see me." "Amen."
> "I am a mirror to you who know me." "Amen."
> "I am a door to you who knock upon me." "Amen."
> "I am a way to you, the traveler." "Amen."[34]

Although the phrase about the mirror could have come straight from the Gospel of Thomas, the primary source for the last two, as well as many of the others, is the Gospel of John.

Whoever composed this hymn, then, clearly found in John's gospel inspiration for the kind of teaching we more often associate with Thomas; for here Jesus invites his disciples to see themselves in him:

> "[W]hich I am about to suffer is your own. For you could by no means have understood what you suffer, unless I had been sent to you as word [logos] by the Father . . . if you knew how to suffer, you would be able not to suffer."[35]

Thus, in the Round Dance of the Cross, Jesus says that he suffers in order to reveal the nature of human suffering, and to teach

the paradox that the Buddha also taught: that those who become aware of suffering simultaneously find release from it. Yet
he also tells them to join in the cosmic dance: "'Whoever dances
belongs to the whole.' 'Amen.' 'Whoever does not dance does
not know what happens.' 'Amen.' "[36]

Those who loved the Acts of John apparently celebrated the
eucharist by chanting these words, holding hands, and circling
in this dance to celebrate together the mystery of Jesus' suffering, and their own—and some Christians celebrate it thus to
this day. In the Acts of John, John tells his fellow disciples that it
is not "strange or paradoxical" that each of them sees Jesus in
different ways, for he explains that what anyone can see depends on that person's expectations and capacity. Once, he says,
Peter and Andrew asked John and James about the young child
they saw calling them from the shore,

> and my brother said . . . to me, "John, what does he want,
> this child on the shore who called us?" And I said, "Which
> child?" And he answered me, "The one beckoning to us."
> And I said, "Because of the long watch at sea, you are not
> seeing well, brother James. Don't you see the man stand-
> ing there who is handsome, with a joyful face?" But he
> said to me, "I do not see him, my brother; but let us dis-
> embark, and see what this means."[37]

John adds, "at another time, he took me and James and Peter
onto a mountain where he used to pray, and we saw him illuminated by a light that no human language could describe." Later,
"Again he took the three of us onto a mountain, and we saw him

praying at a distance." John says, however, that "since he loved
me, I went up quietly to him, as if he did not see, and I stood
there looking at his back." Suddenly, John says, he saw Jesus as
Moses once saw the Lord—"he was wearing no clothes . . . and
did not look like a human being at all . . . his feet shone with
light so brilliant that it lit up the earth, and his head reached
into heaven, so terrifying that I cried out"—whereupon Jesus
immediately turned, was transformed back into the man that
John could easily recognize, and rebuked John in words Jesus
speaks to Thomas in John's own gospel: "John, do not be faithless, but believe."[38]

The Gospel of John inspired yet another example of "evil
exegesis"—the famous and influential Secret Book of John, which
Irenaeus apparently read, and which another anonymous Christian wrote, in John's name, apparently as a sequel to the gospel. The Secret Book opens after Jesus' death, when "John, the
brother of James, the son of Zebedee," walking toward the Temple, is accosted by a Pharisee, who charges that "this Nazarene"
has deceived John and his fellow believers, "filled your ears with
lies, closed your hearts, and turned you from the traditions of
your fathers."[39] John turns away from the Temple and flees to a
desolate place in the mountains, "grieving greatly in [his] heart."
There, as he struggles alone with fear and doubt, he says that
"suddenly the heavens opened, and the whole creation shone,
and the world was shaken."[40] John is astonished and terrified to
see an unearthly light, in which changing forms appear, and to
hear Jesus' voice saying, "John, John, why are you astonished,
and why are you afraid? . . . I am the one who is with you always. I am the Father; I am the Mother; and I am the Son."[41]
After a moment of shock, John recognizes Jesus as the one who

radiates the light of God and appears in various forms, including Father, Son, and Holy Spirit—the last envisioned as feminine
(suggested by the gender of the Hebrew term for spirit, *ruah*) and
so as divine Mother.

But after Jesus consoles John with this vision, he says that
"the God and Father of all things" cannot actually be appre-
hended in anthropomorphic images, since God is "the invisible
one who is above all things, who exists as incorruption, in the
pure light into which no eye may look,"[42] invisible, unimagin-
able, wholly beyond human comprehension. How, then, can one
speak of God at all? To answer this question, the author of the
Secret Book borrows the language of John's gospel: "To the point
that I am able to comprehend him—for who will ever be able
to comprehend him? . . . [God] is the light, the one who gives the
light; the life, the one who gives the life."[43] Yet what follows, as
we shall see in the next chapter, is a remarkable dialogue in
which John questions the risen Savior, who gives him a breath-
taking and wildly imaginative account of what happened "in
the beginning"—mysteries hidden before creation within the
divine being, the origin of evil, and the nature and spiritual
destiny of humankind.

Of all the instances Irenaeus offers of "evil exegesis," however,
his prime example is part of a commentary on John that asks
questions similar to those asked in the Secret Book—what John's
gospel reveals about "the origin of all things." The author of
this commentary, traditionally identified as Ptolemy,[44] says that
"John, the disciple of the Lord, wanting to set forth the origin of
all things, how the Father brought forth all things,"[45] reveals in
his opening lines—although in a way hidden from the casual
reader—the original structure of divine being. This, he says, is

the "primary ogdoad," which consists of the first eight emana-
tions of divine energy, rather similar to what kabbalists later
will call the divine *sephirot*; thus, when Valentinus and his disciples read the opening of John's gospel, they envisioned God,
the divine *word*, and Jesus Christ as, so to speak, waves of divine
energy flowing down from above, from the great waterfall to
the local creek.

Irenaeus rejects this attempt to find hidden meaning in
John's prologue and explains to his reader that he has quoted
this commentary at length so that "you may see, beloved, the
method by which those using it deceive themselves, and abuse
the Scriptures by trying to support their own invention from
them."[46] Had John meant to set forth the primordial structure of
divine being, Irenaeus says, he would have made his meaning
clear; thus "the fallacy of their interpretation is obvious";[47] and
he then, as we shall see, offers the *true* interpretation of John's
gospel.

Yet Irenaeus undertook his massive, five-volume *Refutation
and Overthrow of Falsely So-Called Knowledge* precisely because he
knew that many people might find his conclusions far from obvious. Worse, they might well see him and his opponents as
rival theologians squabbling about interpretation, rather than
as orthodox Christians against heretics. While his opponents
say he reads only the surface, he replies that all of them say different things; not one of them agrees with another, not even
with their own teachers; on the contrary, "each one of them
comes up with something new every day,"[48] as do writers and
artists today, for whom originality is evidence of genuine insight. For Irenaeus, however, innovation proved that one had
abandoned the true gospel. The problem he faced, then, was

how to sort out all those lies, fictions, and fantasies. How to distinguish true from false?

Irenaeus says that there is only one way to be safe from error: go back to what you first learned, and "hold *unmoving* in [your] heart the canon of truth received in baptism."[49] He assumes that his audience knows what this canon is: "This faith, which the church, even when scattered throughout the whole world . . . received from the apostles," and which, he specifies, includes faith in

one God, Father almighty, creator of heaven and earth, and the seas . . . and in one Christ Jesus, the son of God, who became incarnate for our salvation, and in the holy spirit . . . and the birth from a virgin, and the suffering, and the resurrection from the dead, and the heavenly ascension in flesh . . . of our beloved Jesus Christ.[50]

True believers everywhere, he says, share this same faith.

Irenaeus's vision of a united and unanimous "catholic church" speaks more of what he hoped to create than what he actually saw in the churches he knew in Gaul, and those he had visited or heard about in his travels though Gaul, Asia Minor, and Italy. In those travels he encountered resistance from those he called heretics, and when he urged them to return to the simple baptismal faith, he says that they answered in words like this:

We too, have accepted the faith you describe, and we have confessed the same things—faith in one God, in Jesus Christ, in the virgin birth and the resurrection—when we were baptized. But since that time, following Jesus' injunction to "seek, and you shall find," we have been striving to go beyond the church's elementary precepts, hoping to attain spiritual maturity.

Now that the discoveries at Nag Hammadi allow the heretics—virtually for the first time—to speak for themselves, let us look at the Gospel of Philip, to see how its author, a Valentinian teacher, compares his own circle with that of those he considers "simpler" Christian believers. This author, whom we call Philip, and his circle apparently had received baptism in a procedure similar to the one that the church father Justin Martyr describes as customary in Rome;[51] that is, the initiate, having repented of past sins, receives and affirms the teachings of Jesus as taught by his followers, confesses the faith, and promises to live accordingly. Then, led naked into the water, the initiate is baptized as the divine names—God the Father; Jesus Christ, his son; and the holy spirit—are pronounced; and finally, dressed in fresh garments, the new Christian is anointed with oil and invited to participate in the eucharist. Like Justin, Philip says that baptism effects spiritual rebirth; "through this mystery we are *born again* though the holy spirit."[52]

But unlike Justin—or any other early Christian writer known to me—Philip then asks, *What happens—or doesn't happen*—when a person undergoes baptism? Is baptism the same for everyone? Philip suggests it is not. There are many people, he says, whose baptism simply marks initiation; such a person "goes down into the water and comes up without having received anything and says 'I am a Christian.' "[53] But sometimes, Philip continues, the person who undergoes baptism "receives the holy spirit . . . this is what happens when one experiences a mystery."[54] What makes the difference involves not only the mysterious gift of divine grace but also the initiate's capacity for spiritual understanding.

So, Philip writes, echoing Paul's Letter to the Galatians, many believers see themselves more as God's slaves than as God's children; but those who are baptized, like newborn infants, are meant to grow in faith toward hope, love, and understanding (*gnosis*):

> Faith is our earth, in which we take root; hope is the water through which we are nourished; love is the air through which we grow; *gnosis* is the light through which we become fully grown.[55]

Thus, he explains, those who first confess faith in the virgin birth later may come to a different understanding of what this means. Many believers, indeed, continue to take the virgin birth literally, as if Mary conceived apart from Joseph; "some say that Mary conceived through the holy spirit," but, Philip says, "they are in error."[56] For, he explains, "virgin birth" is not simply something that happened once to Jesus; rather, it refers to what may happen to everyone who is baptized and so "born again" through the "virgin who came down," that is, through the holy spirit.[57] Thus, as Jesus was born to Joseph and Mary, his human parents, and later was born *spiritually* when the holy spirit descended upon him at his baptism, so we, too, first born physically, may be "born again through the holy spirit" in baptism, so that "when we became Christians we came to have both a father and mother,"[58] that is, both the heavenly Father and the holy spirit.

But Philip says that many people, whom he calls "the apostles and the apostolic ones,"[59] are "in error," since they remain oblivious of—even offended by—this mystery. Such people, he continues, are also wrong about resurrection, since they take this, too, as if it could be only a unique event in which Christ died and rose bodily from the grave. Philip suggests instead that Jesus' resurrection, like his virgin birth, is not only something that occurred in the past but is a paradigm of what happens to each person who undergoes spiritual transformation. Philip quotes Paul's famous teaching on resurrection ("flesh and blood shall not inherit the kingdom of God," I Corinthians 15:50) to show that those who receive the holy spirit in baptism are not only "born again" but also "raised from the dead."[60]

Someone might object, however, that this cannot be what resurrection means: didn't Jesus rise *in the flesh*? Philip answers that, of course, "one must rise 'in this flesh,' since in this world everything exists in [the flesh]." But he challenges those who take bodily resurrection literally. After all, he asks, "what is flesh?" In answer, he quotes from John's gospel to show that when Jesus told his disciples to "eat my flesh and drink my blood" (John 6:53), he was speaking in metaphor, since what he meant was that they were to partake of the sacred meal of bread and wine, which conveys Jesus' "flesh," that is, Philip suggests, his divine *word*, and his "blood," the holy spirit.[61]

Philip thus discriminates between nominal Christians—those who claim to be Christians simply because they were baptized—and those who, after baptism, are spiritually transformed. He sees himself among the latter but does not congratulate himself for belonging to a spiritual elite; instead, he concludes by anticipating that ultimately *all* believers will be transformed, if not

in this world then in eternity. Whoever undergoes such transformation, he says "no longer is a Christian, but a Christ."[62]

If Irenaeus read the Gospel of Philip, he must have sharply
rejected such teaching; for, as we have seen, when he demands
that the believer "hold *unmoving* in his heart the rule of truth received in baptism," he specifically includes the "birth from a
virgin, the passion, and the resurrection from the dead . . . in the
flesh of our beloved Jesus Christ, our Lord";[63] and, like many orthodox believers ever since, Irenaeus accepted these as unique,
revelatory events through which Christ ensured human salvation. Were members of Philip's circle to answer that they confessed the same faith, Irenaeus would have replied, as he did to
other Valentinian Christians, that although they "say the same
things, they mean something different by them." Followers of
Valentinus might readily have admitted that this was true; but,
they asked him, what is *wrong* with that? "When we confess the
same things as you, why do you call us heretics?"[64] No doubt
their interpretations *differed* from his, and from each other's; but
why did Irenaeus think that these differences actually *endangered*
the church?

These questions are hard to answer, for although Irenaeus liked clear boundaries, he was not simply narrow-minded,
and he was by no means intolerant of all difference. In fact, as
he sought to realize his teacher Polycarp's vision of a *universal*
church, he included as "apostolic" a wide range of traditions
that spanned a century and a half and, he claimed, were shared
by Christians scattered from Germany to Spain, Gaul to Asia
Minor, and from Italy to Africa, Egypt, and Palestine. Irenaeus
surely knew that the traditions he accepted—to say nothing of
many more that he disagreed with but allowed—included the

diversity of beliefs and practices that one would expect of what he called "the catholic church . . . scattered throughout the whole world."[65]

In fact, Irenaeus encouraged his fellow believers to tolerate certain variations of viewpoint and practice. For example, he argued against those who accepted only *one* gospel, such as those he calls the Ebionites, who, he says, accepted only Matthew, and followers of Marcion, who accepted only Luke. And while his contemporary Tatian, who, like himself, was a student of Justin, attempted to harmonize the various gospels by rewriting them into one single, composite account, Irenaeus was the first, so far as we know, to urge believers to accept all *four* distinct gospels, despite their obvious differences, and to join them into the collage that he called the "four formed gospel." Furthermore, when Victor, bishop of Rome, demanded that all Christians in the capital city celebrate Easter on the same day, Irenaeus traveled to Rome to urge the bishop not to cause trouble for Greek-speaking Christians, who like Irenaeus himself, had emigrated from Asia Minor and traditionally celebrated Easter on a different day (as Greek, Russian, Ethiopic, Serbian, and Coptic Orthodox Christians still do).[66]

Given, then, that Irenaeus acknowledged a wide range of views and practices, at what point did he find "heterodoxy"—which literally means "different opinions"—*problematic*, and for what reasons? Why does he declare that the Gospel of Truth, like all the "heretical" gospels, "has nothing to do with the apostolic gospel" but is "full of blasphemy"?[67] Why does he insist that the Secret Book of John simply shows "the kind of lies the heretics invent"?[68] To answer these questions, we should recall that Irenaeus was not a theoretically minded philosopher engaging in theological debate so much as a young man thrust into leadership of the survivors of a group of Christians in Gaul after a violent and bloody persecution. As we have seen, Irenaeus could not forget that in Smyrna, where he had grown up in the household of Bishop Polycarp, his aged and renowned spiritual father had been hounded by the police, and after escaping and hiding in a country house, had been captured and brought back to the public amphitheater, where, as the mob shouted insults, he was stripped naked and burned alive. Then, as we noted, about twenty years later (c. 177), in Gaul, where Polycarp may have sent him to work as a missionary, Irenaeus had seen more violence against Christians, some of whom were lynched while dozens of others were arrested and tortured, many strangled to death in prison. According to *The Letters of the Churches of Lyons and Vienne*, some thirty to fifty who survived and refused to renounce their witness were torn apart by wild animals and killed by gladiators in a public spectacle attended by his fellow townspeople. And we have seen that only after the aged bishop Pothinus had died of torture and exposure in prison, Irenaeus, perhaps in his thirties, having somehow escaped arrest, apparently stepped in to serve as leader of those who were left.

As he did so, determined to consolidate these scattered believers and provide them the shelter of a community by joining them into the worldwide network Polycarp had envisioned as a "catholic" church, what concerned Irenaeus was whatever proved seriously divisive. What, then, *did* prove divisive? Irenaeus would have answered *heresy*—and because of the way he characterized it, historians traditionally have identified *orthodoxy* (which literally means "straight thinking") with a certain set of ideas and opinions, and heterodoxy (that is, "thinking other-wise") as an opposite set of ideas. Yet I now realize that we greatly oversimplify when we accept the traditional identifica-tion of *orthodoxy* and *heresy* solely in terms of the philosophical and theological content of certain ideas. What especially con-cerned Irenaeus was the way the activities of these "spiritual teachers" threatened Christian solidarity by offering *second bap-tism* to initiate believers into distinct groups *within* congrega-tions.

The author of the Gospel of Philip, as we have seen, *implicitly* divided the church by discriminating between those who, he says, are "in error" and those who have "come to know the truth"; but Irenaeus knew that many other followers of Valenti-nus divided the church *explicitly*. What he found most objection-able was not so much what they *said* as what they *did*—above all, that many offered believers a *second* baptism in a ritual they called *apolutrosis*—which could take many forms.[69] Irenaeus de-scribes precisely how they operated. First, they called them-selves "spiritual Christians" and attracted unwary people from what they called the "common" and "ecclesiastical" majority, inviting them into private meetings of their own. There they challenged the newcomers—and themselves—to question what their faith meant, and in the process they often discussed pas-sages from the Scriptures. Irenaeus may be speaking from his own experience when he complains that when someone objects to what they say or asks them to explain what they mean, "they claim that he is not a person capable of receiving the truth, since he has not received from above the capacity to under-stand"; thus, he says, "they really give him no answer." But when they find people who prove receptive, they engage them in a long period of preparation and finally declare that these are ready to receive *apolutrosis*, which enables them to move beyond the "common" community to join the more select circles of the spiritually mature. So, Irenaeus complains,

> they call those who belong to the church "common," and "ecclesiastic". . . and *if anyone gives himself up to them like a little sheep, and follows out their practice and their apolutrosis*, such a person is so elated that he imagines he . . . has already entered within the "fullness of God". . . and goes strutting around with a superior expression on his face, with all the pomposity of a cock.[70]

What Irenaeus found most distressing was that those who flocked to the groups gathered around teachers like Ptolemy often heard in these meetings that the baptism all Christians receive in common is, in fact, only the *first step* in the life of faith. Such teachers explained to newcomers that just as John the Baptist baptized with water those who repented, when they themselves first confessed faith in God and in Jesus, they too received, in effect, the "baptism of John" to cleanse them from sin. But such teachers also pointed out how, according to the gospel accounts of Mark, Matthew, and Luke, John the Baptist prophesied that Jesus himself would baptize his followers "with the holy spirit and with fire."[71] They pointed out, too, Jesus' saying that he had "another baptism with which to be baptized,"[72] and they explained that this means that those who advance on the spiritual path are to receive that *second* baptism.

Furthermore, they said, this higher baptism marks a major transition in the initiate's relationship with God. In their first baptism, believers have pledged to serve as Lord the God whom they revere as creator, and fear as divine lawgiver and judge; but now, Ptolemy and his disciples explained, having progressed beyond that level of understanding, they are to come to see God as Father, as Mother, Source of all being—in other words, as One who transcends all such images. Thus Ptolemy invites those who previously saw themselves as God's *servants*—or, more bluntly, his slaves—to come to understand themselves as God's *children*. To signal their release from slavery to become, in Paul's words, God's own children and heirs,[73] Ptolemy calls the second baptism *apolutrosis*, which means "redemption" or "release," alluding to the judicial process through which a slave became legally free.

When we look back to our examples of "evil interpretation," we can see that Irenaeus's characterization, however hostile, nevertheless is accurate. Those who wrote and treasured innovative works such as the Gospel of Truth, the Round Dance of the Cross, the Secret Book of John, and the Gospel of Philip were implicitly criticizing, intentionally or not, the faith of most believers. So, as we noted, Valentinus contrasts those who picture God as a "petty, jealous, and angry" with those who receive "the grace of knowing him" as a loving and compassionate Father. Many scholars believe that the Gospel of Truth was written as an inspirational talk to be delivered at some such baptism among Valentinus's followers, as those who come to know themselves as God's children also come to recognize one another, this gospel says, as "true brothers, upon whom the Father's love is poured out, and among whom He is fully present."[74] So, too, those who participated in the Round Dance of the Cross, circling in the dance and chanting "Amen!" in response to the person chanting Jesus' part, were celebrating their new relationship with Jesus, who here, as we noted, invites them to

> see yourself in Me who am speaking, and, when you have seen what I do, keep silent about my mysteries. You who dance, consider what I do; for this human passion which I am about to suffer is your own.[75]

The dance celebration described in the Round Dance itself may have served as a form of *apolutrosis;* for while virtually all Christians first initiated newcomers through some kind of water baptism, Irenaeus says that these spiritual teachers had not come up with any single way of performing the second baptism: "It has no set form, and every teacher transmits it in his own way, as each is inclined; so there are as many kinds of *apolutrosis* as there are teachers of these mystical insights."[76]

Having carefully investigated these matters, he reports that some of them baptized initiates with water a second time, using different invocations:

> Some . . . bring the initiates to water, and baptizing them, they say these words: *"in the name of the unknown Father of all being; into Truth, the mother of all things; into the One who descended on Jesus [the spirit]; into union; redemption [apolutrosis]; and communion with the powers."*[77]

Others performed *apolutrosis* as a kind of spiritual marriage, which joins a person in union with one's "life hid with Christ in God,"[78] that is, the previously unknown part of one's being which connects one with the divine. Still others, he says, "repeat[ed] certain Hebrew words," and he reports the invocations they used (which are actually not Hebrew words)—"Basema, Chamosse, Baonara, Mistadia, Ruada, Kousta, Babaphor, Kalacheit"[79]—which allude to the hidden names of God. After the invocations and prayers, those who participated pronounced a blessing ("Peace to all upon whom this name rests"), anointed the initiate with balsam oil, and chanted "Amen." There were others, Irenaeus says, who rejected any kind of ritual at all, for they said that "recognizing [God's] ineffable greatness" *itself* constitutes *redemption;* thus whoever recognized this already had been "set free."[80]

Whatever form the ritual took, the candidate usually was required to answer a set of questions. Just as the sacraments of baptism and marriage involve a ritual dialogue that shows what the person intends and pledges ("Do you believe in God, the Father . . . ?" "Do you take this man/this woman . . . ?"), so those who receive *apolutrosis* were asked questions like these: Who are you? Where do you come from? Where are you going? Many religious groups, including the mystery religions, adapted such a set of standard questions—the kind that a local border patrol might ask travelers—to use in their initiations. We have already seen that the Gospel of Thomas shows Jesus teaching his disciples to respond to questions like these, questions that members of Thomas's circle were probably asked during baptism, or second baptism:

> Jesus said, "If they say to you, *'Where do you come from?'* Say, 'We come from the light; the place where the light [first] came into being . . .' If they say to you, *'Who are you?'* Say, 'We are the children [of the light], and we are the chosen

of the living Father.' If they ask you, *'What is the sign of your Father in you?'* Say to them, 'Movement and rest.' "[81]

Those who responded appropriately showed that they knew who they were *spiritually*, and knew how they related to the "living Father" as well as to Jesus, who, like themselves, comes "from the light." Although such teachers practiced *apolutrosis* in many ways, what mattered most to them, Irenaeus says, was that a person experience spiritual rebirth: "They say that it is necessary for those who have received full *gnosis* to be *born again* into the power which is above all things."[82]

But Irenaeus was dismayed at the way such practices were dividing Christians from one another; he declares that "no reform of the church could possibly compensate" for the damage these people were doing as they "cut in pieces and destroy[ed] the great and glorious body of Christ."[83] What *apolutrosis* really means, Irenaeus charges, is not *redemption* at all but something very different—namely, that Satan was inspiring these so-called spiritual teachers to *"deny that baptism is rebirth to God, and to renounce the whole faith."*[84] By devaluing what they held in common with other believers and initiating people into their own smaller groups, such teachers were creating potentially innumerable schisms throughout Christian groups worldwide, as well as in each congregation. Irenaeus concludes by declaring that any spiritual teachers or prophets who do these things are actually heretics, frauds, and liars. He writes his massive, five-volume attack, *The Refutation and Overthrow of Falsely So-Called Knowledge*, to demand that members of his congregation stop listening to any of them and return to the basic foundation of their faith. Irenaeus promises that he will explain for them what the Scriptures really mean and insists that only what he teaches is true.

His primary challenge was this: How could he persuade believers that the "common" baptism, which all believers receive, far from being merely the preliminary step in the life of faith, actually effects, as he claims, "rebirth to God"? And how could he persuade them that it conveys not just the elementary teaching that beginners need but nothing less than the "whole faith"? In response, Irenaeus helped construct the basic architecture of what would become orthodox Christianity. His instructions to congregations about which revelations to destroy and which ones to keep—and, perhaps even more important, how to interpret those they kept—would become the basis for the formation of the New Testament and what he calls its "canon of truth," which, in turn, would become the framework for the orthodox creeds. None of these, of course, were Irenaeus's single-handed accomplishment; on the contrary, as he was the first to point out, he built upon what he loved to call "apostolic tradition" and incorporated the efforts of many others. This does mean, however, that the actions he took, developed by his ecclesiastical successors, proved decisive for what would become Christianity as we know it—as well as what we would not know of it—for millennia to come.

CHAPTER FIVE

ototot

CONSTANTINE AND
THE CATHOLIC CHURCH

When I found that I no longer believed everything I thought Christians were supposed to believe, I asked myself, Why not just leave Christianity—and religion—behind, as so many others have done? Yet I sometimes encountered, in churches and elsewhere—in the presence of a venerable Buddhist monk, in the cantor's singing at a bar mitzvah, and on mountain hikes—something compelling, powerful, even terrifying that I could not ignore, and I had come to see that, besides *belief*, Christianity involves *practice*—and paths toward transformation.

Last Christmas Eve, I went to the midnight service with my sixteen-year-old daughter, Sarah, who, as an infant, when I carried her with me to the Church of the Heavenly Rest in New York, would raise her head to listen intently to the singing cascading down from the choir loft. When she was eight, she joined the choir at Trinity, a Protestant church in Princeton, because, she said, "the music helps my heart." Now, eight years later, after walking in the cold, we slowly pressed our way through the crowded church and found a place to sit close together on the stone stairs behind the lectern, where the choir was standing. This celebration was one that I loved as a child, and had come to love again as an adult, especially since the birth of our first child, Mark, and later of Sarah and David. Since Mark's death, however, I had found participation difficult.

But this year I found myself wholeheartedly singing the carols and listening to the stories of the child born in Bethlehem, angels breaking through darkness to announce the miraculous birth—stories that most New Testament scholars, knowing that we have little or no historical information about Jesus' birth, regard as a mixture of legend and *midrash*, that is, storytelling that draws upon Israel's stories of the miraculous birth of Isaac, of the prophet Samuel, and of the rescue of the infant Moses. On that night, my own associations with those stories seemed to be embraced in the joy and solemnity of the festival, laced, as it is, with intimations of Jesus' impending death as well as the promise of his continuing radiant presence. Attending to the sounds and the silence, the candlelight and darkness, I felt the celebration take us in and break over us like the sea. When it receded, it left me no longer clinging to particular moments in the past but borne upon waves of love and gratitude that moved me toward Sarah, toward the whole community gathered there, at home, or everywhere, the dead and the living. For a moment I was shocked by the thought: We could have made all this up out of what had happened in our own lives; but, of course, we did not *have to* do that, for, as I realized at once, countless *other* people have already done that, and have woven the stories of innumerable lives into the stories and music, the meanings and visions of Jesus' birth. Thus such celebrations are borne along through all the generations that have shaped and re-shaped them, and those that continue to do so, just as encountering the tradition may shape and reshape us.

Many Christians today, however, might ask the same question Irenaeus asked: If spiritual understanding may arise from human experience, doesn't this mean that it is nothing but human invention—and therefore false? According to Irenaeus, it is heresy to assume that human experience is analogous to divine reality, and to infer that each one of us, by exploring our own experience, may discover intimations of truth about God. So, he says, when Valentinus and his disciples opened John's gospel and wanted to understand what *word* means, they reflected on how *word* functions in human experience.[1] What this means, he says, is that they mistook their own projections for theology, so that they found in the Scriptures only what they invented, "each one seeking to validate his own experience."[2] But Irenaeus himself believed that, on the contrary, whatever we might say about our own experience has nothing to do with God:

> So it is that heaping together with a kind of plausibility all human emotions, mental exercises, and formation of intentions, and utterances of words, *they have lied with no plausibility at all against God. For they ascribe the things that happen to human beings, and whatever they recognize themselves as experiencing,* to the divine *word.*[3]

Had those heretics been right, Irenaeus continues, we would have no need of revelation; "the coming of the Lord will appear unnecessary and useless, if, indeed, he did come intending to tolerate and preserve each person's ideas concerning God."

What Irenaeus objected to was the refusal of those he calls heretics to acknowledge how utterly unique Jesus is, and thus their tendency to place him with ourselves on the human side of the equation. Irenaeus proclaims the opposite: that God— and Jesus Christ, God's manifestation on earth—wholly transcends human modes of thought and experience. Against those who emphasize our kinship with Jesus Christ, Irenaeus argues that Jesus' transcendence sets him apart from the rest of humanity:

> I have shown from the scriptures that *no one of all the sons of Adam is, in his own right, called "God" or named "Lord."* But that *He is himself, and in his own right . . . beyond all men who ever lived, God, and Lord, and Eternal King, and Only-begotten, and Incarnate Logos,* is proclaimed by all the prophets, the apostles, and by the Spirit itself, [and] may be seen by all who have attained to even a modicum of truth.[4]

Furthermore, he adds, "those who say that [Jesus] was merely a human being, begotten by Joseph" show themselves ungrateful to the *"word* of God, who *became flesh* [John 1:14] for them."[5] Not only was Jesus' birth—his "spiritual generation from God"— completely different from ordinary human birth but so was his death completely different from ours. For just as he alone was born miraculously from a virgin, so he alone, of the whole human race, having died, rose bodily from the dead—"rose in the substance of flesh, and *pointed out to his disciples the mark of the nails and the wound in his side.*"[6]

Nevertheless Irenaeus had to respond to a question that many people—Jews as well as "heretics"—apparently asked him: What is *wrong* with seeing Jesus as if he were simply "one of us"? Haven't we all—ourselves as well as he—been created in the image of God? Irenaeus agrees but adds that the original affinity between God and ourselves was obliterated when the human race surrendered to the power of evil. "Although by nature we belonged to the all-powerful God," he explains, the devil, whom he calls "the apostasy," captured and came to dominate the human race and "alienated us [from God], contrary to nature, and made us his own."[7] Thus we were all in a desperate situation and would have been utterly destroyed had not the divine *word* descended from heaven to save us; for "there is no other way we could have learned about God unless our Master, existing as the word, had become man"[8] and shed his blood to redeem us from the evil one.

How, then, could Irenaeus safeguard this essential gospel message—upon which he believed salvation depends? As we have seen, when Irenaeus confronted the challenge of the many spiritual teachers, he acted decisively, by demanding that believers destroy all those "innumerable secret and illegitimate writings"[9] that his opponents were always invoking, and by declaring that, of all versions of the "gospel" circulating among Christians, only four are genuine. In taking these two momentous—and, as it turned out, enormously influential—steps, Irenaeus became a chief architect of what Christians in later generations called the

New Testament *canon*, a carpenter's term meaning "guideline"—
often a string with a weight attached—to check that a wall is
straight.[10]

Yet Irenaeus himself never applied the term *canon*, as we do,
to the collection of writings he called the "four formed gospel,"
nor to any other list of writings, since he knew that lists of writings don't prevent heresy. After all, Valentinus and his followers
often drew their inspiration from the same sources that most
Christians revered in common, including Genesis, Paul's letters,
and the gospels of Matthew and Luke. Thus Irenaeus was determined to establish an even more authoritative "canon": it was to
be a guideline for understanding any writing or preaching—any
gospel at all.

Since both he and his opponents started with the "canon
of faith received in baptism,"[11] how could Irenaeus make sure
that all believers would take this to mean what he believed it
meant—that Jesus is God incarnate? To do so, he declares that
he will prove the heretics wrong by using their own favorite
gospel against them. He intends to establish what he calls the
"canon of truth," and to produce from his own reading of
John—by reformulating the baptismal teaching in language he
borrows from that gospel—language that his successors would
build into the Nicene Creed, and the creeds that followed. But
how did John's teaching that Jesus is God's word in human
form become what Irenaeus wanted to make it: the very touchstone of orthodoxy?

This question would be easier to answer if the meaning of
John's gospel were obvious. But we have seen how controver-
sial it was among its earliest readers: Irenaeus complains that
Valentinus's disciples were "always quoting the Gospel of John,"[12]

while, surprisingly, prominent "fathers of the church," including three of his revered mentors, apparently were not.[13] Irenaeus probably was aware that his own teacher, Bishop Polycarp of Smyrna, may not have known John's gospel; at any rate, he chose not to mention it, so far as we know. Nor is John's gospel mentioned by another martyr Irenaeus revered, Ignatius, bishop of nearby Antioch,[14] nor, for that matter, by Justin Martyr, the Christian philosopher in Rome whose works Irenaeus also admired. He does mention that some Christians, including some who opposed the "new prophecy" movement, rejected John's gospel. Perhaps he knew that the Roman teacher Gaius had called the Gospel of John heretical[15] and charged that it was actually written not by Jesus' disciple but by John's worst enemy, the heretic Cerinthus.[16] Irenaeus was not, however, the first to introduce this gospel into circles of "ecclesiastical" Christians; some years earlier, another of Justin's students, the Syrian Tatian, had included it with several others, including Matthew and Luke, when he rewrote these accounts and other sources into his own composite "gospel"; and the many fragments that remain of Tatian's long version show that it was widely read.[17] Irenaeus himself treats the Gospel of John as part of the tradition he received from his home community in Asia Minor; but while he champions this gospel, and repeats the tradition that "John, the disciple of the Lord,"[18] wrote it while he lived in Ephesus, he must have known that many Christians found it problematic, even suspect.

Why, then, did Irenaeus join the Gospel of John with the three much more widely accepted gospels of Matthew, Mark, and Luke, and claim it was an indispensable element of the four formed gospel?[19] And why did he place John not, as Christians did later, as the *fourth* gospel but instead as the *first and foremost* pillar of "the church's gospel"? Irenaeus says that the gospel deserves this exalted position because John—and John alone—proclaims Christ's *divine* origin, that is, his

> original, powerful and glorious generation from the Father, thus declaring, *"In the beginning was the word, and the word was with God, and the word was God* [John 1:1–2]." Also, *"all things were made through him* [*the word*] *and without him nothing was made* [John 1:3]."[20]

Irenaeus tells us that Valentinus's disciple Ptolemy, reading these words, envisioned God, *word*, and finally Jesus Christ as, so to speak, waves of divine energy flowing down from above; thus, he suggests, the infinite divine Source above reveals itself in diminished form in the divine *word*, which reveals itself, in turn, in the more limited form of the human Jesus.[21] But Irenaeus declares that such an interpretation misses what we saw in Chapter 2 as the central conviction John wants to convey—that Jesus embodies the divine *word* that comes forth from God and so, on earth, *is* "Lord and God" to those who recognize him. So Irenaeus challenges Ptolemy's interpretation of John's prologue and argues instead that "God the Father" is equivalent to the *word*, and the *word* is equivalent to "Jesus Christ." He states emphatically that John means there is

> One God all powerful and one Jesus Christ, "through whom all things came into being" [John 1:3]; he says, the *same one* "Son of God" [1:14]; the *same one* "only begotten" [1:14, 18]; the *same one* "Maker of all things"; the *same one*

"true light enlightening everyone" [1:9], the *same one* creator of "all things" [1:3], the *same one* "coming to his own"
[1:11]; the *same one* that "became flesh, and dwelt among
us" [1:14]."[22]

What Irenaeus's successors would derive from this was a kind of
simple, almost mathematical equation, in which God = word =
Jesus Christ.[23] That many Christians to this day consider some
version of this equation the essence of Christian belief is a mark
of Irenaeus's accomplishment—and his success. Irenaeus wants
to emphasize this point when he repeats that Jesus Christ *himself* manifests the "one God almighty" who is the "Maker of the
universe." And because Irenaeus's bold interpretation came virtually to define orthodoxy, those who read John's gospel today
in any language except the Greek original will find that the
translations make his conclusion seem obvious—namely, that
the man "who dwelt among us" was God incarnate (for discussion of the Greek original, see endnote).[24]

   This, then, is the "canon of truth" which Irenaeus reformu-
lates in language he borrows from John's prologue: that "there
is one all-powerful God, who made all things by his word. . . .
So the scripture says, 'all things were made through him and
without him nothing was made' [John 1:3]."[25] Instead of envi-
sioning God on high remote from this world, especially from its
deficiencies and sufferings, Irenaeus declares that God manifests himself in and through this world, even choosing to in-
habit it himself, as Jesus Christ, the "word made flesh."

   Irenaeus argues that this "canon of truth" enables him—and
anyone else who uses it—to read not only the gospels but all
Scripture in the radical way pioneered by some of his Christian

predecessors. Wherever the Jewish Scriptures mention God's *word*, or even where they mention the *Lord God* himself, Irenaeus now claims to find *Jesus Christ*. So, he argues, when God *spoke* to Abraham, it was "our Lord, the *word* of God, who spoke"—not only to Abraham but to all the patriarchs and prophets:

> No doubt . . . the Son of God is implanted everywhere throughout his Scriptures; at one time speaking with Abraham; at another time, with Noah, giving him the dimensions of the ark . . . at another time, he directs Jacob on his journey, and speaks with Moses from the burning bush.[26]

When the prophet Ezekiel saw the Lord surrounded by angels and worshiped in heaven, Irenaeus declares that the One he saw on the throne was *Jesus Christ*.[27] Even when Genesis tells how "the Lord took clay from the earth, and formed *adam*" (Genesis 2:7), Irenaeus declares that "the Lord God" who created humankind in Paradise was "our Lord Jesus Christ, who 'was made flesh' [John 1:14] and was hung upon the cross."[28]

Irenaeus knew that this claim far oversteps anything found in the Gospels of Matthew, Mark, and Luke, where, he notes, each pictures Jesus as a man who receives special divine power, as God's "anointed one." Each of these gospel writers assigns Jesus a somewhat different—human—role. Thus, Irenaeus says, Matthew depicts Jesus as God's appointed king and traces his family back to King David;[29] Luke emphasizes his role as priest;[30] and Mark depicts him primarily as God's prophet.[31] But each of these gospels stops short of identifying Jesus with God, much less *as* God. For Irenaeus, however, the Gospel of John does precisely that; as the church father Origen said later, only John speaks of Jesus' "divinity." Irenaeus, like Origen, took this to mean that John is not only different but also "more elevated," having seen what the others missed; and from this conviction he apparently concluded that only by joining John with the others could the church complete the "fourfold gospel," which teaches that Jesus is God incarnate. Carried away with enthusiasm, Irenaeus identifies personally with the evangelist and declares that "John, the Lord's disciple," wrote this gospel for precisely the same purpose that he himself now was writing his *own* book—namely, to expose "heretics"; to confound those who spread "falsely-called *gnosis*"; and, above all, "to establish the *canon of truth* in the church."[32]

Having set forth his reformulated *canon of truth*—that God the Father is also the Creator who "made all things through his word" (John 1:3), the *word* that became incarnate in Jesus Christ—Irenaeus turns to the practical question: Who worships God rightly, and who does not? First, he says, the Jews do not, since they refuse to see that "the word of the Lord" which spoke to Abraham and Moses was none other than Jesus Christ. Because they do not identify "the word of the Lord" as Jesus Christ, Irenaeus declares,

> the Jews have departed from God, *since they have not received his word*, but they imagined that they could know the Father . . . without the word, *being ignorant of the God who spoke in human form* to Abraham and then to Moses.[33]

Since they fail to recognize Jesus as "the God who spoke in human form" to their ancestors, Irenaeus says that God disinherited the Jews and stripped them of their right to be his priests. Although they continue to worship, God rejects their offerings as he rejected Cain's, since, just as Cain killed Abel, so the Jews "killed the Just One," Jesus, so that "their hands are full of blood."[34]

Thus the Jews worship God in vain, for he has transferred their priesthood to those who *did* recognize his "word"[35]— namely, the apostles whom Jesus taught to offer "the sacrifice of the new covenant," when he told them to offer the bread he called his body and the wine he called his blood. Ever since Jesus' death on the cross, the eucharist that reenacts his sacrifice is the lightning rod that draws God's power down to earth. Not only does the eucharist alone offer access to God but, Irenaeus declares, "this pure sacrifice *only the church offers—not the Jews . . . nor any of the assemblies of the heretics.*"[36]

Since Irenaeus assumed—rightly, no doubt—that few Jews would read what he wrote, much less contest his claim that God rejects their worship, he spent little time arguing that they are excluded. But he did anticipate objections he expected members of his Christian audience to raise: Isn't the eucharist a holy sacrifice when *any* baptized Christian—or, at least, any priest— offers it as Jesus taught his disciples to do? Irenaeus says no: when heretics offer the eucharist, they do so in vain. For those who accept his canon of truth, what matters is not only to be a *Christian* but to be an *orthodox* Christian—that is, one who "thinks straight."

Instead of asserting his own authority to interpret the gospel against that of his opponents, Irenaeus identifies his own belief with that of the whole consensus of what he calls "apostolic tradition." Thus, he insists, "orthodox" Christians are those who uphold the fourfold gospel *together with* the canon of truth—

later to be expanded into the great creeds—that directs how to interpret it. I do not mean to suggest that he set out to deceive his audience. On the contrary, Irenaeus surely shared the conviction that made "orthodox Christianity" so compelling to him, as well as to many other Christians to this day: that "the faithful," as trustworthy stewards, hand down only what they, in turn, received from the apostles, without adding or subtracting anything from what Irenaeus and others call the *depositum fidei*—the faith that the apostles deposited, as in a bank. By invoking the authority of the ancient consensus of the apostles they can claim, then, that what they teach is not only the *unchanging truth* but absolutely *certain.*[37]

Irenaeus warns that eternal salvation depends on discriminating between which priests in Christian churches are "genuine" and which are, in his words, "heretics, schismatics, or hypocrites," and he calls on believers to *obey* the former and *shun* the latter:

> Therefore it is necessary to *obey the priests who are in the church*—those who have received the succession from the apostles, as we have shown, and who have also received. . . . the *certain gift of truth . . . but to hold in suspicion those who stand apart from the primary line of succession, and who gather in any place whatsoever, [and to regard them] either as heretics with evil intentions or as schismatics, puffed up with themselves, or as hypocrites.*[38]

Irenaeus knew that the "disciples of Valentinus" did not oppose the clergy. On the contrary, what made them especially hard for him to discredit was the fact that many of them were priests themselves. Yet he warns believers to beware of those whose claims to priestly office are virtually identical to any others' but who actually are *heretics* who "serve only themselves," and not God. He says that believers must be careful to associate only with priests who worship God *rightly.* This means not only that they "teach sound doctrines" but that they speak "sound words" and display "blameless conduct"—in short, they do not hold unauthorized meetings, or claim access to secret teaching, or perform special initiations.

Irenaeus ends his five-volume *Refutation* calling upon his fellow believers to judge and excommunicate heretics. Recalling how God's wrath falls upon the Jews "who became the killers of their Lord," he declares that truly spiritual Christians must also condemn "all the followers of Valentinus," since, although many believers see them as fellow Christians, they actually subvert the faith and, like the Jews, have become "sons of the devil." Finally he contrasts those who take "many deviant paths" with those who "belong to the church," who share

> one and the same faith, observe the same precepts, and . . . protect the same form of ecclesiastical constitution . . . in which one and the same path of salvation is demonstrated throughout the world.[39]

Vividly evoking the final judgment pictured in the Revelation, he leaves the reader with visions of the devil, the antichrist, and all their demonic powers being cast into eternal fire along with all of their human offspring, while the heavenly Jerusalem descends to welcome "the priests and the disciples of the apostles" along with "the faithful."[40] For Irenaeus, then, and for his successors, *making a difference* between true Christians and those he calls heretics—and choosing the path of "orthodox" faith and practice—is what ultimately makes the difference between heaven and hell.

We do not know how members of Irenaeus's own congregation reacted to his pleas, although we *do* know how distressed he was that the great majority of Christians initially accepted the Valentinians' view of themselves. While Irenaeus, as bishop, was working to expose them as "wolves in sheeps' clothing"[41] and expel them from the churches, he wrote that most Christians regarded them as among their most influential and advanced members. In his own time, Valentinus had been widely respected as a teacher by his fellow Christians in Rome,[42] and even a generation later Irenaeus's contemporary the famous Egyptian teacher Clement of Alexandria, as well as Clement's brilliant successor, Origen, engaged in discussion and argument with prominent disciples of Valentinus, and regarded them as fellow Christian teachers. Although Clement and Origen often criticized aspects of Valentinian theology, they also adopted elements of it into their own teaching.[43]

About twenty years after Irenaeus wrote, Tertullian described how his fellow believers in Carthage reacted when he warned them against joining circles he called heretical:

> "How does it happen," they ask, "that this woman or that man, who were *the most faithful, the most circumspect, and the most respected in the church*, have gone over to the other side?"[44]

But Irenaeus was convinced that the presence of the Valentinian Christians was dangerously divisive—that it undermined the preaching of the gospel and the authority of its leaders. He wanted them either to abandon their "heresy" or be cut off from the churches. We do not know how his contemporaries responded; I would guess that the majority, moved by his concern, rallied around Irenaeus and, rather than risk expulsion, chose the safer shelter of the church community and what Irenaeus insisted was the stable authority of the "catholic" consensus of churches and their clergy. In any case, we know that Christians in later generations increasingly followed his lead, as many tried to compel those who persisted in "heresy" either to conform or to separate themselves from the churches. For during the following century and a half, as rapidly growing numbers of converts joined Christian churches despite sporadic outbursts of violent persecution, many bishops adopted and developed the safeguards Irenaeus had outlined to strengthen what he had called the "same form of ecclesiastical constitution" by standardizing basic Christian instruction and excluding those who deviated from the "one . . . path of salvation." During the fourth century, when persecution suddenly gave way to official toleration of Christians under Constantine, and then to the construction of a Christian empire, a coalition of bishops would take up Irenaeus's agenda and attempt to realize his vision of a catholic—that is, universal—orthodox church.

During Irenaeus's lifetime, of course, this astonishing turn of events lay a hundred and fifty years in the future. As we have seen, his Valentinian opponents had never intended to go their own separate way. But many of them rejected the alternatives Irenaeus placed before them: either accept the common faith as "the whole faith" or reject it entirely. Instead, they continued to affirm the common faith as a first step toward truth but questioned not only what it means but what lies beyond it. Among themselves they not only recognized diversity but expected and welcomed it, as philosophers did in their discussions, as evidence of original and creative insight.[45] So, Tertullian wrote caustically,

> When they consider that "spiritual seed in everyone," whenever they hit upon something new, they immediately call their audacity a spiritual gift—no unity, only diversity! And so we see clearly that most of them disagree with one another, since they are willing to say—and even sincerely—of certain points, "This is not so," and "I take this to mean something different," and "I do not accept that."[46]

Tertullian expressed shock, too, that, as in some philosophic circles, women participated with men: "These heretical women— how audacious they are! They are bold enough to teach, to preach, to take part in almost every masculine function—they may even baptize people!"[47] While they appreciated diverse viewpoints within their own circles, such Christians may have extended less tolerance and generosity toward the "simple" believers who followed the bishop. Irenaeus wrote that when he directly questioned Valentinians and challenged them, they either remained silent or said that he was simply wrong, since he had not yet advanced beyond a naïve level of understanding.[48]

Irenaeus, for his part, says that when these "absolutely foolish and stupid people" were threatened with excommunication, they sometimes replied that they no longer believed in the God whom he invoked as an angry judge ready to cast unbelievers into the fires of hell. Moreover, they questioned his understanding of the Scriptures. Some asked, for example, how one could worship a God who first "hardened the heart of Pharaoh and his servants"[49] and then punished them by drowning them in the sea. Or how could a just God *refrain* from condemning Lot for impregnating his own daughters when he was drunk?[50] As we have seen, the author of the Gospel of Truth says that those who come to know the infinite goodness and compassion that belong to "the fullness of God" no longer think of God in terms of such deficient and anthropomorphic images.

Others, including Valentinus's disciple Heracleon, interpreted disparity between Christians in terms not unlike what the psychologist William James would call "varieties of religious experience."[51] Heracleon contrasts two qualitatively different types of conversion experience. He says that the great majority of Christians appeal to God only when they are desperate, and turn to faith only when they see miracles; thus the gospels often depict Jesus as a wonder-worker who heals the sick, raises the dead, and walks on water. Since they experience the human situation—their own situation—as pervaded by suffering and threatened by death, these Christians see Jesus above all as a healer and savior. Heracleon says that John characterizes this kind of conversion when he tells how Jesus, traveling to Galilee, met a ruler who begged him to come down and heal his son, who was desperately ill. Although Jesus rebuked him for the deficiency of his faith ("Unless you see signs and wonders, you will not believe"), the ruler renewed his pleas: "Sir, come down before my child dies." But after Jesus challenged him to have faith ("Go: your son will live") and his son recovered, the story concludes that "he himself believed, and all his household."[52]

This type of conversion experience, Heracleon says, is familiar to those Christians who see God as John pictures this ruler—as a strict, limited, but well-meaning master and father, who has decreed the death penalty for every one of his children who sins and yet loves them and grieves when they perish. But they also believe that, apart from Jesus' sacrificial death on the cross, God does not forgive his own children; he actually saves only those who "believe."

One might ask, how *else* could one see God than as divine ruler, father, and judge? And how else could one see Jesus, except as a miracle worker and savior? Isn't that how the gospels depict him? Heracleon says that John tells the story of the "woman at the well" to show, by contrast, how a person gifted with grace experiences conversion. Here John recounts how Jesus, tired from travel, sits down to rest near a well, asks a Samaritan woman who comes to draw water to give him a drink, and offers her, in return, "living water":

The woman said to him, "Sir, you have nothing to draw with, and the well is deep; where do you get that living water?" . . . Jesus said to her, *"Whoever drinks from this water will thirst again, but whoever drinks from the water that I shall give him will never thirst; the water that I give will become in him a spring of water, welling up to eternal life."*

The woman said to him, "Sir, give me this water, so that I may not be thirsty, nor come here to draw." Jesus said, "Go, call your husband, and come here." . . . Jesus said to her, *"Woman, believe me, the*

> *hour is coming . . . and is now, when the true worshipers will worship*
> *the father in spirit and in truth. . . . God is spirit, and those who wor-*
> *ship him must worship in spirit and truth."*[53]

Heracleon explains that for John, as for the prophet Isaiah, *water* means "spiritual nourishment"; thus, the story shows that the woman is aware of spiritual thirst and, not knowing how to satisfy it, she has come to draw water from the "well of Jacob," which signifies traditional ways of worshiping God. But since these leave her thirst unsatisfied, when Jesus offers to reveal the source of a wellspring within herself, she immediately grasps what he means and responds, "Give me this water!"

Heracleon points out that Jesus' answer ("Go, call your husband, and come here")[54] makes no sense: not only does he not respond to her request but, as the story shows, he knows that she is not married. Bewildered by his words, the woman initially takes them literally and admits that she is unmarried but has lived with six men. Heracleon says that Jesus reveals to her that she has lived this way "through ignorance of God and the needs of her own life."[55] When he tells her to "call her husband," he is showing her that she already has a "partner" in divine being—that is, a relationship to God of which she is not yet aware. He directs her to call upon resources she already has been given, and to discover her spiritual counterpart, her "fulfillment" (*pleroma* in Greek). Once she recognizes this as an essential part of her being, she may celebrate communion with God as the divine "marriage."

Different as these two types of conversion experience are, they are by no means mutually exclusive. The first sees salvation as deliverance from sin and death; the second shows how

CONSTANTINE AND THE CATHOLIC CHURCH | 163

someone "ignorant of God and of [one's] own nature," and mired in destructive activity, eventually develops a growing awareness of—and need for—relationship with God. Heracleon explains that whoever experiences the first type of conversion may— eventually will—also experience the second, which is what Augustine, writing two centuries later, meant when he spoke of "faith seeking understanding."

Heracleon explains that most Christians tend to take literally the images they find in the Scriptures: they see God as the *creator* who made this present world, the *lawgiver* who gave tablets to Moses on Sinai, the divine *father* who begot Jesus. But those who experience God's presence come to see these traditional images of God for what they are—human creations. One need not *reject* such images, Heracleon says, since they provide an essential way of pointing toward divine reality that words cannot express; but one may come to see that all religious language— and much other language—consists of such images. Whoever realizes this comes to worship God, as Jesus says, "in spirit and in truth."[56]

While Irenaeus sought to clarify basic convictions about God and Jesus Christ in theological statements that would become the framework of the fourth-century creeds, Valentinian Christians accorded such theological propositions a much less important role. Instead of regarding these as the essential and certain basis for spiritual understanding—and instead of rejecting them—they treated them as elementary teachings and emphasized instead what Irenaeus mentions only in passing—how far God surpasses human comprehension.

The Secret Book of John, similarly, sets forth what theologians call the *via negativa*, recognizing what *cannot* be known and

discarding misapprehensions about God. Nevertheless, the Secret Book says that human beings have an innate capacity to
know God but one that offers only hints and glimpses of divine
reality.[57] The Secret Book suggests that the story of Eve's birth
from Adam's side speaks of the awakening of this spiritual capacity. Instead of simply telling about the origin of woman, this
story, symbolically read, shows how the "blessed one above, the
Father" (or, in some versions of the text, the "Mother-Father"),
feeling compassion for Adam, sent him

> a "helper"—luminous *epinoia* ["creative" or "inventive"
> consciousness] which comes out of him, who is called Life
> [Eve]; and she "helps" the whole creation, by working with
> him, and by restoring him to his full being, and by teach-
> ing him about the descent of his kind, and by showing the
> way to ascend, the way he came down.[58]

Thus Eve symbolizes the gift of spiritual understanding, which
enables us to reflect—however imperfectly—upon divine reality.
Another book discovered at Nag Hammadi, On the Origin of
the World, says that when the first man and woman recognized
their nakedness, "they saw that they were naked of spiritual understanding [*gnosis*]." But then the luminous *epinoia* "appeared to
them shining with light, and awakened their consciousness."[59]

The Secret Book intends this story to show that we have a la-
tent capacity within our hearts and minds that links us to the
divine—not in our ordinary state of mind but when this hidden capacity awakens. Because the term *epinoia* has no precise
equivalent in English, I shall leave it in Greek. To speak of various modes of consciousness susceptible to revelation, the au-

thor of the Secret Book invokes a cluster of words related to the Greek verb *noein*, which means "perceive," "think," or "be aware." The Secret Book explains that, although God is essentially incomprehensible, the powers that reveal God to humankind include *pronoia* (anticipatory awareness), *ennoia* (internal reflection), and *prognosis* (foreknowledge or intuition), all personified as feminine presences, presumably because of the gender of the Greek words. But according to the Secret Book it is, above all, the "luminous *epinoia*" that conveys genuine insight. We might translate this as "imagination," but many people take this term as Irenaeus did, to refer to fantasy rather than conscious awareness. Yet as the Secret Book envisions it, *epinoia* (and related modes of awareness) remains an ambiguous, limited—but indispensable—gift. When John asks whether everyone receives the luminous *epinoia*, the savior answers yes—"The power will descend *upon every person*, for without it, no one can stand"—[60] and adds that *epinoia* strengthens those who love her by enabling them to discriminate between good and evil, so that moral insight and ethical power are inseparable from spiritual understanding: "When the spirit of life increases, and the power comes and strengthens that soul, no one can any longer deceive it with works of evil."[61]

The author of the Secret Book stresses that the insights this spiritual intuition conveys are neither complete nor certain; instead, *epinoia* conveys hints and glimpses, images and stories, that imperfectly point beyond themselves toward what we cannot now fully understand. Thus the author knows that these very stories—those told in the Secret Book—are to be taken neither literally nor too seriously; for these, too, are merely glimpses that, as Paul says, we now know only "in a mirror, darkly."[62] Yet, however incomplete, these glimpses suffice to reveal the presence of the divine, for the Secret Book says that, apart from spiritual intuition, "people grow old without joy . . . and die . . . without knowing God."[63]

How is it, then, that many people remain oblivious to *epinoia*? To answer this question, the Secret Book tells a story intended to show that although the creator–god pictured in Genesis is *himself* only an anthropomorphic image of the divine Source that brought forth the universe, many people mistake this deficient image for God. This story tells how the creator–god himself, being unaware of the "blessed one, the Mother–Father, the blessed and compassionate One" above, boasted that he was the only God ("I am a jealous God; there is none other besides me").[64] Intent on maintaining sole power, he tried to control his human creatures by forbidding them to eat the fruit of the tree of knowledge. But when Adam and Eve disobeyed him, and chose to seek knowledge of the divine Source above, he realized that they had listened to their inner resource, the luminous *epinoia*. As soon as the creator–god realized what they had done, he retaliated; first he punished them both, and even cursed the earth itself because of them;[65] then he tried to force the woman to subject herself to the man, saying, "Your husband shall rule over you";[66] and, finally, "all his angels cast them out of Paradise,"[67] burdening them with "bitter fate" and with daily cares to make them oblivious to the "luminous *epinoia*."[68]

But this is a mythical explanation. Can we find a more practical reason for the suppression of the "luminous *epinoia*"? I suggest that the author of the Secret Book knew how Christians like Irenaeus challenged those who spoke of the "God beyond God," and insisted that everyone worship only the creator. But while Valentinus's followers often met such challenges with silence, the author of the Secret Book returns the challenge in stories such as this one that are meant to show how—and why—such leaders, in the name of the God they serve, consign spiritual Christians to hell. The Secret Book suggests that those who worship God only as creator—including most Christians—share his animosity toward spiritual awareness, and also toward those who speak for its presence in human experience. The story of the creator's hostility to *epinoia*, then, is a parable, both comic and painful, of conflict between those who seek spiritual intuition and those who suppress it.

Irenaeus, shocked and distressed by such readings of Genesis, protests that his opponents place far too little confidence in traditional sources of revelation—and far too much in their own imagination:

> *To what distance above God do you lift up your imaginations, you rash and inflated people?* . . . God cannot be measured in the heart, and in the mind he is incomprehensible—he who holds the earth in the hollow of his hand. Who knows the measure of his right hand? Who knows his finger? Or do you understand his hand—that hand which measures immensity? For his hand lays hold of all things, and illumines the heavens, and also the things below the heavens, and tests the reins and the hearts, and is present in mysteries and in our secret thoughts, and does openly nourish and sustain us. . . . Yet, *as if now they had measured and thoroughly investigated him . . . they pretend that beyond [God] there is . . . another Father—certainly they are not looking up to heavenly things, as they claim, but really descending into a profound abyss of insanity.*[69]

But it would take more than theological argument for Irenaeus's viewpoint to prevail in churches throughout the world: it would take, in fact, the revolution initiated by the Roman emperor Constantine. In his famous *History of the Church*, Eusebius of Caesarea, a bishop in Palestine who survived years of persecution in which many of his friends and fellow Christians died, wrote how God miraculously intervened on October 28, 312, by revealing Christ's sign in the heavens to the pagan emperor Constantine and gaining his allegiance.[70] Eusebius then tells how, in the years that followed, Constantine declared amnesty for Christians and became their imperial patron. But this practical military leader chose to recognize only those who belonged to what may have become, by his time, the best-organized and largest group, which he called the "lawful and most holy catholic church."[71]

Constantine's recognition carried with it, of course, enormous benefits. In 313 the emperor ordered that anyone who had confiscated property from "the catholic church of the Christians in any city, or even in other places," during the persecutions of the previous decades must return it immediately to "these same churches"[72] and offer compensation for any damages. Eusebius of Caesarea marveled that in this astonishing new era "bishops constantly received even personal letters from the emperor, and honors, and gifts of money."[73] Eusebius includes in his history a letter Constantine wrote the same year to the proconsul of Africa to say that he was exempting Christian clergy from financial obligations incumbent on ordinary citizens; but, since he knew that the African churches were divided into rival factions, he specified that these privileges applied only to those he called the "ministers of the lawful and most holy catholic religion."[74] The emperor also offered tax relief and, later, tax exemptions to clergy who qualified—while threatening to increase taxes for anyone guilty of founding "heretical" churches. About ten years later, apparently responding to what he considered abuses of these privileges, he wrote a new order to specify that

> the privileges that have been granted in consideration of religion *must benefit only the adherents of the catholic faith* [or "law"]. It is Our will, furthermore, that *heretics and schismatics shall not only be alien from these privileges but also shall be bound and subjected to various compulsory public services.*[75]

Besides allocating money to repair damaged churches, Constantine ordered new ones to be built, including, tradition says, a magnificent Church of St. Peter on the Vatican hill in Rome[76] and the Church of the Holy Sepulcher in Jerusalem. In 324 he wrote to the eastern bishops, urging them to "ask without hesitation whatever [funds] you find to be necessary"[77] from the imperial treasury. He assured them that he had already ordered his finance minister to give them whatever they asked to build new churches and fit them with the splendor appropriate to honor the God of the universe. Constantine also delegated to certain bishops the distribution of the imperial grain supply and other necessities to support people in need, so that they might fulfill Jesus' admonitions to care for the sick, the needy, and the destitute, as well as those who had suffered torture, imprisonment, or exile during the years of persecution.[78] Furthermore, while transforming the status of Christians, Constantine's revolution changed the status of Jews. As Timothy Barnes, one of the foremost contemporary historians of these events, writes, "Constantine translated Christian prejudice against Jews into legal disabilities."[79] He forbade Jews to enter Jerusalem, except on the one day a year they were to mourn for having lost it, and ordered them not to seek or accept converts to Judaism. Moreover, Constantine "prescribed that any Jew who attempted forcibly to prevent conversion from Judaism to Christianity should be burned alive."[80]

To strengthen his own alliance with church leaders and to unify fractious Christian groups into one harmonious structure, Constantine charged bishops from churches throughout the empire to meet at his expense at Nicaea, an inland city, near a large lake, to work out a standard formulation of Christian faith. From that meeting and its aftermath, during the tumultuous decades that followed, emerged the Nicene Creed that would effectively clarify and elaborate the "canon of truth," along with what we call the canon—the list of twenty-seven writings which would become the New Testament. Together these would help establish what Irenaeus had envisioned—a worldwide communion of "orthodox" Christians joined into one "catholic and apostolic" church.

How that happened is far more complex than can be related here. I hesitate even to mention the extraordinary events of the fourth century, since no short sketch can adequately describe them; yet I offer one, since these events no doubt are linked to the history we have been exploring. Fortunately, several outstanding historians have written accounts available for

the interested reader.[81] For our purposes here, even the brief-
est summary would have to note how, during the transitional
decades after 312, Constantine subjected the Roman empire to
a massive restructuring and shifted the underpinnings of imperial power. What he did—and did gradually, in order to minimize
opposition from powerful senators—was transfer the empire's
basic allegiance from the traditional guardians of its welfare, the
gods of Rome, to the foreign god worshiped by those whom his
predecessors had persecuted for atheism.[82] It was at this critical time that Constantine convened the international council of
bishops to meet at Nicaea, "because of the excellent temperature
of the air,"[83] in the early days of June 325. The emperor himself
attended the council and participated in it, telling his guests at
one of the lavish state dinners that he believed God had appointed him "bishop [the Greek term means "supervisor"] of
those outside the church."[84] Although in the past many historians assumed that Constantine directed—even dictated—the entire proceedings, more careful historical investigation has shown
that he not only allowed but expected the bishops themselves
to arbitrate disputes and to forge a working consensus among
rival parties. When he addressed those who gathered at Nicaea,
he urged them to resolve their differences "lest private animosi-
ties interfere with God's business."[85]

One of the conflicts he hoped to resolve had been troubling
churches throughout the empire for several years. As rival Christian groups vied to gain ascendancy in a changed world, the
question was no longer *whether* the "catholic church" would prevail against "heretics and schismatics" but *who* would succeed in
claiming to embody that catholic church. In Egypt, a group of

bishops headed by Alexander, the bishop of Alexandria, and later by his successor Athanasius, took up and extended Irenaeus's agenda. It was he, in fact, who would interpret and update for his contemporaries the "orthodox" side of the controversy earlier engaged in the gospels of Thomas and John. An intense, combative, and single-minded young man, Athanasius, who served as the bishop's secretary, was about eighteen when Alexander engaged in—some would say he started—a conflict that soon divided churches from Egypt to Asia Minor, Syria, and Palestine. Around 318, Alexander had heard that a member of his clergy in Alexandria, a popular Libyan priest named Arius, was preaching that the Word of God, while divine, was not divine in the same way as God the Father. Soon afterward Alexander convened a council of Egyptian bishops to declare Arius's views heretical and excommunicate him, along with all priests and bishops who sided with him, from the church in Alexandria.

This action ignited new controversy. Hearing of Arius's expulsion, bishops in Syria, Palestine, and Asia Minor convened their own councils, several of which declared Arius's teaching not only faithful to catholic tradition but entirely orthodox. Although many bishops urged Alexander to accept Arius back into his church, he adamantly refused. When Alexander and Athanasius received Constantine's summons to Nicaea, to formulate a creed for the "universal" church, they arrived determined to make sure that the carefully chosen—and hotly contested—theological phrases placed there would confess Christ, the Word, as God. They must have been pleased with the result: the formula upon which the majority finally voted, after intense argument, proclaimed that Jesus Christ was "God from God, Light from Light, true God from true God"; that he was "begotten, not made," that is, borrowing John's term, God's "only begotten" offspring (not "made," as were all beings whom God *created*, angels and humans alike).[86]

The next phrase, upon which Alexander and his allies had agreed in advance, proved explosively controversial. To exclude Arius's view that Christ was divine but not in the same sense as God, they insisted on adding that Christ was *"of one being with"*— essentially no different from—God the Father. While the great majority of bishops "were prepared to accept almost any formula that would secure harmony within the church,"[87] those who opposed this phrase pointed out that it occurs neither in the Scriptures nor in Christian tradition. Is it not extreme, they asked, and contrary to the gospels, to say that Jesus Christ is essentially "the same" as God the Father? But those who insisted that he was carried the day; and no doubt it mattered that Constantine, perhaps frustrated by so much time spent wrangling over a phrase, urged the bishops to include it and end the argument. Now that Constantine had endorsed the term, anyone who challenged it might seem to be questioning the orthodoxy of the emperor himself. In any case, all those present signed the document except the few who chose instead to leave: Arius himself, along with some priests and two bishops from Libya who remained loyal to him. Later, however, the inclusion of this phrase intensified controversy among Christians that continued for decades—indeed, for generations (and, some would say, for centuries).

Eventually the Nicene Creed, approved by the bishops and endorsed by Constantine himself, would become the official doctrine that all Christians henceforth must accept in order to participate in the only church recognized by the emperor—the "catholic church." A year before the bishops met at Nicaea, Constantine had tried to legislate an end to "heretical sects," which, by one estimate, may have included about half the Christians in the empire.[88] The emperor ordered all "heretics and schismatics" to stop meeting, even in private houses, and to surrender their churches and whatever property they owned to the catholic church. Although many Christians associated with teachers such as Valentinus, Marcion, and the prophet Montanus ignored the law,[89] and magistrates often failed to enforce it, such legislation lent enormous support to the network of catholic churches.

When Alexander died and Athanasius succeeded him as bishop of Alexandria, Athanasius campaigned tirelessly to induce Christians all over Egypt to unite under this creed, as Irenaeus had envisioned. Constantine's own hopes were more modest; he hoped that the Nicene Creed would offer the basic framework upon which Christians could agree, while allowing room for discussion and disagreement, so long as these did not destroy the fabric of the "universal" church, for, as Barnes observes,

> Constantine believed that all people should be Christian, but that Christians might legitimately hold divergent opinions on theological questions, and that sensible Christians could disagree about doctrine in a spirit of brotherly love.[90]

Some scholars have suggested that these theological disputes were essentially political. The historian Erik Peterson points out that many Christians associated God the Father with the emperor, Jesus Christ with the bishops, and the holy spirit with "the people." Thus, he suggests, Athanasius's claim that the Son is entirely equal with the Father implies that the bishops' authority is equal to that of the emperor himself. Peterson says that this position correlates with Athanasius's refusal to take orders from any emperor, and pervaded the power struggles that characterized the relationship between emperors and bishops in the West throughout the middle ages. Conversely, he says, Arius's formulation, which acknowledges the Father's priority over the Son, survived for centuries in altered form in some of the Eastern churches, which tended to accept imperial power over church affairs, and later would influence the structure of what became "state churches."[91] Whether or not we accept this analysis, we can see that during the decades after the council intense conflict broke out between those who rallied behind Athanasius's position and those who sided with Arius—conflict that engulfed Constantine's sons and grandsons when they succeeded him as emperor and divided bishops and congregations throughout the empire.

As a result, for the next forty years, Athanasius's own position, challenged by those he called Arian Christians—or, as he liked to say, Ariomaniacs—was by no means secure. Although Constantine initially supported Athanasius as Alexander's successor, seven years later he took the side of his opponents and ratified the decision of a council of bishops to depose Athanasius. Forced into exile, Athanasius returned after Constantine's death in 337 to reclaim his position, but two years later he was again deposed by a council of bishops and hid out among his supporters while Bishop Gregory from Cappadocia took over as bishop. Nearly ten years later, when Gregory died, Athanasius returned and reclaimed his office for three more years; but in

349 he was again deposed and replaced by another bishop from Cappadocia. After his third successful rival, having presided as bishop of Alexandria for five years, was lynched in 361, Athanasius succeeded in regaining his position, which he held tenaciously until his death in 373.

Despite such opposition—and perhaps because of it—Athanasius resolved to bring all Egyptian Christians, however diverse, under the supervision of his office. After working to gain the support of ascetic women,[92] he began the more difficult task of establishing his authority over various groups of monks and "holy men," including those who lived in communal monasteries that Pachomius, a former soldier turned monk, had founded throughout Egypt since the legalization of Christianity.[93] In the spring of 367, when Athanasius was in his sixties and more securely established as bishop, he wrote what became his most famous letter. In a world much different from that of Irenaeus, Athanasius included in his annual Easter Letter detailed instructions that would extend and implement the guidelines his predecessor had sketched out nearly two hundred years before. First, he said, since heretics

> have tried to set in order for themselves the so-called apocryphal books and to mix these with the divinely inspired Scripture . . . which those who were eyewitnesses and helpers of the Word handed down to our ancestors, it seemed good to me . . . to set forth in order the canonized and transmitted writings . . . believed to be divine books.[94]

After listing the twenty-two books that he says are "believed to be the Old Testament," Athanasius proceeds to offer the earliest known list of the twenty-seven books he calls the "books of the New Testament," beginning with "the four gospels, Matthew, Mark, Luke, and John," and proceeding to the same list of writings attributed to apostles that constitute the New Testament today. Praising these as the "springs of salvation," he calls upon Christians during this Lenten season to "cleanse the church from every defilement" and to reject "the apocryphal books," which are "filled with myths, empty, and polluted"—books that, he warns, incite conflict and lead people astray. It is likely that one or more of the monks who heard his letter read at their monastery near the town of Nag Hammadi decided to defy Athanasius's order and removed more than fifty books from the monastery library, hid them in a jar to preserve them, and buried them near the cliff where Muḥammad 'Alī would find them sixteen hundred years later.

Although Athanasius intended the "canon of truth," now enshrined in the Nicene Creed, to safeguard "orthodox" interpretation of Scripture, his experience of Christians who disagreed with him showed that these "heretics" could still read the "canonical Scriptures" in ways he considered unorthodox. To prevent such readings, he insists that anyone who reads the Scriptures must do so through *dianoia*—the capacity to discern the *meaning* or *intention* implicit in each text. Above all, he warns believers to shun *epinoia*.[95] What others revere as spiritual intuition Athanasius declares is a deceptive, all-too-human capacity to think subjectively, according to one's preconceptions. *Epinoia* leads only to error—a view that the "catholic church" endorsed then and holds to this day.

Finally, lest anyone seek direct access to God through the "image of God" formed within us in creation, Athanasius took care to block this path as well. In his famous and rhetorically powerful work *On the Incarnation of the Word*, he explains that, although God originally created Adam in his own image, human sin has damaged that image beyond human capacity to repair (a view that Augustine later developed into his understanding of "original sin"). Consequently, there is now only *one* single being who embodies the divine image, and that is the Word of God himself, Jesus Christ:

> Since humankind made in God's image was disappearing, . . . what is the use of humankind originally having been made in God's image? . . . *No one else could re-create the likeness of God's image for human beings except* [*Jesus Christ*], *the Image of the Father.*[96]

While Arius urged believers to emulate Christ, Athanasius declares this effort not only difficult but impossible, even blasphemous: on the contrary, he famously proclaims, "*God became human* so that humankind might become divine." All that a human being can do—*must* do—is believe and receive the salvation that God alone can offer. Thus Athanasius extended what Irenaeus taught: whoever seeks access to God must first have recourse to the Word, whom the believer approaches initially through baptism, by confessing the orthodox faith as contained in the statements of the creed, and by receiving the sacraments—the "medicine of immortality" offered wherever orthodox Christians worship together in church.

Even as a persecuted movement, Christianity had become increasingly visible in cities throughout the empire. During the third and early fourth century, some groups even built their own churches, as the number of converts more than doubled or tripled.[97] Many, no doubt, were persuaded of the truth of Christian faith by the miraculous events that followed Constantine's conversion. No wonder, then, that after 313 many more crowded the churches, not only those seeking some advantage by joining what would become the emperor's church but also, no doubt, others who, although attracted to Christianity, previously had hesitated to receive baptism lest they place themselves and their families in danger. What such converts wanted was not only to share in the promise of divine salvation and eternal life in the next world but also, in this one, to join the "particular Christian society" committed to living according to Christ's precepts—or, at least, according to modified versions of them. Many found in what earlier was a radical alternative to the Roman order a vision of transformed human relationships that now promised to embrace not only home and church but the whole of human society.

This sketch of what happened during the fourth century does not support the simplistic view often expressed by historians in the past—namely, that catholic Christianity prevailed only because it received imperial patronage, or that people participated because their leaders somehow succeeded in coercing them.[98] Several historians have persuasively argued instead that Constantine's decision to affiliate himself with the Christian churches demonstrates the enormous appeal that the Christian movement had held for an increasing numbers of converts long before it was safe to join.[99] Nor does this sketch support the view that Constantine simply used Christianity for cynical purposes.

We do not know his motives, but his actions suggest that he believed he had found in Christ an all-powerful divine patron and the promise of eternal life; and during the thirty years he ruled after that, he legislated, to the extent he considered practical, the moral values he found in biblical sources—the vision of a harmonious society, built upon divine justice, that shows concern even for its poorest members.

Although Constantine's revolution lent support to the claims of catholic bishops that their church, triumphant through God's grace, alone offered salvation, we would be naïve to suppose that Christianity now became, in fact, uniform and homogeneous. Even a glance at the controversies and challenges of the fourth and fifth centuries shows that it did not.[100] What this revolution did accomplish was to enhance the authority of the bishops identified as catholic and to establish their consensus, expressed through the statements of the creed, as defining the boundaries of the newly legitimate faith. To this day, someone who asks, "Are you a Christian?" is likely to follow with questions about propositional beliefs: "Do you believe that Jesus is the Son of God? Do you believe that Jesus Christ came down from heaven to save you from sin?"

The framework of canon, creed, and ecclesiastical hierarchy that Irenaeus and others began to forge in the crucible of persecution and that his successors like Athanasius worked to construct after Constantine's conversion now gained enormous appeal. The "universal" church could invite potential converts to join an assembly that not only claimed to possess certain truth and to offer eternal salvation but had also become socially acceptable, even politically advantageous. Furthermore, the structure of Christian orthodoxy has proven remarkably durable and adaptable through two millennia and is developing new forms even today throughout the world, in areas notably including Africa, North and South America, South Korea, and China.

Scholars who investigate the origins of Christianity now see, however, that the landscape we are exploring has opened up unexpected vistas. The Nag Hammadi discoveries and sources such as the Dead Sea Scrolls, along with the work of many historians today, are opening up not only Christianity as we knew it but much that lay beyond its boundaries—as we used to define them.

———

The events sketched here obviously affect the way we understand our cultural history. But for those of us who find ourselves implicated in this history, as I do, untangling some of its complex strands has practical consequences as well as intellectual ones. In my own case, the hardest—and the most exciting—thing about research into Christian beginnings has been to unlearn what I thought I knew, and to shed presuppositions I had taken for granted.

This research offers new ways to relate to religious tradition. Orthodox doctrines of God—Jewish, Christian, or Muslim—tend to emphasize the separation between what is divine and what is human: in the words of the scholar of religion Rudolph Otto, God is "wholly other" than humankind. Since those who accept such views often assume that divine revelation is diametrically opposed to human perception, they often rule out what

mystically inclined Jews and Christians have always done—
seeking to discern spiritual truth experienced as revelation, truth
that may come from intuition, reflection, or creative imagination. Christian leaders who deny that such experience can teach
us anything about God have often identified themselves as
guardians of an unchanging tradition, whose "faithfulness" consists in handing down only what they received from ancient
witnesses, neither adding nor subtracting anything. And while
church leaders believe that this view of their role expresses appropriate humility, some also understand that it invests them, as
guardians of divine truth, with God's own authority.

Such leaders could not, of course, ban the imagination
entirely—nor was this their intention. But they effectively
channeled the religious imagination of most Christians to
express—and to support—what they already taught. The two-
thousand-year legacy of Christian music, art, architecture, poetry, philosophy, and theology is, of course, enormously rich,
and our culture is inconceivable apart from Christian tradition.

But those who see Christianity as offering, in Irenaeus's words,
a "very complete system of doctrines" that contain "certain truth"
often have difficulty acknowledging—much less welcoming—
diverse viewpoints, which, nevertheless, abound. Anyone who
stands within the Roman Catholic communion, for example,
knows that it embraces members who differ on topics ranging
from doctrine to discipline, and the same applies, of course, to
virtually every other Christian denomination. But since Christians often adopt Irenaeus's view of controversy, many tend to
assume that only one side can speak the truth, while others
speak only lies—or evil. Many still insist that only their church,

CONSTANTINE AND THE CATHOLIC CHURCH | 183

whether Roman Catholic or Baptist, Lutheran or Greek Orthodox, Pentecostalist or Presbyterian, Jehovah's Witness or Christian Scientist—or only the group within their church with which
they agree—actually remains faithful to Jesus' teaching. Furthermore, since Christian tradition teaches that Jesus fully revealed
God two thousand years ago, innovators from Francis of Assisi
to Martin Luther, from George Fox and John Wesley to contemporary feminist and liberation theologians, often have disguised
innovation—sometimes even from themselves—by claiming that
they are not introducing anything new but only clarifying what
Jesus actually meant all along.

Necessary as it seemed to Irenaeus in the second century to
expel Valentinus's disciples as "heretics," doing so not only impoverished the churches that remained but also impoverished
those he expelled. Uprooted from their original home within
Christian churches, those stigmatized as "heretics" often wandered alone—despite the fact that the spiritual inquiry that
engaged them found in Judaism and Christianity not only communities of origin but also primary sources of inspiration.

What such people seek, however, is often not a different "system of doctrines" so much as insights or intimations of the
divine that validate themselves in experience—what we might
call hints and glimpses offered by the luminous *epinoia*. Some
engaged on such a path pursue it in solitude; others also participate in various forms of worship, prayer, and action. Engaging in such a process requires, of course, faith. The Greek term
for *faith* is the same one often interpreted simply as *belief*, since
faith often *includes* belief, but it involves much more: the trust
that enables us to commit ourselves to what we hope and

love.[101] We noted how Tertullian ridiculed those who saw themselves more as seekers than as believers, "Since they are willing to say—and even sincerely— . . . 'This is not so,' and 'I take this to mean something different,' and 'I do not accept that.' "[102] Despite his inference that those who make such discriminations are either foolish or arrogant, it is not only "heretics" who choose which elements of tradition to accept and practice and which to reject. The sociologist Peter Berger points out that everyone who participates in such tradition today chooses among elements of tradition; for, like Judaism and other ancient traditions, Christianity has survived for thousands of years as each generation relives, reinvents, and transforms what it received.[103]

This act of choice—which the term *heresy* originally meant—leads us back to the problem that orthodoxy was invented to solve: How can we tell truth from lies? What is genuine, and thus connects us with one another and with reality, and what is shallow, self-serving, or evil? Anyone who has seen foolishness, sentimentality, delusion, and murderous rage disguised as God's truth knows that there is no easy answer to the problem that the ancients called discernment of spirits. Orthodoxy tends to distrust our capacity to make such discriminations and insists on making them for us. Given the notorious human capacity for self-deception, we can, to an extent, thank the church for this. Many of us, wishing to be spared hard work, gladly accept what tradition teaches.

But the fact that we have no simple answer does not mean that we can evade the question. We have also seen the hazards—even terrible harm—that sometimes result from unquestioning acceptance of religious authority. Most of us, sooner or later, find that, at critical points in our lives, we must strike out on our own to make a path where none exists. What I have come to love in the wealth and diversity of our religious traditions—and the communities that sustain them—is that they offer the testimony of innumerable people to spiritual discovery. Thus they encourage those who endeavor, in Jesus' words, to "seek, and you shall find."[104]

ACKNOWLEDGMENTS

This book is based on research originally presented, for the most part, in scholarly publications (cited in each chapter's notes) and revised to make it more generally accessible. During the seven years of research and writing and revision, I have consulted with many colleagues and friends, from whom I have learned much. First, I am enormously grateful to those who generously took the time to read the manuscript and to offer corrections and criticism, and I mention in particular Glen Bowersock, Karen King, Helmut Koester, and Alexander Nehamas. And I wish to thank those whose comments and criticism helped improve portions of the work as it was in process, especially Daniel Boyarin, Ismo Dunderberg, Father Thomas Keating, Shaya Isenberg, and Stephen Mitchell, as well as April De Conick, Birger Pearson, Louis Painchaud, John Turner, and Robert McLeod Wilson, who commented on the sources presented in chapter 2; members of the Davis Seminar at Princeton University, where the research presented in chapters 3–5 was first presented, especially Anthony Grafton, who chaired the Seminar in 2001–2002, and to those who participated in it, including Peter Brown, Virginia Burrus, Susanna Elm, Rebecca Lyman, and Raymond van Dam, as well as Harry Attridge, Paula Fredriksen, Michael Stone, and Annette Reed. I owe special thanks to my colleagues John Gager, Martha Himmelfarb, and Peter Schafer, for our collegial conversations and for their willingness to check the accuracy of portions of the manuscript, and to Professor Alain Le Boulluec for his helpful comments on an earlier draft, which enabled me to make needed corrections and qualifications. None of us in the Department of Religion at Princeton could accomplish what we undertake without the kindness and invaluable support of department manager Lorraine Fuhrmann, as well as Pat Bogdziewicz and Kerry Smith. I owe many thanks, too, to Margaret Appleby, for her intelligent and resourceful research investigations, and for her expert intervention with the computer.

Research and writing for this book were completed when I was a visitor at the School of Historical Studies at the Institute for Advanced Study in Princeton, during a year of sabbatical from Princeton University in 2001–2002. I am very grateful to the faculty of that school, especially to Giles Constable and Glen Bowersock, who chaired it during the past two years, for their gracious hospitality and for making available to me, as to many others, the serene and collegial environment that the Institute offers. A grant from the Ford Foundation enabled me to take the full year of sabbatical at the Institute; for this I am especially grateful to Constance Buchanan, senior program officer, for the vision, encouragement, and support for which she is well known among our colleagues, and much loved.

There are certain people without whose participation I cannot imagine having written this book. I am very grateful to have worked with Jason Epstein, whose extraordinary gifts as an editor are well known. Over the years, our collaboration and our friendship, with its many conversations, challenges, and marvelous lunches and dinners, has become, for me, an indispensable and enjoyable part of the writing process. John Brockman and Katinka Matson, both longtime friends as well, have contributed to this project in innumerable ways. I am grateful to Ann Godoff, editor in chief and president of Random House at the time the book was written, for her leadership and enthusiastic support, and to Lynn Nesbit, for her generosity of spirit and her enormously perceptive understanding of publishing. I am very grateful to Kate Medina for graciously taking on this book as editor after that time, and contributing to its production her fine insight and generous encouragement. I wish to thank Will Murphy for his excellent suggestions, and for all he has contributed in the process of production; Meredith Blum and Jessica Kirshner, for their care in arranging many details of publication; Benjamin Dreyer, for his careful, excellent supervision of the copyediting; and Catherine Cooney, for her expertise in helping find the Coptic Fayuum portrait on the cover. I owe special thanks to the Rev. Peter Gomes for his invitation to deliver the Noble Lectures at Harvard University, and for the extraordinarily generous hospitality that he offered—along with his colleague the Rev. Dorothy Austin—as well as his helpful and critical comments, and those of other respondents, including Krister Stendahl and Paula Fredriksen, which certainly have helped improve this book.

The most personal gratitude goes to my husband, Kent Greenawalt, for his willingness to read the manuscript in process, and whose incisive understanding and generous encouragement contributed so much to the process; and to members of our family, whose presence offers so much joy: Sarah, Dave, Robert, Carla, Sasha, Claire, and Andrei.

Finally, I am very grateful to those colleagues who have allowed me to read their work in progress in manuscript form, and mention in particular Karen King's important new book, *What Is Gnosticism?*, and her new edition and commentary on *The Gospel of Mary*; Bart Ehrman's forthcoming book, *Lost Christianities*, with his incisive analysis of the sources and their implications; Marvin Meyer's new book, *Secret Gospels*; and Daniel Boyarin's book still, as of this writing, in the process of completion. Having benefited from conversations with Daniel Boyarin about his most recent manuscript, as well as from his earlier publications, I regret that I read *Border Lines: The Idea of Orthodoxy and the Partitioning of Judeo Christianity*, forthcoming in 2004 from the University of Pennsylvania Press, too late to incorporate its insights into this present work.

NOTES

CHAPTER ONE: FROM THE FEAST OF AGAPE TO THE NICENE CREED

1. I Corinthians 15:3–4.
2. So Adolf von Harnack reconstructed the origin of such statements; see *History of Dogma*, volume I, 5–6, and II, 1–2, in Neil Buchanan's translation from the 1900 edition of *Dogmengeschichte* (New York, 1961), volume I, 267–313, and II, 1–29.
3. Irenaeus, *Libros Quinque Adversus Haereses* 2.32.4, ed. W. W. Harvey (Cambridge, 1851), hereafter cited as AH.
4. Tertullian, *Apology* 39.
5. Rodney Stark, *The Rise of Christianity: A Sociologist Reconsiders History* (Princeton, 1996), especially 73–94.
6. From Galen's (lost) summary of Plato's *Republic*, preserved in Arabic and translated by R. Walzer, *Galen on Jews and Christians* (London, 1949), 15.
7. Mark 12:29–31; see also Deuteronomy 6:4.
8. Stark, *Rise of Christianity*, 86–87.
9. Matthew 25:35–49.
10. Tertullian, *Apology* 39.
11. Ibid.
12. Romans 6:3–14.
13. Tertullian, *Apology* 3.
14. Ibid., 2; for Tacitus' views, see his own words in *Annales* 15.44.2–8.
15. *Passio Sanctarum Perpetuae et Felicitatis* 3.1–2.
16. Ibid., 3.3.
17. Ibid., 5.2–4.

18. Ibid., 5:5.
19. Ibid., 6:5.
20. Ibid., 18.2.
21. Justin, I *Apology* 61.
22. Ibid., 14.
23. If, that is, we can take Justin's account as indicating common practice. Scholars often have assumed that Justin described the practices of Roman Christians—indeed, of all Roman Christians—but more recent study has modified this assumption; see, for example, George La Piana, "The Roman Church at the End of the Second Century," *Harvard Theological Review* 17 (1925), 214–277; then A. Hamman, "Valeur et signification des renseignements liturgiques de Justin," *Studia Patristica* 13 (1975), 264–274; also Paul F. Bradshaw's incisive cautionary remarks in *The Search for the Origins of Christian Worship: Sources and Methods for the Study of Early Liturgy* (Cambridge, 1992), 111–113.
24. See Bradshaw's overview of the evidence and the problems in *Search for the Origins.*
25. Here I am following the dating suggested by Jonathan Draper in, for example, his article "Torah and Troublesome Apostles in the *Didache* Community," in J. Draper, ed., *The Didache in Modern Research* (Leiden, New York, and Cologne, 1996), 340–363.
26. Didache 1.2.
27. Ibid., 1.3–5.
28. Ibid., 2.2; 4.8. The view that Didache assumes Matthew is expressed by Helmut Koester in *Synoptische Uberlieferung bei den apostolischen Väter* (Berlin, 1957), 159–241; and Bentley Layton, "The Sources, Dating, and Transmission of the Didache 1:3b–2:4," *Harvard Theological Review* 61 (1968), 343–383. Christopher Tuckett agrees that parallels with Matthew and Luke are best explained on the assumption that the Didache presupposes "the finished gospels of Matthew and Luke," 128, in "Synoptic Tradition in *Di-*

dache," in Draper, *Didache in Modern Research,* 92–128. I find interesting, however, the perspective Draper expresses, for example in "Christian Self-Definition Against the 'Hypocrites' in *Didache* VIII," in the same volume, 223–243, and in "The Jesus Tradition in the *Didache,"* in D. Wenham, ed., *Gospel Perspectives V: The Jesus Tradition Outside the Gospels* (Sheffield, 1985), 269–289.

29. We do not know whether in this case following "the whole divine law" would have required circumcision, but certainly it did require renouncing idolatry—the worship of the gods—and probably also the practice of some version of kosher food laws. In my interpretation here, I follow Draper, "Torah and Troublesome Apostles," 352–359.

30. See also Draper, "Social Ambiguity and the Production of Text: Prophets, Teacher, Bishops, and Deacons in the Development of the Jesus Tradition in the Community of the *Didache,"* in C. N. Jefford, ed., *The Didache in Context: Essays on Its Text, History, and Transmission* (Leiden, 1995), 284–313.

31. Didache 9:4. Scholars have engaged in much discussion of the Didache's account of baptism and eucharist; for a summary of views, see Bradshaw, *Search for the Origins,* 80–82, 132–136; see also Willy Rordorf, "The Didache," in *The Eucharist of the Early Christians* (New York, 1978), 1–23; John W. Riggs, "From Gracious Table to Sacramental Elements: The Tradition History of *Didache* 9 and 10," *Second Century* 4 (1984), 83–101; and Johannes Betz, "The Eucharist in the *Didache,"* in Draper, *Didache in Modern Research,* 233–275.

32. Didache 10.6; see also Enrico Mazza, "Elements of a Eucharistic Interpretation," in Draper, *Didache in Modern Research,* 276–299.

33. Mark 14:22–24; compare Matthew 26:26–29; Luke 22:7–13; I Corinthians 11:23–25.

34. Tertullian, *Apology* 7.

35. Ibid., 8.

36. One contemporary anthropologist has suggested that Paul and his followers adopted this ritual to repel traditionally minded Jews and so to set themselves apart from Jewish communities.

37. Justin, I *Apology* 66. Closer parallels occur within some of the Dead Sea Scrolls; see, for example, Otto Betz, "Early Christian Cult in the Light of Qumran," *Religious Studies Bulletin* 2:2 (April 1982), 73–85.

38. Justin, I *Apology* 54. Many scholars have considered the parallels between the rituals practiced in mystery religions and the Christian eucharist; see, for example, E. Lohse, *The New Testament Environment* (London, 1976), and more recently, A.J.M. Wedderburn, "The Soteriology of the Mysteries and Pauline Baptismal Theology," *Novum Testamentum* 19:1 (1982) 53–72, and "Hellenistic Christian Traditions in Romans 6?" in *New Testament Studies* 29 (1983), 337–355.

39. I Corinthians 1:23. The Greek term is *skandalon*.

40. For the latter phrase, I am indebted to N. T. Wright, *Jesus and the Victory of God* (Minneapolis, 1992).

41. Luke 24:21.

42. Mark 8:31. Mark uses the Greek term *dei*, usually translated "it is necessary."

43. Mark 14:22. See note 50 on references to studies of the "words of institution."

44. Mark 14:24. On the sacrificial imagery, see Edward J. Kilmartin, S.J., "Sacrificium Laudis: Content and Function of Early Eucharistic Prayers," *Theological Studies* 35:2 (June 1974), 268–286.

45. Matthew 26:27–28.

46. Exodus 24:8.

47. On Mark's allusions to the Mosaic covenant, see the summary in Reginald Fuller, "The Double Origin of the Eucharist," in *Biblical Research: Papers of the Chicago Society of Biblical Research VIII* (Chicago, 1963), 60–72; see also Joachim Jeremias, *Die Abendsmahlworte Jesu*

(Göttingen, 1949), translated as *The Eucharistic Words of Jesus* (London and New York, 1966).

48. Jeremiah 31:31–34.

49. On Paul's interpretation of the words, see, for example, Eduard Schweitzer, *The Lord's Supper According to the New Testament* (Philadelphia, 1967); also Paul Neuenzeit, *Das Herrenmahl: Studien zur paulinischen Eucharistieauffassung* (Munich, 1960).

50. For a summary of discussion and for references, see Bradshaw, *Search for the Origins,* 48–51. On sacrifice, see, for example, Robert Daly, *The Origins of the Christian Doctrine of Sacrifice* (London and New York, 1986); and Rowan Williams, *Eucharistic Sacrifice: The Roots of a Metaphor* (Bramcote, Notts, 1982).

51. Justin, I *Apology* 67. But see, for example, the references in note 23, which question whether—or to what extent—Justin describes actual practices, and if so, which he may have in mind.

52. I Corinthians 5:7.

53. Mark 14:12–16.

54. Luke 22:15.

55. Luke 22:19b; I Corinthians 11:24–25.

56. John 13:1.

57. John 19:14.

58. For discussion of John's view of the passion narrative in general, and his special chronology in particular, see Raymond E. Brown, S.J., *The Death of the Messiah: From Gethsemane to the Grave* (New York, London, Toronto, Sydney, and Auckland, 1993).

59. John 19:34.

60. Although John does not offer an account of the "Last Supper," in the John account Jesus does urge his disciples to eat "[his] flesh" and to drink "[his] blood" (6:35–58).

61. Exodus 12:46. The Revised Standard Version offers here a translation that makes the passage sound as if it applied to Jesus, not to a sacrificial animal: "Not a bone of *him* shall be broken."

62. John 19:36.

63. John 6:35–60.

64. I Corinthians 11:26.

65. Apocalypse of Peter 81:10–11. The sign that Constantine later adopted, although often seen as a cross, actually consisted instead of the first two letters of the title *Christ*.

66. See Chapter 4 for discussion and references.

67. Gershom Scholem, the great scholar of Jewish texts, wrote that "myth is the story line to a ritual" (*On the Kabbalah and Its Symbolism* [New York, 1969], 132–133); and while some might object to applying the term *myth* to the gospels, since they relate events attested actually to have happened, the story of Jesus, as the gospels tell it is, if not a myth, a story intended to convey meaning.

68. Professor Helmut Koester, my first and invaluable mentor in the history of Christianity, has demonstrated in a wide range of articles how the early accounts of the gospel are connected with liturgical celebration. See, for example, his recent article "The Memory of Jesus' Death and the Worship of the Risen Lord," *Harvard Theological Review* 91:1 (1998), 335–350.

69. The Greek term *koinonia* can be translated "communion" or "participation," in passages such as I Corinthians 10:16: "The cup of blessing which we bless, is it not a *koinonia* in the blood of Christ: The bread which we break, is it not a *koinonia* in the body of Christ?"

70. I Corinthians 10:17; Galatians 3:28; I Corinthians 10:3–4.

71. Justin, I *Apology* 61; see also 65–66.

72. For discussion, see my earlier book *The Gnostic Gospels* (New York, 1979); and I especially recommend to the interested reader several important recent discussions that, to my regret, were not available to me during the time I was writing: Bart Ehrman, *Lost Christianities* (New York, 2003); Marvin Meyer, *Secret Gospels* (Harrisburg, Pa., 2003); and Richard Valantasis, *The Gospel of Thomas* (London, New York, 1997).

73. The work of many scholars today is changing our earlier, more simplistic picture of the origins of Christianity. Among notable books being published currently see, for example, Daniel Boyarin, *Border Lines: The Idea of Orthodoxy and the Partitioning of Judeo-Christianity* (Pennsylvania, 2004); Bart Ehrman, *Lost Christianities* (New York and London, 2003); Karen King, *What Is Gnosticism?* (Cambridge, 2003); Marvin Meyer, *Secret Gospels* (Harrisburg, Pa., 2003). I am enormously grateful to these colleagues for allowing me to read each of these books in manuscript.

CHAPTER TWO: GOSPELS IN CONFLICT

This chapter condenses and summarizes research that is presented in a fuller and more technical form as Elaine Pagels, "Exegesis of Genesis 1 in the Gospels of Thomas and John," *Journal of Biblical Literature* 118 (1999), 477–496.

1. John 15:12, 17.
2. John 3:18.
3. John 8:44. For discussion and references on how John's gospel, as well as the others, portrays "the Jews," see Elaine Pagels, *The Origin of Satan* (New York, 1995), especially 89–111, and the references cited there.
4. For the authoritative account of the story of the discovery, see James M. Robinson, "The Discovery of the Nag Hammadi Codices," *Biblical Archaeologist* 42 (1979), 206–224.
5. Irenaeus, AH 1, *Praefatio.*
6. Gospel of Thomas 70, in Nag Hammadi Library (hereafter NHL) 126, where this difficult passage is translated differently and, in my view, less lucidly. Throughout the present text, I have taken liberties with NHL translations in the interest of clarity or of preserving the poetic quality of the original text; thus, readers who consult the NHL may note variations.
7. See the incisive book by Michael Williams, *Rethinking Gnosticism:*

An Argument for Dismantling a Dubious Category (Princeton, 1996); and most recently, Karen King's major new book, *What Is Gnosticism?* (Cambridge, 2003). See also Bentley Layton, "Prolegomena to the Study of Ancient Gnosticism," in I. M. White and O. L. Yarbrough, eds., *The Social World of the Early Christians: Essays in Honor of Wayne A. Meeks* (Minneapolis, 1995), 334–350; as well as the thoughtful essay by Antti Marjanen, "Is Thomas a Gnostic Gospel?" in the outstanding collection edited by Risto Uro, *Thomas at the Crossroads: Essays on the Gospel of Thomas* (Edinburgh, 1998), 107–139. James Robinson also edited a one-volume English translation of all the texts discovered as *The Nag Hammadi Library in English* (San Francisco, 1977); Bentley Layton later published another translation as *The Gnostic Scriptures* (New York, 1987). The most complete edition available in English, however, is *The Nag Hammadi Series*, over twenty volumes published by Brill Press in the Netherlands, which include the Coptic texts with English introductions, translations, and notes.

8. See, for example, Steven Davies, *The Gospel of Thomas and Wisdom Tradition* (New York, 1963); Stephen J. Patterson, *The Gospel of Thomas and Jesus* (Sonoma, Calif., 1993); Gregory J. Riley, *Resurrection Reconsidered: Thomas and John in Controversy* (Minneapolis, 1995); April De Conick, *Seek to See Him: Ascent and Vision Mysticism in the "Gospel of Thomas"* (Leiden, New York, and Cologne, 1996); also her fascinating essay " 'Blessed are those who have not seen' (John 20:29): Johannine Dramatization of an Early Christian Discourse," in J. D. Turner and A. McGuire, eds., *The Nag Hammadi Library After Fifty Years* (Leiden, New York, and Cologne, 1997), 381–400.

9. John 20:8; yet see the incisive critique of this kind of usage in Paul-Hubert Poirier, "The Writings Ascribed to Thomas and the Thomas Tradition," in Turner and McGuire, *Nag Hammadi Library After Fifty Years*, 295–397.

10. For discussion, see Chapter 4; also, among the many scholarly

works on this issue, Maurice F. Wiles, *The Spiritual Gospel: The Interpretation of the Fourth Gospel in the Early Church* (Cambridge, 1960); T. E. Pollard, *Johannine Christology and the Early Church* (Cambridge, 1970); C. H. Dodd, *Interpretation of the Fourth Gospel* (Cambridge, 1953); and E. Pagels, *The Johannine Gospel in Gnostic Exegesis* (Nashville, 1973).

11. Mark 11:15–16.

12. Mark 11:18.

13. John 2:15.

14. John 12:10.

15. John 11:48.

16. Origen, *Commentary on John* 10.4–6.

17. John 10:33.

18. John 20:28.

19. Origen, *Commentary on John* 1.6.

20. For discussion of the titles "son of God" and "messiah," see the influential work of Bart Ehrman, *The New Testament: A Historical Introduction to the Early Christian Writings* (Oxford and New York, 2000), 60–84. For an excellent discussion of various Christologies, see Pheme Perkins, "New Testament Christologies in Gnostic Transformation," in *The Future of Early Christianity: Essays in Honor of Helmut Koester* Birger A. Pearson, ed., (Minneapolis, 1991), 422–441.

21. John 20:28.

22. For a masterful discussion of the traditions preserved in Thomas and their relation to the synoptic gospels and to John, see Helmut Koester, *Ancient Christian Gospels: Their History and Development* (London and Philadelphia, 1990), especially 75–127.

23. For an overview of discussion of Thomas tradition, see Poirier, "The Writings Ascribed to Thomas."

24. Koester, *Ancient Christian Gospels*, 78–80; see also the incisive assessment of Philip Sellew, "The Gospel of Thomas: Prospects for Future Research," in Turner and McGuire, *Nag Hammadi Library*

After Fifty Years, 327–346; also Jean-Marie Sevrin, "L'Interprétation de l' évangile selon Thomas, entre tradition et rédaction," in the same volume, 347–360.

25. Gospel of Thomas 1, in NHL 118.

26. Genesis 1:3. For an excellent discussion, see Steven Davies, "Christology and Protology in the Gospel of John," *Journal of Biblical Literature* 111 (1992), 663–683.

27. John 1:3.

28. Koester, *Ancient Christian Gospels*, 86–128; see also Patterson, *Gospel of Thomas and Jesus*.

29. John 1:9; the Greek phrase *phos ton anthropon* can be translated "light of human beings."

30. Genesis 1:26–27; again, for a more detailed and technical version of the discussion presented in this chapter, see Pagels, "Exegesis of Genesis 1."

31. A term that may have been coined by Irenaeus: AH 3.11.8.

32. Ibid., 1.20.1.

33. Mark 8:27–29.

34. Mark 15:39.

35. Psalm 2:7; for discussion of the way such passages are worked into the birth stories of Matthew and Luke, see Raymond E. Brown, S.J., *The Birth of the Messiah: A Commentary on the Infancy Narratives in Matthew and Luke*, 2nd ed. (New York, 1993).

36. Mark 1:1.

37. See, for example, Ezekiel 2:1; 2:8; 3:1; 3:4; 3:10; 3:17; 3:25; and throughout the oracles of Ezekiel.

38. Daniel 7:13.

39. Mark 14:61–62.

40. Most scholars agree that the author of Luke also wrote the New Testament Acts of the Apostles; see Acts 2:22–23, 32–36.

41. John 1.1.

42. Philippians 2:7–8.

43. I Corinthians 12:3.

44. Ignatius, *Letter to the Romans* 6:3.
45. Pliny, *Letter* 10.96.7; see discussion of the pre–Pauline "Christ hymn" of Philippians 2 in Ralph P. Martin's fine monograph *Carmen Christi* (London, 1967).
46. On composition, see Koester, *Ancient Christian Gospels*, 80 ff.; and more recently, the incisive comments of Risto Uro, in his introduction to *Thomas at the Crossroads*, 1–32.
47. Matthew, for example, includes the famous saying that "many are called, but few are chosen" (22:14); Thomas has Jesus say, "I shall choose you, one out of a thousand, and two out of ten thousand" (saying 23, in NHL 121). John's version, too, has Jesus emphasize divine initiative in the process: "You did not choose me, but I chose you" (15:16; see also 13:18).
48. Matthew 16:17.
49. Gospel of Thomas 13, in NHL 119.
50. Ibid., 50, in NHL 123.
51. Mark 1:1–4.
52. Mark 1:15.
53. Mark 9:1.
54. Mark 13:2.
55. Mark 13:8–19.
56. Mark 13:24–26.
57. Mark 13:30–33.
58. John 5:25.
59. John 11:24.
60. Gospel of Thomas 3, in NHL 118.
61. Mark 13:2–37.
62. Gospel of Thomas 51, in NHL 123.
63. Ibid., 113, in NHL 130.
64. Luke 17:20–21.
65. Thomas Merton, quoted by Marcus Borg, in *Meeting Jesus Again for the First Time: The Historical Jesus and the Heart of Contemporary Faith* (San Francisco, 1994).

66. Gospel of Mary 8:15–20. See the major new edition and commentary by Karen King, forthcoming (as of this writing) from Harvard University Press.

67. Luke 21:34–36.

68. John 1:1.

69. Genesis 1:2.

70. Genesis 1:3.

71. John 1:9.

72. Gospel of Thomas 16, in NHL 120.

73. Ibid., 77, in NHL 126.

74. Ibid., 2, in NHL 118.

75. Ibid., 3, in NHL 118.

76. Ibid., 70, translation by Professor George MacRae, offered in class. As stated in note 6, the NHL translation of this difficult saying differs, and I find it less lucid.

77. Ibid., 6, in NHL 118.

78. Matthew 6:3–4.

79. Matthew 6:17.

80. Matthew 7:9–13.

81. Gospel of Thomas 6, in NHL 118.

82. Ibid., 91, in NHL 128.

83. Plotinus, *Ennead* 5, *Against the Gnostics.*

84. Gospel of Thomas 3, in NHL 118.

85. Ibid., 19, in NHL 120.

86. See, for example, On the Origin of the World 108.7–9, in NHL 177; Eugnostos 76.14–81.12, in NHL 228–232; Apocryphon (Secret Book) of John II, 14.13–15.13, in NHL 113; for a more complete edition, comparing the available manuscripts, see Frederick Wisse and Michael Waldstein, eds., *The Apocryphon of John: A Synopsis of Nag Hammadi Codices II, 1; III, 1; and IV, 1 with BG 8502, 2* (Nag Hammadi and Manichaean Studies 33, Leiden, 1995), 82–89.

87. Irenaeus, AH 1.30.1. For references, see Pagels, "Exegesis of Genesis 1," 202–205; and for a masterful discussion, see Hans-Martin

Schenke, *Der Gott "Mensch" in der Gnosis: Ein religionsgeschichtlicher Beitrag zur Diskussion über die paulinische Anschauung von der Kirche als Leib Christi* (Göttingen, 1962); and the fascinating articles by Gilles Quispel, "Der Gnostiche *Anthropos* und die jüdische Tradition," *Eranos Jahrbuch* 22 (1953), 195–234, and "Ezekiel 1:26 in Jewish Mysticism and Gnosis," *Vigiliae Christianae* 34 (1980), 1–13.

88. For a classic discussion see Gershom Scholem, *Major Trends in Jewish Mysticism* (New York, 1965); see also Ithamar Gruenwald, *Apocalyptic and Merkavah Mysticism* (Leiden, 1980), and *From Apocalypticism to Gnosticism: Studies in Apocalypticism, Merkavah Mysticism and Gnosticism* (Frankfurt, Bern, New York, and Paris, 1988); Moshe Idel, *Kabbalah: New Perspectives* (New Haven, 1988); Elliot Wolfson, *Through a Speculum That Shines: Vision and Imagination in Medieval Jewish Mysticism* (Princeton, 1994); and Peter Schäfer, *The Hidden and Manifest God: Some Major Themes in Early Jewish Mysticism* (Albany, 1992).

89. Gospel of Thomas 50, in NHL 123.

90. Ibid., 24, in NHL 121.

91. Ibid., 84, in NHL 127.

92. I am grateful to Stephen Mitchell for his insight and his translation; for this poem, see *Meetings with the Archangel* (New York, 1998), 137.

93. Gospel of Thomas 2, in NHL 118.

94. Ibid., 108, in NHL 129.

95. Book of Thomas the Contender 138.7–19, in NHL 189.

96. John 11:16; for discussion, see Riley, *Resurrection Reconsidered*.

97. For a discussion of the composition of this gospel, see, for example, Raymond E. Brown, S.J., *The Gospel According to John: Introduction, Translation, and Notes* (Garden City, N.Y., 1966).

98. John 21:20–24. Most scholars regard this chapter as an addition to the original text; see, for example, Brown's discussion of chapter 21 in *Gospel According to John*.

99. Matthew 1:18.

100. Matthew 16:17.

101. This disciple appears, for example, in John 13:23.

102. John 13:24–25.

103. John 19:35.

104. John 20:3–8.

105. John 21:7.

106. John 21:17.

107. For discussion, see the forthcoming edition of the Gospel of Mary by Karen King; see also the excellent article by Risto Uro, " 'Who will be our leader?' Authority and Autonomy in the Gospel of Thomas," in *Fair Play: Diversity and Conflicts in Early Christianity: Essays in Honour of Heikki Räisänen* (Leiden and Boston, 2002), 457–485. See also the very interesting work of Richard Valantasis, *Spiritual Guides of the Third Century: A Semiotic Study of the Guide-Disciple Relationship in Christianity, Neoplatonism, Hermetism, and Gnosticism* (Minneapolis, 1991).

108. John 20:30–31.

109. John 20:28.

110. Louis Martyn's groundbreaking work, *History and Theology in the Fourth Gospel* (Nashville, 1979), suggests that the story told in John 9 is, in effect, that of John's community. Martyn's influential thesis has been modified by the critique of other scholars who question especially his assumptions about the formation and use of the so-called *birkat ha mininm*; see Asher Finkel, "Yavneh's Liturgy and Early Christianity," *Journal of Ecumenical Studies* 18:2 (1981), 231–250; William Horbury, "The Benediction of the Minim and Early Jewish–Christian Controversy," *Journal of Theological Studies* 33 (1982); Alan F. Segal, "Ruler of This World: Attitudes About Mediator Figures and the Importance of Sociology for Self–Definition," in E. P. Sanders, ed., *Jewish and Christian Self-Definition*, volume II (Philadelphia, 1980), 245–268; and the very intriguing recently published article by Daniel Boyarin, "The

Gospel of the Memra: Jewish Binitarianism and the Prologue to John," *Harvard Theological Review* 94:3 (2001), 243 ff.

111. John 1:1–41.
112. John 9:7.
113. John 9:22.
114. John 9:38.
115. John 9:39.
116. John 10:8–9.
117. John 8:58.
118. Exodus 3:14.
119. John 19:2.
120. John 3:18.
121. Galatians 3:4.
122. John 1:1–4.
123. John 1:5.
124. John 1:10.
125. John 1:11.
126. John 1:14.
127. Ibid.
128. 1 John 1:1.
129. I am grateful to my colleague Alexander Nehamas for pointing out that this Greek term strongly connotes singularity, a usage that goes back as far as Parmenides' description of what he called being (*tō ōn*).
130. John 14:1.
131. John 15:12.
132. John 15:12–24.
133. Gospel of Thomas 22, in NHL 121.
134. John 8:12.
135. John 8:23.
136. John 8:24.
137. John 1:29.

138. John 3:5.

139. John 6:53–55.

140. In his remarkable monograph *Resurrection Reconsidered*.

141. John 11:16; see Riley's discussion in *Resurrection Reconsidered*, 100–180.

142. John 14:3–4.

143. John 14:6.

144. Luke 24:33–36.

145. Matthew 28:10.

146. John 20:24.

147. John 20:19–23.

148. John 20:28.

149. John 20:29.

150. John 21:24–25.

151. Irenaeus, AH 3.11.1–3.

152. C. H. Dodd, in his commentary on the Johannine gospel, notes that this is what separates John's message from "gnostics"; for Dodd, this secures John's place as an authentically Christian teacher; see *Interpretation of the Fourth Gospel*, 97–114, 250–285.

CHAPTER THREE: GOD'S WORD OR HUMAN WORDS?

For the technical discussion of the research summarized in this chapter, see Elaine Pagels, "Irenaeus, the 'Canon of Truth' and the Gospel of John: 'Making a Difference' Through Hermeneutics and Ritual," *Vigiliae Christianae* 56.4 (2002), 339–371.

1. Theodor Gaster's comment occurred in a conversation; Buber's phrase serves as the title of his book *I and Thou* (translated by W. Kaufmann from *Ich und du* and published in New York, 1970).

2. Raymond E. Brown, S.J.; this paraphrases the end of his review of *The Gnostic Gospels*, *New York Times*, November 1979.

3. Tertullian, *Apology* 1.

4. Ibid., 2.

5. *Martyrdom of St. Polycarp* 3 f.

6. Pliny, *Letter* 10.96.3.

7. *Martyrdom of St. Justin and His Companions*, Recension A, 3.2. The place name has been corrupted in the manuscripts; I follow the reading of Herbert Musurillo, *The Acts of the Christian Martyrs* (Oxford, 1972), 45.

8. Origen, *Contra Celsum* 3.54.

9. Tertullian, *Apology* 50.

10. *Martyrdom of St. Polycarp* 12.

11. So, at least, the author of his Martyrdom represents him; see chapter 8.

12. Irenaeus, AH 3.3.4.

13. Ibid.

14. Polycarp, *Letter to the Philippians* 6.3.

15. Irenaeus, AH 3.3.4.

16. For discussion and references concerning Tatian's *Diatessaron*, see Koester, *Ancient Christian Gospels*, 403–430.

17. Irenaeus, AH 3.11.8.

18. Markus Bockmuehl, " 'To Be or Not to Be': The Possible Futures of New Testament Scholarship," *Scottish Journal of Theology* 51:3 (1998), 271–306.

19. *Martyrdom of St. Polycarp* 6–15.

20. W.H.C. Frend, *Martyrdom and Persecution in the Early Church* (Oxford, 1965; New York, 1967), 5–6.

21. *The Letters of the Churches of Lyons and Vienne*, I.10.

22. Eusebius, *Historia Ecclesiae*, quoting Apollinarius, in 5.16.5.

23. Ibid., 5.17.12; for a careful account of the controversy, see Christine Trevett, *Montanism: Gender, Authority, and the New Prophecy* (Cambridge, 1996); among ancient authors, a primary source is Eusebius's account in 5.16.1–19.2. For an edition of the sayings attributed to the prophets, see Kurt Aland, "Der Montanismus und die Kleinasiatische Theologie," *Zeitschrift für Neue Testamenten Wissenschaft* 46 (1955), 109–116.

24. Eusebius, *Historia Ecclesiae* 5.16.17; Aland, *Montanismus*, saying 16.

25. John 16:4. See the intriguing and provocative article by M. E. Boring, "The Influence of Christian Prophecy on the Johannine Portrayal of the Paraclete and Jesus," *New Testament Studies* 25 (1978), 113–122; see also *Sayings of the Risen Christ: Christian Prophecy in the Synoptic Tradition* (Cambridge, 1982); R. E. Heine, "The Role of the Gospel of John in the Montanist Controversy," *Second Century 6* (1987), 1–18; see also his article "The Gospel of John and the Montanist Debate at Rome," *Studia Patristica* 21 (1989), 95–100; and Dennis E. Groh, "Utterance and Exegesis: Biblical Interpretation in the Montanist Crisis," in D. E. Groh and R. Jewett, eds., *The Living Text* (New York, 1985), 73–95.

26. Irenaeus, AH 3.11.9; Eusebius, *Historia Ecclesiae* 3.28.1; see Dionysios bar Salibi, *Commentary on the Apocalypse* 1.

27. *On Modesty*, 21. On Tertullian, see Timothy D. Barnes, *Tertullian: A Historical and Literary Study* (Oxford, 1971).

28. On the media of revelation, see David E. Aune, *Prophecy in Early Christianity and the Ancient Mediterranean World* (Grand Rapids, 1983); on Valentinus, see the definitive study by Christoph Markschies, *Valentinus Gnosticus? Untersuchungen zur valentinianischen Gnosis mit einem Kommentar zu den Fragmenten Valentins* (Tübingen, 1992).

29. Eusebius, *Historia Ecclesiae* 5.20.4.

30. Mark 1:10–11.

31. Luke 2:8–13.

32. Luke 24:34.

33. Acts 2:17–21; Joel 2:28–32.

34. I Corinthians 1:1; 15:3–11.

35. II Corinthians 12:4.

36. John 16:13.

37. Revelation 1:10–19.

38. Acts 2:1–4.

39. *Martyrdom of Saints Perpetua and Felicitas* 1.

40. So indicates the Muratorian Fragment, a source taken by Harnack and others to be from the late second century but recently dated more persuasively by A. C. Sundberg to the fourth century; see "Towards a Revised History of the New Testament Canon," *Studia Evangelica* 4 (1968), 452–461; and see the fuller study by Geoffrey M. Hahneman, *The Muratorian Fragment and the Development of the Canon* (Oxford Theological Monographs, Oxford, 1992).

41. Acts 1:9–11.

42. *Martyrdom of St. Polycarp* 5.

43. Irenaeus, AH 5.6.1.

44. Ibid., 2.32.4.

45. Ibid.

46. Ibid., 3.11.9.

47. Ibid., 2.13.8.

48. Ibid., 1.13.1. This discussion paraphrases, to some extent, what is described in Pagels, *Gnostic Gospels*, 59–61.

49. Ibid. Marcus's prayer alludes to Matthew 18:10.

50. Irenaeus, AH 1.13.3.

51. Ibid., 1.13.4; see Acts 1:17–26.

52. Irenaeus, AH 1.14.1.

53. Ibid., 1.14.4.

54. See, for more recent discussion, Moshe Idel, *Kabbalah: New Perspectives* (New Haven, 1988). Idel, following previous scholars, including Moses Gaster, sees Marcus's teaching drawing upon Jewish theological speculations and practice. For a major recent contribution, see Niclas Förster's important monograph, *Marcus Magus: Kult, Lehre, und Gemeindeleben einer valentinianischen Gnostikergruppe: Sammlung der Quellen und Kommentar* (Tübingen, 1999).

55. Cf. Genesis 1:3.

56. Irenaeus, AH 1.14.8.

57. Ibid., 1.14.1.

58. Here Irenaeus's polemic echoes that of an admired predecessor whom he calls "the holy elder" (*presbyter*: the term is sometimes translated "priest," but this may be a later connotation); ibid., 1.15.6.
59. Ibid., 1.18.1.
60. Ibid., 1.20.1.
61. For discussion of the Secret Book of John and the Gospel of Truth and how such writings interpret "the Scriptures," see Chapter 4; for some recent articles on gnostic exegesis, see, for example, Pheme Perkins, "Spirit and Letter: Poking Holes in the Canon," *Journal of Religion* (1996), 307–327; Harold W. Attridge, "The Gospel of Truth as an Exoteric Text," in *Nag Hammadi, Gnosticism, and Early Christianity* C. W. Hedrick and R. Hodgson, eds., (Peabody, Mass., 1986), 239–255; Patricia Cox Miller, " 'Words with an Alien Voice': Gnostics, Scripture, and Canon," *Journal of the American Academy of Religion* 57 (1989), 459–483; Robert M. Grant, *Heresy and Criticism: The Search for Authenticity in Early Christian Literature* (Louisville, Ky., 1993); and Louis Painchaud, "The Use of Scripture in Gnostic Literature," *Journal of Early Christian Studies* 4:2 (1996), 129–146.
62. For discussion, see Chapter 5; of the many scholarly discussions, see, among recent articles, David Brakke, "Canon Formation and Social Conflict in Fourth Century Egypt," *Harvard Theological Review* 87:4 (1994), 395–419, as well as his illuminating book *Athanasius and the Politics of Asceticism* (Baltimore and London, 1995).
63. Acts 1:9.
64. Apocryphon of James 2:9–15, in NHL 30.
65. Ibid., 2:19–25, in NHL 30.
66. Ibid., 3:35–4:27, especially 4:19, in NHL 31.
67. Ibid., 5:19–20.
68. Ibid., 15:6–28. In her recent book, April De Conick evaluates this as a vision that both resembles and qualifies those she says were sought in certain circles of Jewish visionaries. See *Seek to See Him*.

69. II Corinthians 12:1–4. April De Conick and Jarl Fossum, "Stripped Before God: A New Interpretation of Logion 37 of the Gospel of Thomas," *Vigiliae Christianae* 45 (1991), 123–150; see also Alan F. Segal, "Heavenly Ascent in Hellenistic Judaism, Early Christianity, and Their Environment," *Aufstieg und Niedergang der Romischen Welt* 2:23:2 (1980), 1333–94; *Paul the Convert: The Apostolate and Apostasy of Saul the Pharisee* (New Haven and London, 1990); and C.R.A. Morray-Jones, "Paradise Revisited (2 Cor. 12:1–12): The Jewish Mystical Background of Paul's Apostolate, Part 2: Paul's Heavenly Ascent and Its Significance," *Harvard Theological Review* 86:3 (1993), 265–292. For a major critical perspective, see Martha Himmelfarb, *Ascent to Heaven in Jewish and Christian Apocalypses* (New York, 1993); "The Practice of Ascent in the Ancient Mediterranean World," in John J. Collins and M. Fishbane, eds., *Death, Ecstasy, and Other Worldly Journeys* (Albany, 1995); "Revelation and Rapture: The Transformation of the Visionary in the Ascent Apocalypses," in John J. Collins and James H. Charlesworth, eds., *Mysteries and Revelation: Apocalyptic Studies Since the Uppsala Colloquium*, JSP Supplements 9 (Sheffield, 1991); and Peter Schäfer, ed., *Synpose zur Hekhalot-Literatur* (Texte und Studien zum Antiken Judentum 2, Tübingen, 1981); *Mystik und Theologie des rabbinischen Judentums* (ed., with M. Schlüter, New York, 1992); and especially *The Hidden and Manifest God: Some Major Themes in Early Jewish Mysticism* (Albany, 1992).

70. Prayer of the Apostle Paul 1:6–9, in NHL 27.

71. Ibid., 1:26–34, in NHL 28; cf. I Corinthians 2:9–10.

72. Carol Newsom, *Songs of the Sabbath Sacrifice: A Critical Edition* (Atlanta, 1985).

73. See note 69 for references.

74. 2 Corinthians 12:3.

75. See references in note 69.

76. Isaiah 6:1–5.

77. This, at any rate, is what many took Genesis 5:24 to mean.

78. See, for example, the Books of Enoch.

79. David J. Halperin, *The Faces of the Chariot: Early Jewish Responses to Ezekiel's Vision* (Tübingen, 1988); Wolfson, *Through a Speculum That Shines.*

80. Apocalypse of Peter 71:15–25, in NHL 341.

81. Ibid., 81.10–82.15, in NHL 344.

82. Gospel of Mary 8.14–20, in NHL 472. For a new translation and discussion, see the forthcoming edition of the Gospel of Mary by Karen King.

83. Gospel of Mary, 10.1–6, in NHL 472.

84. Ibid., 10.10–25, in NHL 472.

85. Ibid., 17.7–15, in NHL 473.

86. Ibid., 17.19–18.19, in NHL 473.

87. Jeremiah 23:25–32.

88. Zechariah 9:9.

89. Matthew 21:6–7.

90. Justin, *Dialogue with Trypho* 7.

91. Ibid., 8.

92. Ibid., 9.

93. Isaiah 7:14.

94. Justin, *Dialogue with Trypho* 43.

95. Irenaeus, AH 1.11.9.

96. Ibid., 1.10.1.

97. Ibid., 1.11.8.

CHAPTER FOUR: THE CANON OF TRUTH AND THE TRIUMPH OF JOHN

For fuller and more technical discussions of the research summarized in this chapter, see Elaine Pagels, "Irenaeus, the 'Canon of Truth' and the Gospel of John: 'Making a Difference' Through Hermeneutics and Ritual," in *Vigiliae Christianae* 56.4 (2002), 339–371; also Pagels, "Ritual in the Gospel of Philip," in Turner and McGuire, *Nag Hammadi Library After Fifty Years*, 280–294; "The Mystery of

Marriage in the Gospel of Philip," in Pearson, *Future of Early Christianity*, 442–452; and *Johannine Gospel in Gnostic Exegesis*.

1. T. S. Eliot, "Ash Wednesday."
2. Irenaeus, AH 1, *Praefatio*.
3. For these fragments, with translation, along with a careful and important recent study, see Christoph Markschies, *Valentinus Gnosticus? Untersuchungen zur valentinianischen Gnosis mit einem Kommentar zu den Fragmenten Valentins* (Tübingen, 1992).
4. The title of this poem, *Theros*, can be translated "harvest" or "summer fruit." The translation I present here is my own; for other translations and for the Greek text, see Christoph Markschies, *Valentinus Gnosticus?* 218–259; see also the incisive response by Andrew McGowan, "Valentinus Poeta: Notes on *Theros*," *Vigiliae Christianae* 51.2 (1997), 158–178.
5. For discussion, see Hans von Campenhausen, *The Formation of the Christian Bible*, trans. J. A. Baker, from *Die Entstehung der christlichen Bibel*, first edited in Tübingen, 1968 (Philadelphia and London, 1972), 80–87.
6. *Letter to Flora* 3.8.
7. Irenaeus, AH 3.11.7.
8. For sources and discussion, see Pagels, *Johannine Gospel in Gnostic Exegesis*.
9. See, for example, Irenaeus, AH 1.9.4; and the discussion by R. L. Wilken, "The Homeric Cento in Irenaeus' *Adversus Haereses* 1.9.4," *Vigiliae Christianae* 21 (1967), 25–33; A. Rousseau and L. Dautreleau, *Irénée de Lyon contre les Hérésies* (Paris, 1965).
10. For an excellent study of such teachings and interpretation, see the recent work of R. M. Grant, *Heresy and Criticism*. See also Robert Lamberton, *Homer the Theologian: Neoplatonist Allegorical Reading and the Growth of the Epic Tradition* (Berkeley, 1986).
11. Irenaeus, AH 2.10.1–4. For a fascinating discussion of parallels between gnostic and patristic exegesis of John's prologue, see Anne Pasquier, "Interpretation of the Prologue of John's Gos-

pel in Some Gnostic and Patristic Writings: A Common Tradition," in Turner and McGuire, *Nag Hammadi Library After Fifty Years*, 484–498.

12. See Perkins, "Spirit and Letter," 307–327.
13. John 2:13 f.
14. Origen, *Commentary on John* 10.4–6; for fuller discussion and references, see Wiles, *Spiritual Gospel*, 96 f., and Pagels, *Johannine Gospel in Gnostic Exegesis*, 66–113.
15. Valentinus 2, in Clement of Alexandria, *Stromateis* 2.14.3–6 (for discussion, see Markschies, *Valentinus Gnosticus?* 54 ff).
16. Valentinus 7, in Hippolytus, *Refutation of All Heresies* 6.42.2.
17. Gospel of Truth 29.9–25, in NHL 43.
18. Opening lines of "Dover Beach."
19. Gospel of Truth 29.9–25, in NHL 43.
20. Ibid., 30.16–21, in NHL 43.
21. Ibid., 24:5–9, in NHL 41.
22. Matthew 18:2–4; Luke 15:3–7.
23. I Corinthians 2:7.
24. Gospel of Truth 18:24–29, in NHL 38.
25. Ibid., 18.29–34, in NHL 38.
26. Ibid., 16.31–33, in NHL 37.
27. Ibid., 42.1–10, in NHL 48.
28. Ibid., 33.35–34.35, in NHL 44.
29. Ibid., 32.35–33.30,
30. I Corinthians 11:23.
31. John 13:4–5.
32. John 13:7–8.
33. "Round Dance of the Cross," in Acts of John 94.1–4. For a recently edited Greek text with French translation and notes, see E. Junod and J. P. Kästli, *Acta Johannis: Praefatio-Textus*, in *Corpus Christianorum* (Turnhout, 1983). Here I am following the recent English translation published by Barbara E. Bowe in her article "Dancing into

the Divine: The Hymn of the Dance in the *Acts of John,*" *Journal of Early Christian Studies* 7:1 (1999), 83–104.

34. "Round Dance of the Cross," in Acts of John 94.9–95.50.

35. Ibid., 96.1–15.

36. Ibid., 95.27–30.

37. Ibid., 88.12–18.

38. Ibid., 90.1–17.

39. Apocryphon of John 1.5–17; see the recent edition already cited, edited by Frederick Wisse and Michael Waldstein; see also the commentary on the Apocryphon of John by Karen King, forthcoming from Harvard University Press in spring 2003.

40. Apocryphon of John, 1.18–33.

41. Ibid., 2.9–14.

42. Ibid., 2.3–10.

43. The latter part of the citation follows BG 25.14–20; cf. John 1:1–4:10.

44. For our purpose here, the precise identity of the author is not the central point—especially because it is not known. We note, however, that Christoph Markschies has persuasively challenged the traditional identification in his important article "New Research on Ptolemaeus Gnosticus," in Zeitschrift für Antike und Christentum 4 (Berlin and New York, 2000), 249–254.

45. Irenaeus, AH 1.8.5.

46. Ibid., 1.9.1.

47. Ibid., 1.9.2.

48. Ibid., 1.18.1.

49. Ibid., 1.9.4.

50. Ibid., 1.10.1.

51. The question of baptismal practice among Valentinian Christians has provoked considerable debate; for discussion and references, and for a fuller discussion of what is briefly summarized in this chapter, see Pagels, "Ritual in the Gospel of Philip." For a differ-

ent viewpoint, see Einar Thomassons's recent studies of Valentinian practice; for example, his article "How Valentinian Is the
Gospel of Philip?" in Turner and McGuire, *Nag Hammadi Library
After Fifty Years*, 251–279; and Martha Lee Turner, "On the Coher-
ence of the *Gospel According to Philip*," 223–250. See also the excellent and detailed study by Peter Lampe, *Die stadtrömischen Christen
in den ersten beiden Jahrhunderten: Untersuchungen zur Sozialgeschichte*
(Tübingen, 1989).

52. Cf. John 3:5; Gospel of Philip 69.4–6, in NHL 141.

53. Gospel of Philip 64.22–26, in NHL 139.

54. Ibid., 64.29–31, in NHL 139.

55. Ibid., 79.25–31, in NHL 147.

56. Ibid., 55.23–24, in NHL 147.

57. Ibid., 71.3–15, in NHL 143.

58. Ibid., 52.21–24, in NHL 132.

59. Ibid., 55.30, in NHL 134.

60. Ibid., 56.26–57.23, in NHL 134–135; for a fuller exposition of the
text, see Pagels, "Ritual in the Gospel of Philip."

61. Gospel of Philip, 57.4–6, in NHL 134.

62. Ibid., 67.26–27, in NHL 140.

63. Irenaeus, AH 1.9.4; 1.10.1.

64. Ibid., 3.15.2.

65. Ibid., 1.10.2.

66. Eusebius, *Historia Ecclesiae* 5.23–26.

67. Irenaeus, AH 1.11.9; however, we cannot be certain that the
Gospel of Truth that Irenaeus mentions here, and ascribes to
"Valentinians," is the same as the text by that name discovered at
Nag Hammadi.

68. Ibid., 1.29.4; most scholars regard the teaching Irenaeus summarizes in AH 1.29.1–4 as a paraphrase of the kind of teaching given
in the Apocryphon of John.

69. For a much fuller discussion and references, see Pagels, "Irenaeus, the 'Canon of Truth' and the Gospel of John."

70. Irenaeus, AH 1.15.2; Tertullian describes similar behavior, but he may be drawing his account from Irenaeus's writings rather than his own encounters with such teachers, in *Adversus Valentinianos* 1–2; however, passages from Tertullian's polemic, especially, for example, in chapter 4, do recall his keen ear for actual dialogue.
71. Mark 1:7–8; Matthew 3:11; Luke 3:16.
72. Mark 10:38.
73. Galatians 4:5–7.
74. Gospel of Truth 43.5–8, in NHL 49.
75. "Round Dance of the Cross," in Acts of John 96.2–8.
76. Irenaeus, AH 1.21.1.
77. Ibid., 1.21.3.
78. Ibid.; cf. Colossians 3:3.
79. Irenaeus, AH 1.21.3.
80. Ibid., 1.21.4.
81. Gospel of Thomas 50, in NHL 123.
82. Irenaeus, AH 1.21.4.
83. Ibid., 4.33.7.
84. Ibid., 1.21.1.

CHAPTER FIVE: CONSTANTINE AND THE CATHOLIC CHURCH

1. Irenaeus, AH 2.13.8.
2. Ibid., 2.13.10.
3. Ibid., 2.13.3; 2.13.10. For discussion, see Pagels, "Irenaeus, the 'Canon of Truth' and the Gospel of John."
4. Irenaeus, AH 3.19.2.
5. Ibid., 3.19.1.
6. John 20:20–28; cited in Irenaeus, AH 5.7.1.
7. Irenaeus, AH 5.1.1.
8. Ibid.
9. Ibid., 1.20.1.
10. The question of canon and its introduction into Christian tradi-

tion is a difficult and disputed one. A. C. Sundberg, in "Canon Muratori: A Fourth Century List," *Harvard Theological Review* 66 (1968), 1–41, offers an incisive critique of the traditional second-century dating of the Muratorian canon list, previously believed to be the earliest known list of the New Testament writings. For a careful and persuasive discussion, see Hahneman, *Muratorian Fragment*. For an excellent and measured review of the question, see Harold Gamble, *The New Testament Canon: Its Making and Meaning* (Minneapolis, 1985); and "The New Testament Canon: Recent Research and the *Status Quaestionis*," a forthcoming article which he kindly allowed me to read in manuscript. For an outstanding introduction to issues in the formation of the New Testament, see David E. Aune, *The New Testament in Its Literary Environment* (Philadelphia, 1987). See also the incisive study by Franz Stuhl-hofer, *Der Gebrauch der Bibel von Jesus bis Euseb: Eine stätistische Unter-suchung zur Kanonsgeschichte* (Wuppertal, 1988); also John Barton, *People of the Book? The Authority of the Bible in Christianity* (Louisville, Ky., 1989).

11. Irenaeus, AH 1.9.4. For discussion, see the classic discussion of "canon" as baptismal confession by Adolf von Harnack, in *History of Dogma*, volume I, chapter 3; also the critique by R. Seeberg in *Lehrbuch der Dogmengeschichte* I–II (Basel, 1953–54), as well as the incisive discussion by D. van den Eynde, "Les Normes de l'Enseignement Chrétien dans la littérature patristique des trois premiers siècles," in J. Duculot, ed., *Ecriture et Tradition*, Catholic University of Louvain, Dissertation Series 2.25 (Paris, 1933), 281–313; also L. William Countryman, "Tertullian and the *Regula Fidei*," *The Second Century* 2 (1982), 201–227.

12. Irenaeus, AH 3.11.7.

13. Scholars have debated the transmission history of John's gospel in sources preceding Irenaeus; see, for example, the discussion in Koester, *Ancient Christian Gospels*, 240–267. In an earlier discussion, Professor Koester apparently agreed with many others that Justin

had alluded to John or Johannine tradition when he apparently
alluded to John 3:5 in his description of baptism (I *Apology* 61).
But in his more recent book, Koester evaluates Justin's version of
this saying as an early, independently transmitted tradition (361).
On manuscript evidence for the Johannine gospel in Egypt, see
Colin H. Roberts, *Manuscript, Society, and Belief in Early Christian Egypt*
(London, 1979). T. E. Pollard, *Johannine Christology and the Early Church*,
says that Theophilus of Antioch is the first Christian writer to at-
tribute the fourth gospel to "John," and "to quote explicitly from
the fourth gospel" (40). See also the important studies by J. N.
Sanders, *The Fourth Gospel in the Early Church* (Cambridge, 1943), and
Maurice F. Wiles, *Spiritual Gospel*.

14. See the later recensions of Ignatius's letters for apparent inser-
tions of Johannine material.

15. For references, see Chapter 3, note 40; also Trevett, *Montanism*,
139–140; see also Charles H. Cosgrove, "Justin Martyr and the
Emerging Christian Community," *Vigiliae Christianae* 36 (1982),
209–232.

16. Irenaeus writes that he had heard from Polycarp that John, "the
disciple of the Lord," was the archenemy of Cerinthus, whom, he
said, John had pronounced "the firstborn of Satan" (AH 3.3.4).

17. For recent discussion, see, for example, T. Baarda, "Diaphonia–
Symphonia: Factors in the Harmonization of the Gospels, Especially in the Diatessaron of Tatian," in W. L. Peterson, ed., *Gospel
Traditions in the Second Century: Origins, Recensions, Text, and Transmission* (Notre Dame, 1989), 133–154; and the recent study by W. L.
Peterson, *Tatian's Diatessaron: Its Creation, Dissemination, Significance,
and History in Scholarship* (Leiden, 1994).

18. Irenaeus, AH 3.11.1; 3.3.4; Irenaeus indicates that Ptolemy's disciples agree (1.8.5).

19. Ibid., 3.11.8–9. As T. C. Skeat writes in "Irenaeus and the Four-
Gospel Canon," *Novum Testamentum* 34 (1992), 194: "Every study of
the Canon of the Four Gospels begins, and rightly begins, with

the famous passage in which Irenaeus, writing about the year 185, seeks to defend the Canon by finding a mystical significance in the number four."

20. Irenaeus, AH 3.11.8–9.

21. Irenaeus quotes a written commentary on the Johannine Prologue in 1.8.5. Although he suggests that what follows is the teaching of Valentinus's disciple Ptolemy, it is more likely a writing by one of Ptolemy's disciples; see Markschies, "New Research on Ptolemaeus Gnosticus," 249–254. See also Pasquier, "Interpretation of the Prologue," 484–498.

22. Irenaeus, AH 1.9.2–3.

23. Thanks to Paula Fredriksen for reminding me that this inference is not what Irenaeus, obviously influenced by Middle Platonic thinking, would have been likely to understand.

24. For fuller discussion of the prologue translations, see Pagels, "Exegesis of Genesis 1," 208–209, and Dodd, *Interpretation of the Fourth Gospel*, 268–269. Many English translations, such as, for example the Revised Standard Version, edited by Herbert G. May and Bruce M. Metzger, not only capitalize the term *logos* (word) but also translate the pronouns in 1:7–10 as "he," as if they referred to *Jesus Christ*, instead of indicating that the Greek can be read as neuter or masculine, depending on whether one reads the pronouns' antecedent as *phos* ("light," neuter in Greek) or *logos* ("word," masculine in Greek). Even the reader who goes back to the Greek original may find, as, for example, in the edition by Nestle–Aland, that the Greek text actually capitalizes the term *logos*, which, in the early manuscripts, would have been indistinguishable from the rest of the text.

25. Irenaeus, AH 1.22.1.

26. Ibid., 4.20.1–10.

27. Ibid., 4.20.10–11.

28. Ibid., 5.15.2.

29. Ibid., 3.11.8. "Matthew, too, relates [Christ's] human generation, saying (Matthew 1:1) . . ."

30. Ibid. "The gospel according to Luke . . . takes up his priestly character."

31. Ibid. "Mark, on the other hand, begins with the prophetic spirit descending from on high" (cf. Mark 1:1).

32. Ibid., 3.11.1.

33. Ibid., 4.7.4.

34. Ibid., 4.18.4.

35. Ibid., 17.4–6.

36. Ibid., 4.18.1–4.

37. A. S. Jacobs, "The Disorder of Books: Priscillian's Canonical Defense of Apocrypha," *Harvard Theological Review* 93:2 (2000), 135–159; see also A. Reed, "Apocrypha, 'Outside Books,' and Pseudepigrapha: Ancient Categories and Modern Perceptions of Parabiblical Literature," paper presented at the Philadelphia Seminar on Christian Origins: Parabiblical Literature, October 10, 2002.

38. Irenaeus, AH 4.36.2–4.

39. Ibid., 5.2.1–2.

40. Ibid., 5.21–34.

41. Ibid., 1, *Praefatio.*

42. See the recent and detailed study by Christoph Markschies, *Valentinus Gnosticus?*; also Lampe, *Die stadtrömischen Christen in den ersten beiden Jahrhunderten,* 251–268.

43. See, for example, Judith Kovacs, "Echoes of Valentinian Exegesis in Clement of Alexander and Origen," paper given at Pisa, August 2000, forthcoming in *Origeniana Octava.*

44. Tertullian, *Prescription Against Heretics* 3.

45. For an incisive and intriguing discussion of correlated fourth-century phenomena, see David Brakke, *Athanasius and the Politics of Asceticism* (Oxford and New York, 1995).

46. Tertullian, *Against the Valentinians* 4.

47. Tertullian, *Prescription Against Heretics* 41.

48. Irenaeus, AH 3.15.2.

49. Exodus 9:35; Irenaeus, AH 4.28.3–30.

50. Genesis 19:33–35; Irenaeus, AH 4.31.1–3.

51. William James, *The Varieties of Religious Experience* (Cambridge, Mass., 1985).

52. John 4:46–53.

53. John 4:11–23; for the fragments that remain from Heracleon's commentary, see Werner Foerster, *Gnosis, Die Fragments Heracleons* (Zürich, 1971), 63–86. For discussion of these fragments, see Pagels, *Johannine Gospel in Gnostic Exegesis;* and more recently the study by J. M. Poffet, *La méthode exégétique d'Héracléon et d'Origène* (Fribourg, 1985).

54. John 4:16.

55. Heracleon, Fragment 19, in Origen's *Commentary on John* 13.15.

56. John 4:23, see Heracleon, Fragments 23–25, in Origen, *Commentary on John* 13.19. For an incisive discussion of "gnostic" views of worship, see Klaus Koschorke, *Die Polemik der Gnostiker gegen das kirchliche Christentum* (Leiden, 1978), especially 142–147.

57. See the edition and translation by Frederick Wisse and Michael Waldstein, *Apocryphon of John: Synopsis of Nag Hammadi Codices II.1; III, 1; and IV.1, with BG 8502, 2,* also the fascinating essay by Waldstein, "The Primal Triad in the *Apocryphon of John*," in Turner and McGuire, *Nag Hammadi Library After Fifty Years,* 154–187, and the commentary forthcoming by Karen King from Harvard University Press.

58. Apocryphon of John 20.15–25, in NHL 110.

59. For this version of the story, see On the Origin of the World, 108–118, in NHL 167–174.

60. Apocryphon of John 26.14–15, in NHL 113.

61. Ibid., 26.15–19, in NHL 113.

62. I Corinthians 13:12.

63. Apocryphon of John 30.2–4, in NHL 115.

64. Ibid., 11.20–21, in NHL 105.

65. Genesis 3:16–19.

66. Genesis 3:16 b.

67. Genesis 3:22–24.

68. Apocryphon of John 28.5–30.11, in NHL 114–115.

69. Irenaeus, AH 4.19.2.

70. Eusebius, *Vita Constantinae* 1.26–29.

71. Eusebius, *Historia Ecclesiae* 10.6.

72. Ibid., 10.5.15–17.

73. For a detailed account, see Timothy D. Barnes, *Constantine and Eusebius* (Cambridge and London, 1981), especially 208–227.

74. Eusebius, *Historia Ecclesiae* 10.7.

75. *Codex Theodosius* 19.5.1.

76. For a forthcoming article that suggests Constantine was *not* the emperor who built the first basilica of St. Peter on the Vatican (as tradition holds), see Glen Bowersock, in the supplement to *Antiquite Tardive* in honor of Lellia Cracco Ruggini, and also in a forthcoming Cambridge University Press volume on the Vatican, edited by William Tronzo.

77. Eusebius, *Vita Constantinae* 2.45–46. See Ramsay MacMullen, *Christianizing the Roman Empire, A.D. 100–400* (New Haven and London, 1884), 43–59; also Barnes, *Constantine and Eusebius*, especially 224–260.

78. On the subsidies of grain, see M. J. Hollerich, "The Alexandrian Bishops and the Grain Trade: Ecclesiastical Commerce in Late Roman Egypt," *Journal of the Economic and Social History of the Orient* 25 (1982), 187–207.

79. Barnes, *Constantine and Eusebius*, 252.

80. Ibid., 252; *Codex Theodosius*, 16.8.6; 16.8.1.

81. The sketch presented here is owed primarily to the careful historiography of Timothy D. Barnes, who has published several

fine histories of this period. Besides his book *Constantine and Euse-bius*, see his more recent *Athanasius and Constantius: Theology and Politics in the Constantinian Empire* (Cambridge and London, 1993). An excellent article that presents an overview of these developments is Glen W. Bowersock, "From Emperor to Bishop: The Self-Conscious Transformation of Political Power in the Fourth Century A.D.," *Classical Philology* 81 (1986), 298–302; see also the important work of Peter Brown, including *Power and Persuasion in Late Antiquity: Towards a Christian Empire* (Madison, Wis., 1992), and *Authority and the Sacred: Aspects of the Christianisation of the Roman World* (Cambridge, 1995); Susannah Elm, *Virgins of God: The Making of Asceticism in Late Antiquity* (Oxford and New York, 1992); and David Brakke, *Athanasius and the Politics of Asceticism*.

82. Glen W. Bowersock offers an excellent survey of these events in "From Emperor to Bishop."

83. Letter, cited in J. Stevenson, *A New Eusebius: Documents Illustrative of the History of the Church to A.D. 337* (London, 1957), 358.

84. Eusebius, *Vita Constantinae* 4.24.

85. Barnes, *Constantine and Eusebius*.

86. Letter of Eusebius of Caesarea to his church, in Socrates' *Historia Ecclesiae* 1.8. For a thoughtful and balanced discussion, see Rowan Williams, *Arius: Heresy and Tradition* (London, 1987).

87. Barnes, *Constantine and Eusebius*, 215.

88. See MacMullen, *Christianizing the Roman Empire*, 59–119; see also Stark, *Rise of Christianity*.

89. See Virginia Burrus, *The Making of a Heretic: Gender, Authority, and the Priscillianist Controversy* (Berkeley, 1998), for a fascinating example of the persistence of groups that catholic Christians regarded as deviant.

90. Barnes, *Constantine and Eusebius*, 213.

91. Erik Peterson, *Monotheismus als politisches problem: ein beitrag zur geschichte der politischen theologie im Imperium romanum* (Leipzig, 1935), later interpreted by George H. Williams, "Christology and Church-

State Relations in the Fourth Century," in two installments in *Church History* 20:4 (1951), 3–33, and 20:4 (1951), 3–33.

92. For an incisive discussion of the evidence, see Susannah Elm, *Virgins of God: The Making of Asceticism in Late Antiquity* (Oxford and New York, 1992).

93. See Philip Rousseau, *Pachomius in the Age of Jerome and Cassian* (Oxford, 1978), and his important book *Ascetics, Authority, and the Church: The Making of a Community in Fourth-Century Egypt* (Berkeley, Los Angeles, and London, 1985); Peter Brown, *Society and the Holy* (London and New York, 1982), and *Power, Politics, and Persuasion;* David Brakke, *Athanasius and the Politics of Asceticism;* Birger A. Pearson and James E. Goehring, *The Roots of Egyptian Christianity* (Philadelphia, 1980), and *The Making of a Church in Fourth-Century Egypt* (Berkeley, 1985); and Samuel Rubenson, *The Letters of St. Anthony: Origenist Theology, Monastic Tradition, and the Making of a Saint* (Lund, 1990); see also Richard Valentasis, *Spiritual Guides of the Third Century: A Semiotic Study of the Guide-Disciple Relationship in Christianity, Neoplatonism, Hermetism, and Gnosticism* (Minneapolis, 1991).

94. Athanasius, *Festal Letter* 39. For discussion, see, for example, Martin Tetz, "Athanasius und die Einheit der Kirche: Zur ökumenisches Bedeutung eines Kirchenväters," Zeitschrift für Theologie und Kirche 81 (1984), 205–207; and Brakke, "Canon Formation and Social Conflict."

95. On Athanasius's use of the term *dianoia* as the standard for exegesis, see T. E. Pollard, "The Exegesis of Scripture and the Arian Controversy," in *The John Rylands Library* 41 (1958–59), 421–429; as in Athanasius, *Or. Contra Ar.* 7 (PG 261); also C. Kannengiesser, *Arius and Athanasius: Two Alexandrian Theologians* (Aldershot, Hampshire, Great Britain, and Brookfield, Vt., 1991).

96. Augustine, *On the Incarnation of the Word* 6:1; 13.2; 10.3; see also 11.3. God "gives [humanity] a share in His own image, our Lord Jesus Christ, and makes them according to His own image and after His likeness, so that, by such grace perceiving the

image, that is, the Word of the Father, they may be able through Him to . . . know their Master and live the happy and blessed life."

97. MacMullen, *Christianizing the Roman Empire*, 86; on the advantages of conversion after that time, see "Nonreligious Factors in Conversion," 52–59; see also Stark, *Rise of Christianity*.

98. I find persuasive the arguments of Timothy D. Barnes, in *Constantine and Eusebius*, 208–260; "The Constantinian Reformation," Crake Lectures, 1982 (Sackville, 1986); and "The Constantinian Settlement," in *Eusebius, Judaism, and Christianity* (Detroit, 1992), 655–657.

99. Jacob Burckhardt's classic book suggests the traditional view; see also Eduard Schwartz, *Zur Geschichte des Athanasius* (Berlin, 1959), *Kaiser Constantin und die christliche Kirche* (Leipzig, 1936), and *Zeit Constantins des Grosses* (Leipzig, 1880).

100. See, for example, Brown, *Power and Persuasion;* Richard Lim, *Public Disputation, Power, and Social Order in Late Antiquity* (Berkeley, 1995); Averill Cameron, *Christianity and the Rhetoric of Empire* (Berkeley, Los Angeles, and Oxford, 1991); and Virginia Burrus, *"Begotten, Not Made": Conceiving Manhood in Late Antiquity* (Stanford, 2000).

101. I am grateful to my friend and colleague Heinrich von Staden for raising this point; for discussion of "the dynamics of faith" in terms of Christian theology, see, for example, Paul Tillich, *The Dynamics of Faith* (New York, 1957). For a Buddhist (and thus non-theistic) view, see Sharon Saltzberg, *Faith: Trusting Your Own Deepest Experience* (New York, 2002).

102. Tertullian, *Against the Valentinians* 4.

103. Peter Berger, *The Heretical Imperative: Contemporary Possibilities of Religious Affirmation* (New York, 1979).

104. Matthew 7:7; note Tertullian's objections to the way that "heretics" use this saying (much as I have here) in his *Prescription Against Heretics* 8–13.

THE GOSPEL OF THOMAS

ⵟⵓⵟⵓⵟ

This text is adapted by Elaine Pagels and Marvin Meyer from
Professor Meyer's translation in *The Secret Teachings of Jesus* (Random
House), in consultation with the Scholars Version published in
The Complete Gospels (Polebridge Press).

These are the secret sayings that the living Jesus spoke and Judas
Thomas the Twin wrote down.

1   And he said, "Whoever finds the interpretation of these sayings
will not taste death."

2   Jesus said, "Let one who seeks not stop seeking until he finds.
When he finds, he will be troubled. When he is troubled, he will be
astonished and will rule over all."

3   Jesus said, "If your leaders say to you, 'Look, the Kingdom is in
heaven,' then the birds of heaven will precede you. If they say to you,
'It is in the sea,' then the fish will precede you. Rather, the Kingdom is
inside you and outside you. When you know yourselves, then you
will be known, and you will understand that you are children of the
living Father. But if you do not know yourselves, then you live in
poverty, and you are poverty."

4   Jesus said, "The man old in days will not hesitate to ask a little
child seven days old about the place of life, and that person will live.
For many of the first will be last and will become a single one."

5   Jesus said, "Recognize what is before your eyes, and the mysteries will be revealed to you. For there is nothing hidden that will not
be revealed."

6   His disciples asked him and said to him, "Do you want us to fast?

How should we pray? Should we give alms? What diet should we observe?"

Jesus said, "Do not tell lies, and do not do what you hate, because all things are revealed before heaven. For there is nothing hidden that will not be revealed, and there is nothing covered up that will not be uncovered."

7 Jesus said, "Blessed is the lion that the human will eat, so that the lion becomes human. Cursed is the human that the lion will eat, and the lion will become human."

8 And he said, "The man is like a wise fisherman who cast his net into the sea and drew it up from the sea full of little fish. Among them the wise fisherman discovered a fine big fish. So the fisherman threw all the little fish back into the sea and with no hesitation kept the big fish. Whoever has ears to hear, let him hear!"

9 Jesus said,

Look, the sower went out, took a handful [of seeds], and scattered them. Some fell on the road, and the birds came and gathered them. Others fell on rock, and they did not take root in the soil or produce any heads of grain. Others fell among the thorns, and the thorns choked the seeds and worms consumed them. Still others fell on good soil, and it brought forth a good crop: it yielded sixty per measure and one hundred twenty per measure.

10 Jesus said, "I have cast fire upon the world, and look, I am guarding it until it blazes."

11 Jesus said, "This heaven will pass away, and the one above it will pass away. The dead are not alive, and the living will not die. During the days when you ate what is dead, you made it alive. When you are in the light, what will you do? On the day when you were one, you became two. But when you become two, what will you do?"

12 The disciples said to Jesus, "We know that you are going to leave us. Who is going to be our leader then?"

Jesus said to them, "Wherever you are, you are to go to James the Just, for whose sake heaven and earth came into being."

13 Jesus said to his disciples, "Compare me to someone and tell me whom I am like."

Simon Peter said to him, "You are like a righteous messenger."

Matthew said to him, "You are like a wise philosopher."

Thomas said to him, "Master, my mouth is utterly unable to say what you are like."

Jesus said, "I am not your master. Because you have drunk, you have become intoxicated from the bubbling spring that I have tended."

And he took him, and withdrew, and spoke three sayings to him.

When Thomas came back to his companions, they asked him, "What did Jesus say to you?"

Thomas said to them, "If I tell you even one of the sayings he spoke to me, you will pick up rocks and stone me. Then fire will come forth from the rocks and devour you."

14 Jesus said to them, "If you fast, you will bring sin upon yourselves. If you pray, you will be condemned. If you give alms, you will harm your spirits. When you go into any country and wander around from place to place, and the people receive you, eat what they serve you and heal the sick among them. For what goes into your mouth will not defile you; rather, it is what comes out of your mouth that will defile you."

15 Jesus said, "When you see one who was not born of woman, bow down and worship. That one is your Father."

16 Jesus said, "Perhaps people think that I have come to cast peace upon the world. They do not know that I have come to cast strife upon the earth: fire, sword, war. For there will be five in a house: there will be three against two and two against three, father against son and son against father, and they will stand solitary."

17 Jesus said, "I shall give you what no eye has seen, what no ear has heard, what no hand has touched, what has never arisen in a human heart."

18 The disciples said to Jesus, "Tell us about the end."

Jesus said, "Have you already found the beginning, then, that you seek for the end? For where the beginning is the end will be. Blessed is the one who stands at the beginning: that one will know the end and will not taste death."

19 Jesus said, "Blessed is the one who came into being before coming into being. If you become my disciples and listen to my sayings, these stones will serve you. For there are five trees in Paradise for you; they do not change, summer or winter, and their leaves do not fall. Whoever knows them will not taste death."

20 The disciples said to Jesus, "Tell us what the Kingdom of Heaven is like."

He said to them,

It is like a mustard seed. [It] is the smallest of all seeds, but when it falls on prepared soil, it grows into a large plant and shelters the birds of heaven.

21 Mary said to Jesus, "What are your disciples like?"
He said,

They are like little children living in a field that is not theirs. When the owners of the field come, they will say, "Give us back our field." They take off their clothes in front of them in order to give it back to them, and they return their field to them. For this reason I say, if the owners of a house know that a thief is coming, they will be on guard before the thief arrives, and will not let the thief break into their house of their domain and steal their possessions. As for you, then, be on guard against the world. Prepare yourselves with great strength, so the robbers cannot find a way to get to you, for the trouble you expect will come. Let there be among you a person who understands. When the crop ripened, he came quickly carrying a sickle and harvested it. Whoever has ears to hear, let him hear!

22 Jesus saw some babies nursing. He said to his disciples, "These nursing babies are like those who enter the Kingdom."

They said to him, "Then shall we enter the Kingdom as babies?"

Jesus said to them, "When you make the two into one, and when you make the inner like the outer and the outer like the inner, and the upper like the lower, and when you make male and female into a single one, so that the male will not be male nor the female be female, when you make eyes in place of an eye, a hand in place of a hand, a foot in place of a foot, an image in place of an image, then you will enter [the Kingdom]."

23 Jesus said, "I shall choose you, one from a thousand and two from ten thousand, and they will stand as a single one."

24 His disciples said, "Show us the place where you are, for we must seek it."

He said to them, "Whoever has ears to hear, let him hear! There is light within a person of light, and it lights up the whole world. If it does not shine, it is dark."

25 Jesus said, "Love your brother like your soul; protect him like the pupil of your eye."

26 Jesus said, "You see the sliver in your brother's eye, but you do not see the timber in your own eye. When you take the timber out of your own eye, then you will see well enough to remove the sliver from your brother's eye.

27 "If you do not fast from the world, you will not find the Kingdom. If you do not observe the sabbath day as a sabbath day, you will not see the Father."

28 Jesus said, "I took my stand in the midst of the world, and in flesh I appeared to them. I found them all drunk, and I did not find any of them thirsty. My soul ached for the children of humanity, because they are blind in their hearts and do not see, for they came into the world empty, and they also seek to depart from the world empty. But meanwhile they are drunk. When they shake off their wine, then they will repent."

29 Jesus said, "If the flesh came into being because of spirit, that is a marvel, but if spirit came into being because of the body, that is a marvel of marvels. Yet I marvel at how this great wealth has come to dwell in this poverty."

30 Jesus said, "Where there are three deities, they are divine. Where there are two or one, I am with that one."

31 Jesus said, "No prophet is welcome in his own village; no physician cures those who know him."

32 Jesus said, "A city built on a high hill and fortified cannot fall, nor can it be hidden."

33 Jesus said, "What you will hear in your ear, in the other ear proclaim from your rooftops. For no one lights a lamp and puts it under a basket, nor does one put it in a hidden place. Rather, one puts it on a lampstand so that all who come and go will see its light."

34 Jesus said, "If a blind person leads a blind person, both of them will fall into a hole."

35 Jesus said, "One cannot enter a strong man's house and take it by force without binding his hands. Then one can loot his house."

36 Jesus said, "Do not worry, from morning to evening and from evening to morning, about what you are going to wear."

37 His disciples said, "When will you appear to us and when shall we see you?"

Jesus said, "When you strip off your clothes without being ashamed, and you take your clothes and put them under your feet like little children and trample them, then [you] will see the son of the living one and you will not be afraid."

38 Jesus said, "Often you have desired to hear these sayings that I am speaking to you, and you have no one else from whom to hear them. There will be days when you will seek me and you will not find me."

39 Jesus said, "The Pharisees and the scholars have taken the keys of knowledge and have hidden them. They have not entered, nor have they allowed those who want to enter to do so. As for you, be as wise as serpents and as innocent as doves."

40 Jesus said, "A grapevine has been planted apart from the Father. Since it is not strong, it will be pulled up by its root and will perish."

41 Jesus said, "Those who have something in hand will be given more, and those who have nothing will be deprived of even the little they have."

42 Jesus said, "Become passersby."

43 His disciples said to him, "Who are you to say these things to us?"

"You do not understand who I am from what I say to you. Rather, you have become like the Jewish people, for they love the tree but hate its fruit, or they love the fruit but hate the tree."

44 Jesus said, "Whoever blasphemes against the Father will be forgiven, and whoever blasphemes against the son will be forgiven, but whoever blasphemes against the holy spirit will not be forgiven, either on earth or in heaven."

45 Jesus said, "Grapes are not harvested from thorn trees, nor are figs gathered from thistles, for they yield no fruit. Good persons produce good from what they have stored up; bad persons produce evil from the wickedness they have stored up in their hearts, and say evil things. For from the overflow of the heart they bring forth evil."

46 Jesus said, "From Adam to John the Baptist, among those born of women, no one is so much greater than John the Baptist that his eyes should not be averted. But I have said that whoever among you becomes a child will know the Kingdom and will become greater than John."

47 Jesus said, "A person cannot mount two horses or bend two bows, and a servant cannot serve two masters, otherwise that servant will honor the one and offend the other. No one drinks aged wine and immediately wants to drink new wine. New wine is not poured into old wineskins, or they might break, and aged wine is not poured into a new wineskin, or it might spoil. An old patch is not sewn onto a new garment, since it would create a tear."

48 Jesus said, "If two make peace with each other in a single house, they will say to the mountain, 'Move from here!' and it will move."

49 Jesus said, "Blessed are those who are solitary and chosen, for you will find the Kingdom. For you have come from it, and you will return there again."

50 Jesus said, "If they say to you, 'Where have you come from?' say to them, 'We have come from the light, from the place where the light came into being by itself, established [itself], and appeared in their image.' If they say to you, 'Who are you?' say, 'We are its children, and we are the chosen of the living Father.' If they ask you, 'What is the sign of your Father in you?' say to them, 'It is movement and rest.'"

51 His disciples said to him, "When will the rest for the dead take place, and when will the new world come?"

He said to them, "What you look forward to has already come, but you do not recognize it."

52 His disciples said to him, "Twenty-four prophets have spoken in Israel, and they all spoke of you."

He said to them, "You have disregarded the living one who is in your presence and have spoken of the dead."

53 His disciples said to him, "Is circumcision beneficial or not?"

He said to them, "If it were beneficial, their father would produce children already circumcised from their mother. Rather, the true circumcision in spirit has become profitable in every respect."

54 Jesus said, "Blessed are the poor, for yours is the Kingdom of Heaven."

55 Jesus said, "Whoever does not hate father and mother cannot be my disciple, and whoever does not hate brothers and sisters, and carry the cross as I do, will not be worthy of me."

56 Jesus said, "Whoever has come to know the world has discovered a carcass, and whoever has discovered a carcass, of that person the world is not worthy."

57 Jesus said,

The Kingdom of the Father is like a person who had [good] seed. His enemy came during the night and sowed weeds among the good seed. The man did not let the workers pull up the weeds, but said to them, "No, otherwise you might go to pull up the weeds and pull up the wheat along with them." For on the day of the harvest the weeds will be conspicuous and will be pulled up and burned.

58 Jesus said, "Blessed is the one who has suffered and has found life."

59 Jesus said, "Look to the living one as long as you live, otherwise you might die and then try to see the living one, and you will be unable to see."

60 [He saw] a Samaritan carrying a lamb as he was going to Judea. He said to his disciples, "[Why is] that person [carrying] the lamb around?"

They said to him, "So that he may kill it and eat it."

He said to them, "He will not eat it while it is alive, but only after he has killed it and it has become a carcass."

They said, "Otherwise he cannot do it."

He said to them, "So also with you, seek a place of rest for yourselves, lest you become a carcass and be eaten."

61 Jesus said, "Two will recline on a couch; one will die, one will live."

Salome said, "Who are you, man? You have climbed onto my couch and eaten from my table as if from one."

Jesus said to her, "I am the one who comes from what is undivided. I was granted from the things of my Father."

[Salome said,] "I am your disciple."

[Jesus said,] "For this reason I say, whoever is [undivided] will be full of light, but whoever is divided will be full of darkness."

62 Jesus said, "I disclose my mysteries to those [who are worthy] of [my] mysteries. Do not let your left hand know what your right hand is doing."

63 Jesus said,

There was a rich man who had a great deal of money. He said, "I shall invest my money so that I may sow, reap, plant, and fill my storehouses with produce, that I may lack nothing." These were the things he was thinking in his heart, but that very night he died. Whoever has ears to hear, let him hear!

64 Jesus said,

A man was receiving guests. When he had prepared the dinner, he sent his servant to invite the guests. The servant went

to the first and said, "My master invites you." The first replied, "Some merchants owe me money; they are coming to
me tonight. I have to go and give them instructions. Please
excuse me from dinner." The servant went to another and
said, "My master has invited you." The second said to the
servant, "I have bought a house, and I have been called away
for a day. I shall have no time." The servant went to another
and said, "My master invites you." The third said to the servant, "My friend is to be married, and I am to arrange the
banquet. I shall not be able to come. Please excuse me from
dinner." The servant went to another and said, "My master
invites you." The fourth said to the servant, "I have bought
an estate, and I am going to collect the rent. I shall not be
able to come. Please excuse me." The servant returned and
said to his master, "Those whom you invited to dinner have
asked to be excused." The master said to his servant, "Go out
on the streets and bring back whomever you find to come to
dinner."

"Buyers and merchants [will] not enter the places of my Father."

65 He said,

A [usurer] owned a vineyard and rented it to some farmers, so they could work it and he could collect its produce from them. He sent his servant so the farmers would
give him the produce from the vineyard. They seized him,
beat him, and almost killed him, and the servant returned
and told his master. His master said, "Perhaps he did not
know them." He sent another servant, and the farmers beat
that one as well. Then the master sent his son and said, "Perhaps they will show my son some respect." Because the
farmers knew that he was the heir to the vineyard, they
seized him and killed him. Whoever has ears to hear, let him
hear!

66   Jesus said, "Show me the stone that the builders rejected: that is the cornerstone."

67   Jesus said, "Whoever knows everything, but is lacking within, lacks everything."

68   Jesus said, "Blessed are you when you are hated and persecuted; wherever you have been persecuted, no place will be found."

69   Jesus said, "Blessed are those who have been persecuted in their hearts: they are the ones who have truly come to know the Father. Blessed are those who hunger, that the belly of the one in need may be filled."

70   Jesus said, "If you bring forth what is within you, what you have will save you. If you do not have that within you, what you do not have within you [will] destroy you."

71   Jesus said, "I shall destroy [this] house, and no one will be able to build it [again]."

72   A [person said] to him, "Tell my brothers to divide my father's possessions with me."

He said to the person, "Man, who made me a divider?"

He turned to his disciples and said to them, "I am not a divider, am I?"

73   Jesus said, "The harvest is great but the workers are few, so ask the master of the harvest to send workers to the fields."

74   Someone said, "Lord, there are many around the drinking trough, but there is nothing in the well."

75   Jesus said, "There are many standing at the door, but only those who are solitary will enter the bridal chamber."

76   Jesus said,

> The Kingdom of the Father is like a merchant who had a supply of merchandise and then found a pearl. That merchant was prudent; he sold the merchandise and bought the single pearl for himself.

"So also with you, seek his treasure that is unfailing, that is enduring, where no moth comes to eat and no worm destroys."

77 Jesus said, "I am the light that is over all things. I am all. From me all came forth, and to me all extends. Split a piece of wood, and I am there. Lift up the stone, and you will find me there."

78 Jesus said, "Why have you come out to the countryside? To see a reed shaken by the wind? And to see a person dressed in fine clothing, [like your] rulers and your powerful men? They are dressed in fine clothing, and they cannot understand truth."

79 A woman in the crowd said to him, "Blessed are the womb that bore you and the breasts that nourished you."

He said to [her], "Blessed are those who have heard the word of the Father and have truly kept it. For there will be days when you will say, 'Blessed are the womb that has not conceived and the breasts that have not given milk.'"

80 Jesus said, "Whoever has come to know the world has discovered the body, and whoever has discovered the body, of that one the world is not worthy."

81 Jesus said, "The one who has become wealthy should reign, and the one who has power should renounce [it]."

82 Jesus said, "Whoever is near me is near the fire, and whoever is far from me is far from the Kingdom."

83 Jesus said, "Images are visible to people, but the light within them is hidden in the image of the Father's light. The Father will be revealed, but his image is hidden by his light."

84 Jesus said, "When you see your likeness [in a mirror], you are pleased. But when you see your images that came into being before you and that neither die nor become visible, how much you will have to bear!"

85 Jesus said, "Adam came from great power and great wealth, but he was not worthy of you. For had he been worthy, [he would] not [have tasted] death."

86 Jesus said, "[Foxes have] their dens and birds have their nests, but the son of man has no place to lie down and rest."

87 Jesus said, "Miserable is the body that depends on a body, and miserable is the soul that depends on these two."

88 Jesus said, "The messengers and the prophets will come to you and give you what belongs to you. You, in turn, give them what you have, and say to yourselves, 'When will they come and take what belongs to them?'"

89 Jesus said, "Why do you wash the outside of the cup? Do you not understand that the one who made the inside is also the one who made the outside?"

90 Jesus said, "Come to me, for my yoke is easy and my rule is gentle, and you will find rest for yourselves."

91 They said to him, "Tell us who you are so that we may believe in you."

He said to them, "You search the face of heaven and earth, but you have not come to know the one who stands before you, and you do not know how to understand the present moment."

92 Jesus said, "Seek and you will find. In the past, however, I did not tell you the things about which you asked me then. Now I am willing to tell them, but you are not seeking them.

93 "Do not give what is holy to dogs, or they might throw them upon the manure pile. Do not throw pearls [to] swine, or they might make [mud] of it."

94 Jesus [said], "One who seeks will find, and for [one who knocks] it will be opened."

95 [Jesus said], "If you have money, do not lend it at interest. Rather, give [it] to someone from whom you will not get it back."

96 Jesus [said], "The Kingdom of the Father is like [a] woman who took a little leaven, [hid] it in dough, and made it into large loaves of bread. Whoever has ears to hear, let him hear!"

97 Jesus said,

> The Kingdom of the [Father] is like a woman who was carrying a [jar] full of meal. While she was walking along [a] distant road, the handle of the jar broke and the meal spilled behind her [along] the road. She did not know it; she noticed no accident. When she reached her house, she put the jar down and discovered that it was empty.

98 Jesus said,

> The Kingdom of the Father is like a person who wanted to kill a powerful man. While still at home he drew his sword and thrust it into the wall to find out whether his hand would go in. Then he killed the powerful man.

99 The disciples said to him, "Your brothers and your mother are standing outside."

He said to them, "Those here who do what my Father wants are my brothers and my mother. They are the ones who will enter the Kingdom of my Father."

100 They showed Jesus a gold coin and said to him, "Caesar's men demand taxes from us."

He said to them, "Give Caesar what belongs to Caesar, give God what belongs to God, and give me what is mine.

101 "Whoever does not hate [father] and mother as I do cannot be my [disciple], and whoever does [not] love [father and] mother as I do cannot be my [disciple]. For my mother [gave me falsehood], but my true [mother] gave me life."

102 Jesus said, "Woe to the Pharisees. For they are like a dog sleeping in the cattle manger: the dog neither eats nor [lets] the cattle eat."

103 Jesus said, "Blessed are those who know where the robbers will enter, so that [they] may prepare, collect their resources, and be ready before the robbers come."

104 They said to Jesus, "Come, let us pray today and let us fast."

Jesus said, "What sin have I committed, or how have I been undone? Rather, when the groom leaves the bridal chamber, then let people fast and pray."

105 Jesus said, "Whoever knows the father and the mother will be called the child of a whore."

106 Jesus said, "When you make the two into one, you will become children of humanity, and when you say, 'Mountain, move from here!' it will move."

107 Jesus said,

> The Kingdom is like a shepherd who had a hundred sheep.
> One of them, the largest, went astray. He left the ninety–nine
> and looked for the one until he found it. After his toil, he
> said to the sheep, "I love you more than the ninety–nine."

108 Jesus said, "Whoever drinks from my mouth will become like me;
I myself shall become that person, and the mysteries will be revealed
to him."

109 Jesus said,

> The Kingdom is like a man who had a treasure hidden in his
> field but did not know it. And [when] he died, he left it to his
> [son]. The son [did] not know [about it either]. He took over
> the field and sold it. The buyer went plowing, [discovered]
> the treasure, and began to lend money at interest to whom-
> ever he wished.

110 Jesus said, "Whoever has found the world and has become
wealthy, let him renounce the world."

111 Jesus said, "The heavens and the earth will roll up in your presence, and whoever is living from the living one will not see death."
Does not Jesus say, "Those who have found themselves, of them the
world is not worthy"?

112 Jesus said, "Woe to the flesh that depends on the soul. Woe to the
soul that depends on the flesh."

113 His disciples said to him, "When will the Kingdom come?"

"It will not come by watching for it. They will not say, 'Look, it is
here!' or 'Look, it is there!' Rather, the Kingdom of the Father is spread
out upon the earth, but people do not see it."

114 Simon Peter said to them, "Make Mary leave us, for females are
not worthy of life."

Jesus said, "Look, I shall guide her to make her male, so that she

too may become a living spirit resembling you males. For every female who makes herself male will enter the Kingdom of Heaven."*

ʇoʇoʇoʇ

I am grateful to Random House and Polebridge Press, and especially
grateful to Professor Marvin Meyer, who has graciously granted permission to consult the translation he published, with Professor Stephen
Patterson, as the Scholars Version in *The Complete Gospels,* and extended
to me, as to many of our colleagues, the benefit of his expertise.

Those who wish further to investigate the Gospel of Thomas and
the meaning of particular sayings (including the enigmatic saying 114)
may find the following publications especially useful:

Marvin Meyer, *The Gospel of Thomas: The Hidden Sayings of Jesus* (San
Francisco, 1992)

Marvin Meyer, *Secret Gospels: Essays on Thomas and the Secret Gospel of
Mark* (Harrisburg, Pa., 2003)

Willis Barnstone and Marvin Meyer, *The Gnostic Bible* (Boston, 2003)

Andrew Harvey, Stevan Davies (trans.), *The Gospel of Thomas: Anno-
tated and Explained* (London, 2003)

Stephen J. Patterson, *The Gospel of Thomas and Jesus* (Sonoma, Calif.,
1993)

Gregory J. Riley, *Resurrection Reconsidered: Thomas and John in Controversy* (Minneapolis, 1995)

Risto Uro, ed., *Thomas at the Crossroads: Essays on the Gospel of Thomas*
(Edinburgh, 1998)

Richard Valantasis, *The Gospel of Thomas* (London, 1997)

—*Elaine Pagels*

---

*The words *female* and *male* are not to be taken literally (as if they referred to woman
and man) but rather as characterizing respectively what is human and what is divine. See M. Meyer, *The Gospel of Thomas* (San Francisco, 1992), note on saying 114.

INDEX

diversity and factionalism in, 28,
  62–63, 65–66, 79–80, 81,
  84–97; *see also specific sects and
  texts*
dying cared for by, 8–9
Ebionite, 111, 134
evangelical, 30–31
as family, 3, 6, 7, 10, 13, 14
Johannine, 62
legalization of, 6, 158, 168, 176,
  179–80
money as viewed in, 6–9, 13,
  16
mystery cults compared with,
  19–20
mysticism in, 41, 51, 74–75, 182
new morality in, 9–10
origins of, 31–34
orthodox, 33, 113, 117, 119, 128,
  133, 135–36, 142, 148, 151,
  154–58, 170–81
persecution of, 5, 11–13, 59, 68,
  73, 78–79, 82–84, 86, 135, 158,
  168, 169, 178–79
Peter, 61, 62, 81
political factors in shaping of,
  33, 79, 168–75, 179–80
practice vs. belief in, 143
as seekers, 29, 34, 53, 57, 75–76,
  96, 97, 99, 100–101, 130,
  183–85
sick cared for by, 8–10, 169
spiritual, 136–37, 156
Thomas, 38–39, 58, 66, 72, 81
transformation of, 29
in transition to creed, 5–6,
  27–28, 33, 45, 148, 155,
  170–74, 178
Valentinian, 116–19, 128, 130–33,
  138, 145, 148, 150, 155–63,
  166
see also specific topics
Christian Scientist, 183
christos ("anointed one"), 42

church:
  catholic, 80, 129, 134, 135, 158,
    168–81
  four pillars of, 111
  state, 175
  universal, 133
Church of Jesus Christ of Latter-day
  Saints (Mormons), 23, 123
Church of St. Peter, 169
Church of the Heavenly Rest, 3–6,
  27, 29, 143–45
Church of the Holy Sepulcher, 169
Clement of Alexandria, 157
clothing, 9, 85, 126
  baptism and, 14, 130
coercion, giving up, 51
Commentary on John (Heracleon),
  116–17
Commodus, Emperor, 77
communion, eucharist as, 27
compilers vs. authors, 46
consciousness:
  "creative" or "inventive" (*epinoia*),
    164–67, 177, 183
  as mind, 104, 108
Constantine, Roman emperor, 28,
  158, 168–75
  attempt to end heretical sects
    by, 174
  conversion of, 6, 179–80
  letter to proconsul of Africa by,
    168–69
  Nicaea council and, 6, 170–74
conversion experience, Heracleon
  on types of, 160–63
Coptic Orthodox Christians, 134
Corinth, Paul's letters to Christians
  in, 88, 99, 100
covenant, 21
creeds, Christian, transition to, 5–6,
  27–28, 33, 45, 148, 155,
  170–74, 178
criminals, crimes:
  burial of, 7–8

Luke, Gospel of (cont'd):
  dreams and visions in, 87, 88
  followers of Marcion and, 111,
    134
  in four formed gospel, 81,
    111–13, 153
  Gospel of John compared with,
    35–40, 60–61, 62, 68, 69, 118,
    122
  Gospel of Thomas compared
    with, 40, 46, 48, 53–54
  Jesus as characterized in, 41,
    43–45, 121, 152
  kingdom of God in, 50
  last supper in, 22, 25
  sacrifice in, 22
  son of man in, 51
Luther, Martin, 183
Lutheran Church, 183
Lyons, 80, 82–83, 92

MacRae, George, 31–32
magic, giving up of, 13, 16
Marcion, 6, 80–81, 111, 134, 174
Marcus, 92–97, 105, 106
  as Satan's apostle, 96, 103
Marcus Aurelius, Roman emperor,
    8, 83
Mark, Gospel of, 20–23, 33, 45, 87,
    108, 137, 149
  as basis for New Testament
    canon, 26
  in four formed gospel, 81,
    111–13, 153
  Gospel of John compared with,
    35–38, 40, 60–61, 68, 69, 118
  Gospel of Thomas compared
    with, 40, 46, 48
  Jesus as characterized in, 41–43,
    152
  kingdom of God in, 48, 69
  last supper in, 22–23, 25
  sacrifice in, 20–21, 22
Mark (disciple), 50

marriage, 85
  ritual dialogue of, 140
  spiritual, 139, 162
Martha, 49
Martyn, Louis, 63
Mary, Virgin, 61, 87, 109–10, 131
Mary (sister of Lazarus), 49
Mary Magdalene, 61–62, 65, 66, 72
Mary Magdalene, Gospel of, 51, 63,
    103–5, 111
Matthew, 66
  wise philosopher answer of, 47
Matthew, Gospel of, 18, 23, 33, 45,
    93, 110–13, 137, 148, 149
  Didache compared with, 15, 16
  Ebionites and, 111, 134
  events that bear out prophecy
    and, 107–8, 110
  in four formed gospel, 81,
    111–13, 153
  Gospel of John compared with,
    12, 35–40, 60–61, 68, 69, 118
  Gospel of Thomas compared
    with, 40, 46, 48, 53–54
  Jesus as characterized in, 41, 43,
    121, 152
  last supper in, 22, 25
  new morality in, 9–10
  sacrifice in, 21, 22
Maximilla, 84–85, 91–92
Merkabah (chariot) literature, 101
Merton, Thomas, 51, 76
messiah:
  as "anointed one," 42, 47
  as christos, 42
  Jesus as, 20, 38, 42, 43, 44, 46, 47,
    63, 64, 67, 108
  as title, 38, 42
mind (consciousness), 104, 108
miracles, 7, 63–64, 79, 91, 160
Mithras, 9, 19
money, 85
  in Christianity vs. pagan
    religions, 6–9